DROUGHT

Drought is the most complex of all natural hazards. Resulting in serious economic, social and environmental costs and losses in both developed and developing countries, drought has severely affected most countries in recent years, and on multiple occasions in many cases. Drought risks are escalating in response to many factors, including the increasing and shifting population that leads to expanding pressure on water and other natural resources.

Drought draws together contributions from over 75 leading international researchers in the field, to present the most comprehensive volume of research on the physical and social dimensions of drought to date. Including an extensive range of case studies covering the most drought-prone and most drought-affected countries, the contributors examine new technology, planning methodologies, and mitigation actions from recent drought experiences worldwide.

Following a discussion of the critical concepts of drought, the book is divided into seven additional parts which address causes and predictability; monitoring and early warning techniques; impacts and assessment methodologies; adjustment and adaptation strategies; policy, mitigation techniques and preparedness methodologies; links between drought and other global issues; and conclusions and future challenges.

To reduce the risk associated with drought hazard, societies must assess their exposure to drought and identify where, when, and who is vulnerable. This action can lead to the development of mitigation programmes and policies and preparedness plans aimed at reducing the risks of future drought events. Discussing both the physical and social dimensions of drought and proposed management actions and policies, this volume will prove invaluable to all those seeking a greater understanding of this complex natural hazard.

Donald A. Wilhite is Director of the National Drought Mitigation Center, University of Nebraska, Lincoln, USA.

Routledge Hazards and Disasters Series

Published to mark the end of the International Decade for Natural Disaster Reduction, this important new series of definitive works spans major hazards and disasters worldwide. Bringing together both new and landmark research from leading experts worldwide, each volume in the series represents a unique achievement, spanning the breadth of disaster-prone regions and the spectrum of themes at the core of current research. Each volume is introduced and collated by specialist editors renowned in the field.

Series Advisory Board:

Henry Quarantelli, DRC, University of Delaware, USA
Dennis Mileti, Natural Hazards Research Center, University of Colorado, USA
Earnest Paylor II, Office of Mission to Planet Earth, NASA, USA
Earl Jay Baker, Florida State University, USA
Robert Simpson, Washington, DC, USA
Keith Smith, University of Stirling, UK
John Handmer, Flood Hazard Research Centre, University of Middlesex, UK
Eric Alley, Institute of Civil Defence & Disaster Studies, UK
Keith Cassidy, Major Hazards Assessment Unit, Health & Safety Executive, UK
Denis Smith, Durham University Business School, Durham, UK
Terry Jeggle, IDNDR Secretariat, Switzerland
S.W.A. Gunn, President World Association of Disaster & Emergency Medicine, Switzerland
Herbert Tiedermann, Germany
Aniello Amendola, Joint Research Centre, Ispra, Italy
Hayim Granot, Bar-I-Lan University, Israel
Neil Britton, Emergency Management Office, Wellington, New Zealand
Kyoji Sassa, Disaster Prevention Institute, Kyoto University, Japan
Lianshou Chen, Chinese Academy of Meteorological Sciences, Beijing

Titles already published in the series:

Drought
Storms

Forthcoming titles planned for the series:

Floods
Earthquakes
Volcanoes
Geological Hazards
Hazards, Environment and Sustainability

DROUGHT
A Global Assessment

VOLUME I

EDITED BY
DONALD A. WILHITE

London and New York

First published 2000
by Routledge
11 New Fetter Lane, London EC4P 4EE

Simultaneously published in the USA and Canada
by Routledge
29 West 35th Street, New York, NY 10001

Routledge is an imprint of the Taylor & Francis Group

Typeset in Galliard by Solidus (Bristol) Limited
Printed and bound in Great Britain by
Butler and Tanner Ltd, Frome and London

British Library Cataloguing in Publication Data
A catalogue record for this book is available from the British Library

Library of Congress Cataloging in Publication Data
Drought : a global assessment / edited by Donald A. Wilhite.
p. cm. — (Hazards and disasters : v. 2)
1. Droughts. I. Wilhite, Donald A. II. Series.
QC929.24.D74 2000
363.3′929—dc21 99–10302

ISBN 0-415-16833-3 (2-volume set)
ISBN 0-415-16834-1 (Volume I)
ISBN 0-415-21418-1 (Volume II)

CONTENTS

VOLUME I

VOLUME II

FIGURES

TABLES

BOXES

CONTRIBUTORS

Karen Bakker is affiliated with the Climate Impacts and Responses Programme of the Environmental Change Unit at the University of Oxford, United Kingdom.

A. Mestre Barceló is affiliated with Servicio de Aplicaciones Climatológicas, Instituto Nacional de Meteorologia, in Madrid, Spain.

Charles Batchelor is head of the Agrohydrology Section of the Institute of Hydrology in Wallingford, Oxfordshire, United Kingdom.

Grant Beard is a meteorologist with the National Climate Centre, Bureau of Meteorology, in Melbourne, Victoria, Australia.

Abdellatif Bencherifa is vice president for Student Affairs at Al Akhawayn University in Ifrane, Morocco.

Charlotte Benson is a research fellow with the Overseas Development Institute in London.

Hendrik J. Bruins is affiliated with the Social Studies Centre of the Jacob Blaustein Institute for Desert Research, the Department of Geography and Environmental Development, and the Negev Center for Regional Development at Ben-Gurion University of the Negev, Israel.

Iracema F.A. Cavalcanti is affiliated with Instituto Nacional de Pesquisas Espaciais in São Paulo, Brazil.

Chaoying Huang is affiliated with the National Climate Centre in Beijing, People's Republic of China.

Edward Clay is a research fellow with the Overseas Development Institute in London.

H.P. Das is the director of the Division of Agricultural Meteorology, Meteorological Office, India Meteorological Department, in Pune, India.

Susanna Davies is deputy director of the Institute of Development Studies at the University of Sussex, Brighton, East Sussex, United Kingdom.

G.C. de Hoedt is affiliated with the National Climate Centre of the Bureau of Meteorology, Melbourne, Victoria, Australia.

J.M. de Jager is Special Professor in the Department of Agrometeorology, Faculty of Agriculture, at the University of the Orange Free State in Bloemfontein, South Africa.

Ariel Dinar is senior economist with the Agriculture and Natural Resources Department of the World Bank in Washington, DC, USA.

Randall M. Dole is affiliated with the National Oceanic and Atmospheric Administration's Environmental Research Laboratories, Climate Diagnostics Center, in Boulder, Colorado, USA.

Thomas E. Downing is programme leader of the Climate Impacts and Responses Programme of the Environmental Change Unit at the University of Oxford, United Kingdom.

H.E. Dregne is Horn Professor Emeritus and special consultant at the International Center for Arid and Semiarid Land Studies at Texas Tech University in Lubbock, Texas, USA.

J.A. Dyer is retired from the International Affairs Division, Markets and Industry Services Branch, Agriculture and Agri-Food Canada, in Ottawa, Ontario, Canada.

Benedykt Dziegielewski is director of the International Water Resources Association and associate professor of geography at Southern Illinois University in Carbondale, Illinois, USA.

William Easterling is a professor in the Department of Geography at Pennsylvania State University in University Park, Pennsylvania, USA.

Neil J. Ericksen is director of the International Global Change Institute at the University of Waikato in Hamilton, New Zealand.

John Osgood Field is retired from the School of Nutrition Science and Policy at Tufts University in Medford, Massachusetts, USA.

C.K. Folland is the leader of the Climate Variability Group in the Hadley Centre for Climate Prediction and Research, United Kingdom Meteorological Office, in Bracknell, England.

H.J. Fouché is assistant director of the Free State Department of Agriculture, Section Pasture Science, in Glen, Free State Province of South Africa.

C. Peral Garcia is affiliated with Servicio de Aplicaciones Climatológicas, Instituto Nacional de Meteorologia, in Madrid, Spain.

W.J. Gibbs is retired director of the Australian Bureau of Meteorology, Melbourne, Victoria, Australia.

Michael H. Glantz is senior scientist in the Environmental and Societal Impacts Group, National Centre for Atmospheric Research, in Boulder, Colorado, USA.

Lisa J. Graumlich is the deputy director and dean of the Earth Learning Center, Biosphere 2 Center, Columbia University, Oracle, Arizona, USA.

Michael Hayes is a climate impacts specialist with the National Drought Mitigation Center at the University of Nebraska–Lincoln, USA.

Heather Haylock is a planner with City Planning, Department of Planning and Regulatory Services, Auckland City Council, Auckland, New Zealand.

R.L. Heathcote is Visiting Scholar in the School of Geography, Population and Environment Management at Flinders University in Adelaide, South Australia.

Richard R. Heim, Jr is affiliated with the Climate Perspectives Branch of the Global Climate Laboratory, National Climatic Data Center, National Oceanic and Atmospheric Administration, in Asheville, North Carolina, USA.

M.D. Howard is senior lecturer in the Department of Agrometeorology at the University of the Orange Free State in Bloemfontein, South Africa.

Mrill Ingram is project coordinator of the Forgotten Pollinators Project at the Arizona–Sonora Desert Museum in Tucson, Arizona, USA.

Tijan Jallow is senior technical advisor of the United Nations Development Program in New York, New York, USA.

Andrew Keck is affiliated with the World Bank in Washington, DC, USA.

Kerang Li is affiliated with the Institute of Geography, Chinese Academy of Sciences, in Beijing, People's Republic of China.

W.R. Kininmonth is the general manager of Australasian Climate Research in Kew, Australia.

Felix Kogan is affiliated with the Satellite Research Laboratory of the National Environmental Satellite Data and Information Service of the National Oceanic and Atmospheric Administration in Camp Springs, Maryland, USA.

Mike Laing is Director-Climate, Weather Bureau, Department of Environmental Affairs and Tourism, in Pretoria, South Africa.

Diana M. Liverman is director of the Latin American Studies Program and associate professor in the Department of Geography at the University of Arizona, Tucson, Arizona, USA.

Chris Lovell is affiliated with the Lowveld Research Stations in Chiredzi, Zimbabwe.

S.J. Mason is affiliated with the International Research Institute for Climate Prediction at Scripps Institution of Oceanography at the University of California at San Diego, USA.

Robert Mendelsohn is a professor in the School of Forestry and Environmental Studies at Yale University in New Haven, Connecticut.

J.L. Garcia Merayo is affiliated with Servicio de Aplicaciones Climatológicas, Instituto Nacional de Meteorologia, in Madrid, Spain.

Isiah Mharapara is affiliated with the Lowveld Research Stations in Chiredzi, Zimbabwe.

Kathleen A. Miller is affiliated with the Environmental and Societal Impacts Group, National Center for Atmospheric Research, in Boulder, Colorado, USA.

Karl Monnik is programme manager: AgroMet, Agroclimatological Research, with the ARC–Institute for Soil, Climate and Water in Pretoria, South Africa.

C.E. Mullen is senior meteorologist with the Climate Analysis Section of the National Climate Centre, Bureau of Meteorology, in Melbourne, Victoria, Australia.

Neville Nicholls is group leader of the Bureau of Meteorology Research Centre Climate Group in Melbourne, Victoria, Australia.

Paulo Nobre is affiliated with Centro de Previsão de Tempo e Estudos Climáticos in Brazil.

L.A. Ogallo is a professor in the Department of Meteorology at the University of Nairobi in Kenya.

B. O'Meagher is assistant secretary of the Corporate Policy Division, Department of Primary Industries and Energy, in Canberra, Australia.

Qian Weihong is affiliated with the Department of Geophysics at Peking University in Beijing, People's Republic of China.

Kelly T. Redmond is regional climatologist at the Western Regional Climate Center, Desert Research Institute, in Reno, Nevada, USA.

D. Rind is affiliated with NASA/GISS (Goddard Space Flight Center, Institute for Space Studies) in New York, New York, USA.

John C. Rodda is affiliated with the International Association of Hydrological Sciences, Institute of Hydrology in Wallingford, United Kingdom, and the Institute of Geography and Earth Sciences at the University of Wales at Aberystwyth, United Kingdom.

C.F. Ropelewski is affiliated with the International Research Institute for Climate Prediction, Lamont-Doherty Earth Observatory of Columbia University, Palisades, New York, USA.

Alvin Z. Rubinstein is affiliated with the Department of Political Science at the University of Pennsylvania in Philadelphia.

A.S.R.A.S. Sastri is associate director of research and head of the Department of Physics and Agrometeorology at Indira Gandhi Agricultural University in Raipur, India.

M. Stafford Smith is affiliated with the CSIRO National Rangelands Program in Alice Springs, Northern Territory, Australia.

A.R. Subbiah is affiliated with the Rajiv Gandhi National Drinking Water Mission, Department of Rural Development, Ministry of Rural Areas and Employment, in New Delhi, India.

Mark Svoboda is a climate/water resources specialist with the National Drought Mitigation Center at the University of Nebraska–Lincoln, USA.

Will D. Swearingen is research associate professor of geography and director of the International Environmental Technologies Program in the Earth Sciences Department at Montana State University in Bozeman, Montana, USA.

Tsegaye Tadesse is affiliated with the National Meteorological Services Agency in Addis Ababa, Ethiopia. He is also a graduate student in the School of Natural Resource Sciences at the University of Nebraska–Lincoln, USA.

P.D. Tyson is affiliated with the Climatology Research Group of the University of Witwatersrand in Johannesburg, South Africa.

Olga Vanyarkho is a graduate student in the School of Natural Resource Sciences at the University of Nebraska–Lincoln, USA.

Coleen Vogel is with the Climatology Research Group, Department of Geography and Environmental Studies, at the University of the Witwatersrand, Johannesburg, South Africa.

M.E. Voice is superintendent of the National Climate Centre of the Bureau of Meteorology, Melbourne, Victoria, Australia.

Wang Shaowu is a professor in the Department of Geophysics at Peking University in Beijing, People's Republic of China.

E.E. Wheaton is lead scientist and climatologist of the Climatology Section of the Saskatchewan Research Council in Saskatoon, Saskatchewan, Canada.

D.H. White is director of ASIT Consulting (Agro-ecological Systems and Information Technology) in Canberra, Australia.

Donald A. Wilhite is the director of the National Drought Mitigation Center and International Drought Information Center and a professor at the University of Nebraska–Lincoln, USA.

Jim Williams is business development coordinator for the Environmental Sciences Department of the Natural Resources Institute at the University of Greenwich in Chatham, United Kingdom.

Ye Jinlan is affiliated with the Department of Geophysics at Peking University in Beijing, People's Republic of China.

Yufeng Chen is affiliated with the Institute of Geography, Chinese Academy of Sciences, in Beijing, People's Republic of China.

Igor Zonn is affiliated with the Russian Engineering Academy, Foreign Relations Office, Soyuzvodproject in Moscow.

SERIES FOREWORD

At the beginning of the 1990s the International Decade for Natural Disaster Reduction (IDNDR) was established by the member states of the United Nations General Assembly. Its objective was straightforward: by concerted international action, to protect people and property from the worst effects of natural hazards through the wider application of existing scientific and technical knowledge. During the course of the decade, and spurred on by several very costly natural disasters, a greater awareness has developed about humankind's own role in creating, or tolerating, unacceptable vulnerability to natural hazards. The social and economic implications of such risks has given a much greater importance to public policy decisions and local community responsibilities in preventing natural disasters.

Disasters are costly. Hundreds of millions of dollars are spent each year on immediate, short-term emergency relief. It is more recently that we have become fully aware of the consequences of natural disasters over time, and of the fact that long-term effects are measured in *billions* of dollars in losses.

The consequences of the Mt. Pinatubo volcanic eruption in the Philippines, for example, continue to be felt ten years after the event. Similarly, the dramatic floods during the decade – many of which were the worst in a century – have had long-lasting effects on the populations of Western Europe, North America, India, China, and Bangladesh.

It is evident that natural disasters respect no national borders. The consequences of wildfire, smoke and haze have been felt on three continents; the devastation of Hurricane Mitch was experienced in countries throughout Central America. The effects of El Niño were seen around the world.

Hazardous natural phenomena will continue to occur, as they shape the environments on which our societies depend, but there is much that scientific knowledge, the decisions of public authorities and professional skills can do to prevent them from becoming human disasters.

Fortunately, we have learned that there is much that we can do to prevent natural hazards from turning into human disasters. Modern, global economic relationships, driven by the complexity of our societies, provide an imperative to become more attentive to the potential losses of natural disasters. However, recent advances in transmitting information, news or scientific data, provide us with the opportunities to realise that disaster prevention *is* both necessary *and* feasible. We are rapidly moving towards a global recognition that there is a need to concentrate public awareness and professional resources in all countries to make disaster prevention a public value. Prevention becomes possible.

The IDNDR has sought to focus attention through its international framework of collaborating scientific institutions, national authorities, commercial endeavour and public interests on the basic fact that 'prevention pays'. The present publication, a volume of a series, Hazards and Disasters, is an admirable example of that framework at work in bringing together the many professional interests necessary for successful disaster prevention. The comprehensive scientific information provided, together with the wide-ranging examples of professional experience, will serve students and practitioners alike in translating their professional dedication into applied disaster mitigation. Furthermore, as a commercial venture that draws upon scientific endeavour for the wider understanding of natural hazards and risk at local levels of activity, it is an example of a working partnership that has been able to draw on the various sectors of society essential for taking sustained disaster prevention into the twenty-first century.

Together, we are working for a common purpose through advocacy, the application of effective policies, and the continuation of assured coordination to create a Culture of Prevention for a Safer Twenty-first Century. The publication of the Hazards and Disasters Series to mark the conclusion of the International Decade for Natural Disaster Reduction is a noteworthy, and above all practical, example of the vision that all societies can indeed insure their social investments and protect their economic assets, given the commitment to do so. We have the comprehensive knowledge, and professional skills – which this series makes widely available to all.

Philippe Boulle, Director, IDNDR Secretariat, Geneva, Switzerland

FOREWORD

As one who has been interested for more than forty years in the study of climate, climate change, rainfall, and drought in what has been called the world's driest continent, I feel privileged to write a foreword for the drought volume of the ambitious *Hazards and Disasters: A Series of Definitive Major Works*.

The simple definition of drought is 'shortage of water to meet essential needs'. This definition highlights the complex nature of drought, the impact of which depends to a considerable extent on how water is used. Human communities have a wide variety of demands for water. The different uses of water by urban communities, pastoralists, agriculturalists, horticulturalists, commerce and industry, and desert nomads graphically illustrate why each group will have a different perception of drought.

How should we measure drought? One convenient and readily available measure is rainfall. In Australia we have found a close correspondence between the occurrence of rainfall in the lowest ten percentile range and an awareness among pastoralists and agriculturalists that they are experiencing drought. That awareness generally emerges when the total rainfall of a period of some three months or more falls in the first decile range (lowest ten percentile range).

Other definitions and measurements of drought appear in this volume. I am reminded of Schneider's remarks in 1977: 'I was in a group of modellers who wanted to address all these issues about the theories of climate. Before we did that we thought we might spend a minute and dismiss the issues of the definition of climate. I remember that about three hours later we were still heatedly discussing the definition and concluded it is a time series which is a long record of some climatic event.' Finding agreement on the definition and measurement of drought is likely to be similarly difficult but should not be our goal. The main objective should be to exchange ideas and increase awareness of various strategies for reducing drought impacts. The information in this volume should help us reach this goal.

What should we do to reduce the effects of drought? The statement (wrongly attributed to Mark Twain) that 'everyone complains about the weather but no one does anything about it' has a particular relevance to drought. In studying drought, one must realise that, like many other potential disasters, it is not 'an act of God' but one of the manifestations of the climate of our planet. Perhaps more importantly, we must remember that we possess the knowledge, wisdom, and foresight to take action to reduce drought's deleterious effects.

To begin our study of drought, we must ensure that we have an adequate data base of drought and its impact. This must include a long-term record of monthly rainfall and other meteorological elements for as many locations as possible. A data base of at least 100 years is desirable. It should also include information on drought impacts on numbers and conditions of livestock, grain harvests, water conservation and supply, industry and commerce, and the national economy. In Australia in the 1950s, Foley documented drought impacts using newspaper reports spanning many decades. More recent Australian studies have considered a wider range of specific information on drought impacts.

Governments should promote awareness campaigns to inform and educate all sectors of the community (and relevant arms of their bureaucracy) on the nature of drought and on strategies to prepare for and combat drought when it arrives. Such cam-paigns, to be effective, should be relaunched about every ten years.

Humans tend to have short-term memories. In looking to the future, we tend to neglect the disasters that might befall us. But if we look at rainfall records of the last 100 years, it becomes readily apparent that drought (like death and taxes) is inevitable. In a world where an exponential increase in population is occurring, we must prepare ourselves to deal with drought and other potential disasters.

W.J. Gibbs
Melbourne
April 1997

REFERENCES

Foley, J.C. (1957) 'Droughts in Australia', *Bulletin 43*, Melbourne, Australia: Bureau of Meteorology.
Schneider, S.H. (1977) 'What climatologists can say to planners', in *Living with Climate Change, Phase II*, McLean, Virginia: The Mitre Corporation.

PREFACE

Drought is a global phenomenon that can and does occur in virtually all landscapes, resulting in significant economic, social, and environmental costs and losses. These costs and losses have risen dramatically in recent decades. Drought is an insidious hazard of nature which is considered by many to be the most complex but least understood of all natural hazards.

History tells us that societies have seldom been prepared for the inevitable recurrence of drought. It is often considered to be a rare and random event, certainly not one that could be anticipated, planned for, and its impacts effectively managed. In recent decades, the impacts of drought have escalated in response to increasing population, misdirected or nonsustainable government policies and programs, environmental degradation, new technologies, and fragmented government authority in water and natural resources management. These escalating impacts have increasingly drawn the attention of both the scientific and policy community, not only because

of the frequency and severity of recent droughts in both developing and developed countries, but also because of the complexity of economic impacts associated with the phenomenon and its far-reaching social costs and environmental damages.

The goal of this book is to provide the scientific and policy community with information in the form of new technologies and methodologies, as well as lessons learned, that will help nations define a new paradigm for drought planning and management in the 21st Century. The overview chapters and case studies included in this book provide information to scientists, policy makers, and planners that, if implemented, can reduce the devastation of drought through improved prediction and monitoring techniques, mitigation programs and policies, and contingency planning. The completion of the International Decade for Natural Disaster Reduction provides a unique opportunity to implement this new paradigm for drought management in the 21st Century.

ACKNOWLEDGEMENTS

Drought is the culmination of nearly two years of work and could not have been completed without the time and effort of many persons. First, I would like to thank the authors of each of the chapters. They contributed their time and expertise to this effort and are largely responsible for the final product. I have had the privilege to work with many of them on previous occasions and appreciate their dedication to improving our understanding of drought and its impacts on societies worldwide. I trust that we will have the opportunity to work together again as my quest for enhanced awareness and understanding of drought issues continues.

Second, I would like to express my appreciation to my publications specialist, Deborah A. Wood. Deborah has worked with me at the University of Nebraska for nearly two decades and has assisted with many projects and publications. This project is certainly the most ambitious of all that we have attempted. I would have never undertaken a project of this magnitude without her excellent editorial and organisational skills. Thanks, Deborah, for all of your assistance.

Finally, I would like to express my appreciation to Vicki Wilcox for her word processing skills and sense of humour for the hours that she spent incorporating the thousands of editorial changes in these volumes.

PART I

BACKGROUND AND CONCEPTS

I

DROUGHT AS A NATURAL HAZARD

Concepts and definitions

Donald A. Wilhite

INTRODUCTION

Worldwide, economic damages attributed to natural disasters tripled from the 1960s (US$40 billion) to the 1980s (US$120 billion) (Domeisen 1995). The 1990s have witnessed a continued escalation of economic damages, reaching US$400 billion through 1996 (Carolwicz 1996). Between 1992 and 1996, losses associated with natural disasters in the United States averaged US$54.2 billion per week (Carolwicz 1996).

The economic, social, and environmental costs and losses associated with drought are also increasing dramatically, although it is difficult to quantify this trend precisely because of the lack of reliable historical estimates of losses. White and Haas estimated in 1975 that the average annual crop losses associated with drought in the Great Plains region of the United States were about US$700 million. In 1995, the US Federal Emergency Management Agency (FEMA) estimated annual losses attributable to drought at US$6–8 billion (FEMA 1995).

More specific figures from recent drought episodes in the United States provide a clearer picture of the magnitude of drought losses and our continuing vulnerability. The southwestern and southern Great Plains states experienced dramatic impacts on agriculture, water supply, wildfires, transportation, and tourism and recreation in 1996 and 1998. For example, the impacts of the 1996 and 1998 droughts in Texas have been estimated at US$6 billion (Boyd 1996) and US$5.8 billion (Chenault and Parsons 1998), respectively. The 1998 drought in Oklahoma resulted in estimated agricultural losses of more than US$2 billion

(Thurman 1998). These estimated losses in 1996 do not include losses that occurred in New Mexico, Oklahoma, Kansas, Colorado, Utah, Arizona, and Nevada. Likewise, significant losses also occurred in 1998 in Florida, South Carolina, Georgia, and Louisiana.

The estimated losses further illustrate the trend in vulnerability in the United States. Factors that may explain this trend are numerous; they include deficiencies in monitoring and early warning systems and the application of this information by decision makers, urbanisation, population growth and regional population shifts to more drought-prone areas, outdated or inappropriate water management policies and practices, lack of contingency planning, fragmented responsibilities in water/drought management by government agencies, and poor coordination within and between levels of government. Thus, vulnerability is increasing in the United States despite dramatic technological advances and the availability of large financial resources (Riebsame *et al.* 1991). The series of drought years that occurred in the United States between 1986 and 1992, as well as severe drought conditions that prevailed in 1994, 1996, and 1998, has further reinforced the reality of the nation's vulnerability. What concerns many scientists and decision makers is the diversity and complexity of drought impacts and the low level of preparedness for future events. The ongoing debate about climate change and its potential effects on the frequency and severity of extreme climatic events is adding further to the concerns of scientists and decision makers.

The concerns about the trends in losses associated with natural disasters in developed countries are magnified when placed in the context of developing nations. Natural hazards result in significant loss of life and serious economic, environmental, and social impacts that greatly retard the development process. Figure 1.1 illustrates the trend of major natural disasters between 1963 and 1992, expressed as the number of disasters affecting 1 per cent or more of the total annual gross national product. Figure 1.2 ranks these disasters by type, illustrating that drought, floods, and tropical storms were the most frequent disasters occurring during this period. The Centre for Research in the Epidemiology of Disasters (Blaikie *et al.* 1994) grouped natural disaster occurrence by decade and has shown that the number of droughts increased from 62 in the 1960s to 237 during the 1980s. However, these figures for drought are misleading. Drought is one of the most underreported natural disasters because the sources of most of these statistics are international aid or donor organisations. Unless countries

afflicted by drought request assistance from the international community or donor governments, these episodes are not reported. Thus, severe droughts such as those that occurred in Australia, Brazil, Canada, Spain, England, the United States, and many other countries in recent years are not included in these statistics.

BACKGROUND

Drought is considered by many to be the most complex but least understood of all natural hazards, affecting more people than any other hazard (Hagman 1984). For example, in sub-Saharan Africa, the droughts of the early to mid-1980s are reported to have adversely affected more than 40 million people (Office of Foreign Disaster Assistance 1990). The 1991–2 drought in southern Africa affected 20 million people and resulted in a deficit of cereal supplies of more than 6.7 million tonnes (SADCC

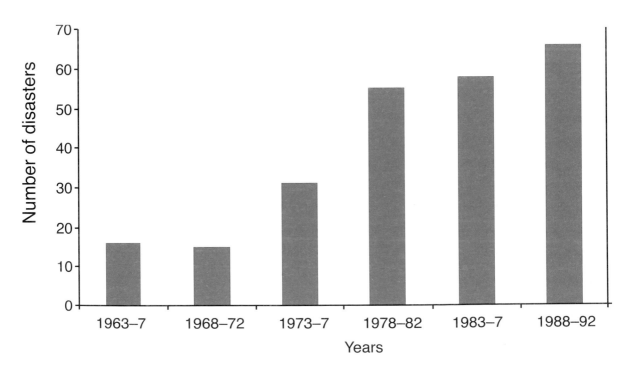

* = 1% or more of total annual GNP

Figure 1.1 Number of disasters causing significant damage, 1963–92*. The figure was created from data provided by the UN/Secretariat, International Decade for National Disaster Reduction

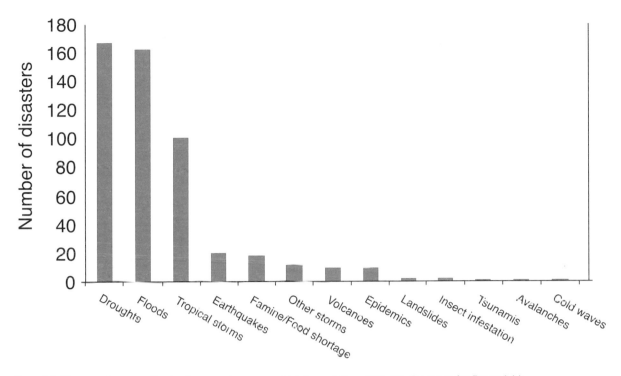

Figure 1.2 Disasters, by type, affecting 1 per cent or more of total population, 1963–92. (Source as for Figure 1.1.)

1992). In the United States, the drought of 1988 resulted in estimated impacts of nearly US$40 billion (Riebsame *et al.* 1991), making this single-year drought the costliest disaster in American history. Drought results in significant impacts regardless of the level of development, although the character of these impacts will differ profoundly.

Drought is a normal feature of climate and its recurrence is inevitable. However, there remains much confusion within the scientific and policy community about its characteristics. It is precisely this confusion that explains, to some extent, the lack of progress in drought management in most parts of the world. The purpose of this chapter is to provide a foundation for the concept of drought that will help readers understand the complex aspects of this natural hazard as they are discussed in subsequent chapters. More specifically, the chapter will articulate the differences between drought and other natural hazards, the types and definitions of drought, and definitions of key components of the cycle of disaster management. Enhancing understanding of drought concepts should

help readers understand why, according to Hagman (1984), the phenomenon is not better understood by scientists and policy makers. Through an improved understanding and awareness of the concept and characteristics of drought and its differences from other natural hazards, both scientists and policy makers will be better equipped to establish much-needed policies and plans whereby vulnerability can be reduced or stabilised for future generations.

DROUGHT: THE CONCEPT

Drought differs from other natural hazards (e.g., floods, tropical cyclones, and earthquakes) in several ways. First, since the effects of drought often accumulate slowly over a considerable period of time and may linger for years after the termination of the event, the onset and end of drought is difficult to determine. Because of this, drought is often referred to as a creeping phenomenon (Tannehill 1947). Tannehill notes:

We have no good definition of drought. We may say truthfully that we scarcely know a drought when we see one. We welcome the first clear day after a rainy spell. Rainless days continue for a time and we are pleased to have a long spell of such fine weather. It keeps on and we are a little worried. A few days more and we are really in trouble. The first rainless day in a spell of fine weather contributes as much to a drought as the last, but no one knows how serious it will be until the last dry day is gone and the rains have come again . . . we are not sure about it until the crops have withered and died.

(Tannehill 1947)

Although Tannehill's book was written more than fifty years ago, climatologists continue to struggle with recognising the onset of drought and scientists and policy makers continue to debate the basis (i.e., criteria) for declaring an end to a drought.

Second, the absence of a precise and universally accepted definition of drought adds to the confusion about whether or not a drought exists and, if it does, its degree of severity. Realistically, definitions of drought must be region and application (or impact) specific. This is one explanation for the scores of definitions that have been developed. Wilhite and Glantz (1985) analysed more than 150 definitions in their classification study, and many more exist. Although the definitions are numerous, many do not adequately define drought in meaningful terms for scientists and policy makers. The thresholds for declaring drought are arbitrary in most cases (i.e., they are not linked to specific impacts in key economic sectors). For example, what is the significance of a threshold of 75 per cent of normal precipitation over a period of three months or more? A definition of this type would be especially misleading for locations with a strong seasonal component of annual precipitation. These types of problems are the result of a misunderstanding of the concept by those formulating definitions and the lack of consideration given to how other scientists or disciplines will eventually need to apply the definition in actual drought situations (e.g., assessments of impact in multiple economic sectors, drought declarations or revocations for eligibility to relief programmes).

Third, drought impacts are nonstructural and spread over a larger geographical area than damages that result from other natural hazards. For example, a recent analysis of drought occurrence by the (US) National Drought Mitigation Center for the forty-eight contiguous states in the United States demonstrated that severe and extreme drought affected more than 25 per cent of the country in twenty-seven of the past one hundred years. This represents an area of 750,000 mi^2 (1,942,500 km^2) or more.

Drought seldom results in structural damage, in contrast to floods, hurricanes, and tornadoes. For these reasons, the quantification of impacts and the provision of disaster relief are far more difficult tasks for drought than they are for other natural hazards. Emergency managers, for example, are more accustomed to dealing with impacts that are structural and localised, responding to these events by restoring communication and transportation channels, providing emergency medical supplies, ensuring safe drinking water, and so forth. These characteristics of drought have hindered the development of accurate, reliable, and timely estimates of severity and impacts and, ultimately, the formulation of drought contingency plans by most governments.

Hazard events have been ranked by Bryant (1991) on the basis of their characteristics and impacts. This ranking is summarised in Table 1.1. Key hazard characteristics used for this evaluation include an expression of the degree of severity, length of event, total areal extent, total loss of life, total economic loss, social effects, long-term impact, suddenness, and occurrence of associated hazards for thirty-one hazards. Although the ratings of the various hazards in Table 1.1 are subjective, the overall rank is useful because it provides an integrated assessment of hazard characteristics and the relationships between hazards. Because of the intensity, duration, and spatial extent of drought events and the magnitude of associated impacts, drought ranks very high. One can make a cogent argument, however, that total loss of life associated with drought in this case is significantly overrated. Loss of life that is directly associated with drought is rare in most settings. The ranking by Bryant attributes loss of life because of famine to drought. This is inappropriate since the primary cause of famine in recent decades has been civil war or political strife, both of which heighten vulnerability to drought. Drought events disrupt food production systems and can be a significant natural trigger for famine.

Table 1.1 Ranking of hazard events by characteristics and impacts

Overall rank[b]	Event	Grading of characteristics and impacts[a]								
		Degree of severity	Length of event	Total areal extent	Total loss of life	Total economic loss	Social effect	Long-term impact	Suddenness	Occurrence of associated hazards
1	Drought	1	1	1	1	1	1	1	4	3
2	Tropical cyclone	1	2	2	2	2	2	1	5	1
3	Regional flood	2	2	2	1	1	1	2	4	3
4	Earthquake	1	5	1	2	1	1	2	3	3
5	Volcano	1	4	4	2	2	2	1	3	1
6	Extra-tropical storm	1	3	2	2	2	2	2	5	3
7	Tsunami	2	4	1	2	2	2	3	4	5
8	Bushfire	3	3	3	3	3	3	3	2	5
9	Expansive soils	5	1	1	5	4	5	3	1	5
10	Sea-level rise	5	1	1	5	3	5	1	5	4
11	Icebergs	4	1	1	4	4	5	5	2	5
12	Dust storm	3	3	2	5	4	5	4	1	5
13	Landslides	4	2	2	4	4	4	5	2	5
14	Beach erosion	5	2	2	5	4	4	4	2	5
15	Debris avalanches	2	5	5	3	4	3	5	1	5
16	Creep and soilifluction	5	1	2	5	4	5	4	2	5
17	Tornado	2	5	3	4	4	4	5	2	5
18	Snowstorm	4	3	3	5	4	4	5	2	4
19	Ice at shore	5	4	1	5	4	5	4	1	5
20	Flash flood	3	5	4	4	4	4	5	1	5
21	Thunderstorm	4	5	2	4	4	5	5	2	4
22	Lightning strike	4	5	2	4	4	5	5	1	5
23	Blizzard	4	3	4	4	4	5	5	1	5
24	Ocean waves	4	4	2	4	4	5	5	3	5
25	Hail storm	4	5	4	5	3	5	5	1	5
26	Freezing rain	4	4	5	5	4	4	5	1	5
27	Localised strong wind	5	4	3	5	5	5	5	1	5
28	Subsidence	4	3	5	5	4	4	5	3	5
29	Mud and debris flows	4	4	5	4	4	5	5	4	5
30	Air-supported flows	4	5	5	4	5	5	5	2	5
31	Rockfalls	5	5	5	5	5	5	5	1	5

Source: Summarised from Bryant (1991)
Notes:
a Hazard characteristics and impacts are graded on a scale of 1 (largest or greatest) to 5 (smallest or least significant)
b Overall rank is based on average grading

Drought is a normal, recurring feature of climate; it occurs in virtually all climatic regimes. It occurs in high as well as low rainfall areas. It is a temporary aberration, in contrast to aridity, which is a permanent feature of the climate and is restricted to low rainfall areas. Many people associate the occurrence of drought with most of Africa, India, China, the Great Plains of North America, and Australia; they have more difficulty visualising drought in Southeast Asia, Brazil, western Europe, or the eastern United States, regions perceived by many to have a surplus of water. This fact emphasises both the regional and relative nature of drought, a characteristic that will be discussed in more detail later in this chapter.

Drought is the consequence of a natural reduction in the amount of precipitation received over an extended period of time, usually a season or more in length, although other climatic factors (such as high temperatures, high winds, and low relative humidity) are often associated with it in many regions of the world and can significantly aggravate the severity of the event. Drought is also related to the timing (i.e., principal season of occurrence, delays in the start of the rainy season, occurrence of rains in relation to principal crop growth stages) and the effectiveness of the rains (i.e., rainfall intensity, number of rainfall events). Thus, each drought year is unique in its climatic characteristics and impacts. For example, Magalhães *et al.* (1988) have vividly pointed out the climatic differences between five consecutive drought years that occurred in northeast Brazil between 1979 and 1983, noting the critical linkages between the timing of rainfall and impacts.

Drought severity is dependent not only on the duration, intensity, and geographical extent of a specific drought episode, but also on the demands made by human activities and vegetation on a region's water supplies. The characteristics of drought, along with its far-reaching impacts, make its effects on society, economy, and environment difficult, though not impossible, to identify and quantify.

Many people consider drought to be largely a natural or physical event. Figure 1.3 illustrates that, in reality, drought has both a natural and social component. The risk associated with drought for any region is a product of both the region's exposure to the event (i.e., probability of occurrence at various severity levels) and the vulnerability of society to the event. The natural event (i.e., meteorological drought) is a result of the occurrence of persistent large-scale disruptions in the global circulation pattern of the atmosphere. Exposure to drought varies spatially and there is little, if anything, that we can do to alter drought occurrence. Vulnerability, on the other hand, is determined by social factors such as population, demographic characteristics, technology, policy, and social behaviour. These factors change over time, and thus vulnerability is likely to increase or decrease in response to these changes. Subsequent droughts in the same region will have different effects, even if they are identical in intensity, duration, and spatial characteristics, because societal characteristics will have changed. However, much can be done to lessen societal vulnerability to drought, and subsequent chapters will discuss these actions from many regional and disciplinary perspectives.

DEFINING DROUGHT

Because drought affects so many economic and social sectors, scores of definitions have been developed by a variety of disciplines. In addition, because drought occurs with varying frequency in nearly all regions of the globe, in all types of economic systems, and in developed and developing countries alike, the approaches taken to define it also reflect regional and ideological differences (Wilhite 1992). Impacts also differ spatially and temporally, depending on the societal context of drought. A universal definition of drought is an unrealistic expectation. Wilhite and Glantz (1985) concluded that definitions of drought should reflect a regional bias since water supply is largely a function of climatic regime.

Definitions of drought can be categorised broadly as either conceptual or operational (Wilhite and Glantz 1985). Conceptual definitions are of the dictionary type, generally defining the boundaries of the concept of drought, and thus are generic in their description of the phenomenon. For example, the Encyclopedia of Climate and Weather (Schneider 1996) defines drought as 'an extended period – a season, a year, or several years – of deficient rainfall relative to the statistical multi year mean for a region'. These types of definitions are useful for furthering

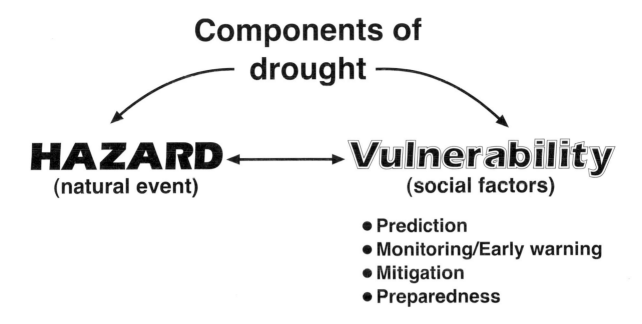

Figure 1.3 Components of drought

our description of the phenomenon, but cannot be used to detect the onset of drought because of their lack of specificity. They do, however, incorporate the concept of the intensity and duration of the event and the need for regional bias.

Tannehill uses another conceptual definition that incorporates key elements of drought: a deficiency of precipitation from expected or normal that, when extended over a season or longer period of time, is insufficient to meet the demands of human activities, resulting in economic, social, and environmental impacts.

Operational definitions attempt to identify the precise characteristics and thresholds that define the onset, continuation, and termination of drought episodes, as well as their severity. These definitions are the foundation of an effective early warning system. They can also be used to analyse drought frequency, severity, and duration for a given historical period. An operational definition of agricultural drought might be one that compares daily precipitation to evapotranspiration (ET) rates to determine the rate of soil water depletion and then expresses these relationships in terms of drought effects on plant behaviour at various phenological stages of development. The effects of these meteorological conditions on plant growth would be reevaluated continuously by agricultural specialists as the growing season progresses.

Many disciplinary perspectives of drought exist. Each discipline incorporates different physical, biological, and/or socioeconomic factors in its definition of drought. Because of these numerous and diverse disciplinary views, considerable confusion often exists over exactly what constitutes a drought (Glantz and Katz 1977). Research has shown that the lack of a precise and objective definition in specific situations has been an obstacle to understanding drought, which has led to indecision and/or inaction on the part of managers, policy makers, and others (Wilhite and Glantz 1985, Wilhite *et al.* 1986). It must be accepted that the importance of drought lies in its impacts. Thus definitions should be region and impact or application specific in order to be used in an operational mode by decision makers. A comprehensive review of drought definitions and indices can be found in a technical note published by the World Meteorological Organization (WMO) (1975). Other sources, such as Subrahmanyam (1967), Glantz and Katz (1977), Sandford (1979), Dracup *et al.* (1980), and Wilhite and Glantz (1985), can be consulted for a thorough discussion of the difficulties in defining drought.

Drought has been grouped by type as follows: meteorological, hydrological, agricultural, and socio-economic (Wilhite and Glantz 1985). Figure 1.4 explains the relationship between these various types of drought and the duration of the event. Droughts

usually take three or more months to develop, but this time period can vary considerably, depending on the timing of the initiation of the precipitation deficiency. For example, a significant dry period during the winter season may have few, if any, impacts for many locales. However, if this deficiency continues into the growing season, the impacts may magnify quickly since low precipitation during the fall and winter season results in low soil moisture recharge rates, leading to deficient soil moisture at spring planting.

Meteorological (or climatological) drought is expressed solely on the basis of the degree of dryness

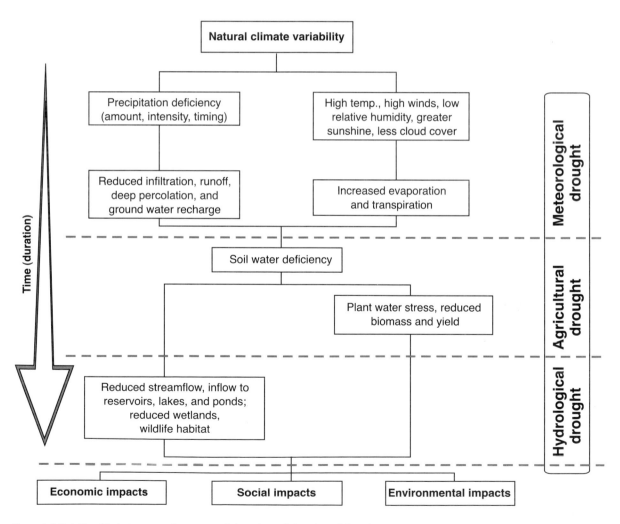

Figure 1.4 Relationship between various types of drought and duration of drought events

(often in comparison to some normal or average amount) and the duration of the dry period. Thus, intensity and duration are the key characteristics of these definitions. Meteorological drought definitions must be considered as region specific since the atmospheric conditions that result in deficiencies of precipitation are climate regime dependent. For example, some definitions differentiate meteorological drought on the basis of the number of days with precipitation less than some specified threshold rather than the magnitude of the deficiency over some period of time (e.g., for Britain, fifteen days, none of which received as much as 0.25 mm of precipitation [British Rainfall Organization 1936]). Such a definition is unrealistic in those regions where precipitation distribution is seasonal and extended periods without rainfall are common. Most meteorological drought definitions relate actual precipitation departures to average amounts on monthly, seasonal, water year, or annual time scales. Human perceptions of these conditions are equally variable.

Agricultural drought links various characteristics of meteorological drought to agricultural impacts, focusing on precipitation shortages, differences between actual and potential evapotranspiration (ET), soil water deficits, and so forth. A plant's demand for water is dependent on prevailing weather conditions, biological characteristics of the specific plant, its stage of growth, and the physical and biological properties of the soil. An operational definition of agricultural drought should account for the variable susceptibility of crops at different stages of crop development. For example, deficient subsoil moisture in an early growth stage will have little impact on final crop yield if topsoil moisture is sufficient to meet early growth requirements. However, if the deficiency of subsoil moisture continues, a substantial yield loss may result.

The impacts of drought are crop specific because the most weather-sensitive phenological stages vary between crops. Planting dates and maturation periods also vary between crops and locations. A period of high temperature stress that occurs in association with dry conditions may coincide with a critical weather-sensitive growth stage for one crop while missing a critical stage for another crop. Agricultural planning can often reduce the risk of drought impact on crops by altering the crop, genotype, planting date, and cultivation practices.

Agriculture is usually the first economic sector to be affected by drought because soil moisture supplies are often quickly depleted, especially if the period of moisture deficiency is associated with high temperatures and windy conditions. The timing of rainfall during the growing season is critical in the determination of impacts. Crop or forage yields may be normal or above normal during a drought if rainfall is timely (i.e., coinciding with critical phenological stages) and effective (i.e., low intensity and high soil infiltration rate).

Hydrological droughts are associated with the effects of periods of precipitation shortfall on surface or subsurface water supply (i.e., streamflow, reservoir and lake levels, groundwater) rather than with precipitation shortfalls (Dracup et al. 1980, Klemeš 1987). Hydrological droughts are usually out of phase or lag the occurrence of meteorological and agricultural droughts. Meteorological droughts result from precipitation deficiencies; agricultural droughts are largely the result of soil moisture deficiencies. More time elapses before precipitation deficiencies are detected in other components of the hydrological system (e.g., reservoirs, groundwater). As a result, impacts are out of phase with those in other economic sectors. Also, water in hydrological storage systems (e.g., reservoirs, rivers) is often used for multiple and competing purposes (e.g., power generation, flood control, irrigation, recreation), further complicating the sequence and quantification of impacts. Competition for water in these storage systems escalates during drought, and conflicts between water users increase significantly.

The frequency and severity of hydrological drought is often defined at the river basin scale. Whipple (1966) defined a drought year as one in which the aggregate runoff is less than the long-term average runoff. Low-flow frequencies have been determined for many streams. If the actual flow for a selected time period falls below a certain threshold, then hydrological drought is considered to be in progress. However, the number of days and the level of probability that must be exceeded to define a hydrological drought period is somewhat arbitrary. These criteria will vary between streams and river basins.

The impacts of hydrological drought in an

upstream portion of a river basin can also extend downstream as reduced streamflow may result in lower reservoir and groundwater levels at downstream locations, even though meteorological drought does not exist in this portion of the basin. Reductions in reservoir and groundwater levels in downstream portions of the basin may result in serious impacts on public water supplies, hydroelectric power production, recreation, transportation, agriculture, and other sectors. Conflicts between upstream and downstream water users may result, as has been the case in many river basins in the United States (see Opper 1994 for an example from the Missouri River Basin). International water disputes often arise in situations where rivers transcend national borders, such as in the Middle East or between the United States and Mexico.

The discussion up to this point has focused on the distinctions between the types of drought during its onset or development phase. During the termination phase of drought, the interrelationships between these drought types may differ. Figure 1.4 is also useful in understanding the termination phases of drought. During drought onset, agriculture is usually the first sector to experience drought because soil moisture will normally be the first component of the hydrological system to be affected. When the rains return, however, soil moisture levels may dramatically improve, and over a short time frame. Thus, agricultural drought, particularly on rain-fed cropland, may end abruptly. Depending on the timing of these rains, however, impacts may linger because potential crop yields may already have been reduced substantially. Hydrological drought may continue for many months or years, since recharge of reservoirs and groundwater is a long process. For example, following the series of severe drought years between 1987 and 1992 in the Missouri River basin, it was estimated that four to five years of normal precipitation over the basin would be required to bring reservoirs back to normal levels.

Finally, socioeconomic drought associates the supply and demand of some economic good or service with elements of meteorological, hydrological, and agricultural drought. Some scientists suggest that the time and space processes of supply and demand are the two basic processes that should be included in an objective definition of drought (Yevjevich 1967).

For example, the supply of some economic good (e.g., water, hay, hydroelectric power) is weather dependent. In most instances, the demand for that good is increasing as a result of increasing population and/or per capita consumption. Therefore, drought could be defined as occurring when the demand for that good exceeds supply as a result of a weather-related supply shortfall (Sandford 1979). This concept of drought supports the strong symbiosis that exists between drought and human activities. Thus, the incidence of drought could increase because of a change in the frequency of the physical event, a change in societal vulnerability to water shortages, or both. For example, poor land-use practices such as overgrazing can decrease animal carrying capacity and increase soil erosion, which exacerbates the impacts of and vulnerability to future droughts. This example is especially relevant in semiarid regions (e.g., South Africa, Australia) and in areas of hilly or sloping terrain (e.g., Lesotho).

DROUGHT CHARACTERISTICS AND SEVERITY

Droughts differ from one another in three essential characteristics: intensity, duration, and spatial coverage. Intensity refers to the degree of the precipitation shortfall and/or the severity of impacts associated with the shortfall. It is generally measured by the departure of some climatic index from normal and is closely linked to duration in the determination of impact. The simplest index in widespread use is the percentage of normal precipitation. With this index, actual precipitation is compared to normal or average precipitation for time periods ranging from one to twelve or more months. Actual precipitation departures are normally compared to expected or average amounts on a monthly, seasonal, annual, or water year (October–September) time period. One of the principal difficulties with this (or any) index is the choice of the threshold below which the deficiency of precipitation must fall (e.g., 75 per cent of normal) to define the onset of drought. Thresholds are usually chosen arbitrarily. In reality, they should be linked to impact. Many indices of drought are in widespread use today, such as the decile approach (Gibbs 1967, Lee 1979, Coughlan 1987) used in Australia, the

Palmer Drought Severity Index and Crop Moisture Index (Palmer 1965 and 1968, Alley 1984) in the United States, and the Yield Moisture Index (Jose *et al.* 1991) in the Philippines and elsewhere. A relatively new index that is gaining increasing popularity in the United States is the Standardized Precipitation Index (SPI), developed by McKee *et al.* (1993 and 1995). A discussion of climatic indices for monitoring drought is included in several chapters in this volume in Part III (Monitoring and early warning techniques). For a comparison of several popular meteorological indices, see Olidapo (1985).

Another distinguishing feature of drought is its duration. Droughts usually require a minimum of two to three months to become established but then can continue for months or years. The magnitude of drought impacts is closely related to the timing of the onset of the precipitation shortage, its intensity, and the duration of the event. The five-year (1979–83) drought in northeast Brazil is a good case in point. In this series of years, 1979 and 1980 were both drought years in the classic sense (i.e., a significant deficiency during the principal rainy season). In 1981, the seasonal rainfall totals were slightly above normal, but the temporal distribution resulted in agricultural drought. In 1982, the rainfall totals were below normal, but the temporal distribution of precipitation was conducive to crop development. Agricultural impacts were less adverse. These four 'drought' years were followed by the most severe drought year (1983) of the previous twenty-five years, with dramatic agricultural impacts (Magalhães *et al.* 1988).

Droughts also differ in terms of their spatial characteristics. The areas affected by severe drought evolve gradually, and regions of maximum intensity shift from season to season. In larger countries, such as Brazil, China, India, the United States, or Australia, drought would rarely, if ever, affect the entire country. During the severe drought of the 1930s in the United States, for example, the area affected by severe drought never exceeded 65 per cent of the country (see Figure 1.5). By contrast, drought affected more than 95 per cent of the Great Plains region in 1934. In India, the droughts of this century have rarely affected more than 50 per cent of the country. An exception occurred in 1918–19, when 73 per cent of the country was affected (Sinha

et al. 1987). On the other hand, it is indeed rare for drought *not* to exist in a portion of these countries in every year. For example, Figure 1.5 illustrates that in the United States, the percentage area affected by drought is often greater than 10 per cent. Thus, the governments of these larger countries are more accustomed to dealing with water shortages and have established an infrastructure to respond, albeit reactively. For smaller countries, it is more likely that the entire country may be affected since droughts are usually regional phenomena – they result from large scale anomalies in atmospheric circulation patterns that become established and persist for periods of months, seasons, or longer.

From a planning perspective, the spatial characteristics of drought have serious implications. Nations should know the probability that drought may simultaneously affect all or several major crop-producing regions within their borders and develop contingencies if such an event were to occur. Likewise, it is important for governments to know the chances of a regional drought simultaneously affecting agricultural productivity in their country as well as adjacent or nearby nations on whom they are dependent for food supplies. In some instances, a nation's primary drought mitigation strategy may be to import food from nearby nations, ignoring the likelihood that a drought may have significant regional impacts on food supplies. Likewise, the occurrence of drought worldwide or in the principal grain-exporting nations, such as occurred during the ENSO event of 1982–3 (Glantz *et al.* 1987, Glantz *et al.* 1991), may significantly alter a developing country's access to food from donor governments.

DROUGHT AND THE CYCLE OF DISASTER MANAGEMENT

Although drought is a natural hazard, the term drought management implies that human intervention can reduce vulnerability and impacts. To be successful in this endeavour, many disciplines must work together in tackling the complex issues associated with detecting, responding to, and preparing for the inevitability of future events. Disaster management, of which drought management is a subset, requires that scientists and policy makers focus on

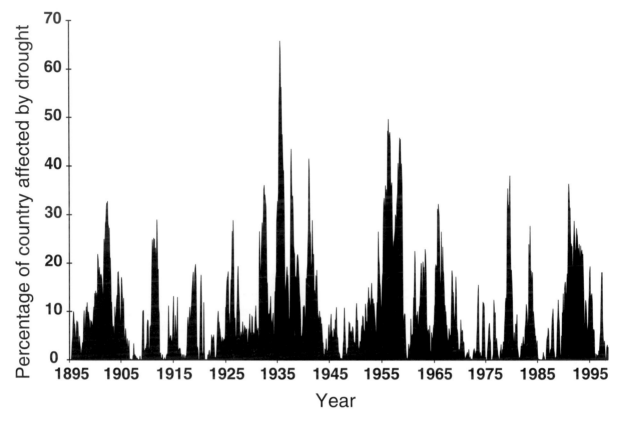

Figure 1.5 Percentage area of the United States (48 contiguous states) in severe and extreme drought (i.e., ≤ −3.0), according to the Palmer Drought Severity Index, during the period 1895–1995

both the protection and recovery/rehabilitation portion of the cycle shown in Figure 1.6. In the past, the emphasis in disaster management has been placed largely on the response and recovery portion of this cycle, which explains why society has generally moved from disaster to disaster with little or no attention to mitigation, preparedness, and prediction and monitoring. This approach is commonly referred to as crisis management. This volume attempts to integrate all components of disaster management.

The remainder of this book will be devoted to the presentation of case studies for many countries and regions. These case studies will focus on the causes of drought and prediction methods, alternative monitoring and impact assessment methodologies, responses, and mitigation and preparedness strategies and technologies. For this reason, it is imperative that key terms be defined at the outset so that the reader

understands each of the concepts highlighted by the disaster management cycle. Definitions of these and other these key terms and phrases are given below.

• *Hazard* is the potential for a major incident. To elaborate, the term refers to the probability of occurrence, within a specified period of time in a given area, of a potentially damaging natural phenomenon. Each hazard poses a level of risk that varies spatially and temporally and occurs with varying degrees of intensity and severity. Extreme natural events may affect different places singly or in combination at different times. Drought, from a meteorological perspective, is a natural event, and little can be done to reduce the frequency or severity of the event. A critical component of drought management is the characterisation of the risk (i.e., drought climatology) associated with the hazard. The chapters included in

Risk management

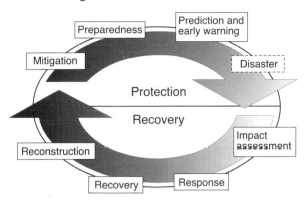

Crisis management

Figure 1.6 The cycle of disaster management

the monitoring and early warning section (Part III) of this volume discuss the historical frequency and severity of drought events and operational monitoring programmes to detect the onset or emergence of drought conditions.

• *Vulnerability* refers to the characteristics of a person or group in terms of their capacity to anticipate, cope with, resist, and recover from the impact of a natural hazard. It involves a combination of factors that determine the degree to which someone's life and livelihood is put at risk by a discrete and identifiable event in nature or in society. Vulnerability exists in a continuum from high to low and can be voluntary or involuntary. Vulnerability may exist because of high exposure to the hazard, sociocultural factors, or a combination of the two. This topic is treated in various ways by many authors in this volume. Chapter 45 by Tom Downing and Karen Bakker is a discussion of the complex issues associated with vulnerability.

• *Risk* is the product of hazard and vulnerability. Exposure to the natural event (i.e., hazard) is relatively constant, but vulnerability is dynamic in response to changes in societal characteristics, including technologies, policies, population changes resulting in changes in demand, changes in social behaviour, and so forth. Activities such as mitigation, preparedness, monitoring/early warning, and prediction are all directed at reducing the risk associated with future drought events either through a better understanding of the hazard or a reduction in vulnerability, or both.

• *Disaster* is the actual historical event. Disasters can be the result of natural or environmental causes and can be human-induced. Greater emphasis on prediction, monitoring, mitigation, and preparedness can greatly reduce the frequency and severity of natural disasters. Many of the case studies included in this volume provide documentation of previous drought-related disasters in developing and developed countries.

• *Impact assessment* refers to actions that allow for early estimates of the costs and losses associated with the occurrence of drought. Impacts are generally classified as economic, social, and environmental and are difficult to quantify because of their nonstructural nature. Methodologies or techniques for estimating impacts, and the reliability of those estimates, are highly variable from one natural hazard to another. Case studies of the impacts of drought events and methodologies for understanding and quantifying impacts are discussed in the section on impacts and assessment methodologies (Part IV).

• *Response* refers to post-impact interventions by government and others that are usually implemented during or following an emergency and directed at saving lives, minimising property damage, or improving or shortening the post-disaster recovery process. For drought, most response efforts are in the form of emergency assistance programmes or low-interest loans. Response to previous drought events is discussed in many of the case studies presented in this volume.

• *Recovery and rehabilitation* are actions or activities that restore critical life-support systems or return life to normal for persons in the affected area, such as transportation and communication services, emergency medical care, temporary housing, and water supplies. Many response, rehabilitation, and mitigation programmes are directed at reducing impacts and minimising recovery time.

• *Mitigation* is short- and long-term actions, programmes, or policies implemented during and in advance of drought that reduce the degree of risk to human life, property, and productive capacity. These actions are most effective if done in advance of the event. The types or forms of mitigation activities vary from one natural hazard to another. Drought-related mitigation actions are, for the most part, different from those used for other natural hazards because of the insidious nature of hazard. A first step in mitigation is the identification of the impacts associated with previous droughts and an assessment of whether these impacts (and others) are likely to be associated with future drought events. From this point, specific actions can be identified to reduce the impacts of future drought events. Part IV emphasises the range of impacts associated with drought in various geographical settings as well as methodologies to quantify these impacts. Part V considers adjustment and adaptation strategies employed to reduce impacts and Part VI concentrates on preparedness methodologies, institutional arrangements/capacities, mitigation programmes and actions, and policies that have been or could be employed to reduce the impacts of drought.

• *Preparedness* refers to predisaster activities designed to increase the level of readiness or improve operational and institutional capabilities for responding to an emergency (e.g., early warning systems, operational plans). For drought, contingency plans are useful for denoting programmatic responsibilities; improving information flow on severity, impacts, and policies between and within levels of government; and coordination between levels of government.

• *Prediction* refers to activities that provide users and decision/policy makers with advanced forecasts of the occurrence of drought. These forecasts can take many forms, but probability of occurrence (time, duration, and intensity or severity) is usually associated with the predictions. Forecast accuracy is highly variable between natural hazards and is particularly limited for droughts in most parts of the world. Lead time is an important consideration for drought forecasts as well, so decision makers are given ample opportunity to incorporate this information in planning strategies and the implementation of mitigation programmes. There is also an important distinction between forecasts of meteorological drought and those of hydrological drought, especially in regions where snowpack

is a critical element of the hydrological system. Information on the status of snowpack conditions can provide considerable advanced lead time for reliable forecasts of below-normal streamflow and reservoir levels.

• *Monitoring and early warning* refers to activities that provide information that can be used to alert decision makers at all levels of the onset of drought. This information can be used by planners, emergency managers, policy and decision makers, and others to implement programmes and policies that will help to reduce the risk associated with the hazard. Monitoring activities include the collection and analysis of data, data product development, and the communication of data products to decision makers and other users. Data includes not only physical data related to hazards but also social and biological data that assist in the definition of vulnerability. A comprehensive drought monitoring system would include the collection of climatological data (e.g., temperature and precipitation) as well as streamflow, reservoir and groundwater levels, soil moisture, snowpack, and remotely sensed data from satellites. This information is useful in forecasts of agricultural and hydrological drought. Monitoring and early warning techniques, including the use of indices to track current drought conditions and to view them in a historical context, is the subject of Part III.

SUMMARY

Drought is an insidious natural hazard that is a normal part of the climate of virtually all regions. It should not be viewed as merely a physical phenomenon. Rather, drought is the result of an interplay between a natural event and the demand placed on water supply by human-use systems. Drought should be considered relative to some long-term average condition of balance between precipitation and evapotranspiration.

Many definitions of drought exist; it is unrealistic to expect a universal definition to be derived. Drought can be grouped by type of disciplinary perspective as follows: meteorological, hydrological, agricultural, and socioeconomic. Each discipline incorporates different physical, biological, and/or socioeconomic factors in its definition. It must be accepted that the importance of drought lies in its impacts. Thus definitions should be impact or application specific and reflect unique regional climatic characteristics in order to be used in an operational mode by decision makers.

The three characteristics that differentiate one drought from another are intensity, duration, and spatial extent. Intensity refers to the degree of precipitation shortfall and/or the severity of impacts associated with the departure. Intensity is closely linked to the duration of the event. Droughts normally take two to three months to become established but may then persist for months or years, although the intensity and spatial character of the event will change from month to month or season to season.

The impacts of drought are diverse and generally classified as economic, social, and environmental. Impacts ripple through the economy and may linger for years after the termination of the drought episode. Impacts are often referred to as direct or indirect. Because of the large number of groups and economic sectors affected by drought, the nonstructural nature of its impacts, its spatial extent, and the difficulties in quantifying environmental damages and personal hardships, the precise calculation of the financial costs of drought is difficult. Drought years frequently occur in clusters, and thus the costs of drought are not evenly distributed between years. It appears that societal vulnerability to drought is escalating, and at a significant rate.

It is imperative that increased emphasis be placed on mitigation, preparedness, and prediction and early warning if society is to reduce the economic and environmental damages associated with drought and its personal hardships. This will require interdisciplinary cooperation and a collaborative effort with policy makers at all levels.

REFERENCES

Alley, W.M. (1984) 'The Palmer Drought Severity Index: Limitations and assumptions', *Journal of Climate and Applied Meteorology* 23, 1: 100–9.

Blaikie, P., Cannon, T., Davis, I., and Wisner, B. (1994) *At Risk: Natural Hazards, People's Vulnerability, and Disasters*, London: Routledge.

Boyd, J. (1996) 'Southwest farmers battle record drought', United Press International.

British Rainfall Organization (1936) *British Rainfall*, Air Ministry, Meteorological Office, London, cited in World Meteorological Organization (1975), 'Drought and agriculture', *WMO Technical Note* 138.

Bryant, E.A. (1991) *Natural Hazards*, Cambridge: Cambridge University Press.

Carolwicz, M. (1996) 'Natural hazards need not lead to natural disasters', *EOS* 77, 16: 149, 153.

Chenault, E.A. and Parsons, G. (1998) 'Drought worse than 96; cotton crop's one of worst ever', http://agnews.tamu.edu/stories/AGEC/Aug1998a.htm.

Coughlan, M.J. (1987) 'Monitoring drought in Australia', in D.A. Wilhite and W.E. Easterling (eds), *Planning for Drought: Toward a Reduction of Societal Vulnerability*, Boulder, CO: Westview Press, pp. 131–44.

Domeisen, N. (1995) 'Disasters: Threat to social development', *STOP Disasters: The IDNDR Magazine*, No. 23, Winter, Geneva, Switzerland: IDNDR Secretariat.

Dracup, J.A., Lee, K.S., and Paulson, E.G. Jr. (1980) 'On the definition of droughts', *Water Resources Research* 16, 2: 297–302.

FEMA (1995) *National Mitigation Strategy*, Washington, DC: Federal Emergency Management Agency.

Gibbs, W.J. and Maher, J.V. (1967) 'Rainfall deciles as drought indicators', *Bureau of Meteorology Bulletin No. 48*, Melbourne, Australia.

Glantz, M.H. and Katz, R.W. (1977) 'When is a drought a drought?', *Nature* 267: 192–3.

Glantz, M.H., Katz, R.W., and Krenz, M. (1987) *Climate Crisis: The Societal Impacts Associated with the 1982–83 Worldwide Climate Anomalies*, National Center for Atmospheric Research, Boulder, CO: U.N. Environment Program.

Glantz, M.H., Katz, R.W., and Nicholls, N. (1991) *Teleconnections Linking Worldwide Climate Anomalies*, Cambridge: Cambridge University Press.

Hagman, G. (1984) *Prevention Better than Cure: Report on Human and Natural Disasters in the Third World*, Stockholm: Swedish Red Cross.

Jose, A.M., Magnayon, F.O., and Hilario, F.D. (1991) 'Climate impact assessment for agriculture in the Philippines', unpublished paper, National Workshop on Drought Planning and Management in the Philippines, Quezon City.

Klemeš, V. (1987) 'Drought prediction: A hydrological perspective', in D.A. Wilhite and W.E. Easterling (eds), *Planning for Drought: Toward a Reduction of Societal Vulnerability*, Boulder, CO: Westview Press, pp. 81–94.

Lee, D.M. (1979) 'Australian drought watch system', in M.T. Hinchey (ed.), *Botswana Drought Symposium*, pp. 173–87, Gaborone, Botswana: Botswana Society.

McKee, T.B., Doesken, N.J., and Kleist, J. (1993) 'The relationship of drought frequency and duration to time scales', *Eighth Conference on Applied Climatology*, Boston, MA: American Meteorological Society.

—— (1995) 'Drought monitoring with multiple time scales', *Ninth Conference on Applied Climatology*, Boston, MA: American Meteorological Society.

Magalhães, A.R., Filho, H.C., Garagorry, F.L., Gasques, J.G., Molion, L.C.B., Neto, M. da S.A., Nobre, C.A., Porto, E.R., and Rebouças, O.E. (1988) 'The effects of climatic variations on agriculture in Northeast Brazil', in M.L. Parry, T.R. Carter, and N.T. Konijn (eds), *The Impact of Climatic Variations on Agriculture*, Vol. 2, *Assessments in Semi-Arid Regions*, pp. 273–380, Boston, MA: Kluwer Academic Publishers.

Office of Foreign Disaster Assistance (1990) *Annual Report*, Washington, DC: Office of Foreign Disaster Assistance.

Olidapo, E.O. (1985) 'A comparative performance analysis of three meteorological drought indices', *Journal of Climatology* 5: 655–64.

Opper, R.H. (1994) 'Drought management in the Missouri River Basin', in D. Wilhite and D. Wood (eds), *Drought Management in a Changing West: New Directions for Water Policy*, Lincoln, NE: International Drought Information Center, University of Nebraska, pp. 67–72.

Palmer, W.C. (1965) 'Meteorological drought', *Research Paper* No. 45, Washington, DC: US Weather Bureau.

—— (1968) 'Keeping track of crop moisture conditions, nationwide: The new crop moisture index', *Weatherwise* 21, 4: 156–61.

Riebsame, W.E., Changnon, S.A. Jr., and Karl, T.R. (1991) *Drought and Natural Resources Management in the United States: Impacts and Implications of the 1987–9 Drought*, Boulder, CO: Westview Press.

SADCC (1992) *Food Security Bulletin*, Gaborone, Botswana: SADC.

Sandford, S. (1979) 'Towards a definition of drought', in M.T. Hinchey (ed.), *Botswana Drought Symposium*, Gaborone, Botswana: Botswana Society.

Schneider, S.H. (ed.) (1996) *Encyclopaedia of Climate and Weather*, New York: Oxford University Press.

Sinha, S.K., Kailasanathan, K., and Vasistha, A.K. (1987) 'Drought management in India: Steps toward eliminating famines', in D. A. Wilhite and W. E. Easterling (eds), *Planning for Drought: Toward a Reduction of Societal Vulnerability*, Boulder, CO: Westview Press, pp. 453–70.

Subrahmanyam, V.P. (1967) *Incidence and Spread of Continental Drought*, WMO/IHD Report No. 2, Geneva, Switzerland: WMO.

Tannehill, I.R. (1947) *Drought: Its Causes and Effects*, Princeton, NJ: Princeton University Press.

Thurman, J.N. (1998) 'Oklahoma in grip of new Dust Bowl', *Christian Science Monitor*, 24 August, http://www.csmonitor.com/durable/1998/08/24/pls3.htm.

Whipple, W. Jr. (1966) 'Regional drought frequency analysis', *Proceedings of the American Society of Civil Engineers* 92 (IR2): 11–31.

White, G.F. and Haas, J.E. (1975) *Assessment of Research on Natural Hazards*, Cambridge, MA: The MIT Press.

Wilhite, D.A. (1992) 'Drought', *Encyclopaedia of Earth System Science*, Vol. 2, pp. 81–92, San Diego, CA: Academic Press.

Wilhite, D.A. and Glantz, M.H. (1985) 'Understanding the drought phenomenon: The role of definitions', *Water International* 10: 111–20.

Wilhite, D.A., Rosenberg, N.J., and Glantz, M.H. (1986) 'Improving federal response to drought', *Journal of Climate and Applied Meteorology* 25: 332–42.

World Meteorological Organization (1975) 'Drought and agriculture', *WMO Technical Note* No. 138, Report of the CAgM Working Group on the Assessment of Drought, Geneva, Switzerland: WMO.

Yevjevich, V. (1967) 'An objective approach to definitions and investigations of continental hydrologic droughts', *Hydrology Papers* No. 23, Fort Collins, CO: Colorado State University.

PART II

CAUSES AND PREDICTABILITY

2

PROSPECTS FOR THE PREDICTION OF METEOROLOGICAL DROUGHT

C.F. Ropelewski and C.K. Folland

WHAT IS METEOROLOGICAL DROUGHT?

A comprehensive and widely accepted definition of drought has eluded several generations of meteorologists and hydrologists. Because drought is an applied concept, so its definition varies with its particular impact on society or the environment being evaluated. The most prominent types of drought are meteorological, hydrological, and agricultural drought (e.g., AMS 1997, Meteorological Office 1991, Wilhite and Glantz 1987). Meteorological drought essentially relates to a state of dryness due to a deficiency of rainfall while hydrological drought relates to periods of low river flow or groundwater levels, often caused by a lack of winter rainfall in middle latitudes. Agricultural drought relates to aspects of dryness that affect agricultural crops or forests, particularly the drying of soils. Examples of the integrated near-real time monitoring of both agricultural and meteorological drought are the soil moisture deficit and rainfall calculations for the United Kingdom done routinely from daily synoptic reports by the UK Meteorological Office Evaporation Calculation System (Hough *et al.* 1996). Other examples are the routine computation of the Palmer Drought Index and soil wetness for climate divisions in the United States (Weekly Weather and Crop Bulletin 1997).

A key aspect of all definitions is that drought is characterised by a deviation below normal rainfall conditions for some period of time. Thus drought in a desert where almost no rain normally falls has no meaning. Kogan (1997) brings out the importance of the antecedent precipitation to some drought impacts

as shown by satellite monitoring. For example, he shows that a wet period immediately before severe drought in the growing season may substantially mitigate the observed stress on vegetation. Thus, agricultural drought does not depend solely on the concurrent rainfall deficiency.

The expected average rainfall, and its deviations from the average, before a drought is likely to be experienced varies widely from place to place. A comprehensive analysis of the expectations of given levels of rainfall deficiency from the varying local average is an essential part of the information required for drought assessment. Tabony (1977) provides such an analysis for all parts of the United Kingdom on time scales from one month to five years. From such information, the return period of a rainfall deficiency (or excess) can be assessed at any point or over local areas. Practical definitions of the threshold of drought also depend greatly on typical uses of water resources. A combination of widely varying patterns of expected rainfall and varying use of water resources compared to the availability of water leads to differing perceptions of the threshold for drought. For instance, a month with little rainfall over southeast England in summer (modest water resources, high rate of water use) may cause some alarm with respect to drought conditions, especially if preceding months were fairly dry. However, a similar period over Southern California during summer or in the western Sahel in winter would be well within the statistical envelope of normal conditions and have no practical impact. For all types of drought, both its intensity and the time for which it persists are crucial to impacts (e.g., Gregory 1986). Drought definitions are discussed further in Chapter 1. This chapter is concerned with understanding and predicting meteorological drought. We are concerned in principle with understanding and predicting deficiencies in rainfall from the normal expectation for periods that last from several weeks to decades, though we emphasise durations from one season (three months) to a few seasons, as these have shown the most potential for prediction so far.

The desire to understand and predict the complex temporal behaviour of rainfall has been a motivating force in climate prediction since early recorded history. One of the earliest known references to a raingauge was made in administrative chronicles in India written more than two thousand years ago (Kautilya c. 300 BC). Raingauges were needed because it had been decided to tax agricultural land according to the rainfall received each year. It appears that, during those times, the calamity of drought had the silver lining of a lower tax burden! Sadly, no actual precipitation measurements appear to survive. Records were also taken in Palestine in the first century AD, and later in China in the thirteenth century and in Korea in the fifteenth. The first surviving series of regular rainfall measurements was made by Richard Towneley from 1677 to 1704 near Burnley, Lancashire, northwest England (Towneley 1694, Folland and Wales-Smith 1977). Towneley compared his measurements with those made by a contemporary rainfall observer in Paris, Pierre Perrault (one of the founding fathers of hydrology). Towneley ascribed the generally greater rainfall amounts he measured compared to those measured in Paris (true today) to the effects of the surrounding Pennine Hills. His mechanism was vague, but Towneley appeared to implicitly recognise an orographic enhancement factor in the excess rain, and his work is an early attempt at understanding the causes of rainfall variations. Thus the spatial complexity of rainfall and drought were recognised early on. Biswas (1970) gives further details of early rainfall measurements and why they were made.

The difficult task of understanding the distribution of rainfall and, more recently, understanding and predicting year-to-year variability of precipitation about the mean annual cycle is a problem that continues to challenge and intrigue climate scientists. In this chapter we discuss some of the evidence that major

progress with parts of the epic problem of drought prediction may finally be within our grasp.

A discussion of drought soon turns to the character of precipitation time series. Examination of any long time series reveals a complex and rich mix of variability on all time scales (Figure 2.1). Some have argued (e.g., Mandelbrot and Wallis 1968) that many of the components of the hydrological cycle are self-similar – i.e., that they are fractal and chaotic, and thus may have a large unpredictable component. Key characteristics of many rainfall time series are (1) occurrences of very large extremes, of either sign, in rainfall anomaly and (2) periods of extremes that can sometimes be extremely long and thus establish a new 'climate'. These aspects of historical seasonal rainfall have been dubbed the 'Noah' and 'Joseph' effects, respectively, by Mandelbrot and Wallis.

In principle, meteorological drought is related to the occurrence of rainfall amounts below some relevant threshold value for some period of time. So it is pertinent to ask whether the observed occurrence of such thresholds follows that expected from a random series. A simple measure of the 'Joseph' effect relative to a random expectation is Sherman's $\acute{\omega}$ statistic (Sherman 1950, Craddock 1968: 170):

$$\acute{\omega} = \frac{1}{2D} \sum_{j=1}^{n+1} \left| d_j - d_{j-1} - \frac{D}{n+1} \right| \qquad 0 \le \acute{\omega} \le 1 \quad (1)$$

where $d_1, d_2, \ldots d_n$ are the dates of events drier or wetter than some threshold. D is the total length of the data. The n events $d_1, d_2, \ldots d_n$ divide the data into $n + 1$ intervals, counted from the first observation to the last. If events occur at the beginning or end values of the data, slight modifications to equation 1 are needed. Thus $\acute{\omega}$ is linearly related to the average of the absolute magnitudes of differences in time between successive events relative to the mean length of the intervals. The value of $\acute{\omega}$ varies according to whether the differences in time between successive events are more regular, or less regular, than expected from a random series. For a random series, Craddock (1968) shows that the expected value of $\acute{\omega}$ is about 0.37 for $n \ge 20$. Significantly larger values of $\acute{\omega}$ than 0.37 ($\acute{\omega} = 0.42$ is the 95 per cent confidence value for $n = 40$) indicate that some time intervals

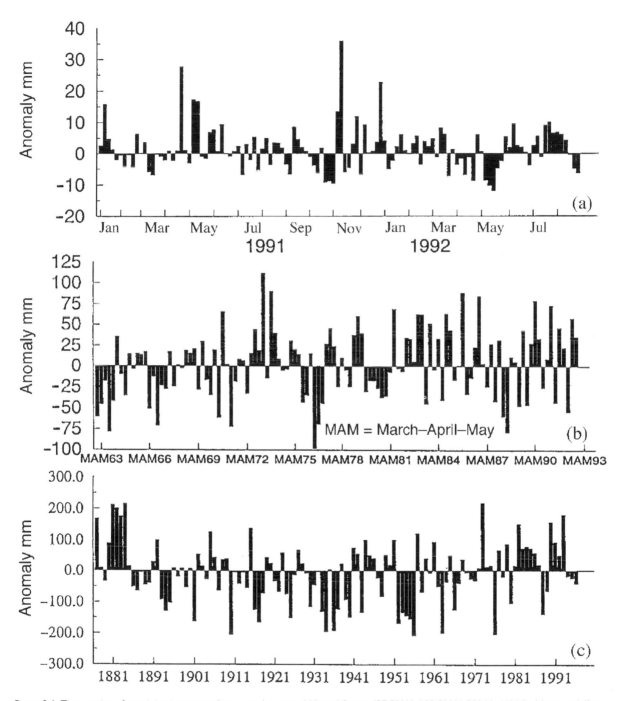

Figure 2.1 Time series of precipitation anomalies over the central United States (87.5° W–102.5° W, 32° N–46° N): (a) pentad (five-day) rainfall anomaly, January 1991 to July 1992; (b) seasonal rainfall anomaly for winter 1962–3 (December 1962–February 1963) to fall 1992 (September–November); (c) annual rainfall anomaly from 1877 to 1996

between threshold events are too short and others too long for all dates of these events to be equally likely. This indicates a tendency to periods of 'different climate'. A value of $\hat{\omega}$ significantly smaller than 0.37 (5 per cent confidence value for $n = 40$ is 0.30) implies that the dates of the events are too regularly spaced for all dates to be equally likely. This value will usually reflect short-lived (relative to the series length) quasi-periodic or chaotic variations and should be the more usual deviation from randomness.

We examined 1,095 values of pentad data (five-day precipitation amounts) for the period 1981–95 taken from a time series for the central United States (Figure 2.1a). These data give $\hat{\omega} = 0.39$ for a threshold of -1σ (one standard deviation below normal), but 0.30 for a more extreme threshold of -1.5σ. Thus by this measure, extremely dry pentads in the central United States do show a tendency to regular spacing, indicating some quasi-periodic behaviour. For much longer unit time scales than pentads, data series are often not long enough to assess this behaviour with confidence. Thus annual rainfall, for events corresponding to smaller negative standard deviation thresholds, gives a value of $\hat{\omega}$ less than the random value, but not significantly so. Values of $\hat{\omega}$ less than the random value, although not always individually statistically significant at the 95 per cent confidence level, were obtained for annual England and Wales rainfall (1766–1996), northwest Indian rainfall for June–September 1871–1994 (Parthasarathy *et al.* 1995), and the December–February North Atlantic Oscillation pressure index (1867–1997), which strongly influences winter rainfall over much of Europe (Figure 3.18 of Nicholls *et al.* 1996a). Taking these results together, the Sherman statistic agrees with our intuitive assessment that significant dry periods are not usually randomly distributed through the time series, although deviations from randomness are often not great.

Annual Sahel rainfall behaves differently. For a threshold of -0.75σ calculated for 1906–95, $\hat{\omega} = 0.51$, giving a highly significantly 'Joseph' effect in the direction of *extended* periods of different susceptibility to drought or to 'different climates'. During the late 1960s and early 1970s, western Africa also experienced individual years of severe drought with magnitudes unprecedented in modern times

(Noah effect) (Figure 2.2, top). Precipitation deficits continued throughout the remainder of the 1970s and 1980s and well into the 1990s (Joseph effect), providing a 'new climate' for the western Sahel (Figure 2.2, bottom). Further discussion of the Sherman $\hat{\omega}$ statistic is given in Folland and Ropelewski (1998).

From the standpoint of those who have been farming and grazing livestock on the African soil for the past twenty years, the question has been not so much 'When will the abundant rains of the 1950s return?' but rather 'How much more, or less, rain will fall this rainy season than last?' Thus the practical definition of drought becomes mixed with sociological issues, and the interannual time scale is especially important. We emphasise the interannual time scale of drought in this chapter, although future anthropogenic climate change may increase the size of changes or variations in rainfall on longer time scales. Thus we might see a widespread tendency to larger values of $\hat{\omega}$ for rainfall series in the next century.

So far, we have discussed departures from the mean precipitation. However, to maximise potential benefits of the skill contained in newly developing precipitation prediction methods, we need to consider their ability to predict seasonal time scale shifts in the probability distribution of precipitation rather than just specific values. This theme will be developed below.

WHAT IS THE EVIDENCE FOR PREDICTABILITY OF DROUGHT?

Understanding and predicting regional interannual climate variations about the mean annual cycle remain among climatology's most challenging problems. Only modest progress with the prediction of seasonal rainfall, and thus meteorological drought, was made until the mid-1980s. Since then the pace of advance has quickened.

The roots of current optimism for improved climate prediction can be traced to the discovery of large-scale atmospheric teleconnection patterns by Sir Gilbert Walker (1868–1958) and his collaborators in the early decades of the twentieth century. An excellent discussion of this work is given in Allan *et al.* 1996. A teleconnection pattern consists of a map

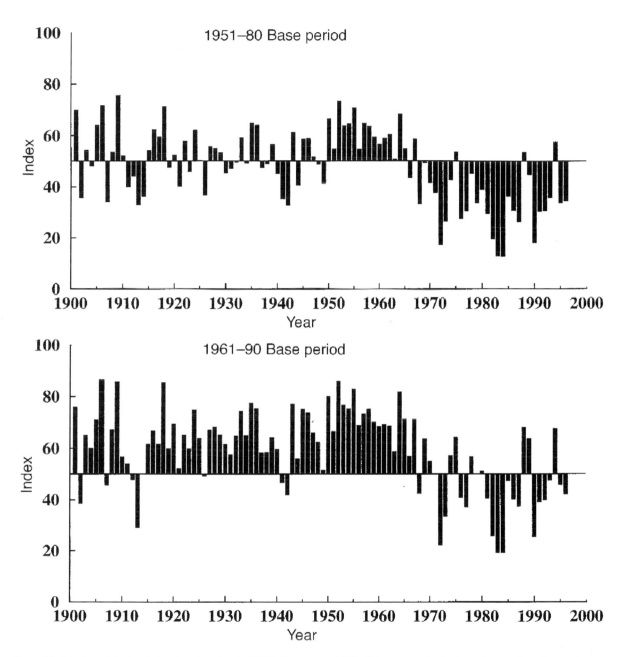

Figure 2.2 Sahel precipitation index, based on Lamb (1982). Top: using a 1951–80 base period, which emphasises drought conditions starting in the late 1960s. Bottom: using a 1961–90 base period, which emphasises earlier wet conditions and recent large interannual variability about a drier climate

of the correlation coefficients between a variable measured at numerous points over a very wide area with a local key variable. Both variables can be of the same or different types. Thus we can correlate rainfall at a specific location (or averaged over a small region) with surface pressure values distributed over much of the globe. If the correlation map shows coherent patterns, which may consist of both positive and negative correlations, these 'teleconnection patterns' are taken to imply a physical link between the local key variable and the widely distributed one (e.g., see Glantz *et al.* 1991). Walker produced teleconnection maps of precipitation, temperature, and surface pressure and was able to identify the largest scale modes of interannual climate variability that we recognise today, including the Southern Oscillation and the North Atlantic Oscillation.

In addition to being a first-rate scientist, Walker was able to carry out his work because of a confluence of fortunate circumstances. First, shortly beforehand, the art of statistics had developed rapidly as a mathematical tool of the observational sciences. Walker was also a very able mathematician who understood statistics (Walker 1997). Having taken the job of head of the Indian Meteorological Department in 1903, he gained the opportunity to carry out his studies, which required a large staff capable of performing manual mathematical operations on extensive data sets. So Walker was able to make a major effort to solve the very practical problem of predicting Indian monsoon rainfall, an activity that had started in the 1870s. Another key factor was that it had just become possible by the early years of the twentieth century to gather sufficient near-global data to describe and analyse large-scale climate variations.

The studies by Walker and others (e.g., Walker 1923 and 1924, Walker and Bliss 1932) showed that relationships existed between large-scale (i.e., near-global) surface pressure patterns and regional rainfall patterns – in particular, the Indian summer monsoon rainfall. Walker's research provided the first observational evidence for the existence of an organised global-scale pattern of interannual climate variability. He called this the Southern Oscillation. Initially his work did not have the impact that might have been expected because, for reasons that remain unclear, the correlations between the pressure patterns and monsoon precipitation weakened about the time they were discovered. The correlations strengthened again at the middle of the twentieth century, but by that time most of the early work had been forgotten.

A crucial part of the picture that remained to be filled in was a physical explanation for the observed teleconnection patterns. A review of knowledge about the Southern Oscillation just as a physical explanation

was on the point of emerging is contained in Lamb (1972). Following some inconclusive work by others (e.g., by Berlage and DeBoer 1960), Professor Jacob Bjerknes at the University of California at Los Angeles made the key step forward by demonstrating that the atmospheric teleconnection patterns were part of a coupled mode of interaction between the equatorial Pacific Ocean and the global atmosphere (Bjerknes 1966, 1969, and 1972). It is now clear that other parts of the global ocean also participate in the Southern Oscillation, manifested through changes in sea surface temperature and the overlying atmospheric circulation.

By the late 1970s and early 1980s, climate scientists were able to document the relationships hypothesised by Bjerknes in more detail (e.g., Rasmusson and Carpenter 1982, who discussed the Southern Oscillation/El Niño as a coupled system). The coupled ocean–atmosphere variation centred on the equatorial Pacific is now commonly referred to as ENSO (El Niño/Southern Oscillation), a phrase coined in planning documents for the international Tropical Ocean Global Atmosphere (TOGA) experiment. During the 1980s and 1990s a series of empirical, modelling, and theoretical studies increased our understanding of the physical mechanisms associated with ENSO. A detailed discussion of recent advances in understanding teleconnection patterns in the TOGA era (1985–94) can be found in Trenberth *et al.* 1998 and Allan *et al.* 1996.

The identification of some of the physical mechanisms associated with ENSO has greatly revitalised interest in Walker's precipitation teleconnection patterns. A series of studies with more complete data sets (e.g., Kiladis and Diaz 1989; Ropelewski and Halpert 1986, 1987, and 1992) reconfirmed several of the teleconnections suggested by Walker and others, and identified additional teleconnections. Ropelewski and Halpert (1987 and 1989) attempted to improve the usefulness of teleconnection patterns for seasonal climate prediction by documenting regions of the globe that, in addition to merely showing statistical ENSO-precipitation links, also had relationships with ENSO that were highly consistent from episode to episode. They particularly identified the seasons and regions of the globe where precipitation was associated with ENSO in at least 75 per cent of the more marked ENSO warm and cold episodes. The quasi-global scale sea surface temperature (SST) patterns associated with ENSO that influence these rainfall patterns appear consistently in many recent studies – e.g., Hsiung and Newell 1983 for recent decades, Parker and Folland 1991 since the late nineteenth century.

Identification of these consistent ENSO-precipitation relationships provides the clearest indication that seasonal meteorological drought in quite extensive areas of the globe may be predictable with useful skill (i.e, in the historical record, ENSO-related dry conditions occur at least 75 per cent of the time in these areas). Figure 2.3 shows those regions, and the appropriate seasons, where precipitation deficits are strongly associated with the warm or cold phase of ENSO – i.e., warm or cold sea surface temperatures in the tropical east Pacific. Although drought may not occur consistently with every warm or cold ENSO episode as appropriate, these regions do have a clearly identified increased probability of drier than-normal seasonal conditions. The link with ENSO can be formalised by calculating precipitation probability distributions conditional on the state of ENSO. Thus precipitation predictions can be based purely on historically observed shifts in the probability distri-

bution of rainfall as a function of ENSO state (e.g., Ropelewski and Halpert 1995). Because the early stages of ENSO can often be identified a season or more before typical ENSO-related droughts commence, recognition of the early stages of a developing ENSO episode has important predictive value.

However, one of the main limitations of ENSO-based seasonal prediction schemes is that, according to the historical record, ENSO is active in its warm or cold phases only about half the time. Since 1900, there have been thirty warm and nineteen cold episode years, according to the Southern Oscillation Index-based criterion of Ropelewski and Jones (1987). The close relationship between the Southern Oscillation Index (SOI) and central equatorial Pacific sea surface temperature anomaly during most of the twentieth century is illustrated in Figure 2.4. If precipitation were skilfully predictable during all such ENSO episodes, but not otherwise, drought prediction would only be possible about half the time. However, crops must be planted and water resources managed every year. As is discussed below, however, ENSO is not the only factor influencing many drought-prone regions. The relatively recent gains in understanding of climate as a coupled ocean–atmosphere system through ENSO studies has led to

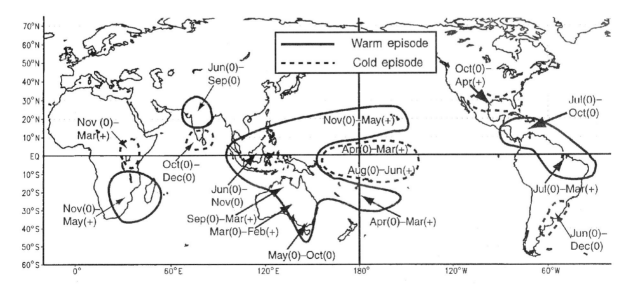

Figure 2.3 Schematic of areas showing consistent occurrence (75 per cent or more) of dry conditions in association with ENSO (El Niño/Southern Oscillation) warm (solid lines) or cold (dashed lines) phases, after Ropelewski and Halpert 1987 and 1989

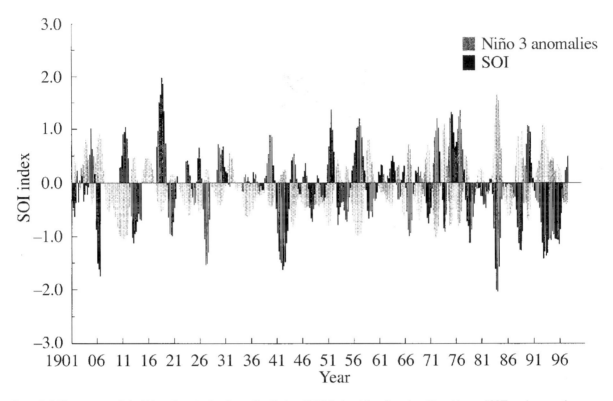

Figure 2.4 Time series of the Tahiti–Darwin Southern Oscillation (SOI) index (after Ropelewski and Jones 1987) and sea surface temperature anomalies for the NIÑO 3 area (150° W–90° W, 5° N–5° S, for the period 1900–7). The SOI is a five-month running mean and is expressed as standardised values computed with respect to the 1951–80 period. Seasonal values of the SOI larger in magnitude than +/–0.5 units are associated with warm or cold ENSO episodes

a broader appreciation of the earth's surface boundary conditions on climate variability. Thus we are hopeful that, as understanding of the ocean (and land surface) boundary influences on climate variability grows, prospects for skilful seasonal rainfall prediction may be greater than for prediction based on ENSO alone.

Although the main focus of this chapter is on seasonal meteorological drought and precipitation, there is evidence linking global ocean SST patterns to regional precipitation variability on decadal scales. This was first pointed out for the sub-Saharan region by Folland *et al.* (1986) and more recently by Ward *et al.* (1993) and Ward (1997). Remarkably strong quasi-bi-decadal variations in southern African rainfall have been known for quite a long time (e.g., Tyson *et al.* 1975). Recently these decadal-scale rainfall variations have been strongly related to a set of global and regional SST patterns (Folland *et al.* 1998). We

return to the decadal time scale in our last section, but already these studies suggest that an ability to separate decadal-scale from interannual variability, where the former is strong, is likely to enhance our skill on interannual scales. Forecast skill on decadal time scales would depend on an ability to skilfully predict patterns of SST on these time scales.

WHAT ARE THE MAIN DROUGHT PREDICTION TOOLS?

Traditionally, operational monthly and seasonal climate prediction has been based on empirically derived statistical relationships (e.g., Gilman 1985, Folland *et al.* 1986, van den Dool 1994, Barnston *et al.* 1994, Krishna Kumar *et al.* 1995). Many examples of current empirical climate prediction techniques appear in the NOAA *Experimental Long-Lead Bulletin* (Climate Prediction Center 1992–7). The statistical techniques draw on many aspects of recorded past variability in the climate system, not just those associated with ENSO. In addition to simple linear correlation and multiple linear regression-based forecasts, a number of other statistical tools are in operational use. These tools include analogs and antianalogs (Livezey and Barnston 1988), Optimal Climate Normals (OCN) (Huang *et al.* 1994), Canonical Correlation Analysis (CCA) (Barnett and Preisendorfer 1987), and eigenvector analysis and linear discriminant analysis (Maryon and Storey 1985, Ward and Folland 1991). More complex methods based on neural networks have also recently been developed (e.g., Long *et al.* 1997). In general, the skill scores of operational precipitation forecasts using these tools has been marginal in the extratropics but much more skilful in parts of the tropics (e.g., Ward *et al.* 1993). In the extratropics, statistical methods offer little encouragement for more reliable drought predictions except when used in conjunction with the current state of ENSO or with ENSO forecasts (e.g., Barnston and Smith 1996). We now focus on statistical drought prediction that relates to ENSO, and the prediction of central and eastern Pacific SST in particular.

Statistical forecasts of sea surface temperature

A number of statistical forecasting methods have shown demonstrable skill in predicting SST for one or more of the equatorial Pacific SST index areas commonly used for monitoring ENSO activity. For example, the CCA method usually gives one- and two-season forecasts with anomaly correlations between observed and forecast standardised SST > 0.7 for much of the year, with higher correlations in northern winter (Barnston and Ropelewski 1992). Similar levels of skill have been obtained by other statistical methods – e.g., linear inverse modelling (Penland and Magorian 1993). Many of the statistical predictions appear regularly in the *Experimental Long-Lead Forecast Bulletin* (Climate Prediction Center 1997). A characteristic of most statistical techniques is that the cross-validated skill scores have a large annual cycle. (Cross validation is a method of estimating forecast skill with minimum statistical bias.) One characteristic of the annual cycle of fore-

cast skill is that the statistical techniques generally perform poorly in northern spring, with cross-validated anomaly correlations < 0.6 for forecasts even just one season ahead and < 0.3 for forecasts two seasons ahead. Simple persistence of the SSTs, or their damped persistence (a combination of persistence and climatology), show just as much, or more, skill at this time of the year.

Even if the statistically based SST forecasts were perfect, however, the historical record shows less-than-perfect relationships between SST anomalies and precipitation even for regions with a strong ENSO influence. In such regions, precipitation anomalies typically show a consistent ENSO relationship in 75–80 per cent of the ENSO episodes this century. However, even the best performing statistical SST prediction schemes have cross-validated correlations between observed and predicted tropical eastern Pacific SST of 0.8–0.9 for two seasons ahead in the northern summer through fall. Thus if the anomaly correlation of the given regional precipitation with the observed SST is 0.8 in strong ENSO years, we might reasonably expect to make predictions of precipitation with anomaly correlations of 0.6–0.7 during such years – i.e., in about half of all years. The average correlation over *all* years will be substantially less; this is consistent with experience (Barnston and Smith 1996). At this relatively low level of overall skill, precipitation forecasts are best couched in terms of probabilities.

Numerical model-based sea surface temperature forecasts

The 1980s witnessed the development of ocean basin-scale numerical models that are coupled to the atmosphere through the surface wind stress (e.g., Philander and Seigel 1985). Soon ocean modellers began to produce experimental coupled ocean–atmosphere model-based forecasts of SST (e.g., Cane *et al.* 1986, Zebiak and Cane 1987). These fairly simple coupled 'anomaly' models were soon followed by more sophisticated models (e.g., Barnett *et al.* 1993; for a review, see Latif *et al.* 1994). All these models predicted the SST anomaly and do not contain full information about the annual cycle in the atmosphere or for SST. Many studies attempted to affect more realistic modelling of ocean–atmosphere interactions by inserting these SST anomaly predictions into global atmospheric circulation models to give a direct forecast of the precipitation (e.g., Ji *et al.* 1994).

Although these developments have resulted in improvements in the skill of predicting ENSO-related SSTs, their greatest contribution has been in diagnosing the coupled ocean–atmosphere system. However, some research has indicated the potential for applications of ENSO SST predictions – e.g., the Cane and Zebiak ENSO SST predictions have been used as the basis for statistical forecasts of maize yield in Zimbabwe (Cane *et al.* 1994). However, it seems that further significant progress requires the inclusion of the mean annual cycle in the models. Inclusion of the annual cycle (i.e., coupling between the full oceanic and atmospheric fields instead of their anomalies) has turned out be exceedingly difficult since the oceanic and atmospheric components of these models tend to have slightly incompatible 'climatologies' and, further, these model 'climatologies' tend to be biased with respect to observations. Even small differences in these 'climate states' tend to create significant imbalances in heat, moisture, and momentum at the sea surface. The flux imbalances must be adjusted in some *ad hoc* manner that may not faithfully account for the real physical interactions at the ocean–atmosphere interface. These nonphysical flux corrections presumably degrade the forecasts. Nonetheless, a key reason for believing that forecasts of the absolute SST are needed is that the main link between tropical SSTs and the atmosphere (local and remote) occurs through overlying deep tropical convection. The geographical position of the deep convection in the tropics is known to be strongly influenced by the areas where the absolute SST exceeds about 28°C (Gadgil 1984).

Because the fully global ocean–atmosphere coupling problem has not yet been solved adequately, other methods are currently used to provide practical seasonal predictions at leading forecast centres. In lieu of running a fully coupled model, operational centres such as the National Centres for Environmental Prediction (NCEP) in the National Weather Service/NOAA run models in a 'sequence'. In this scheme, the observed wind stress drives an ocean model to a new equilibrium (e.g., Figure 2.5). This new ocean state in turn drives a global atmospheric circulation model until it reaches a (near) equilibrium. Wind stress fields are taken from this model output to drive the ocean model again and so on (Ji *et al.* 1994). This is a form of coupled modelling where the atmosphere and ocean are handled as separate components of the climate system. The atmospheric model can be a state-of-the-art global climate model that has the advantage of automatically predicting worldwide precipitation and other elements. Alternatively, it may just be a statistical model (e.g., Barnett *et al.* 1993).

For further information, the reader is directed to three useful reviews of seasonal forecasting: Palmer and Anderson (1994), Davey (1996), and Carson (1998).

WHAT ARE THE PROSPECTS FOR BETTER DROUGHT PREDICTION?

The current state of drought forecasting science suggests strongly that some of the ENSO-based seasonal prediction methods, and methods based on other SST anomaly patterns, can be used for skilful seasonal rainfall prediction and thus for drought prediction. However, significant efforts are required to provide skilful drought predictions in a form that users can readily apply. International efforts are now commencing through the World Meteorological Organization's Climate Information and Prediction Program (CLIPS) and the newly formed International Research Institute (IRI) for Climate Prediction to provide a better feedback between seasonal forecast developers and the user (Carson 1998). Many applications, or potential applications, are discussed in the following chapters of this book. We note here some of the issues in a drought forecasting context.

Most ENSO–precipitation relationships have been defined for broad regions, averaged over several months of the year. Although such information is useful for providing the global precipitation patterns associated with ENSO, it often lacks the required detail for practical application of this information. A multifaceted approach is needed, including more detailed empirical studies, the use of model output

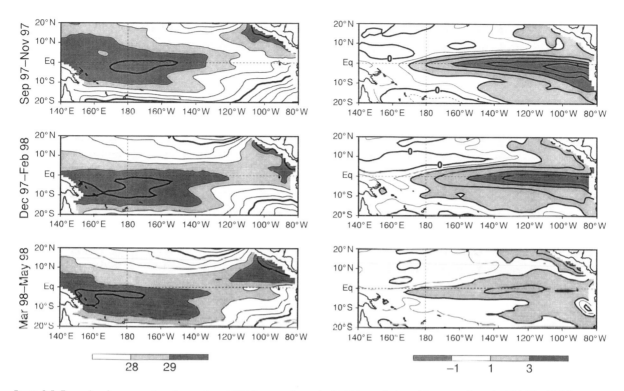

Figure 2.5 Example of an operationally produced SST forecast from the NCEP coupled model system, Ji *et al.* 1994. The SST forecast anomaly pattern is used to force an atmospheric general circulation model. The full seasonal SST fields are shown in the left-hand column and the anomalies are on the right

statistics (MOS) or other statistical adjustments to numerical model forecasts, and investigations of other sources of predictability. These are discussed below.

It cannot be emphasised too strongly that a key requirement for improved seasonal climate predictions is the availability of adequate observed data to monitor current climate and provide the initial conditions for dynamical and statistical forecasting methods (e.g., the Tropical Atmosphere Ocean [TAO] array of moored buoys across the equatorial Pacific). Equally important is the availability of adequate historical data to provide a better understanding of the mechanisms of previous drought episodes and to calibrate the statistical forecasting methods, which will remain essential at least for the near future. Historical data used in conjunction with real time climate monitoring can also provide very useful probability forecasts. For instance, the historically derived shifts in the probability distributions in seasonal rainfall amounts with the state of ENSO can provide a simple conditional probability forecast for many regions of the world (e.g., Figure 2.6). Given an adequately rich data set, these simple techniques can be expanded to provide conditional seasonal probabilities for a number of drought-related variables – e.g., the number of days with no rainfall or the number of consecutive days with rainfall less than some threshold amount. Some initial progress along these lines can be found in Janowiak (1998). It is extremely unlikely that we will be able to go beyond probability forecasts to predict drought on seasonal time scales. The drought prediction problem is inherently probabilistic in large part because of the uncertainties introduced by a substantial unpredictable component in atmospheric variations that influence precipitation on monthly and seasonal scales (Rowell 1998).

The probabilistic approach is extensively exploited in Australia, where drought is the main forecasting problem, through a software package called RAIN-

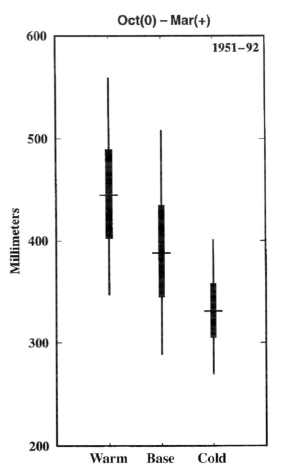

Gulf and Northern Mexico
Oct(0) – Mar(+)

Figure 2.6 Observed distribution of rainfall amounts for warm, non-ENSO, and cold ENSO years for an area including the Gulf Coast of the United States westward through New Mexico for the 1901–50 period (left) and the 1951–92 period (right). The horizontal line on the 'box and whisker' diagrams represents the median; the ends of the boxes, the 30th and 70th percentiles; and the ends of the lines, the 10th and 90th percentiles. Both periods show a clear ENSO influence on October through March precipitation, but the most recent period is clearly wetter in all categories – e.g., median rainfall for cold episodes in the 1951–92 period is about the same as the 70th percentile level for cold episodes during the 1901–50 period

MAN (M. Voice, personal communication, 1997). This is but one example of the potential use of probabilistic forecasts for drought and drought-related impacts. Empirical prediction schemes may also be able to make forecasts of more detailed rainfall statistics such as precipitation rates and the starting and the ending dates of the rainy season, but this is yet to be thoroughly explored.

No numerical model, including coupled ocean–atmosphere models, can in principle provide skilful deterministic day-to-day rainfall predictions on seasonal temporal scales. Despite this, the models, in conjunction with statistical techniques, can be used to predict seasonal differences in the statistical properties of daily precipitation with lead times of a season or more ahead, provided a suitably long time series of past data is available to develop these methods. Statistical methods based on historical data can also be designed to correct the climatology of a dynamical seasonal forecast model for its inevitable biases. The corrected model forecast data are called model output statistics (MOS). Smith and Ropelewski (1997) show that even given a perfect SST forecast – i.e., the observed SST – the current operational atmospheric model used at NCEP needs substantial adjustments to its ENSO-related rainfall patterns for practical use. In their study, forty-five years of seasonal forecasts (hindcasts) based on specified (observed) SST were examined for the period 1950–94. Each seasonal model simulation was repeated thirteen times, where each simulation was started with slightly different initial conditions to estimate the magnitude of unpredictable and therefore random atmospheric variations in the model. The thirteen simulations are averaged to calculate the best model estimate of rainfall for each given seasonal SST pattern. Quite typically, although the model replicated the observed global variations in seasonal rainfall patterns quite well, it showed systematic spatially varying biases. Thus for precipitation-related applications in many regions of the world, the model predictions would require some kind of adjustments, perhaps those generated by a MOS technique. The need for this kind of bias adjustment places a huge burden on the production of operational dynamical forecast models because each time the model is changed, a new set of MOS statistics must be calculated to provide the needed adjustments. This requires the generation and analysis of multidecadal ensembles to obtain the necessary MOS statistics and underscores the need for fundamental improvements to these models, such as those related to the flux adjustments, discussed above.

Knowledge of ENSO is insufficient for regional drought predictions in many parts of the world because in these regions its influence is either small or less important than other factors. For instance, northeast Brazil and west African wet season rainfall are profoundly influenced by tropical Atlantic SST patterns (Folland et al. 1991, Hastenrath 1995, Ward 1997). In addition, parts of the Sahel are affected by SST in the tropical Indian Ocean (Palmer 1986, Folland et al. 1991, Barnston and Smith 1996). Similarly, local SST patterns influence precipitation in Australia, notably in the Indian Ocean north and northwest of Australia in the Australian winter (e.g., Drosdowsky 1993, Fredericksen and Balgovind

1994). The state of ENSO is only one of many factors used to forecast the Indian summer monsoon (Krishna Kumar et al. 1995).

Ward et al. (1993) discuss the useful level of skill of tropical north African forecasts that have been made in real time by the UK Meteorological Office since 1986. These are largely based on statistical relationships with globally distributed SST, SST in the South Atlantic, and a relatively small ENSO component. Over the last decade, the real-time forecasts have had a skill similar to that obtained from cross-validated hindcasts made with the same statistical methods. The chief limitation to further progress is a lack of global tropical SST forecasts valid for the wet season (June through September). Accurate forecasts of ENSO would help, but would in most years be insufficient. Atmospheric dynamical-model-based rainfall forecasts are also used, but they only have useful skill with lead times of a month or less before the rainfall season (Folland et al. 1991). It is also possible that humanity has increased the susceptibility of tropical west Africa to drought through the progressive reduction in near-coastal west African forest cover over recent decades. This change in the land surface boundary has been shown by several authors (e.g., Eltahir and Gong 1996) to have the potential to weaken the north African monsoon. More studies of possible regional anthropogenic influences on tropical north African rainfall, as well as for other regions with marginal seasonal rainfall, are needed.

Ward et al. (1993) also discuss the skill of real-time forecasts for the northeast Brazil wet season made by the UK Meteorological Office since 1987. This is a relatively dry area, subject to intermittent severe drought. These forecasts, as well as those by Hastenrath and collaborators (e.g., Hastenrath 1995), are mainly statistical, although real-time dynamical forecasts have been made since 1994 by the Meteorological Office. The statistical forecasts are based on tropical Atlantic SST anomaly patterns and on ENSO SSTs. On average, tropical Atlantic SSTs have about twice the influence of ENSO for this region of South America, although extreme ENSOs, such as that in 1982–3, can dominate the circulation and precipitation patterns over tropical South America. The real-time forecasts have had a consistently high level of skill, similar to that obtained from both extensive cross-validated hindcasts and global climate model simulations forced with observed SST for 1949–93 (Potts *et al.* 1996). In fact, several atmospheric general circulation models simulate wet season rainfall in this region rather well when given observed sea surface temperatures (Folland and Rowell 1995). Figure 2.7 shows a comparison of the statistical forecasts for the March–May precipitation averaged at two key stations in northeast Brazil to the observations over the 1987–97 period. These have quite similar skill to other forecasts made for the averages of many more stations (Carson 1998).

THE ROAD AHEAD: FUTURE PROSPECTS AND CHALLENGES

The improvements being made to coupled ocean–atmosphere models provide rising expectations for advances in our understanding of the climate system, followed by improved climate predictions, including those of meteorological drought. However, the road toward these improvements may be neither easy nor rapid. Nonetheless, this qualified optimism has contributed to the setting up of a European collaboration on seasonal prediction called PROVOST (Prediction of Climate Variations on Seasonal to Interannual

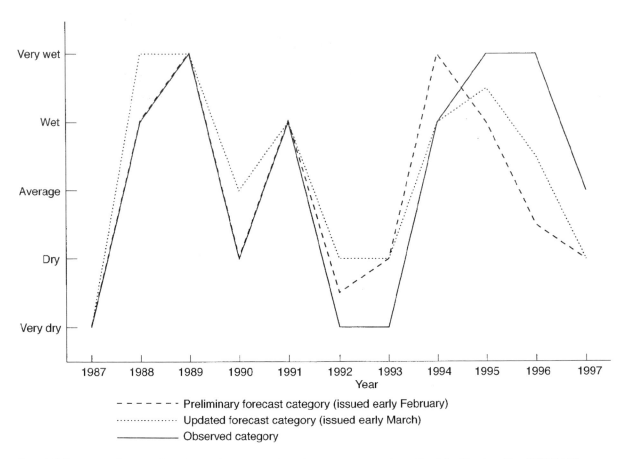

Figure 2.7 Forecast and observed rainfall for the average of two key stations in northeast Brazil for March to May 1987–97. The forecasts are made in five equiprobable categories of rainfall based on past statistics. Observed amounts estimated to fall on the boundary between two categories are placed on that boundary

Time Scales) as well as the multinational IRI, currently headquartered at the Lamont-Doherty Earth Observatory of Columbia University. These efforts have an important coupled model component, although many of the types of methods discussed above are included (Carson 1998).

For ENSO, current coupled models are capable of replicating and, in some cases, improving on the success of empirical/statistical methods. For instance, the current generation of coupled models replicate SST anomaly patterns in the equatorial Pacific that have many characteristics in common with observed ENSO composites. Current models are considerably less successful in the more difficult problem of replicating the specific evolution of the SST and atmospheric circulation patterns in a given ENSO episode. However, it is precisely this problem that must be solved. Just as the 'average' daily weather is rarely observed, the 'canonical' ENSO idea is more a conceptual aid to understanding than a useful construct for prediction. To reach their full potential, coupled models need to be able to replicate the evolution of individual past ENSO episodes and their evolving extratropical atmospheric and ocean interactions.

The most optimistic expectation is that once coupled models have conquered the challenge of ENSO, they will be able to help identify and predict other modes of climate variability. This may include links between ENSO and the climate system not yet discovered in the imperfect observational data. Improved models may aid in investigations of possible climate modes that link ocean basins, such as ENSO-related variations of SST in the tropical North Atlantic, recently discussed by Enfield and Mayer (1997).

In addition to ocean–atmosphere coupling, new generations of models need to include realistic land–atmosphere coupling. Such improvements involve realistic models of the land surface and its vegetation and adequate descriptions based on observed data of the initial vegetation state. Work on land–surface representation in models is currently being mainly driven by the development of coupled models for climate change projection over the next century (Dickinson et al. 1996).

Significant advances in coupled model-based

drought prediction will require the resolution of other major model problems. These advances include extension to forecasting, both the ocean and atmosphere, on a global domain and the resolution of the mismatch between the fluxes at the boundaries of the ocean and atmosphere. For many areas, the addition of realistic land–surface coupling may be essential. All of these will require significant improvements in the model parameterisations of surface processes, boundary layers, clouds, radiation, and convection. None of the required model improvements are likely to yield to a quick solution, but, given the importance of the impact of drought, they are worth pursuing.

It should not be forgotten, however, that not all of the prospects for improved drought predictions reside exclusively on seasonal time scales. Although we do not fully understand the multiannual to decadal scale of climate variability, there is ample evidence for its existence – e.g., in the time series of rainfall (Figure 2.1c) and the secular changes in the probability distributions of rainfall (Figure 2.2). Very recently, new developments in data analysis and in the accuracy of coupled models have started to open up this field. There is some evidence of decadal variations in ENSO that may have a somewhat different character, as measured by the ocean surface temperatures, from the interannual time scales (Kleeman et al. 1996, Zhang et al. 1997, Folland et al. 1998). Modellers are now beginning to find a number of potential mechanisms in the North and tropical Pacific for variability on the decadal to multidecadal time scale (Latif and Barnett 1996). There is also evidence that some ENSO links to rainfall may come and go depending on the secular variability in the strength and magnitude of ENSO itself – e.g., in northern Africa/southern Europe (Ropelewski and Halpert 1987). The predictability of ENSO, one to a few seasons ahead, may also vary on decadal time scales, especially in Northern Hemisphere spring (Balsameda et al. 1995). In addition, secular variability in the climate means (i.e., changes in the 'typical or expected' values over several decades) also influences simple seasonal conditional ENSO probability forecasts. For example, the Gulf Coast of the United States shows a strong ENSO signal for both the first and second half of the twentieth century (Figure 2.6), but because of a long-term increase in precipitation, the probability of drought, measured in absolute rainfall amounts, is different for the two periods. A similar increase in rainfall for a given state of ENSO is seen over Australia in the last twenty-five years (Nicholls *et al.* 1996b).

In the North Atlantic, new evidence has been found for coherent multiannual variations in SST that affect the tropical and extratropical ocean (Sutton and Allen 1997). Potential mechanisms for such variations are being found (Grotzner *et al.* 1998). Variations in North Atlantic sea surface temperature involving Arctic regions have also long been suspected. Recently, intriguing evidence of a coupled ocean–atmosphere mode has been found that has significant potential to affect the climate of Europe on multidecadal time scales (Delworth *et al.* 1997). In the tropical Atlantic, Chang *et al.* (1997) have identified decadal time scale variations in a dipole of SST anomalies between the north and south tropical Atlantic, although there is some controversy about this dipole (Enfield and Mayer 1997). Such variations could be linked to decadal variations in rainfall in both north Africa and northeast Brazil, although the latter are not strong.

On a global scale, there is also ample evidence that decadal and longer-scale variability in the climate system can sometimes confound the interannual climate signal. For instance, Folland *et al.* (1991) and Ward (1997) identify a strong multidecadal signal in tropical west African rainfall. They speculate that this may be linked to variations in the global thermohaline circulation of the oceans. The thermohaline circulation has the potential to change the temperature of some of the Northern Hemisphere oceans relative to the Southern Hemisphere oceans on multidecadal time scales (Schlesinger and Ramankutty 1994). However, large-scale anthropogenic effects related to increases in tropospheric aerosols, mostly in the Northern Hemisphere, have also been implicated in these variations (Santer *et al.* 1996).

A discussion of decadal and longer-scale variations leads naturally to the problem of the possible impact of global anthropogenic climate changes. It has recently been shown that a 'discernible' anthropogenic effect exists in zonally averaged temperature and patterns of surface temperature, though the evidence is not yet conclusive. Some coupled climate model projections indicate that an anthropogenic impact on drought in some parts of the world is likely to be evident in the twenty-first century. This can arise from changes in the atmospheric circulation patterns directly forced by changes in greenhouse gases and other pollutants, possible changes in the behaviour of ENSO (for which the evidence is contradictory at present), or merely because of the direct influence of warming on the surface water balance. In the latter situation, given no or little increase in rainfall, summer soil moisture deficits can rise, giving an increased tendency to drought. From a 'meteorological drought' perspective, combined with expected increases in population, such changes could systematically reduce the rainfall deficiency threshold at which society becomes stressed by the associated agricultural and hydrological droughts, leading to political tensions (Rodda 1995).

Finally, the previously mentioned WMO CLIPS programme has among its objectives an international framework necessary to enhance and promote climate information and prediction. These activities will link to the drought monitoring centres already set up to serve several African countries. The IRI and PRO-VOST will also work toward these objectives. Much more thought is being given to integrating historical climate data information and seasonal predictions within the context of how drought forecasts could be used, especially in developing countries (Frederick H. M. Semazzi, personal communication, 1997). Several of these issues are discussed in detail for north Africa in Hulme *et al.* (1992a and 1992b). Here climatologists, hydrologists, economists, and sociologists came together to identify some of the complex societal issues that may arise once reasonably skilful drought forecasts become possible.

ACKNOWLEDGEMENTS

Many thanks to Mike Halpert at the Climate Prediction Center for providing many of the figures. CFR wishes to thank Vern Kousky at the CPC for many discussions on seasonal prediction and NOAA's Pan American Climate Studies (PACS) program for partial support. CKF is indebted to Mike Davey, Andrew Colman, Mike Harrison, and David Carson for discussions.

REFERENCES

Allan, R., Lindesay, J., and Parker, D.E. (1996) *El Niño Southern Oscillation and Climatic Variability*, CSIRO Publishing, Collingwood, Victoria, Australia.

AMS (1997) 'American Meteorological Society policy statement on drought', *Bulletin of the American Meteorological Society* 78, 5: 847–9.

Balsameda, M.A., Davey, M.K., and Anderson, D.L.T. (1995) 'Decadal and seasonal dependence of ENSO forecast skill', *Journal of Climate* 8: 2,705–15.

Barnett, T.P., Latif, M., Graham, N., Flugel, M., Pazen, S., and White, W. (1993) 'ENSO and ENSO-related predictability. Part I: Prediction of equatorial Pacific sea surface temperature with a hybrid coupled ocean–atmosphere model', *Journal of Climate* 6: 1,545–66.

Barnett, T.P. and Preisendorfer, R. (1987) 'Origins and levels of monthly and seasonal forecast skill for United States surface air temperatures determined by canonical correlation analysis', *Monthly Weather Review* 115: 1,825 50.

Barnston, A.G. (1994) 'Long-lead seasonal forecasts – Where do we stand?', *Bulletin of the American Meteorological Society* 75: 2,097 114.

Barnston, A.G. and Ropelewski, C. F. (1992) 'Prediction of ENSO episodes using canonical correlation analysis', *Journal of Climate* 5: 1,316–45.

Barnston, A.G. and Smith, T.M. (1996) 'Specification and prediction of global surface temperature and precipitation from global SST using CCA', *Journal of Climate* 9: 2,660–97.

Berlage, H.P. and DeBoer, H.J. (1960) 'On the Southern Oscillation, its ways of operation and how it affects pressure patterns in the higher latitudes', *Geofisica Pura e Applicata* 46: 329–51.

Biswas, A.K. (1970) *History of Hydrology*, Amsterdam and London: North Holland Publ. Co.

Bjerknes, J. (1966) 'A possible response of the atmospheric Hadley circulation to equatorial anomalies of ocean temperature', *Tellus* 18: 820–9.

——— (1969) 'Atmospheric teleconnections from the equatorial Pacific', *Monthly Weather Review* 97: 163–72.

——— (1972) 'Large-scale atmospheric response to the 1964–65 Pacific equatorial warming', *Journal of Physical Oceanography* 2: 212–17.

Cane, M.A., Eshel, G., and Buckland, R.W. (1994) 'Forecasting Zimbabwean maize yield using eastern equatorial Pacific sea surface temperature', *Nature* 370: 204–5.

Cane, M.A., Zebiak, S.E., and Dolan, S.C. (1986) 'Experimental forecasts of El Niño', *Nature* 321: 827–32.

Carson, D.J. (1998) 'Seasonal forecasting', *Quarterly Journal of the Royal Meteorological Society* (forthcoming).

Chang, P., Ji, L., and Li, H. (1997) 'A decadal climate variation in the tropical Atlantic Ocean from thermo-dynamic air-sea interactions', *Nature* 385: 516–18.

Climate Prediction Center (1992–7) *Experimental Long-lead Forecast Bulletin*, published quarterly by the Climate Prediction Center, W/NP5, NOAA Science Center, Rm. 800, 4700 Silver Hill Road, Washington, DC, 20233–9910.

Craddock, J.M. (1968) *Statistics in the Computer Age*, London: English Universities Press.

Davey, M. (1996) 'A survey of seasonal forecasting', *Ocean Applications Technical Note* 13, available from the National Meteorological Library, Bracknell, Berkshire, UK, RG12 2SZ.

Delworth, T.L., Manabe, S., and Stouffer, R.J. (1997) 'Multidecadal climate variability in the Greenland Sea and surrounding regions: A coupled model simulation', *Geophysical Research Letters* 24: 257–60.

Dickinson, R.E., Meleshko, V., Randall, D., Sarachik, E., Silva-Dias, P., and Slingo, A. (1996) 'Climate processes', in J.T. Houghton, L.G. Meira Filho, B.A. Callander, N. Harris, A. Kattenberg, and K. Maskell (eds), *Climate Change 1995, The Science of Climate Change*, Cambridge: Cambridge University Press, pp. 193–227.

Drosdowsky, W. (1993) 'An analysis of Australian seasonal rainfall anomalies: 1950 1987. II: Temporal variability and teleconnection patterns', *International Journal of Climatology* 13: 111 19.

Eltahir, E.A.B. and Gong, C. (1996) 'Dynamics of wet and dry years in West Africa', *Journal of Climate* 9: 1,030–42.

Enfield, D.B. and Mayer, D.A. (1997) 'Tropical Atlantic sea surface temperature variability and its relation to El Nino-Southern Oscillation', *Journal of Geophysical Research* 102: 929–45.

Folland, C.K. and Rowell, D.P. (eds) (1995) 'Workshop on simulations of the climate of the twentieth century using GISST', 28–30 November 1994, Hadley Centre, *CRTN* 56, pp. 111.

Folland, C.K. and Wales-Smith, B.G. (1977) 'Richard Towneley and 300 years of regular rainfall measurement', *Weather* 38: 438–45.

Folland, C.K. and Woodcock, A. (1986) 'Experimental monthly long-range forecasts for the United Kingdom: Part I, The Forecasting System', *Meteorological Magazine* 115: 301– 18.

Folland, C.K., Owen, J., Ward, M.N., and Colman, A. (1991) 'Prediction of seasonal rainfall in the Sahel region using empirical and dynamical methods', *Journal of Forecasting* 10: 21–56.

Folland, C.K., Parker, D.E., Colman, A., and Washington, R. (1999) 'Large scale modes of ocean surface temperature since the late nineteenth century', in A. Navarra (ed.), *Beyond El Niño: Decadal and Interdecadal Climate Variability*, Berlin and New York: Springer.

Folland, C.K., Parker, D.E., and Palmer, T.N. (1986) 'Sahel rainfall and worldwide sea temperatures 1901–85', *Nature* 320: 602 7.

Fredericksen, C.S. and Balgovind, R.C. (1994) 'The influence of the Indian Ocean/Indonesian SST gradient on the Australian winter rainfall and circulation in an atmospheric GCM', *Quarterly Journal of the Royal Meteorological Society* 120: 923–52.

Gadgil, S. (1984) 'Ocean-atmosphere coupling over monsoon regions', *Nature* 312: 141–3.

Gilman, D.L. (1985) 'Long-range forecasting: The present and the future', *Bulletin of the American Meteorological Society* 66: 159–64.

Glantz, M.H., Katz, R.W., and Nicholls, N. (eds) (1991) *Teleconnections Linking Worldwide Climate Anomalies*, New York: Cambridge University Press.

Gregory, S. (1986) 'The climatology of drought', *Geography* 71: 97–104.

Grotzner, A., Latif, M., and Barnett, T.P. (1998) 'A decadal climate cycle in the North Atlantic Ocean as simulated by the ECHO coupled GCM', *Journal of Climate* (submitted).

Halpert, M.S. and Ropelewski, C.F. (1992) 'Temperature patterns associated with the Southern Oscillation', *Journal of Climate* 5: 577–93.

Hastenrath, S. (1995) 'Recent advances in tropical climate prediction', *Journal of Climate* 8: 1,519–32.

Hough, M., Palmer, S., Weir, A., Lee, M., and Barrie, I. (1996) 'The Meteorological Office Rainfall and Evaporation Calculation System: MORECS version 2.0 (1995)', *Hydrological Memorandum* 45, updated, available from the National Meteorological Library, Bracknell, Berkshire, UK, RG12 2SZ.

Hsiung, J. and Newell, R.E. (1983) 'The principle nonseasonal modes of variation of global sea surface temperature', *Journal of Physical Oceanography* 13: 1,957–67.

Huang, J., van den Dool, H.M., and Barnston, A.G. (1994) 'Long-lead seasonal temperature prediction using optimal climate normals', *Journal of Climate* 9: 809–17.

Hulme, M., Biot, Y., Borton, J., Buchanan-Smith, M., Davies, S., Folland, C.K., Nicholls, N., Seddon, D., and Ward, M.N. (1992a) 'Seasonal rainfall forecasting for Africa: Part 1. Current status and future developments', *International Journal of Environmental Studies* 39, 4: 245–56.

Hulme, M., Biot, Y., Borton, J., Buchanan-Smith, M., Davies, S., Folland, C.K., Nicholls, N., Seddon, D., and Ward, M.N. (1992b) 'Seasonal rainfall forecasting for Africa: Part 2. Application and impact assessment', *International Journal of Environmental Studies* 40, 2: 103–21.

Janowiak, J.E. (1998) 'ENSO relationships with U.S. precipitation amount and frequency', in *Proceedings of the Twenty-First Climate Diagnostics and Prediction Workshop*, 6–10 October 1997, Lawrence Livermore Laboratory, Berkeley, CA, pp. 165–8. NTIS Publication PB98–13813, National Technical Information Service, US Dept. of Commerce, Springfield, CA.

Ji, M., Kumar, A., and Leetmaa, A. (1994) 'A multiseason climate forecast system at the National Meteorological Center', *Bulletin of the American Meteorological Society* 75: 569–77.

Kautilya (c. 300 BC) *Arthasastra* (The science of politics and administration), translated by R.P. Kangle, Bombay Univ., Bombay: Bombay Press (1963), p. 171.

Kiladis, G.N. and Diaz, H.F. (1989) 'Global climatic anomalies associated with extremes in the Southern Oscillation', *Journal of Climate* 2: 1,069–90.

Kleeman, R., Colman, R.A., Smith, N.R., and Power, S.B. (1996) 'A recent change in the mean state of the Pacific basin climate: Observational evidence and atmospheric and oceanic responses', *Journal of Geophysical Research* 101: 20,483–99.

Kogan, F.N. (1997) 'Global drought watch from space', *Bulletin of the American Meteorological Society* 78: 621–36.

Krishna Kumar, K., Soman, M., and Rupa Kuma, K. (1995) 'Seasonal forecasting of Indian summer monsoon rainfall: A review', *Weather* 50: 449–66.

Lamb, H.H. (1972) *Climate: Past, Present and Future*, Vol. 1, *Fundamentals and Climate Now*, London: Methuen.

Lamb, P.J. (1982) 'Persistence of Subsaharan drought', *Nature* 299: 46–8.

Latif, M. and Barnett, T.P. (1996) 'Decadal variability over the North Pacific and North America: Dynamics and predictability', *Journal of Climate* 9: 2,407–23.

Latif, M., Barnett, T.P., Cane, M.A., Flugel, M., Graham, N.E., von Storch, H., Xu, J.S., and Zebiak, S.E. (1994) 'A review of ENSO prediction studies', *Climate Dynamics* 9: 167–79.

Livezey, R.L. and Barnston, A.G. (1988) 'An operational multi field analog/antianalog prediction system of the United States seasonal temperatures, 1. System design and winter experiments', *Journal of Geophysical Research* 93: 10,953–74.

Long, J., Ying, L., and Zhenshuan, L. (1997) 'Comparison of long-term forecasting of June-August rainfall over Changjiang-Huaihe valley', *Advances in Atmospheric Sciences* 14: 87–92.

Mandelbrot, B.B. and Wallis, J.R. (1968) 'Noah, Joseph, and operational hydrology', *Water Resources Research* 4, 5: 909–18.

Maryon, R.H. and Storey, A.M. (1985) 'A multivariate statistical model for forecasting anomalies of half-monthly mean surface pressure', *Journal of Climatology* 5: 561–78.

Meteorological Office (1991) *The Meteorological Glossary*, Sixth Edition, London: HMSO.

Nicholls, N., Gruza, G.V., Jouzel, J., Karl, T.R., Ogallo, J.A., and Parker, D.E. (1996a) 'Observed climate variability and change', in J.T. Houghton, L.G. Meira Filho, B.A. Callander, N. Harris, A. Kattenberg, and K. Maskell (eds), *Climate Change 1995, The Science of*

Climate Change, Cambridge: Cambridge University Press, pp. 133–92.

Nicholls, N., Lavery, B., Fredericksen, C., Drosdowsky, W., and Torok, S. (1996b) 'Recent changes in relationships between the El Niño–Southern Oscillation and Australian rainfall and temperature', *Geophysical Research Letters* 23: 3,357–60.

Palmer, T.N. (1986) 'Influence of the Atlantic, Pacific and Indian Oceans on Sahel rainfall', *Nature* 322: 251–3.

Palmer, T.N. and Anderson, D.L.T. (1994) 'The prospects for seasonal forecasting – A review paper', *Quarterly Journal of the Royal Meteorological Society* 120: 755–93.

Parker, D.E. and Folland, C.K. (1991) 'Worldwide surface temperature trends since the mid-19th century', in M.E. Schlesinger (ed.), *Greenhouse-Gas-Induced Climatic Change: A Critical Appraisal of Simulations and Observations*, Amsterdam: Elsevier, pp. 173–93.

Parthasarathy, B., Munot, A.A., and Kothwale, D.R. (1995) 'Monthly and seasonal rainfall series for all-India homogeneous regions and meteorological subdivisions: 1871–1994', *Research Report RR-065*, Indian Institute of Tropical Meteorology, Puna, India.

Penland, C. and Magorian, T. (1993) 'Prediction of Niño 3 sea-surface temperature using linear inverse modeling', *Journal of Climate* 6: 1,067–76.

Philander, S.G.H. and Seigel, A.D. (1985) 'Simulation of El Niño of 1982–83', in J. Nihoul (ed.), *Coupled Ocean–Atmosphere Models*, Amsterdam: Elsevier, pp. 517–41.

Potts, J.M., Folland, C.K., Jolliffe, I.T., and Sexton, D. (1996) 'Revised "LEPS" scores for assessing climate model simulations and long range forecasts', *Journal of Climate* 9: 34–53.

Rasmusson, E.M. and Carpenter, T.H. (1982) 'Variations in tropical sea surface temperature and surface wind fields associated with the Southern Oscillation/El Niño', *Monthly Weather Review* 110: 354–84.

Rodda, J.C. (1995) 'Guessing or assessing the world's water resources', *Journal of the Institution of Water and Environmental Management* 9: 360–8.

Ropelewski, C.F. and Halpert, M.S. (1986) 'North American precipitation and temperature patterns associated with the El Niño/Southern Oscillation (ENSO)', *Monthly Weather Review* 114: 2,352–62.

—— (1987) 'Global and regional scale precipitation patterns associated with the El Niño/Southern Oscillation', *Monthly Weather Review* 115: 1,606–26.

—— (1989) 'Precipitation patterns associated with the high index phase of the Southern Oscillation', *Journal of Climate* 2: 268–84.

—— (1995) 'Quantification of ENSO precipitation relationships', *Journal of Climate* 7: 1,041–59.

Ropelewski, C.F. and Jones, P. (1987) 'An extension of the Tahiti-Darwin Southern Oscillation Index', *Monthly Weather Review* 115: 2,161–5.

Rowell, D.P. (1998) 'Using an ensemble of multi-decadal GCM simulations to assess potential seasonal predictability', *Journal of Climate* (forthcoming).

Santer, B.D., Wigley, T.M.L., Barnett, T.P., and Anyamba, E. (1996) 'Detection of climate change and attribution of causes', in J.T. Houghton, L.G. Meira Filho, B.A. Callander, N. Harris, A. Kattenberg, and K. Maskell (eds), *Climate Change 1995, The Science of Climate Change*, Cambridge: Cambridge University Press, pp. 407–43.

Schlesinger, M.E. and Ramankutty, N. (1994) 'An oscillation in the global climate system of period 65–70 years', *Nature* 367: 723–6.

Sherman, R. (1950) 'A random variable related to the spacing of sample values', *Annals of Mathematical Statistics* 21: 339–61.

Smith, T.M. and Ropelewski, C.F. (1997) 'Quantifying Southern-Oscillation-precipitation relationships from an atmospheric GCM', *Journal of Climate* 10: 2,277–84.

Sutton, R.T., and Allen, M.R. (1997) 'Decadal predictability of North Atlantic sea surface temperature and climate', *Nature* 388: 563–7.

Tabony, R.C. (1977) 'The variability of long-duration rainfall over Great Britain', *Met Office Scientific Paper* No. 37, p. 40.

Towneley, R. (1694) 'A letter from Richard Towneley Esq., of Towneley in Lancashire containing observations of rain falling monthly for several years successively', *Philosophical Transactions of the Royal Society* 18, p. 51.

Trenberth, K.E., Branstator, G.W., Karoly, D., Kumar, A., Lau, N.C., and Ropelewski, C.F. (1998) 'Progress during TOGA in understanding and modeling global teleconnections associated with tropical sea surface temperatures', *Journal of Geophysical Research* (forthcoming).

Tyson, P.D., Dyer, T.G.J., and Mametse, M.N. (1975) 'Secular changes in South African rainfall: 1880–1972', *Quarterly Journal of the Royal Meteorological Society* 101: 817–33.

van den Dool, H.M. (1994) 'Long-range weather forecasts through numerical and empirical methods', *Dynamics of Atmospheres and Oceans* 20: 247–70.

Walker, G.T. (1923) 'Correlation in seasonal variations of weather, VIII: A preliminary study of world weather', *Memoirs India Meteorological Department* 24: 75–131.

—— (1924) 'Correlation in seasonal variations of weather, IX: A further study of world weather', *Memoirs India Meteorological Department* 24: 275–332.

Walker, G.T., and Bliss, E.W. (1932) 'World Weather V', *Memoirs of the Royal Meteorological Society* 4: 53–84.

Walker, J.M. (1997) 'Pen portraits of presidents – Sir Gilbert Walker, CSI, ScD, MA, FRS', *Weather* 52: 217–20.

Ward, M.N. (1998) 'Diagnosis and short-lead time prediction of summer rainfall in tropical North Africa at interannual and multi-decadal time scales', *Journal of Climate* 11, 12: 3,167 91.

Ward, M.N. and Folland, C.K. (1991) 'Prediction of seasonal rainfall in the North Nordeste of Brazil using eigenvectors of sea surface temperature,' *International Journal of Climatology* 11: 711–43.

Ward, M.N., Folland, C.K., Maskell, K., Colman, A.W., Rowell, D.P., and Lane, K.B. (1993) 'Experimental seasonal forecasting of tropical rainfall in the UK Meteorological Office', in J. Shukla (ed.), *Predictions of Interannual Climate Variations*, Berlin: Springer-Verlag, pp. 197–216.

Weekly Weather and Crop Bulletin (1997) Available through the Climate Prediction Center W/NP52, NOAA/ NWS/NCEP, Stop 9910, 4700 Silver Hill Rd, Washington, DC 20233–9910.

Wilhite, D.A. and Glantz, M.H. (1987) 'Understanding the drought phenomenon: The role of definitions', in D.A. Wilhite and W.E. Easterling (eds), *Planning for Drought: Toward a Reduction of Societal Vulnerability*, Boulder, CO: Westview Press, pp. 11–27.

Zebiak, S.E. and Cane, M.A. (1987) 'A model El Niño-Southern Oscillation', *Monthly Weather Review* 115: 2,262–78.

Zhang, Y., Wallace, J.M., and Battisti, D. (1997) 'ENSO-like interdecadal variability: 1900–1993', *Journal of Climate* 10: 1,004–20.

3

THE APPLICATION OF EL NIÑO–SOUTHERN OSCILLATION INFORMATION TO SEASONAL FORECASTS IN AUSTRALIA

Neville Nicholls and Grant Beard

INTRODUCTION

Public and political interest in climate in Australia has never been higher. This heightened public interest reflects greater understanding of the climate (e.g., effects of enhanced greenhouse gases, El Niño–Southern Oscillation), improved (faster) monitoring of climate change and variations, and better systems for dissemination of climate information (television, facsimile, World Wide Web), as well as increased recognition of the impact of climate variations on society and the economy.

The effect of these changes on operational climatology can be demonstrated through examining Australian responses to various El Niño–Southern Oscillation episodes. Before the 1972–3 episode, understanding of the effect of the El Niño–Southern Oscillation on Australia was limited, although earlier scientists had studied the phenomenon. Studies in the 1970s and 1980s documented its effects, but even the 1982–3 event caught Australia by surprise, partly because there were no systems in place to rapidly monitor the phenomenon, or to effectively disseminate information and forecasts. By the El Niño events of the early 1990s, a routine seasonal climate prediction service, based on the earlier studies of the El Niño–Southern Oscillation, had been established, and routine monitoring was possible. Buoys moored across the equatorial Pacific allowed the daily monitoring of surface and subsurface temperatures. There were also computer models (as well as statistical models) capable of predicting some aspects of the phenomenon. All this means that Australia now has an 'operational climatology' capability, analogous to

the operational short-range weather prediction, with real-time climate monitoring, scientifically based prediction, and rapid dissemination of information. Much of this is based on the El Niño–Southern Oscillation.

THE IMPACT OF THE EL NIÑO–SOUTHERN OSCILLATION ON AUSTRALIA

Australian droughts generally accompany El Niño episodes (e.g., Allan 1991). Figure 3.1 illustrates the relationship between widespread Australian drought and low values of the Southern Oscillation Index (SOI – the standardised difference in surface atmospheric pressure between Tahiti and Darwin and a simple measure of the El Niño–Southern Oscillation), by comparing time series of the percentage of Australia with annual rainfall in the lowest decile, with annual averages of the SOI. It also indicates that years with little of the country in drought tend to have large positive SOI values, i.e., La Niña episodes.

Figure 3.1 shows data from 1950. Studies have demonstrated the relationship between Australian droughts and the SOI back into the late nineteenth century (see Allan 1991). Before this time, there is not enough information to allow a quantitative comparison of widespread Australian droughts with the El Niño–Southern Oscillation. Documentary evidence of previous droughts is available from before that date. New South Wales, later to become a state of the Commonwealth of Australia, was colonised by Britain in 1788. Nicholls (1988a) searched reports of the governors of the colony to the colonial secretary of the British government in London for references to

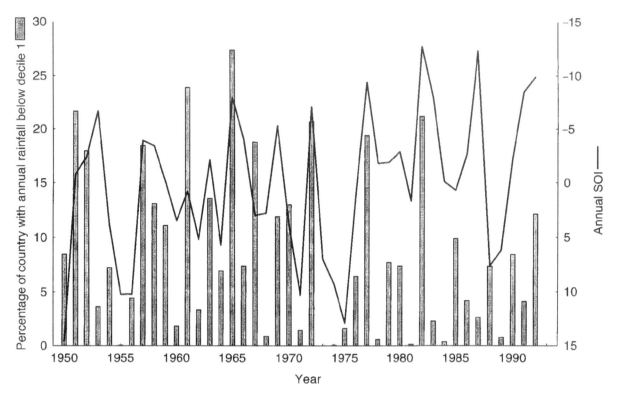

Figure 3.1 Time series of the percentage of Australia with rainfall below the lowest decile (bars) and annual average values of the SOI (line). Note that the SOI scale is inverted

drought from 1788 to 1841. Droughts were mentioned in the El Niño years of 1791, 1804, 1814, 1817, 1819, 1824, 1828, and 1837. Other documentary evidence, such as Russell (1877), indicates that droughts also occurred in concert with El Niño events in the mid-nineteenth century. The coincidence of El Niño events and Australian droughts is identifiable since at least the start of European colonisation in 1788.

The El Niño–Southern Oscillation enhances Australian rainfall variability, as it does wherever it affects climate around the world (Nicholls *et al.* 1997). Australian rainfall is highly variable, largely because of the El Niño–Southern Oscillation phenomenon. The phenomenon also results in Australian droughts typically being long-lived (Nicholls 1992a). Many Australian droughts, and the extensive wet periods, tend to last about twelve months. The 1982–3 drought is a good example, starting early in 1982 and ending in much of the

country in March 1983. El Niño and La Niña episodes both tend to last about twelve months, and this sets the time scale of Australian rainfall fluctuations (Nicholls 1991).

These extended periods of drought or extensive rains do not occur randomly in time, in relation to the annual cycle. The El Niño–Southern Oscillation phenomenon, and the Australian rainfall fluctuations associated with it, is phase-locked with the annual cycle. The heavy rainfall associated with a La Niña episode tends to start early in the calendar year and finish early in the following year (e.g., Nicholls 1992a). The dry periods associated with El Niño episodes tend to occupy a similar period. This means that if an extensive drought or wet period is established by the middle of the calendar year, it is unlikely to 'break' until at least early the following year. The 1982–3 drought again provides a good example.

The link with the El Niño–Southern Oscillation is

most consistent with rainfall in the east and north (e.g., Pittock 1975, McBride and Nicholls 1983, Ropelewski and Halpert 1987 and 1989). Rainfall in the west is less strongly related to phenomenon. Nicholls (1989a) identified a pattern of sea surface temperature variation in the Indian Ocean related to rainfall fluctuations in the central and southern parts of the continent. This pattern is only weakly related to the El Niño–Southern Oscillation and appears to be a somewhat independent factor affecting Australian rainfall.

Not surprisingly, given its effects on Australian climate, the El Niño–Southern Oscillation has a major impact on crop yields, native vegetation, and wildlife. Figure 3.2 shows time series of wheat yields, averaged across Australia, and the SOI. The year-to-year differences in the two variables are plotted, to remove the effects of trends and changes such as the introduction of new cultivars. The relationship is clear –

negative values of the SOI usually coincide with widespread drought (Figure 3.1), which leads to low crop yields (Nicholls 1985). The correlation between the year-to-year differences in yield and the annual SOI is 0.46 (n = 40; significant at 1 per cent). There is ample evidence that the El Niño–Southern Oscillation affects Australian wildlife and vegetation (e.g., Nicholls 1989b, Limpus and Nicholls 1988, Nicholls 1986, Nicholls 1991). For instance, many native Australian plants are remarkably tolerant of severe, extensive droughts. Well-developed tolerance or avoidance strategies are essential because of the frequent severe droughts caused by the El Niño–Southern Oscillation.

How were these relationships between the Australian climate and the El Niño–Southern Oscillation uncovered? How have we progressed to routine issuing of climate forecasts, based on the El Niño–Southern Oscillation?

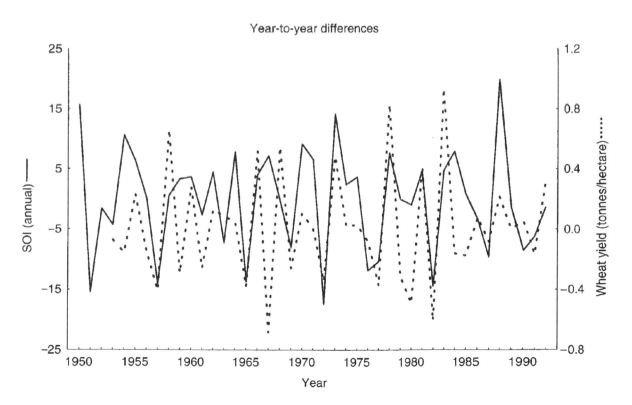

Figure 3.2 Time series of the year-to-year differences in the annual average SOI (full line) and the average Australian wheat yield (dotted line). Year-to-year differences are used to reduce the impact of changes in crop management (e.g., improved cultivars), which tend to result in an upward trend

EARLY AUSTRALIAN WORK ON DROUGHT AND THE EL NIÑO–SOUTHERN OSCILLATION

India suffered a severe drought and famine during 1877 (Kiladis and Diaz 1986). Sir Henry Blandford, the first director of the Indian Meteorological Service, noted the very high atmospheric pressures over Asia at the time and requested pressure information from other meteorologists around the world. Sir Charles Todd, the South Australian government observer, responded by including pressure observations from various Australian stations in an annual series of publications recording monthly observations made in South Australia and the Northern Territory. Pressures during 1877 were also high over Australia, and much of the country suffered from drought that year.

The coincidence of high pressures and droughts in India and Australia obviously stuck in Todd's mind. In 1888, Australia was again struck by a severe drought. An extensive discussion on the cause of drought, between the government observers from South Australia, New South Wales, and Victoria, was published in *The Australasian* on 29 December 1888. Todd suggested that Indian and Australian droughts usually coincided:

> Comparing our records with those of India, I find a close correspondence or similarity of seasons with regard to the prevalence of drought, and there can be little or no doubt that severe droughts occur as a rule simultaneously over the two countries.

By 1896, H. C. Russell, the New South Wales government observer, was also convinced that Indian and Australian droughts often coincided. Russell (1896) attempted to demonstrate the periodicity of droughts but, almost incidentally, indicated the coincidence of droughts in the two countries. This remarkable observation has since been confirmed (e.g., Williams *et al.* 1986) and forms part of the suite of climate linkages we now call the El Niño–Southern Oscillation. Indian and Australian droughts both tend to occur during El Niño episodes (e.g., Ropelewski and Halpert 1987, Kiladis and Diaz 1989).

When Sir Gilbert Walker named and documented the Southern Oscillation (the atmospheric aspects of what was later to be called the El Niño–Southern Oscillation) in the early decades of the twentieth century, its close relationship with Australian rainfall quickly became apparent (e.g., Bliss and Walker 1932). Walker's work indicated that north Australian summer rainfall could be predicted with an index of the Southern Oscillation. Quayle (1910, 1929) indicated that spring rainfall farther south could be predicted in the same way. After that, a trickle of papers discussed the relationship between the Southern Oscillation and Australian climate (e.g., Treloar 1934, Grant 1956, O'Mahony 1961, and Troup 1965), up to the mid-1970s, when the worldwide attention on El Niño led to a resurgence of interest among Australian meteorologists.

The early studies of the possibility that the El Niño–Southern Oscillation could be used in Australian rainfall prediction did not, it appears, lead to the establishment of an operational forecast service. This probably reflects the distrust of the empirical results of studies such as Quayle (1910, 1929), and the absence of any real physical understanding of the El Niño–Southern Oscillation and its effects on Australia. Attempts were made, on occasion, to establish or test methods for seasonal prediction, reflecting the recognised importance of being able to predict drought.

The Bureau of Meteorology prepared experimental long-range (monthly) weather forecasts, for internal assessment, from 1954 to 1971. These were based on an apparent tendency for certain patterns of anticyclonicity to persist for up to a season or longer, rather than any knowledge or understanding of the El Niño–Southern Oscillation. The Extended Period Forecasting Section was established as an operational unit of the Bureau in the late 1960s. Although its main concern was the regular issue of forecasts up to four days ahead, experimental thirty-day forecasts were prepared. These were based on an extension of the methods used in four-day forecasting: a zonal index cycle, blocking patterns, persistence, and the movement of large-scale anomalies. The forecasts were not issued to the public. Analysis revealed that rainfall forecasts were no more accurate than would be expected from chance. Temperature forecasts were slightly (and significantly) more accurate than chance, but not sufficiently accurate to be useful. The experiment was discontinued in 1971.

TOWARD AN OPERATIONAL SEASONAL CLIMATE OUTLOOK SERVICE

By the early 1980s, meteorologists had turned again to the possible use of the El Niño–Southern Oscillation in prediction. Work on the physical cause of the phenomenon had commenced, and several papers describing patterns and relationships between the El Niño–Southern Oscillation, sea surface temperature, and Australian climate had been published (e.g., Priestley 1964, Pittock 1975, Streten 1981, and Coughlan 1979). Some of the earlier (e.g., Quayle) lag relationships had been validated and extended using new data (Nicholls and Woodcock 1981, McBride and Nicholls 1983). New relationships indicating that seasonal temperature, wet-season onset, and even seasonal tropical cyclone activity were predictable, through the El Niño–Southern Oscillation, had been uncovered (Nicholls 1978 and 1979, Nicholls *et al.* 1982). The recognition in mid-1982 that a major El Niño episode was under way led to cautious statements regarding possible implications for Australian rainfall through the remainder of 1982, based on this work (Nicholls 1983). The Bureau's National Climate Centre began preparing and issuing monthly 'Seasonal Climate Outlooks' in 1989.

The basis of the Outlooks was simple linear lagged regression, and variants on this, between the SOI and subsequent rainfall. Trends and phases (Zhang and Casey 1992; Stone and Auliciems 1992) of the SOI are taken into account, as are some patterns of sea surface temperature (Drosdowsky 1993a). The various predictions are combined in a statistically optimal fashion (Casey 1995). Sophisticated time-series methods (Drosdowsky 1996) are also used to project the SOI into the future. These projections can then be used to find analogues – years when the SOI has behaved similarly to the current year. Detailed meteorological data from these analogue years can then be used, for instance, in crop models to examine likely crop yields. By the mid-1980s it was clear that the SOI could be used to produce predictions not just of climate variations, but also of the impact of these variations on the Australian economy and ecology (Nicholls 1988b). A more extensive description of the current Seasonal Climate Outlook service is provided by Kininmonth *et al.* (Chapter 15 of this volume).

One major change since 1989 in the content and presentation of the Outlooks has been the introduction of probabilistic forecasts. At the start, the Outlooks were categorical, providing forecasts, for specific areas, of whether the rainfall in the coming season could be expected to be below, near, or above average. Forecasts were only prepared for those regions and seasons with a substantial lag-correlation between the SOI and rainfall. This caused some confusion, with different areas being forecast for different seasons. The categorical nature of the forecasts may also have led to an overreaction by potential users, without a clear indication of the uncertainties associated with the forecasts. The Bureau now provides forecasts of the probability that an area will receive rainfall in the below-, near-, and above-average categories. Although forecasts presented as probabilities more accurately convey the uncertainty in the forecast, surveys show common customer confusion with this format. The challenge is to improve the presentation of complex probabilistic information.

Dynamical methods, using coupled ocean–atmosphere models, can also provide predictions of the likely future behaviour of the El Niño–Southern Oscillation. The Bureau uses a dynamical model of the coupled ocean–atmosphere system in the tropical Pacific to predict the behaviour of sea surface temperatures related to the El Niño (Kleeman 1996). Six-month-ahead forecasts of east equatorial Pacific sea surface temperatures from this model are included in the Seasonal Climate Outlooks. This coupled model does not include all the complex mechanisms involved in the atmosphere and ocean, but retains the larger-scale mechanisms believed responsible for the El Niño–Southern Oscillation. Similar models were first used to predict the 1986–7 El Niño. They have been used operationally ever since, with increasing sophistication. The models have exhibited some skill in prediction, forecasting the 1991 and (some models) the 1994 El Niño events. They do, however, only forecast ocean conditions – that is, sea surface temperatures. These can then be interpreted in terms of the El Niño and its statistical implications for rainfall over the areas generally affected by the phenomenon. The Kleeman model, unlike some other models of this type, uses subsurface ocean temperature data (Smith 1995). The inclusion of these data has led to improved model predictions, and the model can provide forecasts of El Niño several seasons ahead. The El Niño forecasts from the model can provide guidance, at longer lead times, of the probability of a drought episode commencing in those areas where drought usually accompanies an El Niño.

PROSPECTS FOR IMPROVED FORECASTS

Although the El Niño–Southern Oscillation is a major influence on Australian climate and provides a mechanism for predicting some aspects of droughts, considerable improvement would be needed for the forecasts to reach an acceptable level of skill at all times of the year, and for all of the country. As noted earlier, the effect of the El Niño–Southern Oscillation is clearest in eastern and northern Australia. Further work is needed to provide a system that adequately forecasts rainfall in southern and western parts of the country. More crucially, the El Niño–Southern Oscillation does not provide much skill in prediction around the start of winter (February–June), when many farmers are preparing for planting. Most of Australia's crops are winter cereals, so information about winter and spring rainfall, available before planting, is crucial, if farmers are to profit from insights into the El Niño–Southern Oscillation.

SST-based statistical forecasts

A new statistical forecast system, which uses global and regional patterns of sea surface temperature as predictors, has been developed to replace the current operational technique, which is based largely on the SOI. It is expected that the less variable nature of the sea surface temperature fields should allow for improved predictions, and that patterns of ocean temperature may provide skill in areas where the El Niño–Southern Oscillation is of little help. Nicholls (1989a) and Drosdowsky (1993a and 1993b) indicate that the sea surface temperature fields in the Indian Ocean and Indonesian area may provide predictions for some of the areas where the El Niño–Southern Oscillation is not dominant.

More refined statistical techniques are being used to develop systems for operational prediction. A major problem with improving statistical forecast systems is the few decades of data available. The short period of available data means care is needed, if 'artificial skill' is not to degrade the accuracy of the forecasts. Such artificial skill arises from attempting to use many predictors to improve the apparent skill on the data used to derive the statistical forecast system. The 'increased' skill then usually disappears when the system is used operationally. Inclusion of extra predictors can even degrade the forecasts. The new systems under development take great care to avoid this problem.

Improving content and delivery

Efforts are under way to refine the content and delivery of seasonal predictions. Surveys of potential agricultural users of seasonal climate forecasts have indicated what variables should be predicted, and what level of accuracy and lead time is needed. The Bureau of Meteorology currently only forecasts seasonal (three-month) rainfall. Yet there is a need for temperature forecasts, and for more specific indices, such as the severity of the frost season. Some of these other variables could be forecasted using current techniques and predictors, with a small amount of further development. For instance, Stone *et al.* (1996) suggest that seasonal frost forecasts could be feasible in eastern Australia. Tropical cyclone behaviour is also predictable on seasonal time scales (Nicholls 1992b). Coughlan (1979) demonstrated that the El Niño–Southern Oscillation was related to Australian temperatures, implying that seasonal temperature might be predictable. Nicholls and Kariko (1993) and Suppiah and Hennessy (1996) found that rainfall events were related to the El Niño–Southern Oscillation, suggesting that these were also predictable. Whetton *et al.* (1990) and Allan *et al.* (1996) have documented relationships of the El Niño–Southern Oscillation with streamflow variations, which appear likely to be predictable.

Coupled ocean–atmosphere models

The major hope for improved forecasts, however, lies in the further development of coupled ocean–

atmosphere climate models. Much more detailed than the relatively simple models used routinely since the mid-1980s, they are also much more expensive to run. Rather than simply forecasting El Niño behaviour (e.g., sea surface temperatures in the east equatorial Pacific), they could, in theory, be used to forecast rainfall and temperature over land. The coupling of the ocean to the atmosphere in these models, however, is less than perfect. Improved ocean models (Power *et al.* 1995) are being developed for these coupled models.

One problem with the use of coupled models in seasonal prediction is the difficulty the atmospheric part of the coupled models has in simulating rainfall on the spatial scales important for users, despite their general success in simulating atmospheric variability (Nicholls 1996). Model experiments with specified sea surface temperature anomalies have a long history in the Australian region (Simpson and Downey 1975; Voice and Hunt 1984). The BMRC climate model has been forced with observed sea surface temperatures for the period 1949–91, and the rainfall simulated by the model has been compared with the observed rainfall (Frederiksen *et al.* 1995). The model was run five times, with the same sea surface temperatures but slightly different starting atmospheric conditions. The difference between the runs illustrates the 'noise' in the model. To get much agreement with observed rainfall, we need to average all five runs as an 'ensemble'. The ensemble averages of precipitation show some skill in simulating Australian precipitation, at least over northern Australia. Further south, the models are less successful.

These atmospheric model experiments do a good job of simulating the SOI (Figure 3.3). The SOI therefore probably can be predicted without the need

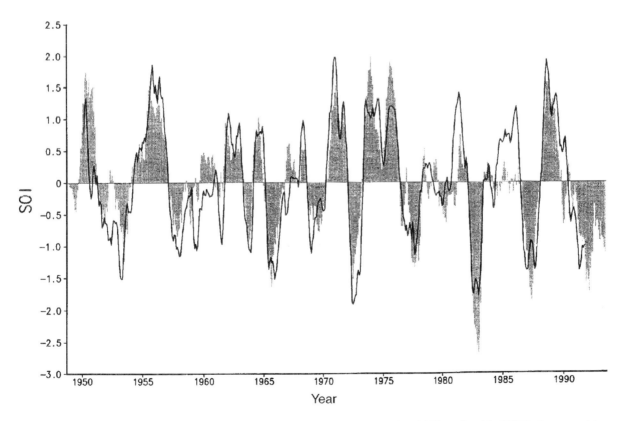

Figure 3.3 Time series of five-month running means of observed SOI (shaded regions) and SOI simulated by BMRC climate model forced with observed sea surface temperatures (line). Note that the scale is in standard deviations, so it is a factor of ten smaller than Figures 3.1 and 3.2

to run expensive ensembles. If so, we could use the coupled ocean–atmosphere models to predict large-scale indices such as the SOI, then use statistical relationships between these forecast indices and the variables we need to predict, such as rainfall at a specific location. Alternatively, we could use the coupled models to predict sea surface temperatures, then use ensemble runs of an atmospheric model forced with predicted sea surface temperatures to prepare predictions of rainfall and other variables of interest. Considerable thought and testing is needed to select the best strategy for using models in seasonal climate prediction.

APPLYING FORECASTS TO AGRICULTURE

Since the 1982–3 El Niño, the influence of this phenomenon on Australian climate has become well recognised. A computer package, 'Australian RAIN-MAN', developed by the Queensland Department of Primary Industries and the Bureau of Meteorology, allows farmers and others to investigate the likely consequences of particular phases or trends of the SOI on rainfall at thousands of locations. When this information is combined with readily available current SOI values, users can prepare their own seasonal climate forecasts.

The availability of forecasts does not necessarily mean that they will be used to change decisions or, even if they are, that the resulting decisions will lead to increased profit or less risk. There must be careful evaluation of how the forecasts might be used to influence farming decisions, and the value of these influences.

Hammer et al. (1996) investigated the value of El Niño–Southern Oscillation-based forecasting methodologies to wheat crop management in northern Australia by examining decisions on nitrogen fertiliser and cultivar maturity using simulation analyses of specific production scenarios. The average profit and risk of making a loss were calculated for the possible range of fixed (i.e., the same each year) and tactical (i.e., varying depending on the El Niño–Southern Oscillation based seasonal forecast) strategies. The technical (forecast-based) strategies would have led to significant increases in profit (up to 20 per cent) and/ or reduction in risk (up to 35 per cent) of making a

loss. The skill in seasonal rainfall and frost predictions, based on the El Niño–Southern Oscillation, generated the value from using tactical management. This study demonstrated that the skill obtainable in Australia was sufficient to justify, on economic grounds, their use in crop management. Presumably these forecasts could also be useful in drought-management decision making, for instance in determination of appropriate stocking rates on pastoral properties (McKeon et al. 1990).

CLIMATE CHANGE AND SEASONAL FORECASTING

The Australian forecast techniques depend on historical climate data. The statistical techniques use lag relationships between indicators of the state or phase of the El Niño–Southern Oscillation and rainfall. If the relationships between these variables change, perhaps as a result of climate change, then their use in seasonal climate prediction may be jeopardised. Even the climate models used to predict the El Niño rely to some extent on assumptions that the climate is not changing as a result of human interference. Their forecasts would also be undermined if the climate were changing. Nicholls (1984) investigated the stability, over time, of the forecasts based on the El Niño–Southern Oscillation. Forecasts were more skilful if only a relatively short (fifteen years) period was used in their derivation. This suggests that decadal scale changes in the climate have been affecting the forecast relationships. Nicholls (1992b) found that the relationship between the number of tropical cyclones in the Australian region and the El Niño–Southern Oscillation changed in the early 1980s, although this seems more likely to represent changes in analysis techniques or data availability than a real climate change.

Nicholls et al. (1996) found that relationships between Australian climate variables (specifically maximum temperature and rainfall) had changed, apparently rather abruptly, in the early 1970s. They also noted an apparent change in the relationship between Australian rainfall and the SOI. This change may to some extent invalidate the use of statistical relationships developed using earlier historical data. The change in relationship can be seen in Figure 3.1.

After the mid-1970s, the low values of the SOI were not accompanied by droughts as widespread as would have been the case before that time. At the very least, these apparent changes demand some study of the implications for seasonal prediction, whether with statistical methods or climate models.

THE FUTURE

The strength of the relationships between the El Niño–Southern Oscillation and Australian climate variations means that it is relatively simple to develop systems for climate prediction, and several different forecast schemes are emerging. So, in the future, different organisations – some government agencies, some private organisations – will be preparing and distributing forecasts for drought. This seems likely to lead to confusion, since the systems and forecasts will differ. In the past, such confusion has at times led consumers to doubt the credibility of the forecasts; such doubts will continue to arise. We must devise strategies to deal with an increasing number of (potentially conflicting) forecasts of drought, if Australia is to benefit from the predictability provided by the El Niño–Southern Oscillation. If this challenge is not overcome, Australia will continue to be subject to the excess climate variability produced by El Niño–Southern Oscillation without gaining from the positive aspects of the phenomenon's influence.

ACKNOWLEDGEMENTS

Beth Lavery provided the drought time series for Figure 3.1. Carsten Frederiksen provided Figure 3.3. The SOI values for the figures were provided by the Bureau of Meteorology's National Climate Centre.

REFERENCES

Allan, R.J. (1991) 'Australasia', in M. Glantz, R. Katz, and N. Nicholls (eds), *Teleconnections Linking Worldwide Climate Anomalies*, Cambridge: Cambridge University Press, pp. 73–120.

Allan, R.J., Beard, G.S., Close, A., Herczeg, A.L., Jones, P.D., and Simpson, H.J. (1996) *Mean Sea Level Pressure Indices of the El Niño–Southern Oscillation: Relevance to Stream Discharge in South-Eastern Australia*, Divisional Report 96/1, CSIRO Division of Water Resources, Canberra, Australia.

Bliss, E.W. and Walker, G.T. (1932) 'World Weather V', *Memoirs of the Royal Meteorological Society* 4: 52–84.

Casey, T. (1995) 'Optimal linear combination of seasonal forecasts', *Australian Meteorological Magazine* 44: 219–24.

Coughlan, M.J. (1979) 'Recent variations in annual-mean maximum temperatures over Australia', *Quarterly Journal of the Royal Meteorological Society* 105: 707–19.

Drosdowsky, W. (1993a) 'Potential predictability of winter rainfall over southern and eastern Australia using Indian Ocean sea surface temperature anomalies', *Australian Meteorological Magazine* 42: 1–6.

—— (1993b) 'An analysis of Australian seasonal rainfall anomalies: 1950–1987. II: Temporal variability and teleconnection patterns', *International Journal of Climatology* 13: 151–70.

—— (1996) 'Analogue (non-linear) forecasts of the Southern Oscillation Index time series', *NOAA Experimental Long-lead Forecast Bulletin* 5: 49–50.

Frederiksen, C.S., Indusekharan, P., Balgovind, R.C., and Nicholls, N. (1995) 'Multidecadal simulations of global climate trends and variability', *Proceedings TOGA95 International Scientific Conference*, Melbourne, Australia, 2–7 April 1995.

Grant, A.M. (1956) *The Application of Correlation and Regression to Forecasting*, Meteorological Study No. 7, Bureau of Meteorology, Melbourne.

Hammer, G.L., Holzworth, D.P., and Stone, R. (1996) 'The value of skill in seasonal climate forecasting to wheat crop management in a region with high climatic variability', *Australian Journal of Agricultural Research* 47: 717–37.

Kiladis, G.N. and Diaz, H.F. (1986) 'An analysis of the 1877–78 ENSO episode and comparison with 1982–83', *Monthly Weather Review* 114: 1,035–47.

—— (1989) 'Global climatic anomalies associated with extremes in the Southern Oscillation', *Monthly Weather Review* 2: 1,069–90.

Kleeman, R. (1996) 'Forecasts of Nino 3 SST using a low-order coupled ocean–atmosphere dynamical model', *NOAA Experimental Long-lead Forecast Bulletin* 5: 21–3.

Limpus, C.J. and Nicholls, N. (1988) 'The Southern Oscillation regulates the annual numbers of green turtles (Chelonia mydas) breeding around northern Australia', *Australian Journal of Wildlife Research* 15: 157–61.

McBride, J.L. and Nicholls, N. (1983) 'Seasonal relationships between Australian rainfall and the Southern Oscillation', *Monthly Weather Review* 111: 1,998–2,004.

McKeon, G.M., Day, K.A., Howden, S.M., Mott, J.J., Orr, D.M., Scattini, W.J., and Weston, E.J. (1990) 'Management of pastoral production in northern Australian savannas', *Journal of Biogeography* 17: 355–72.

Nicholls, N. (1978) 'A possible method for predicting seasonal tropical cyclone activity in the Australian region', *Monthly Weather Review* 107: 1,221–4.

——— (1979) 'A simple air-sea interaction model', *Quarterly Journal of the Royal Meteorological Society* 105: 93–105.

——— (1983) 'Predictability of the 1982 Australian drought', *Search* 14: 154–5.

——— (1984) 'The stability of empirical long-range forecast techniques: A case study', *Journal of Climate and Applied Meteorology* 23: 143–7.

——— (1985) 'Impact of the Southern Oscillation on Australian crops', *Journal of Climatology* 5: 553–60.

——— (1986) 'A method for predicting Murray Valley Encephalitis in southeast Australia using the Southern Oscillation', *Australian Journal of Experimental Biology and Medical Science* 64: 587–94.

——— (1988a) 'More on early ENSOs: Evidence from Australian documentary sources', *Bulletin of the American Meteorological Society* 69: 4–6.

——— (1988b) 'El Niño–Southern Oscillation impact prediction', *Bulletin of the American Meteorological Society* 69: 173–6.

——— (1989a) 'Sea surface temperature and Australian winter rainfall', *Journal of Climate* 2: 965–73.

——— (1989b) 'How old is ENSO?', *Climatic Change* 14: 111–15.

——— (1991) 'The El Niño–Southern Oscillation and Australian vegetation', *Vegetatio* 91: 23–36.

——— (1992a) 'Historical El Niño/Southern Oscillation variability in the Australasian region', in H.F. Diaz and V. Markgraf (eds), *El Niño – Historical and Paleoclimatic Aspects of the Southern Oscillation*, Cambridge: Cambridge University Press, pp. 151–73.

——— (1992b) 'Recent performance of a method for forecasting Australian seasonal tropical cyclone activity', *Australian Meteorological Magazine* 40: 105–10.

——— (1996) 'Modelling climatic variability', in T.W. Giambelluca and A. Henderson-Sellers (eds), *Climate Change: Developing Southern Hemisphere Perspectives*, New York: John Wiley and Sons, pp. 131–43.

Nicholls, N. and Kariko, A.P. (1993) 'East Australian rainfall events: Interannual variations, trends, and relationships with the Southern Oscillation', *Journal of Climate* 6: 1,141–52.

Nicholls, N. and Woodcock, F. (1981) 'Verification of an empirical long-range weather forecasting technique', *Quarterly Journal of the Royal Meteorological Society* 107: 973–6.

Nicholls, N., Drosdowsky, W., and Lavery, B. (1997) 'Australian rainfall variability and change', *Weather* 52: 66–72.

Nicholls, N., Lavery, B., Frederiksen, C., Drosdowsky, W., and Torok, S. (1996) 'Recent apparent changes in relationships between the El Niño–Southern Oscillation and Australian rainfall and temperature', *Geophysical Research Letters* 23: 3,357–60.

Nicholls, N., McBride, J.L., and Ormerod, R.J. (1982) 'On predicting the onset of the Australian wet season at Darwin', *Monthly Weather Review* 110: 14–17.

O'Mahony, G. (1961) *Time Series Analysis of Some Australian Rainfall Data*, Meteorological Study No. 14, Bureau of Meteorology, Melbourne.

Pittock, A.B. (1975) 'Climatic change and the patterns of variation in Australian rainfall', *Search* 6: 498–504.

Power, S.B., Kleeman, R., Tseitkin, F., and Smith, N.R. (1995) *BMRC Technical Report on a Global Version of the GFDL Modular Ocean Model for ENSO Studies*, BMRC, October 1995.

Priestley, C.H.B. (1964) 'Rainfall–sea surface temperature associations on the New South Wales coast', *Australian Meteorological Magazine* 47: 15–25.

Quayle, E.T. (1910) *On the Possibility of Forecasting the Approximate Winter Rainfall for Northern Victoria*, Bulletin No. 5, Commonwealth Bureau of Meteorology, Melbourne.

——— (1929) 'Long range rainfall forecasting from tropical (Darwin) air pressures', *Proceedings of the Royal Society of Victoria* 41: 160–4.

Ropelewski, C.F. and Halpert, M.S. (1987) 'Global and regional scale precipitation patterns associated with the El Niño–Southern Oscillation', *Monthly Weather Review* 115: 1,606–26.

——— (1989) 'Precipitation patterns associated with the high index phase of the Southern Oscillation', *Journal of Climate* 2: 268–84.

Russell, H.C. (1877) *Climate of New South Wales*, Sydney: Government Printer.

——— (1896) 'On periodicity of good and bad seasons', *Journal of the Royal Society of New South Wales* 30: 70–115.

Simpson, R.W. and Downey, W.K. (1975) 'The effect of a warm mid-latitude sea surface temperature anomaly on a numerical simulation of the general circulation of the southern hemisphere', *Quarterly Journal of the Royal Meteorological Society* 101: 847–67.

Smith, N.R. (1995) 'The BMRC ocean thermal analysis system', *Australian Meteorological Magazine* 44: 93–110.

Stone, R.C. and Auliciems, A. (1992) 'SOI phase relationships with rainfall in eastern Australia', *International Journal of Climatology* 12: 625–36.

Stone, R., Nicholls, N., and Hammer, G. (1996) 'Frost in northeast Australia: Trends and influences of phases of the Southern Oscillation', *Journal of Climate* 9: 1,896–909.

Streten, N.A. (1981) 'Southern Hemisphere sea surface temperature variability and apparent associations with Australian rainfall', *Journal of Geophysical Research* 86: 485–97.

Suppiah, R. and Hennessy, K.J. (1996) 'Trends in the intensity and frequency of heavy rainfall in tropical Australia and links with the Southern Oscillation', *Australian Meteorological Magazine* 45: 1–18.

Treloar, H.M. (1934) *Foreshadowing Monsoonal Rains in*

Northern Australia, Bulletin No. 18, Bureau of Meteorology, Melbourne.

Troup, A.J. (1965) 'The Southern Oscillation', *Quarterly Journal of the Royal Meteorological Society* 91: 490–506.

Voice, M.E. and Hunt, B.G. (1984) 'A study of the dynamics of drought initiation using a global general circulation model', *Journal of Geophysical Research* 89: 9,504–20.

Whetton, P., Adamson, D., and Williams, M. (1990) 'Rainfall and river flow variability in Africa, Australia and East Asia linked to El Niño–Southern Oscillation events', *Geological Society of Australia Symposium Proceedings* 1: 71–82.

Williams, M.A.J., Adamson, D.A., and Baxter, J.T. (1986) 'Late Quaternary environments in the Nile and Darling basins', *Australian Geographical Studies* 24: 128–44.

Zhang, X.-G. and Casey, T.M. (1992) 'Long-term variations in the Southern Oscillation and relationships with Australian rainfall', *Australian Meteorological Magazine* 40: 211–25.

4

PREDICTING DROUGHT IN KENYA

Prospects and challenges

L.A. Ogallo

INTRODUCTION

The economy of Kenya relies heavily on exports of rain-dependent agricultural products. Agriculture and its allied industries are also the major employment sectors in Kenya. The major agricultural commodities include maize, wheat, beans, cotton, tea, coffee, sugar cane, pyrethrum, and livestock products. Rainfall is the major natural factor that affects the quality and quantity of the annual productivity of these products. Rainfall further determines water availability for the various socioeconomic uses of water.

Rainfall anomalies like droughts and floods are very common in Kenya every year. Some of these anomalies are mild and are very localised in nature. Others are very severe and sometimes extend over large parts of the country. The chance of any of the extreme rainfall anomalies extending over all parts of the country during a particular rainfall season, however, is very low because of the country's complex topography and large inland water bodies, which introduce significant modifications to the general circulation over the region (Ogallo 1989).

More than 80 per cent of Kenya can be classified as arid and semiarid lands (ASAL). Livestock farming is the major activity in ASAL. Livestock farming practices in ASAL range from zero-grazing (homestead feeding system) to nomadic pasturing in the more arid zones. Large commercial ranges and rain-fed crop farming, however, are very common in the wetter parts of ASAL. A high degree of interannual rainfall variability, including frequent occurrences of droughts, is the major threat to sustainable agricultural productivity of the ASAL.

In recent years, population pressure and changes in land use activities have introduced new dimensions in Kenya's drylands. Population pressure has led to overstocking of livestock, overgrazing, deforestation, desertification, and many other processes of environmental degradation that seem to threaten the traditional survival strategies of the indigenous dryland community. Population pressure has also resulted in the resettlement of settlers from high-potential areas, who often bring their high-potential land use activities to the drylands, including cultivation of high-potential region crops like maize at the expense of drought-resistant crops like sorghum and millet, to sustain their traditional diets and eating habits. This often makes such new settlers more vulnerable to the normal interannual climatic stress of the ASAL, including frequent drought occurrences.

The wetter climate zones of Kenya are generally concentrated near the large water bodies and over the highlands, where a wide range of agricultural activities are being carried out, including the cultivation of both cash and food crops. The high-potential areas provide most of the agricultural exports that form the core of the national economy. The high-potential zones, however, cover less than 20 per cent of the country, signifying that most of Kenya is vulnerable to a high degree of interannual rainfall variability, including drought recurrences.

Apart from drought, other factors that are currently affecting agricultural productivity in the high-potential areas are: the high cost of agricultural inputs; population pressure, including unplanned growth of new urban centres; overuse of fertilisers at some locations, resulting in soil pollution; market/

trade problems; post-harvest losses in the field and through poor storage; water erosion of the soil; and many other processes of environmental degradation.

Drought, however, is the major natural disaster that has been associated with annual deficits in agricultural productivity; shortages of energy, food, and water; famine; and devastating impacts on many other sectors/services that form integral components of national socioeconomic development. Some of these drought impacts linger for several years, and no sustainable socioeconomic development can therefore be achieved without proper planning and management strategies for coping with such droughts. The major components of such disaster management strategies must include drought monitoring, diagnosis, prediction, efficient early warning systems, and drought preparedness policies.

This review of predictability of Kenyan drought has addressed four key drought issues, namely:

- dynamics and causes;
- socioeconomic impacts, including the recent integrated global efforts to address such problems;
- predictability prospects; and
- challenges to drought prediction in Kenya.

DYNAMICS AND CAUSES OF DROUGHT IN KENYA

Droughts in Kenya have been associated with anomalies in the spatial and/or temporal characteristics of the systems that control the regional climate. The major systems that control rainfall variability in Kenya include:

- the Inter Tropical Convergence Zone (ITCZ)
- east African monsoon winds
- subtropical anticyclones over Africa
- tropical cyclones
- easterly/westerly waves
- jetstreams
- extratropical weather systems
- thermally induced mesoscale systems
- teleconnections with global and regional scale circulation anomalies like those associated with El Niño/Southern Oscillation (ENSO), quasi-biennial oscillation, and intraseasonal wave

The major transports of moisture inland for rainfall formation in Kenya are the regional monsoonal wind systems. The direction and speed of these winds also affect the patterns of the convective processes inland. Two distinct monsoonal wind systems are common over the region, namely north and south easterlies. Both converge over Kenya and other parts of equatorial eastern Africa during the autumn and spring seasons. However, Kenya is largely under the dominance of north easterly/south easterly monsoonal winds during the southern/northern summer seasons, respectively. The patterns of the monsoonal wind systems are significantly modified, especially at low levels, by complex topographical patterns.

ITCZ marks the convergence of the low-level interhemispheric north easterly and south easterly monsoonal wind systems. The zone therefore migrates north and south of the equator following the overhead sun, and often lags behind it by three to five weeks. ITCZ is very diffuse at the low levels in Kenya, owing to the existence of complex topographical patterns and many large inland water bodies, which often introduce both zonal and meridional components in the seasonal migration over Kenya. The zonal component of the ITCZ, for example, has been associated with the influx of most westerlies from the Atlantic/Congo/Zaire basins, which dominate the western parts of Kenya during the months of June to August. Easterly/westerly waves are often embedded within the basic tropical monsoonal/midlatitude westerly winds.

The intensity, location, and space-time structure of the subtropical anticyclones not only determine the patterns of the interhemispheric monsoon wind systems, they also determine whether the tracks of the monsoonal winds will be largely continental or maritime, together with overall moisture characteristics of these wind systems. The subtropical anticyclones over the African continent are often centred around four quasi-stationary anticyclones, namely the Arabian, Azores, Mascarene, and St. Helena anticyclones.

Subtropical jetstreams are permanent features above the subtropical front throughout the year, both south and north of the African continent. Three other jetstreams are observed over the continent during the Northern Hemisphere summer months of

June–August. These include the subtropical easterly, east African low level, and west African mid-tropospheric jetstreams. These fast-moving upper level winds have far-reaching impacts with respect to the transport of moisture, momentum, pollutants, and pests, together with many other aspects of the atmospheric dynamics.

Tropical cyclones have both direct and indirect impacts on Kenyan rainfall. The direct impacts are associated with the strong winds, ocean waves, and excessive precipitation that occur when the effects of any cyclone within the western Indian Ocean extend over Kenya. It should be noted that the available climatological records show that no cyclone has ever hit the Kenyan coast. The indirect effects of any cyclone, however, occur when the cyclone is far from the region but still attracts the regional winds towards its centre, thereby interfering with the normal circulation patterns of the regional winds.

Close interactions have been observed between the general circulation over the region and the extra-tropical weather systems like the frontal and blocking systems, midlatitude westerlies, North Atlantic oscillation, east Atlantic patterns, and Eurasia patterns. Teleconnections have also been observed between Kenyan rainfall and ENSO, quasi-biennial oscillation, intraseasonal wave, and so forth. The influence of the complex topographical patterns and the large inland water bodies is very significant in Kenya. The large inland water bodies include Lake Victoria, which has an area of about 70,000 km² and is the second largest freshwater lake in the world. The complex topographical patterns include Mt. Kenya, Mt. Kilimanjaro, and the Great Rift Valley with its attendant chain of mountains. Details of the regional climate processes can be obtained from Ogallo 1993, Anyamba 1992, Fremming 1970, and Findlater 1966.

SOCIOECONOMIC IMPACTS OF DROUGHT

Drought and other extreme climate events are normal components of natural interannual climate variability and common phenomena worldwide every year. The impacts of these natural disasters, however, are minimal in the developed countries where efficient and adequate drought shock absorbers have been developed through sound early warning and disaster preparedness policies.

Societies in developing countries, especially Africa, rely heavily on post-disaster relief and rehabilitation efforts, which make them more and more vulnerable to the severe impacts of drought and other natural disasters. Increased vulnerability of society to the severe consequences of natural disasters led to the declaration of the 1990s as the International Decade for Natural Disaster Reduction (IDNDR) by the United Nations. The major objective of IDNDR is to promote disaster prevention and preparedness through concerted international action, especially in the developing countries, to reduce loss of life, property damage, and socioeconomic disruption, which are often associated with natural disasters. These could help to shift the post-disaster relief and rehabilitation attitudes that are prevalent in many developing countries.

A new dimension to natural climate variability, including the future recurrence of droughts, is the current global concern about the potential change in the traditional space-time patterns of global climate, including the space-time characteristics of extreme climate events through environmental degradation by human activities. Such impacts are currently subjects of many studies and debates, as reflected in the 1995 Intergovernmental Panel on Climate Change (IPCC) scientific assessment of climate change, which indicated 'discernible influence of human activities in the recent climate trends'. IPCC (1995) noted, however, that no conclusive evidence can be derived for human-induced climate change signals until more accurate methods for the detection and attribution of natural/anthropogenic (human-induced) climate change signals are available, together with adequate and accurate climate data for testing various hypothesis. Severe consequences of human-induced climate changes, including changes in the space-time patterns of extreme climate events like drought, would call for clear mitigation and adaptation policies, as highlighted by the IPCC.

Global concern about human-induced environmental degradation processes and sustainability of natural resources vital to most socioeconomic activities led to the organisation of the United Nations Conference on Environment and Sustainable

Development (UNCED), which was held in Rio de Janeiro (Brazil) in June 1995. UNCED action plans into the twenty-first century are summarised in UNCED's publication, which is commonly referred to as 'Agenda 21'. Three conventions related to environmental degradation that were negotiated by UNCED include the United Nations Framework Convention on Climate Change (UNFCCC), United Nations Convention to Combat Desertification (UNCCD), and United Nations Convention on Biodiversity (UNCB).

The global concern about the severe consequences of the alarming rate of increase in population pressure, including the fast growth of unplanned urban centres, has also been addressed at many national, regional, and international fora, including the last two United Nations Conferences on Human Settlement (HABITAT I and II).

The socioeconomic impacts of droughts that were highlighted in this section were based largely on experiences from Kenya.

Kenyan experience

The dynamics and potential causes of droughts in Kenya were highlighted above. It was noted that extreme rainfall anomalies in Kenya are associated with anomalies in the space-time characteristics of the systems that control the regional climate. The impacts of such anomalies, however, vary significantly from year to year, and from one location to another because of modifications of large scale circulation patterns by complex mesoscale systems.

The impacts of complex regional topography and large water bodies on rainfall climatology are quite evident from the annual rainfall patterns given in Figure 4.1. The figure shows that the largest values of annual rainfall are concentrated over the highlands and near the large water bodies. Two rainfall seasons are also common in Kenya, centred around the autumn and spring seasons (Figure 4.2). Parts of western Kenya receive substantial rainfall during the months of June–August as a westerly influx of moist air mass from the Atlantic Ocean and the moist Zaire/Congo basin (Figure 4.2b), while some parts of locations near the large water bodies receive substantial rainfall throughout the year (Figure 4.2b

and 4.2d). Such complex spatial rainfall patterns are also common during anomalous rainfall years. This section highlights the socioeconomic disasters that are often associated with droughts in Kenya. The climatology of the droughts is presented first.

Drought climatology in Kenya

Meteorological drought occurs when precipitation received at any location is significantly less than the normal expectation for any specific (extended) period. This meteorological concept of drought will be maintained throughout this text. Other definitions of drought based on the water balance equation for sectoral water demands and uses can be obtained from many standard references. It should, however, be noted that precipitation deficits are often the trigger of most of the other sectoral droughts.

Figure 4.2 shows that seasonal evolutions of rainfall vary significantly from one location to another in Kenya. Most of the annual rainfall, however, is concentrated within two major seasons – namely, the March–May (long) and October–November (short) rainfall seasons. Any discussion of Kenyan droughts must therefore consider the unique seasonal rainfall cycles of the specific locations. It is not realistic to use annual rainfall records in studying Kenyan droughts since above- and below-normal rainfall may be observed during the two rainfall seasons within the same year. Such anomalies cannot be detected by the use of annual rainfall records. Cumulative effects of rainfall anomalies within any year, however, can be estimated from cumulative annual rainfall total. Figure 4.3 gives examples of the spatial patterns of the cumulative annual drought stress. The values given in the figure represent the probability of occurrence of cumulative rainfall anomalies within the first four lower deciles if annual rainfall observations at the specific locations are ranked from the lowest to the highest values. Low values of drought probabilities are concentrated over areas with high annual rainfall values, while higher probabilities of drought risks are located over the ASAL, which covers 80 per cent of Kenya.

Figure 4.4 shows that the severity of the droughts varies significantly from one year to another. The spatial patterns of the anomalies, however, are very similar in some seasons and years, such as during

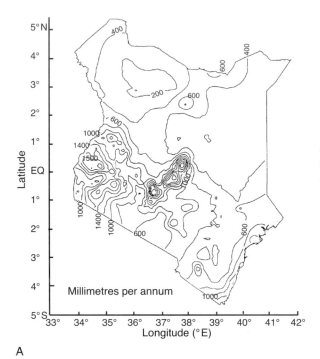

A

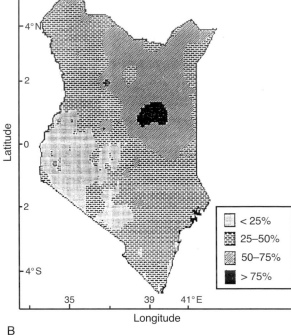

B

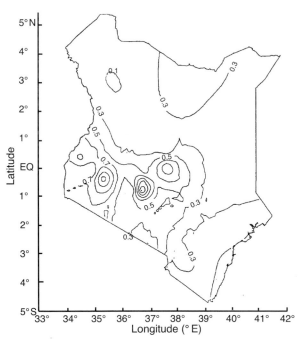

C

Figure 4.1 (a) Mean annual rainfall patterns. (b) Smoothed coefficient of variation map for annual rainfall. (c) Map of aridity patterns in Kenya (P/E$_T$)

some of the strong ENSO events (Figure 4.5). However, it is very clear from Figures 4.5e and 4.5f that not all droughts in Kenya are associated with ENSO. The chance of any year being drought-free throughout the country, or any drought of a particular season extending over all parts of Kenya, are also relatively low (Ogallo 1989).

The vulnerability of the country to high degrees of interannual rainfall variability highlights the need for timely and effective drought monitoring, diagnosis, long-range prediction, and early warning as crucial components of disaster preparedness strategies. The devastating impacts of the droughts in Kenya, together with the post-disaster relief and rehabilitation efforts that are common in many developing countries, are highlighted in the next section, using the most recent (1996–7) drought, which has been considered one of the worst in recent years.

The impacts of the 1996–7 drought

Examples of the time series of the seasonal rainfall anomalies are given in Figures 4.6 and 4.7 for some specific locations. It is evident from the figures that

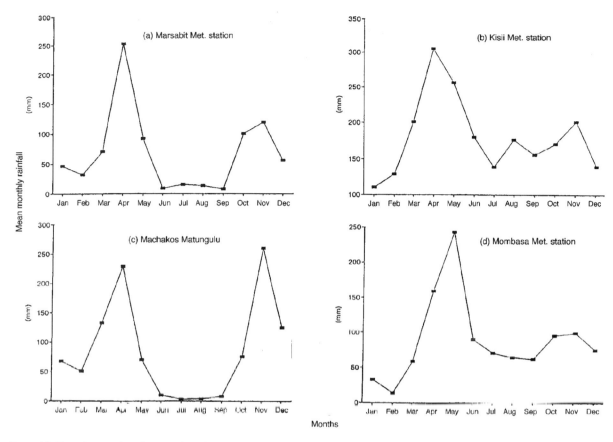

Figure 4.2 Typical examples of seasonal rainfall patterns in Kenya

the most recent severe drought occurred during 1996–7 at a number of locations. The seasonal evolution of this particular drought is shown in Figure 4.8, while Figure 4.9 attempts to compare the 1996–7 drought with some other recent anomalous rainfall periods using cumulative rainfall deficit indices. Under this method, cumulative ten-day rainfall values are plotted and compared for specific years.

Drought occurrences in Kenya are often associated with far-reaching socioeconomic disasters, including: loss of agricultural production; food, energy, and water shortages; mass migration of population and animals; increased insecurity due to inter-clan/tribe cattle rustling; conflicts over limited pastures and water resources within some dryland locations; hoarding and escalating prices of essential commodities; stagnation of many development projects due to the shifting of most of the government resources to

emergency food relief and rehabilitation; loss of life and property; increase in inflation rate; and many other devastating socioeconomic calamities (Ogallo 1997).

The devastating effects of the 1996–7 drought, for example, led to the declaration of a national famine calamity or famine disaster by the government on 28 January 1997 through a legal notice, in order to alleviate the looming natural calamity brought about by the prolonged drought. This involved invoking the Public Security Act for the first time in many years. The legal notice empowered the government to waive duty and value added tax (VAT) on certain essential commodities like maize, milk, and rice for the affected areas, since under Kenyan law, duty on food and VAT can only be waived during a period of national strife or national calamity or disaster (Section 138 of the Customs and Excise, and section 23 of the

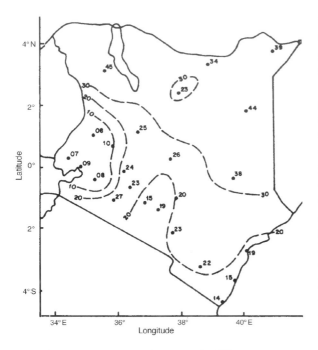

Figure 4.3 Annual probability of droughts (× 100)

Value Added Tax laws). The declaration of the 'national famine disaster' also allowed food relief by religious groups, nongovernmental bodies, and other donors.

The impacts of the 1996–7 drought on the national economy were reflected by the sharp rise in the inflation rate, from 14.7 per cent to 35.4 per cent within a span of few months. Other impacts of inter-annual rainfall variability on agricultural production are highlighted in Figure 4.9 and Table 4.1. Figure 4.9 also highlights the vulnerability of rain-fed agriculture to extreme climate variability for a few other African countries. It is important to note the recent sustainability and increase in grain production in Egypt and Libyan Arab Jamahiraya through the application of irrigation systems. Rainfall and other climate parameters, however, determine water availability for any irrigation system. Long-range climate prediction of rainfall is therefore a crucial component of any sustainable agricultural productivity and national socioeconomic development.

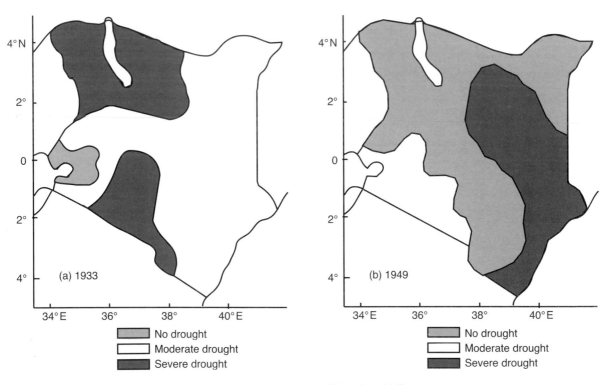

Figure 4.4 (a) Annual patterns of drought in 1933. (b) Annual patterns of drought in 1949

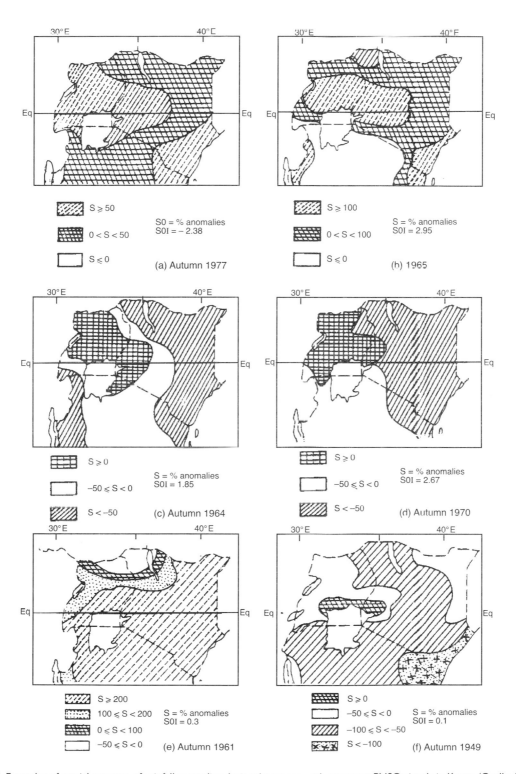

Figure 4.5 Examples of spatial patterns of rainfall anomalies during the season with strongest ENSO signals in Kenya (Ogallo 1988)

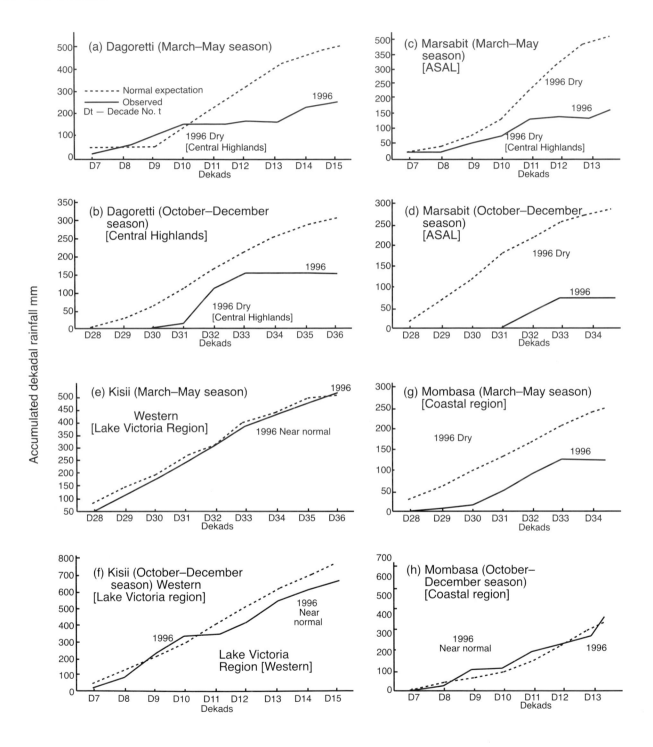

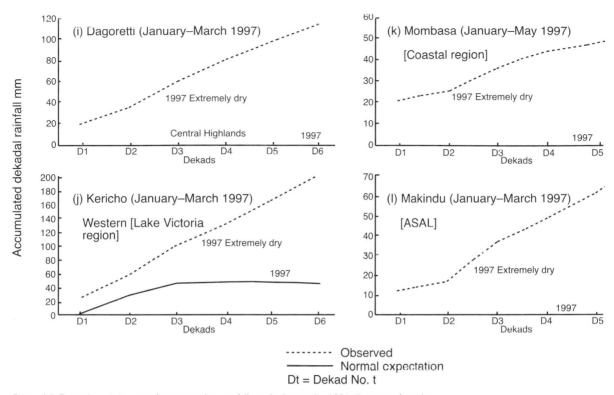

Figure 4.6 Examples of the cumulative ten-day rainfall totals during the 1996–7 severe drought

It should also be noted that not all interannual changes in agricultural productivity can be associated with climate variability. Other causes of reduction in agricultural production in Kenya include poor pricing and marketing, which force farmers to shift to growing better-paying crops in the following season. Global economics, high cost of inputs, external factors, and many other nonclimatic factors have also been associated with reduction in agricultural productivity in Kenya. The ability to predict drought occurrence and associated socioeconomic risks is crucial to any drought preparedness policy.

PROSPECTS AND CHALLENGES OF THE PREDICTION OF DROUGHT IN KENYA

Methods that have been used in long-range prediction of droughts can be classified under three major categories – namely, statistical/empirical, dynamical, and statistical–dynamical. The statistical methods involve the use of statistics derived from climatological records

to extrapolate future expectations. Many such methods assume that the system is stationary (constant mean and variance) to ensure equal chances of occurrences of past fluctuations in the future.

Dynamical methods are based on mathematical equations that govern the dynamics, physics, and other processes that determine the climate of the earth, while the statistical–dynamical (hybrid) methods involve a blending of the statistical and dynamical methods.

Apart from some periods and regions of the world that have strong ENSO signals and other persistent general circulation features, the skill of long-range prediction is still low, especially at regional and local scales. The recently concluded World Climate Research Programme (WCRP) Tropical Ocean Global Atmosphere (TOGA) ten-year programme, however, provided an outstanding insight to the understanding of tropical oceans and the predictability of ENSO signals. From the efforts of TOGA, it is now possible to project ENSO signals several months ahead with reasonable skill (Cane *et al.* 1986). The newly launched programme Climate

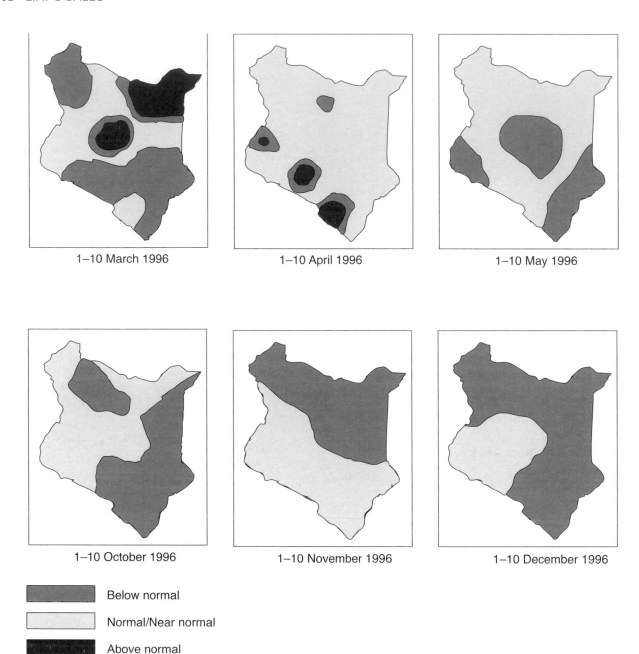

1–10 March 1996   1–10 April 1996   1–10 May 1996

1–10 October 1996   1–10 November 1996   1–10 December 1996

Below normal

Normal/Near normal

Above normal

Figure 4.7 Spatial evolution of the 1996–7 severe drought

Variability and Predictability (CLIVAR) Study by WCRP is expected to extend climate predictability over seasonal to interannual time scales through the development of global coupled predictive models, based on the success of TOGA in the understanding of tropical ocean processes and the extension of ENSO predictability to several months ahead.

At the operational level, most of the long-range prediction methods that have been used in Kenya are largely empirical techniques. Such techniques have

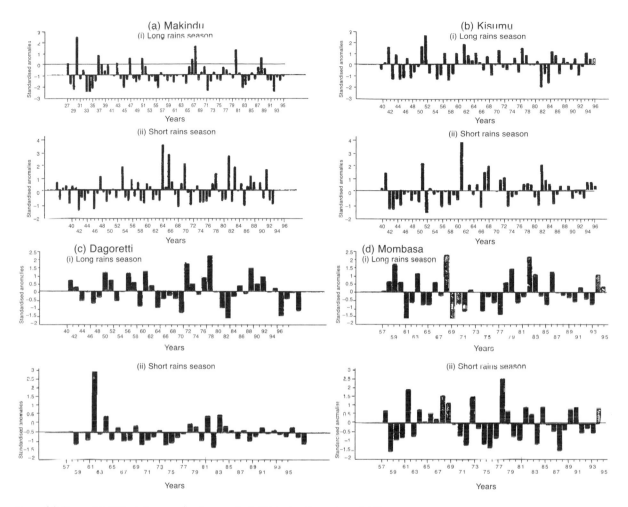

Figure 4.8 Examples of the interannual patterns of rainfall during the major rainfall seasons

included (1) simple conditional probability methods, (2) autoregressive methods based on trends, cyclical fluctuation, and complex autoregressive models like ARIMA, and (3) multiple regression methods. Details of these methods can be obtained from Ogallo 1986, Farmer 1988, Ogallo 1987, and Mutai *et al.* 1996.

The method that has been widely used, however, is multiple regression. Such methods have ranged from the use of simple indices of the regional climate systems as predictors to more complex discriminant analyses to select some optimum number of predictors that must be included in the multivariate prediction equation. The most common empirical predictors have been derived from some indices of

ENSO, sea surface temperatures, quasi-biennial oscillation, intraseasonal wave, and so forth (Ogallo *et al.* 1988, Ogallo 1988, Ogallo *et al.* 1994, Ininda 1995, Okoola 1997, Hastenrath 1995, Mukabana 1992).

The results from most of the empirical forecasting studies have shown that the skill of the prediction by any set of chosen predictors varies significantly from location to location and from one season to another. Maximum predictability skill has been observed over the coastal and Lake Victoria regions during the northern autumn months, when as much as 70 per cent of the total seasonal rainfall variance can be accounted for during strong ENSO signals. Thus, the

Figure 4.9 Interannual variability of annual rainfall and grain production
Source: FAO 1991

Table 4.1 Agricultural production in Kenya, 1993 6

	Annual crop production 1993–6								
	1993 ha	t	b	1994 ha	t	b	1995 ha	t	b
Maize	1.340	–	19.0	1.500	–	34.0	1.440	–	2.9
Wheat	1.540	–	2.30	1.340	–	3.3	1.480	–	3.4
Bean	0.630	–	4.50	0.650	–	3.1	0.700	–	4.9
Rice	0.009	0.044	–	0.010	0.047	–	0.110	0.048	–
Sugar	0.100	0.381	–	0.104	0.303	–	0.123	0.384	–
Fruits	1.300	1.760	–	1.390	1.850	–	1.400	1.910	–
Sorghum	–	0.150	–	–	0.180	–	–	0.130	–
Millet	–	0.520	–	–	0.460	–	–	0.510	–

Source: FAO/WFP, Ministry of Agriculture
Notes: t = tons; b = bags; ha = area cultivated in hectares

recent ability to project ENSO information several months ahead could provide very important information for drought monitoring, diagnosis, and prediction for some parts of Kenya. Such information is currently being used by the National Meteorological Service and the regional Drought Monitoring Centre (DMC), which is located in Nairobi. Such methods were also successfully used to project some of the recent rainfall anomalies in Kenya, including the 1996–7 drought. It was, for example, noted that although the 1996–7 drought was the worst in recent years at many locations in Kenya, the socioeconomic impacts were relatively less severe than those of 1984 (and other years), owing to early warning information provided to the government by the National Meteorological Service, DMC, FAO, and FEWS/USAID. These enabled timely emergency relief and other rehabilitation efforts, which were discussed above.

Long-range prediction of the Kenyan droughts by dynamical and dynamical–statistical methods is still being researched. Most of the recent research has concentrated on the use of general circulation models in examining the predictability potential of monsoonal wind systems, ENSO, sea surface temperatures, and so forth (Mukabana 1992, Hastenrath 1995, Ininda 1995, Sun *et al.* 1997). Such models require special data and other advanced technology facilities, which are often missing within the region.

The major components of a good drought preparedness plan include a data base, timely data acquisition systems, real-time/near real-time monitoring, diagnosis, data/information processing, drought prediction, impact assessment, decision-making mechanisms, user feedback, and evaluation systems. The major challenges for the prediction of droughts in Kenya therefore include:

1 *Data problems* Long periods of high-quality climatological records are required to compute accurate statistics of past droughts as well as indices that will enable comparisons to be made between current and previous droughts.

Apart from rainfall records, the space time distribution of the observation network is relatively poor for the other meteorological parameters in Kenya. Even for rainfall, most of the observations are concentrated in the urban centres, research and administration centres, schools, and other inhabited areas. Relatively few observations are available over the ASAL and mountainous regions.

The observation network for rainfall has decreased substantially, from about 3,000 in the mid-1960s to about 800 by 1996. The rate of the decrease is very alarming and must be addressed to ensure regular maintenance of some crucial minimum raingauge network.

2 *Real-time monitoring systems* The impacts of droughts are often cumulative. Continuous monitoring of drought status can enable the onset, cessation, severity, rate of change, and other drought characteristics to be assessed. Real-time

monitoring is therefore an important component of any drought preparedness strategies. The real-time monitoring methods used in Kenya depend largely on the raingauge network design (discussed above). Some recent methods have included satellite-derived rainfall estimates, but such records have not been calibrated for point rainfall estimates in Kenya. Other drought monitoring methods depend on climate products from the global climate centres (e.g., ENSO forecasts).

3 *Efficient communication facilities* are required for the collection, dissemination, and exchange of data/information. The available communication network is not adequate for an effective drought preparedness and early warning system.

4 *Research* is required to understand the complex drought processes and their socioeconomic interactions. Resources for meteorological research are very limited in Kenya.

5 *Drought monitoring, diagnosis, and prediction require special equipment and high technology facilities* including special instruments and computers, which are limited in Kenya.

6 *Skilled human resources* are required in handling the multidisciplinary dimensions of droughts. Human resources for handling the basic meteorological concepts of drought are available in Kenya. However, they need special training to be able to effectively address the complex multidisciplinary components that could be required to address the basic challenges of drought preparedness.

7 *Mismanagement and abuse of drought information* have been observed in some cases when drought information has been used for economic, political, and other gains by some individual citizens, donors, and others at the expense of the general public. In some cases, drought advisories have been abused through hoarding of essential commodities and introducing them back to the market within a few months at hiked prices. Even after receiving information that one country will experience drought within a few months, some donors have been known to continue pressing that country to export their grain reserves at very minimal prices by guaranteeing they will provide funds for grain imports in case of droughts. The export price for a bag of maize is sometimes as low

as US$5,while the importing price for the same bag of maize during a drought period is sometimes as high as US$20 within a span of two to three months. Such drought industries must be discouraged.

8 *Financial resources* for drought monitoring, diagnosis, prediction, and drought preparedness are limited in Kenya. Kenya has, however, invested heavily in meteorological training, education, and basic facilities.

9 *Timely availability of drought products and services from global climate centres* Many meteorological services in the region rely on drought advisories from the climate centres of the developed world. Such products include ENSO advisories and global circulation data. Such information is sometimes not accessible on time. The installation of the new internet facility at the Kenya Meteorological Department will significantly improve this problem.

10 An educated and well-informed public is likely to respond better to any new policy/methods. *Education and training* of the public, managers, and policy makers is an important component of any drought preparedness strategy. This has not been optimum in Kenya, especially in light of the complex multidisciplinary drought interactions.

11 *Structural adjustment of the World Bank* has introduced a new dimension in the region since it discourages government subsidy, which has been a major post-drought emergency relief strategy for providing basic food in the drought-stricken region. The method was adopted during the drought of 1996–7 by invoking the Public Security Act on 28 January 1997. Without emergency food relief and government subsidy on basic food commodities in the drought-stricken regions, including provision for subsidised seed prices when the rains started, the impacts of the 1996–7 drought would have been very devastating.

It may be concluded that although Kenya has an interministerial disaster management committee under the office of the president, and many other ministerial subcommittees that provide relevant sectoral drought information to the interministerial committee, Kenya does *not* have *an integrated natural disaster preparedness policy* that could be used to minimise devastating post-disaster emergency relief and rehabilitation efforts and optimise the use of recent technological advancements in climate-based technologies for drought monitoring, diagnosis, and prediction. However, Kenya has made many investments in sectoral predisaster planning and management activities. These include the investments that have been made at the Kenya Meteorological Department and Regional Drought Monitoring Centre and in agricultural and water resources activities, among many other sectors. Such efforts must, however, be integrated to avoid sectoral conflicts and provide effective drought preparedness 'shock absorbers'.

REFERENCES

Anyamba, E.K. (1992) 'Some prospects of a 20–30 days oscillation in tropical circulation', *Journal of the African Meteorological Society* 1: 1–19.

Beltrando, G. (1989) 'Space-time variability in April and October–November rainfall over East Africa during the period 1932–83', *Journal of Climatology* 10: 691–702.

Cane, M.A., Zebiak, S.E., and Dolan, S.C. (1986) 'Experimental forecast of El Niño', *Nature* 321: 827–32.

DMC (1997) 'Drought monitoring, February 1997', *Bulletin for Eastern and Southern Africa*, Nairobi: Drought Monitoring Centre.

Farmer, G. (1988) 'Seasonal forecasting of Kenyan coast short rains', *Journal of Climatology* 8: 489–97.

FAO (1991) Computerised Information Series, UN Food and Agriculture Organization, Rome.

Findlater, J. (1966) 'Cross-equatorial jetstream at low level over Kenya', *Meteorological Magazine* 95: 353–64.

Fremming, D. (1970) 'Notes on easterly disturbances affecting East Africa', *Technical Memo* No. 3, East African Meteorological Department.

Hastenrath, S. (1995) 'Recent advances in tropical climate prediction', *Journal of Climate* 8: 1,519–32.

Ininda, J. (1995) 'Numerical simulation of the influence of SST anomalies on the East African rainfall', PhD thesis, Met. Dept. University of Nairobi, Kenya.

IPCC (1995) 'Climate Change 1995', WMO/UNEP Intergovernmental Panel on Climate Change 1995 Working Group I Report.

Mukabana, J. (1992) 'Numerical simulation of the influence of large scale monsoon flow on the diurnal weather patterns over Kenya', PhD thesis, Met. Dept., University of Nairobi, Kenya.

Mutai, C.C., Ward, M.N., and Colman, W. (1996) 'Prediction of East African seasonal rainfall using SST-forced variability', 2nd Conference of the African Met. Soc., 25–28 November 1996, Casablanca, Morocco.

Ogallo, L.A. (1986) 'Stochastic modelling of regional annual rainfall anomalies in East Africa', *Journal of Applied Statistics* 13, 1: 49–56.

—— (1987) 'Relationship between East African rainfall and Southern oscillation', *International Journal of Climatology* 8: 31–43.

—— (1988) 'Spatial and temporal clusters of East African rainfall derived from PCA', *International Journal of Climatology* 9: 145–67.

—— (1989) 'Characteristics of droughts in Kenya', Environment 2000 Conference, 24–26 October 1989, Nairobi, Kenya.

—— (1993) 'Dynamics of the East African climate', *Proceedings of the Indian Academy of Science* 103: 1: 203–17.

—— (1997) 'Post-impacts syndromes and drought response strategies in sub-Saharan Africa', *International Journal of African Studies*, No. 2, pp. 71–9.

Ogallo, L.A., Janowiak, J., and Halpert, M.S. (1988) 'Teleconnections between rainfall over east Africa and global sea surface temperature anomalies', *Journal of the Meteorological Society of Japan* 66, 6: 807–22.

Ogallo, L.A., Okoola, R.E., and Wanjohi, D.N. (1994) 'Characteristics of quasi-biennial oscillation over Kenya and their predictability potential for seasonal rainfall', *Mausam* 45, 1: 57–62.

Okoola, R. (1997) 'Space-time characteristics of the ITCZ over equatorial Eastern Africa during anomalous rainfall years', PhD thesis, Met. Dept., University of Nairobi, Kenya.

Sun, L., Semazzi, F.H.M., Giorgi, F., and Ogallo, L. (1999) 'Application of NCAR regional climate model to Eastern Africa' *Journal of Geophysical Research* 104, D6: 6,529–62.

5

THE PREDICTION OF DROUGHT IN THE BRAZILIAN NORDESTE

Progress and prospects for the future

Paulo Nobre and Iracema F.A. Cavalcanti

INTRODUCTION

Rainfall represents the most important climate phenomenon in the tropics. It constitutes the climatic element that determines a large part of the biological cycles in the tropics, since air temperature is normally high all year. Over the Brazilian northeast (Nordeste), which is located between 4° S and 16° S and 35° W and 46° W (Figure 5.1), just to the east of the Amazon tropical rain forest, rainfall is even more important because of the area's dominant semiarid climate. The annual rainfall over the driest areas of the Nordeste (the 'sertão') is only a fourth of the average annual precipitation over the neighbouring Amazon region, where annual rainfall is more than 2,000 mm (Figure 5.1). The seasons over the Nordeste are characterised by a long stationary dry season, interrupted only by

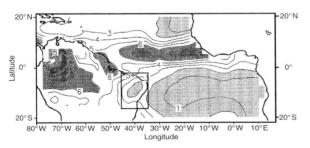

Figure 5.1 Long-term mean annual rainfall (mm/day) over the tropical Atlantic and the northern part of South America. Contour interval is 1 mm/day. Areas less than 2 mm/day and larger than 6 mm/day are shaded. The Nordeste Brazil region is located within the rectangular box over northeastern South America

Source: Adapted from Nobre 1993

the wet season from February to May, concurrent with the southernmost penetration of the inter-tropical convergence zone (ITCZ) over the equatorial Atlantic (Hastenrath 1984). Locally, the rainy season is referred to as the 'winter' season by the native population, the Nordestinos, since air temperatures tend to be lower than during the dry season.

The recurrent droughts over the Nordeste are an old and deeply rooted problem in the Nordeste. Drought is popularly pointed to as the cause for regional poverty and misery, although recent studies challenge this dogma. There are indications that the social and economic impacts of climate variability on the Nordeste are due to the conservative production system that dominates the economical, political, and social structures in the region (Carvalho 1988, Magalhães and Glantz 1992). Furthermore, some entrepreneurs in the Nordeste, as well as in other semiarid regions of the globe, have taken advantage of the Nordeste's dry climate (elevated temperatures and sunshine year round, low relative humidity, and no rains during several months of the year) to produce high-quality irrigated tropical fruits (e.g., mango, grapes, watermelon) of high cash value in the international market.

In adapting human activities to the cycles of nature (i.e., benefiting from an area's natural regional charac-teristics without exhausting its resources), it is possible to use the uniqueness of the Nordeste's highly predictable dry climate as a competitive advantage over other areas of the globe, but not as an excuse for the condition of poverty in which most of its 40 million people live.

The climate variability over the Nordeste has been studied extensively since the late 1800s. Early scientific works tried to link solar activity to the occurrence of droughts over the region (Derby 1885, Kantor 1980, Hull 1942). However, subsequent studies have shown that droughts over the Nordeste are linked to planetary scale atmospheric and oceanic phenomena (Ferraz 1925, Ferraz 1929, Serra 1946, Markham and McLain 1977, Hastenrath and Heller 1977, Kousky 1979, Moura and Shukla 1981, Mechoso *et al.* 1990, Hastenrath and Greischar 1993a, Nobre and Shukla 1996). Nowadays there is a general consensus in the international scientific community that droughts over the Nordeste are the manifestations of planetary-scale oceanic and atmospheric phenomena, for which the distribution of sea surface temperature anomalies (SSTA) over the tropics is the principal forcing (Markham and McLain 1977, Moura and Shukla 1981, Mechoso *et al.* 1990, Chu 1991, Servain 1991, Sperber and Hameed 1991). In particular, the occurrence of positive SSTA over the eastern equatorial Pacific and northern tropical Atlantic and negative SSTA over the equatorial and southern tropical Atlantic constitute favourable conditions for the occurrence of extreme droughts over the northern part of the Nordeste (Hastenrath and Heller 1977, Moura and Shukla 1981, Nobre and Molion 1988). On the other hand, the remarkable predictability of seasonal rainfall anomalies over tropical areas like the Nordeste is linked to the slowly varying distribution of SST over the tropical oceans (Shukla 1981).

The ability to predict the occurrence of droughts over the Nordeste has been a goal of researchers and a desire of the Nordeste's native population for more than a century. Several methods have been developed for this purpose, from the observation of daily weather and nature by native farmers and peasants to the establishment of global arrays of data collection platforms over the continents and the oceans (e.g., the TOGA-type arrays over the equatorial Pacific and the tropical Atlantic) and the formulation of complex dynamical atmospheric and oceanic general circulation models. This chapter describes the state of the art in monitoring and forecasting droughts over the Nordeste region today, as well as methods being developed for monitoring and forecasting seasonal climate variability over the Nordeste in the near future.

THE MEAN CLIMATE OVER THE NORDESTE

The Nordeste is generally known for its dry climate. The annual total rainfall over the semiarid portion of the Nordeste (encompassing most of the northern part of it) varies between 400 mm and 800 mm and is concentrated over three to four months of the year. However, parts of the Nordeste experience quite different climatic conditions than the one just described. For instance, the western portion of the Nordeste, covering the states of Maranhão and part of Piauí, experiences a predominantly Amazonian climate, with annual rainfall of more than 1,500 mm; also, over the eastern shores of the Nordeste, rainfall totals exceed 1,100 mm per year.

The southern part of the Nordeste (encompassing most of Bahia and the southern parts of Maranhão and Piauí) receives most of its annual rainfall during December to February, from the incursion of cold fronts that originate at higher latitudes of the Southern Hemisphere (Kousky 1979). Over the northern part of the Nordeste (encompassing the semiarid portions of Piauí, Ceará, Rio Grande do Norte, Paraíba, Pernambuco, Alagoas, Sergipe, and the northern part of Bahia), however, the principal mechanism organising precipitation is the ITCZ over the equatorial Atlantic. The rainy season over the northern Nordeste is concentrated during February to May, with approximately 80 per cent of the total annual rainfall occurring during this period. The rainy period over the eastern Nordeste occurs during May to August and is related to the seasonal cycle of the southeast trade winds along the shore (Lima 1991). Most of the rainfall over the eastern Nordeste comes from low-level stratiform clouds, covering the eastern coastal zone (the 'zona da mata' and 'agreste') of Rio Grande do Norte, Paraíba, Pernambuco, Alagoas, Sergipe, and Bahia. Kousky (1980) suggested that the diurnal variation of rainfall along the east coast of the Nordeste is related to the moisture convergence in lower levels of the troposphere induced by the interactions between the southeast trade winds and the land–sea breeze.

THE DYNAMICS OF DROUGHTS OVER THE NORDESTE

One of the most important factors that influences the amount of rainfall over the semiarid Nordeste is the latitudinal position of the Atlantic ITCZ. The seasonal meridional migration of the Atlantic ITCZ along the 30° W meridian goes from approximately 14° N during September to 2° S during March. During years of drought over the Nordeste, the ITCZ remains north of the equator and starts its northward migration during mid-March. During wet years, on the other hand, the ITCZ reaches as far south as 5° S and stays south of the equator up to mid-May (Nobre and Shukla 1996). Also, during deficient rainy seasons over the Nordeste (i.e., drought years), the northeast trade winds over the Atlantic are weaker than the mean, sea level pressure (SLP) over the north Atlantic is lower than the mean, and SST over the northern tropical Atlantic is warmer than the mean. Opposite patterns are found over the southern tropical Atlantic: southeast trade winds are stronger, SLP is higher, and SST is cooler than the mean. For wetter-than-normal years, the wind, SLP, and SST anomalous patterns are reversed (Hastenrath and Heller 1977). The patterns of SST, SLP, and surface winds just described are represented in Figure 5.2, adapted from Nobre and Molion (1988).

However, it is not just the tropical Atlantic that plays a role in the dynamics of droughts over the Nordeste region. The El Niño/Southern Oscillation over the equatorial Pacific also contributes to modulating the interannual variability of rainfall over the Nordeste (Bjerknes 1969, Mechoso *et al.* 1990, Chu 1991) and on the SST variability over the tropical Atlantic sector (Hameed *et al.* 1993, Bengtsson *et al.* 1994, Scott and Hastenrath 1995, Nobre and Shukla 1996, Enfield and Enfield 1997).

Although the droughts over the Nordeste are a recurring phenomenon, there is not a satisfactory definition for drought as yet. The main reason for this is the fact that the characterisation of drought does not depend solely on the amount of precipitation, but fundamentally on the spatial and temporal distribution of the rainfall. For example, Magalhães and Rebouças (1988) used the following definition to categorise droughts:

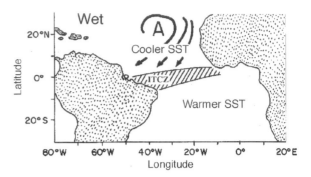

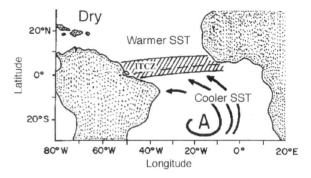

Figure 5.2 Schematic relationships among sea surface temperature, sea level pressure, surface winds, and the position of the Atlantic ITCZ during wet (upper panel) and dry (lower panel) periods over the Nordeste
Source: Adapted from Nobre and Molion 1988

1 An extreme drought occurs when the total precipitation falls below 50 per cent of the annual mean.
2 A drought occurs when the total precipitation is 25 per cent below the climatological normal and the main precipitation period occurs during two months or less.
3 A partial drought occurs when only part of Nordeste is affected by the drought.

During the last 300 years there have been eighteen to twenty droughts per century over the Nordeste (Moura and Shukla 1981, Magalhães and Rebouças 1988). However, there is great spatial variability in the occurrence of droughts over the semiarid Nordeste. The states that are most affected by the occurrence of droughts in the Nordeste region are Piauí, Ceará, Rio Grande do Norte, Paraíba, and Pernambuco (Figure 5.3). Over other states, like low rainfall, covering all of the southern tropical Atlantic. Furthermore, there are observational evidences that the spatial scale of the rainfall anomalies that cause droughts over the Nordeste is much larger than the Nordeste itself. The anomalous rainfall pattern extends from the tropical Atlantic between 5°S and 5° N, extending westward over the central Amazon (Nobre and Shukla 1996).

The large inhomogeneity of the rainfall distribution from state to state in the Nordeste is shown by the histograms of annual rainfall distribution in Figure 5.4. It is readily noticeable in Figure 5.4 that Rio Grande do Norte bears the largest frequency of extreme droughts (annual rainfall less than 50 per cent of the climatological annual precipitation), while Ceará, Paraíba, and Pernambuco experience more years with total annual rainfall slightly above or slightly below normal than years with precipitation around the mean (Figure 5.4). For the sake of comparison, the histogram of annual rainfall

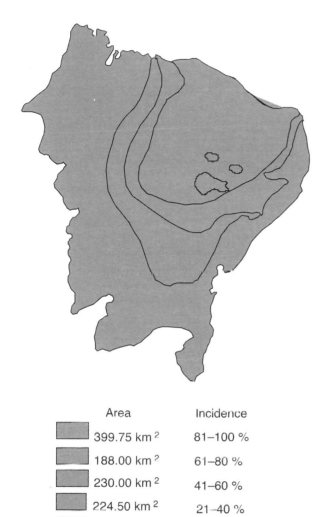

Area	Incidence
399.75 km²	81–100 %
188.00 km²	61–80 %
230.00 km²	41–60 %
224.50 km²	21–40 %
598.75 km²	0–20 %

Figure 5.3 Incidence of droughts over northeastern Brazil relative to the total occurrences of droughts over the region
Source: Adapted from Magalhães and Rebouças 1988

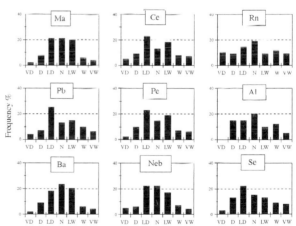

Figure 5.4 Frequency distribution of the total annual rainfall over the northern Nordeste for the period 1910–92. The classes are: (VD) extremely dry (less than or equal to 50 per cent of the climatological mean annual value), (D) dry (51–70 per cent), (LD) slightly dry (71–90 per cent), (N) normal (91–110 per cent), (LW) slightly wet (111–30 per cent), (W) wet (131–50 per cent), (VW) extremely wet (more than 150 per cent of the expected climatological mean). The states' initials are in the inserts at the top of the histogram. They are: (Ma) Maranhão, (Ce) Ceará, (Rn) Rio Grande do Norte, (Pb) Paraiba, (Pe) Pernambuco, (Al) Alagoas, (Se) Sergipe, (Ba) Bahia, and (Neb) for the average of all of the above
Source: Nobre 1997

Maranhão, Alagoas, Sergipe, and Bahia, droughts are normally partial and cause a lesser impact on agriculture and cattle raising (Magalhães and Rebouças 1988).

It is noteworthy that the regions that have the maximum incidence of droughts in Figure 5.3 coincide with an area with low total annual rainfall, as shown in Figure 5.1. Also, the rainfall pattern shown in Figure 5.1 reveals that the low annual totals observed over the Nordeste are part of a much larger area with distribution for the whole semiarid part of the Nordeste is also shown in Figure 5.4.

DROUGHT FORECASTING METHODS FOR THE NORDESTE

There are three main classes of methods for forecasting droughts: purely statistical, statistical–dynamical or conceptual, and numerical. The so-called statistical methods use apparent periodicities in long time series to predict the occurrence of periods of droughts in the near and far future. The forecast skill of this class of methods is generally low. The statistical–dynamical or conceptual methods are based on knowledge of physical mechanisms within the oceans and atmosphere, often inferred from statistical analyses of long atmospheric and oceanic variable time series. Today these methods present the highest forecast skill among the many methods available, but they are generally limited to forecasting area and time-averaged quantities. Lastly, the numerical methods make use of the equations of motion and thermodynamic and physical parameterisations in general circulation models of the atmosphere (AGCM) and of the oceans (OGCM) to forecast seasonal rainfall anomalies with a few months lead time. They require a considerable amount of computer power to integrate the GCMs, and the skill of the numerical forecasts is comparable to or lower than the statistical–dynamical models. However, numerical models represent the most promising class of methods, not only because they have the potential for forecasting the spatial distributions of seasonal rainfall averages, but because of the extended range forecasts (months to seasons lead time) that will be possible in the future, due to the development of coupled ocean–land–atmosphere models.

STATISTICAL METHODS

The statistical methods for drought forecasting are based on the existence of apparent periodicity in long time series. Causal relations among the variables used are neither required nor used. Time series used in the past to generate these types of models include sun spot cycles (Derby 1885, Kantor 1980) and rainfall time series over Fortaleza, in the Nordeste (Kane and Trivedi 1984). Rainfall tendencies for the Nordeste are inferred from months to several years of antecedence by extrapolating the apparent periodicities into the future (Kane and Trivedi 1984). However, although the rainfall time series of Fortaleza presents some low-frequency (interdecade) variability (Markham 1974), it is not physically plausible and statistically justifiable to extrapolate it into the future, since this implies the assumption of stationarity of the rainfall time series. Nobre *et al.* (1984) have shown that the apparent periodicity of the Fortaleza rainfall time series is not statistically significant.

STATISTICAL–DYNAMICAL (OR CONCEPTUAL) METHODS

This class of methods is aimed at forecasting seasonal rainfall anomalies over the Nordeste with a few months lead time. It requires a priori knowledge about physical mechanisms of interaction among the atmosphere, oceans, and biosphere, which are linked to rainfall distribution over the Nordeste. As discussed previously, several studies have shown that seasonal rainfall anomalies over the Nordeste are linked to anomalous distributions of SST over the equatorial Pacific and tropical Atlantic oceans (Moura and Shukla 1981, Hastenrath and Greischar 1993a, Ward and Folland 1991, Nobre and Shukla 1996). Presently, there are several prognostic models based on the interactions among SST, surface winds, sea-level pressure, and rainfall anomalies over the Nordeste. Some of these methods are applied routinely to predicting seasonal rainfall variability over the region. These are described below:

1 University of Wisconsin: Hastenrath and collaborators (1990 and 1993b) use indexes based on pre-rainy season rainfall totals (November to January) over the northern Nordeste, surface winds over the equatorial Atlantic, and SSTA over the tropical Atlantic and equatorial Pacific, as predictors for a multiregression scheme to forecast seasonal rainfall anomalies over the Nordeste in five classes: very dry, dry, normal, wet, very wet. A preliminary forecast is normally issued in mid-February, and the actual forecast is issued in mid-March. Since one of the predictors of

Hastenrath's forecast scheme, namely the Nordeste preseason rainfall, explains nearly 50 per cent of the total interannual variance of the February–September rainfall over the northern Nordeste (with 30 per cent explained by the remainder of the predictors), the forecasts are normally biased toward the preseason rainfall over the region.

2 Hadley Centre: Ward and Folland (1991) use orthogonal empirical functions (EOF) applied on global SSTA fields to forecast March–May rainfall anomalies over the Nordeste. The model consists of projecting the observed SSTA fields over the equatorial Pacific and tropical Atlantic during January and February on the SSTA EOFs, which were previously calculated. Then the most probable seasonal rainfall class (very dry, dry, normal, wet, very wet) is estimated through a linear regression equation. These forecasts are available in mid-February and mid-March.

3 CPTEC/INPE: The conceptual method used in CPTEC is based on the subjective analyses of global atmospheric and oceanic data linked to the modulation of rainfall anomalies over the Nordeste and the result of numerical (AGCM) and statistical–dynamical (canonical correlation analyses) seasonal climate forecasts. All the predictors are analysed subjectively by a team of meteorologists. Each member of the team brings to the monthly general discussion his/her own analyses, and the individual forecasts are brought to a consensus prediction. The forecasts are issued in mid-January, mid-February, and mid-March. The consensus forecast is categorical, and picks the category (very dry, dry, normal, wet, very wet) the coming rainy season is most likely to be.

NUMERICAL METHODS

The most recent and promising class of methods for drought forecasting uses atmospheric and oceanic GCMs to compute ensemble mean forecasts of seasonal climate anomalies. The AGCMs are integrated with prescribed SST boundary conditions and a set of slightly different initial conditions to generate seasonal rainfall forecasts globally. Besides the differences among the AGCM's formulations and resolutions, the main differences among the numerical forecasts are the prescribed SST fields and the number of ensemble members used. A variety of methods are currently being used to generate the SST BC, from persisting last month's SST anomaly fields during the following months (Graham 1993, Graham 1994, Nobre and Cavalcanti 1998) to using more sophisticated statistical prognostic models (Repelli and Nobre 1997) and anomaly and fully coupled ocean–atmosphere GCMs (Barnett et al. 1996, Ji et al. 1996, Kirtman et al. 1996, Zebiak and Cane 1996).

The first results of numerical forecasts of seasonal rainfall anomalies over the Nordeste were obtained at the Scripps Institution of Oceanography in California (Graham 1993, Graham 1994) and at the Center for Ocean Land Atmosphere Studies (COLA) in Maryland before March–May of the 1994 rainy season. Presently, the International Research Institute for climate predictions (IRI) at Scripps, the UK Meteorological Office, and CPTEC generate regular experimental seasonal climate forecasting for the Nordeste using their AGCMs. However, using AGCMs as a tool for climate predictions is limited by the constraints of the necessary prescribed surface boundary conditions.

Looking into the near future, coupled ocean–atmosphere–biosphere GCMs form the next class of models to be used for climate prediction on seasonal to interannual time scales. The coupled models are still in early stages of development, but they address the most important issue for numerical forecasting of climate variability: the interactive exchange of mass, heat, and momentum fluxes at the surface over the oceans (SST) and the continents (soil moisture, albedo, evapotranspiration). Presently, fully coupled and anomaly-coupled ocean–atmosphere GCMs are used to forecast SSTA over the equatorial Pacific with up to one year lead time (Ji et al. 1994, Kirtman et al. 1996, Zebiak and Cane 1996).

Research on coupled ocean–atmosphere modelling also has been done for the tropical Atlantic (Zebiak 1993, Nobre and Kirtman 1996, Chang et al. 1996, Chang et al. 1997), but the results are still incipient for simulating SST interannual variability over the tropical Atlantic. A major research effort and data collection over the tropical Atlantic are needed to understand the genesis of SST interannual variability in the Atlantic Basin.

AGCM SIMULATIONS OF THE NORDESTE RAINY SEASON

The use of AGCMs for studies of precipitation variability over the Nordeste was first performed by Moura and Shukla (1981), who used the Goddard Laboratory for Atmospheric Science (GLAS) model. They applied a dipole pattern of SST anomalies (positive anomalies over the North Atlantic and negative anomalies over the South Atlantic) as a boundary condition to the AGCM and obtained positive precipitation anomalies to the north of the equator and negative anomalies to the south. Positive anomalies of evaporation, vertically integrated moisture flux convergence over the North Atlantic, and the opposite over the South Atlantic were identified in the model results. There were also negative anomalies of sea-level pressure over the North Atlantic and positive anomalies over the South Atlantic. These characteristics and the circulation results were associated with a thermally direct circulation with anomalous ascending motion to the north of the equator and anomalous subsidence south of the equator. They suggested that a possible mechanism for drought over the Nordeste was the intensification of the ITCZ to the north of the equator, where there were positive SST anomalies (warm), and the occurrence of descending motion over the Nordeste and adjoining oceans with negative SST anomalies (cold) and reduced moist convection.

Other numerical AGCM experiments have been done to simulate the interannual variability of precipitation over the Nordeste. The influence of SST anomalies on precipitation over the Nordeste was analysed, with the UCLA GCM, by Mechoso *et al.* (1988), through a simulation of two years (1984 and 1983). These years represented wet and dry conditions, respectively, in the Nordeste rainy season. In the equatorial Atlantic, positive SST anomalies developed during 1984. The model results showed positive anomalies of precipitation over the western Atlantic along the northeast and east coasts of South America in 1984. Negative rainfall anomalies were found over equatorial Brazil. These anomalies were associated with regions of convergence and divergence in the model results. The results of stream function and rotational wind anomalies at 850 hPa for 1984

showed anomalous westerly winds over the equatorial Atlantic and anomalous easterlies over the southeast Atlantic. These were associated with an anomalous cyclonic circulation over the eastern part of Brazil. There were anomalous easterly winds over the equatorial Pacific, consistent with the observed strengthening of the trade winds during 1984. These features were enhanced when the differences between stream function and rotational wind anomalies of 1983 and 1984 were computed. The precipitation difference field over the equatorial Pacific showed the effect of the 1983 El Niño. The anomaly precipitation in the model results during 1983 was negative over the northwest Nordeste and positive over the southern Nordeste. Precipitation differences over the equatorial Atlantic were consistent with a general southward shift of positive precipitation anomalies from north of the equator during 1983 to south of the equator in 1984. They concluded that the good agreement between the simulated and observed anomalies and the interannual differences in the atmospheric circulation over the tropical Atlantic and Pacific were primarily due to SST forcing.

Another AGCM simulation of 1983 and 1984, using the UCLA AGCM, by Mechoso *et al.* (1990) assessed the impact of the Pacific, Atlantic, and Indian oceans on precipitation over the Nordeste and associated atmospheric circulation. The stream function and rotational wind anomalies results over South America and the South Atlantic for 1984 using SST anomalies only over the Atlantic Ocean compare well with the results using global SST anomalies. The pattern was the same found in Mechoso and Lyons 1988. Using only the Pacific SST anomalies, there were similarities with the results using global SST anomalies only near Indonesia and over the extreme west Pacific Ocean. When the Indian Ocean SST anomaly was considered, the similarities with the global SST anomaly results were observed over the Indian Ocean and equatorial Africa. The precipitation anomaly in 1984, using the global SST anomaly, showed enhanced precipitation over northeast Indonesia, a dipole of reduced precipitation over northern Brazil, and enhanced precipitation over the western Atlantic/eastern Nordeste. Using only the Atlantic SST anomalies, the precipitation anomalies were confined to the dipole over South America and the Atlantic, but the positive values were weaker and shifted to the east. The dipole of reduced/enhanced precipitation was associated with the decreased moisture flux from the Atlantic Ocean to the northern part of South America and with the enhanced convergence of the southeast trade winds carrying moisture over the warmer South Atlantic. The model results showed an area of moisture flux divergence over northern Brazil and convergence over the Atlantic/eastern Nordeste, similar to the precipitation anomaly pattern. The patterns of moisture flux and its convergence in 1983 were different. The flux was not well defined, as it was in 1984, and the moisture convergence was found over southeast Brazil. Analyses of remote effects on precipitation over the Nordeste show the influence of the Pacific and Indian Oceans. The sum of the results using Indian Ocean SST anomalies and Pacific SST anomalies showed the dipole of precipitation found when the global SST was used.

Adding a heating term in the thermodynamic equation of the NCAR GCM (community climate model [CCM]), Buchmann et al. (1990) performed experiments in which this heating was maximised at 6.6° S, 30° W, and 6.5° S, 30° W. The model results showed reduced precipitation over the Nordeste in the first case and excess precipitation in the second case.

The northeast rainfall seasons (March–May) of 1987 (dry) and 1989 (wet) were also simulated in an experiment by Richardson and Robertson (1994), using the UK Meteorological Office Unified Model. The model correctly simulated the difference between the negative phase of the Southern Oscillation in 1987 and the positive phase in 1989. Negative and positive anomalies of precipitation over the Nordeste were simulated in 1987 and 1989, respectively, in agreement with the observations. Four long-term integrations (1949–93) showed consistent and skilful simulations of Nordeste rainfall.

A simulation of the interannual rainfall variability in the Nordeste by Harzallah et al. (1996a) with the LMD (Laboratoire de Meteorologie Dynamique) AGCM was performed for the period 1970–88. The seven-member ensemble averages show that the model reproduced the observed rainfall anomalies in a realistic way, especially during the February–May

(FMAM) rainy season, in terms of magnitude and phase of fluctuations. During the nineteen years of the experiment, only in three years was the observed precipitation larger than the model simulation. This fact was related to the occurrence of upper tropospheric cyclones near the Nordeste, which caused convective activity and rain over the Nordeste. They calculated a correlation between the precipitation anomaly over the Nordeste (model results and observed data) and the SST anomaly of all oceans for FMAM. The patterns of both correlations were similar and showed negative correlations in the equatorial central Pacific and a dipole over the North Atlantic and South Atlantic. They also applied the singular value decomposition (SVD) method to SST and precipitation fields. This method provides a measure of the relationship between two variables. Correlations between the SVD time series (first mode) of the model results and observations were 0.98 for SST and 0.8 for precipitation. Another important result found by Harzallah et al. (1996a) was the influence of two oscillatory modes on Nordeste rainfall, one west–east and the other north–south. These were related to the displacement of the Walker cell and the Hadley cell. The second mode was a quasi-decade oscillation, related to the SSTA dipole over the tropical Atlantic. These two modes were associated with the Pacific and Atlantic SST, and the authors suggested that it is a combination of equatorial Pacific, North Atlantic, and South Atlantic influences, organised along the two oscillations, that produces Nordeste rainfall variations.

In Harzallah et al. (1996b), the two circulation cells (Hadley and Walker) were investigated in the GCM model results. During drought years, the upward vertical velocity is displaced northward, corresponding to the migration of the ITCZ to the north. The east–west circulation shows subsiding motion over the Nordeste and ascent motion over the Pacific. This is accompanied by warm waters in the eastern Pacific and warm/cold waters in the northern/southern Atlantic.

A similar experiment to those by Mechoso et al. (1988) and Richardson and Robertson (1994) was done by Cavalcanti et al. (1996), using CPTEC/COLA AGCM, a model derived from the COLA AGCM. Two years of dry (1993) and wet (1994)

conditions over the Nordeste were simulated, and the model results were in good agreement with the observed values. The model does a good job of reproducing the influence of the ITCZ on the precipitation over the Nordeste.

NUMERICAL PREDICTION OF DROUGHTS OVER THE NORDESTE

The good results of statistical models and simulations using AGCMs for the Nordeste rainy season encouraged production of numerical AGCM predictions. The *Experimental Long Lead Forecast (ELLF) Bulletin* has published AGCM predictions for the Nordeste rainy season since 1994. Graham (1994) showed the spatial distribution of estimated correlation skill in predicting March–May precipitation over South America for the period 1970–93. One of the regions with highest forecast skill was Nordeste Brazil, with a value of 0.64. The skill is higher when only the driest and wettest years are forecast. These predictions were made using the Max Planck Institute for Meteorology/ University of Hamburg AGCM, configured with T42L19 resolution. Predictions using this model have been published every year since 1994 in the *ELLF Bulletin*.

The UK Meteorological Office Unified Model was also used to predict the 1994 rainy season of the Nordeste (Richardson and Robertson 1994). The above-normal precipitation results over the Nordeste were verified in the observed data of that year.

Experimental climate predictions have been performed at Centro de Previsão de Tempo e Estudos Climáticos (CPTEC) in Brazil since January 1995, using the CPTEC/COLA AGCM. The numerical seasonal forecast for the Nordeste rainy season of 1995 is discussed in Nobre *et al.* 1995. The predictions using persistent SST anomalies of December, January, and February indicated drier conditions than the observed precipitation during March–May 1995, but when persistent March SST anomalies were applied as boundary conditions, the model response was in good agreement with the observations. The Nordeste rainy season predictions of 1996 and 1997 are discussed in Nobre and Cavalcanti 1998 (in preparation).

Hastenrath and Druyan (1993), based on results

of the Goddard Institute for Space Studies (GISS) AGCM, comment that the GISS AGCM forecasts of seasonal rainfall anomalies over the Nordeste are not as skilful as the predictions for the Nordeste using empirical general circulation diagnostics. The model results were analysed for the period 1980–6 and compared to upper air analyses of ECMWF, COADS surface data, and rainfall measurements in the Nordeste. Only March and April were analysed. The modelled precipitation showed little relation to the observed rainfall. The precipitation was weakly related to the observed interhemispheric SST contrast and to the modelled near-surface meridional wind component. The modelled and observed precipitation were negatively related to the equatorial Pacific SST, a characteristic found in other studies related to ENSO. The poor precipitation results obtained from the model can be linked to its resolution, which was 8° latitude by 10° longitude. Results of AGCMs using higher resolutions showed similarities between modelled and observed precipitation.

To assess the feasibility of seasonal forecasts in multiple GCM simulations, Stern and Myakoda (1995) calculated a measure that they called reproducibility. This measure is the ratio between the standard deviation of a member of an ensemble related to the averaged ensemble, when the observed SST was used, and the standard deviation of the model's climatology. The results of December–February and June–August showed high reproducibility for the Nordeste region. To support the hypothesis that good reproducibility is associated with greater predictability, they showed the coherence between observed precipitation and the ensemble model precipitation.

Brankovic and Palmer (1997), from results of ECMWF AGCM, calculated skill for several areas of the world, one of these being the northern Nordeste. For tropical areas, they used the 200 hPa zonal wind, and they showed high skill for the Nordeste area during December–February of strong ENSO years.

INITIATIVES TO MITIGATE DROUGHTS

The problem of droughts over the Nordeste has received attention from the government of Brazil since the late 1800s. The first initiatives to 'combat' droughts over the Nordeste took place during

1884–90 with the construction of the Cedro 1 dam, as a response to the great drought of 1877–9 (SUDENE 1981). The idea of 'fighting the drought' in the sense of 'winning over nature' was a consequence of the basic thought brought to the continent by the pioneer European settlers, for whom development was associated with the 'domination' of natural resources, primarily expressed by clearing forests and replacing them with annual cash crop cultures and pasture. As a consequence, agricultural and cattle raising practices of temperate latitudes were implemented in the emerging nation, the semiarid portions of the Nordeste included. Cultures that demand a regular water supply during the phenological cycle, such as corn and beans, became traditional plantations over the Nordeste. As a consequence, the interannual variability of rainfall distribution, which would have little or no impact on the growth of vegetation types more resistant to the hydric stress that is natural to the dry climate of the region, became a real constraint for the water-demanding agricultural practices of temperate zones introduced in the region.

The actions of the federal government of Brazil toward lessening the scourge associated with droughts materialised with the creation of federal bureaus with the mandate to promote the regional development of the Nordeste. Two such bureaus are the National Department of Works Against the Droughts (DNOCS – Departamento Nacional de Obras Contra as Secas) and the Superintendence for the Development of Nordeste (SUDENE – Superintendência de Desenvolvimento do Nordeste). These institutions adopted what Carvalho (1988) called 'engineering solutions' for the problems related to droughts: implementing a dense network of raingauges, drilling deep water wells, and building a large number of dams for storing rain water and regularising the outflow of some rivers in the region. Those activities brought a great deal of benefits to the region, in the form of hydric and road infrastructure as well as long time series of rainfall data obtained by the network of raingauges operated by SUDENE. However, these actions proved ineffective in reversing the situation of poverty and social convulsion worsened by the occurrence of droughts, since the roots for the misery in the region lie in factors other than the climate (Carvalho 1988, Magalhães and Glantz 1992).

ARTIFICIAL RAINS

Besides the actions taken by SUDENE and DNOCS along the lines of 'combatting droughts', the government of the state of Ceará has implemented a programme of artificial rains. Cloud seeding was done regularly during the rainy seasons, aimed at increasing the amount of rainfall during years of drought. However, although cloud seeding has been conducted in the state for more than twenty years, its efficacy in increasing the amount of rainfall over the region still has not been demonstrated. In this sense, it is unlikely that artificial rains could minimise, much less reverse, the adverse conditions of water supply and agricultural production associated with droughts over the region. On the contrary, even if this process could generate an effective increase on the order of 20 per cent of 'artificial' rains in addition to the rains that would otherwise fall over the region (though such an increase, if indeed not nil, would probably be inferior to 10 per cent of the natural rainfall [Howell 1960]), such an increase would be too small to solve the problems related to the droughts over the Nordeste, where the annual precipitation totals are less than 800 mm. There were other tentative plans to combat droughts over the Nordeste through artificial modification of its weather and climate. However, such initiatives were soon abandoned because of the lack of scientific background and insufficient funding.

In summary, initiatives to 'combat the droughts', in the sense of changing the regional climate in order to supply the water demanded by the traditional agricultural practices over the Nordeste, proved ineffective, even taking into consideration the elevated cash amounts allocated by the federal and state governments specifically for that purpose (and these allocations were only tolerated because of their social appeal).

MONITORING AND PREDICTING DROUGHTS

More recently, information from monitoring and prediction of seasonal climate anomalies over the Nordeste has been used in decision-making processes aimed at minimising the negative socioeconomic impacts normally associated with the occurrence of droughts in the region. Present-day efforts to monitor and forecast climate variability over the Nordeste by the regional states include near-real time rainfall data collection and display as well as analyses of global-scale atmospheric and oceanic variables inferred from meteorological satellite imagery received locally and from global atmospheric and oceanic fields made available by the National Centers for Environmental Prediction (NCEP) in the United States.

To consider the temporal and spatial variability of rainfall over the Nordeste, it is necessary to integrate real time monitoring information extracted from remote sensing data (e.g., meteorological and natural resources satellite imagery, meteorological Doppler radar) and the network of automated data collection platforms, and weather and climate forecasting information. This information allows one to map the areas that are more strongly affected by pluviometric deficit or excess, thus helping to address short-term actions like the determination of areas where soil moisture is adequate for seeding some species of grains or where a shortage of water supply is detected or irrigation is recommended. Also, accurate maps of the areas affected by climate variations in near-real time can influence actions and policies of credit and agricultural insurance.

CURRENT CLIMATE MONITORING OVER THE NORDESTE

The federal and state governments in the Nordeste region have made joint efforts to assemble a regional network of state bureaus of meteorology and water resources. These bureaus have been implemented since 1982, and they use the latest generation of computational equipment; meteorological satellite imagery; a network of automatic data collection platforms (DCP) that relay atmospheric variables in real time via satellite and dial-up phone lines; and, most importantly, an intensive training program to introduce state-of-the-art climate monitoring and forecast tools to the meteorologists and hydrologists of the state bureaus. One of the immediate benefits of this new strategy for climate monitoring and prediction over the Nordeste was the increased interest of state governments and businesses in the use of real time meteorological and hydrological information for orienting planning and actions related to climate variations.

Advances in forecasting and real time evaluation of climate variations similar to those over the Nordeste are also occurring over the tropical Atlantic. Brazil is equipping the Brazilian Islands with automatic DCPs with near-real time data relay via satellite. Brazil also is part of an international consortium with France and the United States, the PIRATA (Pilot Research moored Array over the Tropical Atlantic) project, which is implementing the first array of instrumented anchored buoys over the tropical Atlantic, similar to the TOGA array over the equatorial Pacific. The program is expected to deploy a total of fourteen buoys between 10° S and 15° N until December 1999, of which six have already been deployed.

CASE STUDY: THE USE OF CLIMATE FORECASTS IN CEARÁ

It is interesting to analyse the way climate monitoring and forecasting information has made its way into the decision-making processes of the state government of Ceará in the Nordeste. This case study explored the application of methodology, technology, and knowledge about rainfall variability to the decision-making process and also considered the necessary dialogue between the generators of information and its users.

First, it was clear for all people involved with the business of climate monitoring and forecasting in the Ceará State Bureau of Meteorology and Water Resources (FUNCEME) that information about rainfall distributions over the state (past and future) during the rainy season should be disseminated daily in an easy-to-understand format. This set the highest priority on obtaining data needed to generate daily, weekly, and monthly bulletins. The same is true for the daily collection of rainfall data over the network of conventional raingauges over the state, obtaining satellite imagery over the Nordeste in real time locally, and obtaining global atmospheric and oceanic fields necessary to feed into currently used forecasting techniques. This approach to obtaining all available climate-related data in near-real time and in a form appropriate for government agencies to use in decision making brought FUNCEME and climate information to centre stage in deliberations related to climate-sensitive issues, like agriculture and water supply, with measurable economic and political benefits for the state.

Since 1988, FUNCEME, in cooperation with CPTEC/INPE, has provided climate and water resources monitoring and forecasting information to state government and society. Forecasts about the quality of the rainy season (whether very dry, dry, normal, wet, or very wet) over the state are made and disseminated to the government and mass media on a monthly basis from December to March.

The state secretary of agriculture has begun using climate diagnostics and prognostics information prepared by FUNCEME and CPTEC as an input to planning and scheduling distributions of seeds to farmers. Figure 5.5 shows the percentage of grain production (rice, corn, and beans) and average rainfall totals over the state during pairs of years representative of severe drought years (1983, 1993), moderate drought years (1987, 1992) and years with near-normal total rainfall (1984, 1994), before and after the state started using hydrometeorological information in decision-making processes related to distribution of seeds. During 1983 and 1993, two of the driest years in this century over the Nordeste, annual total rainfall over the state was only 40 per cent of the mean climatological precipitation. The production of grains during 1983 represented only 15 per cent of the annual long-term mean production for the state, whereas it reached 38 per cent of the mean annual production in 1993, when climatic information was being used by the government. During 1987 and 1992, the observed rainfall was 70 per cent of the expected mean annual values, thus characterising years of moderate drought. Production of grains in 1987 was 50 per cent of the long-term mean; in 1992 it was 82 per cent. During 1984 and 1994, average rainfall over the state was near normal. However, grain production in 1984 (106 per cent) was only about half of the production of 1994 (197 per cent). During 1995 (figure not shown), the average rainfall over the state was near the long-term mean average; nevertheless, grain production reached 210 per cent of the state mean production, reproducing the figures observed in 1994.

Although the simple differences in grain pro-

duction in the years mentioned above cannot be attributed solely to the impact of the use of climatic information on the choices of types of seeds (more resistant to water stress) and better timing for planting (based on estimates of soil moisture), it suggests that the systematic use of meteorological information in decision-making processes can result in a measurable difference in the production of grains in the state, relative to years in which climatic information was not taken into consideration. However, a more detailed study is needed to quantify the importance of climatic information relative to other economic factors that influence agriculture over the Nordeste.

The experience of Ceará in using climate information to guide actions that can lessen impacts of droughts on Nordeste society suggests the potential of climate information as a tool to help reverse the historic trend of low productivity associated with droughts over the region. Through a combination of using climate information and choosing economic activities that benefit from the dry climate of the Nordeste – e.g., irrigated fruit culture – it is possible to turn the otherwise 'adverse' climate over the region into a competitive advantage over other regions, where seasonal rainfall distribution during the year, despite being both more abundant and regular, is not as predictable as it is over the Nordeste.

Furthermore, if monitoring and forecasting

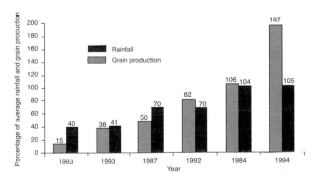

Figure 5.5 Percentage average grain (rice, corn, and beans) production (lefthand bar for each year) and the observed total rainfall (righthand bar for each year) over Ceará during the pairs of years indicated in the horizontal axis. The numbers over the bars are expressed as percentages of the long-term mean annual grain production (650,000 metric tonnes) and annual total rainfall (900 mm) averaged over the state
Source: FUNCEME (personal communication)

climate variability are going to be of any relevance to the Nordeste's economy and society, they must be available in near-real time and in a form that decision makers can use in their decision-making processes. Although necessary, building and operating a dense network of data collection platforms and generating seasonal climate forecasts are not enough to make a difference in lessening the adverse impacts of droughts on the Nordeste's society. Data must be transformed into information that fits the specific needs and terminology of the user community.

CONCLUSIONS

From the scientific standpoint, the interannual variability of the Nordeste's climate is highly predictable. The source of such extraordinary predictability lies in the SST patterns over the tropical oceans. Statistical–dynamical methods for forecasting droughts over the Nordeste have been performing well during the last two decades, but the perspective for the future lies with fully coupled ocean–atmosphere general circulation models, which have the potential of generating skilful seasonal forecasts several months to a year in advance. Today, the most critical issue for developing longer lead times and more skilful predictions of seasonal rainfall anomalies over the Nordeste is the ability to forecast tropical SSTs. Recent developments of coupled modelling and in situ data collection networks over the equatorial Pacific have led to a substantial increase in the ability to forecast SST anomalies over the Pacific, up to a year in advance. The same, however, cannot be said about the Atlantic and Indian oceans as yet. Also, recently there has been a growing interest in the scientific community to better understand the physical processes of ocean–atmosphere interactions over the tropical Atlantic, which will lead to an eventual increase in our capability to forecast Atlantic SSTs as well.

Along with the increased availability of climate information over the Nordeste, both diagnostic and prognostic, there has been a growing awareness among economists and decision makers of the necessity to incorporate climate variability information in the decision-making processes in the region. To accomplish this, it is necessary to invest continually in education (from elementary to graduate levels) in the implementation of real-time data collection networks over both the continent and the adjoining tropical Atlantic, and, most importantly, in generating information that can be digested by the various sectors of the society that are affected by the region's climate variability.

Today, with the advent of computer resources that were unheard of just a few years ago, it is possible and desirable to create a new class of decision-making supporting tools that will allow the ever-growing volume of interrelated information to be assembled into a form decision makers can use. This includes geo-referenced information data bases, also known as 'geographical information systems', which can be used by trained social scientists and economists to make projections and assessments of the implications of specific meteorological forecasts for localised and specific situations.

In the foreseeable future, it is likely that skilful forecasts for seasonal rainfall anomalies will be available with six to twelve months lead time. Also, it is likely that more accurate measurements and forecasts of the intraseasonal variability of rainfall will be available as well. The continuous development and implementation of a variety of automatic observing platforms to sample the three-dimensional structure of the atmosphere and the oceans in near-real time will represent an enormous gain in our ability to understand and predict atmospheric and oceanic variability on seasonal and longer time scales. Also, the continuous and coordinated international efforts to find and implement 'end to end' solutions to climate-related problems, from research to applications, is likely to make a great deal of scientific knowledge available to society in a usable form.

REFERENCES

Barnett, T., Pierce, D., Graham, N., and Latif, M. (1996) 'Dynamically based forecasts for tropical Pacific SST through winter 1997–98 using an improved coupled ocean–atmosphere model', *Experimental Long-Lead Forecast Bulletin*, NWS/NCEP/CPC, pp. 1–3.

Bengtsson, L., Delecluse, P., and Servain, J. (1994) 'On the connection between the 1984 Atlantic warm event and the 1982–83 ENSO', *Tellus – Series A* 46, 448 ff.

Bjerknes, J. (1969) 'Atmospheric teleconnections from the

equatorial Pacific', *Monthly Weather Review* 97: 526–35.

Brankovic, C. and Palmer, T.N. (1997) 'Atmospheric seasonal predictability and estimates of ensemble size', submitted to *Monthly Weather Review* 125, 5: 859–74.

Buchmann, J., Paegle, J., Buja, L.E., and Dickinson, R.E. (1990) 'The effect of tropical Atlantic heating anomalies upon GCM rain forecasts over the Americas', *Journal of Climate* 3. 189–208.

Carvalho, O. (1988) 'A economia política do Nordeste: secas, irrigação e desenvolvimento', Editora Campus.

Cavalcanti, I.F.A., Nobre, P., and Trosnikov, I. (1996) 'Simulação de verão e outono de 92/93 e 93/94 com o GCM CPTEC/COLA', *IX Congresso Brasileiro de Meteorologia*, Campos do Jordão, SP, 1, 807–11.

Chang, P., Ji, L., and Li, H. (1996) 'A decadal climate variation in the tropical Atlantic Ocean from thermodynamic air–sea interactions', *Nature* 385: 516–8.

——— (1998) 'Prediction of tropical Atlantic sea surface temperature', *Geophysical Research Letters* 25, 8: 1,193–6.

Chu, P.S. (1991) 'Brazil's climate anomalies and ENSO', in M.H. Glantz, R.W. Katz, and N. Nicholls (eds), *Teleconnections Linking Worldwide Climate Anomalies*, Cambridge University Press, pp. 43–71.

Derby, O.A. (1885) 'The sun spots and the droughts', *Revista de Engenharia* 8: 112–14.

Enfield, D.B. and Enfield, M.D.A. (1997) 'Tropical Atlantic sea surface temperature variability and its relation to El Nino Southern Oscillation', *Journal of Geophysical Research* 102: 929–45.

Ferraz, J.S. (1925) 'Probable causes of drought occurrences in NE Brazil: Correlation method', Ministério da Agricultura, Diretoria de Meteorologia, Rio de Janeiro, Brazil.

——— (1929) 'Sir Gilbert Walker's formula for Ceara's droughts: Suggestion for its physical explanation', *Meteorological Magazine* 54: 81–4.

Graham, N.E. (1993) 'Experimental predictions of wet season precipitation in northeast Brazil', in NOAA, *Proceedings of the 18th Annual Climate Diagnostics Workshop*, NOAA/NWS/US Department of Commerce, Washington, DC, pp. 378–81.

——— (1994) 'Prediction of rainfall in Northeast Brazil for MAM 1994 using an atmospheric GCM with persisted SST anomalies', *Experimental Long-Lead Forecast Bulletin*.

Hameed, S., Sperber, K.R., and Meinster, A. (1993) 'Teleconnections of the Southern Oscillation in the tropical Atlantic sector in the OSU coupled upper ocean–atmosphere GCM', *Journal of Climate* 6: 487–98.

Harzallah, A., Aragão, J.O.R., and Sadourny, R. (1996a) 'Interannual rainfall variability in Northeast Brazil: Observations and model simulation', *International Journal of Climatology* 6: 861–78.

——— (1996b) 'Vertical motion changes related to

Northeast Brazil rainfall variability: A GCM simulation', *International Journal of Climatology* 16: 879–91.

Hastenrath, S. (1984) 'Interannual variability and annual cycle: Mechanisms of circulation and climate in the tropical Atlantic', *Monthly Weather Review* 112: 1,097–107.

——— (1990) 'Prediction of Northeast Brazil rainfall anomalies', *Journal of Climate* 3: 893–904.

Hastenrath, S. and Druyan, L. (1993) 'Circulation anomaly mechanisms in the tropical Atlantic sector during the Northeast Brazil rainy season', *Journal of Geophysical Research. Atmospheres* 98: 14,917–23.

Hastenrath, S. and Greischar, L. (1993a) 'Circulation mechanisms related to Northeast Brazil rainfall anomalies', *Journal of Geophysical Research. Atmospheres* 98: 5,093–102.

Hastenrath, S. and Greischar, L. (1993b) 'Further work on the prediction of northeast Brazil rainfall anomalies', *Journal of Climate* 6: 743–58.

Hastenrath, S. and Heller, L. (1977) 'Dynamics of climatic hazards in north-east Brazil', *Quarterly Journal of the Royal Meteorological Society* 110: 411–25.

Howell, W.E. (1960) 'Semeação de nuvens em climas tropicais', *Boletim do DNOCS* 10: 347–62.

Hull, F.R. (1942) 'A freqüência das secas no estudo do Ceará e sua relação com a freqüência dosanos de manchas solares mínimas', *Boletim da Secretaria da Agricultura e Obras Públicas* 4: 58–63.

Ji, M., Kumar, A., and Leetma, A. (1996) 'Forecasts of tropical SST using a comprehensive coupled ocean–atmosphere dynamical model', *Experimental Long-Lead Forecast Bulletin*, NWS/NCEP/CPC, pp. 10–14.

——— (1994) 'An experimental coupled forecast system at the National Meteorological Center: Some early results', *Tellus* 46A: 398–418.

Kane, R.P. and Trivedi, N.B. (1984) 'Prediction of drought in the Brazilian Northeast region from an analysis of periodicities in the Fortaleza rainfall data', INPE, 3334-RPI/118, São José dos Campos, SP, Brazil.

Kantor, I.J. (1980) 'Relações estatísticas entre as secas do Nordeste e o ciclo solar', INPE, INPE–1839–RPE/199, São José dos Campos, SP, Brazil.

Kirtman, B.P., Huang, B., Shukla, J., and Zhu, Z. (1996) 'Tropical Pacific SST predictions with a coupled GCM', *Experimental Long-Lead Forecast Bulletin*, NWS/NCEP/CPC, pp. 15–17.

Kousky, V.E. (1979) 'Frontal influences on Northeast Brazil', *Monthly Weather Review* 107: 1,140–53.

——— (1980) 'Diurnal rainfall variation over Northeast Brazil', *Monthly Weather Review* 108: 488–98.

Lima, M.C. (1991) 'Variabilidade da precipitação no litoral leste da Região Nordeste do Brasil', MSc Thesis, Instituto Nacional de Pesquisas Espaciais – INPE, São José dos Campos, SP, Brazil.

Magalhães, A.R. and Glantz, M.H. (1992) *Socioeconomic Impacts of Climate Variations and Policy Responses in*

Brazil, United Nations Environment Program (UNEP), Secretariat for Planning and Coordination State of Ceara (SEPLAN), Esquel Brasil Foundation.

Magalhães, A.R. and Rebouças, O.E. (1988) 'Introduction: Drought as a policy and planning issue in Northeast Brazil', in M.L. Parry, T.R. Carter, and N.T. Konijn (eds), *The Impact of Climatic Variations on Agriculture*, Dordrecht: Kluwer Academic Publishers, pp. 279–304.

Markham, C.G. (1974) 'Apparent periodicities in rainfall at Fortaleza', *Journal of Applied Meteorology* 13: 176–9.

Markham, C.G. and McLain, D.R. (1977) 'Sea surface temperature related to rain in Ceará, northeastern Brazil', *Nature* 265: 320–5.

Mechoso, C.R., Lyons, S.W., and Spahr, J.A. (1988) 'On the atmospheric response to SST anomalies associated with the Atlantic warm event during 1984', *Journal of Climate* 1: 422–8.

———— (1990) 'The impact of sea surface temperature anomalies on the rainfall over Northeast Brazil', *Journal of Climate* 3: 812–26.

Moura, A.D. and Shukla, J. (1981) 'On the dynamics of droughts in northeast Brazil: Observations, theory and numerical experiments with a general circulation model', *Journal of Atmospheric Science* 38: 2,653–75.

Nobre, P. (1993) 'On the genesis of anomalous SST and rainfall patterns over the tropical Atlantic basin', Ph.D. Dissertation, University of Maryland, College Park, MD.

———— (1997) 'O Clima do Nordeste', in *Clima, Recursos Naturais e Sustentabilidade no Nordeste Brasileiro*, Technical Report of ARIDAS Project, IPEA, Brazil.

Nobre, P., Abreu, M.L., Cavalcanti, I.F.A., Quadro, M., and Pezzi, L.P. (1995) 'Climate ensemble forecasting at CPTEC', in National Weather Service, *Proceedings of the Twentieth Annual Climate Diagnostics Workshop*, Washington, DC: National Weather Service, US Department of Commerce, pp. 417–20.

Nobre, P. and Cavalcanti, I.F.A. (1999) 'Seasonal climate prediction over Nordeste Brazil using CPTEC/COLA atmospheric general circulation model', submitted to *International Journal of Climatology*.

Nobre, P. and Kirtman, B.P. (1996) 'Coupled prediction system at COLA/CPTEC', *IX Congresso Brasileiro de Meteorologia*, SBMet, Campos do Jordão, SP, 1, 859–63.

Nobre, C.A. and Molion, L.C.B. (1988) 'The climatology of droughts and drought prediction', in M.L. Parry, T.R. Carter, and N.T. Konijn (eds), *The Impact of Climatic Variations on Agriculture*, Dordrecht: Kluwer Academic Publishers, pp. 305–23.

Nobre, P. and Shukla, J. (1996) 'Variations of sea surface temperature, wind stress, and rainfall over the tropical Atlantic and South America', *Journal of Climate* 9: 2,464–79.

Nobre, C.A., Yanasse, H.H., and Yanasse, C.C.F. (1984) 'Drought prediction in Northeast Brazil by harmonic analysis: Uses and abuses', *Second WMO Conference on Tropical Droughts*, WMO (TPM Report Series No. 15), Fortaleza, pp. 113–15.

Repelli, C.A. and Nobre, P. (1997) 'Statistical prediction of sea surface temperature over the tropical Atlantic', submitted to *Journal of Geophysical Research*.

Richardson, D.S. and Robertson, K.B. (1994) 'A real-time dynamical forecast for the 1994 Nordeste Brazil rainfall season using the Met. Office Unified Model', UK Meteorological Office, *Technical Report* No. 93, Bracknell, United Kingdom.

Scott, C. and Hastenrath, S. (1995) 'Forcing of anomalous sea surface temperature evolution in the tropical Atlantic during Pacific warm events', *Journal of Geophysical Research. Ocean* 100: 15,835–47.

Serra, A.B. (1946) 'The Northeastern Brazil droughts', Serviço de Meteorologia, Rio de Janeiro, Brazil.

Servain, J.M. (1991) 'Simple climatic indices for the tropical Atlantic Ocean and some applications', *Journal of Geophysical Research* 96: 15,137–46.

Shukla, J. (1981) 'Dynamical predictability of monthly means', *Journal of Atmospheric Science* 38: 2,547–72.

Sperber, K.R. and Hameed, S. (1991) 'Resonant modulation of Nordeste precipitation by tropical Atlantic and Pacific sea surface temperatures', *Annual Climate Diagnostic Workshop* 16, 35 ff.

Stern, W. and Miyakoda, K. (1995) 'Feasibility of seasonal forecasts inferred from multiple GCM simulations', *Journal of Climate* 8: 1,071–85.

SUDENE (1981) 'As secas do Nordeste: Uma abordagem histórica de causas e efeitos', Ministério do Interior, CDU 551.577.38(812/814).

Ward, M.N. and Folland, C.K. (1991) 'Prediction of seasonal rainfall in the north nordeste of Brazil using eigenvectors of sea-surface temperature', *International Journal of Climatology* 11: 711–43.

Zebiak, S.E. (1993) 'Air–sea interaction in the equatorial Atlantic region', *Journal of Climate* 6: 1,567–86.

Zebiak, S.E. and Cane, M.A. (1996) 'Forecasts of tropical Pacific SST using a simple coupled ocean–atmosphere dynamical model', *Experimental Long-Lead Forecast Bulletin* 5: 4–9.

6
PROSPECTS FOR PREDICTING DROUGHTS IN THE UNITED STATES

Randall M. Dole

INTRODUCTION

In developing strategies to predict drought, certain fundamental challenges must be recognised. Perhaps the most basic question is, Precisely what is it that we wish to predict? Although there is broad agreement that drought is a prolonged period of anomalous moisture deficiency, identification of the onset, magnitude, and termination of drought varies substantially, depending on the user community or discipline (Wilhite and Glantz 1985). Indeed, even within a particular discipline, identification of drought onset and termination may be quite difficult, leading some to suggest that drought can be identified only retrospectively (Tannehill 1947). In addition, the term 'drought' is applied to phenomena ranging from abnormal dry spells persisting for less than a season to prolonged moisture deficits occurring on decadal or longer periods. This broad range of time scales suggests that an equally broad array of physical mechanisms must be considered in both understanding and predicting droughts.

Further compounding these difficulties is the fundamentally chaotic nature of mid-latitude weather variability, so that small differences in initial states eventually lead to large differences in the evolution of weather patterns. Because the time scales of drought are much longer than estimated limits of a few weeks for deterministic weather predictions (e.g., Lorenz 1983), the ability to predict the precise sequence of events associated with droughts is intrinsically limited. But does this mean that beyond some time period, say a month, all hope for useful predictions is lost?

Emphatically not, if instead of attempting to predict the precise sequence of events, the goal is changed to estimating how given initial and boundary conditions alter the risk of drought – i.e., its event probability, relative to climatological (or current) conditions. This predictability may result from either the presence of certain large-scale components of the atmospheric circulation, or through the effects of lower boundary forcings that evolve on much longer time scales than individual weather systems (e.g., Palmer and Anderson 1994). For operational purposes, the drought prediction problem becomes one of forecasting the probability distribution of some quantitative drought measure or index over a given region and time period. The remainder of this chapter examines the prospects for such predictions in the United States, first by considering factors that produce US droughts and second by discussing possible empirical and modelling approaches to drought predictions.

FACTORS CONTRIBUTING TO US DROUGHTS

Since, by definition, drought is an anomalous water deficit over a given time period and region, a complete mechanistic analysis would consider all factors contributing to the net water balance, including changes in precipitation, evapotranspiration, transports, and storage. The following will provide a brief overview of meteorological processes contributing to droughts over the contiguous United States, focusing principally on changes in precipitation. For further discussions of physical mechanisms for US droughts, particularly over the Great Plains, see also Namias (1983), Chang and Wallace (1987), Trenberth and Guillemot (1996), and Ting and Wang (1997).

General factors

General causes for US droughts are related to changes in vertical motions, horizontal moisture transports, and storm tracks.

Anomalous large-scale subsidence is characteristic of most droughts. Subsidence generally occurs near and downshear (in mid-latitudes, usually eastward) of an upper-level ridge axis (e.g., Holton 1992). Subsidence and associated ageostrophic circulations suppress both large-scale and convective precipitation through several effects, including inhibition of large-scale condensation, mid-tropospheric warming and consequent low-level static stabilisation (convective capping), and suppression of moisture convergence and frontogenesis by low-level divergence. Because specific humidity generally decreases very rapidly with height, anomalous low-level divergence also strongly affects the vertically integrated water vapour budget through changes in moisture-weighted divergence. Suppression of convection and cloudiness by subsidence favour anomalously warm surface temperatures (and in summer, heat waves). Accompanying changes in the surface energy balance due to increased net solar radiation may enhance evapotranspiration during early stages of droughts, accelerating drought development.

Anomalous circulations with droughts often are associated with reduced horizontal moisture transports into the drought region, as in the 1988 drought (Figure 6.1, adapted from Lyon and Dole 1995). In this case, the large-scale flow anomalies opposed the climatological mean flux of water vapour into the drought region from the Gulf of Mexico, which is the primary moisture source for precipitation in much of the central and eastern United States during spring and summer. The anomalous moisture fluxes were related to both the anomalous anticyclonic circulation centred just west of the Great Lakes and the anomalous cyclonic circulation centred off the mid-Atlantic coast.

Storm track shifts are of primary importance for winter and spring droughts, particularly over the western United States, where large-scale winter storm systems account for much of the annual precipitation. Although storm track changes can also be important in summer droughts, such as the 1988 drought (Lyon and Dole 1995, Trenberth and Guillemot 1996, Ting and Wang 1997), the effects are less systematic, particularly in mid to late summer over the central and southern United States. Over most of this region, summer precipitation is predominantly convective and highly intermittent, with the intensity and distribution strongly influenced by mesoscale phenomena such as weak frontal and convective outflow boundaries, mesoscale convective complexes (Maddox 1980 and 1983), and the Great Plains low-level jet (e.g., Bonner 1968, Helfand and Schubert 1995). In addition, the climatological-mean storm track is weak and is shifted well north into Canada. Consequently, relationships between monthly-mean precipitation and upper-level height anomalies are typically significantly weaker in summer than in winter. For example, Klein and Bloom (1987) find that on a nationwide basis, only 30 per cent of the precipitation variance in summer months is explained by the concurrent 700 mb height field, compared with approximately 45 per cent in winter.

In addition to these factors, other mechanisms may contribute significantly to drought. In the western United States, orographic effects strongly influence the intensity and distribution of precipitation, with precipitation markedly suppressed in downslope flow (leeward) regions and enhanced in upslope flow regions. To the extent that the large-scale flow is predictable, this strong orographic effect provides a potentially important source for drought predictability.

Changes in soil moisture, or more generally evapotranspiration, may also contribute to the severity and persistence of drought, particularly in summer in the continental interior. Evapotranspiration is a significant source of moisture for summertime precipitation over continents (e.g., Shukla and Mintz 1982, Mintz 1984), although relative contributions compared to other sources are subject to considerable uncertainty (Brubaker *et al.* 1993). Evapotranspiration anomalies generally result from preceding precipitation anomalies and therefore are unlikely to initiate drought (Trenberth and Branstator 1992, Lyon and

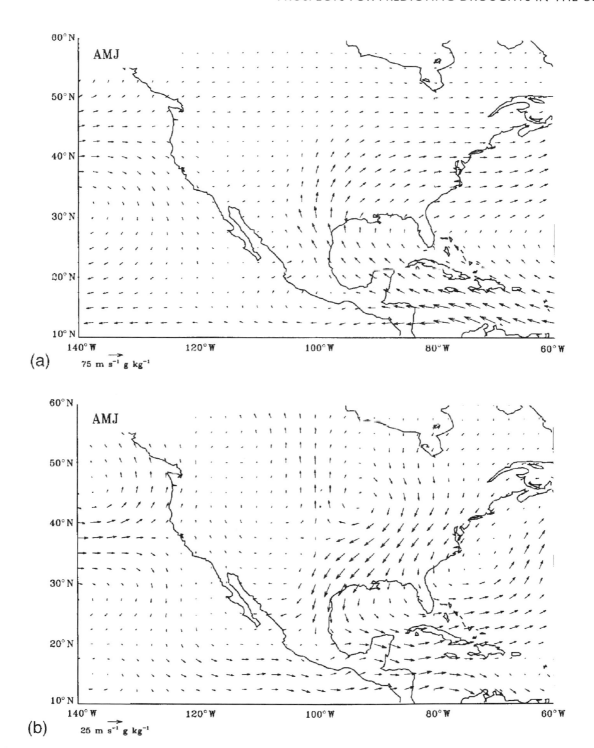

Figure 6.1 (a) April–June climatological 850 hPa moisture fluxes. Units: ms⁻¹ gkg⁻¹, reference vector given at lower left. (b) April–June 1988 anomalous 850 hPa moisture fluxes. Units ms⁻¹ gkg⁻¹, reference vector given at lower left. All figures in this chapter are based on data from the National Oceanic and Atmospheric Administration (NOAA)

Dole 1995); however, both observational (Hao and
Bosart 1987, Kunkel 1989, Namias 1982 and 1991,
Lyon and Dole 1995) and modelling studies
(Ogelsby and Erickson 1989, Atlas *et al.* 1993,
Dirmeyer 1994) indicate that decreases in evapotranspiration may increase the duration and severity
of droughts by reducing local moisture sources in the
desiccated region. Soil moisture anomalies directly
alter the surface energy balance through changes in
evapotranspiration, and therefore significantly influence surface temperatures, particularly during the
warm season over portions of the central United
States (Huang *et al.* 1996a). In particular, reduced
evapotranspiration favours higher maximum surface
temperatures, making concurrent heat wave conditions more likely.

Typical synoptic features of US droughts

The physical factors discussed above are associated with
typical synoptic features, which must be simulated suc-

cessfully for skilful numerical model predictions of
drought. This section presents characteristic synoptic
patterns associated with recent major US droughts.

In their initial stages, most US droughts are
associated with an anomalous upper-level anticyclone
located near or just upstream of the drought region.
Figure 6.2 illustrates such a relationship for the major
drought of 1995–6, which extended across much of
the Southwest and southern Plains and produced
losses estimated in excess of $6.5 billion just for the
state of Texas (Boyd 1996). From the fall of 1995
through summer 1996, the time-mean flow over the
Southwest was dominated by a persistent and
unusually strong high pressure ridge (Figure 6.2).
The anomalous flow opposed moisture inflow from
the Pacific and Gulf of Mexico, produced descending
air motions near and east of the anomalous anticyclone centre, and was accompanied by a shift in the
mean storm track to well north of the region. All of
these factors inhibited precipitation over the Southwest and southern Plains, and the persistence of the

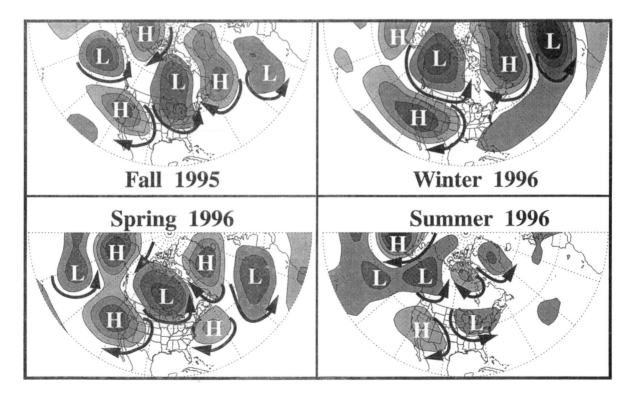

Figure 6.2 Mean upper-level height and wind anomaly patterns from fall 1995 through summer 1996

circulation anomalies over several seasons resulted in severe to extreme drought conditions over much of the area by the spring of 1996.

Figures 6.3 and 6.4 show, respectively, mean upper-level flow patterns associated with the 1980 and 1988 Midwest droughts. The 1980 summer drought had its largest impact on the southern Plains and lower Mississippi Valley (Namias 1982, Hao and Bosart 1987, Wolfson *et al.* 1987, Lyon and Dole 1995). Unlike the 1995–6 drought, the flow anomalies associated with this case developed very rapidly (i.e., essentially within a five- to ten-day period [Namias 1982]), and were characterised by three anomalous ridges located, respectively, over the eastern North Pacific, the southern Plains, and the North Atlantic. This general pattern has been observed during previous droughts in the region, most notably during the summers of 1952 to 1954 (Namias 1982, Chang and Wallace 1987). The rapidity of development and absence of connections to strong sea-surface temperature anomalies, at least in the tropical Pacific, suggest that this case may have been initiated primarily through an internal dynamical mechanism, although the potential importance of North Pacific extratropical sea surface temperature anomalies has been suggested for this case by Namias (1982), and more recently for other

Great Plains droughts by Ting and Wang (1997).

The primary time-mean feature during the 1988 drought was an anomalous anticyclone over the northern United States, which reached maximum intensity over the upper Midwest in June (Figure 6.4). Trenberth *et al.* (1988), Palmer and Brankovic (1989), and Trenberth and Branstator (1992) have suggested that these anomalies were part of a quasi-stationary wavetrain that was forced primarily by tropical heating anomalies associated with a strong La Niña event, although this interpretation has been subject to debate (Mo *et al.* 1991, Namias 1991, Atlas *et al.* 1993, Lyon and Dole 1995, Chen and Newman 1997). For example, studies with general circulation models indicate the importance of both initial conditions (Mo *et al.* 1991) and soil moisture anomalies (Atlas *et al.* 1993) in simulating this event. Chen and Newman (1997) show that major changes in the large-scale flow occurred during the course of the drought, and they argue that this drought should be considered not as a single, quasi-stationary event, but rather as a succession of events that together produced a major hydrological deficit.

As illustrated in these cases, the common synoptic feature in most US droughts is a persistent anomalous anticyclone located near or just upstream of the

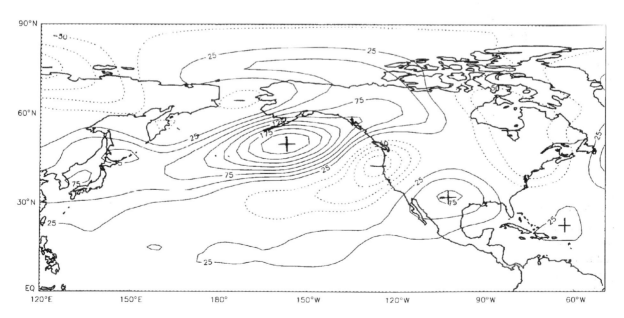

Figure 6.3 Time-average 300 hPa height anomalies for June 1980. Contour interval 25 m, negative anomalies dashed

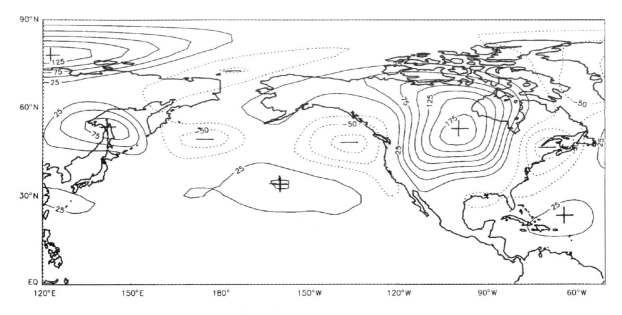

Figure 6.4 Time-average 300 hPa height anomalies for June 1988. Contour interval 25 m, negative anomalies dashed

drought region, particularly during drought development. From a synoptic perspective, this is the critical feature that models must simulate to predict the early stages of drought. As in the cases discussed above, the anomalous anticyclones often appear as part of a wavetrain extending downstream from the Pacific, although in each of these cases the wavetrain differs considerably in structure, as does the timing of onset relative to the season cycle. This timing is potentially quite important for dynamical predictions, because of the sensitivity of Rossby wave propagation to variations in the basic state associated with the seasonal cycle (Newman and Sardeshmukh 1997). Lyon and Dole (1995) show that, by early July in both the 1980 and 1988 cases, the wavetrain patterns weaken considerably, and, based on water vapour budget analyses, they suggest that local boundary conditions played an important role in prolonging drought-heat wave conditions. Several other studies have also emphasised the potentially important role of reduced local evapotranspiration in intensifying and perpetuating Midwestern summer droughts (Namias 1982 and 1991, Hao and Bosart 1987, Oglesby and Erickson 1989, Trenberth and Branstator 1992, Dirmeyer 1994, Trenberth and Guillemot 1996).

Relationships of US droughts to large-scale modes of variability

The previous section presented typical examples of jetstream variations associated with droughts in various parts of the United States. A more difficult, but crucial, question is, What are the causes for the observed jetstream variations?

On seasonal-to-interannual time scales, the El Niño–Southern Oscillation (ENSO) phenomenon significantly influences the large-scale flow, and hence temperature and precipitation patterns, over the continental United States, particularly in winter and spring (for a thorough review of ENSO, see, e.g., Philander 1990). Indeed, ENSO research has been the primary driving force and basis for optimism in the development of seasonal to interannual forecasting capabilities in the United States and elsewhere, particularly because of emerging capabilities to predict tropical Pacific sea surface temperatures out to approximately a year in advance (Barnston *et al.* 1994, Latif *et al.* 1994). This optimism must be tempered by the knowledge that the estimated mean signal from ENSO over the United States is not large compared to natural variability (Madden 1976,

Chervin 1986, Kumar and Hoerling 1995) and, partly as a consequence, there is considerable variability in US climate from one ENSO event to another that appears unrelated to tropical Pacific sea surface temperatures (Kumar and Hoerling 1997).

Nevertheless, systematic ENSO signals have been identified in a wide range of US climate variables. For example, Ropelewski and Halpert (1986, 1989, and 1996) and Kiladis and Diaz (1989) document in detail the composite-mean relationships between ENSO and seasonal-mean anomalies in US temperatures and precipitation. These studies show that ENSO cold conditions (La Niña events) are associated with below-normal precipitation in winter and spring over the Gulf Coast and Southeast, suggesting a predisposition toward drought under these circumstances.

Hydrological studies have also identified ENSO influences on regional streamflow variability. Cayan and Webb (1992) and Kahya and Dracup (1994) document relationships between ENSO and streamflow over parts of the western United States, while Kahya and Dracup (1993) discuss statistically significant responses in streamflow to El Niño and La Niña events over four core regions: the Gulf of Mexico, the Northeast, the north central plains, and the Pacific Northwest. Guetter and Georgakakos (1996) identify a strong association between La Niña and below-normal streamflows in the Iowa River basin. These studies support the idea that, in some seasons and regions, ENSO conditions alter the risk of drought. Further evidence for this viewpoint will be presented in the following section.

In addition to ENSO, other low-frequency atmospheric phenomena may significantly influence North American climate, such as the North Atlantic Oscillation (Hurrell 1995) and decadal variability in the North Pacific (Latif and Barnett 1994 and 1996, Trenberth and Hurrell 1994). The significance of relationships between these phenomena and US droughts remains to be established, although a recent study (Ting and Wang 1997) suggests that a decadal trend in Great Plains precipitation during the period 1950–90 was correlated to North Pacific sea surface temperature (SST) variations. Prolonged drought on decadal and longer time scales is certainly an important feature of US climate, as is evident from

the 'Dust Bowl' droughts of the 1930s and other droughts in this century (Diaz 1983), as well as longer-term records based on paleoclimate evidence (e.g., Bark 1978, Cook et al. 1997). Both solar and lunar forcing have been suggested as related to approximately bi-decadal variations in drought over the western United States, although interpretations have been controversial, and convincing mechanisms for such relationships have yet to be identified.

On seasonal to interannual time scales, North Pacific SSTs may also influence summer precipitation variability over the Great Plains. Ting and Wang (1997) find that dry summers over the Great Plains are associated with below-normal SST over the central North Pacific and above-normal SST over both the eastern and western Pacific. It remains to be determined whether the extratropical SST are forcing an atmospheric response favourable for Great Plains droughts, as suggested by Ting and Wang, or instead are predominantly a response to such a circulation, as might be anticipated from some studies of extratropical air-sea interactions (e.g., Davis 1976).

On shorter time scales, intraseasonal changes in tropical convection over the tropical Pacific affect low-frequency variability over the North American sector, particularly in winter and spring (Weickmann et al. 1985, Madden and Julian 1994). To the extent that such variations are predictable, they may be useful in anticipating possible changes in short-term moisture conditions and related indices, such as the Crop Moisture Index (Palmer 1968).

POSSIBLE APPROACHES TO PREDICTING US DROUGHTS

At present, the US National Weather Service (NWS) does not issue routine drought forecasts or outlooks. Rather, for lead times beyond five days, official forecasts provide the most probable categories in average temperatures and precipitation over given time periods. For seasonal forecasts, this corresponds to a three-categorical forecast of above-normal, near-normal, or below-normal conditions for seasonal-mean temperatures and precipitation extending out to four seasons in advance (Barnston et al. 1994). These forecasts are based on a combination of empirical statistical methods, such as canonical correlation analysis (Barnston 1994) and optimal climate normals (Huang *et al.* 1996b), model forecasts with the National Centers for Environmental Prediction (NCEP) coupled ocean–atmosphere model (Ji *et al.* 1994a and 1994b), and modifications based on experience by forecasters at the Climate Prediction Center.

As discussed earlier, for operational drought forecasting, the basic problem is to predict the probability distribution of some quantitative drought measure or index over a given region and time period. The specific parameter will depend on the time scale and desired application. For example, for short time scales or agricultural applications, this measure may be the Crop Moisture Index (CMI), while for longer periods the modified Palmer Drought Severity Index (PDSI) or some other index may be used that is better suited for specific purposes (for discussions of the various drought indices, see Palmer 1968, Alley 1984, Karl and Knight 1985, McKee *et al.* 1993). The remainder of this section discusses possible approaches to estimating future risks of droughts, with primary emphasis on seasonal time scales. Two basic approaches will be considered: empirical forecasts and ensemble model predictions.

Before discussing specific examples, however, it is helpful to consider why even apparently modest climate signals may significantly influence the risks of drought and therefore provide potentially useful predictability. Figure 6.5 illustrates the basic concept of conditional risks of extreme events, which is at the heart of the drought prediction problem. The top curve in this figure represents the climatological distribution of a particular drought index, and the bottom curve represents the conditional distribution of this index related to some climate forcing, such as ENSO. What is striking is that even a relatively modest shift in the mean, such as occurs over parts of the continental United States in association with ENSO, can substantially change the probabilities at the extremes of the distribution – for example, severe droughts (or floods). In particular, extreme events on one side of the distribution become much more likely, while those on the other side become much less likely. Such shifts in probabilities have important implications, and any foreknowledge of such a shift would have potentially useful applications.

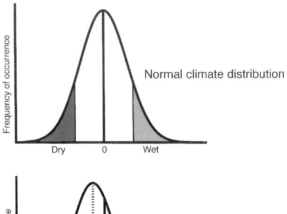

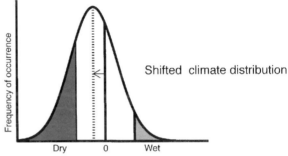

Figure 6.5 Schematic showing the effect on the relative frequencies of extreme dry events (dark shading) and wet events (light shading) resulting from a small shift in the mean of a normal distribution

Empirical approach

To illustrate possible prospects of drought prediction using empirical methods, a few results will be presented from ongoing studies at the NOAA–CIRES Climate Diagnostics Center (CDC) on how ENSO affects the frequency of occurrence of climate extremes over the continental United States. These results are based on collaborative work at CDC involving the present author, C. Smith, and K. Wolter. The examples to be discussed below are based on data over the 100-year period from 1896 to 1995. Precipitation data for this period were derived from the National Climate Data Center (NCDC) US climate division data.

For each climate division and standard season, rankings were first determined from driest to wettest seasons, and the twenty driest seasons and twenty wettest seasons were then selected for more detailed study. Note that these lowest and highest quintiles correspond, respectively, to commonly used thresholds for 'much below normal' and 'much above normal' precipitation. Similarly, the Southern Oscillation Index (SOI) values for the corresponding time periods were ranked from lowest to highest values over the 100-year period, with the twenty lowest values (generally corresponding with ENSO warm-phase, or El Niño, conditions) and twenty highest values (usually corresponding with ENSO cold-phase, or La Niña, conditions) selected to evaluate possible relationships between ENSO and US climate extremes. Estimated changes in the conditional probabilities, or risks, of very dry or very wet seasons associated with ENSO were then evaluated by comparing the observed numbers of extreme seasons occurring with specified ENSO conditions with the expected (i.e., unconditional) values. For further details on the analysis methods, see Wolter *et al.* (1997).

Figures 6.6–6.9 present examples of conditional risk estimates that can be obtained through this procedure. Figure 6.6 shows those areas at significantly increased risks of either very dry or very wet winters, given concurrent El Niño conditions. During El Niño, there are significantly increased risks of very wet winters over the northern and central California coast, much of the Southwest and south central Plains, and the Southeast. Significantly increased risks

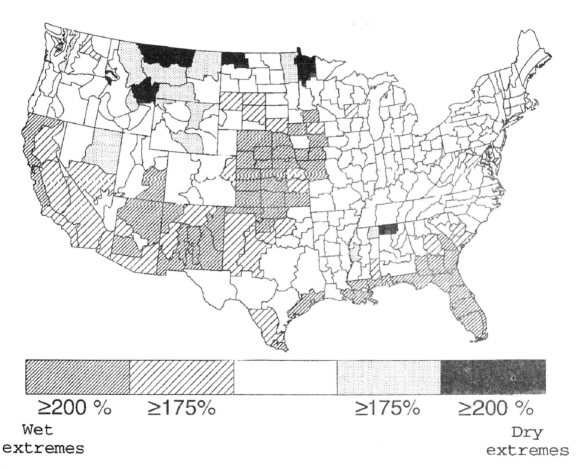

≥200 % ≥175% ≥175% ≥200 %

Wet
extremes

Dry
extremes

Percentage increase in risk relative to climatological average risk

Figure 6.6 Areas of the contiguous United States at significantly increased risk of either very wet winters or very dry winters, given concurrent El Niño conditions. Shading conventions for regions at enhanced risk are given at the bottom. In this figure, ≥ 200 per cent corresponds to a doubling or greater in the number of extreme seasons of that type relative to climatologically expected values

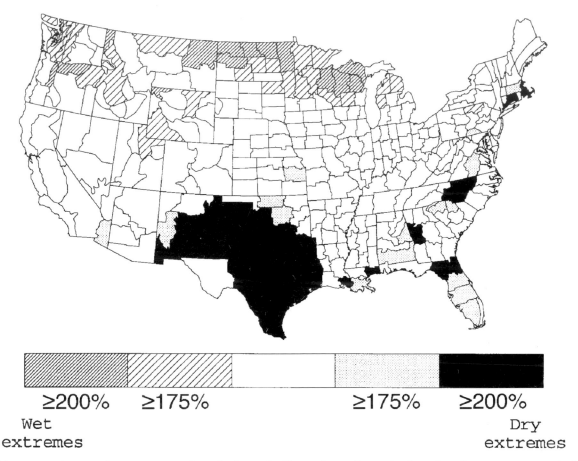

≥200%   ≥175%   ≥175%   ≥200%
Wet   Dry
extremes   extremes

Percentage increase in risk relative to climatological average risk

Figure 6.7 Areas of the contiguous United States at enhanced risk of either very wet winters or very dry winters, given concurrent La Niña conditions. Shading conventions for regions at enhanced risk are given at the bottom. In this figure, ≥ 200 per cent corresponds to a doubling or greater in the number of extreme seasons of that type relative to climatologically expected values

of very dry winters, suggesting a tendency toward drought, cover a substantially smaller area that includes portions of the northern Rockies extending into the far northern Plains. In contrast, for winters with concurrent La Niña conditions (Figure 6.7), areas at greatest risk of very dry conditions include much of Texas and New Mexico, as well as portions of the Southeast and East Coast. Note that the former areas were among those most affected by drought during 1995–6, which occurred in conjunction with weak to moderate La Niña conditions.

In the spring following winter La Niña conditions, the regions of maximum increased risk of very dry conditions shift slightly westward and northward, and include most of New Mexico and parts of Colorado, Arizona, and portions of Texas and the southern Plains (Figure 6.8). Note that much of New Mexico and Texas are at enhanced risk of abnormally dry conditions, suggesting that during La Niña conditions, these areas are at particular risk of multiseason drought. These areas, as well as portions of the southern Plains and Mississippi River basin, are also at increased risk of very dry conditions in fall with concurrent La Niña conditions (not shown).

Figure 6.9 graphically illustrates how ENSO conditions substantially alter the risks of very dry vs. very

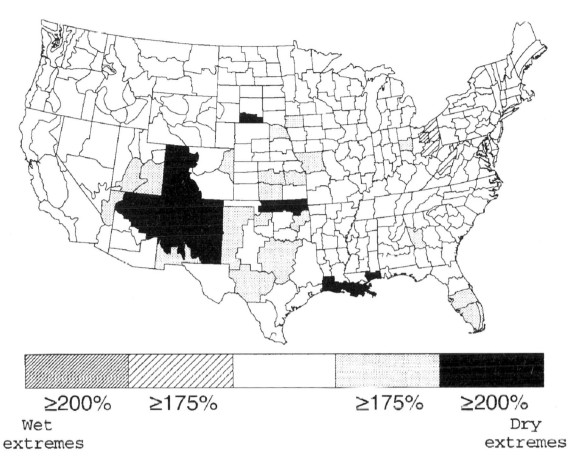

Percentage increase in risk relative to climatological average risk

Figure 6.8 Areas of the contiguous United States at enhanced risk of either very wet springs or very dry springs, given La Niña conditions in the previous winter. Shading conventions for regions at enhanced risk are given at the bottom. In this figure, ≥ 200 per cent corresponds to a doubling or greater in the number of extreme seasons of that type relative to climatologically expected values

wet winters in Texas, an area particularly hard hit by the 1995–6 drought. In particular, during ENSO cold-phase (La Niña) conditions, very dry winters become relatively much more likely, and very wet winters much less likely. Indeed, over the 100 year period, no very wet winters occurred in conjunction with La Niña conditions, although this does not rule out the possibility that this may occur at some future time. Roughly the reverse situation holds during El Niño conditions, with an increased risk of very wet winters and reduced risk of very dry winters. Note that the occurrence of La Niña does not guarantee a very dry winter in this region, but it does shift the

probability distribution in such a way as to make its occurrence, and therefore a possible drought, more likely.

These empirical analyses support the idea that, at least in some seasons and regions, ENSO significantly alters the risks of drought. Further development of such approaches should provide additional prospects for potentially useful predictions of areas at increased risk for drought, based on ENSO (or other) conditions.

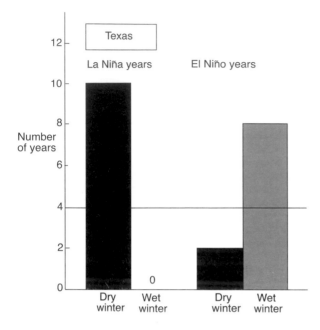

Figure 6.9 Number of very dry vs very wet winters in Texas, 1896–1995, given winter El Niño conditions or La Niña conditions

Modelling approach

One of the disadvantages of empirical techniques is that the data sample size is generally much smaller than desirable for many purposes, including estimations of extreme event probabilities. One consequence is that analyses must generally combine many cases whose differences (for example, in sea surface temperatures) may be physically important, potentially limiting their value for predictive purposes. An alternative approach to estimating shifts in probability distributions is through ensemble predictions derived from numerical prediction models. This is a rapidly developing area of research that holds considerable promise for new operational applications, including drought predictions.

In brief, the basis of this approach is to run numerical prediction models multiple times from slightly different initial conditions, and then to estimate the probability distributions from the outcomes of the different model runs (Figure 6.10). The choice of different initial conditions reflects both the incomplete nature of climate observations and the fact that

the atmosphere's evolution is very sensitive to these uncertainties. In principle, perturbations in physical parameterisations may also be performed, although such an approach has not yet been attempted operationally at NCEP.

At present, NCEP performs ensemble predictions for medium-range forecasts (out to approximately two weeks) with the Medium Range Forecast (MRF) model (Tracton and Kalnay 1993), and out to six months with the NCEP coupled ocean–atmosphere model system (Ji *et al.* 1994a and 1994b). The latter system includes a Pacific basin ocean model derived originally from the Geophysical Fluid Dynamics Laboratory modular ocean model, and an atmospheric general circulation model (AGCM) that is a modified version of NCEP's operational global MRF model (Ji *et al.* 1994a, Kumar *et al.* 1996). The AGCM contains modifications of certain physical parameterisations designed to improve climate simulations of tropical deep convection and precipitation, as well as the mid-latitude response to tropical SST forcing.

For the seasonal forecasts, the NCEP coupled model ensembles currently consist of eighteen members. It remains to be determined whether this sample size is sufficient for estimating possible influences of tropical SSTs on droughts and other extreme climate events. However, scientists at NCEP and CDC have been performing collaborative studies with substantially larger ensemble sizes to study a variety of ENSO-climate sensitivity issues (see, e.g., Hoerling *et al.* 1997). Figure 6.11 provides one example of results obtained from such studies. The particular example was kindly provided by Dr. M. Hoerling of CDC, and shows histograms of winter-season rainfall amounts for California, given climatological SST (Figure 6.11a) and El Niño conditions (Figure 6.11b), as derived from forty-member ensembles.

Figure 6.11 shows that, although there is considerable overlap between the distributions obtained from the climatological and El Niño runs, there are also systematic differences in the mean precipitation and relative frequencies of extreme seasons. In particular, seven of the members in the El Niño runs have mean daily rainfall rates in excess of 5 mm per day^{-1}, while only one such member exceeds this value in the climatological SST runs. Such a shift in distributions is consistent with the increased risk of very

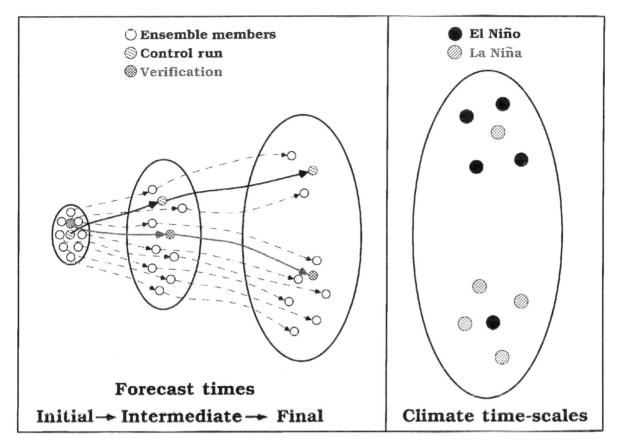

Figure 6.10 Schematic diagram of the basic ensemble prediction technique. Forecasts are started from slightly different sets of initial conditions, with the ellipses showing the general dispersion of forecasts with increasing forecast lead time. The right-hand panel shows how, on climate time scales, anomalous boundary conditions (in this case, either El Niño or La Niña) may alter the conditional probabilities toward certain preferred states

wet winters over much of California during El Niño conditions that was identified earlier in the empirical analyses (Figure 6.6). Note also that the model runs (and empirical analyses) indicate that drought risk, although reduced, is not entirely eliminated during El Niño (see also Kahya and Dracup 1994). Such results, while preliminary, are encouraging in indicating that ensemble model predictions may also provide useful information on possible future risks of droughts and other extreme climate events.

SUMMARY

The science of drought prediction is still in its earliest stages. Although skill in such forecasts will likely always be modest, even marginal skill may have substantial social and economic value. The challenge in predicting droughts is due in part to the complexity of the phenomenon itself. As discussed above, droughts are influenced by a wide range of dynamical and physical processes, whose importance varies substantially during the course of the events. Further, many droughts develop and evolve through processes of natural climate variability, which may be partly or entirely unpredictable at extended ranges. Nevertheless, continuing advances in understanding the mechanisms for drought, together with the emergence of new forecasting approaches, suggests that potentially useful US drought predictions are possible.

Because of the chaotic nature of the climate

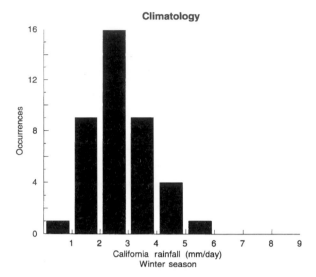

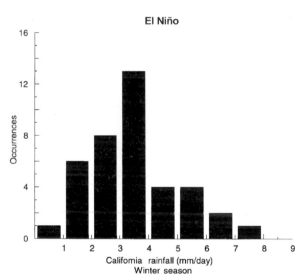

Figure 6.11 Numbers of winter seasons where California rainfall was within indicated categories (units: mm day[-1]), as obtained from two forty-member ensemble simulations with the NCEP seasonal prediction model for (a) climatological sea surface temperature conditions and (b) El Niño conditions

emphasising ensemble prediction techniques. For operational purposes, it is likely that a blending of the two approaches would be most useful for forecasting drought risks.

In developing new drought forecast products, the best immediate prospects for skill appear to be on seasonal to interannual scales, where significant seasonal and regional ENSO influences on drought probabilities may be usefully exploited. On shorter time scales, predictions may be feasible of drought indices that respond quite rapidly to precipitation and temperature variations, such as the CMI, using parameters derived from ensemble forecasts with the Medium Range Forecast model. At present, prospects for drought predictability on longer scales are much more difficult to assess, as causal mechanisms on these time scales are inadequately understood and predictive skill for regional climate variations is yet to be demonstrated. In addition to natural mechanisms, long-term drought variations may be influenced by anthropogenic climate change. Although some model studies suggest that there may be more frequent or severe droughts in a warmer climate, confidence in projecting any regional changes is presently very low (IPCC 1995, Gregory *et al.* 1997).

Several areas of research may contribute to developing skilful drought forecasts. In particular, although a major emphasis has been on identifying ENSO influences on US droughts, other boundary variations, such as in soil moisture, vegetation, and North Pacific SSTs, are likely to be important in many cases. Although predictability due to these factors is yet to be demonstrated, the possibility deserves further investigation.

ACKNOWLEDGEMENTS

Thanks to Mr. Andy Loughe and Ms. Cathy Smith of the Climate Diagnostics Center for help in preparing figures, and to Drs. Henry Diaz, Martin Hoerling, Mathew Newman, and Jeffrey Whitaker of CDC for helpful discussions and suggestions on an earlier version of this manuscript. The author is supported through the National Oceanic and Atmospheric Administration Environmental Research Laboratory (ERL). Work at CDC related to this review is supported through NOAA ERL and the NOAA Office of Global Programs.

system, drought predictions are fundamentally probability forecasts, with the basic problem being to estimate how particular initial and boundary conditions alter drought risks over a given region and time period. To illustrate possible approaches to obtaining such estimates, two basic prediction methods were discussed: empirical and modelling, with the latter

REFERENCES

Alley, W.M. (1984) 'The Palmer Drought Severity Index: Limitations and assumptions', *Journal of Climate and Applied Meteorology* 21: 1,100–9.

Atlas, R., Wolfson, N., and Terry, J. (1993) 'The effect of SST and soil moisture anomalies on GLA model simulations of the 1988 US summer drought', *Journal of Climate* 6: 2,034–48.

Bark, L.D. (1978) 'History of American droughts', in N.J. Rosenberg (ed.), *North American Droughts*, Boulder, CO: Westview Press, 9–23.

Barnston, A.G. (1994) 'Linear statistical short-term climate predictive skill in the Northern Hemisphere', *Journal of Climate* 7: 1,513–64.

Barnston, A.G., van den Dool, H.M., Zebiak, S.E., Barnett, T.P., Ji, M., Rodenhuis, D.R., Cane, M.A., Leetmaa, A., Graham, N.E., Ropelewski, C.R., Kousky, V.E., O'Lenic, E.A., and Livezey, R.E. (1994) 'Long-lead seasonal forecasts – Where do we stand?', *Bulletin of the American Meteorological Society* 75: 2,097–114.

Bonner, W.D. (1968) 'Climatology of the low-level jet', *Monthly Weather Review* 96: 833–49.

Boyd, J. (1996) 'Southwest farmers battle record drought', United Press International, 30 May.

Brubaker, K.L., Entekhabi, D., and Eagleson, P.S. (1993) 'Estimation of continental precipitation recycling', *Journal of Climate* 5: 1,077–89.

Cayan, D.R. and Webb, R.H. (1992) 'El Niño–Southern Oscillation and streamflow in the United States', in H.F. Diaz and V. Markgraf (eds), *El Niño: Historical and Paleoclimate Aspects of the Southern Oscillation*, New York: Cambridge University Press, pp. 29–68.

Chang, F.C. and Wallace, J.M. (1987) 'Meteorological conditions during heat waves and droughts in the United States Great Plains', *Monthly Weather Review* 115: 1,253–69.

Chen, P. and Newman, M. (1998) 'Rossby-wave propagation and the rapid development of upper-level anomalous anticyclones during the 1988 US Drought', *Journal of Climate* 11, 10: 2,491–504.

Chervin, R.M. (1986) 'Interannual variability and seasonal climate variability', *Journal of the Atmospheric Sciences* 43: 233–51.

Cook, E.R., Meko, D.M., and Stockton, C.W. (1997) 'A new assessment of possible solar and lunar forcing of the bidecadal drought rhythm in the western United States', *Journal of Climate* 10: 1,343–56.

Davis, R.E. (1976) 'Predictability of sea surface temperature and sea level pressure over the North Pacific Ocean', *Journal of Physical Oceanography* 6: 249–66.

Diaz, H.F. (1983) 'Some aspects of major dry and wet periods in the contiguous United States', *Journal of Climate and Applied Meteorology* 22, 1: 3–16.

Dirmeyer, P.A. (1994) 'Vegetation stress as a feedback mechanism in midlatitude drought', *Journal of Climate* 7, 10: 1,463–83.

Gregory, J.M., Mitchell, J.F.B., and Brady, A.J. (1997) 'Summer drought in northern mid-latitudes in a time-dependent CO$_2$ climate experiment', *Journal of Climate* 10, 4: 662–86.

Guetter, A.K. and Georgakakos, K.P. (1996) 'Are the El Niño and La Niña predictors of the Iowa River seasonal flow?', *Journal of Applied Meteorology* 35: 690–705.

Hao, W. and Bosart, L.F. (1987) 'A moisture budget analysis of the protracted heatwave in the southern Plains during the summer of 1980', *Weather and Forecasting* 2: 269–88.

Helfand, H.M. and Schubert, S.D. (1995) 'Climatology of the simulated Great Plains low-level jet and its contribution to the continental moisture budget of the United States', *Journal of the Atmospheric Sciences* 8: 784–806.

Hoerling, M.P., Kumar, A., and Zhong, M. (1997) 'El Niño, La Niña, and the nonlinearity of their teleconnections', *Journal of Climate* 10: 1,769–86.

Holton, J.R. (1992) *An Introduction to Dynamic Meteorology*, New York: Academic Press, Inc.

Huang, J., van den Dool, H.M., and Georgakakos, P. (1996a) 'Analysis of model-calculated soil moisture over the United States (1931–1993) and applications to long-range temperature forecasts', *Journal of Climate* 9, 6: 1350–61.

Huang, J., van den Dool, H.M., and Barnston, A.G. (1996b) 'Long-lead seasonal temperature prediction using optimal climate normals', *Journal of Climate* 9: 809–17.

Hurrell, J.W. (1995) 'Decadal trends in the North Atlantic Oscillation: Regional temperatures and precipitation', *Science* 269: 676–9.

IPCC (1995) *Climate Change 1995. The Science of Climate Change* (J.T. Houghton, L.G. Meira Filho, B.A. Callander, N. Harris, A. Kattenberg and K. Maskell, eds), Cambridge: Cambridge University Press.

Ji, M., Kumar, A., and Leetmaa, A. (1994a) 'A multiseason climate forecast system at the National Meteorological Center', *Bulletin of the American Meteorological Society* 75: 569–77.

—— (1994b) 'An experimental coupled forecast system at the National Meteorological Center: Some early results', *Tellus* 46A: 398–418.

Kahya, E. and Dracup, J.A. (1993) 'US Streamflow patterns in relation to the El Niño–Southern Oscillation', *Water Resource Research* 29: 2,491–503.

—— (1994) 'The influences of Type 1 El Niño events on streamflows in the Pacific Southwest of the United States', *Journal of Climate* 7: 965–76.

Karl, T.R. and Knight, R.W. (1985) 'Atlas of monthly Palmer Hydrological Drought Indices (1931–1983) for the contiguous United States', *Historical Climatology Series* 3–7, Asheville, NC: National Climatic Data Center.

Klein, W.H. and Bloom, H.J. (1987) 'Specification of monthly precipitation over the United States from the surrounding 700 mb height field', *Monthly Weather Review* 115: 2,118–32.

Kiladis, G.N. and Diaz, H.F. (1989) 'Global climate anomalies associated with the Southern Oscillation', *Journal of Climate* 2: 1,069–90.

Kumar, A. and Hoerling, M.P. (1995) 'Prospects and limitations of seasonal atmospheric GCM predictions', *Bulletin of the American Meteorological Society* 76: 335–45.

—— (1997) 'Interpretation and limitations of observed inter-El Niño variability', *Journal of Climate* 10: 83–91.

Kumar, A., Hoerling, M., Ji, M., Leetmaa, A., and Sardeshmukh, P.D. (1996) 'Assessing a GCM's suitability for making seasonal prediction', *Journal of Climate* 9: 115–29.

Kunkel, K.E. (1989) 'A surface energy budget view of the 1988 midwestern United States drought', *Boundary-Layer Meteorology* 48: 217–25.

Latif, M. and Barnett, T.P. (1994) 'Causes of decadal climate variability over the North Pacific and North America', *Science* 266: 634–7.

—— (1996) 'Decadal climate variability over the North Pacific and North America: Dynamics and predictability', *Journal of Climate* 9: 2,407–23.

Latif, M., Barnett, T.P., Cane, M.A., Fluegel, M., Graham, N.E., von Storch, H., Xu, J.S., and Zebiak, S.E. (1994) 'A review of ENSO prediction studies', *Climate Dynamics* 9: 167–79.

Lorenz, E.N. (1983) 'Estimates of atmospheric predictability at medium range', in *Predictability of Fluid Motions*, New York: American Institute of Physics, pp. 133–40.

Lyon, B.F. and Dole, R.M. (1995) 'A diagnostic comparison of the 1980 and 1988 U.S. summer heat wave-droughts', *Journal of Climate* 8, 6: 1,658–75.

Madden, R. (1976) 'Estimate of natural variability of time-averaged sea level pressure', *Monthly Weather Review* 104: 942–52.

Madden, R. and Julian, P.R. (1994) 'Observations of the 45–50 day tropical oscillation – A review', *Monthly Weather Review* 122: 814–37.

Maddox, R.A. (1980) 'Mesoscale convective complexes', *Bulletin of the American Meteorological Society* 61: 1,374–87.

—— (1983) 'Large-scale meteorological conditions associated with midlatitude, mesoscale convective complexes', *Monthly Weather Review* 111: 1,475–93.

McKee, T.B., Doesken, N.J., and Kleist, J. (1993) 'The relationship of drought frequency and duration to time scales', *Preprints, 9th Conference on Applied Climatology* (15–20 January, Dallas, TX), Boston, MA: American Meteorological Society, pp. 233–6.

Mintz, Y. (1984) 'The sensitivity of numerically simulated climates to land-surface boundary conditions', in J.T. Houghton (ed.), *The Global Climate*, Cambridge: Cambridge University Press, pp. 79–106.

Mo, K.C., Zimmerman, J.R., Kalnay, E., and Kanamitsu, M. (1991) 'A GCM study of the 1988 United States drought', *Monthly Weather Review* 119: 1,512–32.

Namias, J.R. (1982) 'Anatomy of Great Plains protracted heat waves (especially the 1980 US summer drought)', *Monthly Weather Review* 110: 824–38.

—— (1983) 'Some causes of United States drought', *Journal of Climate and Applied Meteorology* 22: 30–9.

—— (1991) 'Spring and summer 1988 drought over the contiguous United States – Causes and prediction', *Journal of Climate* 4: 54–65.

Newman, M. and Sardeshmukh, P.D. (1998) 'The impact of the annual cycle on the North Pacific-North American response to remote low frequency forcing', *Journal of the Atmospheric Sciences* 55, 8: 1,336–53.

Oglesby, R.J. and Erickson, D.J. (1989) 'Soil moisture and the persistence of North American drought', *Journal of Climate* 2: 1,362–80.

Palmer, W.C. (1968) 'Keeping track of crop moisture conditions, nationwide: The new Crop Moisture Index', *Weatherwise* 21: 156–61.

Palmer, T.N. and Anderson, D.L.T. (1994) 'The prospects for seasonal forecasting – A review paper', *Quarterly Journal of the Royal Meteorological Society* 120: 755–93.

Palmer, T.N. and Brankovic, C. (1989) 'The 1988 U.S. drought linked to anomalous sea surface temperature', *Nature* 338: 54–7.

Philander, S.G. (1990) *El Niño, La Niña, and the Southern Oscillation*, New York: Academic Press.

Ropelewski, C.F. and Halpert, M.S. (1986) 'North American precipitation and temperature patterns associated with the El Niño–Southern Oscillation', *Monthly Weather Review* 115: 1,606–26.

—— (1989) 'Precipitation patterns associated with the high index phase of the Southern Oscillation', *Journal of Climate* 2: 268–84.

—— (1996) 'Quantifying Southern Oscillation–precipitation relationships', *Journal of Climate* 9: 1,043–59.

Shukla, J. and Mintz, Y. (1982) 'Influence of land-surface evapotranspiration on the earth's climate', *Science* 215: 1,498–501.

Tannehill, I.R. (1947) *Drought, Its Causes and Effects*, Princeton, NJ: Princeton University Press.

Ting, M. and Wang, H. (1997) 'Summertime U.S. precipitation variability and its relation to Pacific sea surface temperature', *Journal of Climate* 10, 8: 1,853–73.

Tracton, M.S. and Kalnay, E. (1993) 'Ensemble forecasting at NMC: Operational implementation', *Weather and Forecasting* 8: 379–98.

Trenberth, K.E. and Branstator, G.W. (1992) 'Issues in establishing causes of the 1988 drought over North America', *Journal of Climate* 5: 159–72.

Trenberth, K.E., Branstator, G.W., and Arkin, P.A. (1988) 'Origins of the 1988 North American drought', *Science* 242: 1,640–5.

Trenberth, K.E. and Guillemot, C.J. (1996) 'Physical processes involved in the 1988 drought and 1993 floods in North America', *Journal of Climate* 9, 6: 1,288–98.

Trenberth, K.E. and Hurrell, J.W. (1994) 'Decadal ocean–atmosphere variations in the Pacific', *Climate Dynamics* 9: 303–19.

Weickmann, K., Lussky, G.R., and Kutzbach, J.E. (1985) 'Intraseasonal (30–60 day) fluctuations of outgoing longwave radiation and 250 mb stream function during northern winter', *Monthly Weather Review* 113: 941–61.

Wilhite, D.A. and Glantz, M.H. (1985) 'Understanding the drought phenomenon: The role of definitions', *Water International* 10, 3: 111–20.

Wolfson, N., Atlas, R., and Sud, Y.C. (1987) 'Numerical experiments related to the summer 1980 U.S. heat wave', *Monthly Weather Review* 115: 1,345–57.

Wolter, K., Dole, R.M., and Smith, C.A. (1999) 'Short-term climate extremes over the continental U.S. and ENSO. Part I: Seasonal temperatures', *Journal of Climate* 12.

7

PREDICTABILITY OF DROUGHT IN CHINA

Wang Shaowu, Ye Jinlan, and Qian Weihong

INTRODUCTION

China is located in a monsoon region where droughts and floods occur with very high frequency. For example, the cultivated area during 1978–89 averaged 112.6 million ha, about one-third of which usually suffered from assorted disasters. Among these disasters, drought predominated (Wang *et al.* 1991). The sown area and the area affected by disasters for the period 1978–89 are outlined in the first and second columns of Table 7.1. The percentage of the sown area affected by disasters is shown in parentheses. This number varies between 22.1 per cent in 1984 and 35.1 per cent in 1988. The figures show a steady pattern: the area affected by disasters remained

between 20 per cent and 40 per cent in this period. The next two columns show the area affected by drought and flood, respectively. The figures in parentheses are the percentage of the sown area affected by drought or flood. Droughts and floods account for 60.6 per cent and 23.2 per cent, respectively, of the total area affected by disasters. The area affected by drought makes up more than half of the area affected by disasters. It identifies the predominance of droughts over other disasters, including floods (Figures 7.1 and 7.2). Figure 7.1 shows the annual average crop yield. For the entire country, it increased from 2.6 t/ha in 1978 to 3.6 t/ha in 1989. Technological progress and improvement of societal conditions are respon-

Table 7.1 Sown area and area affected by disasters (in million hectares)

Year	1 Area sown	2 Area affected by disaster (col. 2/col. 1) %	3 Area affected by droughts (col. 3/col. 2) %	4 Area affected by floods (col. 4/col. 2) %
1978	150.10	50.79 (33.8)	40.17 (79.1)	2.85 (5.6)
1979	148.48	39.37 (26.5)	24.65 (62.6)	6.67 (17.2)
1980	146.38	44.53 (30.4)	26.11 (58.6)	9.15 (20.5)
1981	145.16	39.79 (27.4)	25.69 (64.6)	8.62 (21.7)
1982	144.75	33.13 (22.9)	20.70 (62.5)	8.36 (25.2)
1983	143.99	34.71 (24.1)	16.09 (46.4)	12.16 (35.0)
1984	144.22	31.89 (22.1)	15.82 (49.6)	10.63 (33.3)
1985	143.63	44.37 (30.9)	22.99 (51.8)	14.20 (32.0)
1986	144.20	47.14 (32.7)	31.04 (65.8)	9.16 (19.4)
1987	144.96	42.09 (29.0)	24.92 (59.2)	8.69 (20.6)
1988	144.87	50.87 (35.1)	32.90 (64.7)	11.95 (23.5)
1989	146.55	46.99 (32.1)	29.36 (62.5)	11.33 (24.1)
Mean	145.61	42.14 (28.9)	25.87 (60.6)	9.49 (23.2)

Source: Department of Statistics of China (1991). A Statistical Survey of China, Chinese Statistics Press, Peking, p. 56 (in Chinese)

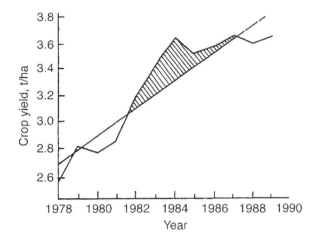

Figure 7.1 Crop yield in China, 1978–89 (in t/ha), from Wang *et al.* 1991

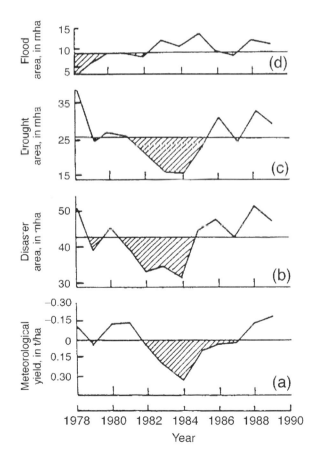

Figure 7.2 Meteorological yields (a), area affected by disasters (b), area affected by droughts (c), and area affected by floods (d), 1978–89, from Wang *et al.* 1991

sible for the generally increasing trend of the crop yield. Therefore, the linear trend was removed from the original series, although it is impossible to determine if the trend is linear. Then the residual of the series is examined as the meteorological yield, which is postulated to depend mainly on the meteorological conditions. The area with positive anomaly in Figure 7.1 is shaded. In Figure 7.2, meteorological yield (a) is compared with the total area affected by disasters (b) and the area affected by drought (c) or flood (d), where the scale of the ordinate of meteorological yield is reversed downward to meet the negative correlation of it with the area affected by disasters. Close agreement of meteorological yield with the drought area is obvious. The correlation coefficient between them reaches −0.77, although we must note that the series is very short. The aforementioned data provide good evidence of the predominant role of droughts in controlling the crop yield in China.

Li *et al.* (1996) have studied droughts during the growing season in China. The calendar months of the growing season and a definition of drought are given in Tables 7.2 and Table 7.3.

The total number of droughts, including serious and severe droughts from 1951 to 1991, is shown in Figure 7.3. The greatest number of droughts (areas where more than fifty droughts occurred) was observed in the Huabei region (north China), including Beijing, Hebei, and Shanxi provinces, and parts of Henan and Shandong provinces. Drought occurs more than once a year in this area. Another maximum was observed in extreme southeast China. This chapter will concentrate on studies of summer drought in north China.

Table 7.2 Growing season in various regions

Region	Months
Northeast	April–September
Huang, Huai, and Hai Rivers	March–October
Changjiang River	March–November
South and southwest	entire year

Source: Li *et al.* 1996

Table 7.3 Definition of drought with anomaly of rainfall in percentage according to rainfall anomaly (%)

Spell	Drought	Serious drought	Severe drought
One month	−80%		
Two months	−51% ~ −80%	−80%	
Three months	−26% ~ −50%	−51% ~ −80%	−80%
Four months	−1% ~ −25%	−26% ~ −50%	< −50%
Five months		−1% ~ −25%	< −25%
Six months or more			−1% ~ −25%

Source: Li *et al.* 1996

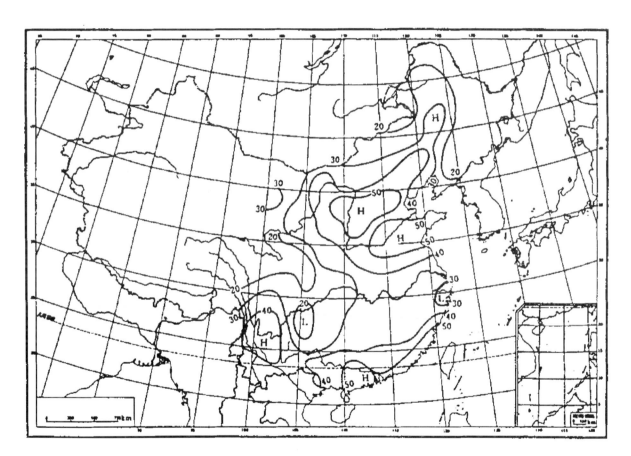

Figure 7.3 Frequency of total drought occurrences, 1951–91, from Li *et al.* 1996

PREDICTABILITY OF SUMMER DROUGHTS IN NORTH CHINA

Summer rainfall of north China

Observational data was analysed to study the atmospheric circulation mechanism responsible for the summer rainfall anomaly. The 5 key stations selected to form a series representative of summer rainfall in north China were Beijing, Shijiazhuang, Taiyuan, Jinan, and Zhengzhou. Figure 7.4 shows the correlation coefficients between the mean summer rainfall series averaged for the 5 key stations and 160 stations over the mainland area of China. The shaded area represents a correlation coefficient of 0.3 or more; the correlation coefficient in the central part of the shaded area reaches 0.5 or more. Key stations are denoted by small squares in Figure 7.4. Other stations used in the present study are shown with dots. The mean rainfall series of north China is generally representative of a great deal of northern

China. The shaded area is more or less in accordance with the area of the greatest frequency of drought (Figure 7.3). Therefore, this mean summer rainfall series is representative for north China.

Atmospheric circulation mechanism responsible for summer rainfall

The atmospheric circulation mechanism related to the summer rainfall anomaly of north China was examined by studying the correlation coefficients between 500 hPa level heights and the mean rainfall series of north China. Figure 7.5 indicates that two positive correlation centres occur on the east coast of the Asian continent and in the eastern Tibet Plateau. Correlation coefficients between mean summer rainfall of north China and 500 hPa level heights at 30° N, 120° E and 30° N, 90° E reach 0.43 and 0.40, respectively. It infers that summer rainfall will be greater when the subtropical high in the western Pacific and the high over the Tibet Plateau are stronger than the

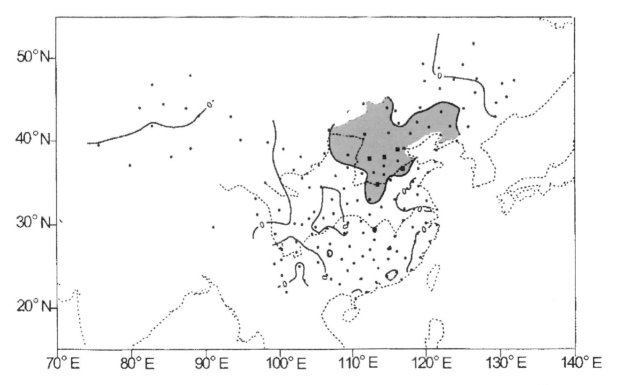

Figure 7.4 Correlation coefficients between summer rainfall in north China and the mainland area of China; area with 0.3 or more correlation is shaded

normal. Negative correlation was found south of Lake Baikal. This indicates the important role of cold air currents in forming summer rainfall in north China. The factors controlling summer rainfall in north China can be divided into two groups: the first relates to the subtropical high in the western Pacific, the second is associated with cold air currents in the middle latitudes of East Asia. To quantify the relationship between the atmospheric circulation and rainfall in north China, correlation coefficients were calculated by using circulation indices popularly accepted in Chinese meteorology (Wang and Zhao 1987). Correlation coefficients are given in Table 7.4.

Table 7.4 shows that summer rainfall in north China is greater when the subtropical high moves to the north and west more than normal. Also, summer rainfall increases when the trough over Lake Baikal is deep and the high over the Tibet Plateau is strong.

Stepwise regression equation analysis was carried out to isolate the independent circulation indices responsible for variations of summer rainfall in China. Results are shown in Table 7.5.

Table 7.5 indicates that the westward extension of the subtropical high in the western Pacific predominated over the others; this explains about one-third of the variance of summer rainfall in north China. The subtropical high provides warm and moist air to the area under examination. At the same time, the trough over Lake Baikal supplies cold air through the cold front. The convergence of warm and cold currents generates large-scale precipitation and stimulates the development of middle-scale and mesoscale disturbance, resulting in heavy rainfall in north China. X7 and X2 infer that favourable conditions for summer rainfall also exist when the meridional circulation is strong but the subtropical high is not too strong. Altogether, about half of the total variance of summer rainfall can be interpreted. It suggests that the seasonal predictability of summer rainfall using a general circulation model (GCM) depends both on the skill of prediction of monthly or seasonal mean of 500 hPa level heights and the skill of prediction of rainfall anomaly from predicted 500 hPa level heights.

Table 7.4 Correlation coefficients between atmospheric circulation indices and summer rainfall

No.	Index	Correlation coefficient
X1	Area of subtropical high	0.01
X2	Intensity of subtropical high	−0.04
X3	Latitude of subtropical high	0.27
X4	North border of subtropical high	0.27
X5	West border of subtropical high	−0.44
X6	Zonal index of westerlies in East Asia	−0.21
X7	Meridional index of westerlies in eastern Asia	0.15
X8	Trough over the Bay of Bengal	0.16
X9	High over the Tibet plateau	0.29
X10	Trough over Lake Baikal	−0.30

Notes:
X1 Numbers of grid points with 588 dm or more of 500hPa heights from 180° to the west
X2 Weighting sum of grid points, 588 = 1, 589 = 2, and so on
X3 Latitude of ridge of subtropical high between 110° E and 150° E
X4 Average latitude of 588 dm contour line between 110° E and 150° E
X5 West border of 588 dm contour line in longitudes
X6 Difference of 500 hPa heights between 40° N and 60° N in 90° E–150° E
X7 Difference of 500 hPa heights between 90° E and 150° E in 40° N–60° N
X8 Average 500 hPa heights over the Bay of Bengal
X9 Average 500 hPa heights over the eastern Tibet Plateau
X10 Average 500 hPa heights south of Lake Baikal

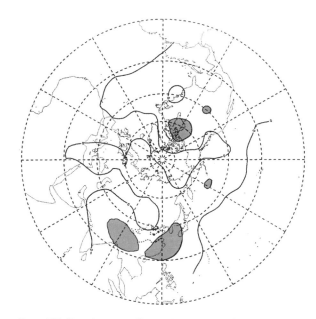

Figure 7.5 Correlation coefficients between rainfall in north China and mean 500 hPa heights in summer

Seasonal forecasting of summer rainfall of north China

Routine long-range forecasting of summer rainfall in China is done mainly based on statistical models, although recently more GCMs are being used. For example, nine GCMs, including both atmospheric GCMs and ocean–atmosphere coupled GCMs, were integrated to predict the rainfall anomaly of summer 1997. However, the skill of GCM prediction is still unknown, so the results of the GCMs were only used as a reference to the forecasting. Seasonal forecasting

of summer rainfall in China is mainly based on inter-seasonal correlation between summer rainfall and predictors, usually 500 hPa heights or SST in winter. This kind of correlation has been called rhythm in China. For example, Table 7.2 indicates that 500 hPa heights over the Tibet Plateau positively correlate to summer rainfall in north China. Zhao (1996) found significant interdecadal variability of the Tibet Plateau. The 500 hPa level height averaged for the Plateau area was greater in each year for 1958–67, but lower than the normal in seventeen years during the next twenty years, 1968–87. In seven of the first ten years, the predominant summer rain belt occurred in north China, but in fourteen of the next twenty years, the rain belt was found in southern China, the Huai River, or the Changjiang River valley. This means that 500 hPa height over the Plateau positively correlates to summer rainfall in north China. The positive correlation centre over the Plateau in Figure 7.5 and the correlation of summer rainfall in north China with circulation index X_9 in Table 7.4 proves again the reality of this relationship. However, the aforementioned relationship only refers to the summertime.

Wang (1984) has indicated that strong rhythm was found over the Plateau. A 500 hPa height rhythm is demonstrated in Figure 7.6, where the lag correlation coefficients between the heights of January (H_1) and other months (March to December, H_3 to H_{12}) over the Plateau (30°–40° N, 70°–100° E) are shown. Maxima of correlation are found in June to August; these are significant at the 95 per cent confidence level. It means that 500 hPa height anomaly in summer closely correlates to that in winter. Correlation

Table 7.5 Circulation mechanism responsible for the summer rainfall anomaly in north China

No.	Circulation mechanism	Correlation coefficient with summer rainfall	Percentage of the variance explained
X2	Intensity of subtropical high	−0.04	1.7
X5	West border of subtropical high	−0.44	33.0
X7	Meridional circulation index	0.15	3.0
X10	Trough over Lake Baikal complex	−0.3	9.3
	Total	0.68	47.0

coefficients between H_1 and $H_3 \sim H_5$ are negative or insignificant. The differences of correlation $(r_2 - r_1 \sim)$ were calculated (Figure 7.7), where r_1-correlation coefficient is between H_1 and $H_3 \sim H_5$ and r_2-correlation coefficient is between $H\sim$ and $H6 \sim Ha$. In Figure 7.7, a contour line of 2,000 m was drawn and areas with elevations of 2,000 m or more were shaded. Configuration of the 0.2 line of $r_2 - r_1$ is in good agreement with the shaded area, the Tibet Plateau. It suggests that this kind of rhythm may associate with the surface characteristics of the Plateau.

It has long been proposed that snow cover over the Plateau plays an important role in the formation of the rhythm (Wang 1984). The physical process responsible for the 500 hPa height rhythm includes

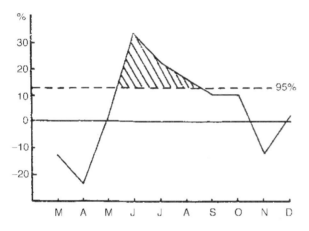

Figure 7.6 Lag correlation between January 500 hPa heights over Tibet Plateau (30–40° N, 70–100° E) and March–December, from Wang 1984

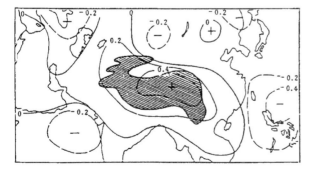

Figure 7.7 Differences of r_2 and r_1, r_1–correlation between H_1 and H_{3-5}, r_2–correlation between H_1 and H_{6-8}, from Wang 1984

deeper and more frequent than normal occurrences of troughs at the 500 hPa level over the Plateau. These produce heavy snow, which usually remains until early summer. The greater than normal snow cover reduces the heat source for greater albedo and melting, resulting in a negative anomaly of 500 hPa height in early summer over the Plateau. Synoptic study suggests that eastward migration of the high centre over the Plateau is one of the favourable factors for the seasonal jump of the subtropical high to the north. A negative anomaly of 500 hPa height weakens the high centre over the Plateau in early summer, then delays the seasonal development of the subtropical high and the northward jump of the rain belt to north China. In contrast, a positive anomaly of 500 hPa level height corresponds to light snow in winter, faster than normal warming in spring and early summer, and, finally, a positive anomaly of 500 hPa level height in early summer over the Plateau, which is favourable to the seasonal development of a subtropical high and increasing summer rainfall in north China.

Much of the rhythm phenomena has been found in China for the last forty years or so, and it is accepted generally as a basic guide in long-range or climatic forecasting. Unfortunately, the physical processes and mechanisms responsible for the formation of most of the rhythm phenomena are yet to be understood. It is believed that improving numerical simulation through coupled GCMs and skill core of climatic prediction by AGCM will increase understanding of the mechanism and raise the skill of seasonal prediction of summer rainfall.

HISTORICAL DOCUMENTATION OF DROUGHT FOR THE LAST MILLENNIUM

Observational data of summer rainfall in China is usually limited to the twentieth century or the period since 1950, except in Beijing and a few stations in the coastal region. The series of summer rainfall is not long enough for studying climatic change or interdecadal variability. However, experience in long-range forecasting suggests that seasonal forecasting can hardly be successful without consideration of decadal variability. Therefore, great efforts have been made in China to lengthen the series of summer rainfall (Wang and Zhao 1981). Fortunately, historical docu-

Table 7.6 Classification of summer rainfall grades of north China, 1951–96

Grade	Climate characteristics	Number of years	Frequency %	Average anomaly %
1	Severe flood	4	8.7	67.3
2	Flood	13	28.3	25.6
3	Normal	16	32.6	0.3
4	Drought	10	23.9	–2.8
5	Severe drought	3	6.5	–47.0

mentation of droughts and floods is plentiful. There-fore, a series of studies have been carried out to quantify and digitise documentary data and assimilate it with instrumentally observational data of summer rainfall. Finally, a series of drought/flood grades for the last millennium was reconstructed. That recon-struction is briefly described below.

Identification of drought/flood grades according to observational data of summer rainfall is a very important step in correlating historical documentary data with modern observations, because most of the documentation came from archives of county gazetteers or memorials to the throne. These consisted of a lot of qualitative description, such as flood, severe drought, and bad yield or harvest. It is impossible to estimate monthly or seasonal rainfall anomaly directly from historical documents. Therefore, the reconstructed series should consist of grades rather than anomaly values in mm. To get a proper basis for the grades, rainfall anomalies for the last forty-six years (1951–96) were examined and classified into five grades according to the anomaly value. Rainfall anomaly percentages for 1951–96 are shown in Figure 7.8. Four maxima are classified in the first grade. These are greater than 50 per cent and are separated clearly from other positive anomalies. Three minima around –50 per cent are grouped into the fifth grade. Thirteen years with anomalies of 12–37 per cent, and eleven years with anomalies of 12–29 per cent, are classified into the second and fourth grades, respec-tively. The others are classified into the third grade, or the normal grade. Average anomalies for each of the grades are given in Table 7.6. It agrees in general with the definition shown in Table 7.3 and with the widely accepted concept that +25 per cent (–25 per cent) and +50 per cent (–50 per cent) can be used as

the threshold of flood (drought) and severe flood (severe drought) (Feng et al. 1985).

The next step in reconstructing the drought/flood series is the identification of the grades in years when observational data were not available (Wang and Zhao 1979 and 1981). An example from Baoding, near the centre of north China, is shown in Table 7.7, and its series is characteristic of north China (Wang and Zhao 1987). From Table 7.7, one can get a gen-eral idea of the identification of drought/flood grades according to documentary data. Following a similar procedure, grades of 124 stations for 1470 to 1979 were identified, and a series of drought/flood maps for the last 500 years was published (CNMA 1981).

The final step in the reconstruction of a drought/flood series of north China was to combine the grades of the five stations in north China into one grade. This procedure is outlined in Table 7.8. Conse-quently, a drought/flood series of north China was reconstructed for the years 1000–1996.

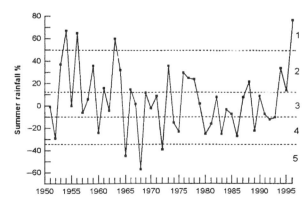

Figure 7.8 Summer rainfall anomalies of north China, 1951–96 (in percentage)

Table 7.7 Classification of drought/flood grades for Baoding near the centre of north China

Documentary record	Grade	Frequency
Sail a boat over the land	1	12
Prolonged rain in summer and autumn	1	17
Rainfall persisted for a month	1	16
Flood with water 1 m deep over the land	1	8
Flood in summer	2	18
Local heavy rainfall	2	11
Drought in summer, flood in autumn	2	38
Drought in spring, flood in summer	2	3
Local flood	2	14
Local harvest with flood	3	7
Harvest	3	29
No record	3	140
Local harvest with locusts	3	7
Hail	4	24
Locusts	4	28
Local drought in summer	4	10
Local drought	4	17
Drought	4	20
Severe drought	5	6
Heat, drought	5	7
Severe drought, no rain	5	11

Table 7.8 Definition of average drought/flood grade of north China

Average grade	Grades of five stations
1	1 and 2 predominate; no 4 or 5
2	2 predominates; no 4 or 5, or only one 4
3	3 predominates; no 1, 2 or 4, 5, or with both 2 and 4 or 1 and 5
4	4 predominates; no 1 or 2, or with only one 2
5	5 and 4 predominate; no 1 or 2

DROUGHTS IN NORTH CHINA DURING THE PERIOD 1000–1996

Frequencies of the five grades for each century are given in Table 7.9. Figure 7.9 shows the series with an eleven-year weighting mean. The ordinate indicates the grade, so the upper portion of the figure indicates drought and severe drought (grades 4 and 5, respectively). The frequency of grades 4 and 5 in each century is shown in Figure 7.10 in columns and shaded columns. The maximum frequency of drought and severe drought occurs in the twelfth, thirteenth,

fifteenth, and twentieth centuries. (Data for the twentieth century is of course incomplete, consisting of only 97 years rather than 100 years as in other centuries.) Relatively wet periods with fewer droughts and severe droughts occurred in the fourteenth and nineteenth centuries.

This is clearly manifested in the wavelet transformation shown in Figure 7.11, where the high frequency variability was cut down to emphasise the large time scale of climatic change. The shaded area in Figure 7.11 shows a negative anomaly of grade,

Table 7.9 Frequency of grades

Year	1	2	3	4	5
1000–99	10	28	27	25	10
1100–99	11	22	29	28	10
1200–99	10	24	30	24	12
1300–99	12	32	27	21	8
1400–99	10	25	27	25	13
1500–99	9	29	27	21	14
1600–99	13	16	36	20	15
1700–99	10	30	28	24	8
1800–99	14	28	28	18	12
1900–96	7	23	32	26	9
Total	106	257	291	232	111

meaning that the drought/flood grade here is lower than the normal, and it corresponds to a wetter climate. In contrast, the blank area represents dry periods. Alternation between wet and dry periods indicates the predominance of interdecadal variability of drought/flood. The power spectrum of the drought/flood grades is shown in Figure 7.12. The peaks significant at the 95 per cent confidence level are labelled with the length of the period. It indicates that 10.2a, 33.3a (interdecadal variability), 2.4a, and 2.0a (QBO) cycles are significant. However, interdecadal variability among cycles provides more important information that is critical for climatic forecasting of drought. Table 7.10 shows the drought/flood grade for 1800–1996, in which the dry period is outlined. It indicates that the last dry period started in 1965 and ended in 1986. This prolonged dry period is clearly demonstrated in Figure 7.8. It is impossible to study variations of the dry period with limited observational data. However, Table 7.10 documents the alternation of dry and wet periods. Six dry periods occurred in the last two centuries, approximately in agreement with the 33a cycle on the power spectrum diagram.

Table 7.10 Drought/flood grade for 1800–1996

Year	0	1	2	3	4	5	6	7	8	9
1800	3	1	4	4	4	5	3	3	2	2
1810	3	5	6	5	4	2	1	5	2	1
1820	2	2	1	1	2	5	4	4	2	3
1830	3	3	5	3	3	4	4	4	3	3
1840	1	2	3	2	2	3	3	5	2	2
1850	3	1	2	1	2	2	4	5	4	5
1860	3	4	3	2	3	4	3	4	2	3
1870	4	1	1	2	3	4	5	5	4	2
1880	3	3	3	1	3	2	2	2	3	2
1890	1	3	2	1	1	2	2	3	2	4
1900	5	2	5	3	3	3	3	4	4	3
1910	2	1	2	3	2	3	4	1	3	3
1920	5	4	2	2	2	3	4	4	4	4
1930	4	4	2	3	4	5	5	2	3	3
1940	2	5	4	4	3	4	3	4	4	1
1950	3	3	4	2	1	3	1	3	3	2
1960	4	2	3	1	2	5	2	3	5	2
1970	3	3	5	2	4	4	2	2	2	3
1980	4	4	3	4	3	3	4	3	2	4
1990	3	3	4	3	2	2	1			

Table 7.11 Dry periods in north China, 1800–1996

Years	1	2	3	4	5	Total
1802–14	0	2	3	4	4	13
1825–37	0	1	5	5	2	13
1856–78	2	3	6	8	4	23
1899–09	0	1	5	3	2	11
1926–48	0	3	5	12	3	23
1965–86	0	6	7	6	3	22

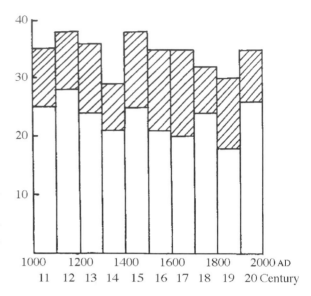

The frequency of the five grades for each of the dry periods is given in Table 7.11. Droughts and severe droughts in the dry period account for 40–65 per cent of the total, but the sum of the normal frequency of grade 4 and grade 5 is only about 34 per cent. This suggests that interdecadal variability should be considered in making long-range forecasts of droughts. Unfortunately, understanding of the physical causes and mechanisms responsible for the interdecadal variability of droughts is still limited, and more study should be devoted to these areas.

Figure 7.10 Frequency of drought (blank area) and severe drought (hatched area) in the eleventh to twentieth centuries

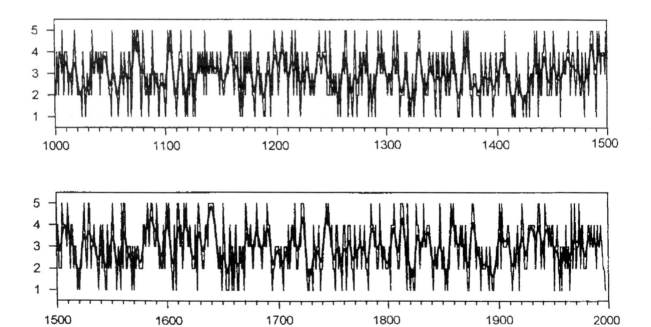

Figure 7.9 Drought/flood grade series, 1000–1996. Smooth curve shows eleven-year weighting mean

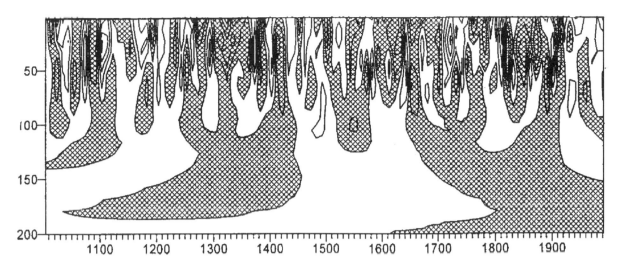

Figure 7.11 Wavelet transformation of drought/flood grade series in north China, 1000–1996

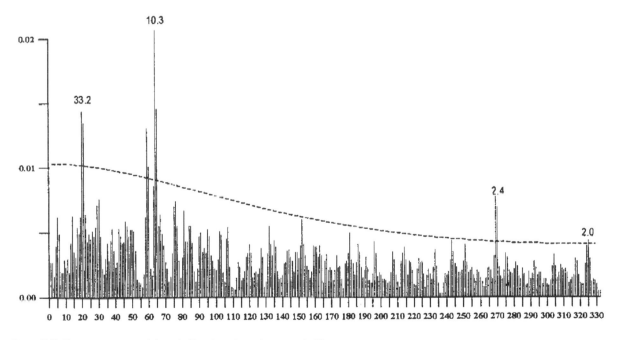

Figure 7.12 Power spectrum of drought/flood grade series in north China

SUMMARY

1 Drought damage to crop yields was greater than damage caused by other natural disasters. Droughts account for an average of 60.6 per cent of the total area affected by disasters.

2 The greatest frequency of droughts during the growing season is found in north China.

3 The subtropical high and meridional circulation in the middle latitudes over East Asia are responsible for the occurrence of summer rainfall in north China.

4 Seasonal forecasting of summer rainfall anomaly in China is based on interseasonal correlation between winter and summer.

5 The mechanism responsible for the interseasonal correlation may be linked to feedback between snow cover over the Tibet Plateau or SST over the western and equatorial eastern Pacific and the atmosphere.

6 Historical documents were used to extend the observational rainfall series back to 1000.

7 Analysis of a 997-year series revealed long-term climatic change and periodicity, especially a 33a cycle.

8 Alternation of dry and wet periods indicates that north China is in a relatively wet period. The last dry period ended in 1986. The dried-up Lake Baiyangdian has stored water again in 1988.

REFERENCES

CNMA (Chinese National Meteorological Administration), Peking University (1981) *Atlas of Droughts and Floods in China during the Last 500 Year Period*, Peking: China Atlas Press.

Feng Peizhi, Li Cuijin, and Li Xiaoquan (1985) *Analysis of Staple Meteorological Disasters in China, 1951–1980*, Peking: China Meteorological Press.

Li Kerang, Yin Siming, and Sha Wanying (1996) 'Characters of time-space of recent drought in China', *Geographical Research* 15, 3: 6–15.

Wang Shaowu (1984) 'The rhythm in the atmosphere and oceans in application to long-range weather forecasting', *Advances in Atmospheric Sciences* 1, 1: 7–18.

Wang Shaowu, Wang Guoxue, and Zhang Zuomei (1991) 'Droughts and floods in North and East China, AD 1880–1989', in *Proceedings of the United States–People's Republic of China Bilateral Symposium on Droughts and Arid-Region Hydrology*, 16–20 September 1991, Tucson, AZ, pp. 255–60.

Wang Shaowu and Zhao Zongci (1979) 'An analysis of historical data of droughts and floods in last 500 years in China', *Acta Geographica Sinica* 34, 4: 329–41.

Wang Shaowu and Zhao Zongci (1981) 'Droughts and floods in China, 1470–1979', in T.N.L. Wigley, M.J. Ingram, and G. Farmer (eds), *Climate and History*, Cambridge: Cambridge University Press, pp. 271–88.

Wang Shaowu and Zhao Zongci (1987) *Foundation of Long-Range Weather Forecasting*, Shanghai: Shanghai Science and Technology Press.

Zhao Zhenguo (1996) 'Progress of seasonal forecasting on summer drought and flood in China', in Wang Shaowu (ed.), *Studies on Climatic Prediction*, Peking: China Meteorological Press, pp. 84–93.

8

THE OCCURRENCE AND PREDICTABILITY OF DROUGHTS OVER SOUTHERN AFRICA

S.J. Mason and P.D. Tyson

INTRODUCTION

Southern Africa lies within the subtropical high pressure belt of the Southern Hemisphere between about 15° and 35° S (Figure 8.1). Subsidence of air in large anticyclones predominates for most of the year, resulting in arid or semiarid conditions throughout much of the subcontinent. During the first half of summer (October–December), the southward migration of the locus of tropical convection provides early-season rainfall to the northern parts of the subcontinent, while the development of a subtropical trough within the quasi-permanent high pressure belt facilitates the occurrence of rainfall farther south from midlatitude systems. By January, the tropical atmosphere is usually dominant over most of the sub-

continent, often bringing good rains, especially when links with westerly troughs form.

The interannual rainfall variability of the region is high, with the coefficient of variation exceeding 40 per cent in the drier western areas (Onesta and Verhoef 1976, Tyson 1986). Droughts are an inherent feature of the climate, and water resources are under growing pressure from population and industrial expansion, being particularly strained during drought years when demand for water increases (Mason and Joubert 1995). Given the high degree of interannual rainfall variability in the southern African region, skilful seasonal forecasts could greatly assist in water resource planning and the amelioration of drought and flood impacts (Vogel 1994). Since the 1991–2 drought, long-range seasonal forecasts for southern Africa using statistical methods have been produced by universities, the national meteorological services, and drought monitoring centres in South Africa and neighbouring countries (Mason *et al.* 1996). More recently, statistical forecasts have been supplemented by real-time general circulation model ensemble seasonal forecasts. In this chapter, progress in the understanding of droughts and predictability over southern Africa is reviewed.

DROUGHT OCCURRENCE AND FREQUENCY

Droughts are as old as Africa (Tyson 1986) and are a prominent feature of the meteorological record for southern Africa (Figure 8.2). In the twentieth century, they have occurred over South Africa and parts of neighbouring countries with great regularity in an

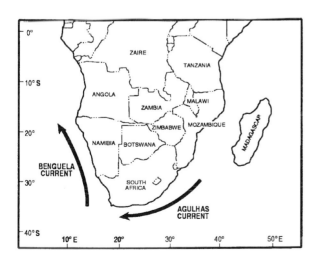

Figure 8.1 Location map of southern Africa showing the political boundaries, islands, and major ocean currents

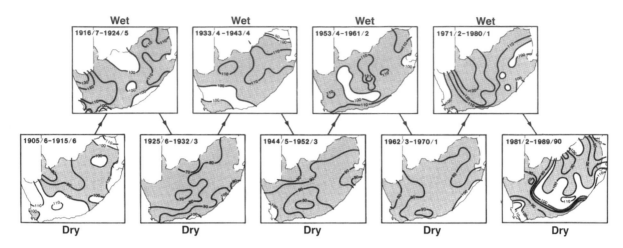

Figure 8.2 Percentage of mean annual rainfall for designated wet and dry spells based on an analysis of October–September rainfall data for the period 1905–90 (modified after Tyson 1986). Shaded areas indicate above-normal rainfall in wet spells and below-normal rainfall in dry spells

oscillation with a period of eighteen to twenty years. In South Africa, five major drought periods, in which the major part of the country has experienced below-normal rainfall, have been observed since 1905. The most severe drought year during the dry spell of 1925–33 occurred in 1932–3. The year 1944–5 was the driest during the spell between 1944 and 1953, 1965–6 the driest between 1963 and 1972, and 1982–3 the driest in the dry spell that began in 1982. During the early nineties, a reversion to normal or wetter conditions might have been expected, but 1991–2 was a particularly bad year and was followed by three further years of less than average rains.

Quasi-periodic variability in drought occurrence

That the interannual rainfall variability over southern Africa exhibits statistically significant quasi-periodic variability was first identified more than 100 years ago (Tripp 1888) and initiated active research over the next few decades (Nevill 1908, Cox 1925, van Reenen 1925, Peres 1930, de Loor 1948). Renewed interest in the oscillatory nature of South African rainfall developed in the early seventies (Tyson 1971 and 1986, Tyson *et al.* 1975). Over South Africa, distinctive oscillations have been verified and from the mid-1970s have been used in long-range seasonal forecasting models (Dyer and Tyson 1977, Tyson and

Dyer 1978 and 1980, Louw 1982, Currie 1993). Of greatest significance is an eighteen- to twenty-year oscillation in the northeast part of the country, shown in Figure 8.3 (Tyson 1971, 1978, 1980, and 1986; Dyer 1975, 1980a, and 1981a; Tyson *et al.* 1975; van Rooy 1980; Vines 1980; Kelbe *et al.* 1983; Lindesay 1984; Currie 1991 and 1993; Jury and Levey 1993a and 1993b). It extends into Zimbabwe (Ngara *et al.* 1983, Makarau and Jury 1997) and Botswana (Jury *et al.* 1992) and possibly into southern Zambia. The eighteen- to twenty-year oscillation is likewise apparent in streamflow records (Abbott and Dyer 1976, Partridge 1985, Alexander 1995), the temperature record, and tree-ring data (Tyson 1986). In the early nineties, the oscillation faltered owing to the occurrence of consecutive/persistent El Niños (Mason 1997a). It may have resumed from the beginning of the 1995 summer rainfall season.

The oscillation in rainfall has been attributed to the eighteen-year cycle in the luni-solar tide (Currie 1991 and 1993); sunspot variability (Alexander 1995); and similar oscillations in sea-surface temperatures in the South Atlantic (Mason 1990, Shinoda and Kawamura 1996), the central Indian (Cadet and Diehl 1984, Jury *et al.* 1996), and eastern equatorial Pacific oceans (Hurrell and van Loon 1994, Mason and Jury 1997, Tyson *et al.* 1998). The Pacific sea-surface temperature oscillation is out of phase with

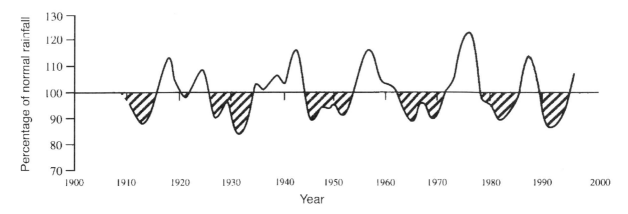

Figure 8.3 An area-averaged time series of rainfall for the summer rainfall region of South Africa, smoothed by a five-term binomial filter (modified after Tyson 1986)

the rainfall, implying that above-average temperatures in the eastern Pacific Ocean are associated with below-average rainfall over southern Africa (Figure 8.4). Although such a phase relationship is consistent with El Niño–southern African rainfall associations, the eighteen- to twenty-year oscillation in sea-surface

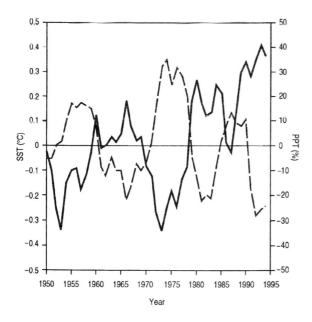

Figure 8.4 Seven-year running mean sea-surface temperature anomalies (SST) averaged over the eastern equatorial Pacific Ocean (180°–90° W, 10° S–5° N) (solid line) and percentage rainfall (PPT) over South Africa (dashed line) (after Mason and Jury 1997)

temperatures is only weakly reflected in the Southern Oscillation Index. That is not to say that the sea temperature oscillation does not have a significant impact: given the weak orographic forcing of the standing waves compared to the Northern Hemisphere (Pittock 1973 and 1980), such interdecadal variability can have an important influence on the waves in middle and high latitudes of the Southern Hemisphere (Hurrell and van Loon 1994).

It has been suggested that the oscillation in the eastern Pacific sea-surface temperatures affects southern Africa via the temperate atmosphere involving variability in wave 3 of the Southern Hemisphere atmospheric circulation (Tyson *et al.* 1998). The sensitivity of the midlatitude atmosphere to tropical heat anomalies is greatest during January (Albrecht *et al.* 1986, Meehl and Albrecht 1988), when rainfall over most of southern Africa is at its peak. More specifically, a warming of sea-surface temperatures in the eastern Pacific is thought to result in a weakening of the semiannual oscillation in the midlatitudes (van Loon and Rogers 1984). The implications for southern Africa are significant because the total annual rainfall of the region is strongly influenced by the amplitude of the semiannual cycle, rainfall being higher when the amplitude is greater (Theron and Harrison 1991). The sea temperature variability in the eastern Pacific Ocean could therefore have a maximum impact on rainfall in the region, which lends credence to the proposed teleconnection, despite the fact that the observed interdecadal changes in wave 3 are greatest during the austral winter (van Loon *et al.* 1993). Further research is required to resolve these uncertainties in the mechanisms of teleconnections in interdecadal variability in the Southern Hemisphere.

A ten- to twelve-year oscillation accounts for more than 30 per cent of the interannual rainfall variance along the south coast of South Africa and has been linked to sea-surface temperatures to the south of the subcontinent (Mason 1990), solar variability (Vines 1980, Currie 1991 and 1993, Mason and Tyson 1992), and changes in the phase of standing wave 3 (Vines 1980, Tyson 1981 and 1986). There is coherence between the eleven-year rainfall oscillation over South Africa and similar oscillations in New Zealand and South America (Vines 1980 and 1982). In southeast Australia and New Zealand, the oscillation is related to variability in standing wave 3 as a result of its important influence on blocking in this sector (Trenberth 1975 and 1980a, Trenberth and Mo 1985). Although atmospheric blocking is generally weak and infrequent in the vicinity of southern Africa at intraseasonal time scales (Trenberth and Mo 1985, Kidson 1988), a regular variation, with a periodicity of about ten years, in the longitudinal position of the first ridge of wave 3 is evident and may be related to the oscillation in rainfall (Tyson 1981).

Higher frequency rainfall variability with periods of about 2.3 years is identifiable over South Africa, Zimbabwe, and Madagascar (Tyson 1971, Nicholson and Entekhabi 1986, Jury *et al.* 1992 and 1995, Jury and Levey 1993a and 1993b, Makarau and Jury 1997). Similar quasi-biennial oscillations in rainfall in the New Zealand sector are associated with variability in wave 3 (Trenberth 1975 and 1980b), but such an association is less well defined near southern Africa (Mason and Jury 1997). Instead, the stratospheric Quasi-Biennial Oscillation (QBO) of equatorial zonal winds is implicated (Mason and Tyson 1992, Mason and Lindesay 1993, Mason *et al.* 1994) through a hypothesised interaction with the Walker circulation over eastern southern Africa (Jury *et al.* 1994). During the easterly phase of the QBO, upper-tropospheric easterlies off the east coast of southern Africa are thought to strengthen (Figure 8.5), resulting in upper-level convergence and subsidence over the subcontinent (Jury 1992, Jury *et al.* 1994, Jury

and Pathack 1993 and 1997). However, upper-tropospheric near-equatorial easterly anomalies are not a consistently observed feature of dry conditions over the subcontinent (Tyson 1986, Lindesay 1988, Mason *et al.* 1994, Rocha and Simmonds 1997a and 1997b, Jury 1996a, Mason and Jury 1997), and the mechanisms of stratospheric-tropospheric interaction in the region have yet to be verified. Further work is required to investigate the possibility of an alternative influence of tropospheric QBOs (Trenberth 1979 and 1980b, Ropelewski *et al.* 1992).

As a reflection of the influence of El Niño–Southern Oscillation events on rainfall variability in the region, rainfall oscillations with periods of 3.5–7 years are evident throughout most of the subcontinent (Vines and Tomlinson 1985, Nicholson 1986, Nicholson and Entekhabi 1986 and 1987,

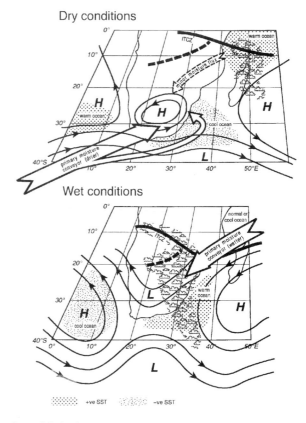

Figure 8.5 A schematic conceptual model to illustrate changing circulation controls, sea-surface temperatures, moisture transport conveyors, and loci of tropical convection in extended wet and dry spells over southern Africa

Tyson 1986, Lau and Sheu 1988, Jury *et al.* 1992 and 1995, Jury and Levey 1993a and 1993b, Makarau and Jury 1997). Oscillations with periods of 2.7 and 6 years over Namibia have not been explained (Dyer and Marker 1978).

Long-term trends in drought frequency and intensity

Whether southern Africa has been experiencing progressive desiccation has been debated for more than 100 years (Wilson 1865, Barber 1910, Schwarz 1919, Cox 1926, Thompson 1936, Vorster 1957, Brook and Mametse 1970), and opinion is still somewhat divided. No evidence of progressive desiccation has been reported for Zimbabwe (Marume 1992, Unganai 1992), Botswana (Nicholson 1989), and the summer rainfall region of South Africa (Dyer 1976b, Tyson *et al.* 1975, Tyson 1980, Mason 1996). Notwithstanding, averaging over a wider area of southern Africa as a whole reveals that the period since the late 1970s has been considerably drier than any earlier period over the last century (Nicholson 1993, Hulme *et al.* 1996). A decrease of approximately 10 per cent in mid-summer rainfall (December–February) has been observed between 1931–60 and 1961–90 over northern Botswana, Zimbabwe, and eastern South Africa (Hulme 1992 and 1996, Gondwe *et al.* 1997, Hulme *et al.* 1996, Mason 1996, Makarau and Jury 1997). This has been accompanied by a decrease in the effectiveness of rainfall for maize growing in southern Zambia (Kruss *et al.* 1992). The effects of abrupt warming in tropical sea-surface temperatures in the mid-1970s and an increase in the frequency of El Niño events (Trenberth 1990, Kerr 1992, van Loon *et al.* 1993, Graham 1994 and 1995, Allan *et al.* 1995, Wang 1995, Trenberth and Hoar 1996) have probably been significant in causing the altered conditions after the 1970s (Mason 1996 and 1997a).

An increase in the interannual variability of rainfall appears to have occurred over Zimbabwe (Unganai 1992), eastern South Africa (Mason 1996), and other parts of southern Africa (Hulme 1992). The implications are that droughts (and flood years) are becoming more frequent and severe. Such an occurrence is consistent with those expected for the region as a result of an enhanced greenhouse effect (Joubert *et al.* 1996).

ATMOSPHERIC CIRCULATION DURING DROUGHT YEARS

Distinctive changes in the large-scale atmospheric flow fields take place over southern Africa and adjacent oceans during periods of prolonged below-normal rainfall and during severe short-term droughts. The standing wave structure of the Southern Hemisphere circumpolar westerlies undergoes systematic change in the vicinity of Africa. The oceanic semipermanent subtropical high pressure cells weaken and are displaced equatorward, the intertropical convergence zone is similarly affected, moisture fluxes alter significantly, and moisture transport patterns change radically. The development of weather-producing quasi stationary easterly waves is curtailed over southern Africa and the locus of tropical convection moves eastward and often offshore. An attempt is made to capture these changes schematically in Figure 8.5 by comparing the conditions conducive for droughts with those responsible for extended wet spells. It is necessary to consider in more detail each of the component factors interacting to produce droughts.

The eastward shift in the locus of tropical convection during droughts (Harangozo and Harrison 1983, Harrison 1983a, Tyson 1986, Jury 1992 and 1996, Jury and Pathack 1991 and 1993, Jury *et al.* 1992 and 1994) is evident in patterns of outgoing long-wave radiation (Jury *et al.* 1992, 1993a, and 1995; Jury and Waliser 1990) and has been ascribed to a reversal in the Walker circulation over the east coast (Harrison 1983a, Lindesay 1986, Jury 1992, Jury *et al.* 1994, Shinoda and Kawamura 1996). Confluent upper winds associated with this reversal of the western Indian Ocean Walker cell contribute to the general weakening of tropical convection over the subcontinent in dry summers and to subsidence and positive pressure anomalies (Hofmeyr and Gouws 1964; Taljaard 1981 and 1989; Tyson 1981, 1984, and 1986; Matarira 1990; Matarira and Jury 1992; Shinoda and Kawamura 1996; Rocha and Simmonds 1997a). The structure of the Walker circulation over the east coast is complicated (Tyson 1986, Lindesay 1988, Mason *et al.* 1994, Janicot *et al.* 1996, Jury 1996, Rocha and Simmonds 1997a and 1997b), and further work is required to clarify more precisely the details and mechanisms of variability in the region.

With the suppression of convection over the sub-continent, Hadley cell mass overturning weakens, but becomes more vigorous to the east (Lindesay 1988, Lindesay and Jury 1991, Jury 1996). A weakening, and possibly a northward shift, of the tropical convergence zones occurs over the subcontinent (Torrance 1979, Lindesay and Jury 1991, van den Heever 1994, Shinoda and Kawamura 1996), but the significance of latitudinal displacements of convection is less clear than that of longitudinal displacements (Nicholson and Chervin 1983).

During wet spells (Figure 8.5), the interaction between quasi-stationary tropical easterly waves and transient temperate westerly waves produces tropical-temperate troughs that contribute significantly to the excess rainfall characteristic of wet spells (Harangozo and Harrison 1983; Harrison 1984a, 1984b, and 1984c; Smith 1985; Tyson 1986; Diab et al. 1991; Lyons 1991; van den Heever 1994; Jury 1997a). This is particularly so in eastern areas of the continent where the locus of convective activity is to be observed. By contrast, during droughts the preferred location of tropical-temperate troughs and their associated cloud bands shifts eastward over the western Indian Ocean. The systems are less frequent and more diffuse during dry conditions. The eastward shift in convection is manifest in part as an increase in the frequency of tropical disturbances in the southwest Indian Ocean to the east of Madagascar (Jury 1993). The subsidence in the easterly outflow from disturbances that occur in the Mozambique Channel to the west of the island causes dry conditions over southern Africa. In both cases, low-level westerlies or westerly anomalies to the west of the disturbances inhibit moisture convergence over the land from the Indian Ocean (Matarira 1990, Jury and Pathack 1991, Jury 1992 and 1993, Rocha and Simmonds 1997a and 1997b).

During wet conditions, moisture transport is almost exclusively in a slowly ascending conveyor from the northeast and the tropical Indian Ocean (D'Abreton and Lindesay 1993, D'Abreton and Tyson 1995 and 1996) (Figure 8.6). By contrast, in droughts, and even on no-rain days generally, moisture transport is primarily in a descending dry conveyor from the southwest and from the South Atlantic Ocean. Low-level westerly wind anomalies over the east coast of southern Africa are a consistent feature

of dry conditions over the subcontinent (Jury and Lutjeharms 1993, Rocha and Simmonds 1997a). Northeasterly transport is weakened not only when tropical cyclones form frequently over the western tropical Indian Ocean, but also when the south Indian Ocean anticyclone weakens (Matarira 1990, Jury and Pathack 1993, Jury et al. 1992 and 1995, Matarira and Jury 1992, Hastenrath et al. 1993, Jury 1996). Variability in the strength and position of the South Indian anticyclone is relatively high compared to the South Atlantic anticyclone (Vowinckel 1955, McGee and Hastenrath 1966, Dyer 1981b).

The southeast Atlantic Ocean becomes the dominant moisture source during dry years (Figure 8.6). Being colder and subsiding, the Atlantic moisture conveyor is considerably drier than its wet-spell Indian Ocean equivalent. It is also more stable (Miron and Lindesay 1983, Harrison 1988, Barclay et al. 1993). During drought years the dominance of westerly flow is indicative of the persistence of the temperate circulation throughout the summer season (Taljaard 1989). The westerlies prevail anomalously far north (Tyson 1986) and are an expression of a weakening in the semiannual oscillation (Harrison 1984b, Lindesay 1988, Theron and Harrison 1991).

In the equatorward-shifted westerlies during drought years, changes in amplitude and phase of standing westerly waves are of considerable importance (Hofmeyr and Gouws 1964). For good rains, a northwest- to southeast-aligned trough needs to be located over the western half of the subcontinent to facilitate advection of tropical moisture ahead of the trough (Harrison 1986, D'Abreton and Lindesay 1993, D'Abreton and Tyson 1995 and 1996, van den Heever 1994, Jury 1996). If the trough is displaced toward the east coast or has a low amplitude, or if the trailing ridge is weak, equatorward, or weakened, poleward transport occurs and rainfall occurs less easily (King and van Loon 1958, Longley 1976, Taljaard 1981, Tyson 1981, Miron and Tyson 1984, Lyons 1991, Taljaard and Steyn 1991). With a weakening in the amplitude of the westerly waves, the formation of cut-off lows (van Loon 1971, Dyer 1982, Taljaard 1985 and 1986) and ridging of anticyclones south of the subcontinent (Taljaard 1986, Tyson 1986, Triegaardt et al. 1988) is curtailed. The coupling of tropical and temperate disturbances (Tyson 1986, Barclay et al. 1993) is less frequent. With more zonal westerlies, blocking to

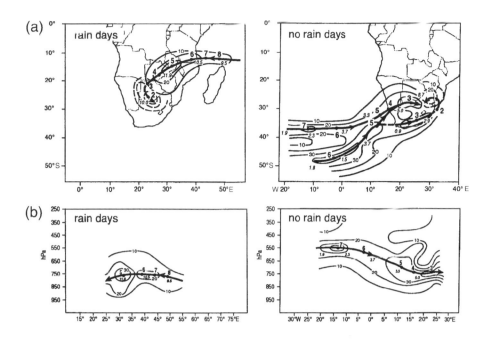

Figure 8.6 Mean moisture transport fields in the horizontal and vertical on rain and no-rain days in mid-summer (January) over southern Africa (after D'Abreton and Tyson 1996). Heavy lines denote maximum frequency transport pathways, along which mean times of transit (in days) from receptor points and specific humidities (g.kg^{-1}) are indicated; contours enclose percentage air transported

the southeast of the subcontinent weakens (Tyson 1984) and the persistence of westerly disturbances over the sub-continent diminishes (Tyson 1986).

Over the winter rainfall region in the extreme southwestern part of the subcontinent, rainfall is almost exclusively from midlatitude disturbances (Taljaard 1981, Muller and Tyson 1988). The atmospheric circulation controls of drought are different from those affecting the summer rainfall areas of the rest of the subcontinent. In fact, the relationship between droughts in the latter region and wet spells in the former is inverse (Lindesay 1984 and 1988, Muller and Tyson 1988). Atmospheric variability in the midlatitudes of the South Atlantic Ocean is weaker than over the Indian Ocean (Physick 1981), and so drought conditions over the winter rainfall region are generally not as severe as over the rest of the subcontinent. Drier conditions are usually experienced when temperate cyclones are anomalously far south and when wet conditions are prevailing elsewhere in the subcontinent (Taljaard 1989, Brundrit and Shannon 1989).

CAUSES OF DROUGHTS AND EXTENDED DRY PERIODS

Droughts over southern Africa are caused by decreases in the frequency, duration, and/or intensity of large-scale weather systems that are responsible for sig-nificant rainfall in the region (Harrison 1983b, Taljaard 1989, Mason and Jury 1997) rather than by a simple decrease in the number of rain days (Rubin 1956, Harrison 1983b) or in the length of the rainfall season (Nicholson and Chervin 1983, cf. Waylen and Henworth 1996). To some extent, the variability of the atmosphere over southern Africa may be attri-buted to internal variability of the circulation in the region, but boundary layer forcing both locally and from far afield has a significant effect.

El Niño–Southern Oscillation events

El Niño–Southern Oscillation (ENSO) warm events are frequently associated with drought over much of southern Africa (Stoeckenius 1981, Mo and White 1985, Nicholson and Entekabi 1986, Ropelewski and Halpert 1987 and 1989, Janowiak 1988, Halpert and Ropelewski 1992, Main and Hewitson 1995, Moron *et al.* 1995, Shinoda and Kawamura 1996, Mason and Jury 1997, Nicholson and Kim 1997, Rocha and Simmonds 1997a) and are partly responsible for continental and global-scale climate anomaly teleconnections (Nicholson 1981 and 1986, Nicholson and Chervin 1983, Harnack and Harnack 1985). The influence of ENSO warm events on rainfall is strongest in the southeastern part of the subcontinent (Ropelewski and Halpert 1987 and 1989, Matarira 1990, Rocha and Simmonds 1997a, Shinoda and Kawamura 1996, Nicholson and Kim 1997). Near the border between Zimbabwe and South Africa, correlations between the Southern Oscillation Index and rainfall are reduced (Harrison 1984d, Waylen and Henworth 1996), but the association strengthens again in a northwest to southeast band across South Africa (Dyer 1979, Lindesay *et al.* 1986, Lindesay 1988, van Heerden *et al.* 1988, Jury and Pathack 1993, Jury *et al.* 1994, Hastenrath *et al.* 1995, Jury 1996). The association with rainfall over South Africa has occurred for at least the last 200 years (Lindesay and Vogel 1990), although El Niño years are not always synchronous with dry conditions in the region (Mason and Mimmack 1992).

The influence of ENSO warm events on the atmosphere over southern Africa occurs mainly, though not exclusively, via the tropical atmosphere. The predominance of the tropical response in turn defines the spatial and seasonal variation of the rainfall associations in the region (Mason *et al.* 1996, Nicholson and Kim 1997). Over South Africa the influence is strongest during the peak summer rainfall months of December–March, when warm and cold events have typically reached maturity and when the tropical atmospheric circulation is usually dominant over most of the subcontinent (Lindesay 1988, Mason and Jury 1997). Over Zimbabwe, it is the early- and late-season rains that are more severely affected, suggesting an impact on the timing of the southward and northward migration of the tropical convergence zones (Waylen and Henworth 1996, Makarau and Jury 1997). Differences between the timing of the rainfall deficits associated with ENSO warm events between

South Africa and Zimbabwe suggest that different synoptic climatological responses are involved (Waylen and Henworth 1996) and would help to explain the weakening of the ENSO influence near the border of the two countries (Harrison 1984d). The tropical atmosphere in the southern African region during the austral summer responds to ENSO warm events in a manner largely consistent with the characteristics associated with dry conditions as discussed above and as summarised in Figure 8.5. An eastward shift in the preferred longitude of tropical convection occurs (Lindesay *et al.* 1986, Mason and Jury 1997). Similar eastward shifts in convection have been observed in the Australasian sector during Pacific warm events (Allan 1988 and 1991). Warming in the tropical western Indian Ocean during ENSO warm events appears to be largely responsible for the teleconnection between the Pacific signal and the tropical atmosphere over southern Africa (Goddard and Graham 1997, Nicholson 1997, Nicholson and Kim 1997, Rocha and Simmonds 1997b), and so details of the mechanisms involved are discussed in the section on sea-surface temperatures below.

It would be incorrect to state that the ENSO signal in the southern African region is detectable only in the tropical atmosphere. The Southern Hemisphere standing waves are known to respond to ENSO events (Pittock 1973; Trenberth 1975, 1979, and 1980a; Rogers and van Loon 1982; Karoly *et al.* 1996). In the southern African sector, a northward shift of the westerlies and a weakening of amplitude of the waves occur during warm events (Lindesay 1988) and are typical features of dry conditions over the subcontinent (Figure 8.5).

Sea-surface temperature anomalies

Higher-than-average sea-surface temperatures in the central and western tropical Indian Ocean are frequently responsible for dry conditions over southern Africa (Walker 1990; Jury 1992, 1995, and 1996; Walker and Shillington 1990; Jury and Pathack 1993 and 1997; Mason 1995; Makarau and Jury 1997; Rocha and Simmonds 1997a). Although occasional independent Indian Ocean warm events occur, typically they follow shortly after a peak in warm events in the Pacific Ocean (Cadet 1985, Suppiah 1988, Meehl

1993, Jury *et al.* 1994, Mason 1995, Nicholson 1997) The warming of the Indian Ocean is probably in response to associated changes in wind stress and the radiation budget (Cadet 1985, Hastenrath *et al.* 1993, Latif *et al.* 1994, Latif and Barnett 1995, Nagai *et al.* 1995, Nicholson 1997). This sympathetic response in the Indian Ocean may be essential in the transmission of the El Niño signal to southern Africa since it provides the mechanism for an eastward shift in the preferred longitude of tropical convection (Goddard and Graham 1997, Nicholson 1997, Nicholson and Kim 1997, Rocha and Simmonds 1997b). Increased sensible and latent heat fluxes over the warmer oceanic areas of the tropical Indian Ocean increase the atmospheric instability in the vicinity of the heat anomaly and weaken the pressure gradient onto the subcontinent. The influx of moisture over the land by the tropical easterlies therefore weakens and a strengthening of convection over the ocean occurs (Jury 1992, 1995, and 1996; Jury and Pathack 1993; Jury *et al.* 1993b and 1996; Mason *et al.* 1994; Mason 1995; Tennant 1996; Crimp 1997; Rocha and Simmonds 1997a and 1997b) The variance of sea surface temperatures of the Indian Ocean is low during the summer rainfall season (Streten 1981) and so the association with rainfall over the subcontinent is possibly weaker than it otherwise would be (Shinoda and Kawamura 1996).

As discussed, dry conditions over southern Africa are frequently associated with a warmer-than-average western tropical Indian Ocean (Figure 8.5). However, this area is an important source of atmospheric moisture throughout the summer rainfall season and becomes the dominant source in the second half of summer. Increases in sea-surface temperatures in the same region have therefore been observed to enhance rather than reduce rainfall over southern Africa (Lindesay and Jury 1991, Hulme *et al.* 1996). Similarly, modelling studies fail to produce much enhancement of rainfall over southern Africa given negative sea-surface temperature anomalies, nor much weakening of convective activity over the Indian Ocean (Tennant 1996, Jury *et al.* 1996).

Farther south, a decrease in the surface temperatures of the Agulhas Current may have a negative effect on moisture fluxes into the overlying atmosphere, particularly with the occurrence of ridging anticyclones (Lutjeharms *et al.* 1986, Walker and Mey 1988, Mey *et al.* 1990, Jury and Levey 1993b, Jury 1994, D'Abreton and Tyson 1995 and 1996, Rouault *et al.* 1995). Dry conditions may result over eastern southern Africa as a consequence (Walker 1990, Mason 1990 and 1995, Mason and Tyson 1992, Jury 1992, Jury and Pathack 1991 and 1993, Jury *et al.* 1993c, Hastenrath *et al.* 1995, Rocha and Simmonds 1997a, Shinoda and Kawamura 1996). Possibly of greater importance than the sea-surface temperature anomalies *per se* is their influence on the meridional sea-surface temperature gradients to the south and southeast of the subcontinent. Weaker-than-average sea-surface temperature gradients that would be associated with negative temperature anomalies in the Agulhas region could weaken baroclinic disturbances passing over the area (Sanders and Gyakum 1980, Brundrit and Shannon 1989).

Changing temperature gradients in the South Atlantic Ocean may have a similar effect on the baroclinicity of disturbances (Walker and Lindesay 1989). The variability in the westerly waves and the surface passage of cyclones and transient anticyclones is likely to be a reflection of such sea surface temperature modulation on the systems (Mason *et al.* 1994, Mason 1995).

Sea-surface temperature variability in the tropical Atlantic Ocean illustrates some similarities to the Pacific El Niño phenomenon (Weare 1977, Gillooly and Walker 1984, Walker *et al.* 1984, McLain *et al.* 1985, Lamb *et al.* 1986, Lough 1986, Shannon *et al.* 1986, Parker *et al.* 1988, Taunton-Clark and Shannon 1988, Agenbag 1996, Jury 1997b, Nicholson 1997) and has been linked to drought conditions over the Sahel (Semazzi *et al.* 1988 and 1996, Ward 1992, Nicholson and Kim 1997). The impact of changes in this oceanic region on rainfall over southern Africa is insignificant in comparison to the impacts of changes in the Pacific and the Indian Oceans (Walker 1990, Mason *et al.* 1994, Mason 1995, Jury 1997b, Mason and Jury 1997), except over Angola and Namibia, where near-coastal precipitation is enhanced (Hirst and Hastenrath 1983a and 1983b). Theoretically, tropical Atlantic sea-surface temperature variability could have an important influence on moisture flux convergence over southern Africa during early summer, but further work is required to confirm this (D'Abreton and Lindesay 1993, D'Abreton and Tyson 1995).

South of about 15°S in the eastern Atlantic Ocean, sea temperatures are relatively low. The Walker cell over the South Atlantic Ocean consequently lies farther north than its western Indian Ocean counterpart. Walker cell variability is therefore of less significance over the west coast of southern Africa than it is over the east coast (Mason and Jury 1997). Temperature contrasts between the tropical Atlantic and eastern Pacific oceans may be partly responsible for Walker cell variability over the Atlantic (Park and Schubert 1993, Jury 1996, Janicot *et al.* 1996). The variability may explain westerly upper zonal wind anomalies over the equatorial Atlantic that frequently precede a dry rainfall season over southern Africa (Jury *et al.* 1994 and 1995).

The Quasi-Biennial Oscillation

The ENSO influence on rainfall over southern Africa is stronger when the stratospheric QBO is in its westerly phase (Mason and Lindesay 1993). When the QBO is in easterly phase, the influence of ENSO variability on rainfall in the region becomes insignificant (Figure 8.7). The 1991–2 season provides an exception (Jury 1995). The mechanism by which the QBO possibly modulates the ENSO–southern African rainfall association is poorly understood. The Oscillation is thought to interact with the Walker circulation over the western Indian Ocean (Jury and Pathack 1993 and 1997, Jury *et al.* 1994). Lower stratospheric easterly zonal winds would provide

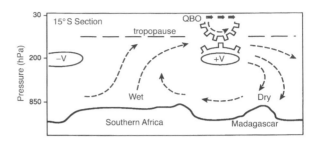

Figure 8.8 A possible mechanism for the interaction of the stratospheric Quasi-Biennial Oscillation of zonal winds and the Walker circulation over eastern southern Africa (after Jury *et al.* 1994)

upper-tropospheric wind stress that would enhance Walker cell overturning with a descending limb over southern Africa and a rising limb over the ocean to the east (Figure 8.8). During westerly phase years, the Walker cell would be reversed, and with a rising limb over southern Africa, convection and rainfall over the subcontinent would be enhanced. Whichever way the mechanism operates, the influence of the stratospheric QBO on rainfall over southern Africa is significant (Mason and Tyson 1992, Jury 1993, Mason *et al.* 1994). This is further illustrated by the modulating effect brought about on the associations between sea-surface temperatures and rainfall. In the case of a sensitive area of the southwest Indian Ocean (Figure 8.9, *upper*), the anomalously warm sea-surface occurs during droughts over South Africa when the QBO is easterly, but during wet years when it is westerly (Mason 1992). Similar modulation, though not as pronounced, occurs in the cases of other designated regional sea-surface temperature effects in the Indian and South Atlantic oceans (Mason 1992). There is evidence to suggest that tropical forcing by sea-surface temperatures (e.g., in the Indian Ocean to the north of Madagascar) may be little influenced by changes in the phase of the QBO (Figure 8.9, *lower*).

FORECASTING DROUGHTS

Interannual rainfall variability over southern Africa is largely determined by the preferred longitude of subtropical convection and by shifts and changes in amplitude of the westerly waves. These features of atmospheric variability respond in part to changes in boundary-layer forcing associated with sea-surface

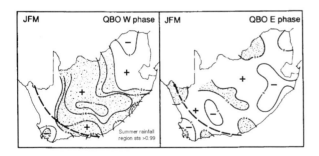

Figure 8.7 January–March correlation between the seasonal mean SOI and rainfall by phase of the QBO. Point correlations in shaded areas are significant at the 90 per cent level. Statistical field significance (sfs) for the region as a whole is indicated where it exceeds 90 per cent. The dashed line indicates the boundary between the summer (to the northeast) and winter (to the southwest) rainfall regions (after Mason 1992)

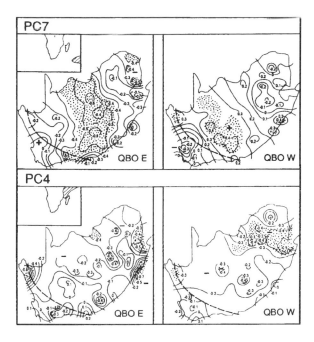

Figure 8.9 Correlations, stratified by the phase of the QBO, between January–March sea-surface temperature principal component scores in the indicated areas of the Indian Ocean and rainfall (after Mason 1992). Areas with positive correlations are shaded light gray. Areas with significant correlations (positive and negative) are shaded dark grey. In the case of the association between the southwestern Indian Ocean temperatures (*upper*) and rainfall, statistical field significance exceeds 90 per cent for the summer rainfall region of South Africa taken as a whole; in the case of the tropical Indian Ocean temperatures (*lower*), the combined set is field significant, but the component fields, split by the phase of the QBO, are not

temperatures in the oceans surrounding southern Africa and farther afield in the equatorial Pacific Ocean. Skilful seasonal forecasts of rainfall over the subcontinent depend on an ability to explain such variability and on the memory of the atmosphere (Palmer and Anderson 1994, Kumar and Hoerling 1995, Mason *et al.* 1996, Mason 1997b and 1998). The sensitivity of the atmosphere to boundary conditions is usually the main source of seasonal predictability, although the large-scale atmospheric components, such as westerly waves, may have some influence on the probability of individual synoptic weather patterns, thus providing an additional ability to make probabilistic forecasts of general conditions beyond two weeks.

Models developed during the late 1970s and early 1980s for long-range rainfall forecasting were based on statistical extrapolation of observed oscillations of rainfall (Dyer and Tyson 1977, Tyson and Dyer 1978 and 1980, Louw 1982), surface pressure variations (Dyer 1976a and 1976b, Howes and Dyer 1982), the use of sunspots (Dyer 1977, Dyer and Gosnell 1978), and antecedent winter temperatures (Dyer 1980b). They had limited success. In response to a better understanding of the atmospheric response to boundary-layer forcing (Mason *et al.* 1996), current operational seasonal forecasting is more soundly based. The method relies on statistical associations between sea-surface temperatures, outgoing long-wave radiation, and atmospheric circulation indices in the tropics, subtropics, and midlatitudes (Mason 1995, 1997b, and 1998, Barnston *et al.* 1996, Jury 1996, Mason *et al.* 1996, Makarau and Jury 1997, Mattes and Mason 1998, Landman and Mason 1999). In October 1994, the South African Long-lead Forecast Forum (SALFF) was founded with the purpose of developing the seasonal forecasting capabilities in South Africa. Many of the national meteorological services of countries to the north of South Africa have also established long-range forecasting units (Mason *et al.* 1996, Mason 1997b).

Predictability

The World Climate Research Programme's Atmospheric Modelling Intercomparison Project (AMIP) has provided an opportunity for using general circulation models to estimate the potential predictability of the atmosphere from boundary-layer forcing associated with sea-surface temperature variability. By varying initial conditions slightly, an ensemble of predictions is prepared. By comparing simulated ensemble variability for various AMIP experiments with the ensemble variability of control runs, and by using unvarying climatological sea-surface temperatures, estimates of predictability can be derived (Dix and Hunt 1995). In those regions where sea-surface temperatures provide a source of atmospheric predictability, correlations between individual runs constituting an ensemble should be significant. The average correlations between monthly rainfall anomalies of three ensemble members for the CSIRO nine-level

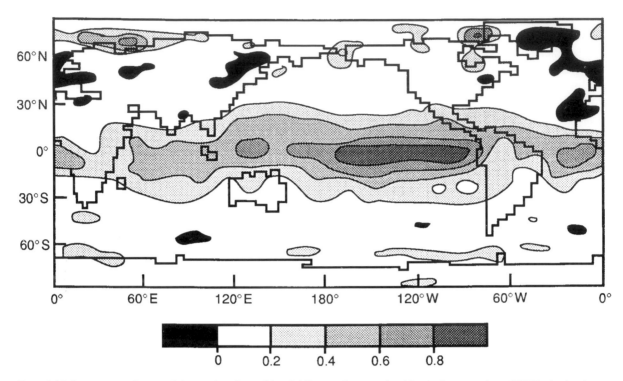

Figure 8.10 Average correlations of time series of monthly rainfall anomalies at each grid point between three CSIRO nine-level model AMIP runs. The three runs differ only in their initial conditions (after Dix and Hunt 1995). High correlations indicate areas with a reproducible atmospheric response to sea-surface temperature forcing

general circulation model are illustrated in Figure 8.10 (Dix and Hunt 1995). Most predictability lies within 20° of the equator, and is greatest in areas where rainfall is predominantly from a single well-organised quasi-permanent circulation system, such as the intertropical convergence zone (Hastenrath 1995). Tropical sea-surface temperatures are the main source of predictability, even within the midlatitudes (Lau and Nath 1994). Unfortunately, even within the tropics, estimated potential predictability is disproportionately small over land areas (Dix and Hunt 1995). This has been confirmed for southern Africa (Harrison 1996).

Given the seasonal variability of the predictability of the atmosphere, which is marked over southern Africa (Mason *et al.* 1996), estimates of annual predictability may be misleading. Reasonably successful hindcasts of rainfall variability for some extreme drought years over southern Africa have been produced using general circulation models forced by forecasted and observed sea-surface temperatures (Hunt *et al.* 1994,

Semazzi *et al.* 1996, Goddard and Graham 1997). In some years, as was the case for the 1991–2 drought, results were less satisfactory (Hunt 1997). The models appear to perform poorly where the model climatology is not sufficiently realistic (Hunt 1997). Over southern Africa, the control rainfall simulations by general circulation models generally reproduce the broad-scale features of spatial and seasonal variability, but significant weaknesses are apparent (Joubert 1997, Mason and Joubert 1997). Accordingly, seasonal forecasting skills for the region may suffer.

The general circulation models probably underestimate the predictability of the atmosphere because of inadequately or incorrectly simulated responses to sea-surface temperature anomalies (Latif *et al.* 1994) and because of an exaggeration of the importance of atmospheric chaos (Dix and Hunt 1995). Modelled tropical convection responses to positive sea-surface temperature anomalies are generally too weak (Mo and Wang 1995). Most models simulate an atmospheric response that is correspondingly weak, as was the case for southern Africa with the 1982–3 warm El Niño–Southern Oscillation event (Smith 1995, Joubert 1997). Given the limitations of general circulation models, it has been suggested that a variety of different forecasting models be used (Vislocky and Fritsch 1995) in conjunction with statistical models that are currently claiming relatively high levels of predictability (Mason 1998, Mattes and Mason 1998).

Operational ensemble seasonal forecasting for southern Africa

From the onset of the wet season in 1995, operational seasonal forecasts for southern Africa derived from ensemble general circulation model forecasts and sea-surface temperatures have been produced by the United Kingdom Meteorological Office (UKMO) and the Scripps Institute of Oceanography. Preliminary assessments of the operational performance of the UKMO model have been made, and these suggest that the statistical models may be performing slightly better. For both the 1995–6 and 1996–7 seasons, the UKMO forecasts were for average or drier conditions for the second half of the season (January–April). Wetter-than-average conditions were experienced. The model simulated an early start of the northward advance of the westerlies, characteristic of the onset of winter, for the 1995–6 season. As discussed earlier, the westerlies bring relatively dry, often descending, air over southern Africa. The westerlies in the late-summer control climate of the UKMO model are too strong (Joubert 1997), and so on average the model will simulate a late-season decrease in rainfall that is too early and too rapid. A similar problem was experienced during the 1996–7 season: the UKMO model indicated a drier-than-average January–April, but exceptional rains in March pushed the seasonal total above average. Given this limitation in the control climate, the UKMO model may be inherently unable to simulate adequately wet conditions in late summer. Numerical modelling holds great promise for the future, but until the forecasting can be improved, statistical modelling remains essential.

Statistical modelling

Statistical models have been used in operational seasonal forecasts of southern African rainfall since 1991. Various measures of ENSO variability are important, but not primary, inputs into the models (Cane et al. 1994, Hastenrath et al. 1995, Jury 1996, Mason et al. 1996, Makarau and Jury 1997, Mason 1998, Mattes and Mason 1998, Landman and Mason 1999). Other important variables for the southern African region include sea-surface temperatures in the Indian and South Atlantic oceans, outgoing long-wave radiation and tropospheric atmospheric circulation indices (zonal and meridional wind components), and the Quasi-Biennial Oscillation (Mason et al. 1996). Within South Africa there are three active forecasting groups, each of which uses different sets of predictors and different statistical approaches. At the University of Zululand, forecasts are produced using a multiple regression model relating a full range of atmospheric and oceanic predictors to rainfall over regions throughout southern Africa (Jury 1996). The Research Group for Seasonal Climate Studies of the South African Weather Bureau uses a canonical correlation analysis model to relate sea-surface temperatures in the Atlantic, Indian, and Pacific oceans to rainfall variability in eight regions of the country (Landman and Mason 1999). Atmospheric variables are not used as predictors. Similarly, the Climatology Research Group uses principal components of sea-surface temperatures as the only predictors in a quadratic discriminant analysis model (Mason 1998) and has investigated the possibility of constructing models using canonical discriminant analysis and logistic regression. In all instances, lead times are restricted to about six months, although efforts are being made to extend lead times to nine months or longer by forecasting sea-surface temperature anomalies in a two-tiered approach. The model has been adapted for use on Namibian rainfall (Mattes and Mason 1998).

The Pacific Ocean is the main source of predictability for southern African six-month rainfall forecasts. The Indian and South Atlantic oceans are important for forecasts with shorter lead times (Mason 1998, Mattes and Mason 1998, Landman and Mason 1999). The spatial and temporal variability of forecast skill over southern Africa is largely a reflection of the fundamental differences in 'forecastability' between the tropical and temperate atmospheres and the seasonal dependence of ENSO influences in the region. Highest forecast skill accordingly is achieved after the austral summer rainfall season has started. As an example, the seasonal variation of skill scores for cross-validated six-month rainfall hindcasts over the period 1951–95 for the northeastern interior of South Africa are illustrated in Figure 8.11. Statistically significant hindcast skill levels can be achieved throughout most of the year, and similar results are evident for other regions (Mason 1998). Linear error in probability space (LEPS) scores (Potts *et al.* 1996) for six-month hindcasts and for the northeastern interior peak in December (Figure 8.11), when forecasts for December–May rainfall can be released. Recently, it has appeared that it will be possible to develop useful forecast skill shortly before the start of the summer rainfall season (Mason 1998, Landman and Mason 1999) as indicated by a secondary peak in hindcast skill scores in July and August (Figure 8.11). Indications are that drought years are more forecastable than flood years, since individual flood-

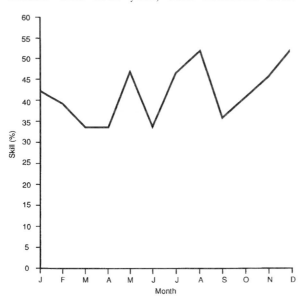

Figure 8.11 Seasonal variation of the LEPS score for the cross-validated six-month rainfall hindcasts over the training period 1951–95 for the northeastern interior of South Africa (after Mason 1998)

producing synoptic systems, such as tropical cyclones or extreme cut-off lows in the westerlies, may significantly distort annual rainfall statistics in particular wet years (Landman and Mason 1999). Droughts, on the other hand, require persistent forcing of atmospheric conditions that are unfavourable for the development of rainfall over the subcontinent.

CONCLUSIONS

Droughts and extended spells of dry years are an endemic feature of the climate of southern Africa. They are more persistent and homogeneously dry spatially than their wet-spell counterparts. Extended spells of wet years have a higher internal variability than their dry-spell counterparts. All current predictions of the effects of global warming suggest that extremes of climate, including droughts, are likely to be a feature of the twenty-first century.

The variations in the large-scale flow fields of the Southern Hemisphere that affect southern Africa and adjacent ocean areas in extended dry spells have been thoroughly investigated and are well understood. Moisture transport patterns have been shown to vary significantly between wet and dry periods. The degree of external forcing of southern African climate by sea-surface temperature changes in the Pacific, Indian, and Atlantic oceans has been established to the extent that the spatial variance in southern African rainfall associated changes in each ocean domain is known. External forcing by the Quasi-Biennial Oscillation has been shown to imprint a distinctive modulation on other forcing mechanisms.

Extended dry spells and droughts are typically associated with warming of the eastern Pacific Ocean, the occurrence of El Niños, and positive sea-surface temperature anomalies north of Madagascar in the Indian Ocean and over the South Atlantic Ocean. At the same time, negative anomalies prevail over the Agulhas current, and beyond, off the east coast of South Africa. Such changes are linked either directly or indirectly to distinctive adjustments in the general circulation over the region. These include strengthening of the subcontinental anticyclone over southern Africa, while the equivalent South Atlantic and south Indian anticyclones weaken relatively and are displaced equatorward. Moisture transport in less stable air from tropical Africa and the western tropical Indian Ocean diminishes significantly and is replaced by a predominance of transport of drier, more stable, subsided air from the South Atlantic Ocean. The circumpolar westerlies expand equatorward and the disturbances therein penetrate farther north over southern Africa (but are associated with less rainfall than the tropical systems that are more prevalent in wet spells).

Prediction of seasonal conditions, including the forecasting of droughts, using sea-surface temperature, circulation indices, outgoing long-wave radiation and the Quasi-Biennial Oscillation in statistical models is performed routinely, and encouraging levels of skill are being achieved in the southern African region. Notwithstanding, much work remains to be done to refine and improve the models. The use of ensemble forecasting based on general circulation models is in its infancy, but is being developed rapidly. Ultimately, all seasonal and interannual prediction of droughts will have to be based on this approach. Before this can happen, however, uncertainties associated with the models need to be minimised and the models need to be upgraded significantly. While this is being done, statistical modelling will retain a central role in forecasting conditions over a subcontinent beset by drought occurrence and facing an uncertain future in respect of its water resources.

ACKNOWLEDGEMENTS

P. Stickler, W. Job, and W. Phillips drew the diagrams. The figures have been reproduced with the permission of *International Journal of Climatology*, published by the Royal Meteorological Society, Oxford University Press; *Progress in Physical Geography*, published by Edward Arnold Limited; *Theoretical and Applied Climatology*, published by Springer-Verlag; and *WaterSA*, published by the Water Research Commission.

REFERENCES

Abbott, M.A. and Dyer, T.G.J. (1976) 'The temporal variation of rainfall over the summer rainfall region of South Africa', *South African Journal of Science* 72: 276–8.

Agenbag, J.J. (1996) 'Pacific ENSO events reflected in meteorological and oceanographic perturbations in the southern Benguela', *South African Journal of Science* 92: 243–7.

Albrecht, B.A., Ramanathan, V., and Boville, B.A. (1986) 'The effects of cumulus moisture transports on the simulation of climate with a general circulation model', *Journal of the Atmospheric Sciences* 43: 2,443–62.

Alexander, W.J.R. (1995) 'Floods, droughts and climate change', *South African Journal of Science* 91: 403–8.

Allan, R.J. (1988) 'El Niño Southern Oscillation influences in the Australasian region', *Progress in Physical Geography* 12: 4–20.

—— (1991) 'Australasia', in M.H. Glantz, R.W. Katz, and N. Nicholls (eds), *Teleconnections Linking Worldwide Climate Anomalies: Scientific Basis and Societal Impact*, Cambridge: Cambridge University Press, pp. 73–120.

Allan, R.J., Lindesay, J.A., and Reason, C.J.C. (1995) 'Multidecadal variability in the climate system over the Indian Ocean region during the austral summer', *Journal of Climate* 8: 1,853–73.

Barber, F.H. (1910) 'Is South Africa drying up?', *Agricultural Journal of the Cape of Good Hope* 86: 167–70.

Barclay, J.J., Jury, M.R , and Landman, W. (1993) 'Climatological and structural differences between wet and dry troughs over southern Africa in the early summer', *Meteorology and Atmospheric Physics* 51: 41–54.

Barnston, A.P., Thiao, W., and Kumar, V. (1996) 'Long-lead forecasts of seasonal precipitation in Africa using CCA', *Weather and Forecasting* 11. 506–20.

Brook, G.A. and Mametse, M.N. (1970) 'Rainfall trend patterns in South Africa', *South African Geographical Journal* 52: 134–8.

Brundrit, G.B. and Shannon, L.V. (1989) 'Cape storms and the Agulhas Current: A glimpse of the future?', *South African Journal of Science* 85: 619–20.

Cadet, D.L. (1985) 'The Southern Oscillation over the Indian Ocean', *Journal of Climatology* 5: 189–212.

Cadet, D.L. and Diehl, B.C. (1984) 'Interannual variability of surface fields over the Indian Ocean during recent decades', *Monthly Weather Review* 112, 1,921–35.

Cane, M.A., Eshel, G., and Buckland, R.W. (1994) 'Forecasting Zimbabwean maize yield using eastern equatorial Pacific sea surface temperature', *Nature* 370: 204–5.

Cox, G.W. (1925) 'Periodicity in rainfall', *Transactions of the Royal Society of South Africa* 12: 295–9.

—— (1926) 'Some notes on the circulation of the atmosphere over Southern Africa', *South African Journal of Science* 23: 103–67.

Crimp, S.J. (1997) 'A sea-surface temperature sensitivity test using the Colorado State University Regional Atmospheric Modelling System', *South African Journal of Science* 93: 133–41.

Currie, R.G. (1991) 'Deterministic signals in tree-rings

from Tasmania, New Zealand and South Africa', *Annales Geophysicae* 9: 71–81.

——— (1993) 'Luni-solar 18.6- and 10–11-year solar cycle signals in South African rainfall', *International Journal of Climatology* 13: 237–56.

D'Abreton, P.C. and Lindesay, J.A. (1993) 'Water vapour transport over southern Africa during wet and dry early and late summer months', *International Journal of Climatology* 13: 151–70.

D'Abreton, P.C. and Tyson, P.D. (1995) 'Divergent and non-divergent water vapour transport over southern Africa during wet and dry conditions', *Meteorology and Atmospheric Physics* 55: 47–59.

——— (1996) 'Three-dimensional kinematic trajectory modelling of water vapour transport over southern Africa', *WaterSA* 22, 297–305.

de Loor, B. (1948) 'Die ontleding van Kaapstad reenval (1938–1946)', *Tydskrif vir Wetenskap en Kuns* New Series 8: 34–6.

Diab, R.D., Preston-Whyte, R.A., and Washington, R. (1991) 'Distribution of rainfall by synoptic type over Natal, South Africa', *International Journal of Climatology* 11: 877–88.

Dix, M.R. and Hunt, B.G. (1995) 'Chaotic influences and the problem of deterministic seasonal predictions', *International Journal of Climatology* 15: 729–52.

Dyer, T.G.J. (1975) 'The assignment of rainfall stations into homogeneous groups: An application of principal component analysis', *Quarterly Journal of the Royal Meteorological Society* 101: 1,005–13.

——— (1976a) 'Meridional interactions between rainfall and surface pressure', *Nature* 264: 48.

——— (1976b) 'On the components of time series: The removal of spatial dependence', *Quarterly Journal of the Royal Meteorological Society* 102: 157–65.

——— (1977) 'On the application of some stochastic models to precipitation forecasting', *Quarterly Journal of the Royal Meteorological Society* 103: 177–89.

——— (1979) 'Rainfall along the east coast of southern Africa, the Southern Oscillation, and the latitude of the subtropical high pressure belt', *Quarterly Journal of the Royal Meteorological Society* 105: 445–51.

——— (1980a) 'The distribution of rainfall over the sugar region of South Africa', *Transactions of the Royal Society of South Africa* 44: 257–67.

——— (1980b) 'On August mean temperature and the succeeding season's rainfall over South Africa', *South African Journal of Science* 76: 85–7.

——— (1981a) 'A description of interannual rainfall variance over space and time for South Africa: 1921–1975', *Transactions of the Royal Society of South Africa* 44: 453–64.

——— (1981b) 'The apparent absence of the quasi-biennial oscillation in sea-level pressure in the South Indian Ocean and South Atlantic Ocean', *Quarterly Journal of the Royal Meteorological Society* 107: 461–7.

——— (1982) 'On the intra-seasonal variation in rainfall over the subcontinent of southern Africa', *Journal of Climatology* 2: 47–64.

Dyer, T.G.J. and Gosnell, J.M. (1978) 'Long term rainfall trends in the South African sugar industry', *Proceedings of the South African Sugar Technologists Association*, pp. 1–8.

Dyer, T.G.J. and Marker, M.E. (1978) 'On the variation of rainfall over South West Africa', *South African Geographical Journal* 60: 144–9.

Dyer, T.G.J. and Tyson, P.D. (1977) 'Estimating above and below normal rainfall periods over South Africa, 1972–2000', *Journal of Applied Meteorology* 16: 145–7.

Gillooly, J.F. and Walker, N.D. (1984) 'Spatial and temporal behaviour of sea surface temperatures in the South Atlantic', *South African Journal of Science* 80: 97–100.

Goddard, L. and Graham, N.E. (1997) 'GCM-based climate forecasts over southern Africa', *Preprints of the Fifth International Conference on Southern Hemisphere Meteorology and Oceanography*, pp. 87–8.

Gondwe, M.P., Jury, M.R., and Mulenga, H.M. (1997) 'Sensitivity of vegetation (NDVI) to climate over southern Africa: relationships with rainfall and OLR', *South African Geographical Journal* 79: 52–60.

Graham, N.E. (1994) 'Decadal-scale climate variability in the tropical and North Pacific during the 1970s and 1980s: Observations and model results', *Climate Dynamics* 10: 135–62.

——— (1995) 'Simulation of recent global temperature trends', *Science* 267: 666–71.

Halpert, M.S. and Ropelewski, C.F. (1992) 'Surface temperature patterns associated with the Southern Oscillation', *Journal of Climate* 5: 577–93.

Harangozo, S.A. and Harrison, M.S.J. (1983) 'On the use of synoptic data in indicating the presence of cloud bands over southern Africa', *South African Journal of Science* 79: 413–14.

Harnack, R.P. and Harnack, J. (1985) 'Intra- and inter-hemispheric teleconnections using seasonal Southern Hemisphere sea level pressure', *Journal of Climatology* 5: 283–96.

Harrison, M.S.J. (1983a) 'The Southern Oscillation, zonal equatorial circulation cells and South African rainfall', *Preprints of the First International Conference on Southern Hemisphere Meteorology*, pp. 302–5.

——— (1983b) 'Rain day frequency and mean daily rainfall intensity as determinants of total rainfall over the eastern Orange Free State', *Journal of Climatology* 3: 35–45.

——— (1984a) 'A generalised classification of South African summer rain-bearing synoptic systems', *Journal of Climatology* 4: 547–60.

——— (1984b) 'The annual rainfall cycle over the central interior of South Africa', *South African Geographical Journal* 66: 47–64.

——— (1984c) 'Comparison of rainfall time series over

South Africa generated from real data and through principal component analysis', *Journal of Climatology* 4: 561–4.

—— (1984d) 'Note on the origins of the dry Limpopo Valley', *South African Journal of Science* 80: 333–4.

—— (1986) 'A Synoptic Climatology of South African Rainfall Variability', unpublished PhD thesis, University of the Witwatersrand.

—— (1988) 'Rainfall and precipitable water relationships over the central interior of South Africa', *South African Geographical Journal* 70: 100–11.

—— (1996) 'Seasonal prediction of southern African rainfall using the UK Meteorological Office unified model', *Proceedings of the Seasonal Rainfall Forecasting Workshop*, pp. 27–34.

Hastenrath, S. (1995) 'Recent advances in tropical climate prediction', *Journal of Climate* 8: 1,519–32.

Hastenrath, S., Nicklis, A., and Greischar, L. (1993) 'Atmospheric-hydrospheric mechanisms of climate anomalies in the Western Equatorial Indian Ocean', *Journal of Geophysical Research* 98: 20,219–35.

Hastenrath, S., Greischar, L., and van Heerden, J. (1995) 'Prediction of the summer rainfall over South Africa', *Journal of Climate* 8: 1,511–18.

Hirst, A.C. and Hastenrath, S. (1983a) 'Ocean–atmosphere mechanisms of climate anomalies in the Angola–tropical Atlantic sector', *Journal of Physical Oceanography* 13: 1,146–57.

—— (1983b) 'Diagnostics of hydrometeorological anomalies in the Zaire (Congo) basin', *Quarterly Journal of the Royal Meteorological Society* 109: 881–92.

Hofmeyr, W. L. and Gouws, V. (1964) 'A statistical and synoptic analysis of wet and dry conditions in north-western Transvaal', *Notos* 13: 37–48.

Howes, C. and Dyer, T.G.J. (1982) 'On the spatial variation of an apparent relationship between monthly rainfall over southern Africa and sea-level oceanic barometric pressure', *Transactions of the Royal Society of South Africa* 44: 513–22.

Hulme, M. (1992) 'Rainfall changes in Africa: 1931–1960 to 1961–1990', *International Journal of Climatology* 12: 685–99.

—— (1996) 'Recent climatic change in the world's drylands', *Geophysical Research Letters* 23: 61–4.

Hulme, M., Conway, D.D., Joyce, A., and Mulenga, H. (1996) 'A 1961–90 climatology for Africa south of the Equator and a comparison of potential evapotranspiration estimates', *South African Journal of Science* 92: 334–43.

Hunt, B.G. (1997) 'Prospects and problems for multi-seasonal predictions: Some issues arising from a study of 1992', *International Journal of Climatology* 17: 137–54.

Hunt, B.G., Zebiak, S.E., and Cane, M.A. (1994) 'Experimental predictions of climatic variability for lead times of twelve months', *International Journal of Climatology* 14: 507–26.

Hurrell, J.W and van Loon, H. (1994) 'A modulation of the atmospheric annual cycle in the Southern Hemisphere', *Tellus* 46A: 325–38.

Janicot, S., Moron, V., and Fontaine, B. (1996) 'Sahel droughts and ENSO dynamics', *Geophysical Research Letters* 23: 515–18.

Janowiak, J.E. (1988) 'An investigation of interannual rainfall variability in Africa', *Journal of Climate* 1: 240–55.

Joubert, A.M. (1997) 'AMIP simulations of atmospheric circulation over southern Africa', *International Journal of Climatology* 17: 1,129–54.

Joubert, A.M., Mason, S.J., and Galpin, J.S. (1996) 'Droughts over southern Africa in a doubled-CO_2 climate', *International Journal of Climatology* 16: 1,149–58.

Jury, M.R. (1992) 'A climatic dipole governing the interannual variability of convection over the SW Indian Ocean and SE Africa region', *Trends in Geophysical Research* 1: 165–72.

—— (1993) 'A preliminary study of climatological associations and characteristics of tropical cyclones in the SW Indian Ocean', *Meteorology and Atmospheric Physics* 51: 101–15.

—— (1994) 'A thermal front within the marine atmospheric boundary layer over the Agulhas Current south of Africa: Composite aircraft observations', *Journal of Geophysical Research* 99: 3,297–304.

—— (1995) 'A review of research on ocean–atmosphere interactions and South African climate variability', *South African Journal of Science* 91: 289–94.

—— (1996) 'Regional teleconnection patterns associated with summer rainfall over South Africa, Namibia and Zimbabwe', *International Journal of Climatology* 16: 135–53.

—— (1997a) 'Inter-annual climate modes over southern Africa from satellite cloud OLR 1975–1994', *Theoretical and Applied Climatology* 57: 155–63.

—— (1997b) 'South-east Atlantic warm events: Composite evolution and consequences for southern African climate', *South African Journal of Marine Science* 17: 21–8.

Jury, M.R. and Levey, K.M. (1993a) 'The Eastern Cape drought', *WaterSA* 19: 133–7.

—— (1993b) 'The climatology and characteristics of drought in the eastern Cape of South Africa', *International Journal of Climatology* 13: 629–41.

Jury, M.R. and Lutjeharms, J.R.E. (1993) 'Die struktuur en moontlike aandrywingskragte van die 1991–1992-droogte in suidelike Afrika', *Suid Afrikaanse Tydskrif vur Natuurwetenskap en Techologie* 12: 8–16.

Jury, M.R. and Pathack, B.M.R. (1991) 'A study of climate and weather variability over the tropical southwest Indian Ocean', *Meteorology and Atmospheric Physics* 47: 37–48.

—— (1993) 'Composite climatic patterns associated with extreme modes of summer rainfall over southern Africa:

1975–1984', *Theoretical and Applied Climatology* 47: 137–45.

——— (1997) 'Climatic patterns associated with the 1992 drought over southern Africa: Observations and GCM results', *Journal of the African Meteorological Society* (forthcoming).

Jury, M.R. and Waliser, D. (1990) 'Satellite microwave measurements of atmospheric water vapour and marine wind speed, case study application', *South African Journal of Marine Science* 9: 309–16.

Jury, M.R., Pathack, B., and Sohn, B.J. (1992) 'Spatial structure and interannual variability of summer convection over southern Africa and the SW Indian Ocean', *South African Journal of Science* 88: 275–80.

Jury, M.R., Pathack, B., and Waliser, D. (1993a) 'Satellite OLR and microwave data as a proxy for summer rainfall over sub-equatorial Africa and adjacent oceans', *International Journal of Climatology* 13: 257–69.

Jury, M.R., Pathack, B., Wang, B., Powell, M., and Raholijao, N. (1993b) 'A destructive tropical cyclone season in the SW Indian Ocean, January–February 1984', *South African Geographical Journal* 75: 53–9.

Jury, M.R., Valentine, H.R., and Lutjeharms, J.R.E. (1993c) 'Influence of the Agulhas Current on summer rainfall along the southeast coast of South Africa', *Journal of Applied Meteorology* 32: 1,282–7.

Jury, M.R., McQueen, C.A., and Levey, K.M. (1994) 'SOI and QBO signals in the African region', *Theoretical and Applied Climatology* 50: 103–15.

Jury, M.R., Parker, B.A., Raholijao, N., and Nassor, A. (1995) 'Variability of summer rainfall over Madagascar: Climatic determinants at interannual scales', *International Journal of Climatology* 15: 1,323–32.

Jury, M.R., Pathack, B.M.R., Rautenbach, C.J. de W., and van Heerden, J. (1996) 'Drought over South Africa and Indian Ocean SST: Statistical and GCM results', *Global Atmosphere Ocean System* 4: 47–63.

Karoly, D.J., Hope, P., and Jones, P.D. (1996) 'Decadal variations of the Southern Hemisphere circulation', *International Journal of Climatology* 16: 723–38.

Kelbe, B.E., Garstang, M., and Brier, G. (1983) 'Analysis of rainfall variability in the northeastern region of South Africa', *Archiv für Meteorologie, Geophysik und Bioklimatologie* 32A: 231–52.

Kerr, R.A. (1992) 'Unmasking a shifty climate system', *Science* 255: 1,508–10.

Kidson, J.W. (1988) 'Indices of the Southern Hemisphere zonal wind', *Journal of Climate* 1: 183–94.

King, J.A. and van Loon, H. (1958) 'Weather of the 1957 and 1958 winters in South Africa', *South African Geographical Journal* 40: 62–7.

Kruss, P.D., Mukhala, E., and Muchinda, M.R. (1992) 'On trends in the Zambian precipitation maize crop index: 1950–1990', *Preprints of the Fifth International Meeting on Statistical Climatology*, pp. 115–16.

Kumar, A. and Hoerling, M.P. (1995) 'Prospects and limitations of seasonal atmospheric GCM predictions', *Bulletin of the American Meteorological Society* 76: 335–45.

Lamb, P.J., Peppler, R.A., and Hastenrath, S. (1986) 'Interannual variability in the tropical Atlantic', *Nature* 322: 238–40.

Landman, W.A. and Mason, S.J. (1999) 'Operational long-lead prediction of South African rainfall using canonical correlation analysis', *International Journal of Climatology*, forthcoming.

Latif, M. and Barnett, T.P. (1995) 'Interactions of the tropical oceans', *Journal of Climate* 8: 952–64.

Latif, M., Sterl, A., Assenbaum, M., Junge, M.M., and Maier-Reimer, E. (1994) 'Climate variability in a coupled GCM. Part II: the Indian Ocean and monsoon', *Journal of Climate* 7: 1,449–62.

Lau, K.M. and Sheu, P.J. (1988) 'Annual cycle, Quasi-biennial Oscillation and Southern Oscillation in global precipitation', *Journal of Geophysical Research* 93: 10,975–88.

Lau, N.-C. and Nath, M.J. (1994) 'A modelling study of the relative roles of tropical and extratropical SST anomalies in the variability of the global ocean–atmosphere system', *Journal of Climate* 7: 1,184–207.

Lindesay, J.A. (1984) 'Spatial and temporal rainfall variability over South Africa, 1963 to 1981', *South African Geographical Journal* 66: 168–75.

——— (1986) 'Relationships between the Southern Oscillation and Atmospheric Circulation Changes over Southern Africa', unpublished PhD thesis, University of the Witwatersrand.

——— (1988) 'South African rainfall, the Southern Oscillation and a Southern Hemisphere semi-annual cycle', *Journal of Climatology* 8: 17–30.

Lindesay, J.A. and Jury, M.R. (1991) 'Atmospheric circulation controls and characteristics of a flood event in central South Africa', *International Journal of Climatology* 11: 609–27.

Lindesay, J.A. and Vogel, C.H. (1990) 'Historical evidence for Southern Oscillation–southern African rainfall relationships', *International Journal of Climatology* 10: 679–89.

Lindesay, J.A., Harrison, M.S.J., and Haffner, M.P. (1986) 'The Southern Oscillation and South African rainfall', *South African Journal of Science* 82: 196–8.

Longley, R.W. (1976) 'Weather and weather maps of South Africa', *South African Weather Bureau Technical Paper* No. 3.

Lough, J.M. (1986) 'Tropical Atlantic sea surface temperatures and rainfall variations in subsaharan Africa', *Monthly Weather Review* 114: 561–70.

Louw, W.J. (1982) 'Oscillations in Orange Free State rainfall', *South African Weather Bureau Technical Paper* No. 11.

Lyons, S.W. (1991) 'Origins of convective variability over equatorial southern Africa during austral summer', *Journal of Climate* 4: 23–39.

Lutjeharms, J.R.E, Mey, R D., and Hunter, I.T. (1986) 'Cloud lines over the Agulhas Current', *South African Journal of Science* 82: 635–40.

Main, J.P.L. and Hewitson, B.C. (1995) 'Regionalisation of daily precipitation in Botswana 1972–1989', *South African Geographical Journal* 77: 51–5.

Makarau, A. and Jury, M.R. (1997) 'Predictability of Zimbabwe summer rainfall', *International Journal of Climatology* 17: 1,421–32.

Marume, W. (1992) 'Desiccation in the Lowveld area of Zimbabwe', *Preprints of the Fifth International Meeting on Statistical Climatology*, pp. 133–6.

Mason, S.J. (1990) 'Temporal variability of sea surface temperatures around southern Africa: A possible forcing mechanism for the eighteen-year rainfall oscillation?', *South African Journal of Science* 86: 243–52.

—— (1992) 'Sea surface temperatures and South African rainfall variability', unpublished PhD thesis, University of the Witwatersrand, Johannesburg.

—— (1995) 'Sea-surface temperature–South African rainfall associations, 1910–1989', *International Journal of Climatology* 15: 119–35.

—— (1996) 'Rainfall trends over the Lowveld of South Africa', *Climatic Change* 32: 35–54.

—— (1997a) 'Recent changes in El Niño–Southern Oscillation events and their implications for southern African climate', *Transactions of the Royal Society of South Africa* 52: 377–403.

—— (1997b) 'Review of recent developments in seasonal forecasting of rainfall', *WaterSA* 23: 57–62.

—— (1998) 'Seasonal forecasting of South African rainfall using a non-linear discriminant analysis model', *International Journal of Climatology* 18: 147–64.

Mason, S.J. and Joubert, A.M. (1995) 'A note on inter-annual rainfall variability and water demand in the Johannesburg region', *WaterSA* 21: 269–70.

—— (1997) 'Simulated changes in extreme rainfall over southern Africa', *International Journal of Climatology* 17: 291–301.

Mason, S.J. and Jury, M.R. (1997) 'Climatic variability and change over southern Africa: A reflection on underlying processes', *Progress in Physical Geography* 21: 23–50.

Mason, S.J. and Lindesay, J.A. (1993) 'A note on the modulation of Southern Oscillation–southern African rainfall associations with the Quasi-biennial Oscillation', *Journal of Geophysical Research* 98: 8,847–50.

Mason, S.J. and Mimmack, G.M. (1992) 'The use of bootstrap correlation coefficients for the correlation coefficient in climatology', *Theoretical and Applied Climatology* 45: 229–33.

Mason, S.J. and Tyson, P.D. (1992) 'The modulation of sea surface temperature and rainfall associations over southern Africa with solar activity and the Quasi-biennial Oscillation', *Journal of Geophysical Research* 97: 5,847–56.

Mason, S.J., Lindesay, J.A., and Tyson, P.D. (1994) 'Simulating drought in southern Africa using sea surface temperature variations', *WaterSA* 20: 15–22.

Mason, S.J., Joubert, A.M., Cosijn, C., and Crimp, S.J. (1996) 'Review of the current state of seasonal forecasting techniques with applicability to southern Africa', *WaterSA* 22: 203–9.

Matarira, C.H. (1990) 'Drought over Zimbabwe in a regional and global context', *International Journal of Climatology* 10: 609–25.

Matarira, C.H. and Jury, M.R. (1992) 'Contrasting meteorological structure of intra-seasonal wet and dry spells in Zimbabwe', *International Journal of Climatology* 12: 165–76.

Mattes, M. and Mason, S.J. (1998) 'Evaluation of a seasonal forecasting procedure for Namibian rainfall', *South African Journal of Science* 94: 183–5.

McGee, O.S. and Hastenrath, S. (1966) 'Harmonic analysis of the rainfall over South Africa', *Notos* 15: 79–90.

McLain, D.R., Brainard, R.E., and Norton, J.G. (1985) 'Anomalous warm events in eastern boundary current systems', *CalCOFI Report* 26: 51–64.

Meehl, G.A. (1993) 'A coupled air-sea biennial mechanism in the tropical Indian and Pacific regions: Role of the oceans', *Journal of Climate* 6: 31–41.

Meehl, G.A. and Albrecht, B.A. (1988) 'Tropospheric temperatures and Southern Hemisphere circulation', *Monthly Weather Review* 116: 953–60.

Mey, R.D., Walker, N.D., and Jury, M.R. (1990) 'Surface heat fluxes and marine boundary layer modification in the Agulhas retroflection region', *Journal of Geophysical Research* 95: 15,997–16,015.

Miron, O. and Lindesay, J.A. (1983) 'A note on changes in airflow patterns between wet and dry spells over South Africa, 1963 to 1979', *South African Geographical Journal* 65: 141–7.

Miron, O. and Tyson, P.D. (1984) 'Wet and dry conditions and pressure anomaly fields over South Africa and the adjacent oceans, 1963–79', *Monthly Weather Review* 112: 2,127–32.

Mo, K.C. and Wang, X.L. (1995) 'Sensitivity of the systematic error of extended range forecasts to sea surface temperature anomalies', *Journal of Climate* 8: 1,533–43.

Mo, K.C. and White, G.H. (1985) 'Teleconnections in the Southern Hemisphere', *Monthly Weather Review* 113: 22–37.

Moron, V., Bigot, S., and Roucou, P. (1995) 'Rainfall variability in subequatorial America and Africa and relationships with the main sea-surface temperature modes (1951–1990)', *International Journal of Climatology* 15: 1,297–322.

Muller, M.J. and Tyson, P.D. (1988) 'Winter rainfall over the interior of South Africa during extreme dry years', *South African Geographical Journal* 70: 20–30.

Nagai, T., Kitamura, Y., Endoh, M., and Tokioka, T. (1995) 'Coupled ocean–atmosphere model simulations of El Niño/Southern Oscillation with and without an active

Indian Ocean', *Journal of Climate* 8: 3–14.

Ngara, T., McNaughton, D.L., and Lineham, S. (1983) 'Seasonal rainfall fluctuations in Zimbabwe', *Zimbabwe Agricultural Journal* 80: 149–50.

Nevill, E. (1908) 'The rainfall in Natal', *Agricultural Journal of Natal* 11: 1,531–3.

Nicholson, S.E. (1981) 'The historical climatology of Africa', in T.M.L. Wigley, M.J. Ingram, and G. Farmer (eds), *Climate and History*, Cambridge: Cambridge University Press, pp. 249–70.

—— (1986) 'The nature of rainfall variability in Africa south of the equator', *Journal of Climatology* 6: 515–30.

—— (1989) 'Long-term changes in African rainfall', *Weather* 44: 46–56.

—— (1993) 'An overview of African rainfall fluctuations of the last decade', *Journal of Climate* 6: 1,463–6.

—— (1997) 'An analysis of the ENSO signal in the tropical Atlantic and western Indian Oceans', *International Journal of Climatology* 17: 345–75.

Nicholson, S.E. and Chervin, R.M. (1983) 'Recent rainfall fluctuations in Africa–interhemispheric teleconnections', in A. Street-Perrott, M. Beran, and R. Ratcliffe (eds), *Variations in the Global Water Budget*, Dordrecht, The Netherlands: D. Reidel, pp. 221–38.

Nicholson, S.E. and Entekhabi, D. (1986) 'The quasi-periodic behaviour of rainfall variability in Africa and its relationship to the Southern Oscillation', *Archiv fur Meteorologie, Geophysik und Bioklimatologie* 34A: 311–48.

—— (1987) 'Rainfall variability in equatorial and southern Africa: Relationships with sea surface temperatures along the southwestern coast of Africa', *Journal of Climate and Applied Meteorology* 26: 561–78.

Nicholson, S.E. and Kim, J. (1997) 'The relationship of the El Niño–Southern Oscillation to African rainfall', *International Journal of Climatology* 17: 117–35.

Onesta, P.A. and Verhoef, P. (1976) 'Annual rainfall frequency distributions for 80 rainfall districts in South Africa', *South African Journal of Science* 72: 120–2.

Palmer, T.N. and Anderson, D.L.T. (1994) 'The prospects for seasonal forecasting – A review paper', *Quarterly Journal of the Royal Meteorological Society* 120: 755–93.

Park, C.K. and Schubert, S.D. (1993) 'Remotely forced intraseasonal oscillations over the tropical Atlantic', *Journal of the Atmospheric Sciences* 50: 89–103.

Parker, D.E., Folland, C.K. and Ward, M.N. (1988) 'Sea-surface temperature anomaly patterns and prediction of seasonal rainfall in the Sahel region of Africa', in S. Gregory (ed.), *Recent Climatic Change*, London: Belhaven Press, pp. 166–78.

Partridge, T.C. (1985) 'Spring flow and tufa accretion at Taung', in P.V. Tobias (ed.), *Past, Present and Future of Hominid Evolution*, New York: Alan R. Liss, pp. 171–82.

Peres, M.A. (1930) 'Preliminary investigations on the rainfall of Lourenco Marques', *South African Journal of Science* 27: 132–5.

Physick, W.L. (1981) 'Winter depression tracks and climatological jet streams in the Southern Hemisphere during the FGGE year', *Quarterly Journal of the Royal Meteorological Society* 107: 883–98.

Pittock, A.B. (1973) 'Global meridional interactions in stratosphere and troposphere', *Quarterly Journal of the Royal Meteorological Society* 99: 424–37.

—— (1980) 'Patterns of climatic variation in Argentina and Chile – I. Precipitation, 1930–1960', *Monthly Weather Review* 108: 1,347–61.

Potts, J.M., Folland, C.K., Jolliffe, I.T., and Sexton, D. (1996) 'Revised "LEPS" scores for assessing climate model simulations and long-range forecasts', *Journal of Climate* 9, 34–53.

Rocha, A. and Simmonds, I. (1997a) 'Interannual variability of southern African summer rainfall. Part I: Relationships with air-sea interaction processes', *International Journal of Climatology* 17: 235–65.

—— (1997b) 'Interannual variability of southern African summer rainfall. Part I: Modelling the impact of sea surface temperatures on rainfall and circulation', *International Journal of Climatology* 17: 267–90.

Rogers, J.C. and van Loon, H. (1982) 'Spatial variability of sea level pressure and 500 mb height anomalies over the Southern Hemisphere', *Monthly Weather Review* 110: 1,375–92.

Ropelewski, C.F. and Halpert, M.S. (1987) 'Precipitation patterns associated with El Niño/Southern Oscillation', *Monthly Weather Review* 115: 1,606–26.

—— (1989) 'Precipitation patterns associated with the high index phase of the Southern Oscillation', *Journal of Climate* 2: 268–84.

Ropelewski, C.F., Halpert, M.S., and Wang, X. (1992) 'Observed tropospheric variability and its relationship to the Southern Oscillation', *Journal of Climate* 5: 594–614.

Rouault, M., Lee-Thorp, A.M., Ansorge, I., and Lutjeharms, J.R.E. (1995) 'Agulhas Current air-sea exchange experiment', *South African Journal of Science* 91: 493–6.

Rubin, M.J. (1956) 'The associated precipitation and circulation patterns over southern Africa', *Notos* 5: 53–9.

Sanders, F. and Gyakum, J.R. (1980) 'Synoptic-dynamic climatology of the "bomb"', *Monthly Weather Review* 108: 1,589–1,606.

Schwarz, E.H.L. (1919) 'The progressive desiccation of Africa: The cause and the remedy', *South African Journal of Science* 15: 139–90.

Semazzi, F.H.M., Mehta V., and Sud, Y.C. (1988) 'An investigation of the relationship between sub-Saharan rainfall and global sea surface temperatures', *Atmosphere Ocean* 26: 118–38.

Semazzi, F.H.M., Burns, B., Lin, N.-H., and Schemm, J.-K. (1996) 'A GCM study of the teleconnections between the continental climate of Africa and global sea surface temperature anomalies', *Journal of Climate* 9: 2,480–97.

Shannon, L.V., Boyd, A.J., Brundrit, G.B., and Taunton-

Clark, J. (1986) 'On the existence of El Niño-type phenomenon in the Benguela System', *Journal of Marine Research* 44: 495–520.

Shinoda, M. and Kawamura, R. (1996) 'Relationships between rainfall over semi-arid southern Africa and geopotential heights, and sea surface temperatures', *Journal of the Meteorological Society of Japan* 74: 21–36.

Smith, A.V. (1985) 'Studies of the effects of cold fronts during the rainy season in Zimbabwe', *Weather* 40: 198–202.

Smith, I.N. (1995) 'A GCM simulation of global climate interannual variability: 1950–1988', *Journal of Climate* 8: 709–18.

Stoeckenius, T. (1981) 'Interannual variations of tropical precipitation patterns', *Monthly Weather Review* 109: 1,233–47.

Streten, N.A. (1981) 'Southern hemisphere sea surface temperature variability and apparent associations with Australian rainfall', *Journal of Geophysical Research* 86: 485–97.

Suppiah, R. (1988) 'Relationships between Indian Ocean sea surface temperature and rainfall of Sri Lanka', *Journal of the Meteorological Society of Japan* 66: 103–11.

Taljaard, J.J. (1981) 'The anomalous climate and weather systems of January to March 1974', *South African Weather Bureau Technical Paper* No. 9.

—— (1985) 'Cut-off lows in the South African region', *South African Weather Bureau Technical Paper* No. 14.

—— (1986) 'Change of rainfall distribution and circulation patterns over Southern Africa', *Journal of Climatology* 6: 579–92.

—— (1989) 'Climate and circulation anomalies in the South African region during the summer of 1982/83', *South African Weather Bureau Technical Paper* No. 21.

Taljaard, J.J. and Steyn, P.C.L. (1991) 'Relationships between atmospheric circulation and rainfall in the South African region', *South African Weather Bureau Technical Paper* No. 24.

Taunton-Clark, J. and Shannon, L.V. (1988) 'Annual and interannual variability in the south east Atlantic during the twentieth century', *South African Journal of Marine Science* 6: 97–106.

Tennant, W.J. (1996) 'Influence of Indian Ocean sea-surface temperature anomalies on the general circulation of southern Africa', *South African Journal of Science* 92: 289–95.

Theron, G.F. and Harrison, M.S.J. (1991) 'The atmospheric circulation over Gough and Marion Islands', *South African Journal of Science* 87: 331–8.

Thompson, W.R. (1936) 'Moisture and farming in South Africa', *South African Agricultural Series* 14: 1–260.

Torrance, J.D. (1979) 'Upper windflow patterns in relation to rainfall in south-east central Africa', *Weather* 34: 106–15.

Trenberth, K.E. (1975) 'A quasi-biennial standing wave in the Southern Hemisphere and interrelations with sea surface temperature', *Quarterly Journal of the Royal Meteorological Society* 101: 55–74.

—— (1979) 'Interannual variability of the 500 mb zonal mean flow in the Southern Hemisphere', *Monthly Weather Review* 107: 1,515–24.

—— (1980a) 'Planetary waves at 500 mb in the Southern Hemisphere', *Monthly Weather Review* 108: 1,378–89.

—— (1980b) 'Atmospheric quasi-biennial oscillations', *Monthly Weather Review* 108: 1,370–77.

—— (1990) 'Recent observed interdecadal climate changes in the Northern Hemisphere', *Bulletin of the American Meteorological Society* 71: 988–93.

Trenberth, K.E. and Hoar, T.J. (1996) 'The 1990–1995 El Niño–Southern Oscillation event: Longest on record', *Geophysical Research Letters* 23: 57–60.

Trenberth, K.E. and Mo, K.C. (1985) 'Blocking in the Southern Hemisphere', *Monthly Weather Review* 113: 3–21.

Triegaardt, D.O., Terblanche, D.E., van Heerden, J., and Laing, M.V. (1988) 'The Natal flood of September 1987', *South African Weather Bureau Technical Paper* No. 19.

Tripp, W.B. (1888) 'Rainfall of South Africa, 1842–1886', *Quarterly Journal of the Royal Meteorological Society* 14: 108–23.

Tyson, P.D. (1971) 'Spatial variation of rainfall spectra in South Africa', *Annals of the Association of American Geographers* 61: 711–20.

—— (1978) 'Rainfall changes over South Africa during the period of meteorological record', in M.J.A. Werger (ed.), *Biogeography and Ecology of Southern Africa*, The Hague: W. Junk, pp. 53–69.

—— (1980) 'Temporal and spatial variation of rainfall anomalies in South Africa south of latitude 22° during the period of meteorological records', *Climatic Change* 2: 363–71.

—— (1981) 'Atmospheric circulation variations and the occurrence of extended wet and dry spells over southern Africa', *Journal of Climatology* 1: 115–30.

—— (1984) 'The atmospheric modulation of extended wet and dry spells over South Africa, 1958–1978', *Journal of Climatology* 4: 621–35.

—— (1986) *Climatic Change and Variability over Southern Africa*, Cape Town, Oxford University Press.

Tyson, P.D. and Dyer, T.G.J. (1978) 'The predicted above-normal rainfall of the seventies and the likelihood of droughts in the eighties in South Africa', *South African Journal of Science* 74: 372–7.

—— (1980) 'The likelihood of droughts in the eighties in South Africa', *South African Journal of Science* 76, 340–1.

Tyson, P.D., Dyer, T.G., and Mametse, M.N. (1975) 'Secular changes in South African rainfall: 1880 to 1972', *Quarterly Journal of the Royal Meteorological Society* 101: 817–33.

Tyson, P.D., Sturman, A.P., Fitzharris, B.B., Mason, S.J., and Owens, I.F. (1998) 'Circulation changes and teleconnections between glacial advances on the west coast of New Zealand and extended spells of drought years in South Africa', *International Journal of Climatology* 17, 14: 1,499–1,512.

Unganai, L.S. (1992) 'Changes in Zimbabwe's rainfall regime and the effect on the climatological means ("normals")', *Preprints of the Fifth International Meeting on Statistical Climatology*, pp. 133–6.

van den Heever, S.C. (1994) 'Modelling Tropical–Temperate Troughs over Southern Africa', unpublished MSc dissertation, University of the Witwatersrand.

van Heerden, J. and Terblanche, D.E. (1988) 'Some popular beliefs on South Africa rainfall prediction investigated', *South African Weather Bureau Newsletter* 265: 57–60.

van Heerden, J., Terblanche, D.E., and Schulze, G.C. (1988) 'The Southern Oscillation and South African summer rainfall', *Journal of Climatology* 8: 577–97.

van Loon, H. (1971) 'A half-yearly variation of the circumpolar surface drift in the Southern Hemisphere', *Tellus* 23: 511–16.

van Loon, H. and Rogers, J.C. (1984) 'Interannual variations in the half-yearly cycle of pressure gradients and zonal wind at sea level on the Southern Hemisphere', *Tellus* 36A: 76–86.

van Loon, H., Kidson, J.W., and Mullan, A.B. (1993) 'Decadal variation of the annual cycle in the Australian dataset', *Journal of Climate* 6: 1,227–31.

van Reenen, R.J. (1925) 'Note on the apparent regularity of the occurrence of wet and dry years in South West Africa', *South African Journal of Science* 22: 94–5.

van Rooy, M.P. (1980) 'Extreme rainfall anomalies over extensive parts of South Africa during periods of 1 to 5 successive "summer years"', *South African Weather Bureau Technical Paper* No. 8.

Vines, R.G. (1980) 'Analyses of South African rainfall', *South African Journal of Science* 76: 404–9.

—— (1982) 'Rainfall patterns in southern South America, and possible relationships with similar patterns in South Africa', *South African Journal of Science* 78: 457–9.

Vines, R.G. and Tomlinson, A.I. (1985) 'The Southern Oscillation and rainfall patterns in the Southern hemisphere', *South African Journal of Science* 81: 151–6.

Vislocky, R.L. and Fritsch, J.M. (1995) 'Improved model output statistics forecasts through model consensus', *Bulletin of the American Meteorological Society* 76: 1,157–64.

Vogel, C.H. (1994) '(Mis)management of droughts in South Africa: Past, present and future', *South African Journal of Science* 90: 4–5.

Vorster, J.H. (1957) 'Trends in long range rainfall records in South Africa', *South African Geographical Journal* 34: 61–6.

Vowinckel, E. (1955) 'Southern Hemisphere weather map analysis: Five-year mean pressures', *Notos* 4: 17–50.

Walker, N.D. (1990) 'Links between South African summer rainfall and temperature variability of the Agulhas and Benguela Current Systems', *Journal of Geophysical Research* 95: 3,297–319.

Walker, N.D. and Mey, R.D. (1988) 'Ocean/air energy fluxes within the Agulhas retroflection region', *Journal of Geophysical Research* 93: 15,473–83.

Walker, N.D. and Lindesay, J.A. (1989) 'Preliminary observations of oceanic influences on the February–March 1988 floods in central South Africa', *South African Journal of Science* 85: 164–9.

Walker, N.D. and Shillington, F.A. (1990) 'The effect of oceanographic variability on South African weather and climate', *South African Journal of Science* 86: 382–6.

Walker, N.D., Taunton-Clark, J., and Pugh, J. (1984) 'Sea temperatures of the South African west coast as indicators of Benguela warm events', *South African Journal of Science* 80: 72–7.

Wang, B. (1995) 'Interdecadal changes in El Niño onset in the last four decades', *Journal of Climate* 8: 267–85.

Ward, M.N. (1992) 'Provisionally corrected surface wind data, world wide ocean–atmosphere surface fields and Sahelian rainfall variability', *Journal of Climate* 5: 454–75.

Waylen, P.R. and Henworth, S. (1996) 'A note on the timing of precipitation variability in Zimbabwe as related to the Southern Oscillation', *International Journal of Climatology* 16: 1,137–48.

Weare, B.C. (1977) 'Empirical orthogonal analysis of Atlantic Ocean surface temperatures', *Quarterly Journal of the Royal Meteorological Society* 103: 467–78.

Wilson, J.F. (1865) 'Water supply in the basin of the River Orange or "Gariep South Africa"', *Journal of the Royal Geographical Society* 35: 106–29.

9

DROUGHT AND ITS PREDICTABILITY IN ETHIOPIA

Tsegaye Tadesse

INTRODUCTION

The catastrophic droughts that tortured Africa in the 1980s were the subject of many newspaper and magazine articles and international television programmes. This forced African governments to establish a strategy, with international cooperation, to combat these disastrous phenomena. In Ethiopia, one of the drought-stricken countries in Africa, the need to predict drought is very high because of its consequences for the country's large population and their dependence on marginal and subsistence agriculture. Moreover, considerable efforts have been made worldwide to understand and predict drought. This chapter discusses drought and its predictability in Ethiopia.

Historical documentation of drought in Ethiopia

Ethiopia has often suffered from acute droughts and famines that have caused unprecedented misery for the people. In the 1980s, the damage of recurring drought in Ethiopia left millions homeless, and several hundred persons perished. The country's political situation and various other conditions may have exaggerated these numbers; nevertheless, the recurring drought in those years left an indelible impression.

The historical evidence of drought is mostly qualitative in nature, such as levels of reservoirs and river flow. The sources of information are mainly from local chronicles, archived data, historical texts and literature, travellers' diaries, European settlers' notes, folk songs, and so on.

Documentation of droughts and famines based on historical and scientific data has been done by a study known as the NMSA–SAREC project in 1989 (NMSA 1996). This report, based on the historical records of the chronological events of droughts in Ethiopia, showed that:

1 During the period from 253 BC to AD 1, one drought/famine was reported in a seven-year period.
2 From AD 1 to AD 1500, there were 177 droughts/famines, one every nine years, over the country.
3 In the sixteenth, seventeenth, eighteenth, and nineteenth centuries and the first half of the twentieth century, ten, fourteen, twenty-one, sixteen, and eight droughts/famines, respectively, were reported, suggesting sixty-nine events in the 450-year period – an average of one disaster every seven years.
4 In the period between 1950 and 1987, eighteen droughts/famines were reported, suggesting one event every two years. The decadal analyses of the historical records show that the decade 1960–9 was the worst, having seven disaster years. The study indicated that the maximum number of events occurred during the second century AD, followed by the first part of the twentieth century. It further showed an apparent increasing trend in the occurrence of droughts over Ethiopia from the sixteenth century onward.

Seasonal weather prediction experiences in Ethiopia

Rainfall is the most important climatic parameter influencing the economy of Ethiopia, an economy that is highly dependent on agriculture. There are two rainy seasons. The longest and most important one occurs from June to September and is known as *kiremt*; the short rainy period occurs between February and May and is known as *belg*. Because of uncertain and variable rains over drought-prone areas, agriculture became a gamble in most years. The years of bad rainfall led not only to droughts but also to famines in Ethiopia. This clearly shows the importance of the prediction of monthly and seasonal rainfall distribution.

The recurring droughts led Ethiopian meteorologists to establish an early warning system in the mid-1980s to issue at least a general outlook for the forthcoming rainy season so that farmers and policy makers can take appropriate measures. Thus, the prediction of seasonal rainfall was started in Ethiopia in 1986 at the experimental level by a small group of Ethiopian experts. The outlook issued at the beginning of the rainy seasons constituted a spatial and temporal analysis of rainfall. Having made a good start by accurately forecasting the 1987 drought, this group of experts formed a small unit under the Research and Studies Team of the National Meteorological Services Agency (NMSA) to issue experimental and semioperational weather outlooks. What was then known as the Ethiopian Relief and Rehabilitation Commission (RRC) managed to take necessary measures, using the forecast given by NMSA, to combat the 1987–8 famine and was awarded the SASAKAWA–UNDRO prize for its efforts. Having thus gained experience, this unit was transferred to the Weather Forecast and Analysis Team in 1990 to issue weather outlooks routinely for every season. At present, with a wider range of responsibilities, it is operating within the Weather Forecast and Early Warning Team under the Meteorological Analysis and Forecast Department.

The methods used to prepare and issue the seasonal weather outlook are analogue, trend, statistical, and teleconnection methods. Based on the international definitions and use that have been adopted by NMSA, the methods can briefly be explained as follows:

1 The analogue method is based on the assumption that a current synoptic situation will likely develop in the same way as similar synoptic situations of carefully selected past years. In this case, synoptic situations from the surface up to the upper tropospheric levels will be carefully examined. Moreover, the Southern Oscillation index (SOI) and other conditions, like frequency of tropical cyclone and rainfall during the months of the preseasonal and main season, are considered thoroughly to select the best analogue year.

2 Using the trend method, the trends of the major synoptic systems are analysed in the preseasonal period and the result is compared with the current year.

3 The statistical method is an objective method of forecasting based on a statistical examination of the past behaviour of the atmosphere using regression formulas, probabilities, and other statistical measures.

4 The teleconnection method is based on the ocean–atmosphere interaction and its influence on the areas far from the field of action. Thus, in this method the condition of the sea surface temperature (SST) over the central and eastern equatorial Pacific Ocean (i.e., the field of action) and the SOI data are used to predict the spatial and temporal distribution of rainfall based on the studies of their correlation. The SST and SOI data are also used to facilitate the selection of analogue years.

Using the above-mentioned methods, outlooks for the spatial and temporal distributions of rainfall are prepared and issued to users and policy makers. Rainfall distribution is categorised as normal, above-normal, or below-normal, as compared to the long-term mean (i.e., below 50 per cent of the long-term mean is considered to be much below normal, 50–75 per cent is below normal, 75–125 per cent is within the normal range, and more than 125 per cent is above normal). In terms of time, the outlooks constitute the monthly rainfall situations within the season. Verification of the forecasts indicates that more than 80 per cent of the outlooks issued are correct.

DROUGHT INDICATORS

There are many reasons for the occurrence of droughts. From the meteorological point of view, it is known that the intensity and movement of synoptic systems over the country and adjoining regions characterises the type and nature of the rainfall. The irregularities of these systems cause rainfall activity to be deficient or excessive. Prolonged deficient and uneven rainfall due to these irregularities can lead to droughts.

Synoptic systems dominant in drought years

Although the amount and distribution of rainfall varies because of topography, the principal factors that influence its spatial variations are changes in the intensity, position, and direction of movement of rain-producing atmospheric systems over the country.

According to various research findings, the following generalisations about the synoptic system are true when droughts occur during the long rainy season.

1 At the surface level, the South Atlantic and South Indian Ocean (Mascarine) anticyclones become weak, and frequent extratropical cyclones will be observed over these areas. This suggests that a decrease in moisture incursion to Ethiopia and adjoining regions occurs with such conditions. Relatively weak cross-equatorial flow over the Somali Coast, weaker monsoon heat low over the Arabian peninsula, and a relatively stronger ridge along western Europe toward the Horn of Africa are typical conditions during drought years. Moreover, the winds over the north and northwestern parts of Ethiopia are strong during drought years (compared to other years).
2 At the middle tropospheric level (500 hPa), the circulation over the Indian subcontinent and adjoining areas becomes weak in drought years.
3 At the upper tropospheric level (200 hPa), the tropical easterly jet stream (TEJ) is located over the southern parts of the Arabian peninsula during drought years, which is south of its normal position.

Generally, stronger surface winds, less moisture incursion over the country, feeble cross-equatorial flow, weaker Indian monsoon and Sudan thermal lows, an intense ridge from the Sahara, weaker tropospheric circulation, and deeper longitudinal penetration of the northern hemispheric trough are characteristics of drought years. Moreover, the westerly and easterly jets are displaced south of their normal positions.

Ocean–atmosphere interaction and its relation to drought

A phenomenon that is produced as a result of changes in the ocean–atmospheric interaction over the eastern equatorial Pacific Ocean, induced by the anomalous behaviour of the sea surface temperature, is known as El Niño/Southern Oscillation (ENSO). The effect of ENSO events on the global atmospheric circulation has been the occurrence of drought in many areas and floods in other areas. Since meteorological drought is based on deficient rainfall and its distribution in time and space, this type of drought occurs when rainfall is well below expectation in any large area for an extended period.

Ocean–atmosphere interaction and its relation to drought has been the subject of a number of studies. Several of these studies have indicated that ENSO is a useful climate signal that may affect atmospheric circulation in a reliably predictable way. These studies have stated that the principal cause of drought is the quasi-periodic oscillation of rain-producing weather systems, triggered by the combined effects of ENSO events.

The findings have revealed that, in Ethiopia, many of the ENSO episodic years have coincided with deficient rainfall, leading to drought (Tadesse 1996). The normalised rainfall anomaly has been calculated for Ethiopia in ENSO episodic years (see Figure 9.1). The results of this study showed that eight out of twelve ENSO years (67 per cent) had below-normal rainfall in the period 1952–92. Moreover, ten out of twelve ENSO years had a negative anomaly, meaning that 83 per cent of ENSO years had deficient rainfall in Ethiopia (Tadesse 1994). This suggests that ENSO events have a great impact on the recurrence of droughts in Ethiopia.

SOI and SST indices

The Southern Oscillation is an important atmospheric phenomenon in the tropics. It is characterised by the exchange of air between the eastern and western hemispheres. The pressure changes occur in a see-saw fashion and are represented by a parameter (the Southern Oscillation Index) that measures the difference in pressure between the two regions. During

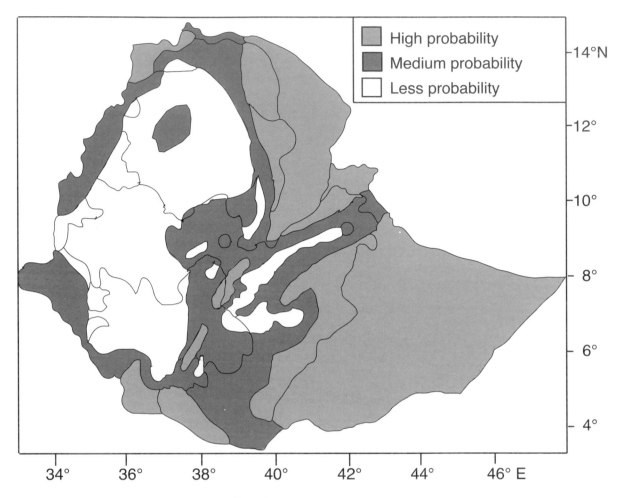

Figure 9.1 Drought-prone areas of Ethiopia (after Haile 1988)

the strong or normal period of Southern Oscillation, the westward trade winds converge on the north Australia-Indonesian low pressure zone, where the air rises with considerable cloudiness and rainfall. The air returns coastward at high altitudes and sinks over the cold, dry southeast Pacific high pressure belt. During an El Niño event, the normal circulation is disturbed, leading to changes in the rainfall patterns of some countries. This index has a strong correlation with Ethiopian rainfall (Tadesse 1994). Similarly, the results of preliminary studies confirm that there is a strong relation between the equatorial eastern Pacific SST anomaly and belg and kiremt rain in Ethiopia

(Yeshanew 1989, Bekele 1993). These indices are used extensively by experts in NMSA when preparing the seasonal outlook of rainfall.

The drought-prone areas of Ethiopia

Comparing the seasons, belg is more susceptible to droughts because of the uncertain behaviour of rains during this season.

Studies (Danielov 1987, Mersha 1996) revealed that, generally, the northeastern and southeastern parts of the country are highly drought-prone, with frequent occurrence of droughts. Using the decile method as an indicator of drought, a map has been prepared to show the probability of drought occurrences in Ethiopia (see Figure 9.2). This figure shows areas with values less than 0.3, between 0.3 and 0.5, and greater than 0.5 designated as low, medium, and high probability zones, respectively.

Case studies of drought periodicity

Case studies of drought have shown that the occurrence of drought in Ethiopia exhibits a quasi-periodic oscillation of roughly eight to ten years (Haile 1988). However, further thorough studies are needed to generalise this periodicity.

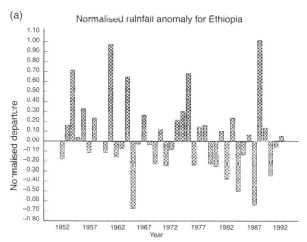

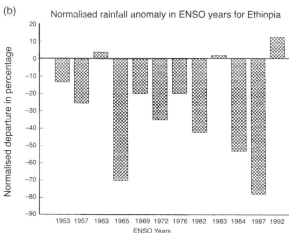

Figure 9.2 Normalised rainfall in ENSO episodic years (based on NMSA data)

ASSESSMENT OF THE OUTCOMES OF DROUGHT

Drought has a big impact on rain-fed agriculture. The seasonal rainfalls during kiremt and belg account for 75 per cent to 90 per cent of annual rainfall in Ethiopia (Degefu 1987). The fluctuations of these rains in time and space have greater repercussions. Often the failures of the rains lead to drought and famines.

In Ethiopia, the adverse impacts of recurrent drought result in an increasing demand for food. Moreover, the alarming trend of population growth makes the problem more severe. Wherever drought occurs, almost all agricultural products are affected, and there is no food reserve because most people are living at a subsistence level. Consequently, this leads to famine. Historical documentation shows that most of the drought years were linked with famines, leading to the death of thousands of people and cattle, in addition to heavy losses to agriculture. The documentation also shows that droughts prolonged for years have occurred many times, crippling the country's fragile economy.

USEFULNESS AND LIMITATIONS OF THE PREDICTABILITY OF DROUGHT

Usefulness and limitation of long-term predictions

Predicting drought is extremely important; it allows policy makers and others to take appropriate measures to combat drought's effects. It saves lives and reduces property damage. However, no perfect method exists to reliably predict the occurrence, persistence, cessation, or recurrence of drought. NMSA issues seasonal outlooks with a precaution: 'As weather systems are variable in time and space, users are advised to follow up dekadal and monthly weather outlooks'. This precaution is given to users to advise them of the limitation of long-range prediction and to make them aware that they need to watch for amendments to the outlooks. Regardless of the limitations, the predictions that are being issued by NMSA have a good skill score so far. Further studies are being carried out to identify the onset and succession of rainy periods so that drought can be identified and predicted as accurately as possible. Research is still under way to understand the causes of drought and improve the reliability of predictions.

Prediction of ENSO as one indicator of drought

The association between Ethiopia's seasonal rainfall and global features is a useful input for long-range prediction of the country's deficient rainfall and drought. According to a recent study (Tadesse 1996), it has been confirmed that there is a strong correlation between ENSO and droughts over the Horn of Africa. This study suggests that ENSO can be one of the indicators of drought over Ethiopia and adjoining regions. Studies are still under way to scientifically show how far these results are useful to predict and monitor droughts in a better way.

Modern methods of data acquisition and communication

Modern methods of data acquisition via satellites and remote sensing help provide early warnings of threats from drought and famine. The satellite pictures are very useful for detecting rain-producing systems over the country. For example, METEOSAT and NOAA (NDVI) satellite images are used in actual weather assessment and forecasting. The meteorological data distribution (MDD) of METEOSAT is also a practical example of efficient and cost-effective satellite communication. Therefore, the use of satellites in communication, especially in meteorological communication, should be further strengthened in national drought early warning and food security improvement in Ethiopia.

INFORMATION DISSEMINATION AND NATIONAL WARNING SYSTEM

Because of the growing public interest in and need for seasonal rainfall outlooks and drought prediction, NMSA is making the information available through newspapers, radio, and television. Daily summaries of weather reports and forecasts are also issued to different governmental (and, on request, nongovernmental) bodies as well as decision makers. These are followed by the regular agrometeorological ten-daily, monthly, and seasonal bulletins, which consist of necessary information, advisories, and outlooks for the next period.

The information is disseminated to many socioeconomic sectors, including the following:

1 Prime Minister's office and regional states' offices: These offices are issued daily weather reports and ten-daily, monthly, and seasonal outlooks for policy making and other decisions at the national level.
2 Disaster Prevention and Preparedness Commission (DPPC): DPPC is one of the most important customers using NMSA meteorological information in disaster early warning and relief activities. DPPC uses the information for assessing crop condition (using vegetation maps), making food security improvements, assessing pastoral condition, and determining water requirements to enable them to take appropriate action before human and material loss occurs.
3 Other governmental offices: These include offices such as the Ministries of Education, Health, and Water Resources.
4 International governmental and nongovernmental organisations: These include organisations like CARE (Ethiopia), Catholic Relief and Development Association (CRDA), Food and Agricultural Organization (FAO), ACTIONAID (Ethiopia), US Agency for International Development (USAID), European Economic Community (EEC), and French Veterinary Project.

It should be noted here that dissemination of drought early warning information is not an easy task. It might cause political, social, and economical problems. For example, the possibility that private economic sectors and individual merchants would withhold the supply of food to the market to take advantage of the situation makes it very complicated to issue drought predictions to the public. The normal procedure in this case is that NMSA gives the information to the Minister of Water Resources, who is in charge of NMSA, and advises the appropriate officials, who then decide whether to release the information, based on consideration of the possible impacts. The information dissemination might, in some cases, be delayed until top officials of the government decide that the time is appropriate.

FUTURE PROSPECTS AND REMARKS

Upgrading drought prediction methods

Prediction of drought is still a fascinating problem. Current knowledge needs to be improved, and all drought detection and monitoring methods have to be upgraded. Advances in technology should also allow the discovery of new methods. With the existing technology, new findings are emerging for monitoring and forecasting the global climate system in near-real time. Modern, fast communication technology is also being developed to allow distribution of climate information all over the world. Climate Information and Prediction Services (CLIPS), which was formulated by the World Meteorological Organization (WMO), is one example of this technology.

Investigations are needed to achieve better prediction of drought. All national meteorological services, the scientific community, and individual citizens should contribute to upgrading drought prediction. For example, considering ENSO as one of the predictors of drought, investigations are being carried out in NMSA to improve its understanding of the detailed effects of ENSO on Ethiopia's seasonal rainfall, with particular reference to drought. That is expected to upgrade Ethiopia's seasonal forecast capabilities in the future.

Raising awareness of disaster reduction at the level of decision and policy makers

Drought is undoubtedly one of the worst enemies of human beings. Governments should always be aware of and prepared for these calamities. The national meteorological services and other concerned early warning units should always ensure that policy makers and national and international communities that are responsible for natural disaster reduction are kept informed. The public should also be made aware, via the media, that they need to take appropriate actions. Long-term planning is necessary if any country is to deal with drought effectively. This has to be done collectively by different organisations associated with drought management and mitigation.

Therefore, governments as well as organisations and individuals concerned with disaster prevention should always be prepared to respond to the early identification of drought with both short-term preparedness measures and emergency plans and long-term preventive measures. Moreover, a considerable emphasis should always be given to impact assessment and response strategies to reduce societal vulnerability to drought.

International cooperation

International cooperation is essential to better prediction of drought by the national meteorological centres. The fast exchange of information in near-real time contributes to an improved forecast. Upgrading the knowledge and skill of the developing nations will inevitably involve the assistance of the international community.

CONCLUSIONS

The complex nature of the causes of drought, coupled with its adverse consequences, still provides a challenge to many scientists to investigate the problems of drought in Africa. In Ethiopia, the need to predict drought is very high because severe and prolonged droughts have multidimensional impacts on the progress and development of the country's economy, including suffering and death for thousands of human beings and animals.

The historical documentation of drought shows recurrent drought in Ethiopia for many years. Compared to the previous centuries (starting from 253 BC), drought appears to show an increasing trend since 1950. Could global climate change be responsible for this? Studies are under way to respond to this question. However, it is clear that global conditions caused by ocean–atmosphere interaction affect synoptic systems like pressure systems; location, intensity, and movement of the Inter Tropical Convergence Zone (ITCZ); cross-equatorial flow; easterly jet stream; and so forth. Several findings indicate that in ENSO episodic years, these systems change and have an influence on rainfall activities, leading to drought in areas like Ethiopia and flooding in other parts of the world. Thus, an ENSO condition that includes SOI and SST indices can be taken as an indicator of drought in Ethiopia. Nevertheless, a closer look at these systems is useful for qualitative assessment of seasonal rainfall and to predict the likely dry spells and their duration.

In Ethiopia, the current status of predictability of drought is reasonably good. However, with the advance of technology, it is expected to improve. It should be noted that not all parts of the country are affected by drought at the same time in the same year. Moreover, the severity and frequency of drought varies over different parts of the country. Thus, drought predictability in Ethiopia should further be designed so that predictions can be issued for particular areas and products can be tailored to users. Research activities that are under way today give hope for a better quality of predictions.

REFERENCES

Bekele, F. (1993) 'The use of ENSO information in Ethiopia', paper presented at the Workshop *Usable Science: Food Security, Early Warning and El Niño*, 25–28 October 1993, Budapest, Hungary.

Danielov, S.A. (1987) 'Preparation of drought probability map of Ethiopia', NMSA memo.

Degefu, W. (1987) 'Some aspects of drought in Ethiopia', in M.H. Glantz (ed.), *Drought and Hunger in Africa*, Cambridge: Cambridge University Press, pp. 23–36.

Haile, T. (1988) 'Causes and characteristics of drought in Ethiopia', *Ethiopian Journal of Agricultural Sciences* 10, 1–2: 85–97.

Mersha, E. (1996) 'Drought prone areas and crop failure risk in Ethiopia', paper presented at the Commission for Disaster Prevention and Preparedness (CDPP) regional training programme on early warning systems, 15–20 April 1996, Addis Ababa, Ethiopia.

NMSA (1996) *Drought Assessment in Ethiopia*, Vol. 1, No. 2, National Meteorological Services Agency, Addis Ababa, Ethiopia.

Tadesse, T. (1994) 'Summer monsoon seasonal rainfall of Ethiopia in ENSO episodic years', in *Proceedings of the International Conferences on Monsoon Variability and Prediction*, WMO/TD No. 619, pp 48–55.

—— (1996) 'ENSO – An indicator of drought over horn of Africa?', paper presented at the third *Kenya Meteorological Society Workshop on Meteorological Research and Applications and Services*, 7–11 October 1996, Mombasa, Kenya.

Yeshanew, A. (1989) 'Meteorological drought in Ethiopia – Chronology, characteristics, frequency, proneness, causes and impacts', paper presented at the *Second Workshop on Applicability of Environmental Physics and Meteorology in Africa*, 14–25 August 1989, Addis Ababa, Ethiopia.

PART III

MONITORING AND EARLY WARNING TECHNIQUES

10

INTEGRATED CLIMATE MONITORING FOR DROUGHT DETECTION

Kelly T. Redmond

WHY SHOULD WE MONITOR?

Droughts develop slowly There is thus no fundamental reason why the appearance of drought has to
come as a surprise. However, as with all accumulative
phenomena, without constant monitoring, an attendant
set of escalating indicators, and an effective means of
distributing the information, significant thresholds
can be crossed without notice. Monitoring is needed
for several interlinking purposes:

- To determine the current status of specific resources.
- To detect changes and long-term trends.
- To obtain knowledge of fundamental linkages and
  processes at work.
- To enable development and implementation of
  early warning indicators.
- To assess the efficacy of regulatory and mitigative
  actions.

Monitoring is an indispensable part of resource
management. Human and natural resources are significantly affected by variations in the physical
environment. Over time, water management decisions
can be no better than their input information.
Because we cannot now (nor will we ever be able to)
predict climate behaviour beyond some limited
degree, and because we cannot predict the consequences of climatic fluctuations on human and natural
systems beyond some other limited degree (even if we
had perfect climate forecasts), we are left with no
alternative but to continue to monitor.

A primary need in monitoring is to keep testing
how closely our perceptions match the observations
about the status of systems of interest. This is particularly necessary if buffering processes produce
temporal lags in system behaviour, or if remote conditions are relevant to local assessments. Both circumstances arise frequently in drought monitoring.
For example, summer irrigation water in arid regions
may have fallen months ago and far away as mountain
snowfall. In arid regions, water 'source' regions are
frequently out of sight (sometimes by hundreds or
thousands of kilometres) of the 'demand' regions.
The mismatch between perception and reality can
also be large in very dry or wet climates, in regions
that have large precipitation seasonality, or in regions
that have large horizontal or vertical gradients in
climate behaviour. For example, in a wet climate, such
as the US Pacific Northwest, it may 'seem' wet even
in a dry winter. Conversely, a wet month in an arid
climate may 'seem' dry. In other locations a wet (dry)
season in a lowland valley may be a dry (wet) season
in nearby mountains.

A second need in monitoring is to improve our
understanding of how natural processes function.
Statistical associations among long time series of
interrelated variables can lead the way to needed
insights into cause-and-effect relationships. Retrospective case studies of the consequences of particular
sequences of dry conditions, and post mortems on
recent episodes, also contribute to the knowledge
base. In many such cases, it is not clear until during
or even after an event, sometimes well after, that
retrospective monitoring information will be needed
to understand an episode. Many of the manifestations
of drought on living systems are subtle, and only
come to light long afterward.

Despite a long-recognised need for monitoring,

the United States still does not have a comprehensive national climate monitoring programme in place to meet the needs of all sectors (Diaz and Karl 1994).

WHAT DO WE WANT TO KNOW?

Which facets of natural and human systems should be monitored to adequately assess drought status? Some quantities are directly related to the physical state of the system, and others to the impacts of this physical state on human systems.

Physical environmental data

Atmospheric   The factors of most interest are those that affect the water budget of the soil. Naturally, precipitation is the primary quantity of interest. Evaporation and transpiration are the primary loss mechanisms for soil water. These processes are affected by temperature, wind speed, humidity, and solar radiation. Water in the soil contributes to deep aquifer recharge and discharge to streams.

Of the various atmospheric elements, precipitation is more closely tracked because its relative variability in time is greater than the relative variability of evapotranspiration. For example, Kunkel (personal communication 1990) has shown that over a forty-year time span in the US Corn Belt, the coefficient of variation (mean divided by standard deviation) for annual precipitation in Illinois is about 17 per cent, whereas the corresponding figure for potential evapotranspiration is only about 8 per cent, and the actual rate is somewhat lower than the potential rate. Precipitation is easier to measure and is more tangible and visible, and we often pay much more attention to it on that basis alone.

In topographically diverse climates, especially in midlatitudes, snow plays a very important role. In mountainous locations, a high percentage of the annual precipitation can fall as snow. The storage of water in snowpack at temperatures below freezing (sometimes referred to as 'nature's white reservoir') and the subsequent slow (usually) and controlled release via the melting process introduce a substantial lag. Snow can also play a significant role in extremely flat terrain (e.g., the Red River floods in North Dakota and Minnesota in 1997).

Hydrologic   The movement of water in and on the upper layers of the earth's surface can be measured in various ways. Streamflow is the most visible expression of this movement, and it is a primary measured quantity. Surface elevation of standing bodies of water and its time rate of change are two other desired quantities. Groundwater levels in wells change more slowly, but serve as an important indicator for drought. Soil moisture can be measured directly with various types of probes, but simple, cheap, reliable, and accurate devices to determine soil moisture profiles that can be deployed in quantity do not yet exist. The spatial variability in soil characteristics does not make this problem any easier.

Soil and vegetation   One way to estimate soil moisture status is to measure proxy quantities that depend on soil moisture, such as the health of plants. For example, various indices have been constructed that describe the health of 'green' plants by measuring the reflectivity of leaf surfaces, which respond differently at different wavelengths to water stress. The Normalized Difference Vegetative Index (NDVI) is one such measure in widespread use. These measurements can be made from aircraft or (usually) satellite, and thus consist of spatial snapshots.

Impact-related information

In addition to information about the state of the physical climate system, information is needed about the effects of variations in this system on water supplies, plants, and so forth. A medical analogy might be that a person notices symptoms such as tiredness, inattention, or irritability before causal factors become apparent; indeed, the detection of drought is not unlike other slow-onset phenomena such as a developing chronic disease. It is important to determine the linkages between causes (i.e., variations in the climate system) and the effects of these variations.

A wide array of economic, social, or environmental indicators, including market prices, unemployment, labour supply imbalances, water quality, wildlife mortality, wildfire incidence, and demographic changes throughout various human and natural systems, are available to assist with this task. The relative magnitude of quantitative measures of these phenomena, and of the causative climate system phenomena, provides clues to sensitivities and to inference of linkages.

Degree of summarisation

Needs exist for data that have been subject to different amounts of summarisation.

1 Original data. This includes the primary 'currency' in use in different disciplines. Examples for physical systems could include the daily precipitation amounts, weekly well water levels, and streamflow values; or, for human systems, the price of futures markets, number of bankruptcy declarations, or hydroelectric replacement costs, to name a few.

2 Products. This includes summarised or manipulated data, which in some way contain added value because the original data have either been manipulated or combined with other data. In mathematical terminology, products are functions of the original data. The simplest product could thus also be thought of as the original data themselves, where output equals input. Examples could include various drought indices (see below) such as the Standardized Precipitation Index or the Palmer Drought Index, or measures of economic loss. New combinations are constantly being invented, so it is important that there be access to the original data.

TEMPORAL VERSUS SPATIAL DESCRIPTIONS OF DROUGHT STATUS

At various times we want to know (1) what is happening through time at a given point, (2) what is happening across space at a given time, or even (3) how a spatial pattern has evolved in time. Unfortunately, we only have limited information for discrete points, not necessarily uniformly distributed, in space and time.

Temporal domain issues

Typically, in the time domain, we would like to know the answers to a series of related questions:

1 Where are we now?
2 How did we get here?
3 What is the historical perspective for the current situation?
4 What are the most likely outcomes from the current situation?

Drought doubt

The first two questions posed above are interconnected. It is sometimes difficult to portray time-scale-dependent behaviour to decision makers. It is quite possible to simultaneously experience wet and dry conditions at different time scales; in fact, this situation has often been observed. For example, an extended wet spell (the last year or two) may have been interrupted by a short but very dry period (the last month or two). The extended wet spell may itself be occurring in a climatically dry regime (the last decade or two). All of the above circumstances matter, but for different reasons for different sectors. Are we in drought, or not?

The answer to such a question is usually ambiguous. Different parts of the various human and natural systems are responding to climatic phenomena on different time scales. A residential well of 100 m depth will not respond to yesterday's precipitation. A dryland wheat crop may see severe water stress from a sixty-day dry period while a neighbouring irrigated field is green and healthy because of a previous wet winter in far-off mountain headwaters. A dry period during critical phenological stages (e.g., planting, spring greenup, seed filling) can be more damaging than the same dry period a month earlier or later. In the western United States, very dry summers may have little impact on those users with senior water rights and access to stored water accumulated over the past twelve to twenty-four months. Moist volcanic islands with porous soil can quickly lapse into drought conditions when normally abundant rains fail to materialise (e.g., Giambelluca *et al.* 1991), whereas other soils are not as affected by the same event. What is drought from one standpoint is not drought from another.

Drought can be broadly defined as a shortage of water to meet present needs. Since 'need' varies considerably from sector to sector, different time and space scales are important for different purposes. Drought monitoring should be designed to address the entire spectrum of needs. These vary greatly, depending on the seasonality and the horizontal and vertical gradients in precipitation, the phase (liquid or solid) of the water resource, soil properties and moisture content, underlying geology, land use practices, and other conditions. It is quite possible for one sector to be experiencing drought on its own terms while another sector in essentially the same location is relatively unaffected. Drought status is *sector-dependent*, and it therefore seems pointless to adopt a detailed specific definition of drought. The definitional question has been dealt with extensively elsewhere (e.g., Dracup and Lee 1981, Dracup *et al.* 1980a and 1980b, Jackson 1981, Wilhite and Glantz 1987).

Establishing historical perspectives

It is important to understand the historical context for current conditions. Is the current situation extremely rare, or something frequent enough that we shouldn't be surprised by its presence? Several criteria must be satisfied if we are to adequately assess historical perspective.

1   The records should be homogeneous in time. Whether that record is climatic, economic, or some other type, consistent methodology should be employed in measuring or determining the quantity in question. This has been a constant concern in climatology, and a difficult issue. It is even more difficult in social and economic matters, where it is much harder to hold other factors constant.
2   Records should be as long as possible. A century of consistent records is very desirable. Because record lengths vary from station to station, one or more particularly noteworthy past droughts may not be present in a shorter record, which can lead to inconsistencies in the interpretation of the historical perspective for a given current situation. This becomes a very important design issue when developing structural responses to water management needs.
3   Even a century is a fairly short time, and it is helpful to know how representative the historical record is of longer time periods. This can only be done with proxy evidence. For example, Hughes and Brown (1992) used sequoia tree rings to infer that the twentieth century appears to be the wettest in the Sierra Nevada in the past 2,000 years. Although confirmatory studies are desirable, such perspectives are invaluable.
4   The notion that climate transits between 'regimes' of

behaviour on the scale of decades has recently regained popularity (e.g., Mantua *et al.* 1997, Latif and Barnett 1996, Zhang and Levitus 1997). Climate fluctuations (lasting a few years), regimes (lasting a few decades), and natural or human-induced trends (decade to century scale) may all be present at once. If so, the statistical properties of climate elements, which include drought characteristics, may be drawn from two or more populations.

These climatic histories should be free from artificial trends and other temporal inhomogeneities, such as changes in location or observational practices. Since this information can seldom be developed adequately in a short-term emergency mode, the necessary background information must be prepared ahead of time, and the monitoring system must be up and running well before the problem develops.

Spatial domain issues

Ideally, we would like to be able to assess drought status at all points in a geographical domain of interest. Because a limited number of point measurements in time are available, both topography and the physical characteristics of precipitation-producing systems place practical limits on the extent of spatial interpolation that can successfully occur.

Convective precipitation often has a significant degree of fine structure on spatial scales of a few kilometres, even over flat terrain. To some extent, the movement of individual cells, and their tendency toward organisation into lines and other groupings, smear out the effects of the small dimensions of the active precipitation-producing regions, but these effects are partially counteracted by the rapid growth and decay cycle of the individual components. For spotty summertime convection, observing networks would have to be very dense to capture all of the spatial variability.

In topographically diverse terrain, stratiform and convective precipitation both can exhibit very strong horizontal and elevational gradients in both amount and frequency. Only in a few specialised cases, covering small watersheds, are there dense surface observing networks. In general, however, the number of surface-based sampling points is usually not adequate to fully interpolate to a few-kilometre scale. In addition, because of elevational effects, the background reference climatologies can vary greatly (by one or two orders of magnitude) over relatively short horizontal distances (10–20 km). In contrast to flat terrain, there is more tendency toward 'anchoring' at preferred spots. The elevational relationships to climate statistics vary from place to place and season to season, and there is typically a dearth of the basic information with the required spatial density on the fine scale needed to establish these relationships.

In some parts of the world (e.g., the eastern United States), new tools such as the National Weather Service WSR-88D (NEXRAD) radars can give reasonable estimates of convective precipitation on a few-kilometre spatial scale. But in other areas, particularly those that are arid or topographically diverse, these estimates have serious problems. As an example, in the Reno (Nevada) area, with present algorithms, significant radar underestimations and overestimations (multiples of ten or one hundred) have been documented in winter stratiform and summer convective situations, respectively. In other radarless parts of the world, or in mountainous regions, such options are not available. Even in locations where reliable and credible estimates are produced, such products are only available for the past few years, historical probabilities on climatic time scales do not exist on the same spatial scale, and rapid access to the high volume of data poses an almost insurmountable problem with present technology.

ACCESS TO INFORMATION

Much more climate information exists than is commonly recognised. However, unless there is access to this information, it is of little value. Conversely, the most readily accessible data and information is not always the most appropriate or accurate; rapid access to bad information is no better than slow access to good information.

This point is particularly germane to precipitation. Measurements of precipitation that are both automated (and therefore readily transmissible) and accurate (enough to meet a wide variety of additional nondrought climatological needs) have proven extremely difficult to make. This is especially true for frozen precipitation, whose importance ranges from nil in tropical climates to overriding in northern or elevated climates where streamflow is driven largely by snowmelt. The least expensive and most cost-effective all-purpose measurements are generally regarded to be those made manually with a wind-shielded gage. They are also the most numerous and have the longest records, the latter an important characteristic for drought monitoring. The principal difficulty with manual measurements is the lack of a rapid and reliable method to introduce the values into an efficient electronic transmission system without introducing new errors, and the further coordination needed to place the values in proper historical context. A frequent complication in many cases (for example, the US cooperative climate network) is the administrative separation between the observational functions and the storage, distribution, and analysis functions.

The meteoric rise in the popularity and use of the World Wide Web makes this a natural choice for a tool for improving the distribution of drought-related weather observations. The technology for initial transference (brief human involvement is still needed) of manual measurements into electronic format, via either voice synthesisers or web-based form entry, is well within reach. Once in this form, many more possibilities arise. The Unified Climate Access Network, an initiative involving regional and national climate entities within the US Departments of Agriculture and Commerce, is attempting to define how the necessary coordination would be accomplished in a practical setting.

Nevertheless, the collection and flow of current climatic, hydrologic, and vegetative information; their merging with historical archives; the subsequent distillation of this combination into products; and the dissemination of these products must take place smoothly if the output is to be helpful in the decision-making process.

VISUALISATION AND PRESENTATION OF INFORMATION

A related problem to data access is its form of presentation. How do we portray this complexity to decision and policy makers? Simpler methods are better, to aid typically overwhelmed decision makers, but oversimplification is dangerous, too. If information is not presented effectively, its content and implications may not be fully understood or appreciated, leading to less than optimal use, or even disuse or misuse. To illustrate, where hydrologic lags are significant (for example, snowmelt systems) and a strong seasonal cycle is present (wet winters and arid summers), and if the current situation (for example, summer water availability) has its roots in past behaviour (for example, winter snowfall), it is helpful for the presentation format to strengthen the perception that relief is climatologically not likely in the near future.

As noted earlier, drought status may simultaneously show conflicting or paradoxical behaviour at different time scales. Such complexity should be preserved as much as practical without becoming incomprehensible to managers and decision makers. Thoughtfully designed graphical portrayals of such circumstances are likely to be considerably more effective than textual or narrative presentations. The Standardized Precipitation Index, discussed below and in Chapter 12, represents one attempt to directly address this issue. The use of colour and animation, using the capabilities of the World Wide Web, offers a substantial prospect for improving the presentation of complex drought information, including the evolution that has resulted in the present situation, and the likelihood of various outcomes.

Although well understood by the climatology and hydrology community, many issues concerning drought and its perception are often interpreted for the public in simplistic or unnecessarily fuzzy terms, especially when hydrologic lags, remote water sources, artificial manipulation of water systems by human actions, or multiple time scale climatic phenomena are acting to differentially affect water supplies to different sectors. Since decision makers, especially in the political arena, tend to originate from this broad pool of citizens and respond to its perceptions, the role of public education in fostering a deeper understanding of drought is clearly both very desirable and also a continuing long-term challenge.

THE USE OF INDICES

One way to depict situations in simplified ways is to develop indices that distill complex behaviour into one or a few numbers. The widespread adoption of this approach is indicative of its broad appeal. Some of the desirable properties of indices are elaborated in Redmond (1991). As noted there, all indices have strengths and weaknesses, and no one index is suitable to address every user and use. However, if their limitations are borne in mind, indices can play a very useful role. Nonetheless, everyday experience indicates that these limitations are not always remembered or heeded.

The Palmer Drought Index family

Palmer (1965) formulated a drought index for use in the US Great Plains, based on a simplified water balance. One intent was to normalise to the background climatology so that values were more directly comparable across differing climates. Variants such as the Palmer Drought Severity Index and Palmer Hydrological Drought Index have been defined, differing largely in their degree of 'memory' of past climate behaviour. The computations are very nonlinear, and the method was the subject of an excellent critique by Alley (1984). For practical reasons, the calculation is driven only by monthly precipitation and temperature. Guttman (1991) has investigated the sensitivity of the Palmer Index to isolated climatic 'shocks' (unbroken strings of specified climatological monthly values interrupted by a single month with unusual precipitation or temperature). His studies reveal a wide variety of unusual and even bizarre responses, some of which occur many months or even a few years after the causative event. These undesirable characteristics are not widely known, and the method has come into wide use, in large part because of the lack of a suitable substitute, and also because it is considered to be a 'known quantity'.

The Standardized Precipitation Index

McKee et al. (1993 and 1995), in a study of the characteristic time scales of the Palmer Index at more than 1,000 US stations, found that the Palmer Index was highly correlated to precipitation accumulated over the past six to twelve months, depending on season and location, especially in the eight- to twelve-month time frame. Temperature seemed to add little information. This motivated them to propose a Standardized Precipitation Index (SPI). An incomplete gamma function is fitted to the distribution of nonzero monthly values (zero values are accounted for separately). Points on the cumulative distribution function thus defined are then mapped to their corresponding points on the cumulative distribution function for a normal distribution, which could be interpreted in terms of the number of equivalent standard deviations for a normal distribution.

The SPI calculation is much more straightforward than the Palmer, and depends only on precipitation. Subsidiary values from the SPI calculation address the five main quantities identified by McKee (personal communication 1993) as being most requested by users for water supply issues:

• What is the absolute accumulated precipitation amount?
• What is the absolute accumulated precipitation departure from expected?
• What is the percentage of average precipitation?
• How frequently does the accumulated precipitation amount occur?
• What is a simple measure that can encapsulate the above information?

In addition, the SPI is capable of portraying situations that are simultaneously wet on one time scale and dry on another.

The capabilities associated with the SPI can be illustrated with examples taken from Oklahoma Climate Division 4 (West Central). That area experienced a significant winter/spring drought in 1995–6. That was followed by a very wet late summer. Figures 10.1–10.5 illustrate the five quantities referred to above. The accumulated precipitation, accruing backward in time from the end of March 1997 (at the left) up to seventy-two months earlier (on the right) is shown in Figure 10.1. Note that almost no precipitation accumulated from twelve to eighteen months ago, and also that little has accumulated in the previous six months. But is this above or below normal?

The accumulated precipitation departure from long-term means (102 years in this case) is shown for each time scale in Figure 10.2. Thus, the latest month has been about an inch below normal, the latest two months (combined) have been near average, and the

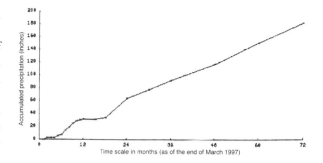

Figure 10.1 Accumulated precipitation over the seventy-two months extending back in time from the end of March 1997. West Central Oklahoma climate division. Expressed in inches

latest six months have been slightly below average. However, the latest seven months were much more above average than the latest six, and the latest eight months and nine months even more above average. The upward slope of the departures as one progresses to the right indicates that the months seven, eight, and nine months ago were well above average. The declining slope from ten to eighteen months indicates that those months averaged below normal, and, finally, the past year and a half has been rather close to average, masking the significant variability that occurred during that interval. It can also be seen that the past several years are quite a bit wetter than the century-long average, even out to the past six years. These amounts are given in absolute units – what about their relative size?

Figure 10.3 shows the percentage of average

Figure 10.2 Departure of recent precipitation from Figure 10.1 from long-term 102-year average precipitation for each time scale. Expressed in inches

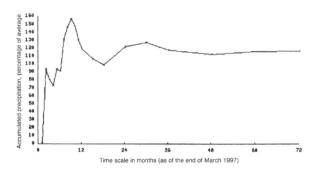

Figure 10.3 Accumulated precipitation shown in Figure 10.1 divided by the corresponding long-term mean, expressed as per cent

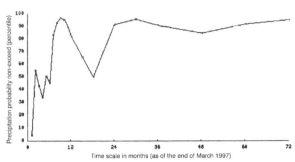

Figure 10.4 Probability that the accumulated precipitation from Figure 10.1 will not be exceeded in a randomly selected year, for each time scale, expressed in per cent. 0 = lowest rank, 100 = highest rank

precipitation for each time scale. It can be seen that the one-inch deficit for the latest one month is near zero per cent of average, and that the very slight deficit for the latest two months from Figure 10.2 translates into about 95 per cent of average for February–March. The precipitation for the latest ten months is about 160 per cent of average, and for the latest eighteen months it is near 100 per cent. Over the past several years, totals have been about 10–15 per cent higher than the average over the entire historical record.

Figure 10.4 portrays the rank, or the likelihood, that a randomly selected month from the record would have a lower value (i.e, the percentile). The near-zero value for the most recent month is within the lowest 5 per cent of the distribution. (In some arid locations and during some or all of the year, zero monthly precipitation is the most common value, but the SPI accounts for this.) The latest ten months (June–March) are in the upper 5 per cent, compared with all other June–March periods in the past 102 years, and this includes the recently concluded very dry month. The past eighteen months are average, a value that is exceeded about 50 per cent of the time, as one would expect. The past sixty and seventy-two months are among the 10 per cent wettest such 5- to 6-year-long periods recorded. So, a wet regime has been interrupted by a dry period occurring some twelve to eighteen months ago, and later by a very wet period last summer (about seven to ten months ago).

Finally, the SPI (Figure 10.5) shows corresponding ups and downs, but the values are rescaled to be comparable or akin to standard deviations.

Thus, a value of plus or minus 1.0 occurs about once in three years, and a value of plus or minus 2.0 should occur about once in twenty years.

A map of SPI for the time scale of one month is shown in Figure 10.6. The SPI value is very low for the division discussed above in west central Oklahoma for just this one month, but that is different from claiming that a drought is present. Whether drought is considered to be present in this case depends very much on which sector is making the assessment.

On the basis of studies by McKee *et al.* (1993 and 1995) and Guttman (1991, 1998 and 1999) and Guttman *et al.* (1992), the National Drought Mitigation Center and the Western Regional Climate Center have begun to place more emphasis on the SPI than on the Palmer Index family (Redmond *et al.* 1997). With the wide variety of climates and

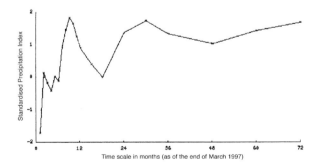

Figure 10.5 Standardized Precipitation Index for each time scale for the same precipitation data as in Figure 10.1. Dimensionless

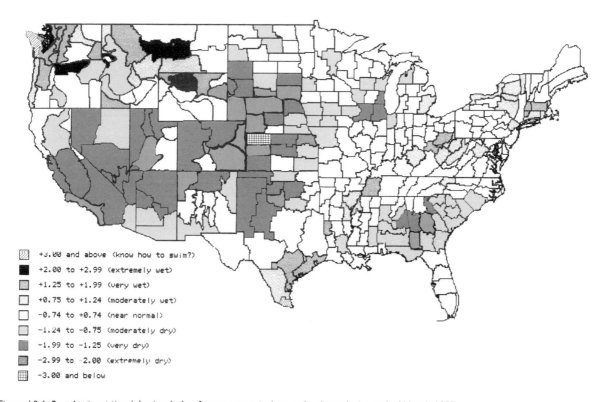

Figure 10.6 Standardized Precipitation Index for one-month time scale, through the end of March 1997

Legend:
- +3.00 and above (know how to swim?)
- +2.00 to +2.99 (extremely wet)
- +1.25 to +1.99 (very wet)
- +0.75 to +1.24 (moderately wet)
- -0.74 to +0.74 (near normal)
- -1.24 to -0.75 (moderately dry)
- -1.99 to -1.25 (very dry)
- -2.99 to -2.00 (extremely dry)
- -3.00 and below

climate behaviours in the West, the SPI seems particularly suitable as a monitoring tool.

Surface Water Supply Index

Another index that is in use is the Surface Water Supply Index (SWSI) (Schafer and Dezman 1982). This measure was formulated for use in mountainous areas where snowpack plays a significant role. Percentiles of seasonal (winter) precipitation, snowpack, streamflow, and reservoir storage are determined separately and combined into a single weighted index, which is scaled and constrained to lie in the range –4 to +4, a typical range of the Palmer Index. The question of how to determine the weights remains open; they need to vary during the year to account for elements such as snowpack, which disappears in summer, or for elements that have small or artificially manipulated values, such as reservoir storage. How to combine the effects of large reservoirs with small

relative variability and small reservoirs with large variability in the same drainage basin is also a problem. The SWSI is most sensitive to changes in its constituent values near the centre of its range, and least sensitive near the extremes. This measure is in use at this writing for drought monitoring in several states, including Oregon, Montana, and Colorado.

Normalized Difference Vegetative Index

Chlorophyll absorbs most light in the middle of the visible spectrum. At wavelengths of light between 500 nm and 700 nm, centred on green, only about 20 per cent is reflected. However, at longer wavelengths, in the near infrared from 700 nm to 1,300 nm, chlorophyll reflects about 60 per cent of the incident light. Several National Oceanic and Atmospheric Administration (NOAA) satellites in near polar orbits have been equipped with the Advanced Very High Resolution Radiometer (AVHRR), which can measure brightness in five spectral bands. Channel 1 senses radiation in the 580–680 nm wavelength band, and Channel 2 senses radiation in the 730–1,100 nm radiation band. The difference in brightness between these two bands (Ch 2 minus Ch 1) is a measure of how much chlorophyll is contained in a pixel, which averages about 1 km on a side. Because changing relations between illumination, surface slope, and aspect cause slight changes in the overall radiation sensed by the satellite, this difference can be divided by the sum ('normalized'), and a new index can be defined, the Normalized Difference Vegetative Index (see, for example, Tarpley *et al.* 1984), as

$$NDVI = (Ch\ 2\ minus\ Ch\ 1) / (Ch\ 2\ plus\ Ch\ 1)$$

The index is more positive the more dense and green the plant canopy, with NDVI values typically 0.1–0.6. For this reason the NDVI is sometimes called a greenness index. Rock and bare ground have NDVI near zero, and clouds, water, and snow have NDVI less than zero.

Weekly images of the surface of the earth which consist of mapped NDVI values can be prepared. To be useful for drought monitoring, allowance must be made for the natural differences in vegetative type associated with background climate. Desert vegetation is always less green than lush forests, and has more soil in between plants, so its NDVI naturally will be less. Some plants, such as grasses, mature and turn brown each year, and thus have a seasonal cycle. With about a decade of observations, an approximate daily climatology can be formed, and current NDVI at each pixel subtracted from the long-term average for this time of year at that pixel, to obtain a departure from average. These departures can then be mapped. Complications to simple straightforward interpretation can arise from slow trends in satellite orbit characteristics, differential degradation or drift of sensors, long-term wet or dry spells, trends in scene blockage by clouds, and other conditions. Clouds pose a constant problem, and a number of adjustments are made to account for their effects. An example is shown in Figure 10.7 (see colour section between pp. 160–1) for the week 18–24 April 1997. This shows that much of Texas, Minnesota, and North Dakota, and western Pennsylvania, are

considerably greener than average for this time of year. The white areas had significant snow or cloud cover during the orbits when the satellite passed overhead.

INTEGRATED CLIMATE MONITORING

Utilisation and coordination of existing networks and resources

It is most unlikely that dense new regional or national networks will be deployed for the express purpose of monitoring for drought and other climate phenomena. Even if this is done, the establishment of the requisite historical context for a new network is usually difficult and laborious. In relatively flat terrain, the station separation of the US national cooperative climate network, typically 40 km, appears adequate. In mountainous terrain, with an abundance of sharp climate gradients, each climate zone needs to be sampled adequately. Valley and mountain stations often do not experience the same climate anomalies, even when separated by only 5 or 10 km, and sometimes their respective climatic departures from average can be radically different. In such regions, the problem of establishing the historical context, which can vary significantly on scales of a few kilometres or less, is much harder.

A western US prototype

Recognising recent fiscal constraints, aware of changing interagency interrelationships and possibilities, and faced with rapidly developing new technologies, a group of interested representatives met at a workshop preceding the Western Drought Conference held in May 1994 in Portland, Oregon, to discuss ways of coordinating monitoring activities in the western United States (see Redmond 1994a for a summary). In this region, several major federal networks, funded by the US Departments of Commerce, Interior, and Agriculture, are in operation:

1 The National Weather Service daily historical cooperative network. About 2,500 current sites (including Alaska and Hawaii). All-purpose manual climatological stations, mostly temperature and

precipitation, with records stretching a century or more. Average elevation 3,300 feet.

2 The Bureau of Land Management/US Forest Service (custodians for about 90 per cent of the sites) Remote Automatic Weather Station/Remote Environmental Monitoring Station (RAWS/REMS, hereafter RAWS) network. About 700 current sites with hourly measurements of the typical meteorological elements (wind, temperature, humidity, precipitation). Average elevation 4,600 feet.

3 The Natural Resources Conservation Service Snowpack Telemetry (SNOTEL) network. About 700 current automated sites for measuring and reporting daily snowpack, precipitation, and temperature in high mountain headwaters basins, with records of about twenty years. Average elevation 7,100 feet.

Other smaller or regional networks also exist, such as the Bureau of Reclamation Agrimet Network in the Pacific Northwest. Although maps (Figures 10.8–10.11) of the networks show a high density of sites, a look at the elevational characteristics of the three largest networks (Table 10.1) shows that their stations are concentrated in different ecological zones.

The networks mentioned above are managed by different agencies for different purposes, have different pathways for data flow, vary widely in real time accessibility, measure different properties of the climate system with different instrument packages, have differing types of station history files, treat quality control in quite different ways, were not coordinated in their development or operation, and heretofore have only been accessible separately.

Before the data can be combined for climate monitoring purposes, various network-specific limitations must be addressed. The cooperative network data are extremely useful, but very cumbersome to obtain within a day or two. The SNOTEL network needs a better station history, more rapid access to the historical data base, and some quality control (now under way). The RAWS network also needs improvements to its station histories, a thorough quality control of the historical data base, and a derived data base (daily from hourly) for more

Figure 10.8 Locations of National Weather Service cooperative network daily observations in the eleven western states, December 1991

Figure 10.9 Locations of Bureau of Land Management/US Forest Service Remote Automatic Weather Stations (RAWS) in the eleven western states, March 1994

Figure 10.10 Locations of Natural Resources Conservation Service SNOTEL sites in the eleven western US states, March 1994

Figure 10.11 Locations of Bureau of Reclamation Agrimet stations, a regional network, February 1994

Table 10.1 Percentage of current stations in various elevational bands in the western United States (including Alaska/Hawaii). NWS Cooperative Network values are from December 1991, RAWS values are from June 1994, SNOTEL values are from 1993

Elevation (feet)	Observational network		RAWS		SNOTEL	
	%	Sum	%	Sum	%	Sum
−300–1,000	27.7	27.7	8.0	8.0	2.2	2.2
1,000–2,000	9.3	37.0	7.0	15.0	2.6	4.8
2,000–3,000	10.3	47.3	11.3	26.3	1.1	5.9
3,000–4,000	10.1	57.4	13.2	39.5	4.2	10.1
4,000–5,000	16.1	73.5	17.1	56.6	7.5	17.6
5,000–6,000	11.3	84.8	16.3	72.9	11.6	29.2
6,000–7,000	8.3	93.1	12.7	85.6	13.4	42.6
7,000–8,000	3.8	96.9	7.0	92.6	16.0	58.6
8,000–9,000	2.0	98.9	5.4	98.0	17.3	75.9
9,000–10,000	0.7	99.6	1.5	99.5	14.9	90.8
10,000–15,000	0.2	99.8	0.5	100.0	9.2	100.0
Number of stations		2,514		743		544
Average elevation		3,300		4,600		7,100

Source: Redmond 1994a
Notes: % = percentage of stations. Sum = cumulative sum of percentages

efficient access. Daily background climatologies are needed from all sites for all networks, adjusted to allow for the relatively short records from the SNOTEL and RAWS networks.

In addition, not all networks measure the same elements, or in the same way. For example, among the three networks covering the west, only RAWS measures wind and humidity. All measure precipitation, but RAWS precipitation is unusable when temperatures are below freezing. All of the networks are capable of providing maximum and minimum temperature information, or a close approximation; RAWS only reads once an hour, and cooperative climate stations more often record from morning to morning rather than evening to evening. Agrimet quantities, including wind, are measured at just 2 m above ground to be near the plant canopy.

The use of multiple overlapping networks for climate monitoring has several considerations not unlike those for quality control (see Redmond 1994b: 3–5). In particular, a very substantial amount of infrastructure development is needed before starting: sufficient storage, efficient access, quality metadata, interagency coordination, smooth pathways for data flow, ingestors to process incoming data, and ways to produce and display products. The entire process should be automated to the extent possible.

In spite of these difficulties, much of the basic structure for making this capability a reality already exists. There is a desire to cooperate and agreement among the agencies that the goal is worthwhile (Redmond 1994a). Many of the supportive activities needed are under way in some fashion. At least in the West, there is strong incentive and a burgeoning demand for environmental monitoring information for a growing variety of natural resource management needs. Efforts are proceeding to reach the goals of integrated climate monitoring.

DATA ISSUES

Several needs must be met for integrated climate monitoring to be successful. A linked infrastructure is needed to obtain recent or current data in a timely manner. In addition to hardware and software, and network connections, this entails people-to-people and agency-to-agency coordination. Data quality

needs to meet standards, and methods to assess data quality should be in place. A flagging system is very helpful. Retrospective (for the historical data base) and operational (for the incoming data stream) quality control can be handled separately. Descriptive information about the station ('metadata') constitutes a separate area of concern.

Unique site identification numbers need to be assigned to every station in every network; often this necessitates substantial consultation with network managers. Typically, there are numerous points of disagreement between the actual contents of a climatic data base and what the metadata indicate ought to be present. Like the climate data it pertains to, the metadata data base must exist in digital form, should be accessible, should be accurate, and needs to be kept current. The development of adequate metadata is not trivial, but is often treated as being a relatively simple and straightforward matter to handle, and the magnitude of work needed is almost always underestimated. See Redmond (1994b) for elaboration on these points.

LONG-TERM COMMITMENT

Above all, for climate monitoring to be most effective, a long-term commitment is needed to sustain the activity. If the view is adopted that climate never strictly repeats and thus that climatic processes are non-stationary (e.g., Bryson 1997), there is no point at which we can say that we have finally monitored enough and can stop. The need will exist indefinitely. To ensure the necessary degree of confidence that the variability that monitoring activities bring to our attention is truly a feature of the climate system, rather than an artifact of the observational system, it is imperative that sufficient resources be allocated to the monitoring enterprise to be able to distinguish between the behaviour of the observed and the behaviour of the observer. This is accomplished most effectively if monitoring, like quality control, is viewed as an end-to-end process, and not simply as a series of isolated, disconnected activities. A strong appreciation of the need for consistency through time should guide all such efforts. Environmental monitoring systems function as our extended human sensory system, and ultimately all that we know about the world is acquired or validated through observation.

REFERENCES

Alley, W.M. (1984) 'The Palmer Drought Severity Index: Limitations and assumptions', *Journal of Climate and Applied Meteorology* 23: 1,100–9.

Bryson, R.A. (1997) 'The paradigm of climatology: An essay', *Bulletin of the American Meteorological Society* 78: 449–55.

Diaz, H.F. and Karl, T.R. (eds) (1994) 'Information needs for precipitation-sensitive systems', Boulder, CO, 4–6 May 1993, Workshop report, *NOAA Environmental Watch Report 94.1*, May 1994.

Dracup, J.A. and Lee, K.S. (1981) 'Reply to D.R. Jackson comment on "On the definition of droughts"', *Water Resources Research* 17, 4: 1,240.

Dracup, J.A., Lee, K.S., and Paulson, E.G. Jr. (1980a) 'On the statistical characteristics of drought events', *Water Resources Research* 16, 2: 289–96.

——— (1980b) 'On the definition of droughts', *Water Resources Research* 16, 2: 297–302.

Giambelluca, T.W., Nullett, M.A., Ridgley, M.A., Eyre, P.R., Moncur, J.E.T., and Price, S. (1991) *Drought in Hawaii*, Honolulu: Commission on Water Resource Management, Department of Land and Natural Resources, State of Hawaii.

Guttman, N.B. (1991) 'A sensitivity analysis of the Palmer Hydrologic Drought Index', *Water Resources Bulletin* 27, 5: 797–807.

——— (1998) 'Comparing the Palmer Drought Index and the Standardized Precipitation Index', *Journal of the American Water Resources Association* 34, 1: 113–21.

——— (1999) "Accepting the Standardized Precipitation Index: A calculation algorithm", *Journal of the American Water Resources Association* 35, 2: 311–22.

Guttman, N.B., Wallis, J.R. and Hosking, J.R.M. (1992) "Spatial Comparability of the Palmer Drought Severity Index", *Water Resources Bulletin* 28, 6: 1,111–19.

Hughes, M.K. and Brown, P.M. (1992) 'Drought frequency in central California since 101 B.C. recorded in giant sequoia tree rings', *Climate Dynamics* 6: 161–7.

Jackson, D.R. (1981) 'Comment on "On the definition of droughts" by J.A. Dracup *et al.*', *Water Resources Research* 17, 4: 1,239.

Latif, M. and Barnett, T.P. (1996) 'Decadal climate variability over the North Pacific and North America: Dynamics and predictability', *Journal of Climate* 9: 2,407–23.

Mantua, N.J., Hare, S.R., Zhang, Y., Wallace, J.M., and Francis, R.C. (1997) 'A Pacific interdecadal climate oscillation with impacts on salmon production', *Bulletin of the American Meteorological Society*.

McKee, T.B., Doesken, N.J., and Kleist, J. (1993) 'The relation of drought frequency and duration to time scales', *Proceedings, AMS Eighth Conference on Applied Climatology*, 17–22 January 1993, Anaheim, CA, pp. 179–84.

——— (1995) 'Drought monitoring with multiple time scales', *Proceedings, Ninth Conference on Applied Climatology*, 15–20 January 1995, Dallas, TX, pp. 233–6.

Palmer, W.C. (1965) 'Meteorologic drought,' *Research Paper* No. 45, US Department of Commerce, Weather Bureau, Washington, DC.

Redmond, K.T. (1991) 'Climate monitoring and indices', in D.A. Wilhite, D.A. Wood, and P.A. Kay (eds), *Drought Management and Planning: Proceedings of the Seminar and Workshop*, IDIC Technical Report Series 91–1, Lincoln, NE: International Drought Information Center, University of Nebraska, pp. 29–33.

——— (1994a) 'Workshop report: An integrated climate monitoring system for the West', in D.A. Wilhite and D.A. Wood (eds), *Proceedings, Drought Management in a Changing West: New Directions for Water Policy*, IDIC Technical Report Series 94–1, Lincoln, NE: International Drought Information Center, University of Nebraska, pp. 1–17.

——— (1994b) 'Quality control of manual fire weather data', *Western Regional Climate Centre Report #94–01*, Western Regional Climate Centre, Desert Research Institute, Reno, NV.

Redmond, K.T., Svoboda, M., and Stimson, J. (1997) 'Operational use of the Standardized Precipitation Index for drought monitoring', *Proceedings, Thirteenth Conference on Hydrology*, Long Beach, CA, 2–7 February 1997, pp. 21–2.

Shafer, B.A. and Dezman, L.E. (1982) 'Development of a Surface Water Supply Index (SWSI) to assess the severity of drought conditions in snowpack runoff areas', in *Proceedings of the 50th Annual Western Snow Conference*, pp. 164–75.

Tarpley, J.D., Schneider, S.R., and Money, R.L. (1984) 'Global vegetation indices from the NOAA–7 meteorological satellite', *Journal of Climate and Applied Meteorology* 23: 491–4.

Wilhite, D.A. and Glantz, M.H. (1987) 'Understanding the drought phenomenon: The role of drought definitions', in D.A. Wilhite and W.E. Easterling (eds), *Planning for Drought: Toward a Reduction of Societal Vulnerability*, Boulder, CO: Westview Press, pp. 11–27.

Zhang, R.H. and Levitus, S. (1997) 'Structure and cycle of decadal variability of upper-ocean temperature in the North Pacific', *Journal of Climate* 10: 710–27.

11
DROUGHT INDICES
A review

Richard R. Heim, Jr

THE NATURE OF THE PROBLEM

Some numerical standard is needed for comparing droughts from region to region, as well as for comparing historical drought events. However, the considerable disagreement that has existed, and still exists, about the definition of drought makes it difficult to devise a universal index for the phenomenon. Furthermore, drought's characteristics and the wide range of economic sectors it has an impact on make its effects difficult, though not impossible, to quantify.

The World Meteorological Organization (WMO) defines a drought index as 'an index which is related to some of the cumulative effects of a prolonged and abnormal moisture deficiency' (WMO 1992). When devising a drought index, Friedman (1957) noted that it should meet four criteria: (1) the time scale should be appropriate to the problem at hand; (2) the index should be a quantitative measure of large-scale, long-continuing drought conditions; (3) the index should be applicable to the problem being studied; and (4) a long accurate past record of the index should be available or computable. The first and third criteria are somewhat related. For example, what is useful for long-term paleoclimatic studies (e.g., indices based on glaciological and alluvial evidence, oceanic and lake sediments, tree-ring and pollen analysis, or proxy evidence such as historical documents and annual crop yield) would not be applicable for the operational monitoring of drought because of the nature of paleoclimatic indices and the difficulty involved in collecting paleoclimatic data on a real-time operational basis.

EARLY DROUGHT INDICES

Common to all types of drought is the fact that they originate from a deficiency of precipitation that results in water shortage for some activity or some group (Wilhite and Glantz 1985). Reliable observations of rainfall became available about two centuries ago. As a result, practically all drought indices and drought definitions used this variable either singly or in combination with other meteorological elements (WMO 1975).

Early drought definitions readily incorporated some measure of precipitation over a given period of time (Tannehill 1947, Friedman 1957, WMO 1975, Wilhite and Glantz 1985). A drought would exist if the criteria were met, and the index would then be a measure of the drought's duration and/or intensity.

For example, during the first decade of the twentieth century, the US Weather Bureau identified drought as occurring during any period of twenty-one or more days with rainfall 30 per cent or more below normal for the period (Henry 1906, Steila 1987). A drought measure frequently used at that time was accumulated precipitation deficit, or accumulated departure from normal. Other examples of early criteria include:

1 fifteen consecutive days with no rain;
2 twenty-one days or more with precipitation less than one-third of normal;
3 annual precipitation that is less than 75 per cent of normal;
4 monthly precipitation that is less than 60 per cent of normal; and

5   any amount of rainfall less than 85 per cent of normal.

Even as late as 1957, Friedman used annual rainfall as his drought index in a study of drought in Texas. Similar criteria have been employed in other countries:

6   Britain: fifteen consecutive days with less than 0.25 mm (0.01 inch) [or 1.0 mm (0.04 inch)];
7   India: rainfall half of normal or less for a week, or actual seasonal rainfall deficient by more than twice the mean deviation;
8   Russia: ten days with total rainfall not exceeding 5 mm (0.20 inch);
9   Bali: a period of six days without rain; and
10 Libya: annual rainfall that is less than 180 mm (7 inches).

Most of these definitions/indices were valid only for their specific application in their specific region. Indices developed for one region may not be applicable in other regions because the meteorological conditions that result in drought are highly variable around the world. Indices developed to measure the intensity of meteorological drought, for instance, were inadequate for agricultural, hydrological, or other applications.

These deficiencies were recognised early. The problems with developing an agricultural drought index, for example, include consideration of vegetation, soil type (which determines soil moisture capacity), antecedent soil moisture, and evapotranspiration as influenced by wind speed and the temperature and humidity of the air. Many of these climatic elements were not widely measured or could not be incorporated into a drought index. For example, Abbe (1894) noted:

> From an agricultural point of view, a drought is not merely a deficiency of rainfall, but a deficiency of water available for the use of the growing crops ... Thus a drought affecting agriculture is a complex result of many considerations ... Therefore, both from an agricultural and engineering point of view, it is impracticable to define the intensity of a drought in general and exact terms.

In the US Weather Bureau's *Bulletin Q: Climatology of the United States*, A. J. Henry (1906) concluded that, 'in general, climatological statistics alone fail to give a sufficient accurate conception either of the duration or intensity of [agricultural] drought. Supplementary observations upon the condition of vegetation in each locality are especially needed'.

During the first half of the twentieth century, scientists focused their efforts on addressing the inadequacies noted above, as well as continuing to develop drought indices relevant to the specific application being considered.

Munger (1916) developed an objective measure of the comparative forest fire risk for year to year and region to region. After determining that the single factor that has the most important influence on the fire hazard in the Pacific Northwest is the infrequency of soaking rains, Munger used, as his drought index, the length of the period without a twenty-four-hour rainfall of 0.05 inch. He devised a graphical technique to represent the intensity of the drought. The technique used the area of a right-angle triangle, whose height and base were both proportional to the duration of the drought. Expressed mathematically:

$$\text{severity of drought} = \frac{L^2}{2}$$

where L is the length of the drought in days.

Kincer (1919) prepared, for the first time, a series of much-needed maps and charts showing the seasonal distribution of precipitation in the contiguous United States. Included were maps showing the frequency of subnormal precipitation (i.e., droughts) for the United States east of the Rockies for the warm season (March–September). Kincer defined a drought as thirty or more consecutive days with less than 0.25 inch of precipitation in twenty-four hours.

In a study of the climatic requirements of the bean beetle in the eastern United States, Marcovitch (1930) devised an equation incorporating both temperature and precipitation to compute a drought index:

$$\text{drought index} = \frac{N^2(100/R)^2}{2}$$

where N is the total number of two or more consecutive days above 90°F, and R is the total summer rainfall for the same months.

Blumenstock (1942) applied probability theory to compute drought frequencies in a climatic study. For his index, he used the length of the drought in days, with a drought considered terminated by the occurrence of at least 0.10 inch of precipitation in forty-eight hours or less.

Efforts to measure soil moisture depletion focused on evaporation, and efforts to measure moisture use by plants focused on transpiration. Evaporation and transpiration (or, collectively, evapotranspiration [ET]), according to Thornthwaite (1931), depend on solar radiation, wind speed, humidity, nature of vegetation, and condition of the soil, with solar radiation being the dominant factor. However, since direct measurements of solar radiation are not generally available, it was found that the mean daily temperature, latitude, and time of year could be used to approximate the amount of water loss to the atmosphere by evaporation when it is assumed that there is an adequate supply of moisture in the soil for the vegetation at all times. This measure is called potential evapotranspiration; the difference between actual and potential evapotranspiration depends on the availability of moisture in the soil.

With this foundation, Thornthwaite (1931) developed the precipitation effectiveness index, which is the sum of the twelve monthly precipitation effectiveness ratios, where the monthly effectiveness ratio is the monthly precipitation divided by the monthly evaporation. He also (Thornthwaite 1948) proposed using precipitation minus evapotranspiration as a drought index.

It should be pointed out that Thornthwaite's work furthered the development of drought indices, but he, along with Koeppen and others, also did much to lay the groundwork for the modern climate classification system. As noted by the World Meteorological Organization (1975), a distinction should be made between *drought* and *aridity*. Aridity is usually defined in terms of low average rainfall or available water and, setting aside the possibility of climatic change, is a permanent climatic feature of a region. Drought, on the other hand, is a temporary feature in the sense that, considered in the context of variability, it is experienced only when rainfall deviates appreciably below normal. Aridity is, by definition, restricted to regions of low rainfall and usually high temperature, whereas drought is possible in virtually any rainfall or temperature regime. With this distinction

in mind, Thornthwaite's two indices are more climatological aridity indices than drought indices.

McQuigg (1954) and Waggoner and O'Connell (1956) incorporated both the amount and timing of precipitation in their Antecedent Precipitation Index (API). Originally designed to estimate soil moisture content for use in flood forecasting, the API was computed on a daily basis by multiplying the index for the previous day by a factor, usually 0.90. If rain occurred on any day, the amount of rainfall observed was added to the index. Snowfall was included on the day it melted. They obtained good results for the eastern and central United States. Iowa corn yields were poor when the API dropped below 0.10 and in the wet years when it failed to go below 0.50 during mid-May to mid-August.

Thornthwaite's work prompted van Bavel and Verlinden (1956) to develop the concept of an agricultural drought-day, a period of one day during which a drought condition exists (i.e., a day for which the available soil moisture is zero). They estimated soil moisture conditions using daily precipitation and evapotranspiration (computed using Penman's formula, which incorporated solar radiation, sunshine duration, air temperature, relative humidity, and wind speed). Dickson (1958) used the drought-day concept, but experimented with a different way of computing evapotranspiration (i.e., making it proportional to the total moisture content of the soil). This different methodology resulted in a computed agricultural drought-day quantity that was considerably less (by up to 55 per cent) than the quantity computed with the method used by van Bavel and Verlinden.

The 1960s saw the development of the moisture stress-day as a drought index for corn (WMO 1975). A moisture stress-day (i.e., corn plants lost turgor) occurred if (1) potential evapotranspiration (PE) exceeded 6.4 mm (0.25 inch) per day when soil water was below 85 per cent of available capacity, or (2) PE exceeded 5.1 mm (0.20 inch) per day when soil water was below 50 per cent of capacity, or (3) PE exceeded 1.3 mm (0.05 inch) per day when soil water was less than 10 per cent of available capacity.

Meanwhile, Thornthwaite and others developed the water budget accounting method to keep track of soil moisture. Various assumptions were made about soil moisture field capacity, and monthly values of precipitation and potential evapotranspiration were used. They emphasised that, to determine how severe a drought may be in a place, one must compare water need with water supply in individual years.

> We cannot define drought only as a shortage of rainfall, [they said] because such a definition would fail to take into account the amount of water needed. Furthermore, the effect of a shortage of rainfall depends on whether the soil is moist or dry at the beginning of the period. . . . [Agricultural] drought does not begin when rain ceases but rather only when plant roots can no longer obtain moisture in needed amounts.
> (Thornthwaite and Mather 1955)

One attempt to address these needs was the idea of 'moisture adequacy'. This index, developed by McGuire and Palmer (1957) as an outgrowth of the concept of potential evapotranspiration, compared a location's moisture need to the actual moisture supply (rainfall plus available soil moisture). The moisture adequacy index, then, is the per cent sufficiency of the actual moisture supply toward meeting the need. They plotted a map of these index values to show the general spatial pattern of drought during 1957 in the eastern United States.

Drought identification and evaluation procedures thus slowly evolved during the first half of the twentieth century from simplistic approaches that considered the phenomenon to be a rainfall deficiency to problem-specific models of limited applicability. The stage was set for the development of a more sophisticated technique to quantitatively appraise what Steila (1987) termed the total environmental moisture status.

PALMER'S DROUGHT INDEX

In 1965, Wayne Palmer published his model for a drought index that incorporated antecedent precipitation, moisture supply, and moisture demand (based on the pioneering evapotranspiration work by Thornthwaite) in a hydrologic accounting system (Palmer 1965). He used a two-layered model for soil moisture computations and made certain assumptions concerning field capacity and transfer of moisture to and from the layers. Palmer applied what he called CAFEC (*Climatologically Appropriate for Existing Conditions*) quantities to normalise his computations, thus enabling comparison of the dimensionless index across space and time. This procedure enables the index to measure abnormal wetness as well as dryness, with persistently normal precipitation and temperature theoretically resulting in an index of zero in all seasons in all climates.

The computation of Palmer's index consists of the following steps:

1 Carry out a monthly hydrologic accounting for a long series of years (other time frames, such as weeks or days, could be used instead). The accounting involves five parameters: precipitation, evapotranspiration, soil moisture loss and recharge, and runoff. Potential and actual values are computed for the last four.
2 Summarise the results to obtain certain coefficients that are dependent on the climate of the location being analysed.
3 Reanalyse the series using the derived coefficients to determine the amount of moisture required for 'normal' weather during each month. These 'normal', or CAFEC, quantities are computed for each of the parameters listed in step 1.
4 Compute the precipitation departure (precipitation minus CAFEC precipitation) for each month, then convert the departures to indices of moisture anomaly. This moisture anomaly index has come to be known as the *Palmer Z index* and reflects the departure of the weather of a particular month from the average moisture climate for that month, regardless of what has occurred in previous or subsequent months.
5 Analyse the index series to determine the beginning, ending, and severity of the drought periods.

In Palmer's computations, the drought severity for a month is dependent on the moisture anomaly for that month *and* on the drought severity for the previous and subsequent months. This has come to be known as the *Palmer Hydrological Drought Index* (PHDI) and reflects the long-term *hydrologic* moisture conditions.

There is a lag between the time that the drought-inducing meteorological conditions end and the environment recovers from the drought. In his effort to create a *meteorological* drought index, Palmer expressed the beginning and ending of drought (or wet) periods in terms of the *probability* that the spell has started or ended. A drought or wet spell is definitely over when this probability reaches or exceeds 100 per cent, but the drought or wet spell is considered to have ended the *first month* that the probability became greater than zero per cent and then continued to remain above zero per cent until it reached 100 per cent. This meteorological drought index has come to be known as the *Palmer Drought Severity Index* (PDSI).

This back-stepping procedure of ending droughts or wet spells cannot be satisfactorily used for real-time calculations of PDSIs (i.e., operational PDSIs) since one cannot know in advance whether a few months of wet or dry weather are the beginnings of a new spell of wet or dry weather or merely a temporary interruption of the current drought or wet spell (Karl 1986). During the period of 'uncertainty' when an existing drought (or wet spell) may or may not be over, the model computes an index value for the established drought (X1) and an index value for an incipient wet spell (X3). Similar computations are made for an established wet spell (X2) and incipient drought (also X3). Which term (X1, X2, or X3) the model selects for the PDSI depends on the probability that the established spell is over. The US National Weather Service (NWS) incorporated this feature in a modification of the PDSI in the 1990s (Heddinghaus and Sabol 1991). The NWS modification allows computation of the PDSI operationally by taking the sum of the wet and dry terms after they have been weighted by their probabilities (P and 100 per cent – P, where P is the probability that the spell is over).

At the time of its introduction, Palmer's procedure was hailed as 'the most satisfactory solution to the problem of combining precipitation and temperature as predictor variables' (Julian and Fritts 1968). The Palmer index became widely used in the United States. It was applied to other areas of the world, but the results have been mixed (WMO 1975, Kogan 1995).

The Palmer index was a landmark in the development of drought indices. However, it was not without critics. Several scientists have offered criticism of the model and its assumptions and have discussed its limitations. The criticisms fall into two broad categories, concerning water balance models in general and Palmer's model in particular.

Alley (1984) had reservations concerning how water balance models treat potential evapotranspiration, soil moisture, runoff, and distribution of precipitation and evapotranspiration within a month or week, and how they do not consider seasonal or annual changes in vegetation cover and root development. He criticised the Palmer model in particular for not incorporating a lag to account for the delay between generation of excess water and its appearance as runoff, and for making no allowance for the effect of snowmelt or frozen ground. He was also concerned about the arbitrary designation of the drought severity classes (see Table 11.1) and the transition index values indicating an end to an established drought or wet spell.

Although Palmer tried to normalise for location and season, his index is not spatially comparable across the contiguous United States (Alley 1984, Guttman *et al.* 1992) or directly comparable between months (Alley 1984). Concern was raised about the possible asymmetrical and bimodal statistical distributions of the PDSI and PHDI index values (Alley 1984, Guttman 1991).

Sensitivity studies have found that the value of the PDSI is highly dependent on (1) the weighting factor used to make it comparable between different months and regions and (2) the value specified for the available water capacity in the soil (Karl 1983), as well as (3) the calibration period used to compute the

Table 11.1 Palmer drought index categories

Moisture category	PDSI
Extremely wet	≥4.00
Very wet	3.00 to 3.99
Moderately wet	2.00 to 2.99
Slightly wet	1.00 to 1.99
Incipient wet spell	0.50 to 0.99
Near normal	0.49 to −0.49
Incipient drought	−0.50 to −0.99
Mild drought	−1.00 to −1.99
Moderate drought	−2.00 to −2.99
Severe drought	−3.00 to −3.99
Extreme drought	≤−4.00

Source: Based on Palmer 1965

CAFEC quantities (Karl 1986), with longer calibration periods providing more consistent estimates of the *CAFEC* quantities and index values. If the calibration period is changed, the Palmer indices for the entire period of record should be recomputed to maintain consistency through time. Guttman (1991) found that the period of time required for the PHDI to reflect actual rather than artificial initial conditions could be more than four years, and that the effects of temperature anomalies are insignificant compared to the effects of precipitation anomalies.

The index was specifically designed to treat the drought problem in semiarid and dry subhumid climates, with Palmer himself cautioning that extrapolation beyond these conditions may lead to unrealistic results (Palmer 1965, Guttman 1991).

In spite of these criticisms, the Palmer drought index is widely used by a variety of people (hydrologists, foresters, field meteorologists, economists, policy decision makers, news media, private consultants, researchers) as a tool to monitor and assess long-term meteorological drought and wet spell conditions. As pointed out by the National Drought Mitigation Center (web site http://enso.unl.edu/ndmc/) and Willeke *et al.* (1994), it is most effective measuring impacts sensitive to soil moisture conditions, such as in agriculture, and it has also been used to start or end drought response actions.

Three years after the introduction of his drought index, Palmer (1968) introduced a new drought index based on weekly mean temperature and precipitation, as an outgrowth of his PDSI work. This Crop Moisture Index (CMI) was specifically designed as an agricultural drought index. It depends on the drought severity at the beginning of the week and the evapotranspiration deficit or soil moisture recharge during the week. It measures both evapotranspiration deficits (drought) and excessive wetness (more than enough precipitation to meet evapotranspiration demand and recharge the soil). The CMI has been adopted by the US Department of Agriculture and is published in its *Weekly Weather and Crop Bulletin* as an indicator of the availability of moisture to meet short-term crop needs (Wilhite and Glantz 1985).

As part of a PHDI study to aid planners during recovery from severe droughts, Karl *et al.* (1986) computed the precipitation required to end or ameliorate an existing drought, and the climatological probability of receiving at least this required amount of precipitation, for the 344 climate divisions of the contiguous United States.

THE POST-PALMER ERA

In the decades since Palmer introduced the PDSI, several other drought indices have been developed and adopted, but none has had an impact large enough to relegate Palmer's index to the dusty annals of history. Some of the subsequent indices applied old concepts to new applications, while others addressed inadequacies in the Palmer model.

Shear and Steila (1974) and Steila (1987) proposed an alternate approach (to Palmer's) of using water budget analysis to identify moisture anomalies. Their procedure, like Palmer's, accounts for precipitation, potential evapotranspiration, and soil moisture but yields moisture status departure values that are expressed in the same units as precipitation – i.e., they are areally applicable water-depth measures having equivalent meteorological significance in diverse climatic realms.

Keetch and Byram (1968) developed an index of drought for use by fire control managers. Based on an 8-inch soil moisture storage capacity, the Drought Index (DI) is expressed in hundredths of an inch of soil moisture depletion, ranging from 0 (no moisture deficiency) to 800 (absolute drought). Computation of the DI is based on a daily water-budgeting procedure whereby the drought factor is balanced with precipitation and soil moisture.

In a 1980 study of economic sectors affected by drought, Changnon linked drought thresholds and impacts in Illinois using departure of precipitation from normal over a twelve-month period as his index (Wilhite and Glantz 1985).

The Surface Water Supply Index (SWSI), a hydrologic drought index developed for Colorado in 1981, was designed to complement the PDSI by integrating snowpack, reservoir storage, streamflow, and precipitation at high elevation (Wilhite and Glantz 1985). The SWSI has a similar scale, and the SWSI and PDSI are used together to trigger Colorado's Drought Assessment and Response Plan. The index has been modified and adopted by other western states.

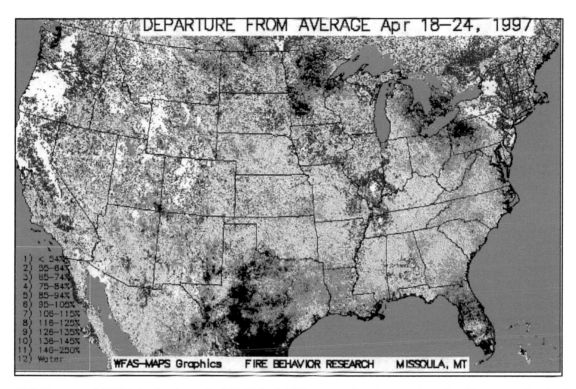

Figure 10.7 Greenness (NDVI) index for the week of 18–24 April 1997, expressed as departure from decadal average values for this time of year. Green areas have greener vegetation, red areas less green than usual, and white either cloudy or snow-covered. Courtesy US Forest Service Fire Lab, Missoula, Montana

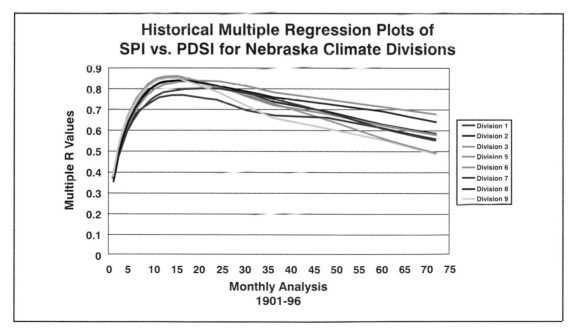

Figure 12.11 Historical multiple regression plots of the Standardized Precipitation Index vs the Palmer Drought Severity Index for Nebraska climate divisions (adapted from McKee *et al.* 1995)

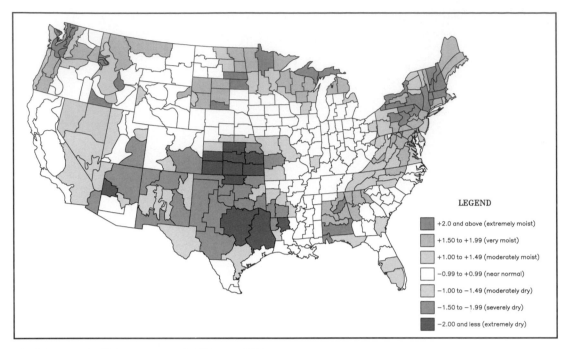

LEGEND

■ +2.0 and above (extremely moist)
■ +1.50 to +1.99 (very moist)
■ +1.00 to +1.49 (moderately moist)
□ −0.99 to +0.99 (near normal)
■ −1.00 to −1.49 (moderately dry)
■ −1.50 to −1.99 (severely dry)
■ −2.00 and less (extremely dry)

Figure 12.13 Five-month SPI through the end of February 1996
Sources: Map prepared by the National Drought Mitigation Center from data provided by the National Climatic Data Center and the Western Regional Climate Center

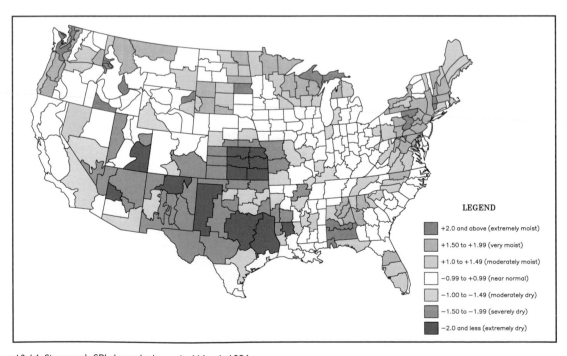

LEGEND

■ +2.0 and above (extremely moist)
■ +1.50 to +1.99 (very moist)
■ +1.0 to +1.49 (moderately moist)
□ −0.99 to +0.99 (near normal)
■ −1.00 to −1.49 (moderately dry)
■ −1.50 to −1.99 (severely dry)
■ −2.0 and less (extremely dry)

Figure 12.14 Six-month SPI through the end of March 1996
Sources: Map prepared by the National Drought Mitigation Center from data provided by the National Climatic Data Center and the Western Regional Climate Center

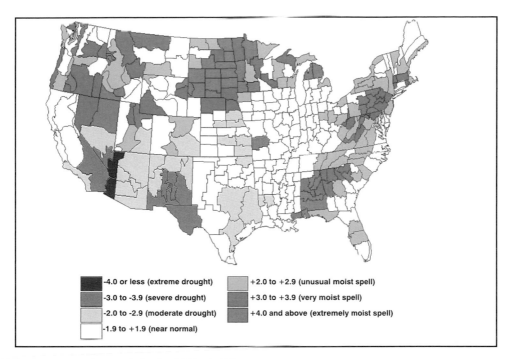

Figure 12.15 Palmer Drought Severity Index for 30 March 1996
Source: Climate Prediction Center, NOAA

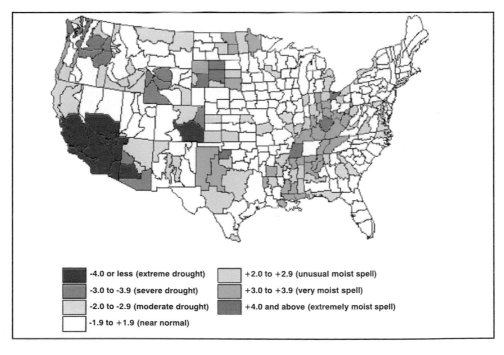

Figure 12.16 Palmer Drought Severity Index for 5 July 1997. Source as Figure 12.15

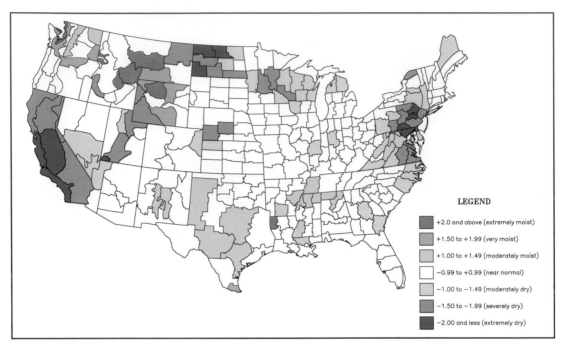

Figure 12.18 Five-month SPI through the end of June 1997

Sources: Map prepared by the National Drought Mitigation Center from data provided by the National Climatic Data Center and the Western Regional Climate Center

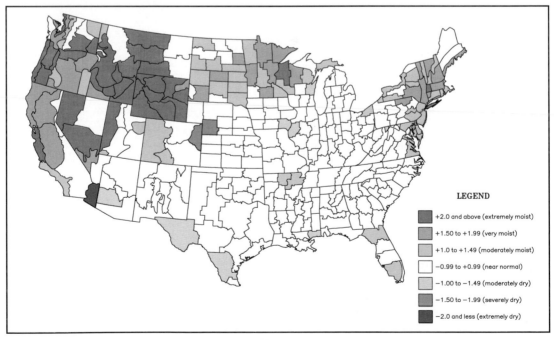

Figure 12.19 Three-month SPI through the end of December 1996

Sources: Map prepared by the National Drought Mitigation Center from data provided by the National Climatic Data Center and the Western Regional Climate Center

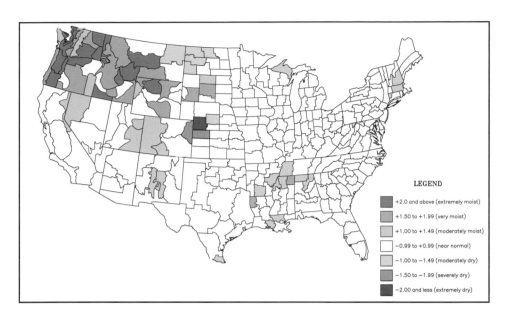

Figure 12.20 Nine-month SPI through the end of June 1997

Sources: Map prepared by the National Drought Mitigation Center from data provided by the National Climatic Data Center and the Western Regional Climate Center

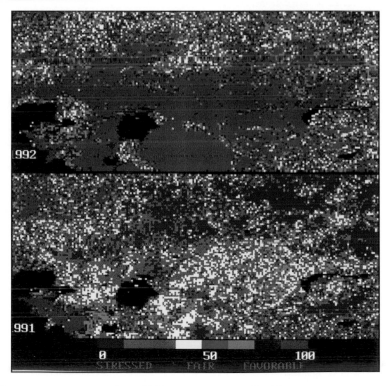

Figure 14.3 Colour-coded maps of vegetation condition (VCI) at the end of June, Kazakh

Source: Gitelson and Kogan 1995

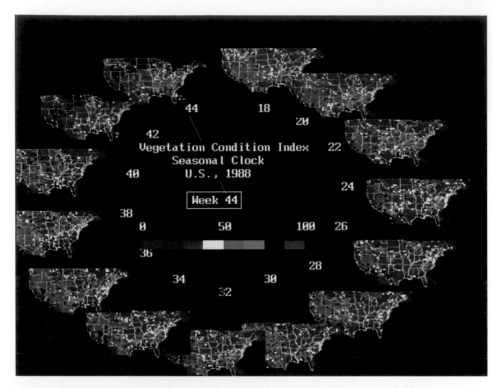

Figure 14.5 Colour-coded maps of the 1988 biweekly vegetation condition (VCI), based on the average VCI for each 1° by 1° box, United States
Source: Kogan 1997

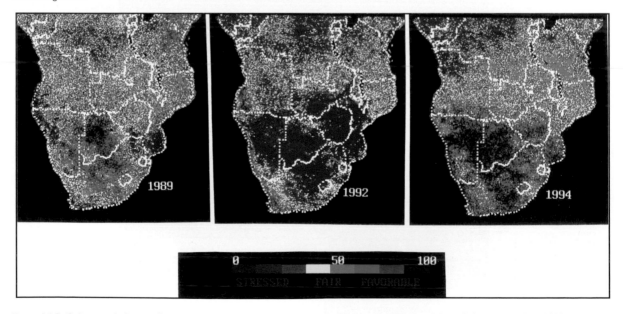

Figure 14.7 Colour-coded map of vegetation condition (VT) at the end of February 1989 (local drought), compared to 1992 (large area drought) and 1994 (favourable condition), southern Africa
Source: Unganai and Kogan 1998

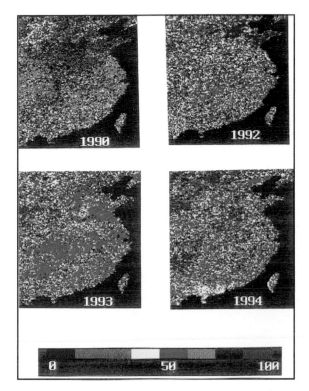

Figure 14.8 Colour-coded map of vegetation condition (VT) at the end of July, southeastern China
Source: Kogan 1997

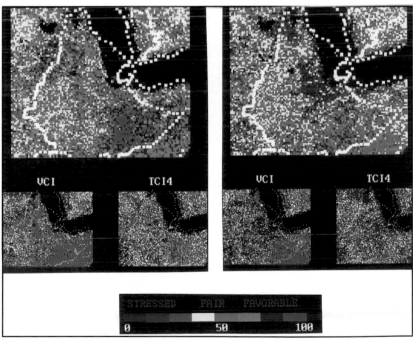

Figure 14.11 Colour-coded map of vegetation condition (VT, VCI, and TC14) at the end of June (week 26) and August (week 36) 1987, Ethiopia
Source: Kogan 1997

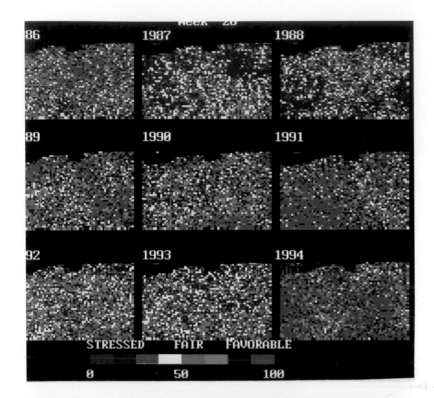

STRESSED   FAIR   FAVORABLE

0   50   100

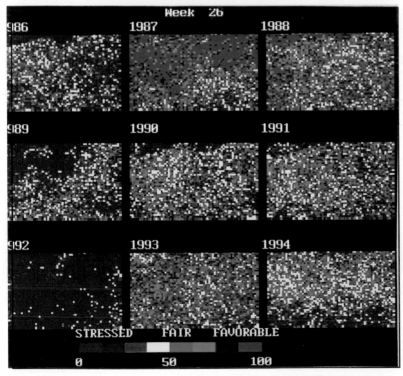

Week 26

STRESSED   FAIR   FAVORABLE

0   50   100

Figure 14.13 Colour-coded map of VCI (a) and TCI (b) at the end of June (week 26), Poland

McKee *et al.* (1993) developed the Standardized Precipitation Index (SPI) as an alternative to Palmer's index for Colorado. Historical data are used to compute the probability distribution of the monthly and seasonal (the past two months, three months, etc. – up to forty-eight months) observed precipitation totals, and then the probabilities are normalised. The methodology allows expression of droughts (and wet spells) in terms of precipitation deficit, per cent of 'normal', and probability of nonexceedance as well as the SPI. Drought intensity, magnitude, and duration can be determined, as well as the historical data-based probability of emerging from a specific drought. The different time scales (seasons) for which the index is computed address the various types of drought: the shorter seasons for agricultural and meteorological drought, the longer seasons for hydrological drought. Although developed for use in Colorado, the SPI can be applied universally to any location.

As noted by the National Drought Mitigation Center on their web site, new drought indices have been developed by researchers in other countries for applications and locales where the Palmer index proved inadequate. Dependable rains (DR), defined as the amount of rainfall that occurs statistically in four out of every five years, have been applied by Le Houorou *et al.* (1993) to the African continent. The National Rainfall Index (RI), used by Gommes and Petrassi (1994) in another study of precipitation patterns in Africa, allows comparison of precipitation patterns across time and from country to country. The RI is a national scale index, computed by weighting the national annual precipitation by the long-term averages of all of the stations within the nation. The Australian Drought Watch System is based on consecutive months (at least three) with precipitation below a certain decile threshold, where the deciles are determined from the cumulative frequency of the distribution of ranked monthly and annual precipitation totals (Wilhite and Glantz 1985).

The US National Oceanic and Atmospheric Administration has applied satellite-based technology to the real-time monitoring of drought. The vegetation condition index (VCI), computed from satellite AVHRR radiance (visible and near infra-red) data and adjusted for land climate, ecology, and weather conditions, showed promise when used for drought detection and tracking (Kogan 1995). The VCI uses the close dependence of vegetation on climate, which harks back to the principles that guided German biologist Wladimir Koeppen in his development of a vegetation-based climate classification system some ninety years earlier. The VCI allows detection of drought; it also allows (and is a potential global standard for) measurement of the time of its onset and its intensity, duration, and impact on vegetation.

There are several extensive reference lists (Friedman 1957, Palmer and Denny 1971, WMO 1975, Hasemeier 1977, Wilhite and Hoffman 1980, Wilhite and Wood 1983, NOAA 1989) that the reader may consult for additional information about drought and drought indices.

SUMMARY

The monitoring and analysis of drought have long suffered from the lack of an adequate definition of the phenomenon. This has affected the development of drought indices, which have slowly evolved during the last two centuries from simplistic approaches based on some measure of rainfall deficiency to more complex problem-specific models. These models continue to evolve as new data sources become available. The incorporation of evapotranspiration as a measure of water demand by Thornthwaite led to the landmark development by Palmer of a water budget-based drought index, which is still widely used thirty years later.

REFERENCES

Abbe, C. (1894) 'Drought', *Monthly Weather Review* 22: 323–4.
Alley, W.M. (1984) 'The Palmer Drought Severity Index: Limitations and assumptions', *Journal of Climate and Applied Meteorology* 23: 1,100–9.
Blumenstock Jr., G. (1942) 'Drought in the United States analysed by means of the theory of probability', *USDA Technical Bulletin* No. 819, Washington, DC: Government Printing Office.
Dickson, R.R. (1958) 'A note on the computation of agricultural drought days', *Weekly Weather and Crop Bulletin* XLV, 1 September 1958, pp. 7–8.
Friedman, D.G. (1957) 'The prediction of long-continuing drought in south and southwest Texas', *Occasional Papers in Meteorology*, No. 1, Hartford, CT: The

Travelers Weather Research Center.

Gommes, R. and Petrassi, F. (1994) 'Rainfall variability and drought in Sub-Saharan Africa since 1960', *Agrometeorology Series Working Paper*, No. 9, Rome: Food and Agriculture Organization.

Guttman, N.B. (1991) 'A sensitivity analysis of the Palmer Hydrologic Drought Index', *Water Resources Bulletin* 27: 797–807.

Guttman, N.B., Wallis, J.R., and Hosking, J.R.M. (1992) 'Spatial comparability of the Palmer Drought Severity Index', *Water Resources Bulletin* 28: 1,111–19.

Hasemeier, A. (1977) 'Drought: A selected bibliography', *Climatological Publications Bibliography Series* No. 3, State of Arizona, Office of the State Climatologist, Arizona State University, Tempe.

Heddinghaus, T.R. and Sabol, P. (1991) 'A review of the Palmer Drought Severity Index and where do we go from here?' in *Proceedings of the 7th Conference on Applied Climatology*, 10–13 September 1991, Boston, MA: American Meteorological Society, pp. 242–6.

Henry, A.J. (1906) 'Climatology of the United States', *Bulletin Q (W.B. No. 361)*, Washington, DC: US Dept. of Agriculture, Weather Bureau, pp. 51–8.

Julian, P.R. and Fritts, H.C. (1968) 'On the possibility of quantitatively extending climatic records by means of dendroclimatological analysis', *Proceedings of the First Statistical Meteorological Conference*, Hartford, CT, 27–9 May 1968, Boston: American Meteorological Society.

Karl, T.R. (1983) 'Some spatial characteristics of drought duration in the United States', *Journal of Climate and Applied Meteorology* 22: 1,356–66.

—— (1986) 'The sensitivity of the Palmer Drought Severity Index and Palmer's Z-Index to their calibration coefficients including potential evapotranspiration', *Journal of Climate and Applied Meteorology* 25: 77–86.

Karl, T.R., Knight, R.W., Ezell, D.S., and Quinlan, F.T. (1986) 'Probabilities and precipitation required to end/ameliorate droughts', *Historical Climatology Series 3–16*, Asheville: National Oceanic and Atmospheric Administration, National Climatic Data Center.

Keetch, J.J. and Byram, G.M. (1968) 'A drought index for forest fire control', *Paper SE-38*, Forest Service Research, US Dept. of Agriculture.

Kincer, J.B. (1919) 'The seasonal distribution of precipitation and its frequency and intensity in the United States', *Monthly Weather Review* 47: 624–31.

Kogan, F.N. (1995) 'Droughts of the late 1980's in the United States as derived from NOAA polar-orbiting satellite data', *Bulletin of the American Meteorological Society* 76: 655– 68.

Le Houorou, H.N., Popov, G.F., and See, L. (1993) 'Agro-bioclimatic classification of Africa', *Agrometeorology Series Working Paper* No. 6, Rome: Food and Agriculture Organization.

Marcovitch, S. (1930) 'The measure of droughtiness', *Monthly Weather Review* 58: 113.

McGuire, J.K. and Palmer, W.C. (1957) 'The 1957 drought in the eastern United States', *Monthly Weather Review* 85: 305–14.

McKee, T.B., Doesken, N.J., and Kleist, J. (1993) 'The relationship of drought frequency and duration to time scales', *Preprints, 8th Conference on Applied Climatology*, 17–22 January 1993, Anaheim, CA, American Meteorological Society, pp. 179–84.

McQuigg, J. (1954) 'A simple index of drought conditions', *Weatherwise* 7: 64–7.

Munger, T.T. (1916) 'Graphic method of representing and comparing drought intensities', *Monthly Weather Review* 44: 642–3.

NOAA (National Oceanic and Atmospheric Administration) (1989) 'Brief bibliography: drought', *Library and Information Services Division Publication* No. 89-4, Washington, DC: National Oceanographic Data Center, National Environmental, Satellite, Data, and Information Service, National Oceanic and Atmospheric Administration, US Dept. of Commerce.

Palmer, W.C. (1965) 'Meteorological drought', *Research Paper* No. 45, US Weather Bureau, Washington, DC.

—— (1968) 'Keeping track of crop moisture conditions, nationwide: The new crop moisture index', *Weatherwise* 21: 156–61.

Palmer, W.C. and Denny, L.M. (1971) 'Drought bibliography', *NOAA Technical Memorandum* EDS 20, Washington, DC: Environmental Data Service, National Oceanic and Atmospheric Administration, US Dept. of Commerce.

Shear, J.A. and Steila, D. (1974) 'The assessment of drought intensity by a new index', *Southeastern Geographer* 13: 195–201.

Steila, D. (1987) 'Drought,' in J.E. Oliver and R.W. Fairbridge (eds), *The Encyclopedia of Climatology*, New York: Van Nostrand Reinhold Company, pp. 388–95.

Tannehill, I.R. (1947) *Drought: Its Causes and Effects*, Princeton, NJ: Princeton University Press.

Thornthwaite, C.W. (1931) 'The climate of North America according to a new classification', *Geographical Review* 21: 633–55.

—— (1948) 'An approach toward a rational classification of climate', *Geographical Review* 38: 55–94.

Thornthwaite, C.W. and Mather, J.R. (1955) 'The water budget and its use in irrigation', *Water – Yearbook of Agriculture 1955*, Washington, DC: US Dept. of Agriculture, pp. 346–58.

van Bavel, C.H.M. and Verlinden, F.J. (1956) 'Agricultural drought in North Carolina', *Technical Bulletin* No. 122, Raleigh: North Carolina Agricultural Experiment Station.

Waggoner, M.L. and O'Connell, T.J. (1956) 'Antecedent precipitation index', *Weekly Weather and Crop Bulletin* XLIII, 15 October, pp. 6–7.

Wilhite, D.A. and Glantz, M.H. (1985) 'Understanding the

drought phenomenon: The role of definitions', *Water International* 10: 111–20.

Wilhite, D.A. and Hoffman, R.O. (1980) *Drought in the Great Plains: A Bibliography*, Lincoln: Nebraska Agricultural Experiment Station Miscellaneous Publication No. 39, University of Nebraska.

Wilhite, D.A. and Wood, D.A. (1983) *Drought in the Great Plains: A Bibliography – Supplement*, Lincoln: Nebraska Agricultural Experiment Station Miscellaneous Publication No. 46, University of Nebraska.

Willeke, G., Hosking, J.R.M., Wallis, J.R., and Guttman, N.B. (1994) *The National Drought Atlas*, Institute for Water Resources, Report 94-NDS-4, Fort Belvoir, VA: US Army Corps of Engineers.

WMO (World Meteorological Organization) (1975) 'Drought and agriculture', *World Meteorological Organization Technical Note* No. 138, WMO Publication No. 392, Geneva, Switzerland: WMO.

——— (1992) *International Meteorological Vocabulary, Second Edition*, WMO Publication No. 182, Geneva, Switzerland: WMO.

12

MONITORING DROUGHT USING THE STANDARDIZED PRECIPITATION INDEX*

Michael Hayes, Mark Svoboda, and Donald A. Wilhite

INTRODUCTION

Because drought is so difficult to define, detect, and measure, researchers have been striving to develop indices to accomplish these tasks. The importance and historical development of drought indices for monitoring drought is emphasised in the chapters by Redmond (Chapter 10) and Heim (Chapter 11). The goal of a drought index is to provide a simple, quantitative assessment of three drought characteristics: intensity, duration, and spatial extent. A drought index should also provide a historical reference that can be used to compare current conditions with past conditions.

In 1993, researchers at Colorado State University developed a new drought index, the Standardized Precipitation Index (SPI) (McKee *et al.* 1993), to improve operational water supply monitoring in Colorado. The need for the new index arose from the limitations of the indices being used at the time. For example, the commonly used Palmer Drought Severity Index (PDSI) has an inherent local time scale that reduces its flexibility in assessing rapidly changing conditions and reduces its use for monitoring longer-term water resources important in Colorado (McKee *et al.* 1993, 1995). Additional weaknesses of the PDSI are discussed by Hayes *et al.* (1998).

The Surface Water Supply Index (SWSI) is also being used in Colorado to monitor water supply. This index is based on an analysis of precipitation, snowpack, streamflow, and reservoir levels within a river basin. The SWSI, however, is difficult to adjust with the development of new water resources, such as a new reservoir, and each SWSI value is unique to the individual river basins, limiting comparisons between basins (Doesken *et al.* 1991). Presently, Colorado is monitoring its water resources using a combination of the SPI, SWSI, and Palmer indices.

Although developed for Colorado, the SPI has attributes that are advantageous for other regions. The National Drought Mitigation Center (NDMC) began creating monthly national maps of the SPI at the climatic division level for the continental United States in February 1996. The precipitation data are collected by the National Climatic Data Center (NCDC) and the SPI values are calculated by the Western Regional Climate Center (WRCC) in Reno, Nevada. The data archive at NCDC extends from 1895 to the present. The NDMC has been making the near real-time SPI maps available over the World Wide Web (http://enso.unl.edu/ndmc/watch/watch. htm#section1a/), with links to NCDC, the Climate Prediction Center (CPC), and the Regional Climate Centers. In February 1997, the WRCC also made near real-time monthly SPI maps, and associated products, available on the Web in the form of a matrix that allows the user the opportunity to choose the SPI map for many time periods (http://wrcc. noaa.gov/spi/spi.html).

---

*NOTE: Figures 12.11, 12.13, 12.16, 12.18, 12.19 and 12.20 can be found in the colour section located between pp. 160–1.

THE STANDARDIZED PRECIPITATION INDEX

The SPI was designed to be a relatively simple, year-round index applicable to all water supply conditions. Simple in comparison with other indices, the SPI is based on precipitation alone. Its fundamental strength is that it can be calculated for a variety of time scales from one month out to several years. Any time period can be selected, often dependent on the element of the hydrological system of greatest interest. This versatility allows the SPI to monitor short-term water supplies, such as soil moisture important for agricultural production, and longer-term water resources such as groundwater supplies, streamflow, and lake and reservoir levels.

Calculation of the SPI for any location is based on the long-term precipitation record for a desired period (three months, six months, etc.). This long-term record is fitted to a probability distribution, which is then transformed into a normal distribution so that the mean SPI for the location and desired period is zero (Edwards and McKee 1997). A particular precipitation total is given an SPI value according to this distribution. Positive SPI values indicate greater than median precipitation, while negative values indicate less than median precipitation. The magnitude of departure from zero represents a probability of occurrence so that decisions can be made based on this SPI value. McKee et al. (1993, 1995) originally used an incomplete gamma distribution to calculate the SPI. Efforts are now in progress to standardise the SPI computing procedure so that common temporal and spatial comparisons can be made by SPI users.

McKee et al. (1993) suggest a classification scale (given in Table 12.1). One can expect SPI values to be within one standard deviation approximately 68 per cent of the time, within two standard deviations 95 per cent of the time, and within three standard deviations 99 per cent of the time. It is considered to be a strength for water management planning that the frequencies of the 'extreme' and 'severe' classifications (Table 12.1) for any location and any time scale are consistent and low. An 'extreme' drought according to this scale (SPI ≤ −2.0) occurs approximately two to three times in 100 years.

The SPI has several limitations and unique charac-

Table 12.1 SPI classification scale

SPI values	Drought category
0 to −0.99	Mild drought
−1.00 to −1.49	Moderate drought
−1.50 to −1.99	Severe drought
−2.00 or less	Extreme drought

Source: McKee et al. 1993

teristics that must be considered when it is used. For example, the SPI is only as good as the data used in calculating it. Near real-time data collected at NCDC are still preliminary. These preliminary data are gathered from 450–550 stations each month across the nation. Climatic divisions in the eastern United States may have several stations used in calculations for that division, while western climatic divisions may not have data available for any stations. In the divisions with no available station data for that month, divisional values are interpolated from surrounding divisions. PDSI values are also calculated this way. Since it normally takes three to four months for all data to be collected and quality-controlled, preliminary data must initially be used by decision makers. The final quality-controlled data base contains approximately 1,200 stations across the country. Coverage is still somewhat limited in the western United States where terrain differences increase the spatial variability of climatic variables. Colorado, Nebraska, and Montana have improved the data coverage by using station networks within their states to calculate the SPI on a site-by-site basis.

Before the SPI is applied in a specific situation, a knowledge of the climatology for that region is necessary. At the shorter time scales (one, two, or three months), the SPI is very similar to the per cent of normal representation of precipitation, which can be misleading in regions with low seasonal precipitation totals. For example, in California during the summer or the Great Plains in winter, low precipitation totals are normal. As a result, large positive or negative SPI values may be caused by a relatively small anomaly in the precipitation amount. Understanding the climatology of these regions improves the interpretation of the SPI values. For this reason, the NDMC has included an interpretation of regional climatology in its presentation of monthly SPI maps on its web site.

HISTORICAL ANALYSES USING THE SPI

McKee *et al.* (1993) and the Colorado Climate Center originally tested the SPI using a historical data base for Fort Collins, Colorado. Since then, interest in the SPI has grown, and the SPI is now being used to monitor water supplies and moisture conditions on state, regional, and national levels.

Historical analyses using the SPI, like the one done for Fort Collins, are useful for illustrating the characteristics of the SPI for locations and comparing the SPI's ability to monitor drought events with the more common PDSI. For this reason, a detailed analysis of the SPI was completed for Nebraska using two different historical data bases. Particular attention was given to those years having significant drought impacts across the state, such as the 1930s, the 1950s, 1985, 1988, and 1989. This historical analysis provides a background for, and illustrates the characteristics of, the SPI and emphasises the importance of the index as a tool to monitor droughts of local, regional, or national scope.

Drought is a common feature of Nebraska's climate. Over the last 100 years, Nebraska has experienced many severe droughts lasting a number of years, along with even more droughts of shorter duration. Substantial impacts have occurred in a number of areas, including the agricultural, energy, environmental, transportation, and social sectors.

Analysis of the SPI for Nebraska was done for twenty time periods (one-month to seventy-two-month) in two data bases. Particular attention was given to the six-, nine-, twelve-, twenty-four-, and forty-eight-month SPI values. The first data set contains SPI values from 1895 to 1996 for the eight climatic divisions in the state; the second data base contains SPI values from 1949 through 1996 for more than 100 climate stations across the state (Figures 12.1 and 12.2 show, respectively, the locations of the eight climatic divisions and the selected climate stations). The shorter six- and nine-month values were examined to capture seasonal trends while the twelve-month SPI serves as a transitional interval to the long-term index values of the twenty-four- and forty-eight-month periods.

Figures 12.3 and 12.4 show time series analyses of the nine-month SPI for the Panhandle and East Central climatic divisions in Nebraska. In the Panhandle, the 1930s stand out, as does a severe drought in the mid-1960s (Figure 12.3). Drought periods are seen during the mid-1930s, 1950s, and 1970s in the East Central Division (Figure 12.4). These time series can be compared to time series of the PDSI for the same two climatic divisions (Figure 12.5 and Figure 12.6). A greater variability exists in the SPI time series, showing that the nine-month SPI is more responsive to changing moisture conditions than the PDSI. The nine-month SPI indicates that during

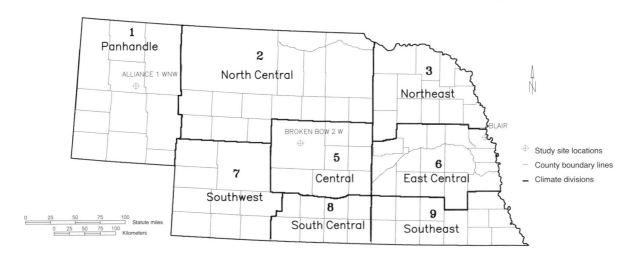

Figure 12.1 Nebraska climate divisions and study sites

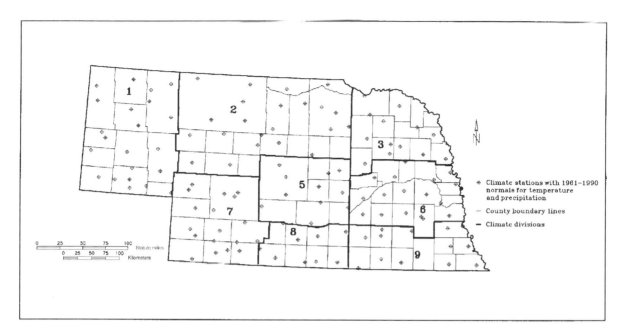

Figure 12.2 Climate stations with thirty-year normals in Nebraska

many 'drought periods' there are periods of wet conditions mixed in for both climatic divisions. An example of this can be seen when examining the mid-1930s for both divisions.

Figures 12.7 and 12.8 show the nine-month SPI time series of wet and dry periods for Alliance and Blair, Nebraska, since 1949. Alliance is in the Panhandle Climatic Division and Blair is in the East Central Division. Although the patterns are similar to the previous figures, there are some important differences. A very severe dry period in Alliance in the late 1980s is not as evident in the other time series (Figures 12.3 and 12.5), illustrating the need for using individual stations to better represent local conditions.

Figure 12.9 is an example of using site data to interpolate SPI values across the state. The two-year period ending in December 1989 indicates that conditions were very dry in both the western and eastern parts of the state. Much of the eastern quarter of the state was in severe drought as defined by the SPI. The drought of 1988–9 was very severe and had a substantial impact on the entire Corn Belt region. The eastern half of Nebraska makes up the western

edge of the Corn Belt. By using the site values, the variability that frequently occurs within each climatic division (Figure 12.1) can be seen.

In the case of Alliance and the Panhandle Division, a small pocket of severe drought is seen in the twenty-four-month SPI values in the immediate area, but most of the Panhandle is experiencing only moderate drought or near-normal conditions. This provides a better picture for local conditions rather than relying on a single representative value for the entire climatic division, and it explains why the SPI time series for Alliance is so low (Figure 12.7) while the climatic division time series is not (Figure 12.3). The use of local SPI information has been very useful for determining the impacts of weather on crop yields (Yamoah *et al.* 1997).

Tables 12.2–12.4 summarise drought occurrences from 1949 to 1996 for Alliance, Broken Bow, and Blair, Nebraska (for locations of these towns, see Figure 12.1). Broken Bow is located in the Central Climatic Division. McKee *et al.* (1993) define a 'drought event' as the period when the SPI is continuously negative and reaches an intensity of –1.0 or less. The drought would then end when a positive

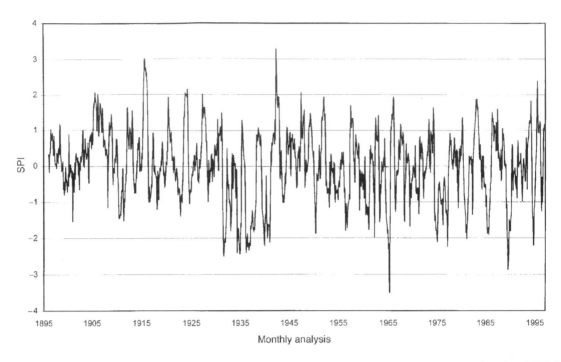

Figure 12.3 Nine-month SPI using monthly precipitation values, 1896–1996, for the Panhandle Climate Division (based on NCDC and High Plains Climatic Centers [HPCC] data)

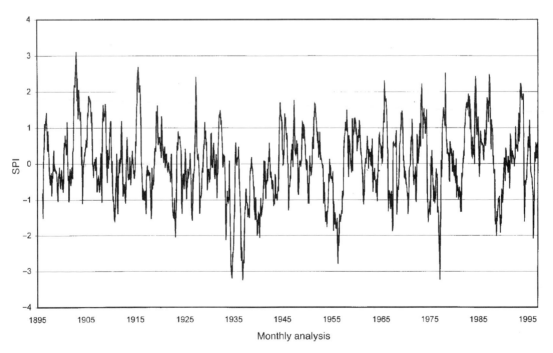

Figure 12.4 Nine-month SPI using monthly precipitation values, 1896–1996, for the East Central Climate Division (sources as for Figure 12.3)

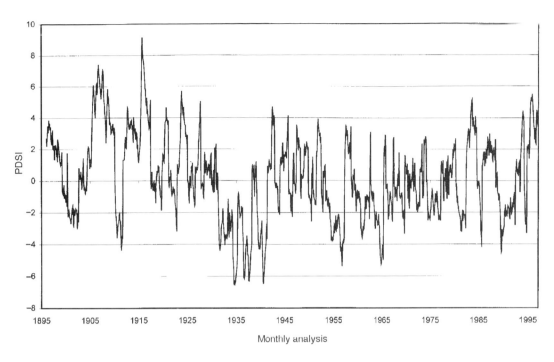

Figure 12.5 Palmer Drought Severity Index (PDSI) using monthly values, 1896–1996, for the Panhandle Climate Division (based on data from the Climate Prediction Center)

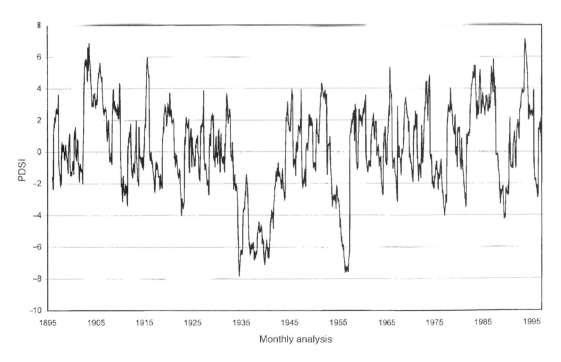

Figure 12.6 Palmer Drought Severity Index (PDSI) using monthly values, 1896–1996, for the East Central Climate Division (based on data from the Climate Prediction Center)

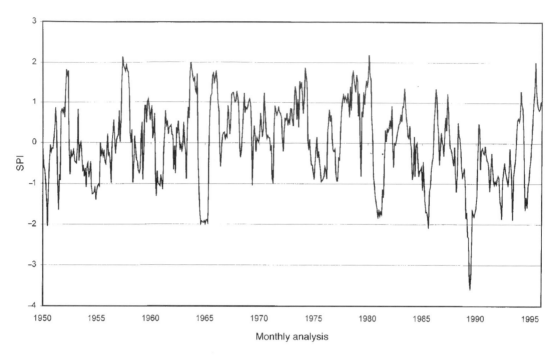

Figure 12.7 Nine-month SPI using monthly precipitation values, 1950–96, for Alliance, Nebraska (Panhandle Climate Division). Sources as for Figure 12.3

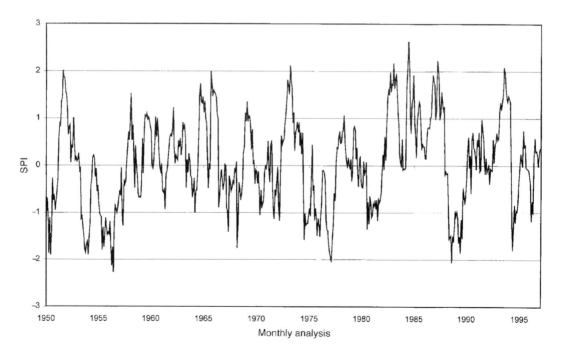

Figure 12.8 Nine-month SPI using monthly precipitation values, 1950–96, for Blair, Nebraska (East Central Climate Division). Sources as for Figure 12.3

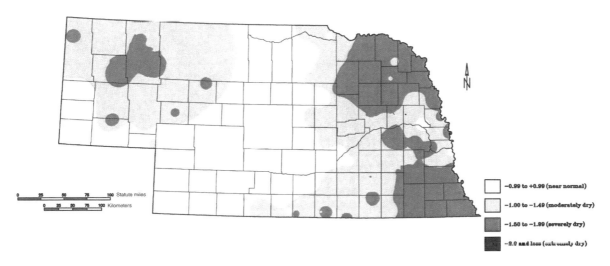

	−0.99 to +0.99 (near normal)
	−1.00 to −1.49 (moderately dry)
	−1.50 to −1.99 (severely dry)
	−2.0 and less (extremely dry)

Figure 12.9 Twenty-four-month SPI through the end of December 1989
Sources: McKee *et al.* 1993, NDMC 1997, High Plains Climate Center 1997

value occurs. These three sites were chosen to provide a cross-section of drought occurrences across the state. For some of the SPI time periods, two droughts are shown to illustrate that the longest droughts are not necessarily the most intense and might not have the largest impacts or damages associated with them. Factors such as the time of onset or the mean intensity instead of the duration should be looked at in addition to the magnitude and peak intensity. For example, the longest drought period at Alliance using the twelve-month SPI lasted 37 months, from 1990 to 1993 (Table 12.2). However, the drought of 1987–90, with a peak intensity of −4.28 (extreme drought) and a mean intensity of −1.27, had a greater impact on the area.

For Broken Bow (Table 12.3), three drought periods during the 1949–1996 period were identified. The drought of longest duration, eighty-one months, began in 1966 and concluded in 1973. However, the drought of 1952–8, lasting sixty-seven months, had a peak intensity of −3.53 (extreme drought) and a mean intensity for the duration of the drought that fell into the severe classification at −1.60. The analysis for Blair, Nebraska, is shown in Table 12.4.

After the Dust Bowl years of the 1930s, the 1950s are generally considered the next worst years in terms of prolonged drought within Nebraska in the modern era. At the drought's peak in the middle of the decade, nearly two-thirds of the state was experiencing severe or extreme drought. Even at the twenty-four-month time period (Figure 12.10), severe drought is evident

Table 12.2 1949–96 SPI drought analysis for Alliance, Nebraska

Years	SPI interval (months)	Duration (months)	Peak intensity	Mean intensity
1990–3	12	37	−1.67	−0.89
1987–90	12	33	−4.28	−1.27
1988–95	24	83	−2.98	−1.23
1983–96	48	153	−3	−1.06

Table 12.3 1949–96 SPI drought analysis for Broken Bow, Nebraska

Years	SPI interval (months)	Duration (months)	Peak intensity	Mean intensity
1952–7	12	58	−2.62	−1.4
1952–7	24	61	−2.88	−1.61
1952–8	48	67	−3.53	−1.6
1966–73	48	81	−1.25	−0.65

Table 12.4 1949–96 SPI drought analysis for Blair, Nebraska

Years	SPI interval (months)	Duration (months)	Peak intensity	Mean intensity
1974–7	12	37	−1.94	−1.15
1953–9	24	69	−2.39	−1.13
1954–60	48	68	−2.67	−1.2
1976–82	48	74	−1.76	−0.89

in all but the Panhandle region in the state. Of course, drought severity levels fluctuated, but a severe or extreme classification (SPI values < −1.5) over a two-year period is a strong signal of persistent drought. Figure 12.10 gives a quick picture of the potential impacts expected given the general lack of irrigation at the time. Shorter-term SPI values (six-, nine-, and twelve-month analysis) during the same time frame (mid-1950s) illustrate the ebb and flow of extreme drought values (SPI < −2.0) and spatial extent across the state.

The tendency of fewer but longer droughts was found in the 24- and 48-month SPI averaging periods (Table 12.5). In the years since 1949, Alliance has experienced ten 12-month SPI drought periods, six

24-month drought periods, and two 48-month drought periods. This trend held true across the other climatic divisions as well. Broken Bow had twelve 12-month, six 24-month, and three 48-month droughts while Blair showed eleven 12-month, seven 24-month, and three 48-month SPI drought periods.

Table 12.6 shows the variation in precipitation both across the state and within the climatic divisions. This table demonstrates why there is a need to use climatic division data with caution, depending on the scale of monitoring efforts. In some years, the divisional data does a good job of representing some of the individual sites; in other years, the departure from the division average can be extreme. This is especially true in the Great Plains region, where convective precipitation is 'hit and miss' for any given location during the spring and summer months.

In comparing the SPI to the PDSI for the Panhandle (Climatic Division 1) and East Central (Climatic Division 6) climatic divisions in Nebraska, initial findings of the relationship for monthly values (1895–1996) are very similar to those that McKee *et al.* (1993, 1995) found for Fort Collins, Colorado (Figure 12.11). Looking at the twelve-month period, the correlation coefficient for the Panhandle was 0.76 while the twenty-four-month value dropped only slightly, to 0.75. For the East Central Division, the

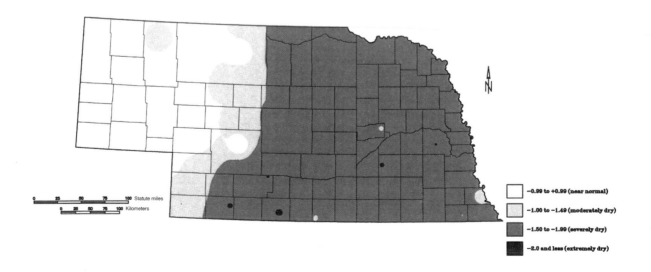

Figure 12.10 Twenty-four-month SPI through the end of December 1956. Sources as for Figure 12.9

Table 12.5 Drought frequency across Nebraska, 1949–96

Location	SPI time period	Number of droughts
Alliance	12	10
	24	6
	48	2
Broken Bow	12	12
	24	6
	48	3
Blair	12	11
	24	7
	48	3

Table 12.6 Annual rainfall by site and climatic division

Location	1934	1953	1965	1989	1993
Panhandle	10.98	17.12	21.67	11.92	21.8
Alliance	8.78	13.89	21.73	9.57	17.52
East Central	15.85	21.38	39.98	22.26	39.71
Lincoln	17.23	17.55	45.15	23.82	39.21

twelve-month correlation was also the strongest, with a value of 0.86. The twenty-four-month value was 0.81. For both divisions, the values were much lower for the nine- and six-month relationships. Thus, the inherent time scale of the PDSI shows a larger lag in response time to current conditions than does the SPI, which can be computed from one to twelve months. As seen in Figure 12.11, the strongest relationship between the PDSI and SPI for all of the climatic divisions was generally found in the twelve- to fifteen-month range, where r^2 values were greater than 0.80.

Mapping various SPI periods within a given year, or years, demonstrates that a site can be classified as either wet or dry (e.g., a short-term [one- to three-month] wet period imbedded in an eighteen-month severe or extreme dry period or vice versa). Analyses of these various maps can be an invaluable tool for planners and decision makers in tracking and triggering mitigative measures.

Interpretation and knowledge of the local climatology plays a key role in interpreting past, present, and future index values at any scale of use. Understanding how the SPI detects, tracks, and depicts his-torical droughts is an important key in recognising and developing triggers for operationally monitoring future droughts.

APPLICATION OF THE SPI: MONITORING THE DROUGHT OF 1995–6

One of the major strengths of the SPI is that its capability to show multiple time scales enables it to detect a drought's onset and development. This ability was demonstrated during the 1995–6 drought in the southern Plains and southwestern United States (Hayes *et al.* 1998). The states most affected by the drought were Kansas, Oklahoma, Texas, New Mexico, and Arizona.

This drought began with a very dry October 1995. The months following October continued to be dry. By February 1996, it was clear that a drought was developing in the southern Plains. During February, dry, hot, and windy conditions caused large wildfires to burn across Texas and Oklahoma. Farmers in the region from southern Nebraska to northern Texas were concerned about the lack of rainfall and its impact on the region's hard red winter wheat crop.

By the end of February, a chart prepared by the Joint Agricultural Weather Facility (Figure 12.12) depicted precipitation for the October 1995–February 1996 period in this winter wheat region as the second lowest over the past 101 years. The five-month SPI map for the country (Figure 12.13) was also clearly showing the dryness for the October–February period in the southern Plains. Most of the climatic divisions from southern Nebraska to northern Texas, which includes the winter wheat region, were at least in the 'severely dry' category (SPI values ≤ -1.5). Dry conditions also appeared in the Southwest from southern California to New Mexico.

The drought situation did not improve in March 1996. By the end of March, the six-month SPI map (Figure 12.14) for October–March showed the same intensity and an increase in spatial extent of the drought into southern Texas. These examples illustrate how the SPI identified the developing drought conditions. At the same time, the PDSI map at the end of March was not accurately representing the drought severity in the southern Plains, and, in fact, barely showed any reason for concern (Figure 12.15).

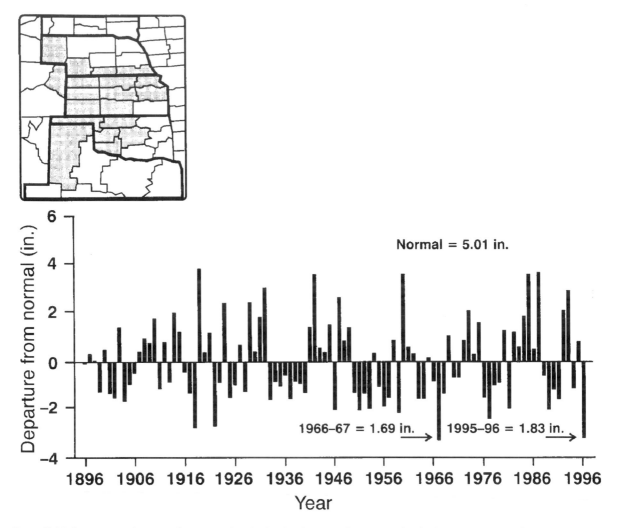

Figure 12.12 Precipitation departure from normal in the hard red winter wheat region for the five-month period October–February for 1896–1996

Sources: Data supplied by NCDC; map prepared by Joint Agricultural Weather Facility

However, farmers and others in the region confirmed the existence of severely dry conditions and potentially larger impacts. Thus, the lead time in recognising drought provided by the SPI, in comparison to the PDSI, was more than a month. This timeliness is an important improvement for making policy decisions concerning drought mitigation and response actions. The PDSI did not depict the true severity of the drought in the southern Plains until mid-May.

APPLICATION OF THE SPI: MONITORING THE WESTERN UNITED STATES IN 1997

In 1997, SPI maps at multiple time scales identified that drought was not a concern in California even though PDSI values, beginning in May and continuing through the summer, showed most of the state experiencing either 'severe' or 'extreme' drought (Figure 12.16). The uniqueness of the 1996–7 winter precipitation season in California provides an excellent example of why the characteristics of the SPI are

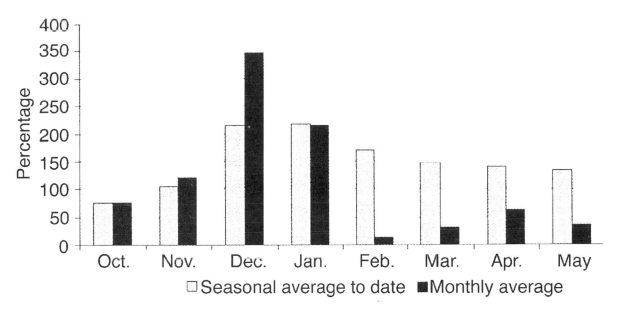

Figure 12.17 Seasonal and monthly percentage of average precipitation for eight stations in the Northern Sierra of California, October 1996–May 1997

valuable in assessing potential drought severity.

Most precipitation in California falls during the winter months (October to April). During the 1996–7 season, extremely heavy precipitation fell during October, November, December, and the first week of January. Dry conditions developed in the weeks that followed and persisted throughout the state for the remainder of the winter season (Figure 12.17).

It is clear that the map of PDSI values (Figure 12.16) is reflecting the dry conditions since the middle of January in the state. But how realistic are the low Palmer values in the 'severe' and 'extreme' drought categories? California depends on snowfall in the mountains to provide runoff to fill the reservoirs around the state. By 1 June 1997, reservoir levels in all areas of the state were adequate. Indeed, precipitation totals for the 1996–7 season were near normal for most of the state because of the combination of the extremely wet first half and dry second half.

The SPI helps to identify the characteristics of the water supply situation in California in 1997. The five-month SPI map at the end of June (Figure 12.18) shows the unusual dryness across California between February and June. Meanwhile, the three-month SPI for December 1996 (Figure 12.19) and

the nine-month SPI for June (Figure 12.20) illustrate how the abnormally wet October December period provided the state with adequate moisture to get through 1997 without serious drought conditions. The low Palmer values, and the low five-month SPI values, are still important to consider. Wildfires play a major role in California. Because of the adequate winter moisture, allowing plentiful vegetative growth, dryness during the spring and summer is a key indicator that wildfires could be a threat in the state. Although this was the situation for California in 1997, only an average number of wildfires was recorded.

CONCLUSIONS

The two SPI applications presented within this chapter illustrate the near real-time monitoring capability of the SPI and the strength of its multiple time scale characteristic. During the 1996 drought in the southern Plains and southwestern United States, the SPI identified regions potentially suffering drought impacts at least one month before other indices did. For California in 1997, the SPI realistically showed that drought was not a concern for water resources in the state although summertime PDSI values por- trayed the state in their 'severe' and 'extreme' drought categories. Thus, the SPI accomplishes the objectives of a drought index in its ability to identify the inten- sity, duration, and spatial extent of droughts as they occur. Meanwhile, the example for Nebraska shows that the SPI can also provide a good historical per- spective of droughts.

Accurate and timely monitoring of dynamic drought conditions is important for reducing the impacts of drought, but this information must be communicated to decision makers. A comprehensive early warning system is considered to be a critical component of a state or regional drought plan. Although no single index can adequately assess all elements of water supply, the characteristics of the SPI illustrate that it can be a valuable component of a drought early warning system.

REFERENCES

Doesken, N.J., McKee, T.B., and Kleist, J. (1991) 'Development of a Surface Water Supply Index for the western United States', Climatology Report Number 91–3, Department of Atmospheric Science, Colorado State University, Fort Collins.

Edwards, D.C. and McKee, T.B. (1997) 'Characteristics of 20th century drought in the United States at multiple time scales', Climatology Report Number 97–2, Department of Atmospheric Science, Colorado State University, Fort Collins.

Hayes, M.J., Svoboda, M.D., Wilhite, D.A., and Vanyarkho, O.V. (1999) 'Monitoring the 1996 drought using the Standardized Precipitation Index', *Bulletin of the American Meteorological Society* 80, 3: 429–38.

McKee, T.B., Doesken, N.J., and Kleist, J. (1993) 'The relationship of drought frequency and duration to time scales', *Proceedings of the Eighth Conference on Applied Climatology*, Boston, MA: American Meteorological Society.

McKee, T.B., Doesken, N.J., and Kleist, J. (1995) 'Drought monitoring with multiple time scales', *Proceedings of the Ninth Conference on Applied Climatology*, Boston, MA: American Meteorological Society.

Yamoah, C., Hayes, M.J., and Svoboda, M.D. (1997) 'Application of the Standardized Precipitation Index to estimate crop yields in Nebraska', *Proceedings of the Tenth Conference on Applied Climatology*, Boston, MA: American Meteorological Society.

13

MONITORING THE INCIDENCE OF LARGE-SCALE DROUGHTS IN INDIA

H.P. Das

INTRODUCTION

During the northern hemispheric summer, the Indian subcontinent witnesses conspicuous seasonal changes in wind systems. Other significant synoptic features are the heat near the surface over northwest India and adjoining Pakistan, the anticyclones in the higher troposphere over Tibet, the intertropical convergence zone over the Indo-Gangetic plains, and the tropical easterly jet in summer. Variations of some of these features from the normal pattern often lead to aberrant weather situations like droughts or floods.

Summer monsoon rains constitute the greatest climatic resource of the Indian subcontinent. For India, traditionally, these rains support not only the country's agriculture and food production, they also contribute substantially to power generation and hence to expanding industrial production for the ever-increasing population and its subsequent demand for more food and power. Our dependence on the monsoon rains has become even more critical and crucial. Success or failure of the crops, and hence the economy, is intimately linked with prospects of good or bad monsoon. No wonder agriculture in India is often seen as a gamble on summer monsoon rainfall.

One of the worst natural calamities that affects India is the large-scale incidence of drought during the summer monsoon season (June to September). In fact, the most common natural cause of Indian famines in the past has been the occurrence of widespread droughts. Droughts create innumerable problems immediately or over time as the economy gradually experiences the adverse shocks of this calamity. If the drought is extensive and prolonged, the cumulative effect is often disastrous. A severe drought not only causes serious damage to the Indian economy but also adversely affects the people. To reduce the effects of droughts on the economy and to mitigate human suffering, the government often has to take extraordinary fiscal and social measures.

DEFINITION OF DROUGHT

The drought problem can be considered basically as a problem of the management and use of limited water resources. It is essentially a 'supply' and 'demand' problem. Any definition that does not include a reference to water 'need' *vis-à-vis* 'demand' must be regarded as inadequate. For this reason, it is rather difficult to come up with a unified definition of the drought phenomenon. Broadly, at least three types of drought are recognised in India.

Meteorological drought

Meteorological drought over an area is defined as a situation in which the seasonal rainfall over the area is less than 75 per cent of its long-term normal. It is further classified as 'moderate drought' if the rainfall deficit is between 26 per cent and 50 per cent and 'severe drought' when it exceeds 50 per cent. There could be meteorological drought on the local, regional, or national scale, varying in horizontal extent, from a cluster of a few districts to several meteorological subdivisions. On a temporal scale, a drought can last for a few weeks or it can be prolonged for a few months or years.

Hydrological drought

If prolonged, meteorological drought can result in hydrological drought, with a marked depletion of surface water and consequent drying of reservoirs, lakes, streams, and rivers, and also a fall in the groundwater table.

Hydrological drought differs from meteorological drought in that the streamflow rate, water reservoir supplies, and groundwater levels are affected by longer durations of unseasonal dryness. Consequently, hydrological drought is often out of phase with meteorological drought.

Agricultural drought

Among the various types of drought, agricultural drought affects the largest section of society. Crop growing periods in the tropics, where dry and wet seasons are well marked, generally coincide with the wet season, which in itself is often subjected to large-scale fluctuations because of vagaries of monsoon rainfall. In definitions of agricultural drought, rainfall deficiency has to take into account physical and biological aspects of the plant, interaction within the soil–plant–atmosphere continuum, and the balance between water demand of plants and water supply.

An agricultural drought occurs when soil moisture and rainfall are inadequate during the growing season to support a healthy crop growth to maturity, causing extreme crop stress and a drastic decrease in yields.

ANALYSIS OF RAINFALL AND DROUGHTS IN INDIA

Droughts and famines have occurred in India for centuries and have even been mentioned in folklore. No precise data of these events are available, however. Since the establishment of the India Meteorological Department in 1875 and systematic data generation, it has been possible to demarcate areas affected by droughts in each year. Some typical cases of significant droughts are depicted in Figure 13.1. The year 1918 appears to have experienced the worst drought the country has ever witnessed in terms of area

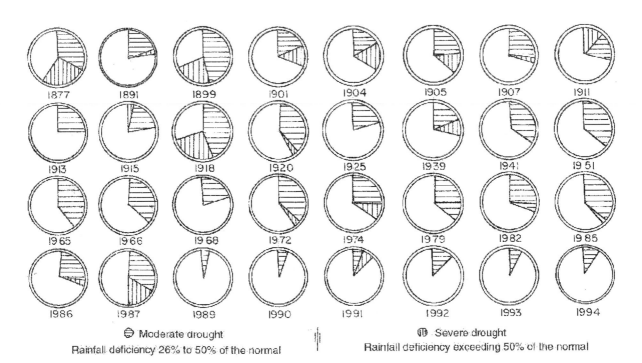

Figure 13.1 Drought years in India, with percentage of the area affected since 1875

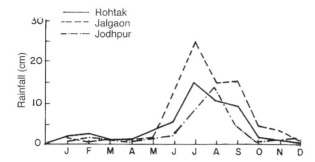

Figure 13.2a First type of rainfall in the problem areas
Source: After Kanitkar 1960

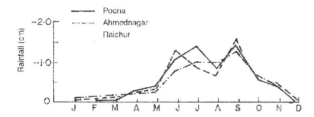

Figure 13.2b Second type of rainfall in the problem areas
Source: After Kanitkar 1960

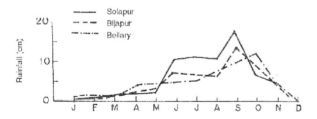

Figure 13.2c Third type of rainfall in the problem areas
Source: After Kanitkar 1960

affected and rainfall departures (Chowdhury *et al.* 1989, Bhalme *et al.* 1990). In terms of area affected, this is followed by droughts in 1899, 1877, 1987, and 1972, in that order. The average seasonal rainfall over the plains of India is a useful tool to determine if the country has suffered from drought. While Koteswaram (1973) estimated this average to be 105 cm, Mooley and Parthasarathy (1983) and Thapliyal (1990) consider the normal seasonal rainfall to be 85.3 and 87.2 cm, respectively.

Regional distribution of rainfall over India is not even and shows wide variations. The principal sources of rain in the Indian subcontinent are the two periodic wind systems known as the southwest monsoon, as mentioned above, and the northeast monsoon. The summer monsoon accounts for about 90 per cent of annual rainfall over different parts of India. The northeast monsoon, which begins in October along the southeast coast and lasts until December, is the principal source of rainfall over this area.

If monthly rainfall distribution data from a few typical stations from the dry and water-scarce areas are carefully examined, three distinct types of rainfall distribution can be easily distinguished (Kanitkar 1960).

In the first type, stations that mainly receive rainfall from the southwest monsoon are included. In this category, as seen in Figure 13.2a, the rainfall has a peak in either July or August. The rainfalls in the remaining months are comparatively lower. At these stations, more than 60 per cent of the annual rainfall usually is received in the first three months (June to August).

The second type of station, although receiving rainfall in the southwest monsoon, also experiences substantial rainfall in the northeast monsoon. Hence, the rainfall pattern shows two peaks of more or less equal magnitude (Figure 13.2b). The rainfall received during the southwest monsoon varies from 40 per cent to 55 per cent of the annual total, while that received during the northeast monsoon amounts to 40–50 per cent.

The third type includes places where the northeast monsoon is more important. The rainfall curve shows only one peak in the latter part of the monsoon (September or October/November – see Figure 13.2c). In this type, the rainfall in the southwest monsoon is further reduced and the northeast monsoon makes up 45–60 per cent of the total rainfall of the year. This type of rainfall distribution is a characteristic feature in dry farming tracts of the Deccan plateau.

Vagaries of rainfall resulting in serious depletion of surface water, drought, or famines have received attention from Indian meteorologists and hydrologists since very early times. Legends of rain-god worship to avert famine and offering prayers are well known in India. Thus, large interannual variability is inherent in Indian monsoon rainfall, and occasions of excess rains and drought events have occurred randomly.

From an analysis of rainfall departure, it is possible

to demarcate areas of different degrees of drought. A drought-prone area is defined as one in which the probability of a drought year is greater than 20 per cent. A chronic drought-prone area is one in which the probability of a drought year is greater than 40 per cent. A drought year occurs when less than 75 per cent of the 'normal' rainfall is received.

Bhalme and Mooley (1980) observed frequent large-scale droughts during 1891–1920 and 1961–75, with only a few isolated instances of major drought between 1921 and 1960. The years of monsoon failure during 1871–1978 have been identified by Mooley and Parthasarathy (1982). The four worst monsoon failures were those of 1899, 1918, 1877, and 1972, in order of decreasing monsoon rainwater deficiency. During 1877, 1899, and 1918, a large part of the country experienced rainfall departures of less than –60 per cent, in contrast to 1972, when the area with –60 per cent or greater deficiency was very small. However, the significant point to be noted here is that the demand for water in 1972 was much larger than that during the earlier years of the worst monsoon failures, the Indian population in 1972 being about 2.4 times the population in 1891. In 1899, there were some pockets in northwest India where the seasonal rainfall was less than even 5 per cent of the normal.

India has been divided into thirty-five meteorological subdivisions that are nearly homogeneous from a rainfall point of view. Kulshrestha and Sikka (1989) found that the number of subdivisions affected by droughts was high during 1871–80, 1891–1900, 1901–10, 1911–20, 1961–70, and 1971–80. When several decades were combined to provide an understanding of the decadal scale variability, they found that the 1891–1920 and 1961–90 periods witnessed frequent droughts while few droughts occurred during 1930–60. This suggests some kind of low-frequency oscillation of the monsoon system on the decadal scale.

DATA AVAILABILITY FOR DROUGHT MONITORING

Most drought monitoring systems are based largely on meteorological data. This data can be used in conjunction with other data and information such as temperature, humidity, and soil moisture to estimate the probable impact of a drought situation. Identification of any type of drought and its extent requires different types of data than that required for research or for the operation of a drought mitigation system. The data requirements are thus interest specific and each type of drought requires different sets of data. The most common element for all types of droughts, however, is rainfall. For hydrological drought, we need rainfall and evaporation data and information on water-holding capacity of the soils in the catchment areas of the water bodies. For agricultural drought, we need data on soil type and texture, water-holding capacity, slope of the ground surface, bulk density, cultivar characteristics, and irrigation and crop management data. (For a broader description of the variables necessary for drought monitoring, see Chapter 1.)

In India, the recurring severe countrywide droughts and ensuing famines during the last quarter of the nineteenth century focused the attention of the government of India on the immediate need for a meteorological service. Systematic instrumental observations in India began toward the end of the eighteenth century during the time of the East India Company with the establishment of meteorological observatories at Madras (1792), Simla (1840), and Bombay (1841). The provincial meteorological services were centralised and the India Meteorological Department came into existence in 1875. This enabled the adoption of uniform methods and standards for collecting, recording, and analysing data. The organisation gradually expanded and presently India has nearly 8,000 reporting and nonreporting raingauge stations.

Thus, India now has more than a century of systematic, accurate, and reliable data for such parameters as rainfall, temperature, atmospheric pressure, and winds for a number of stations. For information regarding earlier centuries, one has to fall back on vague information and cursory records and such indirect information on the weather sequences as may be provided by growth rings of old trees (i.e., dendrochronology), folklore, and so forth.

Without doubt, the most spectacular observing tool in the last few decades is the meteorological satellite. Some of these satellites provide data on 'wetness' of vegetated surfaces and also surface wetness.

These data can be used to depict changes in the photo-synthetic activity of vegetation and thus are useful in the early detection of the onset and spread of drought conditions. These data are now used routinely as part of the National Agricultural Drought Surveillance System in India (Thiruvengadachari 1991).

There should be a concerted effort to develop strategic networks to provide data that support drought detection and monitoring systems. However, no data collection system is complete unless it includes an efficient, timely, and effective means of communication from the observation point to the processing or analysing point. Adequate quality control, regular instrument maintenance, efficient procedures, and communication channels for transmitting advice and warnings to users are also essential.

DROUGHT MONITORING

As noted above, drought is an insidious phenomenon; its onset is gradual and its intensity develops slowly over a prolonged period of time. These features of drought have made monitoring drought conditions a difficult task. In general, two types of monitoring systems exist: surface observations and satellite/remote sensing networks. By suitably integrating these methods, a three-dimensional monitoring system can be established that is characterised by combinations of ground-based observation and space-based and mobile observation facilities. These networks are capable of monitoring all the critical elements associated with any type of drought, including precipitation, surface water, soil moisture, crop water requirement, groundwater irrigation, and drainage. In addition, drought indices can be calculated using data collected from these networks. In drought monitoring, it is essential to establish appropriate and reliable drought indices for different user groups. It is also important to transmit this information in a timely manner via an efficient telecommunication system to its end users. A properly organised delivery system is essential for the monitoring and early warning system to be effective as a disaster mitigation tool.

As has been mentioned above, drought is nothing but rainfall deficiency. Any analysis that progressively describes rainfall activity over a period of time and its deficiency from the long-term normal will indicate

onset, extent, intensity, and cessation of drought conditions.

The India Meteorological Department prepares rainfall maps on a subdivisional basis every week throughout the year. These maps show rainfall received during a week and the corresponding departures from normal. During the rainy season, these maps show the development of drought and its termination.

The India Meteorological Department also monitors drought using a water balance technique. Whereas the method mentioned in the previous paragraph indicates mainly meteorological drought, the water balance technique delineates agricultural drought. This monitoring is done during the kharif crop season (summer crop season) for the country as a whole and during the rabi crop season (winter crop season) for those areas that receive rainfall during post-monsoon/winter seasons. The methodology involves computing an index known as the aridity index (I_a) of the crop season for each week for a large number of stations, using the following formula:

$$\text{Aridity Index} = \frac{\text{Water deficit}}{\text{Water need}}$$

$$= \frac{\text{Actual evapotranspiration} - \text{Potential evapotranspiration}}{\text{Potential evapotranspiration}}$$

The departure of I_a from normal is expressed as a percentage. The following criteria are used to demarcate the area of various categories of agricultural drought:

Drought category	Anomaly value
Mild drought	up to 25 per cent
Moderate drought	26–50 per cent
Severe drought	more than 50 per cent

The anomalies are plotted for more than 250 well-distributed stations. Areas experiencing moisture stress conditions are demarcated and information is passed on to various users.

Typical cases of agricultural drought that occurred in some weeks over different parts of the country during the monsoon period of 1994 are illustrated in Figure 13.3.

The India Meteorological Department follows yet another method in which crop conditions including

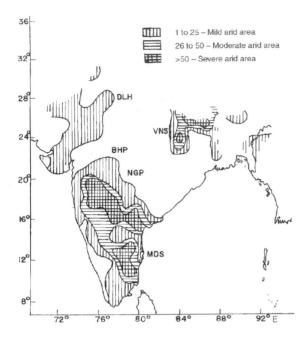

Figure 13.3a Week ending 2/9/94

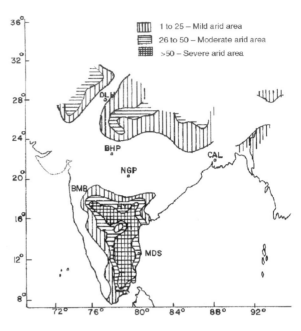

Figure 13.3c Week ending 16/9/94

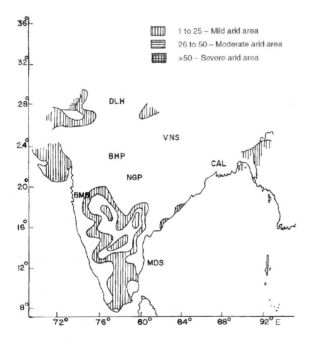

Figure 13.3b Week ending 9/9/94

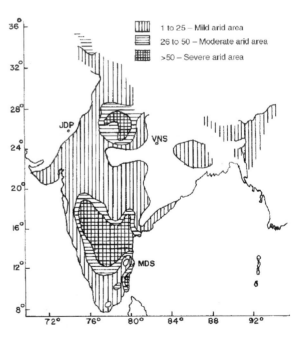

Figure 13.3d Week ending 23/9/94

droughts are monitored and remedial measures are suggested. This system works mostly at the various state capitals, where detailed statewise maps containing weekly rainfall, progressive seasonal rainfall totals and their departures from normal, maximum and minimum temperature, cloud cover, and relative humidity are prepared. These analysed charts are discussed, *vis-à-vis* prevailing crop conditions, incidence of pest disease, and so forth, with agriculture experts (viz., plant pathologists and agronomists from the concerned states). Taking into consideration the actual weather conditions, the outlook, and the crop reports, the 'Agromet Advisory Bulletin' is then prepared.

The bulletins are then disseminated through radio, television, the print media, and village extension workers. Such bulletins are issued from sixteen centres twice a week and one centre once a week. Efficacy of the bulletin is evaluated by sending a set of questionnaires to progressive farmers at the end of the crop season, and the feedback received is kept in mind when preparing future bulletins.

To meet the special requirements of agricultural practices on a medium-range time scale (i.e., three to ten days), the National Centre for Medium Range Weather Forecasting (NCMRWF), with super-computing facility in the form of Cray XMP–14, has also been established. The NCMRWF is providing forecasts based on dynamical models to meet the special requirements of the agricultural community on a medium range scale. Under this scheme, specialists in dynamical meteorology, agrometeorology, agronomy, plant diseases and pests, and other disciplines jointly frame forecasts on the scale of clusters of districts and develop strategies to meet different rainfall situations for the benefit of agriculturists. Presently this is being done from twenty-two centres in India.

Rainfall and crop situations and, indirectly, drought are also monitored by a special task force known as the 'Crop Weather Watch Group' in India under the Central Ministry of Agriculture. This group reviews the progress of monsoons, crop situations, water levels in reservoirs/dams, availability of fertilisers, and so forth. Reports on pest surveillance, locust invasion, and pesticide application are also discussed. Appropriate action on weeding, soil mulching, or thinning plant stands and application of nutrients in areas affected by drought are also suggested. To achieve these objectives, the task force meets every week during the crop season.

Remote sensing and drought monitoring

In recent years, many investigations have demonstrated the capability of satellite-borne sensors to provide information on various drought indicators, which helps to monitor drought more effectively. The following paragraphs discuss remote sensing of rainfall, soil moisture, and vegetation/crop conditions, which are helpful in delineating agricultural drought.

Rainfall estimation by remote sensing

Satellite estimation of rainfall is not likely to be better than rainfall measured through conventional rain-gauges, but nevertheless is useful to fill in spatial and temporal gaps in ground reports. Nageswara Rao and Rao (1984) demonstrated an approach for preparing an indicative drought map based on NOAA AVHRR derived rainfall estimation at the seedling stage of crop growth. For drought monitoring, quantitative point-specific rainfall estimates on a daily basis all over the country may not be required. What is needed, however, is the capability to spatially distribute the point rainfall observations over the areal unit in a qualitative manner.

Remote sensing of soil moisture

Microwave sensors are probably the best soil moisture sensors, considering the strong physical relationship between the microwave response and soil moisture and the capability of microwaves to penetrate clouds, precipitation, and herbaceous vegetation. The principal advantage of active microwave sensors is that high spatial resolution can be obtained even at satellite altitudes.

Microwave sensors can provide estimates of soil moisture only in surface layers up to 10 cm thick. This depth is too shallow, compared to the 1–2 m root zone of many field crops in the tropics. Using the water content in the top 10 cm of the surface layer, the moisture content can be calculated within acceptable limits and with minimum error when the surface soil moisture estimation is made just before dawn.

Some investigations are under way at the National Remote Sensing Agency, Space Application Centre, and elsewhere to evaluate ERS-1 SAR data for soil moisture estimates in the surface layers.

Remote sensing of vegetation status

During periods of drought conditions, physiologic changes within vegetation may become apparent. Satellite sensors are capable of discerning many such changes through spectral radiance measurements and manipulation of this information into vegetation indices, which are sensitive to the rate of plant growth as well as to the amount of growth. Such indices are also sensitive to the changes in vegetation affected by moisture stress.

The visible and near infrared (IR) bands on the satellite multispectral sensors allow monitoring of the greenness of vegetation. Stressed vegetation is less reflective in the near IR channel than nonstressed vegetation and also absorbs less energy in the visible band. Thus the discrimination between moisture stressed and normal crops in these wavelengths is most suitable for monitoring the impact of drought on vegetation.

The National Remote Sensing Agency in India has developed a vegetation index to determine vigour of vegetation. The Normalized Difference Vegetation Index (NDVI) is defined by them as:

$$NDVI = \frac{NIR - VIS}{NIR + VIS}$$

where NIR and VIS are measured radiation in near infrared and visible (chlorophyll absorption) bands.

The NDVI varies with the magnitude of green foliage (green leaf area index, green biomass, or percentage green foliage ground cover) brought about by phenological changes or environmental stresses. The temporal pattern of NDVI is useful in diagnosing vegetation conditions.

Moisture stress in vegetation, resulting from prolonged rainfall deficiency, is reflected by lower NDVI values. Such a decrease could also be caused by other stresses, such as pest/disease infestation, nutrient deficiency, or soil geochemical effects. Discrimination of moisture stress from other effects does not present a problem in coarse resolution data over large areal units, as neither pest/disease attack nor nutrient stress is selective in terms of area or crop type.

National Agricultural Drought Assessment and Monitoring System (NADAMS)

Since 1989, the National Agricultural Drought Assessment and Monitoring System (NADAMS) has been providing biweekly drought bulletins through the kharif season (June to December) for 246 districts in most of peninsular and northern India. The bulletins, which describe prevalence, relative severity level, and persistence through the season at the district level, are being sent to concerned state and central administrators as well as to district-level officers. The drought assessment is based on a comparative evaluation of satellite-observed green vegetation cover (both area and greenness) of a district in any specific time period to cover in similar periods in the previous year. The trend of seasonal vegetation development until the reporting period is also compared with trends of previous years. The drought interpretation takes into account rainfall and aridity anomaly trends (Figure 13.4.) This nationwide early warning service has been found to be useful for providing early assessment of drought conditions.

MONITORING SPATIAL AND TEMPORAL ASPECT OF DROUGHT

The duration, severity, and areal extent of drought are particularly crucial to agriculture. Once a drought condition is established, the duration and areal extent can be monitored closely from the basic meteorological variables. However, drought intensity with respect to potential crop yield needs to be scrutinised using measurements or estimates of plant water demand and soil moisture supply. Timing with respect to stages of crop development also determines the magnitude of agricultural drought.

Short-term episodes of dryness may be of little consequence to crops in a particular phase of their growth cycle, while a similar occurrence during a highly sensitive phase may ultimately ruin the crop and drastically reduce the yield. The type of crop, soil characteristics, and location will determine the effects

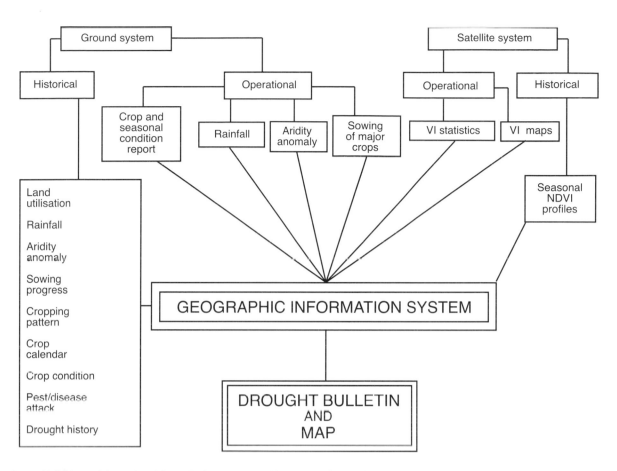

Figure 13.4 National Agricultural Drought Assessment and Monitoring System (NADAMS)

of these episodes. The commencement of drought need not coincide with the commencement of a dry spell, because the crops may survive for some time on stored moisture. The cessation of a drought episode is also difficult to determine because brief intermittent interruptions of the drought event may be of little significance to agriculture.

Five distinct categories of drought affecting crop production in drylands were clearly distinguished (Ramana Rao 1992) in India, depending on the time of occurrence of drought and general climatic conditions of the region. These categories are discussed below.

Early season drought Early season drought occurs when rains necessary for sowing are delayed. Sometimes early rains may occur, tempting the farmers to sow the crops, followed by a long dry spell leading to withering of seedlings and poor crop establishment. Usually, optimum sowing periods are established on the basis of agronomic trials conducted for a period of three to five years in conjunction with critical analysis of the commencement of sowing rains.

Mild season drought These occur in association with the 'breaks' in the monsoon, when the moisture stored in the soil falls short of the water requirement of the crop. If this drought condition occurs during the vegetative phase of crop growth, it might result in stunted growth, low leaf area development, and even reduced plant population. If drought conditions occur after the maximum leaf area development, there is rapid depletion of soil moisture, since the water requirement of the crop depends on the solar radiation intercepted by the crop canopy. When drought conditions occur during the reproductive stage of crop growth, the grain yield will be adversely affected, because the accumulation of dry matter in the storage organs takes place during the post-anthesis period.

Late season drought If the crop encounters moisture stress during the reproductive stage due to early cessation of the rainy season, there is usually a rise in temperature, which hastens the process of crop development to forced maturity. Therefore, late-season droughts must be characterised on the basis of the relationship between water availability to the crop during the reproductive stage and the grain yield.

Permanent drought Permanent droughts are associated with inadequate soil moisture/rainfall to meet the water requirements of the crop during most years. In the arid and semiarid regions of India, crops are grown for subsistence, although the rainfall is not adequate to grow a short duration crop of seventy-five to eighty days. Therefore, the crops are often subjected to moisture stress because of the inadequacy of rainfall to meet the water requirements of crops during most years.

Apparent drought Rainfall in the region may be adequate for one crop but not for others. For example, paddy is grown in some of the dry subhumid regions where it should not be grown. Whenever there is failure of rains in these areas, the rainfall may not be sufficient for paddy. Instead of growing paddy, other crops, like maize, sorghum, and finger millet, could be grown with success. Therefore, apparent drought conditions are encountered because of mismatched cropping patterns in relation to the rainfall/moisture availability patterns.

DROUGHT DURATION

Another distinguishing feature of drought is its duration. Droughts usually require a threshold period of time to become established and usually can last for more than a season. The magnitude of drought impacts is closely related to the timing of the onset of the drought, its intensity, and its duration. Intensity refers to the degree of the precipitation shortfall and/or the severity of impacts associated with the shortfall. Most places in India are subjected to drought in the agricultural sense, but duration and intensity vary

greatly from one climatic zone to other. Drought conditions reach calamitous proportions if the drought occurs for more than one year in the same region. In India, severe droughts occurred in west Rajasthan in 1904 and 1905. The same region experienced moderate droughts consecutively in three years – 1980, 1981, and 1982. Punjab and Haryana states experienced moderate droughts of two consecutive years on two occasions or more. Similarly, moderate droughts occurred in 1965 and 1966 in east Uttar Pradesh, Rajasthan, and east and west Madhya Pradesh. Such consecutive years of drought have a more serious effect than a severe drought of one year. Agro-based industries are the most seriously affected sector.

Droughts also differ in terms of their spatial characteristics. Drought can occur over areas of a few hundred square kilometres, but almost invariably, intensities are not severe and durations are relatively short. The areas affected by severe drought evolve gradually, and regions of maximum intensity shift from season to season.

DROUGHT INDICES

A drought index calculated from known values of selected parameters enables us to evaluate the drought hazard over an area and assess the current extent and severity of drought over a region.

Indices for delineating meteorological drought

In India, Kalyansundram and Ramasastry (1969) modified Van Rooy's (1965) anomaly index by using 25 per cent rainfall departure instead of the mean departures of the ten lowest values. The index, however, could not identify some of the worst drought years in India. The basic difficulty in these studies is that although they were aimed at defining agricultural drought, the water need of the plants in relation to demand was never considered.

Bhalme and Mooley (1980) developed an index, the Drought Area Index, using monthly rainfall deficiency for defining large-scale drought in India. The index is based on the assumption that agriculture in a region is adjusted to average rainfall variability. The criteria that evolved were found to agree well with the actual conditions.

Mooley *et al.* (1981) adopted a percentile method for drought studies in India. They considered a year as having drought when the rainwater deficiency was below the tenth percentile of the normal distribution. With a view to assessing deficiency in monsoon rainfall of India, an index called the Monsoon Deficiency Index was developed by Mooley and Parthasarthy (1982). This index was obtained by expressing the area of the country receiving 80 per cent of the seasonal normal rainfall as a fraction of the total area of the country. In their methodology, however, the authors had ignored year-to-year variations in the area affected. Mooley and Parthasarthy (1983) proposed criteria based on rainfall expressed as a standard deviate, Y_i, given by

$$Y_i = (X_i - \bar{X})/\sigma$$

where X_i is the rainfall of ith year, $\bar{X}$ is the normal rainfall, and σ is the standard deviation. They considered drought to have occurred when $Y_i < -1.28$, the value 1.28 being 10 per cent of the value of the Gaussian distribution. Since districts were used as the basic unit instead of meteorological subdivisions (which are comparatively far larger in area), this approach definitely gives a better representation of subnormal rainfall. A shortcoming in the method is the assumption that the rainfall is normally distributed. It is well known that rainfall over many parts of India is not normally distributed.

Chowdhury and Abhyankar (1984) developed criteria for delineating drought, using 25 per cent as the limit, which is widely assumed to be the threshold for initiating drought conditions in India. This study also does not take the interannual variability into account. Sarker (1988) considered India affected by drought when the departure of rainfall from normal is −11 per cent or less. The value of −11 per cent adopted in the study appears arbitrary. Chowdhury *et al.* (1989) proposed criteria for drought by taking into account rainfall deficiency of 25 per cent or more and the year-to-year variations by computing standard deviation for the area affected. Their definition of drought, however, is based on meteorological subdivisional data. A subdivision comprises a number of districts, and working out the mean for such a vast area (where rainfall is highly spatially variable) does not appear justified.

Indices for delineating and monitoring agricultural drought

The above-mentioned studies are based purely on rainfall deficiency in some way or another. So far as delineating meteorological/hydrological drought is concerned, these definitions may be quite adequate. But for agricultural drought, they are, by and large, of limited use. The beginning of agricultural drought depends on the degree of moistness of the soil at the start of the dry spell. Agricultural drought, therefore, begins when the vegetation cannot extract water from the soil rapidly enough to replace the moisture loss by respiration. It persists when there is no continued replenishment of the water in the soil. In other words, in any delineation of agricultural drought, unless water supply in relation to water need is taken into account, the whole exercise becomes meaningless. This aspect can be solved by a hydrological accounting procedure.

The Gibbs and Maher (1967) approach was used by George and Kalyansundram (1969) for assessing agricultural drought with respect to winter rice yields in India. The method in general was found to furnish critical values of rainfall for different months that would indicate agricultural drought.

Subrahmanyam and Sastri (1969) have computed an aridity index to identify droughts in India. The yearly march of the index was graphically plotted and the amplitude of the departure of the index from its normal value was taken to represent severity of drought on an annual basis. Employing a purely statistical technique, drought years were classified as moderate, large, severe, or disastrous, according to the departure of the aridity index from the normal value: less than $1/2\sigma$ (moderate); between $1/2\sigma$ to σ (large); between σ and 2σ (severe); above 2σ (disastrous), σ being the standard deviation.

The water balance technique was adopted by George and Ramachandran (1969) for drought identification. The date when soil moisture storage falls below half the field capacity after the cessation of monsoon rains was found to give a good indication of whether drought has occurred. In this technique, however, soil moisture storage values were arbitrarily chosen and evapotranspiration loss was calculated on a monthly basis using an empirical relationship.

Different water availability periods like preparatory, intermediate, humid, and moist (Cocheme and Franquin 1967) also provide an indication of crop drought. Agricultural drought has been studied by George and Alda (1969) using this technique for rice. It was found that a significant shortening of the humid period and its early termination led to shortfalls in kharif rice yield, and both kharif rice and wheat yield in rabi season are lowered when the moist period is shortened. Both these studies, however, provide mainly a qualitative idea of drought.

Frere and Popov (1979) developed an index to indicate minimum satisfactory water supply for annual crops. At the end of the growing period, this index, which is calculated for every decade, reflects cumulative stress experienced by the crop during its growth cycle.

Victor and Sastry (1984) worked out weekly soil moisture budgets for five kharif crops during July to October for a semiarid monsoonal climate station. The Soil Moisture Index (SMI) is the ratio of available water to available water capacity in the soil root zone (which is directly related to AE/PE) during different phases of crop production. The frequency distribution of weekly SMI values was computed and compared with a β distribution. The lowest probability of occurrence of agricultural drought was observed in pearl millet. At the flowering stage the probability of occurrence of agricultural drought for pearl millet, sorghum, peanut, corn, and upland paddy ranged from 40–2, 40–7, 40–63, 54–70, and 66–81 per cent, respectively.

Sarker and Biswas (1986) have developed an agroclimatic classification based on the Moisture Availability Index (MAI) to find out the agroclimatic potential of a region in India. MAI is defined as the ratio of assured rainfall (AR) to potential evapotranspiration (PE). This study enables us to identify the core of low crop potential or a scarcity zone.

Das (1987) critically examined agroclimatic potential of the state of Madhya Pradesh in India by working out the weekly MAI and the ratio of the actual evapotranspiration (ET) to potential evapotranspiration (PE). The study makes possible the delineation of the drought-prone area of the state and water stress conditions during the growing period.

Chowdhury and Gore (1989) developed an index

for monitoring agricultural drought. Accordingly, the difference between actual ET and $\acute{E}T$, expected from climatological consideration, is computed. The expected ET is found by multiplying PE by K, where

$$K = \frac{\overline{ET}}{\overline{PE}}$$

The bar denotes the average values. The value ET − $\acute{E}T$ is then weighted, taking into consideration the dry spells. The agricultural drought index Z is

$$Z = \eta(ET - \acute{E}T)$$

where η is a constant.

Agricultural drought is assumed to be experienced when $ET \leq \acute{E}T$. The Crop Moisture Index Υ_i for the ith week is defined as a linear function of Z.

The anomalies are plotted and analysed for every week of the crop-growing seasons. Areas experiencing stress conditions are demarcated using the above criteria, and this information is passed on to various users as another tool for drought monitoring.

IMPACT OF DROUGHT

In order to find ways to monitor drought, it is worthwhile to first determine the impact of drought on the socioeconomic framework of the country. The type of drought that has the most significant effect on a large section of the Indian population is agricultural drought. In economic consequences and human misery, it overshadows other kinds of droughts. It has an immediate effect on the recharge of soil moisture and results in reduction of streamflow and reservoir levels. Since canal irrigation projects in India are diversions from the rivers, a decrease in riverflow further limits irrigation. The availability of water therefore affects crops grown not only in the monsoon season (also known as Kharif crop season) but also in the winter or rabi crop season, since the rabi crops thrive mostly on residual moisture from the kharif season. When drought occurs consecutively for two years, irrigation and hydropower generation are also adversely affected.

Rainfall is the most important meteorological element that significantly influences the crop yield. The effect of drought on crop growth and yield is well known. Moderate water deficiencies during the growing season can result in stunting or distorted development and reduced crop yields. When hardened plants are subjected to drought, their protoplasm shows a lower viscosity and higher permeability to water than that of similar but nonhardened plants. Higher rates of photosynthesis, lower rates of respiration, and a higher root/shoot ratio characterise hardened plants (May and Milthrope 1962), contributing to lower yields.

The impact of droughts on food grain production is considerable since a large portion of the agricultural crops in India depend on rainwater. According to Rao and Manikiam (1985), weather, primarily rainfall, is responsible for a 50 per cent variation in crop yield in India. In the case of rice, which is a rain-fed crop in India and is often grown in hostile environments, the fluctuation is even greater. The kharif crops in India may be exposed to slight or severe water stress, depending on the number of rainless days associated with 'break' or weak monsoon conditions. Crops may also be exposed to waterlogging, in addition to moisture stress. In recent years, the technological advances of better seeds, fertilisers, mechanical tools, better water management, and efficient pest management no doubt have increased the food grain output substantially, yet drought still has an overall impact of reducing production by 8 to 10 per cent.

When we consider percentage change from year to year, the effect of nonmeteorological factors is likely to be eliminated in most cases, and the effect of drought is expected to be prominently noticed in crop yields in years of monsoon failure. A shortfall in food grain production caused by monsoon failure results in a rise in prices in the year following the monsoon failure. However, because of the tendency to hoard, the price rise can sometimes occur in the year of monsoon failure as soon as signs of the failure are noticed or as soon as the monsoon failure is speculated.

The year-to-year changes in food grain production are given in Table 13.1. Crop production invariably falls in a drought year compared to the preceding year, the fall in the monsoon failure year of 1979 being the largest (about 20 per cent). On average, the fall in food grain output in a drought year could be more than 9 per cent greater than the preceding year.

A dramatic rise in food production has generally been noticed (Table 13.1) in the year following the

Table 13.1 Percentage change in food grain production in years of monsoon failures and following years

Year of monsoon failure	% departure	Years following monsoon failure years	% departure
1965	−1.9	1967	24.3
1966	−12.6	1973	15.7
1972	−7.0	1975	25.0
1974	12.8	1980	22.7
1979	−18.9	1983	27.7
1982	−12.0	1988	29.2
1986	−6.7		
1987	−0.7		

drought, with most of the cases registering increases of more than 20 per cent. The largest rise is observed in 1988, when a benevolent and bountiful monsoon increased food output by 29.7 per cent more than in 1987. On average, one can expect a rise in crop output in kharif of 21 per cent in the year following drought.

The impact of the drought on farmers in India is manifested in the following measures adopted by them.

1 Reduce consumption.
2 Postpone social functions such as marriages.
3 Migrate to better areas with livestock, or sell stock.
4 Take consumption loans.
5 Sell assets like gold ornaments as a last resort.

Some farmers develop their own systems of food grains and fodder storage to tide them over during drought years.

CONCLUSIONS

Real-time drought monitoring methods are usually needed to maintain efficient irrigation practices, industrial and domestic water supply, crop and animal protection (e.g., emergency food and water relief), and hydroelectric supply.

Real-time monitoring of weather elements is usually the duty of the national and regional meteorological services. In India this is usually obtained from synoptic records, nonsynoptic records, remote sensing techniques (satellite and radar), and several other standard methods that include empirical techniques.

The real-time reports for hydrological and agricultural droughts can also be obtained from a good network of hydrological and agricultural stations. Records obtained from these stations in India include streamflow, soil moisture, crop growth, lake levels, radiation, evaporation, transpiration, field reports of water management, crops, livestock, and fishing.

ACKNOWLEDGEMENTS

The author wishes to express his gratitude to the Director General of Meteorology, New Delhi, for permission to write this chapter for this volume.

REFERENCES

Bhalme, H.N. and Mooley, D.A. (1980) 'Large scale droughts/floods and monsoon circulation', *Monthly Weather Review* 108: 1,197–211.

Bhalme, H.N., Sikder, A.B., and Jadhav, S.K. (1990) 'Coupling between the El-Niño and planetary-scale waves and their linkage with the Indian monsoon rainfall', *Meteorology and Atmospheric Physics* 44: 293–305.

Chowdhury, A. and Abhyankar, V.P. (1984) 'On some climatological aspects of drought in India', *Mausam* 35, 3: 375–8.

Chowdhury, A. and Gore, P.G. (1989) 'An index to assess agricultural drought in India', *Theoretical and Applied Climatology* 40: 103–9.

Chowdhury, A., Dandekar, M.M., and Raut, P.S. (1989) 'Variability of drought incidence over India: A statistical approach', *Mausam* 40, 2: 207–14.

Cocheme, J. and Franquin, P. (1967) 'An agro-climatological survey of a semi-arid area in Africa, South of Sahara', *WMO Technical Note* No. 86.

Das, H.P. (1987) 'Some aspects of climatological resources and its application to agriculture in Madhya Pradesh', Ph.D. thesis, submitted to the University of Poona.

Frere, M. and Popov, G.F. (1979) 'Agrometeorological crop monitoring and forecasting', *Plant Production and Protection Paper* No. 17, Food and Agriculture Organization, Rome, p. 64.

George, C.J. and Alda, K. (1969) 'Assessment of agricultural drought from water availability period', *Prepublished Scientific Report* No. 95, India Meteorological Department, Pune.

George, C.J. and Kalyansundram, V. (1969) 'A use of monthly rainfall deciles for assessing agricultural droughts in Bihar State', *Prepublished Scientific Report* No. 96, India Meteorological Department, Pune.

George, C.J. and Ramachandran, G. (1969) 'Assessment of agricultural drought from soil moisture deficit', *Prepublished Scientific Report* No. 94, India Meteorological Department, Pune.

Gibbs, W.J. and Maher, J.V. (1967) 'Rainfall deciles as drought indicators', *Bulletin* No. 48, Bureau of Meteorology, Melbourne.

Kalyansundram, V. and Ramasastry, K.S. (1969) 'A drought index based on the rainfall deficiencies as applied to winter Rice yield in Bihar State', *Prepublished Scientific Report* No. 97, India Meteorological Department, Pune.

Kanitkar, V. (1960) 'Dry farming in India', Indian Council of Agricultural Research, New Delhi.

Koteswaram, P. (1973) 'Climatological studies of droughts in Asiatic monsoon area', Proceedings of the India Meteorological Department, Pune.

Kulshrestha, S.M. and Sikka, D.R. (1989) 'Monsoons and droughts in India: Long-term trends and policy choices', Paper submitted to the national workshop on drought management, New Delhi.

May, L.H. and Milthrope, F.L. (1962) 'Drought resistance of crop plants', *Field Crop Abstract* 15: 171–9.

Mooley, D.A. and Parthasarthy, B. (1982) 'Fluctuations in the deficiency of the summer monsoon over India and their effect on economy', *Archiv für Meteorologie, Geophysik und Bioklimatologie Ser. B* 30: 383–98.

——— (1983) 'Variability of the Indian Summer Monsoon and tropical circulation features', *Monthly Weather Review* 111: 967–78.

Mooley, D.A., Parthasarthy, B., Sontakke, N.A., and Munot, A.A. (1981) 'Annual rainwater over India, its variability and impact on economy', *Journal of Climatology* 1: 167–86.

Nageswara Rao, P.P. and Rao, V.R. (1984) 'An approach for agricultural drought monitoring using NOAA/AVHRR and Landsat imagery', in T.D. Guyenne and J.J. Hunt (eds), *IGARSS'84: Remote Sensing – From Research towards Operational Use* (International Geoscience and Remote Sensing Symposium, Strasbourg, France, 27–30 August), Noordwijk, Netherlands: ESA Scientific and Technical Publications Branch, pp. 225–9.

Ramana Rao, B.V. (1992) 'Agrometeorology in drought management in rainfed areas', in L.L. Somani, K.P.R. Vittal, and B. Venkateswarlu (eds), *Dryland Agriculture in India – State of Art of Research in India*, Jodhpur: Scientific Publishers, pp. 9–20.

Rao, N.P.P. and Manikiam, B. (1985) 'Satellite remote sensing for a better disaster forecast and management for agricultural purposes', *Technical Report* TR-56-85, NNRMS, Bangalore, India.

Sarker, R.P. (1988) *Proceedings of the International Conference on Tropical Micro-Meteorology and Air Pollution*, Indian Institute of Technology, Delhi.

Sarker, R.P. and Biswas, B.C. (1986) 'Agroclimatic classification and assessment of crop potential and its application to dry farming tract of India', *Mausam* 37, 1: 27–38.

Subrahmanyam, V.P. and Sastri, C.V.S. (1969) 'Study of aridity and droughts at Vishakhapatnam', *Annals of the Arid Zone* 8: 18–23.

Thapliyal, V. (1990) 'Long range prediction of summer monsoon rainfall over India: Evaluation and development of new models', *Mausam* 41: 339–46.

Thiruvengadachari, S. (1990) 'Satellite surveillance for improved countrywide monitoring of agricultural drought conditions', *Proceedings of the National Symposium on Remote Sensing for Agricultural*

Applications, New Delhi, pp. 389–407.

—— (1991) 'Satellite surveillance system for monitoring agricultural conditions in India', unpublished paper, drought management and preparedness training seminar for the Asia and Pacific regions, Bangkok, Thailand.

Van Rooy, M.P. (1965) 'A rainfall anomaly index independent of time and space', *NOTOS* (Weather Bureau, South Africa) 14: 43–8.

Victor, V.S. and Sastry, P.S.N. (1984) 'Evaluation of agricultural drought using probability distribution of soil moisture index', *Mausam* 35: 259.

14

GLOBAL DROUGHT DETECTION AND IMPACT ASSESSMENT FROM SPACE*

Felix Kogan

INTRODUCTION

Among natural disasters, drought is the most damaging phenomenon that occurs every year across a portion of the world. In the quarter of a century since 1967, droughts have affected 50 per cent of the 2.8 billion people who suffered from all natural disasters. Because of drought's direct and indirect impacts, 1.3 million lives were lost, out of a total number of 3.5 million people killed by disasters (Obasi 1994). In the current decade, large-scale intensive droughts have been observed on all continents. The most memorable droughts affected large and productive agricultural areas of the globe (LeComte 1994 and 1995). Interest in using observations from satellites for drought monitoring has received enhanced attention over the last ten years. Especially successful was a technique developed at the National Oceanic and Atmospheric Administration (NOAA) using measurements of the Advanced Very High Resolution Radiometer (AVHRR) on board NOAA polar-orbiting satellites (Kogan 1987, 1990, and 1995). For the first time, reflectances in the visible, near infrared, and thermal bands were combined into numerical indices (Vegetation Condition Index [VCI] and Temperature Condition Index [TCI]), which considerably improved early drought detection, watch, and monitoring of drought's impacts on agriculture. This chapter presents the new remote sensing technology and its applications worldwide.

---

*NOTE: Figures 14.3, 14.5, 14.7, 14.8, 14.11, 14.13a and 14.13b can be found in the colour plate section located between pp. 160–1.

GENERAL CLIMATOLOGY OF DROUGHTS

The first impression of drought climatology can be obtained from the global distribution of the surface moisture balance (Figure 14.1) expressed as the climatological difference between annual precipitation and annual potential evaporation (Goldsberg 1972). In the areas with a negative moisture balance, vegetation is likely to be potentially vulnerable to drought. Although the farmers often compensate for a lack of water by irrigating crops, the water resources in agricultural areas are generally limited, especially in drought years and over large areas.

Nearly 50 per cent of the world's most populated areas are highly vulnerable to drought. More importantly, almost all of the major agricultural lands are located there (USDA 1994). In the world's two largest agricultural producers, the United States and the former Soviet Union (FSU), droughts occur almost every year. In the past century, the US area affected by severe droughts often exceeded 10 per cent of the entire United States. Every ten to fifteen years, the area exceeded 20 per cent, and in the Dust Bowl years of the 1930s, drought covered 65 per cent of the entire country (Wilhite 1993). Over the past 1,000 years of Russian history, catastrophic droughts occurred eight to twelve times in every century. Severe droughts are more frequent, especially in areas with limited climatic and ecosystem resources.

DROUGHT MONITORING

To reduce drought impacts, the main components of a drought preparedness and mitigation plan should include drought monitoring/early warning, assessment

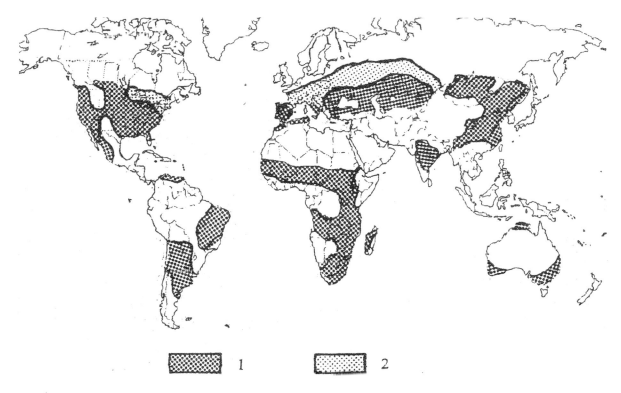

Figure 14.1 Vulnerability of major agricultural areas to drought based on a difference between annual precipitation and potential evaporation (Goldsberg 1972). 1 = frequent intensive drought (difference 10 to –500 mm); 2 = infrequent nonintensive drought (difference 0 to 200 mm)

of impacts, and response (Wilhite 1993). Timely information about the onset of drought and its extent, intensity, duration, and impacts can limit drought-related losses of life as well as human suffering and reduce damage to the economy and environment (Wilhite 1993).

Weather data is normally used for drought monitoring and impact assessment. However, the sparsity of weather stations in some areas makes drought watch a daunting task. Lack of weather information for drought analysis becomes especially acute in areas with limited climatic resources, economic disturbances, and political and military conflicts. Also, telecommunication problems and timely delivery of information to decision and policy makers is a serious concern for an efficient drought watch system.

Africa is the most vulnerable continent. Only a limited amount of weather data is available for the sub-Sahara (Figure 14.2). On average, one weather station is available per 21 million acres, while low-resolution polar orbiting satellite data are available for every 9,000 acres. In Sudan (with an area of about 1 million square miles), a satellite provides information for nearly 10,000 locations, while weather data is not available at all (Figure 14.2).

In addition to the lack of data availability, another constraint to monitoring is weather data that represent point locations rather than areas. Considering sharp spatial weather variability, especially precipitation, impact assessment for crops around a weather station could be very different from a similar assessment a few miles from the station, especially in arid zones. Moreover, weather parameters are physical in nature and are not entirely related to physiological characteristics of vegetation.

Additional constraints appear because of the absence of universal criteria for identifying drought and assessing its development and impacts. In the United

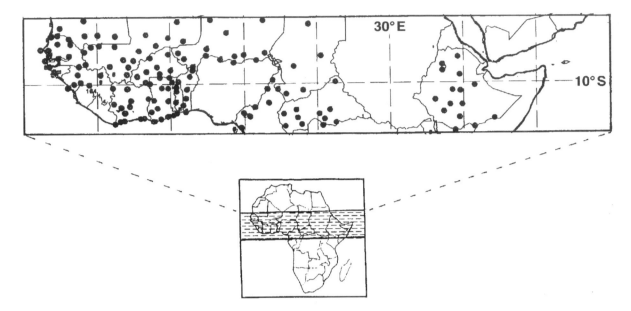

Figure 14.2 Weather station data available to global community on a typical day (9 April 1997), sub-Saharan Africa

States, the weather-based Palmer Drought Index (PDI) is used for this purpose (USDC/USDA 1988). However, the PDI has found little application outside of the United States. The drought watch in other countries is mostly based on domestic indices or weather anomalies (Sastri 1993, White *et al.* 1993, Kerang and Xianchao 1993, Kulik and Sinelshikov 1966). The absence of universal criteria makes it difficult to compare droughts in different continents and countries and to estimate its impacts.

Use of satellite data avoids most of these problems. Moreover, observations from polar-orbiting satellites managed by NOAA provide a unique vantage point, synoptic view, permanent data archive, cost effectiveness, and regular, repetitive view of nearly all of the surfaces.

REMOTE SENSING OF VEGETATION

Satellite remote sensing is based on measurements of electromagnetic radiation, which is reflected, emitted, and scattered by the atmosphere and surface. The intensity of the reflected and emitted radiation from the plant surface is determined by the surface temperature, emissivity, plant physiology, morphology,

chemistry, leaf geometry, fractional vegetation coverage, and soil type and structure (Gates 1970).

By its nature, vegetation has low reflectance in the visible (VIS) and high reflectance in the near infrared (NIR) bands of the solar spectrum. Because plants absorb VIS energy for photosynthesis, this reflectance is very low for normal chlorophyll content but increases when its content drops (Gates 1970, Gitelson and Merzlyak 1994). Water content prevents plants from absorbing high amounts of sun energy (reflecting energy) in the NIR spectral bands, helping them to keep their temperature cooler (Myers 1970, Gates 1970). However, when the amount of water decreases, the NIR reflectance drops, leading to an increase in the vegetation surface temperature and eventually to vegetation stress (Gray and McCrary 1981).

VEGETATION INDEX

The marked difference in vegetation signature to reflect the incident solar light in the VIS and NIR spectral regions was used for constructing the vegetation index (VI) and vegetation monitoring (Tucker 1978). Among many VIs, the Normalized Difference Vegetation Index (NDVI = (NIR − VIS)/(NIR +

VIS)) has been widely adopted and has become the most popular in the scientific and user community.

The NDVI for vegetation is much higher than it is for other entities of the earth (bare soil, rocks, clouds, snow, water), for which NDVI values are close to zero or negative (Holben 1986). More importantly, if vegetation health changes because of stressful environmental conditions, reflectance in the VIS increases while it decreases in the NIR (Gray and McCrary 1981). The opposite directions of these changes magnify the effect of NDVI response to the environmental stress, decreasing the index's value much more than changes in VIS and NIR. These NDVI features make it very useful for monitoring unhealthy vegetation.

DATA DESCRIPTION

Two types of data, satellite and ground, are presented in this chapter. Satellite data were used for drought monitoring and impact assessment, and ground data were applied for calibration of satellite data and result validation.

Satellite data were collected from the Global Vegetation Index (GVI) data set (Kidwell 1994). The GVI is produced by sampling and mapping the 1 km daily radiance in the VIS (Ch1, 0.58–068 μm), NIR (Ch2, 0.72–1.1 μm), and two thermal bands (Ch4, 10.3–11.3 μm, and Ch5, 11.5–12.5 μm) to a 16 km map. To minimise cloud effects, these maps, including the NDVI, are composited over a seven-day period by saving those values that have the largest difference between VIS and NIR reflectance for each map cell. The weekly GVI data for NOAA-9 (1985–8), NOAA-11 (1989–94), and NOAA-14 (1995 to present) were used here. The VIS and NIR channels were corrected for sensor degradation following Rao and Chen (1995). The thermal bands' measurements were converted to brightness temperatures using a look-up table (Kidwell 1994) and a nonlinear correction was applied following Weinreb et al. (1990).

The ground data included rainfall, temperature, vegetation density, biomass, and crop yield. Monthly rainfall and temperature anomalies (deviation from the long-term mean) for each first-order weather station were plotted on a map, and areas of intensive weather anomalies were singled out. Vegetation density was measured by calculating the number of plants per unit area and expressed as a deviation from the multiyear median. The ground data were used to validate satellite data.

AVHRR-BASED ALGORITHM

The VCI and TCI were derived from the NDVI and Ch4 radiance, respectively. The latter was converted to brightness temperature (BT). The NDVI and BT values were screened to eliminate high-frequency noise using statistical filtering of time series (van Dijk et al. 1987, Kogan and Sullivan 1993). This alternative approach completely eliminated the high-frequency outliers, including random outliers; accurately approximated the annual NDVI and BT cycles; and, more importantly, singled out low-frequency weather-related fluctuations (Kogan 1995).

After smoothing, interannual differences in NDVI and BT become more apparent. These differences are due to weather variations. For example, in dry years, the NDVI curve will be lower and the BT curve will be higher than in normal and wet years. This principle of comparing a dry year with other years in the data archive was laid down in the next stage of the algorithm development (Kogan 1994 and 1995).

Therefore, the envelope of the extreme NDVI and BT variations (multiyear maximum and minimum) was determined for each pixel and week. The assumption was that the maximum amount of vegetation is developed in years with optimal weather because such weather stimulates efficient use of ecosystem resources (for example, increase in the rate of soil nutrition uptake). Conversely, the minimum vegetation amount develops in years with extremely unfavourable weather (mostly dry and hot), which suppresses vegetation growth (Kogan 1995).

The condition of vegetation (VCI and TCI) for a particular year was calculated from the NDVI and BT values, which were normalised to their extreme variations (maximum and minimum) derived from multiyear data (equations 14.1–14.3). Since the NDVI and BT interpret extreme weather events in an opposite manner (for example, in case of drought, the NDVI is low and BT is high; conversely, in a nondrought year, the NDVI is high while the BT is low), equation

(14.2) was modified to reflect this opposite response of vegetation to temperature.

$$VCI = 100 \times (NDVI - NDVI_{min})/(NDVI_{max} - NDVI_{min}) \tag{14.1}$$

$$TCI = 100 \times (BT_{max} - BT)/(BT_{max} - Bt_{min}) \tag{14.2}$$

where NDVI, $NDVI_{max}$, and $NDVI_{min}$ are the smoothed weekly NDVI, its multiyear absolute maximum, and minimum, respectively; BT, BT_{max}, and BT_{min} are similar values for BT derived from Ch4 data. The VCI and TCI approximate the weather component in NDVI and BT values. They change from 0 to 100, reflecting variation in vegetation conditions from extremely poor to optimal. In drought years leading to yield reduction, VCI and TCI values drop below 35 (Kogan 1995 and 1997). This level was accepted as a criterion for drought detection. The VCI and TCI were also combined in one index (VT) to express their additive approximation of vegetation stress, as shown by equation (14.3).

$$VT = (VCI + TCI)/2 \tag{14.3}$$

With the development of the validation data set, some weights will be assigned to the VCI and TCI indices.

DROUGHT SPECIFICS

Drought is the most complex but least understood of all natural disasters. Therefore, a universally accepted definition of drought does not exist (Wilhite 1993). The major cause of drought is lack of precipitation. However, the same precipitation deficit could have different impacts, depending on other environmental conditions, type of ecosystem, and economic activities. The most widely used drought categories are meteorological, agricultural, hydrological, and socio-economic (WMO 1975, Wilhite and Glantz 1985). Because the VI characterises vegetation health in response to environmental conditions, the first two types of drought will be discussed further.

Droughts have some specific features that distinguish them from other natural hazards and make them difficult to identify (Wilhite 1993). Drought builds up slowly over a period of time, and its impacts on environment and/or economic activity are cumulative. Thus, the losses from drought are not immediately detectable (i.e., there is a lag time). In addition, the absence of a distinctive criterion for drought creates difficulties in identifying drought and assessing its onset, duration, areal extent, and severity. Drought spreads over a large area that makes it difficult to identify its impacts. In sum, drought is not easily identifiable, especially at its beginning, even if the appropriate weather observations are available.

DROUGHTS DURING 1986–96

In recent years, the VCI and TCI have been used successfully worldwide for detecting drought-related vegetation stress (Kogan 1994, 1995, and 1997; Hayes and Decker 1996; Liu and Kogan 1996). The most interesting cases found in Asia, Africa, Europe, and North and South America are presented here.

Large-area droughts

The following two examples feature Kazakh (from the FSU) and the United States.

Kazakh

Kazakh occupies nearly 1 million square miles (one-third of the area of the United States). The economy of Kazakh is highly dependent on agriculture, which has a grain and livestock orientation. One-tenth of Kazakh's land is sown to grain crops; the rest of the land is range lands providing feed to large herds of sheep that graze year round. A lack of rainfall, high rainfall variability, frequent droughts, and desiccative winds are typical of Kazakh's climate, causing a two- to three-fold variation in agricultural production.

Severe drought struck the newly formed country in 1991, reducing grain yield three-fold compared to the following year. The vegetation stress in 1991 was mostly moisture-related (VCI less than 30). The VCI differences at the end of June between severely stressed vegetation in 1991 and mostly favourable conditions in 1992 were very dramatic (Figure 14.3), although in early May, the 1991 conditions were much better than those of 1992 (Gitelson *et al.* 1996, Kogan 1997). The 1991 drought reached its apogee

(VCI below 15) in July and ceased thereafter.

Satellite-based drought estimates were supported by a considerable contrast in moisture supply from 1991 to 1992. The 1991 rainfall (Figure 14.4a) was much below normal starting in April, while in 1992 it was above normal for most of the growing season (WWCB 1993). In northern Kazakh, the VCI data closely matched wheat density (Gitelson *et al.* 1996) measured in the field during the 1991 and 1992 growing seasons (Figure 14.4b). It is noticeable that in both years, below-normal density in early May (week 18) corresponded to the VCI-derived estimates of vegetation stress (VCI around 20). In early June, both indicators showed that the stress weakened in 1992 and intensified in 1991. At the end of June and in July (weeks 24–30), the conditions continued to improve in 1992 (density above the mean and VCI above 50). They also improved in 1991, although both parameters were below 50. In the range land area of central (Akmola) and southern (Almaty) Kazakh, the VCI and density anomaly also showed a strong correlation (Figure 14.4c).

United States

The 1988 US drought was unique because of its occurrence early in the season as well as its rapid development and expansion and unusual severity, especially in the main agricultural areas.

Satellite data (Figure 14.5) detected a well-formed pattern of stressed vegetation quite early, at the beginning of May (week 18). This drought pattern was persistent, expanding rapidly to the primary agricultural regions by the end of June (week 26). The first weather-based Drought Advisories Report in 1988 was issued by the end of June (NOAA 1988), when the drought had already reached its highest level of development. The changes in the drought-affected area of the United States, estimated from satellite and ground data (Figure 14.6), are very coherent. This coherence is well pronounced during the development stage of drought (May–June). During the drought recovery stage, rainfall, being a physical indicator, indicated improving conditions more quickly than potentials of vegetation to recover. Satellite data provide more reasonable estimates of vegetation recovery during July–September.

Local droughts

Countries of Southern Africa

In recent years, frequent and severe droughts have become a major climatic disaster throughout southern Africa. Such droughts as 1982–4, 1991–2, and 1994–5 affected the region, with devastating impacts on agriculture, water resources, national economies, industry, and the environment. In between the major drought episodes, there were a number of local droughts, which were less destructive but still had serious economic consequences, especially for the developing nations.

Southern Africa's environmental resources are extremely diversified. Annual rainfall ranges from below 20 mm along the western areas of Namibia (Namib desert) to as high as more than 3,000 mm in some highland areas of Malawi (Nicholson *et al.* 1988). The rainy season spans October through April of the following calendar year, with January and February being the peak rainfall months. The vegetation of southern Africa follows the climate pattern quite closely. Corn is the main food crop, grown in areas of quite limited rainfall supply.

Local drought occurred during the principally favourable 1988–9 growing season. Vegetation was stressed only in the northern areas of the Republic of South Africa, southern Zimbabwe, and southern Mozambique (Figure 14.7). In contrast to the 1988–9 local drought, large areas of vegetation stress were identified during 1991–2, while in 1993–4, vegetation conditions were quite favourable across southern Africa. These estimates coincided with the rainfall pattern.

Vegetation stress: cause and effect

China

In 1994, China, which is the world leader in cotton production, unexpectedly purchased a large amount of cotton on the international market. The imports of cotton in 1994–5 were almost twice as large as any imports since 1981. A cotton yield reduction preceded this event three years in a row: 22 per cent in 1992–3, 11 per cent in 1993–4, and 7 per cent in

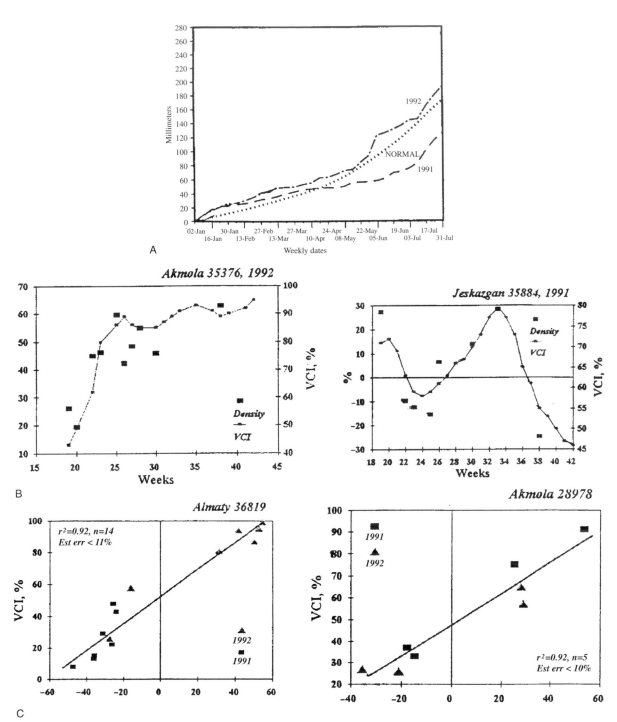

Figure 14.4 Cumulative precipitation (mm) in north central Kazakh (a), growing season dynamics of spring wheat density and VCI (b), and their correlation (c): weather stations 35376 (49.53° N, 69.31° E), 35884 (46.02° N, 70.12° E), 36819 (44.08° N, 75.51° E), and 28978 (52.32° N, 68.45° E)

Source: Kogan 1997, Gitelson and Kogan 1995

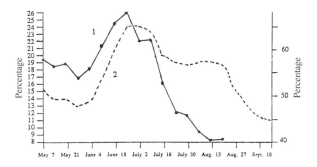

Figure 14.6 Percentage of the US area with less than 50 per cent of normal rainfall (1, left side axis) and with VCI below 10 (2, right side axis)
Source: NOAA 1988

1994–5 (the reduction was estimated relative to the average yield in the highly productive years 1990–1 and 1991–2 [USDA 1994]). AVHRR data showed that the yield reduction can be attributed to vegetation stress in the main cotton-growing areas (Figure 14.8). Of all three years, 1992 had the most severe vegetation stress. Moreover, both VCI and TCI contributed to the stress (VT less than 12) that was typical for severe drought. These results were supported by below-normal rainfall and above-normal temperatures during the summer, particularly in July (WWCB 1992).

Drought-related vegetation stress in the principal cotton-farming area was also observed in 1994. But the unusual weather feature of 1994 was the intensive preseason drought (Figure 14.9a), which resulted in a deficient water supply for irrigated cotton. Fortunately, this deficit was partially offset by a near-normal summer rainfall (Figure 14.9b). Therefore, the 1994 stress was much less intensive, covered a smaller area, and resulted in an insignificant cotton yield reduction compared to 1992. Unlike 1992 and 1994, the 1993 AVHRR-derived vegetation stress in the cotton-growing area was nondrought related because the values of the VCI were very low and TCI values were very high. Weather data support this finding, showing rainfall more than twice the normal amount during the critical period of cotton growth in July and August (Figure 14.9c). Meanwhile, in 1993, vegetation was stressed over a larger area than in 1994, although the stress was less intensive than in 1992, which is consistent with cotton yield reduction.

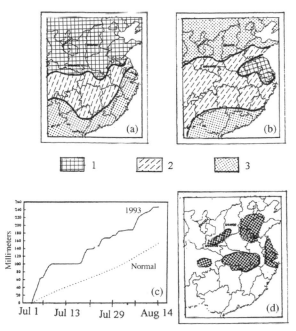

Figure 14.9 Percentage of normal precipitation (a) December 1993–May 1994 and (b) June–August 1994 (WWCB 1994); (c) 1993 cumulative daily rainfall, Hunan province (WWCB 1993); (d) main cotton areas (USDA 1994), southeastern China. For (a) and (b) rainfall: 1 – below normal, 2 – near normal, 3 – above normal

Agricultural versus meteorological droughts

Agriculture of Sahelian Africa's countries is very important for food self-sufficiency and is extremely vulnerable to drought. These countries use meteorological data widely for early drought detection, tracking, mapping, and severity assessment. However, this data is not always reliable for estimation of agricultural drought and its impacts on crops.

Ethiopia

Moisture resources are generally more favourable for agriculture in Ethiopia than in other countries of Sahelian Africa. The Ethiopian climate provides an adequate amount of annual rainfall (500–1,200 mm) in the areas of intensive farming, and numerous rivers have enough water for irrigation. However, weather variability, especially dry and hot weather, is crucial and decisive in labour-intensive farming. Since the

early 1970s, a series of very intense droughts have
affected Ethiopia, causing considerable damage to
crops and the economy, which depends on agriculture. The most memorable droughts, such as
1972, 1984, and 1991 (Yeshanew and Apparao 1989,
Hellden and Eklundh, 1988), resulted in the loss of
natural resources, property, livestock, and thousands
of human lives (Wodajo 1984, DHA 1993).

An interesting case of dryness occurred during
1987 in Ethiopia. As reported by Yeshanew and
Apparao (1989), that year was extremely dry because
precipitation for the entire country was the lowest
since 1969 (Figure 14.10a and 14.10c). Contrary to
the rainfall-derived intense dryness, VT data did not

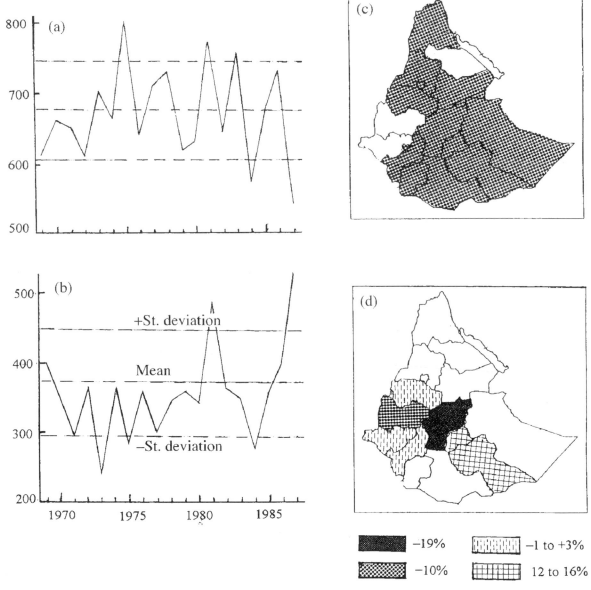

Figure 14.10 1987 cumulative rainfall (mm) during (a) May–September and (b) February–April, (c) area with more than 10 per cent
rainfall deficit during May–September in administrative regions (after Yeshanew and Apparao 1989), and (d) 1987 corn yield anomaly
(departure from the 1979–83 mean yield), Ethiopia

show significant vegetation stress; rather, slightly below-normal vegetation conditions (VT values 40–50) at the end of June 1987 (Figure 14.11a) were observed only in southwestern Ethiopia, mostly due to temperature stress (TCI4 image). In the southeastern pastoral zone, conditions were favourable (VT, VCI, and TCI4 above 75), although severe rainfall deficits were reported there (Yeshanew and Apparao 1989). Only small areas in the farming zone of central Ethiopia indicated vegetation stress (VT values 10–30) at the end of June 1987 (Figure 14.11a). However, the situation changed drastically by the end of August (Figure 14.11b), when a large area of intense vegetation stress appeared (both VCI and TCI4 below 30). This area coincided with an area experiencing a 19 per cent reduction in corn yield (Figure 14.10d). In other regions of Ethiopia, the yield anomaly was also in good agreement with VT estimates at the end of August: in the southeastern pastoral zone, corn yield was above normal and VT estimated favourable conditions; in the western regions, mostly near-normal yield and VT conditions (around 50) were observed.

The discrepancies between weather and satellite data in interpreting the 1987 main season rainfall deficit in Ethiopia appeared because a very intense meteorological drought (Yeshanew and Apparao 1989) did not turn into agricultural drought. This happened because abundant preseason (February–April) rainfall in 1987 (Figure 14.10b) partially compensated for the precipitation deficit during the main season. Vegetation stress did not occur in the majority of regions and vegetation productivity was not reduced. This example emphasises the value of the VCI and TCI tool for identifying agricultural drought and impacts.

DROUGHT AND CROP PRODUCTION

Drought is the main weather-related disaster leading to vegetation stress – especially for crops, which are the most vulnerable type of vegetation. Therefore, world agriculture loses millions of tons of crop production and range land biomass every year. Being an excellent indicator of drought, the new AVHRR-based indices can also be used for estimating losses in agriculture. Average VCI and TCI were calculated for

administrative regions and compared with crop yield anomalies (deviation from the multiyear mean).

South America

Argentina is the second largest agricultural producer in South America. Corn yield statistics for administrative departments of Cordoba, one of the main agricultural provinces in Argentina, were correlated with each department's average VCI and TCI, starting from the first week in July (winter in the Southern Hemisphere) and ending with the last week in June of the next calendar year (a total of fifty-two weeks).

The correlation for the two main departments, Juarez Celmon and Rio Cuarto, is shown in Figure 14.12. This relationship is very strong for both indices (Juarez Celmon). During the critical period of corn growth (January–February), the correlation is much stronger than before or after that time, and the correlation coefficient is slightly larger for VCI than for TCI (in Rio Cuarto, 0.92 versus 0.85). In addition, the time of the highest VCI correlation occurs two to three weeks earlier than for TCI, mid January versus early February, correspondingly. Also, the VCI and TCI value of around 60 is a breaking point, identifying corn yield to be above or below the multiyear mean. If both VCI and TCI are below 35–40 for a few weeks, a reduction of more than 50 per cent of the corn yield can be expected.

Asia

Spring wheat is the principal grain crop in Kazakh. Its growing season starts in May and ends in August. Because winter precipitation in Kazakh is very small, wheat yield is entirely dependent on the growing season rainfall and the time of its arrival. A shortage of rains and/or their late arrival leads to vegetation stress and losses in wheat production. Since droughts are often accompanied by desiccative winds and low air humidity, wheat conditions can deteriorate in a matter of weeks. Therefore, satellite data are extremely useful as an objective source of wheat conditions and production. Average yield for Kazakh administrative regions (*oblast*) during 1985–94 was compared with *oblast* average VCI and TCI.

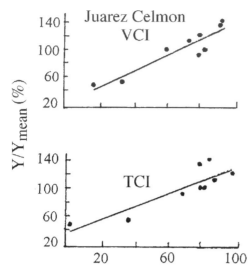
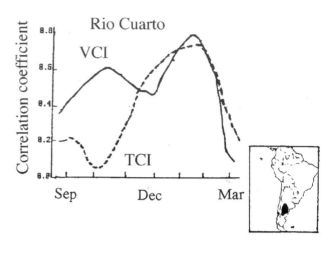

Figure 14.12 Correlation of corn yield (departure from nine-year mean) with region's average VCI and TCI for one week and during the growing seasons in two departments of Cordoba province, Argentina

The correlation between yield anomaly with both the VCI and TCI for northern (Kokchetav) and southern (Jezkazgan) Kazakh is very strong (Table 14.1). However, for the VCI, the correlation is stronger and shifted to the later weeks of the growing season. The critical period in wheat yield response to the indices is clearly defined: around the end of July for the VCI and the end of June for the TCI. The VCI is at its most informative at the end of July for both northern and southern regions, despite the fact that the difference between the regions in precipitable

water supply is 100 mm. For the TCI, pick of the correlation is one month earlier, reflecting enhanced response of wheat to thermal conditions during the period of biomass accumulation (cooler temperatures stimulate larger biomass and [correspondingly] wheat yield). During the yield formation (around and after heading), moisture supply is critical in determining wheat yield.

Europe

One environmental feature of Poland, in comparison with the previously discussed countries of semiarid zones, is much more favourable climatic resources, specifically moisture supply. Most of Poland is located in a zone with a positive balance between moisture supply and demand, especially in the north, where precipitation exceeds potential evaporation by up to 400 mm. Therefore, testing the new algorithms in Poland presented a great opportunity.

Application of the VCI and TCI indices showed that, similar to the other countries, moisture- and temperature-related stress can be identified in some years throughout Poland (Figure 14.13). Vegetation stress can be widespread, as it was in 1992 (TCI), or local, as it was in 1986 (VCI) or 1987 (TCI). The 1992 stress was caused by hot weather, which entirely

Table 14.1 Correlation matrix of mean *oblast* spring wheat yield vs mean *oblast* VCI and TCI, Kazakh

Week	Kokchetav oblast VCI	oblast TCI	Jezkazgan oblast VCI	oblast TCI
24	0.00	0.71	0.72	0.61
25	0.24	0.76	0.74	0.64
26	0.48	0.80	0.76	0.66
27	0.64	0.76	0.77	0.65
28	0.77	0.71	0.79	0.57
29	0.83	0.66	0.80	0.50
30	0.86	0.63	0.82	0.42
31	0.84	0.57	0.82	0.36
32	0.79	0.58	0.81	0.40
33	0.70	0.61	0.80	0.42
34	0.59	0.67	0.77	0.42

covered Poland. However, it is apparent that thermal stress is not always accompanied by moisture-related vegetation stress. In Poland, similar to Ethiopia, pre-season precipitation plays an important role in the accumulation of moisture in the soil and its use during the period of hot weather.

A comparison of average wheat yield with average VCI and TCI in Poznan (southwest) and Zamosc (southeast) *voivodish* (administrative regions) of Poland is shown in Figure 14.14. Although the climate of Poland is more favourable for crop growth, there is a coherence in dynamics of wheat yield and indices during the critical period of yield formation (around heading). The correlation of yield on VCI and TCI is 0.7–0.8.

CONCLUSIONS

The utility of VCI and TCI as the sole source of information about vegetation condition is well documented. Stress conditions (compared to nonstress conditions) are a fairly good source of information about drought, which is normally a major cause of the deterioration of vegetation health. Stress can also be related to excessive wetness, and a combination of low VCI and high TCI is indicative of such conditions. Moreover, VCI and TCI are useful for modelling crop yields, making them good predictors for real-time assessments of conditions and diagnoses of agricultural production. The remote sensing tool is especially beneficial if weather data is not available and/or nonrepresentative due to a sparse weather-observing network. If real-time weather information is reliable, it should be combined with AVHRR-derived characteristics and used as a comprehensive tool for monitoring vegetation stress, estimating drought, assessing weather impacts, and diagnosing crop yield and pasture production.

ACKNOWLEDGEMENTS

The author thanks his colleague Dr. Sullivan for software development and very useful discussions and Drs. J. Tarpley, K. Rao, and G. Ohring for their support. Special appreciation should be given to the author's collaborators, Professor A. Gitelson, Ben-Gurion University of the Negev, Israel; Professor R. Seilers, the University of Rio Cuarto, Argentina; Mr. L. Unganai, Drought Monitoring Center, Zimbabwe; Dr. L. Spivak, the Space Research Institute, Kazakh; Dr. K. Dambrowska-Zelinska, the Institute of Geodezii and Cartography, Poland; and Mr. D. LeComte, NOAA, for contributing their valuable time, data, and expertise and also for testing these indices.

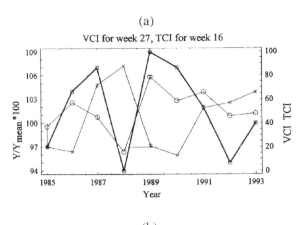

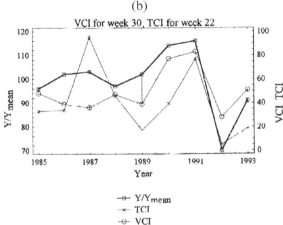

Figure 14.14 Dynamics of wheat yield anomaly, VCI, and TCI, Poznan (a) and Zamosc (b) *voivodish*, Poland

REFERENCES

DHA (*Department of Humanitarian Affairs*) (1993) 'An overview of disasters in 1992: Horn of Africa', United Nations' Department of Humanitarian Affairs, *DHA News*, Special Edition, January/February, pp. 18–20.

Gates, D.M. (1970) 'Physical and physiological properties of plants', in V.I. Myers and D.M. Gates, *Remote Sensing* with *Specific Reference to Agriculture and Forestry*, Washington, DC: National Academy of Sciences, pp. 224–52.

Gitelson, A. and Kogan, F. (1995) *Estimation of seasonal dynamics of arid zone of pasture and crop productivity using NOAA/AVHRR data. Final Report US–Israel AID/CDR/CAD program*, Beer Sheva, Israel.

Gitelson, A. and Merzlyak, M.N. (1994) 'Quantitative estimation of chlorophyll-a using reflectance spectra: Experiments with autumn chestnut and maple leaves', *Journal Photochem. Biol.* 22: 247–52.

Gitelson, A., Kogan, F., Zakarin, E., Spivak, L., and Lebed, L. (1996) 'Estimation of seasonal dynamics of pasture and crop productivity in Kazakhstan using NOAA/AVHRR data', *Proceedings of the IGARSS '96: Remote Sensing for a Sustainable Future*, Vol. 1, pp. 209–11.

Goldsberg, I.A. (ed.) (1972) *Agroclimatic Atlas of the World*, Moscow–Leningrad: Hydrometizdat, pp. 21–2.

Gray, T.I. and McCrary, D.G. (1981) 'The environmental vegetation index, a tool potentially useful for arid land management', *AgRISTARS Report* EW-N1-04076 JSC-17132.

Hayes, M.J. and Decker, W.L. (1996) 'Using NOAA AVHRR data to estimate maize production in the United States Corn Belt', *International Journal of Remote Sensing* 17, 16: 3,189–200.

Helden, U. and Eklundh, L. (1988) *National Drought Impact Monitoring – A NOAA NDVI and Precipitation Data Study of Ethiopia*, Lund, Sweden: Lund University Press, p. 55.

Holben, B.N. (1986) 'Characteristics of maximum-value composite images from temporal AVHRR data', *International Journal of Remote Sensing* 7, 11: 1,417–34.

Kerang Li and Xianchao Lin (1993) 'Drought in China: Present impacts and future needs', in D.A. Wilhite (ed.), *Drought Assessment, Management, and Planning: Theory and Case Studies*, Boston, MA: Kluwer Academic Publishers, pp. 263–91.

Kidwell, K.B. (ed.) (1994) 'Global vegetation index user's guide', US Department of Commerce Technical Report, Washington, DC.

Kogan, F.N. (1987) 'Vegetation index for areal analysis of crop conditions', *Proceedings of the 18th Conference on Agricultural and Forest Meteorology*, Boston, MA: American Meteorological Society, pp. 103–7.

—— (1990) 'Remote sensing of weather impacts on vegetation in non-homogeneous areas', *International Journal of Remote Sensing* 11, 8: 1,405–19.

—— (1994) 'Application of vegetation index and brightness temperature for drought detection', *Advancement in Space Research* 15, 11: 91–100.

—— (1995) 'Droughts of the late 1980s in the United States as derived from NOAA polar orbiting satellite data', *Bulletin of the American Meteorological Society* 76: 655–68.

—— (1997) 'Global drought watch from space', *Bulletin of the American Meteorological Society* 78: 621–36.

Kogan, F. and Sullivan, J. (1993) 'Development of global drought-watch system using NOAA/AVHRR data', *Advancement in Space Research* 13, 5: 219–22.

Kulik, M.S. and Sinelshikov, V.V. (eds) (1966) *Lectures on Agricultural Meteorology*, Moscow–Leningrad: Hydrometizdat.

LeComte, D. (1994) 'Weather highlights around the world', *Weatherwise* 47: 23–6.

—— (1995) 'Weather highlights around the world', *Weatherwise* 48: 20–2.

Liu, W.T. and Kogan, F.N. (1996) 'Monitoring regional drought using the Vegetation Condition Index', *International Journal of Remote Sensing* 17, 14: 2,761–82.

Myers, V.I. (1970) 'Soil, Water, and Plant Relations', in V.I. Myers and D.M. Gates, *Remote Sensing with Specific Reference to Agriculture and Forestry*, Washington, DC: National Academy of Sciences, pp. 253–67.

Nicholson, S.E., Kim, J., and Hoopingarner, J. (1988) *Atlas of African Rainfall and its Interannual Variability*, Dept. of Meteorology, Florida State University, Tallahassee.

NOAA (1988) 'Drought Advisory 88/12: Summary of Drought Conditions and Impacts', September 29, US Department of Commerce, NOAA, Washington, DC.

Obasi, G.O.P. (1994) 'WMO's Role in the International Decade for Natural Disaster Reduction', *Bulletin of the American Meteorological Society* 75: 1,655–61.

Rao, C.R.N. and Chen, J. (1995) 'Inter-satellite calibration linkages for the visible and near-infrared channels of the Advanced Very High Resolution Radiometer on the NOAA-7, -9, and -11 spacecrafts', *International Journal of Remote Sensing* 16, 11: 1,931–42.

Sastri, A.S.R.A.S. (1993) 'Agricultural drought management strategies to alleviate impacts: Examples from the arid and subhumid regions of the Indian subcontinent', in D.A. Wilhite (ed.), *Drought Assessment, Management, and Planning: Theory and Case Studies*, Boston, MA: Kluwer Academic Publishers, pp. 65–87.

Tucker, C.J. (1978) 'A comparison of satellite sensor bands for vegetation monitoring', *Photogrammetric Engineering and Remote Sensing* 44: 1, 369–80.

Unganai, L.S. and Kogan, F.N. (1998) 'Drought monitoring and corn yield estimation in Southern Africa from AVHRR data', *Remote Sensing of Environment* 63: 219–32.

USDA (1994) 'Major world crop areas and climatic profiles', World Agricultural Outlook Board, US Department of Agriculture, *Agricultural Handbook* No. 664, pp. 157–70.

USDC/USDA (1988) *Weekly Weather and Crop Bulletin*, 18 June, Washington, DC, p. 4.

van Dijk, A., Callis, S.L., Sakamoto, C.M., and Decker, W.L. (1987) 'Smoothing vegetation index profiles: An alternative method for reducing radiometric disturbance in NOAA/AVHRR data', *Photogrammetric Engineering and Remote Sensing* 53: 1,059–67.

WWCB (1992) *Weekly Weather and Crop Bulletin* 79, 37: 29.

——— (1993) *Weekly Weather and Crop Bulletin* 80, 33: 23.

——— (1994) *Weekly Weather and Crop Bulletin* 81: 19.

Weinreb, M.P., Hamilton, G., and Brown, S. (1990) 'Nonlinearity correction in calibration of the Advanced Very High Resolution Radiometer infrared channels', *Journal of Geophysical Research* 95: 7,381–8.

White, D., Collins, D., and Howden, M. (1993) 'Drought in Australia: Prediction, Monitoring, Management, and Policy', in D.A. Wilhite (ed.), *Drought Assessment, Management, and Planning: Theory and Case Studies*, Boston, MA: Kluwer Academic Publishers, pp. 213–36.

Wilhite, D.A. (1993) 'The enigma of drought', in D.A. Wilhite (ed.), *Drought Assessment, Management, and Planning: Theory and Case Studies*, Boston, MA: Kluwer Academic Publishers, pp. 3–15.

Wilhite, D.A., and Glantz, M.H. (1985) 'Understanding the drought phenomenon: The role of definitions', *Water International* 10: 111–20.

WMO (World Meteorological Organization) (1975) 'Drought and agriculture', *WMO Technical Note* No. 138, WMO, Geneva.

Wodajo, T. (1984) 'Agrometeorological activities in Ethiopia. Prospects for improving agroclimatic/crop condition assessment', Final Report, September, p. 139.

Yeshanew, A. and Apparao, G. (1989) 'Annual rainfall potential and its variability in drought years over Ethiopia', *Proceedings, Conference on Climate and Water*, 1 September, Helsinki, Finland, pp. 219–35.

15
AUSTRALIAN CLIMATE SERVICES FOR DROUGHT MANAGEMENT

W.R. Kininmonth, M.E. Voice, G.S. Beard, G.C. de Hoedt, and C.E. Mullen

INTRODUCTION

Australia is an ancient land with a mainly semiarid to arid climate. Despite this relatively inhospitable environment, nomadic people have inhabited the continent for at least 40,000 years and adapted to the harsh and variable conditions. As the historian Blainey (1975) writes, 'Nomadic societies in Australia were characterised by an intimate sense of the future and by seasonal planning that was almost rigid . . . season after season they could predict the intimate relationship between climate, the maturing of plant foods, the breeding and migrating habits of birds and reptiles and insects and marsupials.' Nevertheless, according to Blainey, the ability to cooperate across regions in times of regional drought was limited by kinship and nonkinship rules, so that there was generally no sure way of transporting or sharing surpluses.

One of the changes brought by European settlement of the Australian continent was an ability to link regions together for the purposes of drought management. This was a result of national transport infrastructure, communications systems, and the establishment of a national meteorological service. A national cooperative (volunteer) rainfall network has become the foundation on which the Australian Drought Watch Service is built.

The origins of modern knowledge about Australia's climate can be traced to the early European settlements and commencement of systematic meteorological observations (Gibbs 1996). European knowledge of the nature of Australia's climate was hard won because of large differences between the Australian climate and that of the immigrant source region (Figure 15.1). These differences included more variable rainfall, higher evaporation rates, and longer and more frequent droughts. Once knowledge of these differences began to grow, however, a national effort was mounted, culminating in a world-class drought monitoring service by the middle of the twentieth century (Gibbs and Maher 1967).

Over the two centuries of European settlement, the meteorological networks have developed to meet various needs. The current rainfall network (Figure 15.2) serves both water resources and drought management, although the lack of data from the sparsely populated and arid interior is clearly evident. The data from the systematic observations have been recorded and collected, and new analyses of data in the archives continue to provide information for sustainable management of land and water resources.

Soon after the Federation of the Australian Crown Colonies (States) formed the Commonwealth of Australia in 1901, the Bureau of Meteorology was established and commenced operation in 1908. It immediately assumed responsibility for national climate monitoring (with rainfall a key variable) and the publishing of monthly national reports and climate surveys. Its first published monthly map is shown in Figure 15.3. This map shows that meteorologists of the time recognised that users needed to know the historical context of the rainfall values, since the above-average areas have been shaded.

By the middle of the twentieth century, a sufficiently long and geographically distributed rainfall record was available to confidently map the rainfall that is reached in 90 per cent of years and that which is reached in only 10 per cent of years (Figure 15.4).

Figure 15.1 'Learning about drought in Australia: Breaking up of Drought – Reading telegraphic weather reports at Post Office', *Illustrated Sydney News*, 15 September 1877

Figure 15.2 The current Australian rainfall network

This map demonstrates the high variability of Australian rainfall (note how the 400 mm isohyet moves some 600 km inland in Queensland from the driest 10 per cent of years to the wettest 10 per cent of years).

All sectors of the Australian economy are, to varying degrees, dependent on rainfall, but none more so than agriculture. Figure 15.5 shows the close link between average annual rainfall and the estimated value of agricultural production on farms in Australia. The low productivity rates across the tropical north of the continent are due to the high seasonality of the rainfall, high evaporation rates, and lower exploitation of the region. The weakness of the link in the tropical north reminds us that rainfall is not the complete story in agricultural value and hence is not the final arbiter of drought (agricultural use, alternative sources of water supply, and prior conditions all contribute to the impact of a drought on the local enterprise). However, because of the strong first-principle relationship that does exist between rainfall and drought, the Australian drought watch and early warning service has been tailored with the rural sector in mind.

WHAT IS DROUGHT?

There is a vast literature on the definition and classification of drought, most of which acknowledges that no single definition of drought is likely to be uni-

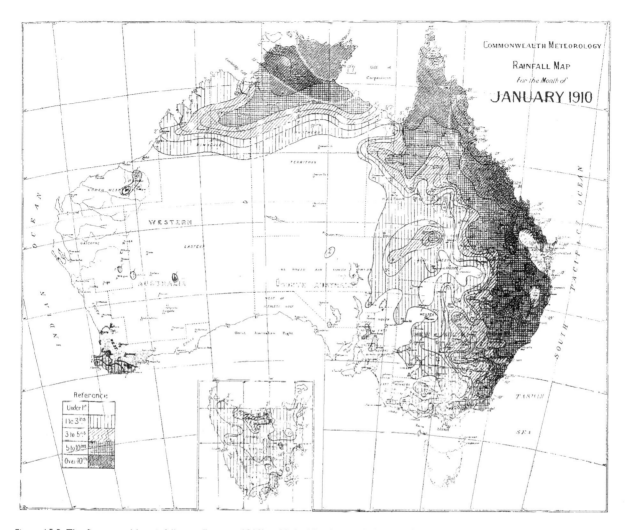

Figure 15.3 The first monthly rainfall map (January 1910) published by the newly formed Australian Bureau of Meteorology

versally acceptable or useful for all purposes and much of which attempts to distinguish between the supply (essentially meteorological) and demand (e.g., agriculture) aspects of drought. Various measures and indices of the severity of drought have been developed and applied in different countries. To the extent that severity of drought is determined by the shortage of rainfall, it may be categorised in terms of various objective measures of rainfall deficiency.

The Bureau of Meteorology drought research programme has evolved from analysis of monthly and annual rainfall. Gibbs and Maher (1967) recognised that common statistical measures such as 'arithmetic mean', 'average', and 'normal' are often poor indicators of rainfall occurrence, particularly since the mean often differs markedly from the median. These researchers proposed that if, as is usually the case, rainfall amounts are not normally distributed, rainfall distribution is best described by quoting the limits of a certain proportion of the occurrences. The method that they chose, and which has been adopted by the Bureau of Meteorology, is to state the limits of each 10 per cent (or decile) of the ordered distribution.

Stating the eleven limits that define the ten decile ranges provides a reasonably complete picture of a

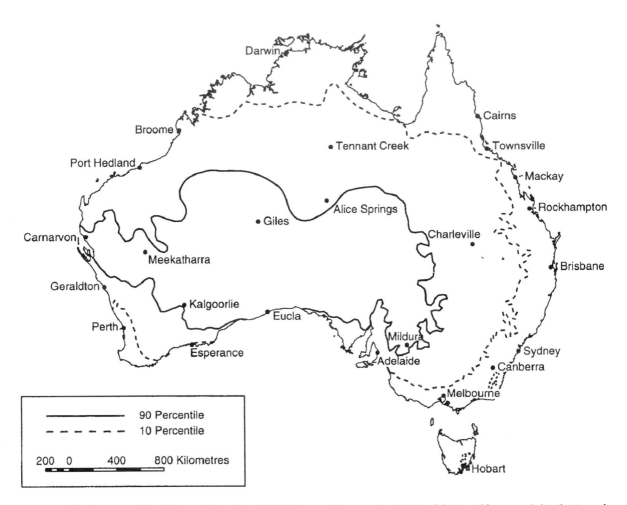

Figure 15.4 The locations of the 400 mm isohyet for decile 1 (lowest 10 per cent) and decile 9 (highest 10 per cent) distributions of rainfall for Australia
Source: Australian Bureau of Meteorology

particular rainfall distribution. The specific decile range within which an individual rainfall total falls provides a useful indication of departure from 'average'. In drier climates, lower decile values are frequently zero, especially when calculated for monthly totals. In such cases, the use of terms such as 'above average' for rainfall in decile 8 loses relevance, and some other form of comment must be used.

Based on the work of Gibbs and Maher, and recognising the problems in drier areas, the Bureau of Meteorology has adopted the following terminology in characterising rainfall amounts.

very much above 'average'	decile range 10
above 'average'	decile ranges 8–9
'average'	decile ranges 4–7
below 'average'	decile ranges 2–3
very much below 'average'	decile range 1

RAINFALL DECILES AS A DROUGHT INDICATOR

Gibbs and Maher (1967) used rainfall data from 100 stations, more or less uniformly distributed over the continent and with long periods of records, to construct maps from 1885 to 1965 showing decile ranges

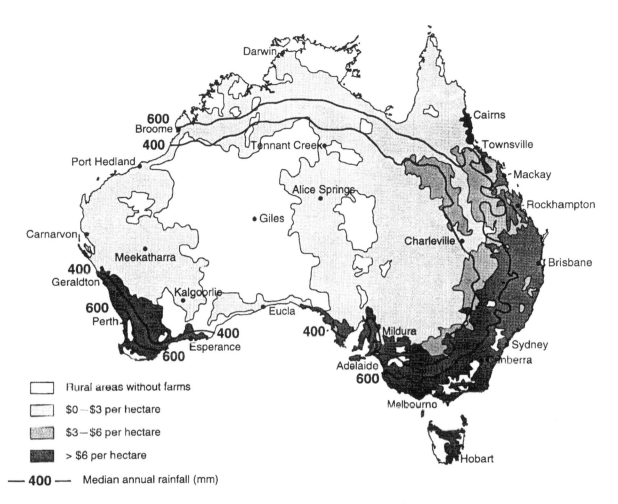

Figure 15.5 Selected contours of Australian median annual rainfall and the estimated value of agricultural production of farms
Source: 1975–6 agriculture data, adapted from map by Australian Natmap

in which annual rainfall occurred. The annual rainfall decile maps provided a consistent assessment of the rainfall situation over areas where the mean or median amounts of rainfall differ greatly. Figure 15.6 is a modern equivalent, for 1996, of the Gibbs and Maher annual rainfall deciles.

The annual rainfall decile maps facilitated study of the spatial distribution of drought. Using the terminology proposed above, the maps identify areas where the annual rainfall is in the first decile range, or *very much below 'average'*. Gibbs and Maher proposed that areas where rainfalls were in the first decile range roughly coincide with 'drought' areas. In making the proposal, they noted that:

- rainfall totals are for calendar years while droughts occur over periods lasting from one month to tens of months;
- in the northern half of the continent, the 'water year' does not coincide with the calendar year;
- drought occurrence depends on land use as well as rainfall.

Despite the recognised deficiencies of the decile maps, they were found to give a useful indication of annual rainfall anomaly and the spatial distribution of areas that are 'very wet' or 'very dry' in the particular year. More recently, Smith *et al.* (1992) examined declared droughts in Victoria and compared these with rainfall

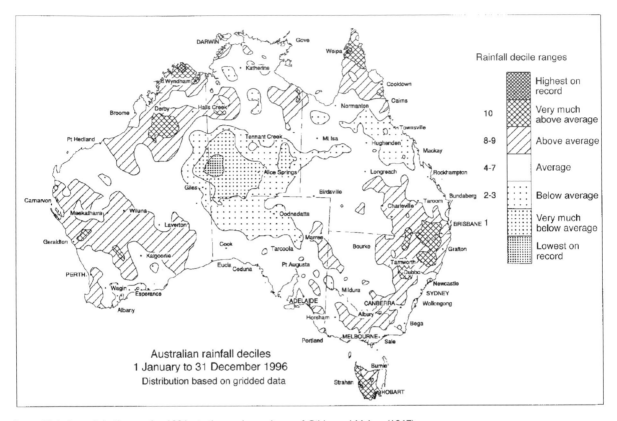

Figure 15.6 Annual decile map for 1996, similar to the analyses of Gibbs and Maher (1967)

percentiles and integrated Palmer Indices. The conclusion drawn was that there is a close correspondence between climatological indices based on rainfall and declared drought periods.

THE AUSTRALIAN DROUGHT WATCH SERVICE

The system eventually adopted by the Australian Bureau of Meteorology for classifying rainfall deficiencies to assist those concerned with managing the effects of drought on the economy and the rural sector generally was as follows:

- A severe rainfall deficiency exists when the rainfall for a period of three months or more falls within the lowest 5 per cent (below the fifth percentile) of recorded rainfalls for the location and period in question.

- A serious rainfall deficiency exists when the rainfall for a period of three months or more falls within the next lowest 5 per cent (between the fifth and tenth percentiles) of recorded rainfalls for the location and period in question.

Once an area is defined as experiencing serious or severe rainfall deficiencies according to the above criteria, it is considered as continuing to experience rainfall deficiencies until:

- The rainfall of the past month already amounts to average or better (i.e., above the third decile) for the three-month period commencing that month.
- Rainfall for the past three months is above average for that period (i.e., above the seventh decile).

Allowance is made for seasonal conditions in regions where there is a marked dry season.

Figure 15.7 is a rainfall deficiency map from the

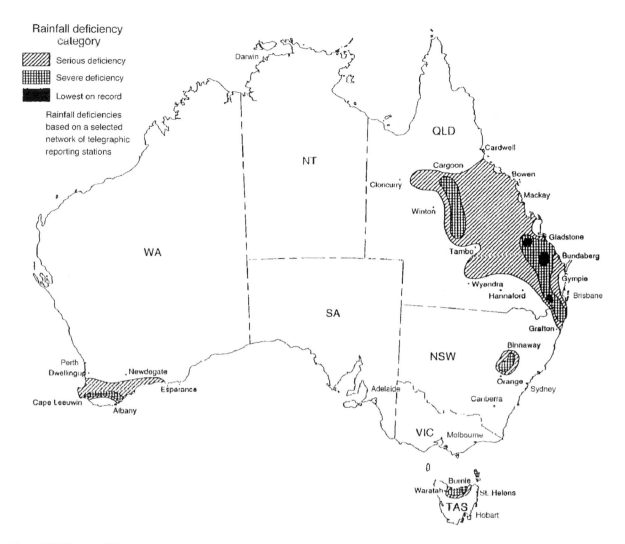

Figure 15.7 Drought Watch map showing areas of severe and serious rainfall deficiency

Drought Watch covering the twenty-month period 1 April 1994 through 30 November 1995. The identified rainfall-deficient areas stem from below-average winter and spring rains across most of Australia, the failure of the 1994–5 summer rains over a large area of eastern Australia, and a successive poor winter rain over the southwest.

This system, the Australian Drought Watch Service, was initiated in June 1965. In the light of analysis of rainfall at the end of each month, if any area of Australia is experiencing serious or severe deficiencies, a 'Drought Statement' is issued from the National

Climate Centre to interested authorities and the media, consisting of:

- a short summary text describing the rainfall deficiency situation nationwide;
- one or more maps delineating the areas of serious and severe rainfall deficiency (as defined above) over time periods that may be chosen differently for different areas to most effectively indicate the duration as well as the intensity of the deficiencies (Figure 15.8).

The Drought Statement is normally issued by the

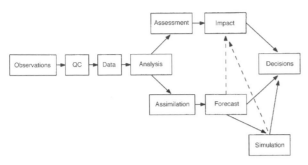

Figure 15.8 Schematic showing the development of information from a meteorological observation network and the use of the various types of information

start of the second week after the end of the month. It can be accessed electronically through the Australian Bureau of Meteorology's 'Weather by FAX' service or through the Bureau's web site (http://www.bom.gov.au/). After release of the 'Drought Statement', a more detailed *Drought Review* booklet is distributed to subscribing organisations. It includes:

- the Drought Statement and maps;
- listing of rainfalls by meteorological district for selected stations in terms of actual values, percentages of normal, and percentile ranking for appropriate periods.

The *Drought Review* booklet is complemented by a companion publication, *Monthly Rainfall Review*, which includes decile and rainfall maps for the most recent month and the most recent three-month period and a series of tables including rainfall amounts, percentiles, and climatological comparisons.

The Australian Drought Watch System was recently streamlined and is now largely automated. The cornerstone of the modernised system is the on-line climate data base ADAM (Australian Data Archive for Meteorology), which allows the efficient retrieval of historical and near real-time meteorological data. The ease of data access from ADAM, together with the creation of an objective scheme for the production of digital analyses, has allowed for the development of a series of comprehensive automated procedures for the routine extraction, analysis, and visualisation of rainfall, rainfall deciles, and temperature data.

An historical rainfall data base, constructed using estimated rainfall at the regular map grid points and

containing monthly data since 1900, has been constructed to generate rainfall decile (or percentile) and deficiency data. This is essentially a process of ranking the current month's rainfall data at map grid points against the historical rainfall data base. The procedure for the automated production of information for the Drought Watch System from near real-time data is:

- collect current station rainfall data;
- validate current station rainfall reports;
- analyse the current rainfall map and estimate grid point values;
- compute the percentile value for estimated current rainfall at each map grid point; and
- analyse the grid point percentiles and map the areas falling in decile ranges.

As part of the visualisation process, colour and black and white maps are generated in a number of formats appropriate for publishing as well as electronic dissemination. For example, both colour and black and white rainfall decile maps for periods of three, six, nine, twelve, eighteen, twenty-four, and thirty-six months are available through the Bureau's Internet site (http://www.bom.gov.au). As well as decile information, rainfall and temperature maps for varying time scales are prepared in electronic format. The information is updated daily, weekly, or monthly, depending on the time scale of the data. In addition to the automated systems for routine data delivery, GIS technology and associated graphics packages are used for tailoring analysed data on a user request basis.

DROUGHT EARLY WARNING

Climate research, particularly over the past two decades and as an outcome of the international Tropical Ocean Global Atmosphere (TOGA) project, has demonstrated the global controls over climate variability on interannual time scales, especially the role of the oceans. The strong coherence of climate anomalies in the Asia–Pacific region is associated with the El Niño/Southern Oscillation phenomenon, and this is the basis for current predictions on the seasonal time scale.

Bureau research in support of the prediction service on seasonal to interannual time scales focuses on:

- better understanding of the role of air–sea interaction over the equatorial Pacific, drawing heavily on the TOGA observations;
- tropical–intratropical interactions and their influence on regional rainfall variability;
- higher level statistical techniques;
- more complex climate parameters as predictors, such as sea surface temperature patterns; and
- development of coupled ocean–atmosphere general circulation models to predict future states of the climate system.

This prediction service is designed to provide information useful in many farm planning operations. It may be used to assist with decisions such as which crops to plant or stocking rates over the coming season, or it might influence decisions at the sale yards (by considering current economics and seasonal expectations). The service has proven useful in managing drought, so common to Australia.

The methodological basis for the Seasonal Climate Outlook (SCO) service is the statistical relationship between grid point rainfall category series, the Southern Oscillation Index (SOI), and global sea surface temperatures. Both displacement from the mean and trend are included as SOI predictors. In addition, the degree of persistence of rainfall anomaly between adjacent but nonoverlapping seasons (e.g., from winter to spring) is also used as input. These predictors, as well as a measure of climatology, form the basis for the current statistical seasonal rainfall prediction issued from the Bureau's National Climate Centre. Each is weighted according to the degree of skill shown over a test period taken from the historical record.

Rainfall outlooks for the following three months covering the whole continent are presented in probability format. For each district and about 250 towns or locations across the country, the outlook consists of two probabilities – the chance that rainfall accumulated over the following three months will fall in either of the end categories, that is, in the below-normal range (less than the thirty-third percentile) or in the above-normal range (greater than the sixty-seventh percentile). These data are presented in tabular and map form. A summary of this information, including a map identifying the areas of sig-

nificant bias in the probabilities, is issued to the news media with an accompanying statement. The probabilities are significantly biased if the predicted outlook of rainfall in either end category exceeds climatology (33 per cent) by at least 11 per cent. This translates to probabilities of 44 per cent or higher for rainfall in either of the end categories.

The summary text in the Seasonal Climate Outlook is usually confined to expected conditions over the upcoming three months. However, there is an important exception, and that is when an El Niño episode is in progress. Each month, the Bureau of Meteorology keeps a close watch on the key indicators from the tropical Pacific. This requires sea surface observations from ships, drifting buoys in the ocean, and satellites; atmospheric observations from satellites, aircraft, and the ground; measurements of tropical winds from Pacific islands, ships, and aircraft; and cloudiness levels from satellites. In most cases, the presence of El Niño can be confirmed by late winter (August), particularly if large areas of eastern Australia have been deficient in rainfall. In such circumstances, the Bureau may issue general advice to the effect that dry or drought conditions may persist in eastern and northern Australia until late summer or early autumn.

Numerous other statistical tables and graphs are also included in each issue of the SCO. These include SOI analogues, rainfall exceedance tables, NINO3 SST prediction, and a summary of recent rainfall patterns. Analogues of the SOI from the historical record are chosen according to how closely they match the most recent nine-month pattern of SOI movement. If they so choose, users can then examine rainfall patterns in the analogue years as a guide to the current year. Exceedance tables show, on a district basis, the percentage of years that the rainfall has exceeded specified totals (e.g., 100 mm) during the coming three months. The years over which these statistics are calculated are selected such that they have a similar SOI to the present. An intermediate coupled ocean–atmosphere computer model is used to predict the sea-surface temperature in the eastern to central equatorial Pacific. This region, known as NINO3, is of critical importance in the generation of El Niño and La Niña events. A predicted NINO3 anomaly is issued six months in advance together with probabilities of the anomaly falling in one of three classes – El Niño (above +1°C), La Niña (below –1°C), or neutral (between –1°C and +1°C).

An assessment of the accuracy of the SCO methodology has been made by cross-validation of the statistics over a set of hindcasts covering a recent period of forty years. A forecast was independently produced for each year within the period based on parameters derived from all other years. Results of cross-validation indicate that the accuracy peaks over eastern and northern Australia and for outlooks issued between July and October. This is particularly so during El Niño and La Niña events, when there is a strong link between the SOI and eastern Australian rainfall. Moderate skill is also obtained in eastern Queensland in the May and November outlooks, as well as over southern South Australia in the March outlook. Other months, apart from a few isolated exceptions, show historical accuracy levels only marginally different from what would be achieved by forecasting climatology. For those periods and locations when the method shows little skill, the outlook reverts to the climatological (or unbiased) assessment.

SERVICE DELIVERY

Presentation issues revolve around how to depict probability information so that it is easily understood, but without compromising its scientific integrity. Clear presentation involves a careful mix of diagrams and text, but in the end it is the education process that is the key. One challenge is to explain the nature of climate variability on time scales from months to decades. This is critical because the SCO is designed to increase the margins of profitability by giving early warning of some of the larger, significant climate variations. These episodic events occur relatively infrequently. Users will gain benefit from the SCO by responding to the predictions over at least five to ten years – that is, the benefits accrue over the long term. An information package called 'Farming a Sunburnt Country' produced by the Bureau of Meteorology in 1994 sought to provide valuable education on 'managing around Australia's high-risk climate'. The package incorporated a manual and video including interviews with farmers and researchers and sold well at a minimal cost of AU$19.95 (1997 prices).

Most subscribers to the SCO service are involved in agriculture or grazing, but a significant number come from the hydrology and water supply industries. Other industries represented in small numbers include mining, scientific research, salt making, fisheries, and manufacturing, to name but a few. Not surprisingly, the uses of seasonal outlooks are many and varied. Apart from the obvious agricultural and pastoral applications, some other examples of usage include engineers estimating construction demand in their forward plans, and water pump manufacturers planning sales requirements and factory production levels.

The Bureau of Meteorology, as the national meteorological authority of Australia, provides (1) climate monitoring and prediction services to assist government, business, and the rural community in better drought preparedness and (2) early assessment of the need for contingency action or drought relief. The Bureau of Meteorology's Drought Watch Service provides a consistent starting point for national action on drought. Declarations of drought by state and territory governments take into account other factors in addition to rainfall. Individuals and businesses can apply to the Commonwealth under the criteria of Exceptional Circumstances for assistance and financial relief when drought is particularly severe and long-lived. Special briefing sessions and additional information are supplied by the Bureau to both state/territory and Commonwealth agencies involved in the assessment process.

Significant upgrades to Bureau systems over the last few years have vastly improved service responsiveness and timeliness, particularly with respect to rainfall analysis services. Until the early 1990s, data collection was slow and laborious; rainfall observations made around the country were first collated in capital city offices before being forwarded to the National Climate Centre in Melbourne for entry into the climate archive. Rainfall maps were manually analysed after collation of data from a variety of sources over a few days. Following improvements to computing and communications systems, these data are now streamed into the national on-line database (ADAM) and are accessible, along with quality control flags, in near real-time by Bureau offices around Australia. Rainfall analyses can be prepared within hours using automated systems. In addition to a range of standard analyses, products can be tailored to users' requirements by varying the period of analysis and the region of interest.

The monitoring service has been enhanced by making standard products more readily available to potential users using a variety of media. Products are provided to the news media for print and electronic distribution. They are also available for electronic access through polling facsimile (locally known as Weather by Fax service) and through the Bureau's web site on the Internet (http://www.bom.gov.au/). Distribution of service products is also made through Bureau Regional Offices. The ability to provide information as a computer file has improved the ease of access and use of the products, and has resulted in better quality maps that are more easily incorporated with other material for decision making. Climate experts in the National Climate Centre, Regional Offices, and Meteorological Information Offices in major provincial centres are available to provide interpretation and advice.

The combination of monitoring and prediction techniques is essential in the provision of a truly integrated service. Information on future rainfall probabilities is as important as analysis of past rainfall in the business of drought management.

Three user-surveys of the SCO service have been conducted in the 1990s to monitor user satisfaction and better tailor the product to users' requirements. Results from a survey conducted in 1996 noted that most subscribers had continued their subscription for more than three years, and that 43 per cent referred to 'every (monthly) edition' to incorporate the information into their farm business strategies.

The Drought Watch Service is now set in a broader framework, with users taking the basic drought monitoring, early warning, and prediction information and applying it to their particular need. Table 15.1 lists some recent examples.

Knowledge of weather and climate provides guidance for those making strategic planning decisions for agricultural systems. Research done by Queensland Department of Primary Industries (QDPI) has shown that over a ten-year period, 78 per cent of farm profit occurs in the three best years. During the time of the extended El Niño sequence of 1991–5, it has been estimated that average production by rural industries fell about 10 per cent while agricultural exports fell by 12 per cent. The direct costs to agriculture totalled some AU$2.4 billion, but because of a 2 : 1 multiplier effect on industries that orbit agriculture, the eventual cost to the Australian economy could be closer to AU$5 billion. Knowing to move resources in the poor years and to maximise resource use in the good years can make all the difference. As summarised by a cattle producer, 'If the Bureau can help us get it right one time when we would have otherwise been wrong, it's saved us money and helped us earn money'.

Work on improved service delivery in the late

Table 15.1 Recent examples of Australian uses of drought watch and probability-based seasonal outlooks

Customer group	Drought watch and/or forecast input	Action
Financiers and banks	Message: high probability that El Niño was over	Revise plans
Some rural users	Seasonal outlook probabilities	Cautious observing the changes vs. their experience
Some rural users	Shift in rainfall probabilities combined with existing soil moisture	Hedge bets, adopt two cropping strategies rather than one
Grain company	Yield forecasts based on recent conditions and seasonal outlooks	Progressive adjustments to storage, marketing, and national distributions
Water industry	Rainfall probabilities combined with recent rainfall anomalies	Incorporation of expected value rainfall into reservoir storage model

Source: Australia Drought Watch Service

1990s has focused on both Internet and Weather by Fax services, recognising the limitations of Internet access in remote localities in Australia. A three-year collaborative development project between the Bureau of Meteorology and Queensland's Department of Natural Resources commenced in 1997 and has, as its objective, to improve the timeliness and tailor presentation of climate information to the agricultural sector. The project has established a web site specifically for the rural community (SILO – http://www.bom.gov.au/silo) and has routinely updated monitoring, prediction, and agricultural impact information to assist with better on-farm decision making. The full SCO is now available on-line via SILO.

Modern needs for information on drought include both past, present, and future information; hence services need to be structured around this need. Decisions are based on climate analyses, assessments, and forecasts (Figure 15.8), but increasingly use outputs of system simulation models, whether they are for agriculture, commodities, markets, or other climate-sensitive human activities.

REFERENCES

Blainey, G. (1975) *Triumph of the Nomads: A History of Ancient Australia*, South Melbourne: Macmillan.

Gibbs, W.J. (1996) 'A mini-history of meteorology in Australia', *Bulletin of the Australian Meteorological and Oceanographic Society* 9: 2 (special publ.)

Gibbs, W.J. and Maher, J.V. (1967) Rainfall deciles as drought indicators, *Bulletin* No. 48, Bureau of Meteorology, Australia.

Hunt, H.A. (1910) *Monthly Meteorological Report of the Australian Commonwealth*, Vol. 1, No. 1, Commonwealth Bureau of Meteorology.

Smith, D.I., Hutchinson, M.F., and McArthur, R.J. (1992) *Climatic and Agricultural Drought: Payments and Policy*, Centre for Resource and Environmental Studies, Australian National University, Australia.

16

DROUGHT MONITORING FOR FAMINE RELIEF IN AFRICA

J.A. Dyer

INTRODUCTION

Drought has a major impact on national food balances throughout Africa. Although food aid helps to reduce the short-term impact of famine, it can be detrimental to long-term sustainable development strategies (Dyer 1989). The real challenge is to ensure that food aid decisions are sound and timely. Although the frequency of food aid programmes may have decreased, drought monitoring systems will continue to play a key role in administering food aid programmes.

In this chapter we will examine the concept and practice of weather-based drought monitoring while accepting that political as well as climatic events cause food shortages. We will evaluate the future role of drought monitoring in food aid to Africa by citing some Canadian experience. Other countries and states, notably the United States, have also successfully developed and operated drought monitoring systems. Examples include work by Motha and Heddinghaus (1986) and Dugas *et al.* (1983), as well as several applications of the Palmer Drought Index (Palmer 1965). This discussion relies heavily on Canadian experience because of the readily available documentation for Canadian work and the drought assistance policy lessons learned in Canada (Dyer 1991). In light of global attention to sustainable food security during 1996 (FAO 1996), these lessons are now highly relevant.

Although the usefulness of satellite information for Africa must be acknowledged (Prince and Justice 1991: 1,137), weather-based monitoring is the most important type of drought monitoring because drought is a weather event. Acquisition of information solely through verbal reports can consume considerable human resources and yield only subjective results. Crop weather monitoring is an operational function that uses weather observations to provide objective information on current crop growing conditions (Dyer and Mack 1984). Weather observations are a convenient and easy type of data to acquire and process in many countries because they are already being collected for other purposes (mainly synoptic forecasting).

Recipients of drought reports include many levels of the agriculture sector (Dyer and Lally 1990). Weather based monitoring provides all participants in drought assistance decisions with a common set of timely and interpretive updates about drought-stricken area(s). Government has an interest in following regional or district issues that confront farmers during the growing season. For producers, weather-based monitoring can guide local decisions about planting, cultivating, harvesting, storage, or trucking products to market, as well as providing market intelligence.

THE DROUGHT MONITORING PROCESS

Dyer and Mack (1984) recognised four phases in crop weather monitoring (Figure 16.1). The first phase, the transmission of weather observations to a central storage facility, can involve some reduction in data volume and selection of measurements for specific applications. If the collection network is created solely for crop monitoring, weather observations can be simplified by ignoring parameters that are primarily of value to synoptic forecasts.

Monitoring System Phases	Operations	Functions
Phase 1	Transmission	selected weather observations to central storage
Phase 2	Pre-processing	editing and extrapolating missing records
Phase 3	Interpretive analysis	models and indices for crop growth and normalizing
Phase 4	Verification	with field observations and other data sources

Figure 16.1 Four generalised phases of a weather-based monitoring system for drought (after Dyer and Mack 1984)

In the second, or pre-processing, phase, current data are edited and sorted by station/site. If missing data are infrequent, they can often be replaced by extrapolations from sites that are reasonably close (Raddatz and Kern 1984) or by values from climate normals. Range testing to guard against unrealistically high or low values is another pre-processing function.

Interpretive analysis takes place in the third phase using models and indices for crop growth or moisture stress to prepare up-to-date maps and reports. Selection of appropriate models is an important aspect of drought monitoring system design. Through agrometeorology, many useful links between weather and crop growth have been established (WMO 1963, Hargreaves 1983) and used in the interpretive phase. Agrometeorological models range from simple empirical indices to complex soil moisture, evapotranspiration, or crop growth simulations (Baier 1973, 1977, and 1989; de Jong 1981). Detailed description of such models is beyond the scope of this discussion.

The fourth phase recognises verification with field observations and other data sources as an ongoing process that extends beyond the scientific development of the models and indices. In spite of the ability to automate through modern technology, there is the human side of the interpretation and feedback. It is

the question, Does this report agree with what we hear is happening out there? that requires skilled crop weather monitoring technicians, particularly in countries critically dependent on their agriculture. Ongoing co-operation and dialogue between those technicians and experts from other disciplines for verification (see Figure 16.1) is essential (FAO 1991a).

DROUGHT MONITORING SYSTEMS FOR AFRICA

Because of the close association of the Food and Agriculture Organization (FAO) of the United Nations (UN) with food security and food aid programmes, FAO has several decades of experience in monitoring drought in Africa under its Global Information and Early Warning System (GIEWS). Although applications of the FAO model have mostly been in Africa, there has been interest in applying this model in South America (FAO 1991b) and India (Reddy 1993: 179). By estimating evapotranspiration rates for different crops and growth stages, crop performance has been expressed through a water satisfaction index (Frere and Popov 1979 and 1986). With a ten-day time step (the dekad), it can be operated with limited weather data, and it has been calculated by hand in many African countries (FAO 1991c).

Following the dramatic impact of the 1984 African droughts on the global community, Canada undertook a pilot project to develop a demonstration weather-based early warning system for drought in Africa. With support from the Canadian International Development Agency (CIDA), Agriculture Canada developed a weather analysis computer package called CANDAF (Canadian Analysis of Drought in Africa) (Dyer and Mack 1986).

CANDAF simulates soil moisture and several related crop indices for both predictive and interpretive applications (Dyer and Cianferro 1988). CANDAF, like the FAO system, uses a forgiving calculation time step, sacrificing temporal precision for reliable supply of weather data and microcomputer operation. CANDAF uses a monthly time step rather than the FAO dekad since it was designed for more remote operation (North America) and broader scale application (African continent). However, country-scale versions of CANDAF were developed for Zambia and Ethiopia (Dyer et al. 1992). CANDAF also allowed flexibility in selecting the monitoring period since peak rainfall seasons vary throughout Africa depending on proximity to the equator (Musembi and Griffiths 1986).

Because weather events are not the only source of temporal variability in agriculture, CANDAF was designed to be verified (phase 4) with agronomic and economic information (Dyer and Mack 1986: 3). Remote sensing-based systems are available for Africa (Hendricksen and Durkin 1986, Prince and Justice 1991), and CANDAF was intended to be used in combination with these systems to provide spatial detail.

EXPERIENCE FROM CANADA

Throughout the 1980s the Canadian government developed several crop weather monitoring systems for subregional or commodity-specific applications. Although shifting economic policies and fiscal restraints have since curtailed the use of these systems, the experience gained through their design and operation is relevant to most drought-affected countries. One such system, the Canadian Agriculture Weather Monitoring System (known as CAWM), provided several crop weather indices on a nationwide reconnaissance level to policy makers. CAWM was unique in making use of second-hand synoptic data, which was transmitted and pre-processed by a private sector partner (Dyer and Lally 1990).

Although CAWM was the only national-scale system serving agriculture in Canada, a number of other systems provided useful service to both federal and provincial governments on a regional scale. The Prairie Provinces received most of the attention because that part of Canada has a long history of droughts that have been very costly to agriculture and government. The Soil Moisture Evaluation Programme (SMEP) was started in the late 1970s by Agriculture Canada (Edey 1980) to monitor soil moisture reserves under small grain cereals (mainly wheat) on a weekly basis throughout the growing season. In 1982, the Forage Drought Early Warning System (FoDEWS) was started to provide late winter and early spring projections of pasture growth in support of the beef industry (Dyer 1984 and 1988). In the late 1980s, soil moisture reports were issued by the Canadian Atmospheric Environment Service – Winnipeg Office (Raddatz 1990).

The Canadian Wheat Board also carried out weather-based estimations of prairie wheat yields (Walker 1989). Weather analysis has been used to trigger crop insurance payments (Selirio and Brown 1979). Most provincial governments also provided precipitation and temperature reports. Although these data were sometimes distributed as part of crop reports, there was no agrometeorological interpretation.

DROUGHT ASSISTANCE POLICY

The key policy question related to drought for all governments is how should government officials react to droughts in support of agriculture. During the 1980s in Canada, major financial drought assistance programmes were frequently initiated in response to calls from the media and the farming community. These programmes were costly and rather ad hoc in nature. Although crop insurance programmes were also in place (Selirio 1984), ad hoc assistance was frequently given over and above crop insurance payments and was often politically driven. Regardless of whether assistance is ad hoc or through an organised system such as crop insurance, the challenge is knowing the right level of drought severity on which to trigger assistance (Dyer 1986).

The main goal of drought monitoring systems should be to make drought policy as effective as possible. An objective decision about assistance to drought victims requires that the criteria for drought severity be both objective and easy to understand and apply. The aim of drought assistance must be to aid the unlucky without subsidising bad management (Dyer 1986). Although there are many ways to define drought, a risk management approach is used for the policy questions being considered here. Drought must first and foremost be considered as an unusual event in which its victims are the unlucky as opposed to the bad managers. Otherwise, drought can become a chronic ailment in agriculture.

By accepting a set of criteria for external assistance which is too lenient, we are setting a precedent for subsidisation (Dyer 1986). When the same conditions recur in future years, the current recipients will expect similar assistance again. The more lenient the drought criteria used, the more frequently will future weather patterns be able to meet these criteria. In the case of beef production, it was realised in Canada that more frequent drought assistance encourages producers to overstock (Dyer 1984). This strategy for beef in developed agriculture is highly applicable to drought strategies in Africa for either pastoral or field crop agriculture.

The options available under this strategy are generalised in the 2×2 decision matrix shown in Figure 16.2 (Dyer 1986). The rows indicate that a high or low impact may be sustained from a particular drought event. Here, impact refers to the damage sustained by a producer from the drought, rather than the meteorological severity. The expected frequency of recurrence of a similar (or more severe) drought is identified in the columns as either high or low.

Figure 16.3 demonstrates the management options and the expected outcomes in qualitative binary form which can be extracted from Figure 16.2. If the drought impact is low, then no action or assistance is required, regardless of whether the recurrence frequency is high or low, thus accounting for both quadrants in row 1 (Figure 16.2). The low frequency–low impact scenario (Quadrant 2) identifies a very robust production system, since the low frequency events are the most severe droughts.

If the impact is high and the frequency with which similar conditions can recur is also high (Quadrant 3), then this producer is too vulnerable to drought, and the appropriate action should be a substantial long-term change in management strategy at the farm level. The economic consequence of not taking this action would be to foster an agricultural system with an expectation of assistance at a high frequency in the future, leading to an increased dependence on government support. For beef production (or pastoral agriculture), this would mean reducing the stocking rates. Under the high impact–low frequency of recurrence situation (Quadrant 4), intervention with some form of external assistance can be justified.

Impact/frequency levels	high frequency of recurrence	low frequency of recurrence
low impact	(Quadrant 1) – robust	(Quadrant 2) – very robust
high impact	(Quadrant 3) – very vulnerable	(Quadrant 4) – vulnerable

Figure 16.2 Binary decision matrix of drought frequency (cumulative) vs drought impact for drought assistance policy decisions
Source: Dyer 1986

DROUGHT DECISION OPTIONS:

LOW IMPACT

- NO ACTION NEEDED

HIGH IMPACT – HIGH FREQUENCY

- MANAGEMENT CHANGE

HIGH IMPACT – LOW FREQUENCY

- EXTERNAL ASSISTANCE

OUTCOMES OF ASSISTANCE:

LOW FREQUENCY DROUGHT VICTIMS

- 'AIDING THE UNLUCKY'

HIGH FREQUENCY DROUGHT VICTIMS

- 'SUBSIDIZING BAD MANAGEMENT'

Figure 16.3 Drought assistance decision options and expected outcomes of external drought assistance (after Dyer 1986)

Special or external assistance to the low-frequency victims is analogous to 'aiding the unlucky' (Outcome 1). Special assistance to high-frequency victims, on the other hand, is analogous to 'subsidising bad management' (Outcome 2). The implementation of this logic in real decision making requires three elements:

1 Decision makers must accept probability (frequency) of recurrence as a basis for defining drought severity.
2 Drought monitoring information must be represented on the basis of frequency of recurrence.
3 In the long term, the agricultural system(s) being assisted must afford the management the latitude needed to shift from a drought-vulnerable state to a more robust state.

Using probability as a basis for defining drought severity does not require the decision maker to have a precise understanding of the parameter used to derive the probability distribution. For example, although an agronomist may fully appreciate the significance of a 20 mm soil moisture reserve to a particular pasture or crop, a political or senior decision maker in charge of external assistance probably would not. The decision maker could, however, understand that 20 mm of reserve might be unusually low for that season and site if shown such a statistic.

Most agrometeorological variables, such as soil moisture reserves, cumulative evapotranspiration, or days without rain (to name a few), can be used as a basis for deriving cumulative drought severity probabilities (Dyer *et al.* 1981). For example, the chance of two days without rain may be the same as four days. However, experiencing at least two days without rain must have a greater probability than experiencing at least four days without rain because the 'at least' two-day case includes the chance of four days without rain as well as two days.

Figure 16.4 demonstrates cumulative probabilities for a distribution of seasonal bare soil evaporation estimates for a South African site (Dyer *et al.* 1988). In this example, a simple sorting process indicates that while a seasonal value should fall below average (normal) in about 50 per cent of the years, a value of less than half of the seasonal average will only occur in about 10 per cent of the years. Clearly, with this basis of estimation, experiencing less than half the seasonal average is an unusual event.

DROUGHT ASSISTANCE AND THE ENVIRONMENT

Although the prime goal of drought intervention in Africa is humanitarian, the impacts illustrated in Figure 16.2 apply to the environmental resource base as well as to the producer. Beef production in Canada demonstrated that being overdependent on government assistance is not environmentally sustainable (Dyer 1984). Although overstocking does not result in overgrazing in all years, stocking rates must allow grassland to recover from being overgrazed during drought years. Herds should be culled during dry periods because carrying capacity will vary from year to year (Lodge *et al.* 1971: 16).

Dryland agriculture is found at the margins of most of the world's deserts (Walton 1969: 116), which occur at a variety of latitudes with varying rainfall and temperature regimes (Arritt 1993: 10). Food aid and timely drought reports can reduce the contribution of

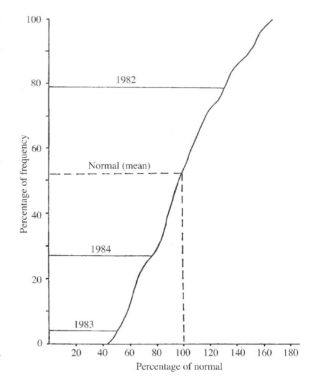

Figure 16.4 Cumulative frequency distribution of simulated bare soil evaporation from 1 January to 30 June for 1936–84, expressed as frequency of equal or less seasonal evaporation (y-axis) and percentage of normal (x-axis). Reprinted with permission from the Canadian Meteorological and Oceanographic Society
Source: Dyer et al. 1988

drought to desertification in any of these zones, since starving people (and their animals) will further degrade an already stressed ecosystem. In Africa, social and environmental health are strongly linked, and drought response strategies need to take social and cultural differences into account (ICIHI 1986: 24). However, unless food aid programmes also take land degradation risks into account, the drought response itself can have major long-term impacts (Dyer 1989). Drought assistance that is too frequent would be a disincentive for many environmentally sound management practices. In Africa, it would also be a production disincentive, keeping many farmers out of the market and at a subsistence poverty level.

Many traditional food production systems are already resilient to drought (Altieri 1987: 71).

High-producing agrotechnologies requiring special drought assistance measures to sustain them should not displace such systems. For example, in Africa, the adoption of high-yielding crop varieties should take drought resistance into account before any local land-races (a nonregistered variety of crop developed by traditional farmers for local conditions) that are already drought-tolerant are replaced. However, low-input farming can also stress the land and lead to desertification through burning, deforestation, and expansion into marginal lands (IGADD 1986: 21). Hence, sustainable agrotechnological advances are needed in the developing countries.

FAMINE CATEGORIES

Although water supply is the dominant environmental factor in determining national food balances in Africa, reduced rainfall is only one aspect of famine. The human tragedy that we associate with famine comes about in a setting of social upheaval, poverty, national debts, and unsustainable land use practices (Timberlake 1985: 7, ICIHI 1985: 26). Three levels of famine, including natural, chronic, and acute, were suggested by Dyer (1989) to integrate social and climatic factors.

Some famines can be considered as natural because they occur as a consequence of natural or meteorological drought, which, in the long term, is a certainty in the African climate. Classifying some famines as natural, however, only reflects their natural causes and does not imply that any human suffering that may result should be accepted as natural, or that no response is justified. On the second level, famines become chronic when population growth or declining economic conditions push land use beyond the limit of sustainable production. In the countries of Africa that cannot grow enough of their own food and whose economies cannot sustain prolonged food imports, food shortages can become chronic. In such cases, the immediacy of food shortages leads to unsustainable land use (overgrazing, etc.), and the environmental damage can reduce food production potential even further. In those countries prone to chronic famine conditions, an extreme drought event can transform chronic shortages into an acute famine in which many human lives are at stake and food aid is the only alternative. The most important characteristic of acute famine is that it is (or should be) unusual.

FAMINE RELIEF AS A STRATEGY FOR FOOD SECURITY

The decision matrix in Figure 16.2 can be applied to food aid by treating the different levels of famine as drought impacts. The victims of acute famine clearly fall into the fourth quadrant (high impact–low frequency), where international food aid is aiding the unlucky. But African countries must acquire the necessary robustness (or drought preparedness) to withstand natural famine conditions without major international intervention. They must develop their own self-sufficient and sustainable safety nets (FAO 1996: 27), as in Quadrant 1 (low impact–high frequency). It is unlikely that many African countries on their own would have the higher degree of robustness implicit in Quadrant 2 (low impact–low frequency).

It is also difficult to apply Quadrant 3 to the African situation, as this would mean withholding aid to victims of chronic famine to avoid subsidising bad management. Although assistance is required, food aid cannot by itself cure chronic food shortages. Food aid in chronic situations must be delivered in coordination with long-term sustainable development strategies that can transform agricultural systems from a vulnerable state to a robust, drought-tolerant state.

Drought monitoring systems play a major role in the set of strategies for responding to famine. A safety net for natural or chronic famine should operate at a national or regional level. Thus, the role of drought monitoring systems at these two levels should be to trigger such domestic safety net actions as financial assistance to drought-stricken farmers, national food reserves, or arrangements with neighbouring states from which food shipments could be acquired. To trigger international intervention with food aid programmes, international organisations should target their drought monitoring systems to acute famine situations. International monitoring systems must provide a common set of information to the numerous nongovernment organisations involved in food aid. At the same time, the international community should focus long-term development on alleviating chronic famine situations.

THE ROLE OF CLIMATE RECORDS IN CLASSIFYING FAMINE

Most famine episodes are brought on by meteorological droughts (political upheavals notwithstanding) whose chances of recurring can be derived by normalising against historical weather records. Normalising is the comparison of current conditions with past conditions to produce a dimensionless parameter. It is an essential interpretive aspect of drought monitoring in all countries (Dyer 1986). The same model, output variable, and estimation date(s) must be used to derive both the current and historical estimates. In the Canadian FoDEWS (Dyer 1988), two methods were used to present normalised estimates. Both methods were also adopted in CANDAF by making use of historical rainfall records and climate normals from more than 1,000 African sites (FAO 1984a and 1984b). In the simpler, more commonly used method, the current condition is presented as a per cent of the long-term average (percentage of normal). Since this method only requires average historical estimates, normals are usually easy to re-estimate as needed.

The second method is to present a current estimate in terms of its return period. For example, in Figure 16.4, because approximately 5 per cent of the years in the distribution were equal to or less than the 1983 value, the 1983 estimate can be said to have a return period of one year in twenty, which can be represented concisely in a map or report as 1/20 (Dyer 1986). Similarly, an evaporation value of 65 per cent of normal would have a return period of 1/5 because approximately 20 per cent of the years analysed gave values equal to or less than 65 per cent of the average (normal). The 1984 return period is 1/4, since it exceeded 25 per cent of the years.

The return period method is more difficult to prepare and less flexible than percentage of normal, since it requires sorting of the historical estimates into ascending or descending order. But it is more policy-relevant because it provides the frequencies of recurrence needed for the decision logic in Figure 16.2. Return periods make probability easier for decision makers to accept as a basis for defining drought severity because they represent the average number of future years in which to expect one recurrence of the current level of severity (or greater). In considering return periods in relation to the above categories of famine:

- acute famines are associated with droughts that have long return periods (low frequency),
- chronic famines occur in conjunction with droughts that have short return periods (recur frequently),
- natural famines are associated with droughts that recur only moderately frequently but whose impacts can be compensated or mitigated to avoid loss of human life without lasting ecological damage.

DROUGHT EARLY WARNING AND LEAD TIME

Drought assistance of any kind is more effective if the information on which it is based is timely (Dyer 1986). Decision makers need lead time to reach a decision and implement the assistance programme (Dyer and De Jager 1986). In developed countries, delays to drought-stricken farmers will limit their cash flow and cause their debts to build up (FPMC 1990: 14). The stakes become higher when assisting subsistence farmers since hungry people cannot defer their needs and food aid shipments can take several months to arrange (ICIHI 1985: 57).

Drought reporting can become timely in two ways. The first way is to ensure that operation of the monitoring system is efficient. Usually the greatest efficiencies are found in the transmission and pre-processing phases (see Figure 16.1), particularly if there is an opportunity to automate (Dyer and Lally 1990). Efficiency can also be improved through electronic distribution of reports. The second way is to provide reliable predictions about future drought conditions, rather than simply reporting the current situation.

Weather-based early warning (prediction) is possible only if an effective and reliable prediction variable can be chosen (Dyer and De Jager 1986). The choice must take into account the correlation over the prediction period and the reliability of the prediction. As well, the variable must be significant to drought impacts, such as the survival and/or growth of a crop. For example, soil moisture reserves at the beginning of the dry season may be the determinant of crop survival at the end of the dry season. Deep soil moisture storage may be more effective than topsoil moisture because the deep moisture is what the crop will likely survive on at the end of the season, and it can be predicted more easily (Dyer and De Jager 1986).

Many early warning systems must use fictitious weather data to keep their models operating during the future prediction period. Systems such as CANDAF or the FAO model, which do not depend on a daily time step, can use monthly climate normals as a proxy for future weather. Although using forecasts of actual future weather events has not been very effective over the long-range periods needed in drought early warning, some climate phenomena, such as the El Niño, may offer potential in some regions of the world.

SUMMARY – THE FUTURE OF DROUGHT MONITORING

This chapter examined the nature and use of the weather-based drought monitoring systems as they would apply to Africa under the new sustainable food security paradigm. Although Figure 16.1 provides a useful framework for a weather based monitoring system, phase 3 should be treated as two sub-phases: (1) actual model operations for current and future conditions and (2) normalising. For systems such FoDEWS and CANDAF, prediction is also part of phase 3. The CANDAF system (Dyer 1989) demonstrated that many weather monitoring concepts used in Canada, including the two methods of normalising and predicting future growing conditions, can be successfully employed in Africa if the social and ecological conditions are also incorporated. FAO should also consider these features in its monitoring system(s).

Given the main drought policy issue considered here, the expectation for future aid created by current assistance, return periods are the best basis for drought definition. However, they are less convenient than per cent of normal. The policy goal of aiding the unlucky without subsidising bad management calls for drought assistance at a predictable frequency. Since in Africa leeway is required for humanitarian needs, short-term drought assistance (food aid) must be integrated with long-term sustainable development and land use. This

integration must focus on the shift from a vulnerable to a robust agricultural system under high impact–high frequency droughts (Figure 16.3). As well, environmental, economic, and social impacts of both the drought and the assistance measures must be assessed in these decisions.

Both national governments and international agencies should carry out drought monitoring, as each level has a specific strategic role in responding to droughts and famine. The international community should react to acute famines with food aid and to other famine situations with development assistance. National governments, assisted by regional organisations (such as east Africa's Intergovernmental Authority for Drought and Development), should take responsibility for droughts that could lead to chronic famine and should ensure against chronic food shortages. Climate analysis is crucial in classifying the droughts that bring about these conditions. The return periods selected to define drought severity and frequencies of intervention in different geographic regions should be similar, even though actual drought severity may vary. For example, droughts with return periods of 1/3 or 1/5 should be handled regionally, while 1/10 to 1/20 return periods would warrant international attention.

Drought monitoring operations in Canada have suffered from both restricted operating resources and a general decrease in government drought assistance. The lesson from this decline for drought analysts is that weather-based monitoring for drought assistance alone can be hard to justify. Other uses should be considered in designing a weather-based monitoring system so that a variety of climatic analysis services are also provided. For example, because CANDAF contains extensive climate reference files, long-term land use planning was recommended as a secondary application (Dyer and Mack 1986, Dyer 1989). Consequently, CANDAF was used to evaluate the climate factors associated with land degradation risks in Ethiopia (Dyer et al. 1993). The real-time function of these systems should include crop yield forecasting in support of agricultural marketing. Helping African farmers turn their crop surpluses into cash would be a substantial long-term development contribution.

REFERENCES

Altieri, M.A. (1987) *Agroecology – The Scientific Basis of Alternative Agriculture*, Boulder, CO: Westview Press, and London: IT Publications.

Arritt, S. (1993) *The Living Earth Book of Deserts*, Pleasantville, NY: The Reader's Digest Association Inc.

Baier, W. (1973) 'Crop-weather analysis models. 1. Summary', *International Journal of Biometeorology* 17, 4: 313–20.

—— (1977) 'Crop-weather models and their use in yield assessments', WMO – No. 458, Technical Note No. 151.

—— (1989) 'Climatic criteria for the maintenance or improvement of soil quality in semi-arid regions', in *Proceedings International Conference on Soil Quality in Semi-arid Agriculture*, June 1989, Saskatoon, Saskatchewan.

de Jong, R. (1981) 'Soil water models: A review', Land Resource Research Institute, Agriculture Canada, Contribution No. 123.

Dugas, W.A., Ainsworth, C.G., and Arkin, G.F. (1983) 'Operational drought evaluations using a crop model', in *Proceedings of 16th Conference on Agriculture and Forest Meteorology* (April 1983, Ft. Collins, CO), Boston, MA: American Meteorological Society.

Dyer, J.A. (1984) 'Monitoring drought for improved grazing land management', *Journal of Soil and Water Conservation* 39, 3: 176–8.

—— (1986) 'Weather based drought early warning and its role in government policy', in *Proceedings of the Canadian Hydrology Symposium*, Regina, Saskatchewan, Canada, June 1986, pp. 123–34.

—— (1988) 'A drought early warning system for prairie pasture land', *Canadian Water Resources Journal* 13, 4: 5–15.

—— (1989) 'A Canadian approach to drought monitoring for famine relief in Africa', *Water International* 14: 198–205.

—— (1991) 'A review of weather based crop monitoring activities by Agriculture Canada,' in *Strengthening National Early Warning and Food Information Systems in Latin America and the Caribbean*, FAO Workshop Report, Santiago, Chile, December 1990, pp. 116–19.

Dyer, J.A. and Cianferro, D.P. (1988) 'System documentation for the Canadian analysis of drought in Africa (CANDAF)', S&C Rprt No. 88–2, Agriculture Canada, Ottawa, Ontario, prepared for the International Development Agency (CIDA).

Dyer, J.A. and De Jager, J.M. (1986) 'The predictability of summer droughts in South African Grassland', *Water International* 11, 3: 78–87.

Dyer, J.A. and Lally, S.K. (1990) 'A Canadian agricultural weather monitoring system using synoptic weather records', *Canadian Water Resources Journal* 15, 1: 67–79.

Dyer, J.A. and Mack, A.R. (1984) 'Weather monitoring, helping agriculture cope', *Agrologist* 13, 2: 14–16.

—— (1986) 'Weather based analysis of drought in Africa', R&E Rprt No. 86–3, Agriculture Canada, Ottawa, Ontario, prepared for the Canadian International Development Agency (CIDA).

Dyer, J.A., Kelbe, B.E., and de Jager, J.M. (1988) 'Lysimetric calibration of a Canadian soil moisture budget model under bare soil in southern Africa', *Climatological Bulletin* 22, 1: 33–47.

Dyer, J.A., Teshome, A., and Torrance, J.K. (1992) 'A climate analysis package for land use planning in Ethiopia', *Canadian Water Resources Journal* 17, 4: 1–12.

—— (1993) 'Agroclimatic profiles for uniform productivity areas in Ethiopia', *Water International* 18, 4: 189–99.

Dyer, J.A., Warner, D.G., and Stewart, R.B. (1981) 'Criteria for drought in spring forage growth', *Canadian Farm Economics* 16, 6: 12–19.

Edey, S.N. (1980) 'SMEP – An approach to aerial assessment of soil moisture reserves in the Prairie Provinces', *Canada Agriculture* 25, 2: 26–9.

FAO (Food and Agriculture Organization) (1984a) *Agroclimatological Data for Africa Volume 1, Countries North of the Equator*, FAO Plant Production and Protection Series No. 22, Rome.

—— (1984b) *Agroclimatological data for Africa Volume 2, countries south of the equator*, FAO Plant Production and Protection Series No. 22, Rome.

—— (1991a) 'Contribution of strengthened agricultural statistical services to crop forecasting', in *Strengthening National Early Warning and Food Information Systems in Latin America and the Caribbean*, FAO Workshop Report (Annex 5 ESC/RLAC/WNES/3), Santiago, Chile, December 1990.

—— (1991b) *Report on the FAO Workshop on Strengthening National Early Warning and Food Information Systems in Latin America and the Caribbean*, Santiago, Chile, 10–14 December 1990, pp. 116–19.

—— (1991c) 'The use of agro-meteorological models for crop monitoring and yield forecasting', in *Strengthening National Early Warning and Food Information Systems in Latin America and the Caribbean*, FAO Workshop Report (Annex 6 ESC/RLAC/WNES/4), Santiago, Chile, December 1990.

—— (1996) 'Rome declaration on world food security', Approved by the World Food Summit, Rome, Italy, 13–17 November.

FPMC (1990) '1990 Cash Flow Situation in the Prairies. A report to the Deputy Ministers of Agriculture', prepared by the Federal–Provincial Monitoring Committee for the Deputy Ministers of Agriculture, Ottawa, Canada.

Frere, M. and Popov, G.F. (1979) 'Agro-meteorological crop monitoring and forecasting', FAO Plant

Production and Protection Paper No. 17, FAO, Rome.

—— (1986) 'Early agro meteorological crop yield assessment', FAO Plant Production and Protection Paper No. 73, FAO, Rome.

Hargreaves, G.H. (1983) 'Practical agroclimatic information systems', in D.F. Cusack (ed.), *Agroclimatic Information for Development – Reviving the Green Revolution*, Boulder, CO: Westview Press.

Hendricksen, B.L. and Durkin, J.W. (1986) 'Growing period and drought early warning in Africa using satellite data', *International Journal of Remote Sensing* 7, 11: 1,583–608.

ICIHI (1985) *Famine – A Man Made Disaster*, Independent Commission on International Humanitarian Issues, Working Group on Disasters report, New York: Vintage Books, Random House Inc.

—— (1986) *The Encroaching Desert – The Consequences of Human Failure*, Independent Commission on International Humanitarian Issues, Working Group on Disasters report, London: Zed Books Ltd.

IGADD (1986) *Assembly of Heads of State and Government – First Session*, Djibouti, January 1986, Intergovernmental Authority for Drought and Development.

Lodge, R.W., Campbell, J.B., Smoliak, S., and Johnston, A. (1971) 'Management of the Western Range', Publ. No. 1425, Agriculture Canada, Ottawa, Canada.

Motha, R.P. and Heddinghaus, T.R. (1986) 'The Agricultural Weather Facility's Operational Assessment Programme', *Bulletin of the American Meteorological Society* 67: 1,114–22.

Musembi, D.K. and Griffiths, J.F. (1986) 'The use of precipitation data to identify soil moisture patterns and the growing seasons in eastern Kenya', *Agricultural and Forest Meteorology* 37: 47–61.

Palmer, W.C. (1965) 'Meteorological drought', *Research Paper* No. 45, Weather Bureau, US Department of Commerce, Washington, DC.

Prince, S.D. and Justice, C.O. (eds) (1991) 'Coarse resolution remote sensing of the Sahelian environment', Special Issue, *International Journal of Remote Sensing* 12 (6).

Raddatz, R. (1990) 'An operational agrometeorological information system for the Canadian Prairies', in *Workshop on the Application of Climate and Weather Information to the Farm*, January 1990, Truro, Nova Scotia, Canada, pp. 122–35.

Raddatz, R. and Kern, J. (1984) 'An assessment of the near real time rainfall network on Canada's Eastern Prairies', *Atmosphere–Ocean* 22, 4: 474–83.

Reddy, S.J. (1993) *Agroclimatic/Agrometeorological Techniques as Applicable to Dry-land Agriculture in Developing Countries*, Secunderabad, India: Jeevan Charitable Trust, Sri Hari Printers.

Selirio, I.S. (1984) 'Weather analysis for crop insurance', *Agrologist* 13, 2: 17–18.

Selirio, I.S. and Brown, D.M. (1979) 'Soil moisture based simulation of forage yield', *Agricultural Meteorology* 20: 99–114.

Timberlake, L. (1985) *Africa in Crisis*, Ottawa: The Common Heritage Programme, Inter Press.

Walker, G.K. (1989) 'Weather sensitivity of Western Canada wheat yields', *Agriculture and Forest Meteorology* 44: 339–51.

Walton, K. (1969) *The Arid Zones*, Chicago: The University Library of Geography Series, Adine Publishing Co.

WMO (1963) 'Guide to agrometeorological practices', WMO No. TP.61, Secretariat of the World Meteorological Organization, Geneva, Switzerland.

17

DROUGHT IN THE CONTEXT OF THE LAST 1,000+ YEARS

Some surprising implications

Lisa J. Graumlich and Mrill Ingram

INTRODUCTION

At the turn of the millennium, scenarios of future threats to the global environment are ubiquitous. A common element of these scenarios is the recognition of the momentum of current trajectories of change, driven by an increasing capacity of humankind to alter the earth in a systemic, global manner (e.g., increasing trace gas concentrations, increasing habitat loss). Dramatic, and often disturbing, trends are extrapolated on the basis of rates observed over the last several decades with the assumption that 'business as usual' will proceed. As a complement to such scenarios, we suggest that by turning our gaze back to times past and exploiting paleoenvironmental records, we can define the envelope of 'natural' environmental variability. The pace and pattern of environmental variability provides critical information necessary to evaluate current trajectories and assess anthropogenic forcings. Toward that end, when we were invited to write a chapter on 'tree rings' for this volume, we interpreted the invitation broadly. In this chapter we suggest that the perspective of the last millennia can provide new insights into the nature of drought as a feature of the climate system as well as a risk to people and institutions. The historical perspective is useful because, even with late twentieth century advances in observational data and numerical climate models, we are still often 'surprised' by the behaviour of the climate system. That is, events in the long-term record confound our expectation of 'normal' climate with events we would not anticipate based on twentieth-century data alone.

Our goal in this paper is to use long-term records to examine our expectation of the nature and consequences of climatic variability, especially drought. Specifically, we are interested in how the long-term perspective provided by tree-ring records alters our expectations about droughts in such a way that we are less likely to be 'surprised' by the events of the next millennium. Initially, we discuss why 'surprise' might be a relevant concept in research on drought, given that the climate system is capable of switching between significantly different modes. We then use two case studies to demonstrate how the theory of surprise can inform our interpretation of droughts as manifestations of the climate system as well as disasters.

WHY MIGHT THE CLIMATE SYSTEM SURPRISE US?

In looking back over the last millennium, we are struck by the number of 'surprises' we see in the long-term record of climate variability and human response. In this context, 'surprise' refers to a set of theories describing how abrupt changes in environmental systems occur and why they pose challenges to those institutions charged with providing the means to cope with change (Holling 1986, Kates and Clark 1996). Surprises result from the interaction between people's expectations and the behaviour of the environment and occur 'when perceived reality departs qualitatively from expectation' (Holling 1986). Surprise confounds our expectations, entailing events that we never imagined could occur (Kates and Clark 1996). Holling (1986) emphasises that our expectations are strongly shaped by underlying metaphors, models, and belief systems, especially fundamental concepts regarding the nature of causality, stability, and change.

The theory of surprise is particularly relevant to research on climatic variability because our most basic beliefs regarding the dynamics of the climate system are in a state of flux, fuelled in large part by new information regarding how the climate system behaves on time scales of decades to centuries. Specifically, our expectation that the climatic system is stationary on time scales of decades to centuries has been discredited based on a growing body of empirical as well as theoretical work (for example, Mandlebrot and Wallis 1969, Mitchell 1976, Lorenz 1986). Recent compilations of climate data clearly indicate that the short (i.e., 50–100 years) instrumental record of climate does not represent a stationary record (Karl 1995, Diaz and Bradley 1995). In particular, the decade of the 1970s witnessed pronounced and rapid shifts or jumps in the climate system, including (1) shifts in the atmospheric circulation patterns in the extra-tropical north Pacific (Trenberth 1990), (2) higher frequency of ENSO conditions in the tropical Pacific (Trenberth and Hurrel 1994), (3) the 'great salinity anomaly' and associated weather events in the north Atlantic (Dickson et al. 1988), and (4) an abrupt decrease in rainfall over the Sahel (greater than 50 per cent) during the period 1968 to 1993 (Nicholson 1995). Evidence for climate 'jumps' is not restricted to this century. High-resolution paleoclimatic studies of the Greenland ice core indicate that mean annual temperature can change up to 10°C in a few years (Grootes et al. 1993, Alley et al. 1995). Further, evidence from the Greenland records implies that rapid 'jumps' in climate may be particularly characteristic of times of changing boundary conditions leading to warmer climates (Broecker 1987, Overpeck 1996).

We are not certain why these shifts occur or the degree to which they represent anthropogenic changes or natural variability (National Research Council 1995). We are certain, however, that the thirty-year time frame over which we define climate 'normals' is not sufficient to characterise climate-related risks, especially in the case of relatively rare, extreme events such as droughts. Thus, the emerging view of the climate system is one in which (1) nonstationary behaviour (i.e., 'jumps' in the system) is probable, especially in times of changing boundary conditions, and

(2) decade scale and longer-scale trends or episodes are an important characteristic of the system.

These new models and metaphors regarding the nature of climatic change call into question the traditional approaches to assigning risk to drought events. The risk of drought as a meteorological event is evaluated in a probabilistic framework in which the severity of a drought event is framed relative to long-term 'normal' conditions and/or the intensity of previous drought events (Wilhite 1993). Drought research often focuses on reducing uncertainty associated with drought – that is, more accurately specifying the probability of occurrence and nature of consequences. Often, a complete knowledge of probabilities and range of potential consequences is poorly known and is sometimes unknowable. Nevertheless, much scientific effort is aimed at reducing uncertainty regarding the probabilities of a given magnitude of drought, with the implicit assumption that reducing uncertainty enhances the generation of sound policies for drought response. This assumption may not hold, especially for climate-related hazards that are regional to global in scale (Waterstone 1993). In Holling's framework, our underlying model for assessing drought hazards has been one of a stable climate system where the biggest challenge to risk assessment was garnering a statistically appropriate data set to characterise a simple system.

Research on global environmental change has raised the spectre that increasing atmospheric trace gases and other similar globally scaled changes may result in nonlinear behaviour in the climate system, resulting in unanticipated climate events or 'surprises'. Further, the societal consequences of climatic 'surprises' may take unanticipated forms because of the increasingly tight linkages between people, institutions, and environmental resources due to increased population and consumption and globalisation of trade. Under such circumstances, research priorities shift from questions of reducing uncertainty to issues of anticipating the unexpected, using techniques based on analyses of historical data, techniques associated with analyses of complex systems, and other methods (Schneider and Turner 1995). Further, in anticipating broad classes of 'surprises', we encounter different challenges in developing responses to reduce vulnerability and enhance societal and environmental resilience with respect to surprises. Kates and Clark (1996) argue that in a world of surprises, policies that increase society's resilience and adaptability are critical. Further, when environmental management is approached using adaptive strategies, surprises serve as useful learning experiences for societies.

In the case studies below, we describe how surprises have resulted in shifts in the models and metaphors that inform our notion of what constitutes a drought and what consequences ensue. The first case study addresses an unexpected event: severe, multidecadal droughts in the Sierra Nevada. The second case study describes unexpected consequences to a drought event, in this case the response of the Anasazi to drought during the late thirteenth century.

MULTIDECADAL DROUGHTS IN THE SIERRA NEVADA AND WESTERN UNITED STATES

Multiple lines of evidence indicate that severe, multidecadal droughts occurred during medieval times (ca. AD 900 to 1400) in the Sierra Nevada (Figure 17.1; see review in Hughes and Graumlich 1996). The Sierra Nevada droughts have been cited in both the scientific and lay press as key evidence that significant shifts in the climate system have occurred in the past and could occur in the future (e.g., Overpeck 1996, Stevens 1994). The 'discovery' of these droughts is illustrative of a common theme in work on environmental surprises: that is, important information was

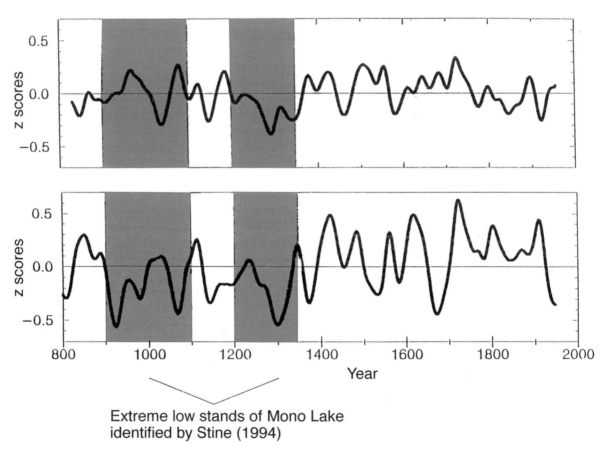

Figure 17.1 Smoothed reconstructions of precipitation as inferred from tree-ring records. The top panel is a reconstruction of winter precipitation for the southern Sierra Nevada (after Graumlich 1993). The lower panel is a reconstruction of annual precipitation for southwestern Nevada (after Hughes and Graumlich 1996). Corroborating evidence for multidecadal droughts as indicated by radiocarbon-dated geomorphic events is indicated for the periods AD 900–1100 and AD 1200–1350 (Stine 1994)

initially discounted as being at odds with conventional expectation. This phenomenon – dismissing data that appear to be outliers – has been most widely discussed as a feature in the delay of the discovery in the seasonal hole in the ozone layer over Antarctica (Pukelsheim 1990). In a similar fashion, the first author (Graumlich; henceforth referred to as 'I') discounted the existence of multidecadal droughts in medieval times in the Sierra Nevada.

About 10 years ago, I initiated what I anticipated would be a conventional study of long-term trends in precipitation in the Sierra Nevada as inferred from tree-ring series over the last 1,000 years. Based on previous tree-ring studies (e.g., Fritts 1991, Earle 1993), I expected to see episodes of drought in the precipitation reconstructions roughly similar in magnitude and duration to those recorded during the twentieth century. I never expected to see what the analyses revealed: two multidecadal droughts (AD 1020–70 and AD 1250–1360), the latter lasting more than 100 years (Graumlich 1993). My initial reaction to these findings was that they represented errors in the analyses. Before writing up the results, I reworked the analyses, checked my data, and examined my assumptions, all of which was motivated by my expectation that such severe droughts were extremely unlikely based on my understanding of climate dynamics.

In the text of the paper reporting these results (Graumlich 1993), I did not call great attention to the droughts, perhaps indicating lingering doubts about the validity of these conclusions. Subsequent to publication, emerging work by others changed my assessment of the validity of my own findings. The most dramatic findings were those of Scott Stine, who found a series of in situ, rooted tree stumps on the shores of Mono Lake, a hydrographically closed lake on the eastern slope of the Sierra Nevada (Stine 1994). Stine's research on long-term fluctuations in Mono Lake has been facilitated by the fact that since the 1940s inflowing streams have been diverted to the city of Los Angeles to meet municipal water demands. As a result, the current lake level of Mono Lake is 14 m below the 'natural', prediversion level. Land surface that is currently exposed as lake shore would be underwater under 'normal' climate conditions. The significance of the Stine stumps thus lies

in the fact that they were rooted at an elevation as much as 15.5 m below the prediversion level of the lake, implying a very large reduction in water supplies to the lake. In addition, each stump has up to fifty annual rings, allowing us to estimate the minimum duration of the droughts. The interpretation of the stumps as indicating large changes in the level of Mono Lake is supported by independent lake-transgressive and lake-regressive sedimentary sequences (Stine 1994). Finally, the most exciting result from my point of view was that the radiocarbon dates for the stumps fell into two periods, AD 900–1100 and AD 1200–1350. Stine's work thus provides independent and conclusive corroboration of the existence of severe and persistent droughts during medieval times in the Sierra Nevada.

Subsequent work has provided additional corroboration of the two severe drought episodes (Hughes and Graumlich 1996; Stine 1997, personal communication). Further, during this period, prolonged disruption of normal precipitation patterns extended over much of the western United States, from southern California (Davis 1992, Jirikowic et al. 1993), across the Colorado Plateau (Dean 1996), and as far east as the Sand Hills of Nebraska (David Loope, personal communication, 1996). The spatial extent of these anomalies implies a persistent northward displacement in the path of the midlatitude storm track over North America. This displacement could have been a result of a contraction of the circumpolar vortex, analogous to the pattern of the California Dust Bowl years of 1928–34. Alternatively, the persistent droughts could reflect a persistent ridge of high pressure steering storm tracks to the north, analogous to the pattern of the 1976–77 drought (Stine 1994). Finally, such severe, multidecadal droughts were not confined to the medieval period. Droughts of similar magnitude and duration occurred six times during the period 6,000 BC to AD 1; they are indicated by reconstructions of precipitation from bristlecone pine in the White Mountains of California and Nevada (Hughes and Graumlich 1996; drought dates are 5970 BC, 5881 BC, 5591 BC, 4058 BC, 3948 BC, and 1257 BC). The dates for previous severe, multidecadal droughts indicate a relatively even distribution of events over the past eight millennia.

The documentation of severe and persistent

medieval droughts in the western United States has implications for our concepts and models of water resource availability in California. Based on the 'drought of record' in the twentieth-century data, our current expectation of extreme drought is that of the Dust Bowl in California from 1928 to 1934. The second most severe drought of record is that of 1987–92. The duration of these two events has lead to an expectation that drought spells will probably not exceed seven years in duration. Observational data have lead to similar expectations with respect to the magnitude of droughts in California. For example, during the Dust Bowl years, runoff from Sierra Nevada streams averaged 70 per cent of normal (Stine 1994). Our findings are sobering in that we see two droughts during medieval times lasting more than fifty years in which runoff was 40 per cent of twentieth-century average values. In the 8,000-year record inferred from bristlecone pine (Hughes and Graumlich 1996), we see further evidence for severe, multidecadal droughts. Ongoing research is seeking to understand how such droughts are related to larger synoptic-scale atmospheric circulation patterns and to assess the potential role of ocean–atmosphere interactions in driving circulation anomalies. The potential payoff for this research will be models with adequate diagnostic power to allow water resource planners to distinguish droughts of moderate severity and duration (i.e., Dust Bowl-type droughts) from droughts of extreme severity and duration (i.e., medieval-type droughts).

ANASAZI PEOPLE AND THE 'GREAT DROUGHT' OF THE THIRTEENTH CENTURY

In the same manner that the discovery of the medieval droughts has implications for drought climatology, the medieval droughts yield insights into droughts as hazards. In most regions where we have strong evidence for medieval droughts, archeological evidence for impacts on the livelihood of people is weak to nonexistent. A spectacular exception to that generalisation is the Colorado Plateau, where more than seventy years of dendrochronological research has yielded absolute calendar dates marking the establishment, growth, and abandonment of prehistoric settlements that can be interpreted in terms of human

population dynamics over the last 2,000 years (Dean et al. 1994). When coupled with long-term, regional records of climatic variability (e.g., Dean 1996), these records offer a unique opportunity to study the interaction between drought, human behaviour, and human demography. As in the previous case study, the narrative of how 'surprise' functioned to reform our models and metaphors of drought as a hazard for prehistoric peoples is instructive.

The late thirteenth century emigration of the Anasazi people of the Colorado Plateau as victims of a 'Great Drought' was a simple but compelling interpretation of two strands of dendrochronological research. The dating of prehistoric Mesa Verde and other sites on the Colorado Plateau provided by tree-rings established that a major demographic dislocation took place during a brief period at the end of the thirteenth century AD (Douglass 1929, Haury 1935). Tree-rings also provided evidence for a 'Great Drought', in the form of a sequence of extremely narrow rings from AD 1276 to 1299 (Douglass 1929, Haury 1935). This conjunction of major climatic and human shifts gave archaeologists reason to identify the 'Great Drought' as the major cause for the Anasazi exodus. This simple and compelling model persisted for several decades in the scholarly literature and has only recently been challenged in the popular press (e.g., Johnson 1996).

Major shifts in the understanding of this event occurred when researchers reconsidered previous assumptions about simple cause-and-effect relationships between society and drought (Jett 1964, Dean et al. 1985, Plog et al. 1988, Petersen 1988, Van West 1994). A rich vein of inquiry is being mined as archaeological data are conceptualised in terms of complex adaptive systems of interacting social and environmental factors. The Anasazi population decline appeared to be a 'surprise' when considered in the context of the increasingly sophisticated understanding of climate and demographic histories of the region. For example, severe dry periods preceded and followed the 'Great Drought' of the late thirteenth century but did not have dramatic effects on populations (Ahlstrom et al. 1995). If the Anasazi had weathered severe droughts in the past, why did this one cause an entire population to abandon settlements that represented large investments of labour and resources? Further, climatological studies raised the possibility that the exodus began before the dry spell set in (Johnson 1996), and that even during the drought, enough moisture fell on the region to grow adequate corn to support the area's population (Van West 1994). Thus empirical data called into question the simple model of a direct linkage between drought and population. On a more theoretical level, it was recognised that 'unless a conceptual scheme existed to relate environmental variability to human behaviour, the effort to identify prehistoric environmental impacts on Southwestern groups would degenerate into an inconclusive exercise in pattern matching' (Dean 1996: 28).

More recent approaches do not completely reject environmental change as a major contributing factor in social transformations (e.g., Ahlstrom et al. 1995). Instead, researchers have moved away from direct cause-and-effect interpretations of the human-environment relationship, toward a view that sees dynamic interactions between a complex and *adaptive* cultural system and environmental conditions that vary at different spatial and temporal frequencies (Dean et al. 1985, Dean 1996). Scale-based complexity in adaptive cultural systems is reflected in the emerging idea that socioeconomic connectivity among Colorado Plateau communities was probably more important to long-term survival than particular agricultural strategies employed by a single community (Wills et al. 1994). Similarly, mobility was fundamental to the adaptive strategies of early southwestern farmers, ranging from movement between upland and lowland settlements to interregional migrations (Dean et al. 1985, Ahlstrom et al. 1995). The movement off parts of the Colorado Plateau during the late thirteenth century can be at least partially explained as a migration into the northern Rio Grande region, driven by changes in rainfall patterns that made the Rio Grande more favourable for agriculture (Ahlstrom et al. 1995). In this light, the social changes that occurred just before AD 1300 were not simply abandonment, but an adaptive strategy to environmental stress. Abandonment implies failure, but these movements of population could be alternatively viewed as shifts in populations within an overall economic system that sustained populations in the face of environmental variation (Wills et al. 1994).

Models of critical environmental conditions for agriculture, and thus human livelihood, during the time of Anasazi population changes have also increased in nuance. In developing complex, behaviour-based models of population dynamics for the prehistoric Colorado Plateau, Dean et al. (1985) argued that environmental conditions encompass many characteristics that affect human adaptation beyond 'wet or dry' and that critical variables interact on differing temporal and spatial scales (Figure 17.2). In this context, predictability is critical: the seasonal timing of precipitation and the amplitude of the variability of precipitation are two important factors in setting up the tension between the expectation of when rain will occur and when it actually occurs. Unpredictable precipitation appears to have posed a greater challenge to prehistoric agriculturists than low levels of precipitation (Ahlstrom et al. 1995, Dean 1996). Further complexity is generated by the interaction of short-term (seasonal to interannual) variation in the climate with long-term environmental trends (e.g., floodplain aggradation and erosion, water table dynamics). Dean et al. (1985) suggest that short-term changes can exacerbate or mitigate the impact of long-term trends and thereby hasten or delay behavioural response to those trends. Finally, a more comprehensive approach to the climate-agriculture relationship of the Anasazi considered a series of adaptive mechanisms that mitigated environmental variability to the extent that Anasazi people were unlikely 'mere pawns of the environment' (Dean et al. 1985: 547). The archaeological record for the Anasazi clearly reflects the varying importance of such adaptations as mobility, shifts in settlement location, changes in subsistence mix, exchange between groups during times of high spatial and temporal variability, and agricultural intensification, especially the development of water control devices.

CONCLUSIONS

What are the implications of the discovery of the severe and prolonged droughts in the western United States for our understanding of the climatology of drought? At the most fundamental level, the paleo-record provides new extremes for assessing the intensity and magnitude of the 'drought of record' in a

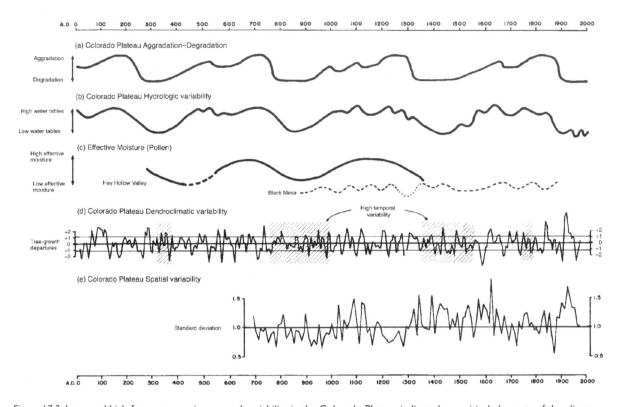

Figure 17.2 Low- and high-frequency environmental variability in the Colorado Plateau indicate how critical elements of the climate system are expressed at different temporal and spatial frequencies (after Dean 1996). All of the variables shown here were important for dryland agriculture. The low-frequency hydrologic and aggradation-degradation curves (a, b) represent, respectively, the rise and fall of alluvial groundwater levels and the deposition and erosion of floodplain sediments. The effective moisture curve (c), derived from analyses of pollen in sediments, represents low-frequency variation in soil moisture. Moisture availability as indicated by tree-ring records (d) reflects decadal scale variability in moisture. The spatial variability of moisture as indicated by a regional network of tree-ring sites (e) indicates the degree of spatial homogeneity or heterogeneity in rainfall patterns. The first three variables are most critical for floodplain agriculture such that environmental deterioration (i.e., floodplain erosion or lower effective moisture) would have created a high degree of resource stress on those groups depending on lowland or floodplain crops. Among groups who used a greater proportion of upland areas for agriculture, high-frequency precipitation would have been more limiting. Note that the Anasazi population decline (after AD 1250) coincides with a time of low temporal and spatial variability in precipitation as well as falling alluvial water tables and floodplain erosion. These factors lowered regional and local carrying capacities at a time when populations had become increasingly aggregated (Dean 1996). Reproduction rights courtesy of Laboratory of Tree-Ring Research, University of Arizona

planning context. If droughts of the severity and persistence observed during medieval times were to occur today, the implications for regional economies and livelihoods would be cataclysmic. Given that such droughts are rare events with serious consequences and little predictability, an appropriate anticipatory response is to strengthen the resilience of social structures and institutions that provide drought relief under a range of drought conditions. A more subtle set of implications is related to Holling's (1986)

observations as to the power of underlying assumptions in influencing how we do scientific research. For example, a critical element in the analyses of the tree-ring data that lead to the 'discovery' of the droughts was recognising and quantifying nonlinear interactions in tree-growth response to multiple climatic variables (Graumlich 1991). The results in Graumlich (1991) were a result of focusing particular attention on anomalies and outliers, reinforcing Kates and Clark's (1996) assertion that attention to anomalies facilitates identification and anticipation of environmental surprise.

What are the implications of the growing appreciation for the complex adaptive strategies of the prehistoric farmers of the Colorado Plateau to a variable and changing rainfall regime? The rethinking of the Anasazi response to drought parallels more general change in concepts regarding the sensitivity of agriculture to climate variability. In the 1980s, many major studies of the potential effects of climate change on modern US agriculture emphasised the use of crop simulation models to predict the effects of various climate-warming scenarios on crop yields. Such work was criticised for failing to include adaptation strategies, including technological changes, into prediction schemes (OTA 1993). More recent studies explicitly recognise possibilities for technological changes in agricultural systems, the adaptive responses of farmers (Easterling 1996), and the multitude of socioeconomic factors that influence the vulnerability of agriculture to drought (Liverman 1990).

ACKNOWLEDGEMENTS

Lisa Graumlich is deeply grateful to Scot Stine and Malcolm Hughes for continued collaboration in unravelling the story of medieval droughts. Jeff Dean provided key references on the question of Anasazi population decline and offered insightful comments on the chapter. We thank Martin Munro and John C. King for technical assistance with data and graphics.

REFERENCES

Ahlstrom, R.V.N., Van West, D.R., and Dean, J.S. (1995) 'Environmental and chronological factors in the Mesa Verde – Northern Rio Grande migration', *Journal of Anthropological Archaeology* 14: 125–42.

Alley, R.B., Meese, D.A., Shuman, C.A., Gow, A.J., Taylor, K.C., Grootes, P.M., White, J.W.C., Ram, M., Waddington, E.D., Mayewski, P.A., and Zielinski, G.A. (1995) 'Abrupt accumulation increase at the Younger Dryas termination in the GISP2 ice core', *Nature* 362: 527–9.

Broecker, W.S. (1987) 'Unpleasant surprises in the greenhouse?', *Nature* 328: 123–6.

Davis, O.K. (1992) 'Rapid climatic change in coastal southern California inferred from Pollen Analysis of San Joaquin Marsh', *Quaternary Research* 37: 89–100.

Dean, J.S. (1996) 'Demography, environment, and subsistence', in J. Tainter and B.B. Tainter (eds), *Evolving Complexity and Environmental Risk in Prehistoric Southwest*, SFI Studies in Complexity, Vol. XXIV, New York: Addison-Wesley, pp. 25–56.

Dean, J.S., Doelle, W.H., and Orcutt, J.D. (1994) 'Adaptive stress, environment and demography', in G.J. Gumerman (ed.), *Themes in Southwestern Prehistory*, Sante Fe: School of American Research Press, pp. 53–86.

Dean, J.S., Euler, R.C., Gumerman, G.J., Plog, F., Hevly, R.H., and Karlstrom, T.N.V. (1985) 'Human behavior, demography, and paleoenviroment on the Colorado Plateaus', *American Antiquity* 50: 537–54.

Diaz, H.F. and Bradley, R.S. (1995) 'Documenting natural climatic variations: How different is the climate of the twentieth century from that of previous centuries?', in D.G. Martinson, K. Bruan, M. Ghil, M.M. Hall, T.R. Karl, E.S. Sarachik, S. Soroohian, and L.D. Talley (eds), *Natural Climatic Variability on Decade-to-Century Time Scales*, Washington, DC: National Academy Press, pp. 17–31.

Dickson, R.R., Meincke, J., Malmberg, S.A., and Lee, A.J. (1988) 'The "Great Salinity Anomaly" in the northern North Atlantic 1968–1982', *Progress in Oceanography* 20: 103–51.

Douglass, A.E. (1929) 'The secret of the southwest solved by talkative tree rings', *National Geographic Magazine* 56: 736–70.

Earle, C.J. (1993) 'Asynchronous droughts in California streamflow as reconstructed from tree rings', *Quaternary Research* 39: 290–9.

Easterling, W.E. (1996) 'Adapting North American agriculture to climate change in review', *Agricultural and Forest Meteorology*, special issue on Adapting North American Agriculture to Climate Change, W.E. Easterling (guest editor), 80: 1–53.

Fritts, H.C. (1991) *Reconstructing Large-Scale Climatic Patterns from Tree-Ring Data: A Diagnostic Analysis*, Tucson: University of Arizona Press.

Graumlich, L.J. (1991) 'Subalpine tree growth, climate, and increasing CO_2: An assessment of recent growth trends', *Ecology* 72: 1–11.

——— (1993) 'A 1000-year record of temperature and precipitation in the Sierra Nevada', *Quaternary Research* 39: 249–55.

Grootes, P.M., Stuiver, M., White, J.W.C., Johnsen, S.J., and Jouzel, J. (1993) 'Comparison of the oxygen isotope records from the GISP2 and GRIP Greenland ice cores', *Nature* 366: 552–4.

Haury, E.W. (1935) 'Tree rings – The archeologist's timepiece', *American Antiquity* 1: 98–108.

Holling, C.S. (1986) 'The resilience of terrestrial ecosystems: Local surprise and global change', in W.C. Clark and R.E. Munn (eds), *Sustainable Development of the Biosphere*, Cambridge: Cambridge University Press, pp. 292–317.

Hughes, M.K. and Graumlich, L.J. (1996) 'Multimillennial dendroclimatic records from the western United States', in R.S. Bradley, P.D. Jones, and J. Jouzel (eds), *Climatic Variations and Forcing Mechanisms of the last 2000 Years*, NATO Advanced Studies Workshop Series, Berlin and New York: Springer-Verlag, pp. 109–24.

Jett, S.C. (1964) 'Pueblo Indian migrations: An evaluation of the possible physical and cultural determinants', *American Antiquity* 29: 281–300.

Johnson, G. (1996) 'Mystery of New Mexico's Anasazis confounds experts again', *New York Times*, 20 August.

Jirikowic, J.L., Kalin, R.M. and Davis, O.K. (1993) 'Tree-Ring 14C as an indicator of climate change. Climatic change in continental isotopic records', *AGU Geophysical Monograph* 78: 353–66.

Karl, T.R. (1995) 'Atmospheric observations', in D.G. Martinson, K. Bruan, M. Ghil, M.M. Hall, T.R. Karl, E.S. Sarachik, S. Sorooshian, and L.D. Talley (eds), *Natural Climatic Variability on Decade-to-Century Time Scales*, Washington, DC: National Academy Press, pp. 12–16.

Kates, R.W. and Clark, W.C. (1996) 'Environmental surprise: Expecting the unexpected', *Environment* 38: 6–34.

Liverman. D. (1990) 'Drought impacts in Mexico: Climate, agriculture, technology, and land tenure in Sonora and Puebla', *Annals of the Association of American Geographers* 80: 49–72.

Lorenz, E.N. (1986) 'The index cycle is alive and well', Namias Symposium, Library of Congress No. 86-50752, pp. 188–96.

Mandlebrot, B.B. and Wallis, J.R. (1969) 'Some long-term properties of geophysical records', *Water Resources Research* 5: 321–40.

Mitchell, J.M. Jr. (1976) 'An overview of climatic variability and its causal mechanisms', *Quaternary Research* 6: 481–93.

National Research Council (1995) *Natural Climatic Variability on Decade-to-Century Time Scales*, Washington, DC: National Academy Press.

Nicholson, S.E. (1995) 'Variability of African rainfall on interannual and decadal time scales', in D.G. Martinson, K. Bruan, M. Ghil, M.M. Hall, T.R. Karl, E.S. Sarachik, S. Sorooshian, and L.D. Talley (eds), *Natural Climatic Variability on Decade-to-Century Time Scales*, Washington, DC: National Academy Press, pp. 32–43.

Office of Technology Assessment (OTA) (1993) *Preparing for an Uncertain Climate*, Office of Technology Assessment, US Congress.

Overpeck, J.T. (1996) 'Warm climate surprises', *Science* 271, 1,820–1.

Petersen, K.L. (1988) *Climate and the Dolores River Anasazi*, University of Utah Anthropological Papers, No. 113, Salt Lake City: University of Utah Press.

Plog, F., Gumerman, F.J., Euler, R.C., Dean, J.S., Hevly, R.H., Karlstrom, T.N.V. (1988) 'Anasazi adaptive strategies: The model, predictions, and results', in G.J. Gumerman (ed.), *The Anasazi in a Changing Environment*, Cambridge: Cambridge University Press, pp. 230–76.

Pukelsheim, F. (1990) 'Robustness of statistical gossip and the Antarctic ozone hole', *IMS Bulletin* 19: 540–5.

Schneider, S. and Turner, B.L. (1995) 'Anticipating global change surprise', in S.J. Hassol and J. Katzenberger (eds), *Anticipating Global Change Surprises*, Aspen, CO: Aspen Global Change Institute.

Stevens, W.K. (1994) 'Severe ancient droughts: A warning to California', *New York Times*, 19 July.

Stine, S. (1994) 'Extreme and persistent drought in California and Patagonia during medieval time', *Nature* 369: 546–9.

Trenberth, K.E. (1990) 'Recent observed interdecadal climate change in the Northern Hemisphere', *Bulletin of the American Meteorological Society* 71: 988–93.

Trenberth, K.E. and Hurrel, J.W. (1994) 'Decadal ocean–atmosphere variations in the Pacific', *Climate Dynamics* 9: 303–19.

Van West, C.R. (1994) 'Modeling prehistoric agricultural productivity in southwestern Colorado: A GIS approach', *Reports of Investigations* 67, Department of Anthropology, Washington University, Pullman, and Crow Canyon Archaeology Center, Cortez.

Waterstone, M. (1993) 'Adrift on a sea of platitudes: Why we will not resolve the greenhouse issue', *Environmental Management* 17, 2: 141–52.

Wilhite, D.A. (1993) 'The enigma of drought', in D.A. Wilhite (ed.), *Drought Assessment, Management, and Planning: Theory and Case Studies*, Boston, MA: Kluwer Academic Publishers, pp. 1–15.

Wills, W.H., Crown, P.L., Dean, J.S., and Langton, C.G. (1994) 'Complex adaptive systems and southwestern prehistory', in G. Gumerman and M. Gell-Mann (eds), *Understanding Complexity in the Prehistoric Southwest*, SFI Studies in the Sciences of Complexity, Proc. Vol. XVI, New York: Addison-Wesley, pp. 297–339.

PART IV

IMPACTS AND ASSESSMENT METHODOLOGIES

18

DROUGHT

Pervasive impacts of a creeping phenomenon

Donald A. Wilhite and Olga Vanyarkho

INTRODUCTION

Throughout human existence, drought has been a threat to the survival of societies. It has often been a trigger for massive human migrations, famines, and wars, altering the course of history itself. Today, as we prepare to enter the twenty-first century, drought continues to affect our global community in countless ways. In fact, we are still discovering the complex inter-relationships between drought and society and grappling with response and mitigation strategies that will lessen impacts and therefore reduce vulnerability for future generations.

A 1984 report by the Swedish Red Cross (Hagman 1984) characterised drought as affecting more people than any other natural hazard; it was also perceived to be the least understood of all natural hazards. This apparent dichotomy is interesting because one might expect governments and international organisations to direct financial and human resources to the most urgent societal needs or problems (i.e., those with the greatest impact). Historically, this has not been the case with respect to drought. Among the principal natural hazards affecting society (i.e., earthquakes, floods, droughts, and typhoons or hurricanes), drought receives less scientific and political attention. This is due largely to its slow-onset nature; cumulative, non-structural impacts; low death toll directly attributable to drought; and extensive areal coverage. The large spatial coverage diffuses relief and recovery efforts.

In recent years, however, there seems to have developed a growing awareness of drought and the need to direct more attention to understanding how its impacts can be reduced. Much of this interest has

been kindled by the increased worldwide presence of drought and famine in recent decades, growing environmental awareness; and concern about desertification, deforestation, and the potential implications of climate change for the frequency and severity of drought.

The purpose of this chapter is to provide an overview of the complexity of impacts associated with drought. This information will be presented in a general context since many of the chapters included in this volume, especially those included in this section, address the complexity of drought impacts and alternative management strategies in the context of specific political, economic, and social settings. A brief case study of the 1996 drought in the United States will be included to illustrate the diversity and complexity of impacts of a recent drought event. Policy responses that have emerged from this event will also be discussed since they may lead to sweeping changes in drought management in the United States in the near future.

DROUGHT IMPACTS OVERVIEW

To more clearly understand the impacts of drought, the phenomenon should not be viewed as merely a natural event. It is the result of an interplay between a natural event (precipitation deficiencies because of natural climatic variability) and the demand placed on water and other natural resources by human-use systems. For example, societies can exacerbate the impacts of drought by placing demands on water and other natural resources that exceed the supply of those resources. This book is replete with examples of this situation in various countries. Societies often plan for normal or above-normal water supplies, ignoring the natural variability of climate systems.

The risk that a society faces from a natural hazard is determined not only by the degree of exposure or frequency of the natural hazard but also by the vulnerability of society. According to Randolph Kent (1987), a disaster occurs when a disaster agent (e.g., drought, earthquake) exposes the vulnerability of a group or groups in such a way that their lives are directly threatened or sufficient harm has been done to economic and social structures, inevitably undermining their ability to survive.

Recent droughts in developing and developed countries and the concomitant impacts and personal hardships that resulted have underscored the vulnerability of all societies to this 'natural' hazard. Recent statistics compiled by the International Decade for Natural Disaster Reduction (IDNDR 1995) indicated that drought accounted for 22 per cent of the damage from disasters, 33 per cent of the number of persons affected by disasters, and 3 per cent of the number of deaths attributed to natural disasters. It is also important to remember that figures on damages resulting from drought include only assistance provided by the international community via international organisations, donor governments, and non-governmental organisations. It does not include relief and recovery funds provided by governments to drought-affected areas within their own borders. For example, the United States expended nearly US$8 billion in responding to the severely affected drought areas in the western and midwestern drought areas between 1974 and 1977 (Wilhite et al. 1986). Another US$6 billion was provided by the federal government in 1988–9 (Riebsame et al. 1991). The Australian government provided assistance to drought-affected areas totalling A$940 million between 1970 and 1984 (Wilhite 1986), and the South African government's expenditures for drought relief in 1984–5 were nearly R450 million (Wilhite 1987).

The number of natural hazard events occurring in most geographic regions over the past three decades has been relatively static for most types of hazards. However, there has been a dramatic increase in the number of reported natural disasters (see Chapter 1). If the number of natural hazard events has not increased dramatically for most hazards, then it is the number of people exposed to these events and their vulnerability that is changing. Vulnerability is defined as people's capacity to anticipate, cope with, and recover from a natural hazard (Blaikie et al. 1994). With the world's population increasing by more than 90 million people annually (Brown et al. 1993), the number of people vulnerable to natural hazards is increasing at an alarming rate. Each year, more people living along coastlines, in flood plains, on hillsides, and in climatically marginal zones are at risk. Environmental degradation is also increasing the risk and impacts of natural hazards at some locations.

In the case of drought and other atmospheric-based natural hazards, projected changes in climate caused by increasing concentrations of CO_2 and other atmospheric trace gases (see Chapter 48) must also be considered when attempting to explain the trend in disasters. In fact, many people already believe the increased number of extreme climatic events recorded over the past decade is an indicator of a changed climate. For example, the recent increase in flood events worldwide has increased speculation that we are already experiencing the impacts of global warming. Increased precipitation amounts and more intense precipitation events are consistent with projections of a changed climate. People also attribute recent drought years to a change in climate, at times without first examining drought occurrence in the context of the historical climatology of the affected area. Attributing a drought event or series of consecutive drought years to climate change also neglects more fundamental questions of vulnerability and how to reduce it (i.e., it is considered only a natural phenomenon). When attempting to explain the causes of an extreme climatic event, such as drought, scientists must clearly distinguish between the causes of the natural event and its social consequences.

THE IMPACTS OF DROUGHT

Drought produces a complex web of impacts that not only ripple through many sectors of the economy but may be experienced well outside the affected region, extending even to the global scale. This complexity is largely caused by the dependence of so many sectors on water for producing goods and providing services.

Impacts from drought are commonly classified as direct or indirect. Reduced crop, range land, and forest productivity; increased fire hazard; reduced water levels; increased livestock and wildlife mortality rates; and damage to wildlife and fish habitat are a few examples of direct impacts. The consequences of these impacts illustrate indirect impacts. For example, a reduction in crop, range land, and forest productivity may result in reduced income for farmers and agribusiness, increased prices for food and timber, unemployment, reduced government tax revenues because of decreased expenditures, increased crime, foreclosures on bank loans to farmers and businesses, migration, and disaster relief programmes. Direct or primary impacts are usually of a biophysical nature. Conceptually, the more removed the impact from the cause, the more complex the link to the cause.

Because of the number of affected groups and sectors associated with drought, the geographic size of the area affected, and the difficulties in quantifying environmental damages and personal hardships, the precise determination of the financial costs of drought is a formidable challenge. The economic costs and losses associated with drought are highly variable from year to year. These costs and losses are also quite variable from one drought year to another in the same place, depending on timing, intensity, and spatial extent of the droughts.

The impacts of drought are commonly classified as economic, environmental, and social (Wilhite 1992). Table 18.1 presents a comprehensive list of the impacts associated with drought. This list represents the experiences of many drought-prone areas of the world, as derived from the literature and from participants of workshops in the United States and regional training seminars in Africa, Latin America, and Asia. These meetings were conducted by the International Drought Information Center at the University of Nebraska–Lincoln between 1989 and 1993. Although drought produces impacts that are regionally distinct, there are many similarities in the types of impacts experienced from one region to another. Many economic impacts occur in broad agricultural and agriculturally related sectors, including forestry and fisheries, because of the reliance of these sectors on surface and subsurface water supplies. In addition to obvious losses in yields in both crop and livestock

production, drought is associated with increases in insect infestations, plant disease, and wind erosion. Droughts also bring increased problems with insects and diseases to forests and reduce growth. The incidence of forest and range fires increases substantially during extended droughts, which in turn places both human and wildlife populations at higher levels of risk.

Income loss is another indicator used in assessing the impacts of drought because so many sectors are affected. Reduced income for farmers has a ripple effect, because their ability to purchase goods and services is limited. Thus, many retailers experience significant reductions in sales. This leads to unemployment; increased credit risk for financial institutions; capital shortfalls; and loss of tax revenue for local, state, and federal government. The recreation and tourism industries are also affected because many consumers have less discretionary income available. Prices for food, energy, and other products increase as supplies are reduced. In some cases, local supply shortfalls for certain goods will result in the importation of these goods from outside the stricken region. Reduced water supply impairs the navigability of rivers and results in increased transportation costs because products must be transported by rail or truck. Hydropower production is also significantly reduced. For example, hydropower generation was 25–40 per cent below average for large sections of the United States in 1988 (Table 18.2), resulting in serious revenue losses for the industry (Wilhite 1993).

Environmental losses are the result of damages to plant and animal species, wildlife habitat, and air and water quality; forest and range fires; degradation of landscape quality; loss of biodiversity; and soil erosion. Some of the effects are short-term and conditions quickly return to normal following the end of the drought. Other environmental effects linger for some time or may even become permanent. Wildlife habitat, for example, may be degraded through the loss of wetlands, lakes, and vegetation. However, many species will eventually recover from this temporary aberration. The degradation of landscape quality, including increased soil erosion, may lead to a more permanent loss of biological productivity of the landscape. Although environmental losses are difficult to quantify, growing public awareness and concern

Table 18.1 Classification of drought-related impacts (costs and losses)

Problem sectors	Impacts

Economic	• loss from crop production
	    annual and perennial crop losses; damage to crop quality
	    reduced productivity of cropland (wind erosion, etc.)
	    insect infestation
	    plant disease
	    wildlife damage to crops
	• loss from dairy and livestock production
	    reduced productivity of range land
	    forced reduction of foundation stock
	    closure/limitation of public lands to grazing
	    high cost/unavailability of water for livestock
	    high cost/unavailability of feed for livestock
	    high livestock mortality rates
	    increased predation
	    range fires
	• loss from timber production
	    forest fires
	    tree disease
	    insect infestation
	    impaired productivity of forest land
	• loss from fishery production
	    damage to fish habitat
	    loss of young fish due to decreased flows
	• loss of national economic growth, retardation of economic development
	• income loss for farmers and others directly affected
	• loss of farmers through bankruptcy
	• loss to recreational and tourism industry
	• loss to manufacturers and sellers of recreational equipment
	• increased energy demand and reduced supply because of drought-related power curtailments
	• costs to energy industry and consumers associated with substituting more expensive fuels (oil) for hydroelectric power
	• loss to industries directly dependent on agricultural production (e.g., machinery and fertilizer manufacturers, food processors, etc.)
	• decline in food production/disrupted food supply
	    increase in food prices
	    increased importation of food (higher costs)
	• disruption of water supplies
	• unemployment from drought-related production declines
	• strain on financial institutions (foreclosures, greater credit risks, capital shortfalls, etc.)
	• revenue losses to federal, state, and local governments (from reduced tax base)
	• deters capital investment, expansion
	• dislocation of businesses
	• revenues to water supply firms
	    revenue shortfalls
	    windfall profits
	• loss from impaired navigability of streams, rivers, and canals
	• cost of water transport or transfer
	• cost of new or supplemental water resource development

Environmental	• damage to animal species
	reduction and degradation of fish and wildlife habitat
	lack of feed and drinking water
	disease
	increased vulnerability to predation (e.g., from species concentration near water)
	• loss of biodiversity
	• wind and water erosion of soils
	• reservoir and lake drawdown
	• damage to plant species
	• water quality effects (e.g., salt concentration, increased water temperatures, ph, dissolved oxygen)
	• air quality effects (dust, pollutants)
	• visual and landscape quality (dust, vegetative cover, etc.)
	• increased fire hazard
	• estuarine impacts; changes in salinity levels, reduced flushing
Social	• increased ground water depletion (mining), land subsidence
	• loss of wetlands
	• loss of cultural sites
	• insect infestation
	• food shortages (decreased nutritional level, malnutrition, famine)
	• loss of human life (e.g., food shortages, heat)
	• public safety from forest and range fires
	• conflicts between water users, public policy conflicts
	• increased anxiety
	• loss of aesthetic values
	• health-related low flow problems (e.g., diminished sewage flows, increased pollutant concentrations, etc.)
	• recognition of institutional constraints on water use
	• inequity in the distribution of drought impacts/relief
	• decreased quality of life in rural areas
	• increased poverty
	• reduced quality of life, changes in lifestyle
	• social unrest, civil strife
	• population migration (rural to urban areas)
	• reevaluation of social values
	• increased data/information needs, coordination of dissemination activities
	• loss of confidence in government officials
	• recreational impacts

Source: Wilhite and Wood 1994

for environmental quality has forced public officials to focus greater attention and resources on these effects.

Social impacts mainly involve public safety, health, conflicts between water users, reduced quality of life, and inequities in the distribution of impacts and disaster relief. Many of the impacts specified as economic and environmental have social components as well. Population outmigration is a significant problem in many countries as people affected by drought choose to migrate to urban areas within the stressed areas or to regions outside the drought area. Food is generally more available in urban areas. However, when drought conditions have abated, these persons seldom return home, placing ever-increasing pressure on the urban environment and infrastructure of the region to which they have emigrated. In the drought-prone northeast region of Brazil, there was a net loss of nearly 5.5 million people between 1950 and 1980 (Magalhães 1988). Although all of this movement was not directly attributable to drought, it was a primary factor in the decision to relocate for many persons. This continues to be a significant problem in

Table 18.2 Hydropower production by selected US power producers in 1988 compared to a ten-year average

Region and producer	Total hydro operating capacity (in MW)	Ten-year average 1983–92 (1,000 Mwh)	Total hydro generation for 1988 (1,000 Mwh)	1988 hydro generation % of ten-year average
Northeast: New York Power Authority	4,068	24,747	22,471	91
South: Corps of Engineers	4,162	11,031	7,560	69
Tennessee Valley Authority	3,346	16,871	9,620	57
Great Lakes: Corps of Engineers	479	1,767	1,041	59
Plains: Corps of Engineers	2,873	9,659	9,949	103
Southwest: Bureau of Reclamation	4,472	15,744	11,304	72
Pacific Gas & Electric	3,904	10,706	7,884	74
Northwest: Corps of Engineers	13,093	55,794	48,507	87
Total/Averages	36,397	146,807	118,335	81

Source: Hydro Review's Hydropower Generation Report database

Brazil and many other drought-prone nations. This shift in population may lead to greater poverty and social unrest.

As with all natural hazards, the economic impacts of drought are highly variable within and between economic sectors and geographic regions, producing a complex assortment of winners and losers with the occurrence of each disaster. For example, decreases in agricultural production result in enormous negative financial impacts on farmers in drought-affected areas, at times leading to foreclosure. This decreased production also leads to higher grain, vegetable, and fruit prices. These price increases have a negative impact on all consumers as food prices increase. However, farmers outside the drought-affected area with normal or above-normal production or those with significant grain in storage reap the benefits of these higher prices. Similar examples of winners and losers could be given for other economic sectors as well. For example, some of the winners associated with the 1988 drought included agricultural producers in nondrought areas; water-producing technologies such as well drilling; weather modification companies; electric utilities; coal companies; Great Lakes ports (lake shipping increased because of decreased river shipping); construction industries; and commercial aviation (Riebsame *et al.* 1991).

THE 1996 DROUGHT IN THE UNITED STATES: CASE STUDY

In 1995, a severe drought developed in portions of western Texas and New Mexico in the American Southwest. This drought carried over into 1996 in these states and expanded into Arizona, central and eastern Texas, and parts of California, Nevada, Utah, Colorado, Oklahoma, and Kansas. The drought area intensified during the late winter and spring months, reaching a peak severity in the May–July period for various portions of the region.

The impacts of drought began in February as the incidence of range fires increased dramatically in Texas, Oklahoma, and Kansas, destroying homes and injuring people. In February, range fires had already caused significant damage in parts of Texas, Oklahoma, and Kansas (O'Hanlon 1996). By March, depletion of groundwater supplies was becoming a problem in parts of Texas, and residents of the Barton Springs/Edwards Aquifer Conservation District were asked to cut water usage by 20 per cent (US Water News Online 1996). By April, the US Department of Agriculture (USDA) reported winter wheat conditions in nineteen states in poor to very poor condition, with the greatest problems in Kansas, Oklahoma, Missouri, and Illinois (Edwards 1996). In May, prices for gasoline, diesel, and liquified petroleum were reported by USDA to be 15 per cent above 1995 levels. Reports from ski resorts in New Mexico indicated reduced revenues of more than 20 per cent (Reuters 1996). Fires increased in central Arizona, California, and New Mexico (Associated Press 1996). Winter wheat production in Texas was reduced to 27 per cent of 1995 production (Houston Chronicle 1996). Agricultural losses for cotton, wheat, feed grains, cattle, and corn were estimated in June at US$2.4 billion in Texas, with an additional US$4.1 billion in losses for agriculturally related industries such as harvesting, trucking, and food processing (United Press International 1996). Reduced irrigation water was responsible for much of the reduction in vegetable production in Texas, with concomitant losses in jobs and income (Antosh 1996). Later estimates of drought losses in Texas were revised downward to about US$5 billion, reflecting lower commodity prices than originally estimated (Fohn 1996). Wheat production in Kansas was estimated at 183 million bushels, only 64 per cent of the 1995 crop (Reuters 1996). Colorado's winter wheat crop was down more than 30 per cent (Algeo 1996); Oklahoma cotton production was down 24 per cent (Stafford 1996).

Water restrictions continued to increase in many cities across the region. Houston residents were forced to cut back on nonessential uses (Houston Chronicle 1996) and Sante Fe was forced to reduce water usage by 25 per cent. Water levels in the Edwards Aquifer, the primary source of water for 1.5 million people in San Antonio and five counties in south Texas, was rapidly reaching the lowest level ever recorded (Smith 1996). Fires continued to be a major problem throughout the drought. In particular, New Mexico, Arizona, Nevada, Colorado, and Utah experienced major forest and wildfires. In Colorado, nearly 68,000 fires burned more than 2 million acres (810,000 ha) (Hillard 1996). Reports of wind and insect damage to crops were being received from Colorado and New Mexico (Reuters 1996a and 1996b). Livestock began to take a toll on range lands in the region as overgrazing began to worsen existing erosion problems in Arizona. A shortage of hay throughout the region reached disastrous proportions in June (Smith 1996), forcing ranchers to sell cattle at the lowest prices in ten years. Environmental damages began to emerge as endangered species were affected, landscapes were eroded, and fires damaged countless areas in the region (Holmes 1996). Nitrate levels in hay rose

dramatically in Oklahoma, reaching toxic or near-toxic levels for livestock (Schafer 1996).

Food prices responded to the lower production levels for milk, meat, produce, and other foodstuffs (Lee 1996, Carrillo 1996). For example, the price of fruit increased more than 22 per cent in June (Carrillo 1996). Fires continued to occur throughout the region and expanded into the Pacific Northwest and the northern Rocky Mountain states (Laceky 1996, Associated Press 1996).

There are no official estimates of the total losses and damages from the 1996 drought. Given the US$5 billion in impacts that occurred in Texas, total regional impacts could be safely estimated in the US$10–15 billion range, although it is difficult to quantify many social and environmental impacts. What was remarkable to many was the significant level of regional vulnerability, the diversity of impacts, and the lack of preparedness to respond to many of these impacts. Many of the states in this region have now initiated longer-term planning efforts directed at improving mitigation and preparedness efforts. Some of the possible policy approaches to dealing with droughts are discussed below.

REDUCING THE IMPACTS OF DROUGHT: IMPLICATIONS FOR POLICY

The increase in the number of natural disasters was documented in Chapter 1. With growing population pressures, more people are exposed to the risks associated with natural hazards each year, leading to a steady increase in the number of natural disasters reported. A concerted effort by governments and the international community is required to reduce this trend. It was for this reason that the decade of the 1990s was designated by the United Nations as the International Decade for Natural Disaster Reduction (IDNDR).

Strategies for responding to and preparing for drought are numerous and range from household or community level to national level. These strategies (discussed in other parts of this volume) take many forms. At the local level, people and communities possess detailed knowledge of the likely occurrence of drought and its effects and have developed (over decades or centuries) a broad range of survival strategies to help them reduce its effects and recover once the rains have returned. These strategies range from a change in cropping or planting patterns to a reduction of assets, such as reducing herd size or selling jewellery or other valuables.

At the state or national level, governments may respond to drought in three ways: predrought mitigation programmes for impact reduction; postdrought relief programmes to provide emergency assistance to victims; and preparedness or contingency planning to develop institutional capacity to respond in a more timely and effective manner and reduce impacts (Parry and Carter 1987). Examples of predrought mitigation programmes include the development of an early warning system, augmentation of water supplies, demand reduction (such as water conservation programmes), and crop insurance. Postdrought interventions refer to those reactive programmes or tactics implemented by government in response to drought. This includes a wide range of reactive emergency measures such as low-interest loans, transportation subsidies for livestock and livestock feed, provision of food, water transport, and drilling wells for irrigation and public water supplies. This reactive crisis management approach has been criticised by scientists, government officials, and many relief recipients as inefficient, ineffective, and untimely. More recently, the provision of emergency relief in times of drought has also been criticised as being a disincentive to the sustainable use of natural resources because it does not promote self-reliance. In fact, this approach may increase vulnerability to drought. Preparedness planning refers to the development of policies and plans that can be useful in preparing for drought. These are usually developed at national and provincial levels with linkages to the local level.

POLICY RESPONSES TO THE 1996 DROUGHT IN THE UNITED STATES: A MODEL FOR OTHER REGIONS?

As described previously, the impacts of the 1996 drought in the United States resulted in diverse and dramatic regional impacts that rippled to both the national and international level. However, the legacy of the 1996 drought is not likely to be the impacts that resulted but rather the policy initiatives that occurred in the post-drought period. These initiatives appear to be changing the way droughts are viewed and managed in the United States. The real question at this point is whether these changes will result in permanent and substantive modifications in the way governmental entities deal with drought.

In June 1996, the Federal Emergency Management Agency (FEMA) was asked to chair a multistate drought task force to address the drought situation in the Southwest and southern Great Plains states. The purpose of the task force was to coordinate federal response to drought-related problems in the stricken region by identifying needs, applicable programmes, and programme barriers. The task force was also directed to suggest ways to improve drought management through both short- and long-term national actions. To accomplish these objectives, a workshop was held in June that included representatives from many federal agencies, the drought-affected states, universities, and the Native American tribal groups. The final report of this workshop (FEMA 1996) divided short- and long-term recommendations and issues into three categories: policy, legislative, and executive branch. These recommendations are the product of intensive discussions and represent the opinions of participating parties.

Several long-term issues and recommendations noted in the FEMA report are relevant to the discussion of policy responses to drought impacts. First, participants recommended the development of a national drought policy based on the philosophy of cooperation with state and local stakeholders. They emphasised that this policy should be developed now even though 'regional interests and states' rights advocates may occasionally throw up roadblocks.' Participants emphasised the need for a contingency plan to help apply lessons from the past to future drought events. This policy should include a national climate/drought monitoring system to provide early warning of the onset and severity of drought to federal, state, and local officials. This policy would also include an institutionalised organisational structure to address the issue of drought on a national scale. Second, it was suggested that a regional forum be created to assess regional needs and resources, identify critical areas and interests, provide reliable and timely information, and coordinate state actions.

It was suggested that multistate and impact-specific working groups be established under this forum to identify critical needs. Third, FEMA was asked to include drought as one of the natural hazards addressed in the National Mitigation Strategy (FEMA 1995), given the substantial costs associated with its occurrence and the numerous opportunities available to mitigate its effects. This report estimated annual losses because of drought at US$6–8 billion. Fourth, states strongly requested that a single federal agency be appointed to coordinate drought preparedness and response. The states recommended that FEMA be given this responsibility; FEMA suggested that USDA be the agency in charge, given its programme responsibilities in agriculture, often the first sector affected. This report was submitted to the president in August 1996.

The second initiative was the development of a drought task force under the leadership of the Western Governors' Association (WGA). This task force was formed in June 1996 as a result of a resolution offered by Governor Gary Johnson of New Mexico. The resolution states, 'The western governors believe that a comprehensive, integrated response to drought emergencies is critical . . . [and that] it is important to work together and cooperatively with other affected entities to plan for and implement measures that will provide relief from the current drought and prepare for future drought emergencies' (WGA 1996).

The WGA Drought Task Force produced a report (WGA 1996) in November that made several important recommendations that were intended to reduce vulnerability to future droughts. First, the task force recommended that a national drought policy or framework be developed that integrates actions and responsibilities among all levels of government and emphasises preparedness, response, and mitigation measures that should be adopted. Second, each state should be encouraged to develop a drought contingency plan that includes early warning, triggers, and short- and long-term planning and mitigation measures. Third, a regional drought coordinating council should be created to develop sustainable policy, monitor drought conditions, assess state-level responses, identify impacts and issues for resolution, and work in partnership with the federal government to address drought-related needs. Fourth, a federal interagency coordinating group should be established with a designated lead agency for drought coordination with states and regional agencies.

A number of important policy initiatives have resulted from the FEMA and WGA reports. First, the National Drought Policy Act of 1997 (Senate Bill 222) was introduced in the US Senate in January 1997. This bill, if passed, would create a commission to make recommendations to the president and Congress on the development of a national drought policy. The bill was passed by the Senate in November 1997. A comparable bill was introduced in the House and will be debated in early 1998. This bill would be the first step in the development of a national drought policy. Second, a memorandum of understanding (MOU) was signed in early 1997 between the WGA and the Departments of Agriculture, Interior, and Commerce; FEMA; and the Small Business Administration. This MOU pledges the development of a partnership between federal, state, local, and tribal governments to reduce the impacts of drought in the western states through improved response and more attention to preparedness and mitigation. This MOU has resulted in the following actions: (1) the western Drought Coordination Council (WDCC) was formed in June 1997 to address the recommendations of the western governors (WGA 1996), and the WDCC is actively working on these recommendations as part of its annual work plan; (2) USDA was designated by the president as the lead federal agency for drought; and (3) USDA has established a federal interagency drought coordinating group to facilitate coordination between the numerous federal agencies with drought-related programme responsibilities.

In addition to these activities, the National Drought Mitigation Center is conducting a series of regional training workshops on drought contingency planning. These workshops are exposing people at various levels of government in all parts of the country to the mechanics of drought contingency planning with the hope of stimulating improved levels of preparedness, the development of better mitigation tools, and networking between levels of governments. States in the 1996 drought-affected area are moving toward the development of plans, as noted by Wilhite (see Chapter 39), so that they will be better prepared to deal with the next episode of severe drought.

CONCLUSIONS

Drought is a pervasive natural hazard that is a normal part of the climate of virtually all regions. It should not be viewed as merely a physical phenomenon. Rather, drought is the result of an interplay between a natural event and the demand placed on water and other natural resources by human-use systems.

The impacts of drought are diverse; they ripple through the economy and may linger for years after the termination of the period of deficient precipitation. Impacts are often referred to as direct or indirect. Because of the number of groups and economic sectors affected by drought, its geographic extent, and the difficulties in quantifying environmental damages and personal hardships, the precise calculation of the financial costs of drought is difficult. Drought years frequently occur in clusters, and thus the costs of drought are not evenly distributed between years. Drought impacts are classified as economic, environmental, and social.

Government response to drought includes a wide range of potential actions to deal with the impacts of water shortages on people and various economic sectors. The types of actions taken will vary considerably between developed and developing countries and from one region to another. Few, if any, actions of government attempt to reduce long-term vulnerability to the hazard. Rather, assistance or relief programmes are reactive and address only short-term emergency needs; they are intended to reduce the impacts and hardship of the present drought.

Developing a drought policy and contingency plan is one way that governments can reduce the impacts of future droughts and improve the effectiveness and efficiency of future response efforts. Drought is a global problem that can only be addressed through a strong interdisciplinary effort from the scientific community, interaction between scientists and policy makers, and the cooperation of international organisations. This is evident for all aspects of drought, including prediction, monitoring, impact assessment, adaptation, response and recovery, and preparedness. A key in this process is the establishment of national and international networks of scientists, natural resource managers, policy makers, and others to foster collaboration on the critical issues associated with

improving predictability, enhancing monitoring and early warning capacity, maintaining and improving observational networks, developing improved models for early estimations of impact, identifying existing (and promoting the development of new and innovative) coping and mitigation strategies, and disseminating methodologies for drought preparedness. These networks will significantly enhance the opportunities for technical cooperation within and between levels of government and between nations. An information clearinghouse that centralises available material from national and international sources on all aspects of drought prediction, monitoring, impact assessment, mitigation, and preparedness would greatly facilitate the transfer of technology between nations and organisations.

REFERENCES

Algeo, D. (1996) 'Winter-wheat harvest varied in Colorado', *Denver Post*, 13 August.
Antosh, N. (1996) 'Water shortages in Texas result in crop cutbacks', *Houston Chronicle*, 18 August.
Associated Press (1996a) 'Emergency declared as Arizona fires rage', 3 May.
Associated Press (1996b) 'Dry weather raises threat as fires burn in western states', 25 August.
Blaikie, P., Cannon, T., Davis, I., and Wisner, B. (1994) *Natural Hazards, People's Vulnerability, and Disasters*, London and New York: Routledge Publishers.
Brown, L.R., Kane, H., and Ayres, E. (1993) *Vital Signs 1993*, Worldwatch Institute, New York: W. W. Norton and Company.
Carrillo, L. (1996) 'Labor Department confirms what consumers know: Food prices increasing', *Sun-Sentinel* (South Florida), 14 July.
Edwards, C. (1996) 'Wheat futures surge amid lack of rain in critical growing period', *Associated Press*, 26 February.
Edwards, C. (1996) 'Wheat futures soar as Kansas crop written off', *Associated Press*, 22 April.
FEMA (1995) *National Mitigation Strategy*, Washington, DC: Federal Emergency Management Agency.
FEMA (1996) 'Drought of '96: Multi-State Drought Task Force findings', Washington, DC: Federal Emergency Management Agency.
Fohn, J. (1996) Agriculture Column, *San Antonio Express–News*, San Antonio, Texas, 21 August.
Hagman, G. (1984) *Prevention Better Than Cure*, Report on Human and Environmental Disasters in the Third World, prepared for the Swedish Red Cross, Stockholm.
Hillard, C. (1996) 'Wildfire threat', Associated Press, 28 June.

Holmes, M. (1996) 'Battling drought, Texas biologists try to save endangered species', *Southwest Sunday*, 27 June.

Houston Chronicle (1996) 'Dow Chemical institutes drought plan to reduce Houston area water use', 2 June.

IDNDR (1995) *Major Disasters Around the World*, Secretariat, International Decade for Natural Disaster Reduction, Geneva, Switzerland.

Kent, R.C. (1987) *Anatomy of Disaster Relief: The International Network in Action*, New York and London: Pinter Publishers.

Laceky, T. (1996) 'Rain, snow, frost helping calm western fires, but winds still threaten', Associated Press, 6 September.

Lee, S.H. (1996) 'Dairy industry cites drought as cause of rising milk prices', *Dallas Morning News*, 8 July.

Magalhâes, A.R. (1988) 'Drought as a policy and planning issue in Northeast Brazil', in M.L. Parry, T.R. Carter, and N.T. Konijn (eds), *The Impact of Climatic Variations on Agriculture* (Volume 2), *Assessments in Semi-arid Regions*, Dordrecht: Kluwer Academic Publishers.

O'Hanlon, K. (1996) 'Texas grass fire burns out of control, dozens of homes destroyed', Associated Press, 23 February.

Parry, M.L. and Carter, T.R. (1987) 'Climate impact assessment: A review of some approaches', in D.A. Wilhite and W.E. Easterling (eds), *Planning for Drought: Toward a Reduction of Societal Vulnerability*, Boulder, CO: Westview Press, pp. 165–87.

Reuters (1996a) 'Drought-hit Texas asks Mexico to enforce water pact', 31 May.

Reuters (1996b) 'Southwest drought threatens broad economic damage', 3 June.

Riebsame, W.E., Changnon, S.A., and Karl, T.R. (1991) *Drought and Natural Resources Management in the United States: Impacts and Implications of the 1987–89 Drought*, Boulder, CO: Westview Press.

Schafer, S. (1996) 'Toxic hay threatens cattle in Oklahoma', *Tulsa World*, 29 July.

Smith, W. (1996) 'Southwestern drought takes toll on farmers, businesses', *Chicago Tribune*, 27 June.

Stafford, J. (1996) 'Rain proves timely for Oklahoma cotton producers', *The Daily Oklahoman*, 30 July.

United Press International (1996) 'Southwest farmers battle record drought', 30 May.

US Water News Online (1996) 'Drought alert sounded in Edwards Aquifer region of Texas', March.

WGA (1996) *Drought Response Action Plan*, Denver: Western Governors' Association.

Wilhite, D.A. (1986) 'Drought policy in the US and Australia: A comparative analysis', *Water Resources Bulletin* 22: 425–38.

Wilhite, D.A. (1987) 'The role of government in planning for drought: Where do we go from here?', in D.A. Wilhite and W.E. Easterling (eds), *Planning for Drought: Toward a Reduction of Societal Vulnerability*, Boulder, CO: Westview Press, pp. 425–44.

Wilhite, D.A. (1992) 'Drought', in *Encyclopedia of Earth System Science* (Volume 2), San Diego: Academic Press.

Wilhite, D.A. (1993) 'Understanding the phenomenon of drought', *Hydro-Review* 12:136–48.

Wilhite, D.A., Rosenberg, N.J., and Glantz, M.H. (1986) 'Improving Federal Response to Drought', *Journal of Climate and Applied Meteorology* 25: 332–42.

Wilhite, D.A. and Wood, D.A. (eds) (1994) *Drought Management in a Changing West: New Directions for Water Policy*, IDIC Technical Report Series 94-1, International Drought Information Center, University of Nebraska–Lincoln, USA.

19

ESTIMATING THE ECONOMIC IMPACTS OF DROUGHT ON AGRICULTURE

William Easterling and Robert Mendelsohn

INTRODUCTION

Drought is a normal feature of our current climate (Rosenberg 1980, Wilhite 1993), a feature that is not likely to disappear with future climate change (Mearns *et al.* 1984). Caused by climate variability, drought imposes heavy costs on farmers, who sometimes lose large amounts of annual crops and revenues. This chapter seeks to measure the economic impact of droughts on US agriculture. First, we seek to determine the magnitude of economic damages from the current rate of droughts. How important are the losses from droughts, given annual net revenues from American farms? Second, what is the value of improved climate forecasting to American farmers? What would be the benefits to American farmers if they could forecast future drought years?

The possibility that the frequencies and magnitudes of future droughts may be changing must be considered. With the accumulation of greenhouse gases in the atmosphere, climate scientists predict that future climates will be warmer (IPCC 1996). Although climatologists are not certain whether climate variability will increase or decrease, greenhouse gases will affect the frequency and severity of droughts. It would therefore be prudent for society to determine the economic impacts that droughts have on the US economy and especially agriculture. In addition, society may be interested in the value of the current frequency of droughts in order to manage crop insurance programs. For example, private insurance companies could offer drought insurance to farmers if the insurance companies knew what the underlying risks were. Similarly, disaster relief officials could determine a fair insurance rate for farmers in return for different levels of relief when drought disasters strike.

Recent advances in climatology have also improved our understanding of how anomalous tropical Pacific Ocean sea surface temperatures known as El Niño–Southern Oscillation (ENSO) events propagate to affect weather conditions in tropical and some subtropical regions. Coupled ocean–atmosphere models using ENSO information provide better predictions of inter-annual precipitation and temperature patterns, enabling climatologists to provide better forecasts of droughts than ever (Sarachik 1992, Sarachik and Shea 1997). Skilful forecasts of climate conditions up to two years ahead are now possible. What is the value of these improved predictions to American farmers? What drought-related costs could be avoided with better forecasts?

In this chapter, we examine two major approaches to measuring the economic value of drought on American farms: the bottom-up and top-down approaches (Root and Schneider 1995). Bottom-up approaches consist of linked biophysical and economic models in a system designed to simulate how the dynamic effects of climate regulate agroecological processes and finally economic activities. The system begins with the manipulation of detailed process-based models of the biophysical mechanisms of climate-crop interactions. The process-based models are forced with climate scenarios (historic and forecasted climate events). They give biophysical estimates (yield, water use, nutrient use) of crop response to climate scenarios. These estimates are then incorporated into socioeconomic models in order to understand the effects of climate-induced yield variability on social welfare. The approaches are labelled 'bottom-up' because they start at the finest level of resolution of process information about the interactions of climate and biophysical processes and then aggregate up to larger-scale socioeconomic processes. For example, a model could start with detailed information about the effects of drought on crop phenology and physiological processes. This information on the plant or field level would then be aggregated to larger areas to predict changes in supply and thus prices.

Top-down approaches examine the outcomes from the biophysical-socioeconomic system. Rather than following the causal chain of events, the top-down approach examines how final outcomes are affected by climate or climate variability. Statistical relations between climate, crop yields, and land values are organised to directly measure the damages/benefits of climate or climate variability. The advantage of focusing on outcomes rather than process is that the approach effectively captures feedbacks within the system since it is systemwide outcomes that are being calibrated. The problem with the 'top-down' approach is that one cannot control for unwanted variation and can be easily misled by omitted variables. Successful examples of the top-down approach include the analysis of the agricultural impact of climate means in Mendelsohn *et al.* 1994 and climate variation in Mendelsohn *et al.* 1996.

We argue that the bottom-up and top-down approaches are complementary methods for quantifying the economic impact of droughts and the potential benefit of using improved drought prediction information to mitigate those impacts. In the remainder of this chapter, we elaborate on the definition of bottom-up and top-down approaches and provide examples of each approach. We conclude with a brief critique of the two approaches.

BOTTOM-UP MODELS

Bottom-up approaches link stand-alone biophysical models with economic models to simulate the economic effects of climate variability on agriculture. Typically, the models begin with a crop simulator that predicts plant growth based on environmental conditions, including climate. The simulator may be used to predict how drought conditions affect crop yields and water use. The simulated changes in crop yields and water use caused by drought conditions are then inserted into an economic model, such as a farm-level decision model, to predict economic consequences. Farm-level decisions are then aggregated to market levels to predict changes in prices and economic welfare. The bottom-up approach explicitly models the chain of causality, beginning with the primary effects of climate variability on physical and biological processes and ending with explicit simulation of the welfare effects from changes in economic activity.

Bottom-up models tend to be static equilibrium analyses. They begin with specific climate patterns, determine equilibrium plant growth, and estimate farm-level activities accordingly. Some models are more dynamic in that biophysical interactions with climate are played out in short time-steps (i.e., days or months), and there are feedbacks from the economic models to the biophysical system in the form of adaptations (Kaiser *et al.* 1993). The biophysical models are most often site specific because of their mechanistic form and large appetite for data on local environmental conditions. The site specific nature of the models, especially the biophysical component models, necessitates the scaling or aggregation of results from individual modelling sites to estimate the regional consequences of climate variability.

Bottom-up approaches have the potential to identify specific management practices (e.g., switching crop varieties, changing crop species, fallowing, stubble mulching, irrigation) that can mitigate climate impacts. Individual strategies can be explored to examine which method effectively reduces the damages of drought. Such a trial-and-error approach would allow analysts to predict the adjustments that individual farmers would undertake when a drought year strikes. These analyses can also shed light on the value to farmers of drought predictions by determining how net revenue changes as farmers make adjustments to lessen the burden of drought years.

Example 1: the MINK analysis of climate change

The Missouri-Iowa-Nebraska-Kansas (MINK) study (Rosenberg 1993) linked a variety of biophysical simulation models to an economic model to explore the effects of a contemporary recurrence of the droughts of the 1930s in the region. Across the MINK region, average annual temperatures during the 1930s ranged from 0.7°C to 1.0°C warmer than the 1951–80 baseline period, and average annual precipitation ranged from 28 to 102 mm less. The crop simulator for the agricultural sector in the MINK study (Easterling *et al.* 1993) was the Erosion Productivity Impact Calculator (EPIC; Williams *et al.* 1984) model. EPIC simulates the impacts of drought on crop growth and yield. The results of the EPIC simulations were then inserted into a county-level economic input-output model known as IMPLAN (USDA–Forest Service 1989) to estimate the effects of the droughts on the regional economy.

EPIC is a crop simulation model developed to estimate the relationships between climate, soil erosion, and crop productivity. The model includes routines for weather simulation, hydrology, nutrient cycling, plant growth, tillage, and crop management. It operates on a daily time-step at the resolution of a hectare. Processes simulated by EPIC are evapotranspiration (based on the Penman-Monteith model), soil temperature, crop potential growth, growth constraints (water stress, stress due to high or low temperature, nitrogen and phosphorus stress), and yield. EPIC uses a single model for simulating all crops, although each crop has unique values for model parameters. The crop growth model relies on radiation-use efficiency in calculating photosynthetic production of biomass. The potential biomass is adjusted daily for stresses mentioned above. Crop yields are estimated by multiplying the above-ground biomass at maturity by a harvest index (defined as economic yield divided by above-ground biomass).

EPIC requires data on soil physical properties (for example, bulk density, water holding capacity, wilting point) and management (for example, fertilisation, tillage, planting, harvesting, irrigation). These data were assembled for a series of 'representative farms' in the MINK study (Table 19.1). The weather variables necessary for driving the EPIC model are daily values of precipitation, minimum/maximum temperature, solar radiation, windspeed, and relative humidity. The weather data were drawn from the historical records of the 1930s and from the 1951–80 period (the baseline) for a distribution of observing stations across the MINK region (Figure 19.1).

Crop yields from individual representative farms were aggregated to make state-level estimates by area-weighted averaging. This method of aggregation was accomplished by weighting the average yields by the size of the area represented by each of the farms. Control yields, against which 'drought-affected' yields were compared, were simulated with the climate of the 1951–80 period. Based on a literature review, interviews with Cooperative Extension specialists, and sensitivity analysis, a number of possible adaptation strategies for coping with drought were identified for testing with EPIC. Earlier planting, use of longer-season cultivars, and furrow diking of warm-season irrigated crops were determined to be most effective in the EPIC model for dealing with the 1930s droughts in the MINK study.

Simulating crop yield response to drought tells only part of the story. The economic consequences of drought-induced changes in crop yields must be estimated too. IMPLAN is an economic input–output model that links inputs and outputs for each sector of the economy (Bowes and Crosson 1993). The model lists the purchases of the various inputs needed in the production of one dollar's worth of a particular commodity in matrix form. An accounting identity reveals overall production of each commodity going either to satisfy intermediate demand (i.e., demand by one industry for the products of another industry) or final demand. The change in overall production resulting from a unit change in the demand for a single output is called a 'multiplier'. The multipliers measure the combined effect of the initial change in final demand caused by some market perturbation plus those changes induced in industries that support the expansion or contraction of the direct or indirect suppliers.

IMPLAN is deterministic in that it does not take into account adjustments by economic agents in response to changes. It is organised with county-level data, and the model can be aggregated to reflect activity at any multiple of counties (i.e., regions, states). In the case of the MINK study, IMPLAN data sets were aggregated for each of the MINK states. The multiplier coefficients were derived from data used in the 1977 Bureau of Economic Analysis input–output tables updated to 1982 by the Forest Service. Bowes and Crosson (1993) manipulated IMPLAN to

Table 19.1 MLRA, weather station, soil type, and crop rotation for each of the representative farms simulated with EPIC

State	Farm #	MLRA	Weather	Station No.	Soil	Crop rotation
Missouri	1	107	Bethany	# 4904	Marshall	Corn-soybean-soybean-wheat
	2					Corn-soybean
	3		Bethany	# 4904	Zook	Corn-soybean-soybean-wheat
	4					Corn-soybean
	5	109	Unionville	# 8523	Grundy	Corn-soybean-soybean-wheat
	6					Corn-soybean
	7	116	Lebanon	# 4825	Huntington	Corn
	50				Clarksville	Alfalfa
Kansas	9	72	St. Francis	# 7093	Ulysses	Wheat-sorghum-fallow
	10					Irrigated corn
	11					Irrigated wheat-corn-sorghum
	12		Ashland	# 365	Ulysses	Wheat-sorghum-fallow
	13					Irrigated corn
	14					Irrigated wheat-corn-sorghum
	42					Wheatgrass
	15	73	Larned	# 4530	Harney	Dryland wheat
	43					Wheatgrass
	16				Uly	Dryland wheat
	17	75	McPherson	# 5152	Irwin	Dryland wheat-sorghum
	44					Alfalfa
	18	106	Horton	# 3810	Marshall	Sorghum-soybean
	19					Corn-soybean
Nebraska	20	65	Atkinson	# 420	Dunday	Irrigated corn
	21				Valentine	Irrigated corn
	45					Wheatgrass
	22	71	Grand Isl.	# 3395	Hord	Irrigated corn
	23				Holdredge	Irrigated corn
	24	72	Gothenburg	# 3365	Keith	Wheat-ecofallow-corn
	25					Wheat-fallow
	46					Wheatgrass
	47				Valentine	Alfalfa
	26	73	Franklin	# 3035	Uly	Dryland wheat
	27					Sorghum
	28	75	David City	# 2205	Hastings	Irrigated corn
	29				Crete	Irrigated Corn
	30	106	Fairbury	# 2820	Wymore	Sorghum-soybean
	31					Corn-soybean
Iowa	32	103	Webster City	# 8806	Nicollet	Corn-soybean
	33				Clarion	Corn-soybean
	34				Webster	Corn-soybean
	35	107	Denison	# 2171	Marshall	Corn-soybean
	36				Zook	Corn-soybean
	37				Ida	Corn-soybean
	48					Alfalfa
	39	108	Maquoketa	# 5131	Tama	Corn-soybean
	40				Drummer	Corn-soybean
	41	109	Fairfield	# 2789	Adair	Corn-soybean
	49					Alfalfa

Source: Easterling et al. 1993

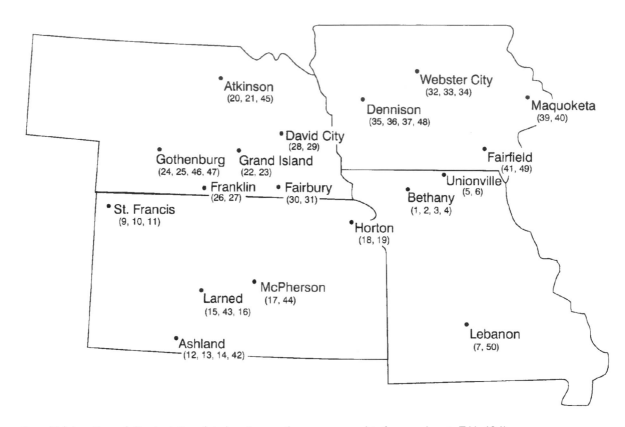

Figure 19.1 Locations of climate stations (numbers in parentheses correspond to farm numbers in Table 19.1)

show how a change in agricultural production caused by climate change affects the demand for agricultural commodities exerted by linked industries in the MINK region. However, these reductions are not welfare measures, but rather changes in gross revenue. To evaluate the welfare effects of these changes, one would also have to calculate changes in net revenue, not changes in gross revenue.

In the absence of adaptations, the droughts of the 1930s caused, on average across the four-state region, simulations of dryland maize to yield 25 per cent less than the control; soybeans to yield 25 per cent less; sorghum and wheatgrass (a forage crop) to yield 24 per cent less; and irrigated maize and sorghum to yield 7 per cent and 10 per cent less, respectively (although increased costs from supplying higher irrigation water demands for both crops counterbalanced the lower yield loss from drought). Dryland wheat yields were essentially unchanged by the 1930s

droughts. By resorting to minor adaptations of planting fourteen days earlier (to avoid the highest heat part of the growing season) and growing longer-season varieties (to take advantage of the longer growing season), the yield losses listed above declined. Here dryland maize yielded 20 per cent less than the control, soybeans yielded 21 per cent less, and sorghum yielded 14 per cent less. No adaptations were practical for wheatgrass, which is a perennial crop. Irrigated maize and sorghum increased in yield by a small amount relative to the control, although their irrigation costs increased dramatically, thus offsetting the yield benefits of the adaptations. With adaptations, irrigated and dryland wheat yields also increased slightly relative to the control yields, although the increases were not statistically significant.

When the yield changes listed in the above paragraph were converted into total agricultural production (i.e., yield per ha times total number of ha planted to the above crops in the states) and inserted into the IMPLAN model, the climate-induced change in the economic value of agricultural production was estimated. The drought-induced average yield changes for all crops, in the absence of adjustments, caused the estimated value of MINK's agricultural production to drop by approximately US$2.7 billion (in 1982 dollars), or a decline of 17 per cent relative to the control value. Had farmers made adjustments to planting dates and varieties grown as described above in advance of each drought year, the estimated value of agricultural production across the MINK region would have declined by an estimated US$1.9 billion (in 1982 dollars), or 12 per cent less than the control value. Hence, the adaptations mitigated 30 per cent of the revenue losses from this extreme drought. Nonetheless, the MINK study indicates that the Dust Bowl climate had a sizable impact on this four-state region.

Example 2: bottom-up analysis evaluating drought predictions

Less severe forms of interannual climate variability than the droughts of the 'Dust Bowl era' are routinely encountered by farmers. They often intermingle with severe droughts. In fact, farmers more often experience mildly disruptive climate conditions than severe droughts. Forecasts of dry years that may not constitute major droughts, but nonetheless cause yield reductions and economic loss to farmers, also may provide adaptive opportunities to farmers. Forecasts of these mild dry events have improved just as have forecasts of more severe forms of climate variability. In this example, we explore the value to farmers of being able to anticipate which years will be normal and which will be dry.

The value of improved forecasts of both mildly dry growing seasons and severe droughts can be gained by seeing what difference it would have made to farmers if they had known in advance when a dry year was coming (i.e., as if they had had a perfect forecast available beforehand). With the advance warning, farmers can adjust their crops and practices and lower their damages from dry years. The difference between the net revenue in the absence of adaptation and the net revenue with adaptation is the maximum benefit of climate forecast information.

We illustrate this principle using EPIC to simulate southeastern Nebraska dryland maize and sorghum over the period 1971–90. We begin by creating a baseline where farmers do not know what weather will be like from year to year. We contrast this outcome to a simulated example where farmers are told whether the next year is a dry or normal year. We predict what farmers will do in response to having this weather forecast. The difference in net revenues from the baseline to the predicted climate outcome quantifies the welfare value of the climate predictions.

Dryland maize and sorghum were modelled at four locations in southeast Nebraska: maize at Mead and Fairbury, and sorghum at Franklin and Pawnee City (Table 19.2). Dry growing seasons occurring over the period 1971–90 at each modelling location were identified by ranking years by their precipitation means and assigning the five years that were driest to the 'dry' category (see Easterling et al. 1996 for a complete description). The middle ten years (neither dry nor wet) were considered 'normal'. The five wettest years were labelled 'wet', but no adaptive analysis of the wet years was done in this example even though adaptations to wet years surely are made by farmers. The division between these categories is somewhat arbitrary, but it definitely provides farmers with information (Easterling et al. 1996). The precipitation ranges for the categories of normal and dry at each location are shown in Table 19.3.

The baseline condition for this period is that the weather is uncertain. That is, the farmer cannot tell whether next year's weather is going to be dry, normal, or wet. The farmer has to choose a management strategy that will maximise expected net revenue given the probability distribution of weather types. With climate forecasts, the farmer will be able to predict whether next year's weather is dry, normal, or wet. For each weather condition, the farmer chooses a strategy that maximises net revenue by changing planting dates and crop varieties. The value of the climate prediction is equal to the increase in net revenue that the farmer can earn by tailoring management to predicted weather.

Without adaptations, simulated maize at Mead in the dry years yielded 23 per cent less than in the normal years and maize at Fairbury yielded 13 per cent less. Simulations also showed that sorghum at

Table 19.2 Representative farm locations, crop type, dryland practice, weather station locations, and soils used in this study

Crop	County	Cooperative weather data	Soil type(s)
Dryland maize	Saunders	Mead	Sharpsburg
Dryland sorghum	Franklin	Franklin	Uly
Dryland maize	Jefferson	Fairbury	Wymore
Dryland sorghum	Pawnee	Pawnee City	Kennebic

Source: Easterling *et al.* 1993

Table 19.3 Precipitation ranges for 'driest' five-years, 'normal' ten-years, and 'wettest' five-years

Cooperative weather data location and county	Precipitation range (mm)
Franklin, Franklin County (dryland sorghum)	299–369
	398–517
	519–686
Mead, Saunders County (dryland maize)	334–387
	394–557
	597–797
Fairbury, Jefferson County (dryland maize)	291–448
	495–671
	678–871
Pawnee City, Pawnee County (dryland sorghum)	339–490
	490–675
	693–785

Source: Easterling *et al.* 1993

Franklin in the dry years yielded 18 per cent less than the normal years and sorghum at Pawnee City yielded 2 per cent less. The adaptations, when applied to the dry years, mitigated some of these yield losses. The adaptations reduced maize loss at Mead by 2 per cent of the yields in normal years and by 3 per cent at Fairbury. The adaptation reduced the sorghum losses at Franklin by 7 per cent of the yields in normal years and offset all of the loss at Pawnee City, resulting in a 4 per cent increase in sorghum yield relative to normal years. Although the reduction in yield loss from adaptation was not large for maize, it was substantial for sorghum. The sorghum yield losses at Franklin were reduced by about one-third by the adaptations and, of course, dryland sorghum at Pawnee actually increased slightly with the adaptations in the dry years. The responsiveness of sorghum to the adaptations in the dry years is not surprising since sorghum is more drought- (and heat-) tolerant than maize and thus is able to take advantage of the adaptations more fully than maize.

Comparing net revenues (using the mean costs and prices for 1984–7) with the predicted climate and adaptation strategy versus the no-adaptation strategy indicates that the climate forecasts increase net revenue over the two maize locations (Mead, Fairbury) by US$7.05[1] per hectare. This is a 12.7 per cent improvement in net revenue. The increase in net revenue over the two sorghum locations (Franklin, Pawnee City) was US$40.83 per hectare. This is a 9.9 per cent improvement in net revenue. If the above modelling sites are representative of all hectares planted to sorghum and maize in their surrounding counties, the value of better climate forecasts for maize and sorghum production in these four counties is US$1,768,000 of regained net revenue.

TOP-DOWN MODELLING

The top-down approach has sought to link economic welfare and climate by directly measuring the effect of climate on economic net welfare. In principle, one is looking for natural experiments where one can observe the outcome from changes in climate on the entire system. Although an active climate change could potentially provide that experiment, the historic record has been so slow and minute that it is very difficult to use intertemporal data to make these estimates. Instead, top-down approaches have tended to rely on cross-sectional experiments.

Building on the Ricardian model of land value, the top-down approach links variations in land values across space with variations in climate. Land values are a good indicator of economic welfare because they reflect the present value of future streams of net revenue. It is changes in these net revenues that we are seeking to measure. Using cross-sectional evidence, the Ricardian technique uses econometric methods to determine the link between climate and economic outcomes.

Because climate is not the only factor that varies across space, one must be careful to control for unwanted variation from other causes. A multiple regression approach is used to estimate the influence of climate versus the control variables. The control variables include soil characteristics such as sand, clay, moisture capacity, and wetlands and economic and environmental controls such as population density, altitude, and latitude. Of course, not all variables can be perfectly measured and accounted for. The possibility that omitted variables may lead to biased estimates is the key weakness of the Ricardian method.

Mendelsohn *et al.* 1994 examined the effect of mean seasonal temperature and precipitation levels on farmland values in each agricultural county across the United States. Climate by county was interpolated from weather station data. The economic data came largely from the US Census. The analysis indicated that climate variables were important determinants of farmland value. Climate had a quadratic 'hill shaped' relation with land value. The optimal temperature configuration involved mean spring temperatures, cool summers, warm falls, and cold winters. The optimal precipitation pattern was wet seasons except for

fall, which should be dry. Although this approach does not model process, it is consistent with basic agronomic results. The cool summers allow crops to mature without heat stress. The warm dry fall allows harvests to ripen. The wet cold winter kills off pests and increases soil moisture for spring planting.

These results suggest that US agriculture is less sensitive to warming than the bottom-up models predicted. There are two reasons for these more optimistic findings from the Ricardian studies. First, the outcome suggests that American farmers will actively adapt to warming and that bottom-up models need to work harder at identifying these adaptations. Second, the Ricardian study captures the entire agricultural sector, whereas most of the bottom-up models had focused exclusively on grains. Because grains are grown in the cooler regions of the country, it is no surprise that they would be heat sensitive. In contrast, fruits and vegetables tend to concentrate in the warmer regions of the country, and these parts of the farm sector would likely benefit from warming.

Example 3: Ricardian analysis of interannual climate variation

As stated in the introduction and in Example 2, droughts are caused by interannual fluctuations in climate. To measure the economic impact of interannual climate variation, one would first have to understand how land values are affected by this variation. In our first example, we present an extended regression that includes not only the level of precipitation and temperature in each season, but also the range of those values over a thirty-year period. This range of values is a measure of the interannual variation in climate. The effect this range has on land values measures how interannual variation affects long-term net revenue.

We predict that interannual variations in winter and spring climates do not have as great an effect on land values as variations in summer and fall. Farmers can observe winter and to some extent spring weather before making planting decisions and so can adjust to these revealed values. However, many decisions by the farmer have to be made before summer and fall weather is known. The uncertainty in these two seasons is consequently expected to be more damaging.

Table 19.4 Multiple regression of climate on land values

Independent variable	Crop land weight	Crop revenue weight
Constant	1,219.0	1,347.0
	(45.91)	(39.68)
Jan. temp.	−55.1	−104.8
	(5.84)	(8.03)
Jan. temp. sq.	−0.024	−1.18
	(0.10)	(3.96)
Apr. temp.	31.7	−3.8
	(2.25)	(5.02)
Apr. temp. sq.	−4.04	−3.75
	(6.11)	(5.02)
Jul. temp.	−77.7	−35.6
	(6.64)	(2.81)
Jul. temp. sq.	1.38	3.31
	(2.15)	(5.14)
Oct. temp.	115.2	87.3
	(5.76)	(3.19)
Oct. temp. sq.	1.48	4.56
	(1.51)	(4.22)
Jan. prec.	−168.3	−200.4
	(6.01)	(4.96)
Jan. prec. sq.	12.0	7.3
	(4.16)	(2.40)
Apr. prec.	157.6	187.4
	(5.00)	(3.71)
Apr. prec. sq.	−22.2	−94.8
	(2.70)	(8.11)
Jul. prec.	72.5	119.1
	(3.42)	(3.61)
Jul. prec. sq.	36.0	26.6
	(6.07)	(3.39)
Oct. prec.	83.4	49.3
	(2.35)	(0.97)
Oct. prec. sq.	−6.6	134.1
	(0.47)	(10.50)
Jan. temp. var.	−31.2	−54.7
	(6.85)	(8.11)
Apr. temp. var.	12.2	21.7
	(1.61)	(2.01)
Jul. temp. var.	−68.8	−85.9
	(8.98)	(6.80)
Oct. temp. var.	−46.7	−35.8
	(6.78)	(3.23)
Jan. prec. var.	59.5	151.6
	(6.87)	(14.60)
Apr. prec. var.	−24.7	−51.9
	(3.16)	(3.93)
Jul. prec. var.	−26.1	−42.9
	(5.00)	(4.73)
Oct. prec. var.	−20.0	−71.8
	(2.78)	(6.90)
Jan. temp. diur. var.	−70.1	−60.8
	(7.15)	(4.71)
Apr. temp. diur. var.	−50.3	−33.2
	(3.84)	(1.85)
Jul. temp. diur. var.	−42.9	−3.2
	(3.56)	(0.23)
Oct. temp. diur. var.	85.2	59.3
	(7.24)	(3.34)
Income per capita	6.61	4.59
	(15.02)	(6.39)
Density	1.17	1.47
	(17.62)	(18.29)
Density sq.	−0.14	−0.17
	(4.75)	(6.84)
Solar radiation	4.5	26.4
	(0.26)	(1.18)
Altitude	76.3	68.6
	(2.67)	(1.89)
Salinity	−442.0	−852.0
	(2.29)	(4.04)
Flooding	−260.0	−699.0
	(5.60)	(9.36)
Wetland	−244.0	821.0
	(2.09)	(5.07)
Soil erosion	−1,496.0	−2,682.0
	(7.68)	(8.52)
Slope length	23.0	51.9
	(4.11)	(6.42)
Sand	−72.9	−251.0
	(1.52)	(3.92)
Clay	79.0	77.5
	(3.97)	(2.34)
Moisture capacity	0.29	0.19
	(7.76)	(3.70)
Permeability	−2.23	−1.50
	(1.03)	(6.95)
R squared	0.81	0.86
# of observations	2,938	2,938

Source: Mendelsohn et al. 1996
Notes: Land values in 1982 dollars. T-statistics in parenthesis

Table 19.4 presents the results of a multiple regression analysis of land values on climate and a large set of controls using the data from all agricultural counties in the United States. For more detail concerning this regression, see Mendelsohn et al. 1996. The model measures the effect of the average level of temperature and precipitation in each season using both a linear and quadratic term. The model also includes the interannual range of temperature and precipitation for each season. Finally, a set of control variables for soils and other factors are included to control for unwanted variation.

Examining the coefficients of the interannual variation variables reveals the effect of climate variation on per-acre farmland values. The April temperature variation term is positive, suggesting farmers adapt well to changes in spring temperatures. The January, July, and October temperature variation coefficients, however, are all negative, implying that farmers are hurt by annual swings in these temperatures. Multiplying these coefficients by the average value of these variables and summing across seasons reveals that without interannual temperature variation, American farmland values would be between US$1,700–2,100 per acre higher than observed. This amounts to an increase of 170–200 per cent of farm value.

With precipitation, the January coefficient is positive, implying that farmers can turn the interannual swings of winter precipitation into an advantage. However, variations in spring, summer, and fall precipitation are all damaging. Multiplying these seasonal coefficients by the average range of precipitation and summing reveals that swings in annual precipitation actually increase land values by US$190–350. Even though the January effect offsets the impact of the other seasons, precipitation variation still has a substantial impact on farm values.

It is commonly thought that the damages from interannual fluctuations – droughts – should be blamed largely on precipitation swings. However, the top-down evidence suggests that the economic damages are largely a result of temperature swings. Further, the evidence suggests that interannual temperature swings are having a large effect on US farms. Aggregating across all farm acreage, existing interannual temperature swings are reducing farm values by US$1.6–1.9 trillion. Multiplying this amount by the real interest rate, climate variation generates an expected annual loss of US$80–95 billion to US agriculture.

Example 4: top-down evaluation of climate predictions

Better forecasts of the pattern of these fluctuations could allow farmers to adjust to the weather they will actually experience. Although forecasts do not change the likelihood of having any particular climate, they allow farmers to anticipate the weather they are about to experience and so adjust to it. To evaluate what improved forecasts would do for farmers, one would have to predict how they are affected today and how they would be affected if they knew in advance what the weather would be like.

The calculation discussed in Example 3 measures the damages from fluctuations without forecasts. We now need to determine how farmers would fare if they knew what weather was coming. Because accurate forecasts of future weather conditions were not available when this data set was collected, we have no direct observations concerning how farmers would do with improved forecasting.

One analogy we could make is that weather predictions would change the coefficients of July and October so that they resembled the coefficients of January and April – recalling from above that January and April are periods when farmers have ample time to adjust their operations. Such an analogy equates having an accurate forecast with having winter and spring flexibility of operations throughout the growing season. Giving summer and fall the average effect of winter and spring implies that precipitation variation would increase farm values US$450–1,300. Even with forecasts, temperature variation would decrease farm values US$710–1,240. Overall, farm values with forecasts would either increase by US$75 or fall by US$262 per acre relative to a world with no climate variation. This aggregates to a net effect of either a US$70 billion gain or a US$244 billion loss relative to a world with no variation. Compared to the estimates of damages from climate variation when there is no forecast, these rough comparisons imply that the value of climate forecasts would be worth US$1.4–1.8 trillion. This amounts to US$70–90 billion a year.

An alternative calculation is to assume that improved weather forecasts would be similar to changing the level of climate. That is, by knowing what weather was coming, farmers could adjust their practices as though next year's weather was normal (average). We assume that farmers have adjusted to the average climate of their location. Thus the coefficients for the climate normals (thirty-year averages) reveal how farmers would react to the climate they can anticipate. We assume that climate forecasts would permit farmers to adjust as though each year was a climate normal in a different location. By exploring the expected outcome from many random years of weather, we can estimate what would have happened to farmers if they could have anticipated next year's weather. Contrasting this expected value with the damages above provides an estimate of the value of climate forecasts.

We begin by creating a distribution of interannual weather patterns consistent with the historical record. For each location, we know the climate normal and the range of climates observed over a thirty-year period. Assuming that this range reflects two standard deviations around the mean, we can generate a distribution of climate outcomes for temperature and precipitation across all four seasons. For this experiment, we assume that temperature and precipitation are independent.

For each weather outcome, we calculate what land values would have been if this outcome was normal for that area. That is, we use the average climate coefficients to predict land values for this weather pattern. We then repeat this exercise for a representative distribution of weather outcomes to get an expected land value. Subtracting this expected land value from the observed land value gives an estimate of the value of anticipated interannual variation. Contrasting this value with the estimate produced in Example 3 provides an estimate of the value of information.

We analyse nine weather alternatives. We begin with the climate normals, then vary temperature, precipitation, and both temperature and precipitation by one standard deviation away from normal. This yields nine combinations of precipitation and temperature alternatives. Farm values are observed to increase with warmer temperatures and higher levels of precipitation. The increases from warmer, wetter years are largely offset by colder, drier years. The expected effect of anticipated climate variation is between a US$63 gain and a US$206 loss per acre. This implies an aggregate effect of between a US$60 billion benefit and a US$192 billion loss. Compared to the predicted damages from unanticipated climate change, these estimates imply climate forecasts could be worth US$1.5–1.7 trillion, or US$75–85 billion a year. These estimates are very close to the earlier estimates of the value of climate forecasts.

CONTRASTING BOTTOM-UP AND TOP-DOWN

The bottom-up and top-down approaches each have strengths and weaknesses as tools for estimating the agroecological and economic consequences of drought. We argue that the weaknesses of the bottom-up approach are the strengths of the top-down approach, and vice versa. Both approaches explicitly acknowledge the certainty that farmers and their supporting institutions adapt to climate variability. The reliance on mechanistic crop simulators gives the bottom-up approach the capability of examining the agronomic and economic efficiency of specific on-farm adaptation strategies. The simulation and testing of new management practices such as crop switching, implementation of irrigation, and moisture conservation can be easily handled. The emphasis on mechanistic relations between climate and biophysical determinants of crop growth gives the bottom-up approach confidence in its estimates of crop response to climate conditions lying outside of the range of historical experience.

In practice, however, the modelling of the totality of farmer adjustments has been the bane of the bottom-up approach. Laden with extensive local environmental detail, the crop models are costly to operate. Running the models many times to explore alternative management strategies is too expensive, except on an individual site basis (Kaiser *et al.* 1993). Many analysts have consequently settled for trying arbitrary adjustments as their adaptation strategy, and the models consequently underestimate the adjustments that farmers would make to climate influences.

By focusing on the economic outcome of the effects of climate variability on the entire agricultural production system, the top-down approach implicitly accounts for the totality of adaptations of farmers and institutions to reduce economic loss or enhance economic gains. The full range of adaptations is, in essence, embedded in the determinants of land value. Hence, the top-down approach reflects the cumulative adaptive experience of American farmers as they established production systems across the many different climatic regimes of the nation.

However, the dependence on data that is highly spatially aggregated denies the top-down approach the capability of examining individual farm-level adaptation strategies. Specific guidance on the efficiency of various adaptations under a range of drought conditions is not possible. Also, the reliance on historic relations between climate and economic performance weakens the ability of the top-down approach to predict the consequences of heretofore unobserved climate conditions.

Reason suggests that the greatest insights into the economic consequences of the impact of drought on American agriculture are to be gained by combining the bottom-up and top-down approaches. The bottom-up approach is most effectively used to gain insights into the specific biological (e.g., net primary productivity, crop water use) and economic (e.g., farm costs, net revenue) effects of drought at the farm-level and in cases where highly detailed information about the impacts of drought is needed at a regional level. An example of the latter is the need to understand the adaptive potential of a new technology, such as a genetically engineered drought-resistant crop, on the overall productivity of a drought-prone region.

The top-down approach is most effectively used to gain insights into the composite of adaptations farmers make in response to climate variation. Adaptive potential in the top-down approach is not biased by the arbitrary selection of adaptation strategies to be included in the modelling and analysis. All agricultural responses to historic climate conditions, even ones that were tried but were not successful, are included in the calculation of drought costs and benefits.

CONCLUSIONS

This study reviews two alternative methods for evaluating the impact of droughts on US farms. The bottom-up approach begins with a climate influence, uses basic agronomic models to calculate changes in yields, and then determines economic impacts using an economic model. In contrast, the top-down approach looks for a direct link between climate and economic impacts. We argue that the advantage of each approach is often the disadvantage of the other approach, so that the two methods complement each other in practice. It is consequently prudent to rely on both methods to calculate economic impacts.

The study develops two bottom-up and two top-down calculations to illustrate each method. The first bottom-up example calculates the economic damages of the Dust Bowl era on Nebraska, Kansas, Iowa, and Missouri. This extreme weather condition resulted in economic damages of about US$1.7 billion to these four states alone. The second bottom-up example places a value on knowing what next year's weather will be for farms in southeastern Nebraska. The study suggests that maize values (using mean 1984–7 costs and prices) would increase by about US$7.05 per hectare, or 12.7 per cent, and sorghum values would increase by about US$40.83 per hectare, or 9.9 per cent, with perfect foresight. The third example uses a top-down approach to put a value on interannual climate variation. The analysis suggests that elimination of interannual climate variation would increase farm values by 170–200 per cent, suggesting annual aggregate values of US$80–95 billion. The fourth example uses a top-down approach to evaluate perfect climate forecasts. Using two alternative methods of calculation, the analysis suggests that perfect climate forecasts would be worth US$70–90 billion annually to farmers. If farmers could anticipate interannual variation, they could largely mitigate its consequences. Perfect climate forecasts would generate substantial benefits. Of course, recent advances in forecasting are still not perfect. These estimates must consequently be viewed as an upper boundary of the value of better climate predictions.

NOTE

1 Maize prices during the 1984–7 period were at historic lows in real terms, hence the large discrepancy between maize and sorghum revenues.

REFERENCES

Bowes, M.D., and Crosson, P.R. (1993) 'Consequences of climate change for the MINK economy: Impacts and responses', *Climatic Change* 24: 131–54.
Easterling, W.E., Crosson, P.R., Rosenberg, N.J., McKenney, M.S., Katz, L., and Lemon, K. (1993) 'Agricultural impacts of and responses to climate change in the Missouri-Iowa-Nebraska-Kansas (MINK) region', *Climatic Change* 24: 23–61.
Easterling, W.E., Chen, X., Hays, C., Brandle, J.R., and

Zhang, H. (1996) 'Improving the validation of model-simulated crop yield response to climate change: An application to the EPIC model', *Climate Research* 6: 263–73.

IPCC (1996) *Climate Change 1995. The Science of Climate Change* (L.G. Meira Filho, B.A. Callander, N. Harris, A. Kattenberg, and K. Maskell, eds), Cambridge: Cambridge University Press.

Kaiser, H., Riha, S., Wilks, D., Rossiter, D., and Sampath, R. (1993) 'A farm-level analysis of economic and agronomic impacts of gradual climate warming', *American Journal of Agricultural Economics* 75: 387–98.

Mearns, L.O., Katz, R.W., and Schneider, S.H. (1984) 'Extreme high-temperature events: Changes in their probabilities with changes in mean temperature', *Journal of Climate and Applied Meteorology* 23: 1,601–13.

Mendelsohn, R., Nordhaus, W., and Shaw, D. (1994) 'The impact of global warming on agriculture: A Ricardian analysis', *American Economic Review* 84, 753–71.

——— (1996) 'Climate impacts on aggregate farm values: Accounting for adaptation', *Journal of Agriculture and Forest Meteorology* 80: 55–67.

Root, T.L., and Schneider, S. (1995) 'Ecology and climate: Research strategies and implications', *Science* 269: 334–41.

Rosenberg, N.J. (ed.) (1980) *Drought in the Great Plains: Research on Impacts and Strategies*, Littleton, CO: Water Resources Publications.

——— (1993) *Towards an Integrated Impact Assessment of Climate Change: The MINK Study*, reprinted from *Climatic Change* 24, Nos. 1–2 (1993), Boston, MA: Kluwer Academic Publishers.

Sarachik, E.S. (1992) 'Climate prediction and the ocean,' *Oceanus* 34: 66–73.

Sarachik, E.S., and Shea, E. (1997) 'End-to-end seasonal-to-interannual climate prediction,' *ENSO Signal* 7: 4–6.

US Department of Agriculture–Forest Service (1989) 'Micro IMPLAN Release 89–03' [a computer program], US Department of Agriculture, Forest Service, Land Management Planning, Fort Collins, CO, March.

Williams, J.R., Jones, C.A., and Dyke, P. (1984) 'A modeling approach to determining the relationship between erosion and soil productivity', *Transactions of the American Society of Agricultural Engineers* 27: 129–44.

Wilhite, D.A. (1993) 'The enigma of drought', in D.A. Wilhite (ed.), *Drought Assessment, Management, and Planning: Theory and Case Studies*, Boston, MA: Kluwer Academic Publishers.

20

COMPUTING DROUGHT SEVERITY AND FORECASTING ITS FUTURE IMPACT ON GRAZING IN A GIS

J.M. de Jager, M.D. Howard, and H.J. Fouché

INTRODUCTION

The nature and severity of drought

Drought is a natural, inevitable, and unpredictable occurrence that is weather controlled. Being a weather phenomenon, drought is stochastic by nature, but highly dependent on the specific environment and type of crop cultivated. The successful monitoring of drought severity and drought forecasting must therefore be stochastically based and climate-soil-crop specific. Such an approach has been adopted here.

Most agricultural areas, and particularly those found in semiarid regions, experience abnormally arid conditions (severe drought) at some time and, less frequently, extremely dry conditions that reach disaster proportions (disaster drought). Hence two significant types of drought situation can be identified, and effective drought monitoring should differentiate between severe and disaster drought.

The primary objective of effective drought management should be the maintenance of the agricultural productive capacity[1] of the region through times of severe drought as well as disaster drought. In the Republic of South Africa, the Provincial Commission of Enquiry into the Re-structuring of Agriculture in the Free State Province (PCERAFS 1996) recognised this dual requirement and has recommended a drought policy aimed at managing both sets of conditions. In essence, it proposed that management for drought be entrusted to two committees, the Drought Risk Management Committee and the Drought Disaster Management Committee.

Management for drought risk entails imple-

mentation of drought policy; monitoring drought severity; technology transfer; researching econometric models; income and tax levelling; and following trends and developments in world trade agreements. On the other hand, management for disaster drought entails delimiting and monitoring the extent of drought areas, expediting the distribution of funds and aid, and fund raising and allocation.

The ideal decision support for drought risk and disaster management is a scientific computerised GIS system for drought severity classification, monitoring, and hazard forecasting. The Drought Monitoring and Forecasting System (DMFS) here described was developed by the Department of Agrometeorology of the University of the Free State and the Section of Pasture Science Research and the Section Information Technology of the Free State Department of Agriculture (FSDA). The latter two sections are successfully implementing a similar system.

Although this chapter will concentrate on analysing drought in grazing in the Free State, the techniques described have been applied to other crops as well (see, for example, Lourens and de Jager 1997 and Van den Berg and Potgieter 1997).

Objectives

The objective of this chapter is to describe the design and performance of a drought monitoring and forecasting system. The specific objectives of the chapter will be to:

- define practical categories of drought severity;
- describe data requirements, database structure,

and a method for monitoring and forecasting drought; and

- illustrate the performance of the DMFS on grassland in the Free State and undertake preliminary tests of the accuracy of its forecasts.

EXPERIMENTAL SITE

Location

The DMFS was developed for Free State Province (FS) of the Republic of South Africa (RSA), located between 26° 40′ and 30° 60′ south latitude and 24° 40′ and 29° 20′ east longitude.

Climate

The province experiences summer rainfall and semiarid to subhumid climatic conditions. Extra-tropical agro-bioclimatic aridity classes for these are defined by Le Houérou, Popov, and See (1993) as follows:

- Class 4 semiarid – Rainfall 200–600 mm/yr; rainfall-to-reference evaporation ratio 20–40 per cent, and rain period duration 100–80 days/yr.
- Class 3 subhumid – Rainfall 400–800; rainfall-to-reference evaporation ratio 30–70 per cent, and rain period duration 180–240 days/yr.

Land use

FS covers approximately 12.94×10^6 ha (Directorate Agricultural Statistics 1996). Although maize is cultivated extensively in the north and northwest and wheat in the west and east, the land surface of the province is predominantly used for range land and livestock farming. Unless effective grassland management is applied, veld deterioration is liable to take place, which will result in marked changes in productive capacity, with serious socioeconomic repercussions (Acocks 1988). This emphasises the need for reliable drought assessment and forecasting. Both short-term management and long-term planning benefit from such decision support.

DEFINITION OF SEVERITY OF AGRICULTURAL DROUGHT

Farming enterprises, particularly in semiarid regions, are planned/budgeted to succeed through protracted periods of unfavourable rainfall. Unfavourable rainfall years (i.e., drought years) are here defined as years in which rainfall is so poor that the farmer cannot make a positive gross margin (gross margin = income – production cost – interest on capital). Drought years include severe and disaster drought situations. It was assumed that climatically and economically sustainable, risk-neutral farming is attainable with strategies planned to ensure survival through drought years (negative gross margins) that occur 25 per cent of the time (i.e., 1 : 4 years, or a success/failure ratio of 3 : 1). Extreme drought situations are deemed to have occurred when yields do not exceed what might be expected 7 per cent of the time (i.e., 1 : 14 years). The latter are highly infrequent acts of nature that threaten preservation of the agricultural productive capacity of a region and warrant being declared disaster situations. Subject to state policy, disaster drought situations could qualify for some form of state assistance. In accordance with these assumptions, disaster, severe, mild, and no agricultural drought are here defined as follows:

- *Disaster* drought is a set of rainfall-soil-crop conditions for which poor rainfall results in crop yields that will not be exceeded 7 per cent of the time (1 : 14 years).
- *Severe* drought is a set of rainfall-soil-crop conditions for which poor rainfall results in crop yields expected to occur 7–25 per cent of the time.
- *Mild* drought is a set of rainfall-soil-crop conditions resulting in yields expected to occur 25–50 per cent of the time.
- *No drought* occurs when rainfall-soil-crop conditions result in yields exceeding the median yield.

DATABASE

Each GIS grid point was assigned a soil clay content for two horizons, the soil rooting depth, the cumulative Probability Distribution Function (CDF) of grassland yield (thirty-six simulated annual yields arranged in ascending order), and current season and median daily weather data (maximum and minimum temperatures, rainfall, and sunshine hours for an entire growing season). *Solar irradiance* was computed from the sunshine duration data using an Ångstrom-type empirical equation (see Reid and Mac 1989). *The soil database* for the GIS was provided by the Section Information Technology of FSDA.

Weather data

The long-term and current season daily weather data were provided by the South African Weather Bureau; the Institute of Climate, Soil and Water Research; the Section Information Technology of the Free State Department of Agriculture (FSDA); and more than 600 Free State farmers who submit real-time rainfall figures to the FSDA.

Real-time drought monitoring and forecasting was carried out at each grid point in daily iterations with a crop growth model (CGM). Each daily weather data value had been interpolated from its three nearest weather stations. Daily weather data series consisted of current season data for 1 July up to the present date, completed with surrogate data compiled from months containing daily median data.

Forecast weather data scenarios

The DMFS required daily data series that could be used as forecast scenarios for each weather element so that crop final yield and biomass status could be computed at some future date. For each element, a forecast scenario, or surrogate weather data series, for a complete year for each given grid point was created. This contained daily weather values that reflect a median weather year. Median data were constructed by searching historical data for each weather station for months yielding median values of the relevant weather variable. These months were then compiled into a one-year data series consisting of daily median values. Grid point daily median values were then interpolated for each day.

COMPUTATIONAL METHOD

Operating procedure

It was practically impossible to obtain measured crop yield data for each GIS grid point. Hence the best, and probably the only, way to achieve the desired type of drought analysis was to use a CGM and weather, crop, and soil data. This enabled the computing and displaying of both long-term crop yield probabilities and current season simulated yield situations.

Computations in the GIS were performed on 1,308 grid points on a $6' \times 6'$ (9 km $\times$ 9 km) raster that was placed over the entire Free State province. This resolution adequately accounts for the existing soil variability. The data base and program occupy 300 megabytes of hard disk space on a Pentium 586, 70 MHz personal computer (PC). Results are presented by the Vertical Mapper routine of the software package MapInfo Professional (see MapInfo Corporation 1992).

Computing present and future drought status involved the following:

Monitoring

1   use of actual weather data commencing from the beginning of the growing season (1 July for range lands in Free State Province) to simulate the natural grassland production status up to the present date for each grid point of the GIS;
2   determination of the probability of this simulated real-time production being exceeded by comparing it against the long-term cumulative probability distribution function of grassland yield (CDF) for the grid point;
3   classification of each grid point as disaster, severe, mild, or no drought, based on the probability of nonexceedence of simulated yield;
4   mapping the output values in the GIS using Vertical Mapper;

Forecasting

5   repeating procedures 1–3 but then completing the growing season using forecasted median daily weather scenarios; and

6 classifying the drought severity of the resulting projected final seasonal yields, as in #3 above.

The sequence and duration of computations 1–6 above is given schematically in Figure 20.1. Overall computing time to complete these actions was approximately four hours. The major decisions necessary when designing the DMFS involved determining the grid size, developing a method for interpolating grid point values of variables (particularly the weather), and creating the forecasting scenarios of daily weather (especially rainfall) for the remaining part of a growing season from any given date.

Interpolation techniques – weather data

Daily weather data values for each grid point were interpolated from the three nearest weather stations using the data point concentration dependent weighting method of Rautenbach (1996). Here, the interpolated grid point value of a variable is given by

$$C_{ij} = \left[\frac{\sum\limits_{k=1}^{3} W(r_{kij}).C_k}{\sum\limits_{k=1}^{3} W(r_{kij})} \right]$$

where $W(r_{kij})$ is the weight function of the kth weather station data value C_k for $k = 1 \ldots 3$ at grid point (i, j). The distance between the position of any data point value C_k and a grid point value C_{ij} is denoted by r_{kij}. The subscripts (i, j) refer to the ith and jth grid point in the x and y direction.

The weight function is then given by:

$$W(r_{kij}) = b \left[\frac{r_{kij} - r_{(\min)ij}}{r_{(\min)ij}} \right]$$

where $r_{(\min)ij}$ is the distance from grid point ij to the nearest weather station. In this technique, the radius of influence of a station daily value decreases with an increase in the value of the parameter b, and increases with an increase in the distance $r_{(\min)ij}$.

Rautenbach (1996) showed that value of b could

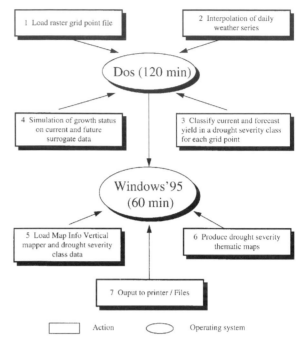

Figure 20.1 Sequence and duration of the various actions carried out by the DMFS

vary between 0.0003 and 0.2, depending on weather station concentration. Scrutiny of the weather station distribution in the FS revealed that weather stations are homogeneously spread over the province, and hence a single value of b was adopted for the province. A preliminary comparison of observed rainfall values versus values interpolated from its three nearest neighbours for a site in the central FS over an eighteen-year period suggested the value of b = 0.00175 to be appropriate.

Interpolation techniques – drought severity

Once each grid point had been awarded a drought severity category, Vertical Mapper applied a smoothing routine to produce maps of the type depicted in Figures 20.3 and 20.4. Of the three smoothing techniques available in Vertical Mapper, inverse distance weighting was selected because it is a type of moving average technique that is usually applied to highly variable data. Rectangular triangulation was discarded because it depicted discrete blocks and discontinuities that are unrealistic in nature, and triangular inter-polation produced unacceptable overshoot and distorted contours.

Probability functions

Climate-soil-crop specific drought assessment is attained by comparison of CGM-computed crop yield against the long-term CDF of yields for each grid point. In this way, it is possible to determine the probability of nonexceedence of the computed yield, and hence the severity of the current drought at the given grid point may be estimated according to the above definitions. Lourens and de Jager (1997) com-pared grid point yield against the CDF for the homoclimatic region within which the grid point resides. It was possible here to determine probabilities of nonexceedence for each grid point and then simply combine them into areas of the same drought severity class using Vertical Mapper. For this, the standard procedures available in MapInfo were used.

Historical weather data were available for the period 1960–95. Unfortunately, the data records for each station were not of equal length. The number of measuring points available over the thirty-six-year study period varied between 20 and 61 for tempera-tures, 333 and 601 for rainfall, and 11 and 46 for sunshine duration. Nonetheless, it was decided to use all available data. Unfortunately, this meant that the CDF for a given grid point was determined from daily data interpolated from the nearest weather stations, which changed with time.

Crop growth model. The Putu grassland, maize, and wheat models have, among others, been used for decision support in the Free State. For these three types of vegetation, Lourens and de Jager (1997) report comparisons of measured versus simulated yields r^2 that vary between 0.74 and 0.94. The grassland ver-sion attained a $r^2 = 0.92$. It was translated into the computer language C for the purpose of this study.

RESULTS AND DISCUSSION

The consequence of using a rate of occurrence of 1 : 14 years as a threshold for defining disaster drought was examined. The proportions of Free State surface area that would have been disaster drought listed

since 1960 were computed. These, together with average seasonal FS rainfall, are illustrated in Figure 20.2. From the point of view of providing drought relief, the magnitudes and frequencies of areas listed appear to be manageable. The extreme drought of 1995 is very evident.

The significance of grazing and livestock farming in the Free State has already been emphasised and so grazing conditions during a time of drought were investigated. The period November 1994 through December 1995 was characterised by possibly the worst drought situation that the RSA and the Free State have ever experienced. This period was thus selected to demonstrate the capabilities of the DMFS. Drought conditions commenced in November 1994, endured until November 1995, and eventually abated in January 1996. Thus the onset and termination of a disaster drought situation are included.

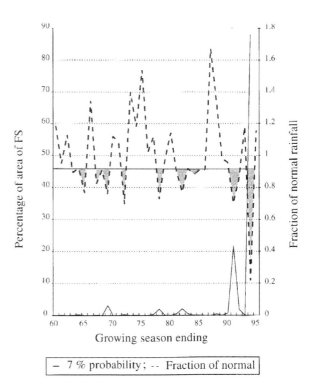

Figure 20.2 Simulated percentage of the area of Free State Province that would have been classified as disaster drought stricken based on a 1 : 14 year rate of occurrence for the period 1960–95

Drought monitoring

Drought monitoring results for 1994–5 are depicted in Figure 20.3, which clearly illustrates how the simulated disaster drought situation worsened, beginning from November 1994. Virtually 70 per cent of the province was affected by the end of December 1994. Simulated disaster conditions worsened and prevailed throughout almost the entire province by the end of November 1995. In December 1995, the rains returned and the drought situation was alleviated. No drought growing conditions were simulated by the end of January 1996. Maps similar to Figure 20.3, but for an improving drought situation, were obtained for December 1995 to January 1996, but are not presented.

Drought severity forecasting

Drought severity was hindcasted[2] two months ahead of time to the last day of November and December 1994 (see Figure 20.4) in situations when drought worsened. Reasonable agreement between hindcasted (Figure 20.4) and simulated conditions (Figure 20.3) is evident. Similar maps and comparisons were obtained for November and December 1995 when drought was abating. They are not shown, but the results were included when testing the forecasting accuracy of the DMFS using hindcasts in Table 20.1.

The reliability of the forecasts was tested by counting the number of grid points for which a hindcasted severity class agreed with the simulated severity class shown in Figure 20.3. The results are reported in

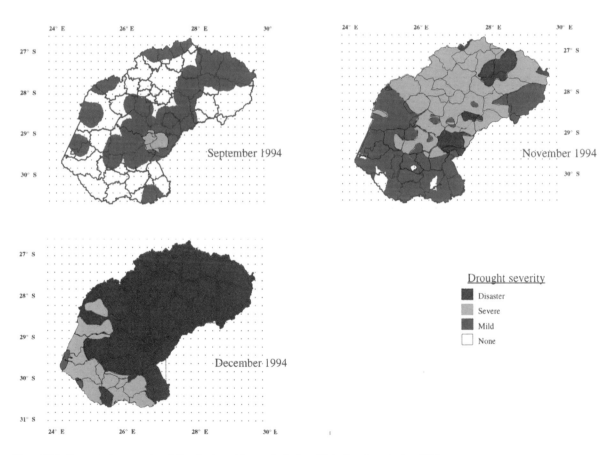

Figure 20.3 Computed seasonal variation in drought severity in Free State Province during 1994

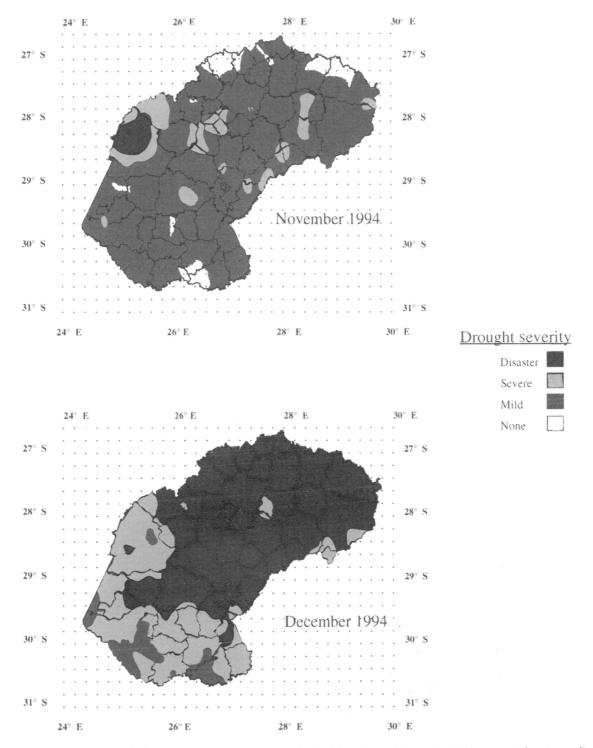

Figure 20.4 Drought severity hindcasted from September and October for November and December 1994, respectively, using median rainfall scenarios

Table 20.1. As might be expected, early in the worsening situation, hindcasts underestimated severity; late in the drought terminating phase, the hindcasts overestimated drought severity. This tendency could have been eliminated, had the Southern Oscillation Index (SOI) been taken into account, a poor (lower quartile) rainfall scenario been used in the worsening situation, and a good (higher quartile) scenario been used in the abating case. This method was followed by Lourens and de Jager (1997), but on only a small portion of the Free State.

In May 1995, the National Drought Advice Committee (NDA) declared a number of magisterial districts in the Free State drought stricken. A comparison of the number of grid points where the DMFS simulated disaster drought agree with the NDA drought classification is given in Table 20.2. It is evident that the DMFS would have listed more magisterial districts than did the NDA. The results do, however, suggest that for disaster drought situations, a threshold probability of 5 per cent yield nonexceedence, rather than the 7 per cent employed here, might be considered.

The overestimate in drought listing by the DFMS was expected. The NDA lists only entire magisterial districts, and then only when a large proportion (> 65 per cent) thereof is drought stricken. There will therefore always be a large number of drought-stricken areas in the province that are not listed by NDA, but which will be classified by the DMFS. Furthermore, the economic situation in the RSA and general lack of funds in 1995 could have had a marked influence in reducing the areas listed by NDA.

Future modifications

Lourens et al. (1995) have developed algorithms for accurately converting METEOSAT imagery values of cloud cover into daily solar irradiance values. Monthly coefficients of determination (r^2) between METEOSAT and surface measurements of solar irradiance ranged between 0.74 and 0.92. More than 90 per cent of model results were within 20 per cent of corresponding measured values. The introduction of such technology needs to be considered.

Table 20.1 Percentages of correct, overestimated, and underestimated hindcasts of drought severity in a worsening (1994) and abating (1995) situation

Situation	Date			Hindcast estimate		
	Year	Month		Correct	Under	Over
Worsening	1994	Nov		33	53	14
	1994	Dec		63	37	0
Abating	1995	Nov		70	21	9
	1995	Dec		63	3	34

Table 20.2 Frequency of DMFS simulated disaster, severe, and mild drought grid points found in NDA listed areas and percentages of Free State province listed by the DMFS and the NDA at the end of May 1995

Drought class	NDA Listed		NDA not listed		Percentage of FS	
	Frequency	(%)	Frequency	(%)	DMFS	NDA
Disaster	487	87	667	89	88	43
Severe	65	12	70	9	11	
Mild	7	1	10	2	1	
None	1	0	1			57
	560	100	748	100	100	100

CONCLUSIONS

To be of practical value to decision makers, and because drought is stochastic, drought analysis must be quantitative and probabilistic-based. The underlying agronomic influences must be adequately accounted for and analyses must be rainfall climate, soil, and crop specific. To meet these prerequisites, it is imperative that the drought assessment be based on a priori definitions of drought severity. This chapter proposes climate-soil-crop specific definitions for disaster, severe, mild, and no-drought situations based on probabilities of nonexceedance of simulated crop yields. Disaster drought was defined as a rainfall-soil-crop situation resulting in crop yields not exceeded 7 per cent the time (i.e., 1 : 14 years)

A drought monitoring and forecasting system based on this type of definition can be created to operate in a GIS environment on a PC. A CGM and historical and current season weather data are required. Monitoring and forecasting consumes approximately four hours of computing time and 300 megabytes of hard disk space if computations are carried out at 1,308 grid points on a $6' \times 6'$ raster covering 12.94×10^6 ha and a data point concentration dependent weighting function is used for interpolating daily weather value. Here, forecasting was undertaken assuming future weather scenarios of median rainfall. However, it became apparent that a DMFS of this type should, in addition to median data, also be provided with upper and lower quartile scenarios. The most appropriate of the latter three may then be selected to predict future weather depending on long-term weather outlooks that could, for example, be based on the current phase of the SOI.

Although no historical data are available, METEOSAT satellite imagery cloud cover data could, in future, improve estimation of spatially distributed solar irradiance.

In a 1995 example on grassland, the DMFS overestimated NDA disaster drought listings. Because of the way NDA listings are made, this was expected. Hindcasted and simulated drought severity agreed reasonably well. The advantage of the DMFS, however, is its capability of forecasting drought situations as well as estimating real-time conditions. The value of this to both farmers and decision makers (such as

grain merchants and the NDA) is great. Furthermore, by including appropriate CGMs, the DMFS can be applied to investigating other cropping situations.

Finally, it may be concluded that a DMFS based on a CGM, historical and current weather data, upper and lower quartile scenarios and median future weather scenarios within a GIS provides an excellent form of technology transfer for drought assessment and decision making.

ACKNOWLEDGEMENTS

The weather data provided by the South African Weather Bureau, the National Institute for Climate Soils and Water Research, the Free State Department of Agriculture, and all cooperating farmers is gratefully acknowledged. Special recognition is accorded the Section Information Technology of FSDA and Johan van den Berg and Andries Potgieter in particular for making available their soil data base. Without these valuable contributions, this chapter would not have seen the light of day.

NOTES

1 Productive capacity: The climatically sustainable agricultural production possible in a given region.
2 Hindcast: Forecasting future conditions from a historical point in time.

REFERENCES

Acocks, J.P.H. (1988) 'Veld types of South Africa', *Memoirs of Botanical Survey of South Africa*, No. 57.
Directorate Agricultural Statistics (1996) *Abstracts of Agricultural Statistics 1996*, Directorate Agricultural Statistics, Pretoria.
Le Houêrou, H.N., Popov, G.F., and See, L. (1993) 'Agro-bioclimatic classification of Africa', FAO, *Agrometeorology Series Working Paper*, No. 6, FAO, Rome, Italy.
Lourens, U.W., and de Jager, J.M. (1997) 'A computerised crop-specific drought monitoring system', *Agricultural Systems* 53, 303–15.
Lourens, U.W., Van Sandwyk, C.M., and de Jager, J.M. (1995) 'Accuracy of an empirical model for estimating daily irradiance in South Africa from METEOSAT imagery', *Agricultural and Forest Meteorology* 74, 1–2: 75–86.
MapInfo Corporation (1992) *MapInfo Professional Users'*

Guide, Troy, New York: One Global View.

PCERAFS (1996) *Provincial Commission of Enquiry into the Re-structuring of Agriculture in the Free State 1995*, report to the Department of Agriculture and Environmental Affairs, Free State Provincial Government.

Rautenbach, C.J. (1996) 'Derivation of a data-point concentration dependent weighting function for interpolation of rainfall grid point fields', *S.A. Journal for Natural Science and Technology* 15, 4: 168–71.

Reid, P.C., and Mac, R. (1989) 'Geographical distribution of monthly mean daily global solar radiation over South Africa', *South African Journal of Plant and Soil* 6, 1: 46–9.

Van den Berg, W.J., and Potgieter, A.B. (1997) *Climatological and Agricultural Conditions in the Free State January 1997*, monthly report, Free State Department of Agriculture Section Information Technology.

21

AN ASSESSMENT OF THE DROUGHT HAZARD IN MOROCCO

Will D. Swearingen and Abdellatif Bencherifa

INTRODUCTION

This chapter examines the drought hazard in Morocco, a representative drought-prone developing country. It demonstrates that this hazard has been increasing over time owing to changes in the socioeconomic context in which drought occurs. The chapter will first present an overview of the basic causes and effects of drought in Morocco. Then it will analyse the historical and contemporary forces that have been contributing to an increase in the drought hazard. Finally, it will present the results of an extensive field survey of farmer responses to increasing vulnerability to drought.[1]

OVERVIEW OF THE DROUGHT HAZARD IN MOROCCO

Drought is Morocco's leading natural hazard (Swearingen 1987a, 1987b, 1992, 1994, 1996). This hazard arises principally from the 'marginal' character of the country's precipitation. Morocco is situated on the southern margins of midlatitude storm systems from the Atlantic, with a Mediterranean-type climate prevailing in the north and desert prevailing in the south. As a result, both the timing and total amounts of rainfall are highly irregular, with dramatic effects on agricultural production.

Morocco is particularly vulnerable to agricultural drought because of the predominance of rain-fed cereal cultivation in its northern half. Since pre-Roman times, this land has specialised in cereal crops, mainly wheat and barley. Cereal crops account for approximately 85 per cent of the country's total cropland and are produced primarily by rain-fed or nonirrigated means. Wheat is the mainstay of the national diet and is consumed mainly as bread and couscous. Nutritional surveys reveal that cereals account for nearly two-thirds of the daily caloric intake and protein supply (Morocco 1988). For rural populations and the urban poor, these percentages are even higher.

Drought in Morocco sharply reduces both cereal acreage and yields, causing total production to plummet. This poses a food security threat, particularly if drought persists beyond a single year. During a typical multiyear drought, cereal imports rise dramatically, substantially increasing foreign debt. Food shortages also develop and rural malnutrition becomes more prevalent. Herds perish or are slaughtered for lack of forage, farmers temporarily abandon their land and flock to the cities, and wind erosion and desertification processes increase.

Good rain-fed cereal harvests in Morocco require adequate rainfall during *both* the planting season (normally from October to December) and subsequent growing season (which extends until harvesting occurs between April and June, depending on the region). Poor harvests or crop failure can result from rainfall shortages during either season. Given the potential for extreme interannual variability in precipitation levels, 400 mm average annual precipitation is normally considered the threshold for viable rain-fed cereal production in Morocco (Bencherifa 1988b, Lery 1982). However, the timing of rainfall is just as critical as the total amount. For example, if Morocco's entire winter precipitation falls during a single intense cloudburst, most will disappear as runoff and be unavailable for crop use. Thus, regardless of the total amount of rain, severe drought conditions will probably develop. However, as little as 250 mm of rain can produce good harvests if it falls at optimal intervals during the agricultural year (Bowden 1979).

Examination of the historical literature reveals that drought has always been frequent in Morocco. For example, an exhaustive historical survey of natural disasters in Morocco from the late ninth century to the early 1900s revealed that there were forty-nine major drought-related famines (Bois 1957). Since 1912, when Morocco was partitioned into French and Spanish protectorates, this country has experienced about twenty-eight years of agricultural drought. The average interval between droughts during the past eighty-five years is only about three years, although there is no detectable periodicity.

Probably at least a third of the total tonnage of cereals in Morocco is still produced by traditional means, including animal traction and the lightweight swing or scratch plough. This traditional technology has two critical and interrelated shortcomings: First, ploughing with the traditional plough is a very slow process. In all, a farmer and his draft animal must travel approximately 60 km to put a single hectare into production (Cleaver 1982). Second, peasants normally cannot begin ploughing until approximately 150 mm of rain have fallen, softening the earth enough to allow the light swing plough to penetrate.

Having to wait for rain presents major problems. The window of opportunity for planting is relatively limited, given the short growing season before the arrival of hot, arid summer conditions. Planting must generally be finished by the end of December or early January. Thus, if the autumn rainy season is delayed or short-lived, the amount of cropland that can be put into production is reduced. The resulting contraction in acreage can be quite substantial. For example, during the 1980s, the area annually cultivated in cereals fluctuated by well over a million hectares in Morocco (Swearingen 1992). This fluctuation was roughly equivalent to a fourth of Morocco's average annual cultivated cereal area during that decade.

Having to wait for rain before ploughing not only reduces crop acreage, it also significantly lowers crop yields. The reason is that a large percentage of the total precipitation has already evaporated before seeds can be planted with the traditional system. The magnitude of this factor is suggested by field tests in Morocco. These tests have demonstrated that planting (with tractor and steel plough) *before* the arrival of the rainy season can improve crop yields by roughly 30 per cent – without any other changes in production methods (Cleaver 1982).

Moroccan farmers and government agronomists are well aware of the constraints of traditional technology. Indeed, soon after the start of the Protectorate, the French administration began to promote agricultural mechanisation in Morocco (Swearingen 1987a). As will be discussed, this policy has continued to the present – with mixed results.

DROUGHT: AN INCREASING HAZARD IN MOROCCO

Before the colonial period, agriculture in most of Morocco consisted of an extensive system of dryland cereal cultivation and animal husbandry (Bencherifa 1986 and 1988a, Swearingen 1987a). Most land was communally owned. Landholdings were usually dispersed to provide for equity and to help counter the risk of crop failure. Surplus grain from bountiful harvests was stockpiled to cover crop failures during drought years. Fallowing (periodically letting cropland lie idle) was widely practised. Fallowing both replenished soil moisture and helped to restore soil fertility.

French colonisation in Morocco (1912–56) dislodged peasants from much of the best land. Europeans acquired approximately 1 million ha (roughly 13 per cent) of Morocco's agricultural land. Exacerbating the effect of European colonisation was land concentration by Moroccan large landowners. During the colonial period, indigenous landowners allied with the French were able to amass sizeable landholdings. Approximately 7,500 Moroccans acquired 1.6 million ha, or 21 per cent of the arable total (Swearingen 1987a and 1987b).

Land concentration during the colonial period had two important consequences: First, as land was expropriated, most peasants became concentrated on a diminished amount of land. This reduced their ability to let part of their land lie fallow (Swearingen 1992, 1994, 1996). With reduced landholdings, many peasants had to put all of their land into cultivation (Bencherifa and Johnson 1990 and 1991).

Reduction of fallow significantly increased the potential for drought, because the primary purpose of fallowing in semiarid regions is to allow soil moisture to accumulate (WMO 1975). Approximately 20–25 per cent of the precipitation falling during the fallow year is retained in the soil. Thus, fallowing substantially boosts the available water supply for subsequent crop use. In low-rainfall areas, this soil moisture component is often the critical difference between a successful harvest and drought. With the reduction of fallowing, this buffer was lost, and vulnerability to drought increased. In addition, excessive land-use pressure caused soil fertility to decline. Declining yields, combined with reduced acreage, made it increasingly difficult for peasants to stockpile grain as a hedge against drought.

Second, large masses of peasants were dislodged to marginal land that was not sufficiently attractive for colonisation. The marginal areas were commonly characterised by a combination of poor soils, unfavourable slope, and deficient rainfall. Previously, most of this land had been used only for livestock grazing. Because of low rainfall levels, much of this land was more vulnerable to drought (Bencherifa 1996).

While land concentration was taking place, other significant changes were occurring. Health measures introduced by the French caused Moroccan death rates to plunge. Morocco's population expanded dramatically, with at least a three-fold increase during colonial times (and a seven-fold increase overall during the present century). This population explosion, combined with land expropriation, intensified pressure on remaining agricultural resources. Fallow was further reduced, peasant landholdings became increasingly fragmented, and more marginal land was put under cultivation.

Colonial agricultural policy, *per se*, also played a major role in deepening Morocco's vulnerability to drought. Between roughly 1915 and 1928, colonial authorities worked hard to increase cereal production for France (Swearingen 1985 and 1987a). Various subsidies and bonuses were offered to encourage cereal cultivation, especially cultivation by mech-

anised means. High market prices were also offered, particularly for wheat. Agricultural mechanisation and high crop prices enabled marginal areas to be profitably cultivated during higher-than-normal rainfall periods. Although Europeans and native Moroccan landowners were the primary beneficiaries of the subsidies and bonuses, lucrative crop prices also enticed peasant farmers into the cash economy and encouraged them to significantly expand their cereal acreage.

The colonial cereal policy produced the desired results. The area planted in cereals in Morocco grew from 1.9 million ha in 1918 to nearly 3 million ha in 1929 (Hoffherr 1932). This was an increase of roughly 60 per cent. However, there were hidden adverse effects. Part of the new cereal acreage came from the reduction of fallow, increasing the potential for drought. Much of the rest came from the extension of cultivation to marginal low-rainfall areas. The proportion of cropland in drought-prone areas steadily increased.

Contributing to Morocco's vulnerability to drought was the fact that the colonial policy favoured wheat production over barley. Previously, barley had been the predominant native cereal. However, wheat now became predominant, and consumer tastes changed to prefer this cereal. With the varieties at the time, the critical rainfall limits for barley were some 30 per cent less than those for wheat (Dresch 1956). In addition, barley ripens earlier and can be harvested significantly sooner than wheat, reducing the risk of late-season drought. In short, by substituting wheat for barley, the colonial wheat policy increased the potential for drought.

Following independence, Morocco gradually recovered ownership of colonial landholdings and engaged in limited land reform. However, much of the former colonial land passed into the hands of more prosperous Moroccan landowners (Swearingen 1987a). Most of the large landholdings acquired by Moroccan landowners during the colonial period were never subject to land reform.

For at least two decades following independence, the Moroccan government seriously neglected rainfed cereal production. As a result, because of population growth, Morocco was experiencing a severe food security crisis by the 1980s. The key symptoms of this crisis were declining per capita cereal production, ever-growing levels of cereal imports, heavy foreign indebtedness related to these imports, and massive food subsidy programmes. By the early 1980s, Morocco was importing more than a third of its cereal grains (FAO, various years) and at least 30 per cent of the population was experiencing mal-nutrition (World Bank 1989). The political implications of this crisis became clear when Morocco experienced serious food-related riots in 1981 and 1984.

Since the early to mid-1980s, Morocco has been engaged in major policy reforms, with the overriding objective of increasing dryland cereal production. Reforms have included privatisation of the state agri-cultural sector to improve efficiency and promotion of modern seed varieties and fertilisers. Of the reforms that have helped increase drought, however, the most significant involve changes in crop prices and pro-motion of mechanisation.

For many years following independence, the Moroccan government maintained tight control over producer prices of basic food crops. Prices for these crops, cereals in particular, were held artificially low until the 1980s. Indeed, for much of this period, crop prices were as low as a fourth to a half of what they would have been without government intervention (Cleaver 1982). The rationale was that low crop prices would enable the government to provide cheap food to its urban populations, helping to keep wages low, thereby assisting industrialisation and other urban development initiatives. An ulterior motive behind the cheap food strategy was to help prevent social unrest among the growing ranks of the urban poor. Unfortunately, low crop prices acted as a major disincentive to farmers (Swearingen 1987b).

Beginning in the late 1970s, fixed producer prices for cereals and other basic food crops were gradually raised. By the mid-1980s, the government had increased producer prices of barley and wheat to approximately twice world market levels. The stimulus effect was remarkable. Assisted by good weather, Moroccan pro-duction of cereals grew from an annual average of 3.8 million tonnes during the 1980–4 period to 6.6 million tonnes during both the 1985–90 and 1988–92 periods (FAO, various years). In part, this growth came from improved yields. In significant part, how-ever, it resulted from an expansion of cereal acreage. Average annual cereal acreage during the 1980–4

period was slightly more than 4.4 million ha – the average that had prevailed for roughly forty years. However, by the 1988–92 period, this average had expanded to 5.4 million ha, an increase of nearly a fourth (FAO, various years).

This increase resulted from the reduction of fallow and the extension of cereal cultivation to marginal range land. Encouraged by extremely high crop prices since the mid-1980s, Moroccan farmers have dra-matically reduced the acreage left in fallow. Because continuously cropped areas are not allowed to accumulate soil moisture, as they do when fallowed, the reduction of fallowing has effectively eliminated an input of water from the cropping system and substantially increased vulnerability to drought.

Besides reducing fallow since the mid-1980s, Moroccan farmers have also substantially extended cultivation of cereal crops within marginal low-rainfall areas. Government efforts to promote mechanisation have facilitated the expansion of cereal cultivation to drought-prone range land. Generous subsidies have enabled many more-prosperous farmers to fully mechanise their operations. Often, they gain extra income from ploughing the fields of neighbours who cannot afford farm machinery. In addition, ploughing services are provided by rural entrepreneurs who have purchased equipment to plough others' fields. Smaller or poorer landowners who cannot afford to purchase tractors and modern ploughs usually find it cheaper to hire ploughing services than hand labour. This, too, has contributed to the expansion of mechan-isation. As a result, the tractor and disc plough have converted large stretches of range land to cereal acreage. Some of these new lands normally receive as little as 200 mm of annual rainfall (Dresch 1986).

Within Morocco as a whole, well over half of the cereal acreage is now located in low rainfall zones receiving less than 400 mm per year. In the govern-ment's survey of agricultural areas during the 1983–4 season, it found that 51 per cent of the country's cereal crops were being grown in low-rainfall areas (AID 1986). Since then, the percentage of drought-prone land has continued to increase.

Ironically, the Moroccan government has pro-moted mechanisation as a way to help drought-proof the country's rain-fed cereal production (Swearingen 1987a and 1992). Expansion of mechanisation has helped overcome the traditional technology-related problem of reduced cereal acreage from sparse or late rains during the planting season. Modern farm machinery also allows for quick planting of late crops in the case of spring rain. In these ways, mechanisation has helped to mitigate the drought hazard. However, through facilitating cultivation of marginal areas, mechanisation is substantially increasing the drought hazard in Morocco.

FIELD RESEARCH TO ASSESS SOCIETAL RESPONSES TO INCREASING DROUGHT

To evaluate farmer responses to increasing vulnerability to drought, the authors organised an extensive field research project in Morocco during the early 1990s. A project team led by one of the authors (Bencherifa), which consisted of professors and graduate students from the Université Mohammed V in Rabat, intensively interviewed farmers about farming practices and drought coping strategies. These interviews were conducted in three different regions of Morocco: the Chaouia (near Benslimane), the Chichaoua (west of Marrakech), and the Northeast, usually referred to as Maroc oriental (near Taoucherfi).

The team purposely selected study sites that are differentiated by average precipitation levels. The Chaouia site is subhumid, Maroc oriental is semiarid, and the Chichaoua site is arid. In addition, they selected sites with different population-density levels in order to compare the effects of different levels of population pressure. The Chaouia site has relatively high population densities ($80–120/km^2$), as opposed to Maroc oriental and the Chichaoua, where densities are relatively low ($30–40/km^2$). Finally, researchers considered historical factors. Throughout Morocco, a long-term trend has been the transition from extensive nomadic pastoralism into settled, more intensive farming. An attempt was made to select sites with different histories of sedentarisation. The Chaouia has relatively old, settled agricultural communities, whereas sedentarisation is relatively recent in the Chichaoua and still in progress in Maroc oriental.

The research team surveyed a total of 335 households or production units: 194 in the Chaouia, 101 in the Chichaoua, and 40 in Maroc oriental. The survey consisted of a series of six questionnaire interviews, which were administered orally to the same household units over a period of approximately twenty months, from September 1992 to May 1994.

The interview protocol was intended to capture information about dynamic responses of producers to specific climate conditions, including both drought and abundant rainfall. By coincidence, the survey covered periods of highly variable weather. The agricultural seasons of 1991–2 and 1992–3 were characterised by extreme drought conditions (following the exceptionally rainy 1990–1 season, for which data were also gathered). By contrast, the 1993–4 season was unusually humid. These highly variable conditions allowed project researchers to observe, first-hand, farmer responses to both drought and abundant rainfall conditions as well as to interrogate these responses.

The first survey, conducted in September 1992, consisted of questions designed to gather fundamental socioeconomic data for each study site and production unit, such as household size and composition, land size and tenure, herd size and composition, grain and fodder storage facilities, and production resources (including machinery, draft animals, and equipment). Subsequent surveys addressed strategies and responses related to environmental conditions. These included land use, livestock management patterns, allocations of labour, and alternative income-generating activities. The successive interviews enabled the researchers to track both structural and process-related changes over the entire survey period.

In all three study areas, it quickly became clear that rainfall variability is well accounted for in production strategies. The historical backgrounds of the communities in these study areas provide a reservoir of memories that allows drought to be regarded as a normal rather than exceptional event. Farmers expect periodic drought and plan for it in their production strategies.

However, the survey also revealed that traditional drought coping strategies have been losing their effectiveness. They have been weakened by increasing population pressure and more intensive use of agricultural land. In addition, increasing inequalities between producers (a result of the unequal penetration of market-oriented farming practices) have increased the vulnerability of the poorest farming households to the impacts of drought.

From this extensive field survey, the research team was able to make several generalisations:

1 *Fallow has a critical role within the agropastoral system* Fallow has an essential, polyfunctional role in both crop production and livestock rearing. Fallowing is universally recognised by farmers to be a major determinant in increasing crop output. During the fallow year (as previously noted), fields not only accumulate soil moisture but also nitrogen, leading to increased yields when these fields are again cultivated. In addition, fallow is an essential part of livestock production. This is because farmers obtain fodder both from stubble remaining from the previous year's cultivation and from weeds that grow on fallowed fields. When fallow disappears from the agropastoral system because of demographic pressure, farmers become more vulnerable to drought. In all three regions, fallow has been steadily decreasing.

2 *Livestock raising is a basic drought coping strategy* In all three study regions, livestock play a key role in farmer survival strategies and are not merely a relic of the former pastoralist culture. Despite environmental and demographic differences, all three study regions are characterised by combined animal herding and cultivation. Rarely is a purely farming or a purely pastoralist production unit found in any of these regions. However, agropastoral systems in these regions differ considerably in terms of herd composition. Differences are due both to the availability of arable land versus range land (in part, the result of different levels of population pressure) and the quality of the range land. In the Chaouia, the most prevalent herd consists of cattle; in the Chichaoua, combined cattle and sheep; and in Maroc oriental, sheep and goats.

In all cases, because of strong market demand and relatively high prices, livestock production is regarded as the key way to maximise farm incomes during years of adequate or abundant rainfall. However, this integration of livestock production and cultivation increasingly is becoming dysfunctional in the case of multiyear droughts. This is because it relies heavily on the use of by-products from cultivation for animal fodder (hay, straw, stubble, and weeds from fields in fallow). Available fodder has largely disappeared from most farms following a single year of drought. Because of population pressure and the conversion of higher-quality range land to cultivation, the agropastoral system has become increasingly vulnerable.

3 *Farmers employ a traditional suite of other strategies to cope with drought* The traditional suite of drought coping strategies includes the following: (a) Grain and animal fodder are stockpiled using a variety of traditional storage systems, including *nader*, which are conical stacks of hay and straw, and *matmora*, which are underground grain storage pits. Stockpiling grain and fodder is an effective way to buffer drought's impacts, particularly if it does not continue for more than a single year. (b) Farmers reduce their herd size to a level that can be sustained through the drought. However, even in severe drought conditions, they attempt to maintain a small herd of breeding stock. This core herd allows a new start once rainy conditions return. Insistence on retaining a herd during drought might appear to be irrational (e.g., during severe drought, a day's worth of fodder per animal may be roughly equal to a fourth of the value of the animal). However, farmers recognise that they need to retain core breeding stock to quickly rebuild their herds when better conditions return. (c) Farmers often adopt a relatively mobile, pastoral-nomadic stock-raising pattern to seek grazing resources elsewhere if they run out of fodder on their own farms. (d) Farmers take advantage of rainfall whenever it occurs. If the normal cereal crops cannot be planted in fall or early winter because of drought, and if late-season rain occurs, they plant late crops (*mazouzi*) such as chickpeas or lentils. The multiyear drought during the first half of the 1990s revealed the limitations of these traditional drought coping strategies. As this drought continued through a second year, severe socioeconomic impacts were felt at the rural household level in most of northern Morocco.

4 *During the early 1990s, farmers progressively*

adopted new drought coping strategies Strategies adopted in response to the multiyear droughts during the early 1990s included the following: (a) Farmers almost universally adopted mechanisation wherever possible. When farm income did not allow them to purchase their own farm machinery, they hired ploughing services. Mechanisation of ploughing, in particular, has become a general drought coping strategy because it allows both for rapid planting following the first rains and for quick response to late rainfall. For example, in case of late spring rain after previously planted crops have failed, modern farm machinery allows for rapid replanting. Mechanisation also dramatically increases farm output during favourable rainfall years by allowing farmers to maximise the cultivated area. This increased production can be stockpiled as a hedge against future drought. As previously noted, however, mechanisation also has increased the negative impacts of drought. In short, it has helped agricultural production in Morocco become a 'high risks, high rewards' game. (b) Farmers also adopted fertiliser use as a way to increase production during good years to stockpile in preparation for future drought. (c) Farmers adopted intensive livestock raising of cattle in stables as a way to increase farm income. (d) Wherever possible, they attempted to develop irrigation through digging of new wells, use of motor-pumping, and use of diversion devices to concentrate runoff to their plots. (e) Farm families increasingly relied on off-farm income to supplement their farming resources. This strategy included temporary migration to urban areas by one or more family members during drought years. In the severe three-year drought in the Chichaoua during the early 1990s, about 80 per cent of a typical family's resources came from outside the farm.

5   *Vulnerability to drought is related to a variety of agronomic factors* Agronomic factors that help determine vulnerability to drought include the following: (a) The actual time of ploughing and planting. These operations need to be keyed to the timing of the first fall rains in the October to November period. Farmers need to make basic decisions about when to plant, which entails risks. Farmers who achieve optimal timing in planting are less likely to be affected by drought than farmers who plant either too early or too late. (b) The specific crops grown. Barley is the most drought-resistant cereal crop – thus its domination in arid and semiarid conditions. Hard and soft wheat are more sensitive to shortfalls of precipitation. (c) The preceding land use. Fallow, particularly ploughed fallow (*jachère travaillée*), helps to mitigate the effects of drought because of the accumulation of soil moisture in fallowed fields. (d) The amount and type of labour inputs. Labour inputs allocated for preparation of soils (most importantly, animal traction versus modern machinery) have a major influence on vulnerability to drought. As previously noted, mechanisation assists in rapid planting, enabling crops to benefit from rainfall before it evaporates from the soil. (e) The type of soil. Heavy soils are excellent agronomically when rainfall is above average. However, light soils have advantages during years of below-average rainfall.

6   *The socioeconomic impacts of drought are related to its duration* The duration of drought is a major determinant of its socioeconomic impacts. One year of drought following a normal rainfall year has far fewer negative impacts at the household level than is commonly assumed. This is because of the effectiveness of traditional drought coping strategies, including stockpiling of grain and fodder during higher-than-normal rainfall years. The general calculation among the farmers surveyed is that 'good years cover the bad years'. It is only when drought lasts more than a single year that its effects generally become critical at the household level. When drought lasts more than a single year, stockpiles of grain and fodder become exhausted, throwing household economies into crisis and threatening starvation for both livestock and people.

CONCLUSION

The extensive field survey confirmed that a highly vulnerable agricultural system has emerged in

Morocco. In all three regions surveyed, increasing population pressure and higher market demand have exerted pressure on local natural resources, resulting in the extension of cultivation to lower-rainfall areas and the reduction of fallowing. Data collected suggest that most Moroccan farmers can successfully endure only a single year of meteorological drought without significant hardship. If drought continues through a successive year or even longer, socioeconomic impacts become critical, even disastrous.

NOTE

1   This research was supported, in part, by grants from the Human Dimensions of Global Change initiative of the National Science Foundation and the Program in Science and Technology Cooperation of the US Agency for International Development.

REFERENCES

AID (1986) *Morocco: Country Development Strategy Statement (FYs 1987–1991). Annex C: The Agricultural Sector in Morocco: A Description*, unpublished report, Washington, DC: United States Agency for International Development.

Bencherifa, A. (1986) *Agropastoral Systems in Morocco. Cultural Ecology of Tradition and Change*, unpublished Ph.D. thesis, Clark University, Worcester, MA, USA.

—— (1988a) 'Agropastorale Organisationsformen im Atlantischen Marokko', *Die Erde* 119: 1–13.

—— (1988b) 'Le Monde rural marocain', in T. Agoumy and A. Bencherifa (eds), *La Grande Encyclopédie du Maroc. Géographie Humaine*, Cremona, Italy: GEP.

—— (1996) 'Is sedentarization of pastoral nomads causing desertification? The case of the Beni Guil of Eastern Morocco', in W. Swearingen and A. Bencherifa (eds), *The North African Environment at Risk*, Boulder, CO: Westview Press, pp. 117–30.

Bencherifa, A., and Johnson, D. (1990) 'Adaptation and intensification issues in pastoral systems. Observations in Morocco', in J.G. Galaty and D. Johnson (eds), *The World of Pastoralism*, New York: Guilford Press, pp. 394–416.

—— (1991) 'Resource management changes in the Middle Atlas Mountains: From extensive pastoralism to intensive cash production', *Mountain Research and Development* 3:183–94.

Bois, C. (1957) 'Années de disette, années d'abondance: Sécheresses et pluies au Maroc', *Revue Pour l'Etude des Calamités* 26, 35: 33–71.

Bowden, L. (1979) 'Development of present dryland farming systems', in A.E. Hall, G.H. Cannell, and H.W. Lawton (eds), *Agriculture in Semi-Arid Environments*, Berlin: Springer-Verlag.

Cleaver, K. (1982) *The Agricultural Development Experience of Algeria, Morocco and Tunisia: A Comparison of Strategies for Growth*, staff working paper 552, Washington, DC: World Bank.

Dresch, J. (1956) *L'Agriculture en Afrique du Nord*, Paris: Centre de Documentation Universitaire.

FAO (various years) *Production Yearbook*, Rome: Food and Agriculture Organization.

Hoffherr, R. (1932) *L'Economie Marocaine*, Paris: Recueil Sirey.

Lery, F. (1982) *L'Agriculture au Maghreb*, Paris: G.-P. Maisonneuve et Larose.

Morocco (1988) Consommation et Dépenses des Ménages 1984–85. Premiers Résultats. Vol.1, Rapport de Synthèse, Rabat: Direction de la Statistique.

Swearingen, W. (1985) 'In pursuit of the granary of Rome: France's wheat policy in Morocco, 1915–1931', *International Journal of Middle East Studies* 17: 347–63.

—— (1987a) *Moroccan Mirages: Agrarian Dreams and Deceptions, 1912–1986*, Princeton, NJ: Princeton University Press.

—— (1987b) 'Morocco's agricultural crisis', in I.W. Zartman (ed.), *The Political Economy Of Morocco*, New York: Praeger, pp. 159–72.

—— (1992) 'Drought hazard in Morocco', *Geographical Review* 82: 401–12.

—— (1994) 'Northwest Africa', in M.H. Glantz (ed.), *Drought Follows the Plow*, Cambridge: Cambridge University Press, pp. 117–33.

—— (1996) 'Is drought increasing in Northwest Africa? A historical analysis', in W. Swearingen, and A. Bencherifa (eds), *The North African Environment At Risk*, Boulder, CO: Westview Press, pp. 17–34.

WMO (1975) 'Drought and agriculture', *Technical Note* No. 138, Geneva: World Meteorological Organization.

World Bank (1989) *Social Indicators of Development*, Baltimore: Johns Hopkins University Press.

22

THE ECONOMIC DIMENSIONS OF DROUGHT IN SUB-SAHARAN AFRICA

Charlotte Benson and Edward Clay

INTRODUCTION[1]

Drought is Africa's principal type of natural disaster. Droughts, however defined, are frequent and severe in many countries as a result of the extreme rainfall variability in the extensive arid and semiarid areas of the continent and the poor moisture retention capacity of most African soils. Widely quoted estimates suggest that at least 60 per cent of sub-Saharan Africa is vulnerable to drought and perhaps 30 per cent is highly vulnerable (IFAD 1994). Moreover, parts of the Sahelian belt have been coping with an increasingly dry regime, with rainfall significantly below the norms of the period before the 1960s (Hulme 1992).

Yet, despite the potentially serious nonagricultural and economy-wide or macroeconomic impacts of drought, there has been little research to date in this area in sub-Saharan Africa, either *ex post* or *ex ante*. This appears to reflect the fact that drought has typically been perceived as a problem principally of agriculture and, particularly, food supply, with economies automatically and immediately restored to their longer-term growth paths upon the return of improved rains.

In contrast, the physical phenomenon of drought, rural household coping mechanisms or survival strategies,[2] and government and donor responses have been extensively studied. This body of research is important in contributing to a broader understanding of drought and to the design of more appropriate relief and rehabilitation responses. At the aggregate level, it also has important implications for the macroeconomic and financial impacts of drought. However, it does not directly address these latter issues.

In terms of drought relief and rehabilitation programmes, the economy-wide impacts of drought have also often been largely ignored. Sub-Saharan African governments and the international community have typically responded to drought events by mounting large-scale relief operations. These absorb a substantial share of resources both of the affected countries and the international community. For instance, 7.5 per cent of the UK aid programme was expended on the British response to the drought and famine crisis in Africa during the fiscal years 1984–5 and 1985–6 (Borton *et al.* 1988). The primary objective of such assistance invariably has been to minimise suffering and loss of human life. Food aid, much of it for use in direct, free distribution programmes within the affected areas, has bulked large in relief efforts. For example, some US$4 billion, including associated logistical costs, in food aid and government-organised commercial grain imports, was provided in response to the 1991/92 (i.e., July 1991 to June 1992) drought in southern Africa (Collins 1993). In contrast, the importance of nonfood items, such as water equipment, essential drugs, livestock feed, and agricultural inputs, has apparently been less fully recognised (Thompson 1993, DHA and SADC 1992). Moreover, efforts designed expressly to mitigate the impacts of droughts before their onset have generally been accorded even lower priority.

The response to the severe 1991/92 drought in southern Africa was somewhat different. Some members of the international donor community displayed a far greater willingness to provide balance-of-payments support in response to that crisis than to any previous drought.[3] This modified approach partly reflected concern about the threat to ongoing economic reform and structural adjustment programmes, in which donor agencies had committed significant resources. Indeed, the structural adjustment programmes implied that several of the affected economies were already being closely monitored, throwing the issue of the economic impact of droughts into sharper focus than was perhaps the case in earlier droughts in the Sahel and the Horn of Africa. They also underscored the need for a higher level of contingency planning. Nevertheless, many other donors continued to overlook or give only limited attention to the economy-wide impacts of the drought – for instance, on foreign-exchange availability and government expenditures.

Scope of chapter

This chapter presents the findings of an exploratory study to examine the macroeconomic and financial impacts of drought in sub-Saharan Africa in more detail, drawing on evidence from a range of countries with varying agroecological zones and economic structures.[4] The chapter focuses particularly on the factors determining an economy's vulnerability to drought and its scope for adaptive behaviour, both *ex ante* and *ex post*, with the broader objective of contributing to a deeper understanding of the consequences of drought and the formulation of more appropriate and effective drought contingency planning and responses.

There are considerable methodological difficulties in isolating the impact of a particular exogenous shock, such as drought, from underlying trends and other internal and external factors influencing economic performance, such as movements in prices of major imports and exports, changes in government economic policy, booms and slumps in the world economy, or effects of civil or international conflict. In view of such constraints, this chapter shows how it is possible to adopt an eclectic approach, using a mixture of quantitative and qualitative analysis. The quantitative analysis is partial, involving a combination of regression analysis of relationships between economic aggregates and variability in rainfall and an examination of movements around trends, 'before and after' impacts, and forecasts versus actual performance of key economic indicators.

POTENTIAL IMPACTS OF DROUGHT ON SUB-SAHARAN AFRICAN ECONOMIES

A preliminary review of the impacts of drought in Africa suggests that the interactions between drought shocks and the economy are complex, rather than direct and straightforward. But before exploring that complexity, a working definition of drought that focuses on economic rather than physical or social impacts is required. These conceptual issues are also considered in this section. The main factors determining the nature of the interaction between drought and the economy also need to be taken into account. Those concerning the role of the physical environment, the financial system, and public policy are discussed before exploring the relationship between economic structure and drought in more detail in the following section.

An economic definition of drought

This chapter adopts a probabilistic concept of drought, encapsulating concepts of hydrological, meteorological, agricultural, and social dimensions to postulate an economic definition. *Meteorological drought* has been defined as a 'reduction in rainfall supply compared with a specified average condition over some specified period' (Hulme 1995). In an African context, this is typically a period of a year or more. *Hydrological drought* pertains to the impact of a reduction in precipitation on surface or subsurface water levels, thus possibly lagging behind periods of agricultural or meteorological drought (Wilhite 1993). *Agricultural drought* is defined as a reduction in moisture availability below the optimum level required by a crop during different stages of its growth cycle, resulting in impaired growth and reduced yields.[5] Finally, *social drought* relates to the impact of drought on human activities, including indirect as well as direct impacts.

As with agricultural and social definitions, an economic drought concerns the impacts of precipitation-related reductions in water availability on productive activities, including the provision of water for human consumption, rather than water availability *per se*. Recurrent, predictable seasonally low levels or low mean rainfall in arid areas do not constitute drought. Such events are associated with well-established, predictable climatological patterns that occur with a high degree of probability, say 80 per cent. Thus, these are phenomena to which local economies have adapted by selecting less water-intensive types of agricultural and nonagricultural activities and by investing in water storage to smooth seasonal variations in supply.

An economic drought, by contrast, involves low rainfall that is outside the normal, expected parameters with which an economy is equipped to cope. Such an event typically results in sharp reductions in agricultural output, related productive activity, and employment. In turn, this is likely to lead to lower agricultural export earnings and other losses associated with a decline in rural income, reduced consumption and investment, and destocking. Meteorological drought may also result in hydrological conditions that have a direct adverse impact not only on irrigated agriculture but also on nonagricultural production, including hydroelectric power generation (which is an increasingly important source of energy in a number of African countries) and certain industrial processes, as well as human water supply. Droughts have additional potential multiplier effects on the monetary economy: the rate of inflation, interest rates, credit availability, levels of savings, the government budget deficit, and external debt stocks. Indeed, the combination of these direct impacts, indirect linkages, and multiplier effects implies that the economy-wide consequences of a drought may be considerable.

The probabilistic nature of drought as an economic phenomenon should be stressed for a number of reasons. First, it does not involve a simple technical relationship that can be characterised with any certainty. It is contingent on the interaction of a meteorological event or anomaly with the changing or dynamic conditions of the economy. The impact depends partly on the expectations of the various economic enterprises, ranging from largely self-provisioning, peasant households to large private and public corporations, which are affected by events, and also the immediate economic conditions, which, in turn, are determined by a number of other factors. These considerations suggest a working definition of an economic drought as a meteorological anomaly or

extreme event of intensity and/or duration outside the normal range of events, which enterprises and public regulatory bodies have taken into account in their economic decisions, and which therefore results in unanticipated, usually negative, impacts on production and the wider economy.

According to this definition, a drought can therefore be viewed as a form of internal supply-side shock – that is, as a severe disturbance that has direct, nonmarginal impacts on the real domestic economy.

Environmental diversity and the rural economy

As already indicated, from an economic perspective, a country's drought vulnerability is not approximately synonymous with that of its aridity. Countries with a higher proportion of arid lands unsuited to rain-fed cereal and other agricultural production are likely to experience frequent and severe droughts, precluding significant rain-fed production. However, communities in such countries are also likely to have well-developed coping mechanisms, having adapted to the marginal rainfall conditions through appropriate investments, water resource management, and agricultural practices over time. In contrast, predominantly semiarid countries with largely rain-fed agricultural sectors are likely to experience nationwide droughts only as an extreme event, perhaps as in the case of Zimbabwe and Zambia in 1991/92. Other economies again, including possibly Ethiopia and Kenya, are, according to historical record, highly unlikely to experience nationwide droughts affecting most of their agricultural economy at all. Socio-economic systems in these latter two categories of country are less well equipped to cope with droughts, implying that they may, in fact, have a larger economic impact in less drought-prone regions. This view of adaptation introduces the possibility of non-linearities, whereby only extreme, more improbable drought events involve significant economy-wide impacts.

Longer-term climatic trends

Interseasonal or annual fluctuations in levels of precipitation may fluctuate around particular trends or cyclical patterns in the longer term, rather than remaining within certain parameters. The extent of economic vulnerability to drought is therefore partly dependent on the extent to which such patterns and trends are both recognised and taken into account by various economic agents and decision makers.

The various regions of Africa have displayed differing climatic trends over the period since decolonisation – i.e., broadly since the early 1960s. Figure 22.1 compares three regions: the Sahel, east Africa, and southeast Africa.[6] The Sahel has experienced a significant decline in average rainfall levels, defined in terms of a comparison between the three decades before and after 1960. In contrast, for more than a century, the southeast African region of southern summer rainfall has experienced a quasi 18–20 year cycle of one relatively wet and one relatively drier decade (Tyson and Dyer 1978). Meanwhile, the east African region is not affected by either significant trends or cyclical patterns in rainfall regime.

The distinct regional climatic differences have potential implications for agriculture, water management (more generally), and the possible economic consequences of drought. In some sense, the stationary if random rainfall patterns of east Africa are the simplest because the probability distribution of monthly and annual levels of precipitation can be directly calculated from historical records. Farmers, water sector managers, and others have a good grasp of the risks of drought based on their individual experience (assuming little impact of environmental degradation) and thus, from a longer-term perspective, are able to make rational cropping and other decisions based on approximately complete information. In contrast, the Sahelian economies have, in effect, been confronted with an increasingly unfavourable environment that requires and rewards adaptation through risk-reducing strategies in the rural economic systems.[7] Meanwhile, the quasi-cycles of southeastern Africa may pose particularly difficult problems in making appropriate hazard management and investment decisions. Decisions based on rainfall or hydrological information such as river flows or recharge of aquifers for only part of one or more full cycles (ten to fifteen or thirty years), or which assume random distribution of drought years rather than taking into account the actual rainfall cycle, could involve greater than intended exposure to drought hazards. The assessment of

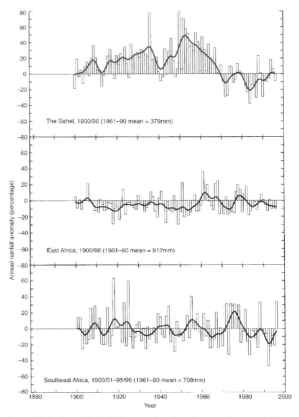

Figure 22.1 Annual rainfall anomalies for three regions in Africa from 1990 to 1996: the Sahel, east Africa, and southeast Africa. The regions are defined in Hulme (1995).

Notes: The annual anomalies are calculated as per cent departures from the 1961–90 average annual rainfall. The respective mean annual 1961–90 rainfall for each region is indicated. The smooth curve results from applying to the annual values a ten-point low-pass Gaussian filter which emphasises variations on time scales of ten years or more. The data derive from the global gridded rainfall data set held by the Climatic Research Unit. The rainfall year for southeast Africa is from July to June

Source: Mike Hulme, Climatic Research Unit, University of East Anglia, Norwich

drought risk in southern Africa is further complicated by as yet highly tentative indications at the level of regional analysis of small future reductions in mean annual rainfall and an associated increase in the expected frequency of extreme events such as the 'one in fifty year' drought of 1991/92 (Hulme 1996).

Role of financial systems

The evolution of a country's financial systems is not linked in any simple linear way to levels of GDP. However, the size and structure of the private financial sector, involving banks, other intermediaries, and elements of a private capital market, will have potentially significant implications for the way an economy responds to drought and other economic shocks and the types of adaptive behaviour available to both individual households and public authorities. Following a drought shock, both demand for agricultural credit and defaults on previous loans are likely to rise. In countries where extensive formal savings institutions for smaller savers exist, substantial internal flows of resources may occur, as those in less-affected areas transfer remittances to their relatives in greater need, effectively spreading the household impacts of drought. For example, the transfer of remittances from urban- to rural-based relatives was also facilitated by the well-articulated system for small savings provided by the Post Office Savings Bank in Zimbabwe in the aftermath of the 1991/92 drought. Affected enterprises are likely to face reductions in their financial balances and therefore to seek further loans or extended credit. Increased public sector budgetary pressures and parallel pressures on the public foreign-exchange account due to increased public sector imports could also place additional strains on the financial system. Increased pressure on financial markets may be partly offset by reduced rates of investment borrowing and by possible declines in private sector demand for imported raw materials and intermediate goods. However, there is likely to be some remaining financial gap that, depending on how it is met, will have varying implications for the impact of the drought on the economy.

Role of public policy

At independence, most African economies inherited public enterprises with responsibility for agricultural marketing, electricity supply, water supply, waste disposal, and transport. Public institutions were also heavily involved in formal human resource development and social welfare provision through education, health, and other social services. Public sector involvement in both agricultural and nonagricultural sectors increased in the early post-colonial period, bringing many problems of economic efficiency and public finance which are now widely recognised. Subsequent economic reforms and the growth of both informal and regulated sectors have further modified, and sometimes reduced, the role of the public sector in the production and distribution of goods and the provision of public services. These gradual changes imply that the role of the public service, and thus the effects of a drought shock, have varied both over time and between countries. For example, parastatal marketing depends to differing and changing degrees on large-scale commercial production and the surpluses of small-scale self-provisioning peasant farmers. The effects of drought shocks may be amplified where marketing is dependent on the production surpluses of small-scale farmers, as discussed in the next section.

To summarise, this preliminary review indicates that the economic implications of a drought are dependent on a complex set of environmental and economy-specific factors. Indeed, as discussed in further detail below, in the early stages of development an economy may actually become more vulnerable to drought and therefore potentially more severely affected by drought shocks.

ECONOMIC STRUCTURE AND THE IMPACT OF DROUGHT

In developing a conceptual framework for analysing drought shocks, it is useful to differentiate between four types of economy in terms of the role of rain-fed and irrigated agriculture, intersectoral linkages in production and final expenditure, intensity of water usage, levels of gross domestic product (GDP) per capita, and natural resource endowments:[8]

1 *Simple economies* – predominantly rain-fed agricultural and livestock semisubsistence economies with a limited functioning infrastructure, low levels of per capita income, and high levels of self-provisioning in the rural population. To the extent that a modern sector exists, there are few links between this and the agricultural sector. Commodity and factor markets may be incomplete and poorly integrated, at least at a national level. These characteristics may be further

exaggerated where conflict results in a disarticulation or loss of economic complexity in both the real and monetary systems (Clay 1998).

2 *Intermediate economies* – more diversified economies with economic growth occurring via the development of labour-intensive, low-technology manufacturing sectors, typically dependent on a combination of domestically produced renewable natural resources and imported inputs and capital equipment, but with natural resources still representing a relatively important part of export earnings.

3 *Complex economies* – developed economies with a relatively small agricultural sector and proportionately small forward and backward linkages between the agricultural sector and other water-intensive activities and the rest of the economy. As yet, no sub-Saharan African country could be viewed unambiguously as a complex economy.

4 *Dualistic economies with large extractive minerals sectors* – economies consisting of a 'traditional' low (labour) productivity rural economy, entailing a high level of self-provisioning, which coexists with a 'modern' economy involving an export-oriented sector closely integrated with a service sector but which is relatively immune to performance in other sectors. Drought will affect only part of a dualistic economy unless the export-oriented extractive sector is water-intensive. Such dualism is a characteristic feature of many sub-Saharan African economies, including drought-prone Botswana, Namibia, and Niger, as well as South Africa, which has the highest per capita GDP in the region.

In reality, this typology is highly simplified, and specific structural characteristics are not unique to economies lying within a particular category. For example, Australia is a complex economy with a large mineral sector while India and Argentina, although falling into the second category, have substantial industrial sectors. Regional dimensions can also be important. For instance, the Namibian economy is not particularly vulnerable to the direct impacts of drought. However, it is being closely integrated into the wider South African Development Corporation (SADC) region, where drought can have profound impacts with multiplier implications for Namibia.

Another major caveat of the typology is that it ignores the fact that economies are dynamic, rather than static, entities and that the impact of a particular drought is therefore partly time-dependent. In particular, economic restructuring, financial deepening, urbanisation, and increasing regional integration have all been important trends in sub-Saharan Africa in recent years and, as already indicated, have played a role in altering the nature of the economic impact of droughts. Conflict also involves a loss of complexity, whereas with peace and rehabilitation, countries acquire more complex characteristics. Nevertheless, the typology is useful in focusing attention on how drought shocks interact with economies differentiated by their economic structures.

The initial direct or physical effects of drought on the productive sector are similar regardless of the type of economy, although the relative and absolute magnitude of each shock will depend on specific country characteristics. A decline in rainfall has an initial adverse impact on the agricultural and livestock sectors, hydroelectric power generation, and other water-intensive activities. Domestic availability of water is also restricted, with implications for health and household activities, including the time required to collect water. Increased competition for more limited water resources may also occur, possibly requiring important policy decisions (for example, on the relative allocation of water resources to hydroelectric power generation and irrigation).

Droughts then have a range of second- (and subsequent) round effects, the broad schema of which is indicated in Figure 22.2.[9] However, the precise nature and magnitude of these impacts depends on particular country circumstances, as discussed in further detail below.

Simple economies

The economic impact of drought is largely felt via its direct impact on the agricultural sector. This is reflected in substantial percentage declines in GDP, agricultural exports, and employment opportunities as well as widespread sale of assets. Severe drought also results in widespread nutritional stress, higher morbidity, and, possibly, higher mortality. However, because of weak intersectoral linkages, a high degree

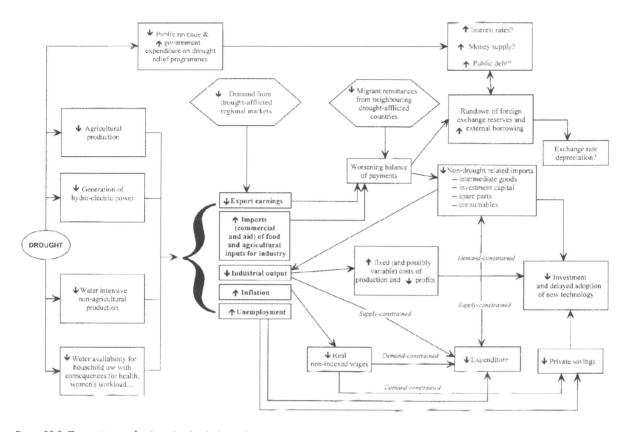

Figure 22.2 Transmission of a drought shock through an economy
Source: Benson and Clay 1998

of self-provisioning, relatively small nonagricultural sectors, and (often) poor transport infrastructure, the multiplier effect through the rest of the economy is fairly limited, largely occurring through a decline in consumer expenditure. The effects of drought are likely to be concentrated in the rural economy.

Recovery is relatively fast. Assuming the timely availability of sufficient seed, draught animals or agricultural machinery, other agricultural inputs and tools, and predominantly annual cultivation cycles, the restoration of good rains can restore levels of GDP to predrought levels almost immediately, although recovery will be slower in the cases of livestock production and sugar cane, coffee, and other crops with a multiyear production cycle. However, drought may leave a legacy of higher levels of internal and external indebtedness, larger balance-of-payments deficits, and reduced and less equitably

distributed capital assets, such as livestock and household items.

Intermediate economies

The effects of drought are diffused more widely through the economy, reflecting greater overall integration and stronger intersectoral linkages than displayed in simple economies. Droughts affect the (larger) manufacturing sector as well as the agricultural and livestock sectors as lower domestic production of agroprocessing inputs reduces nonagricultural production whilst forcing up the cost of agro-inputs. Intermediate goods are also likely to form a larger share in total imports, implying that any drought-related import squeeze will have additional multiplier implications for domestic production. Consumer purchasing power is also likely to decline because of some combination of higher food prices, job losses in both agricultural and nonagricultural industries,[10] nominal wage freezes, and the reduced availability and higher cost of credit (see below). Falling markets, rising input costs, and, possibly, higher interest rates can result in delayed investment in new capital and technology, with longer-term growth implications.

In the aftermath of a drought, as in a simple economy, the agricultural sector will recover relatively quickly. However, recovery of the manufacturing sector may be slower because of the combined impacts of various difficulties such as continued input shortages, in turn reflecting ongoing foreign exchange problems and thus continued shortages of imported inputs, and only a slow pickup in demand (see Box 22.1).

The structure of financial sectors and government financial policy are also likely to be more important in shaping the impact of a drought shock than in a simpler economy. The government is likely to meet a larger share of the costs of the relief efforts itself, rather than relying almost entirely on international grant assistance. This will be financed by some combination of the reallocation of planned expenditure, government borrowing, and monetary expansion, with various indirect longer-term implications, as discussed in further detail below. Large interannual fluctuations in economic performance, such as drought can cause, could also create economic management difficulties – e.g., in controlling public expenditure. For example, the transfer of remittances from urban to rural-based members of households was facilitated by the well-articulated system for small savings in Zimbabwe in the aftermath of the 1991/92 drought. This mitigated the impact of the drought on the rural areas but at the same time effectively spread its impact

---

BOX 22.1   IMPACT OF DROUGHT ON THE MANUFACTURING SECTOR IN ZIMBABWE

Largely as a result of the 1991/92 drought, Zimbabwean manufacturing GDP declined by 9.5 per cent in 1992. The drought alone led to a minimum 25 per cent reduction in the volume of manufacturing output, a 6 per cent fall in manufacturing export earnings, and a 2 per cent reduction in total export receipts. The textiles (including cotton ginning), clothing and footwear, nonmetallic mineral product, metal and metal product, and transport equipment subsectors were particularly severely affected. The drought affected the manufacturing sector in a variety of ways:

Water shortages – most municipalities imposed rationing, with particularly severe water shortages experienced in the cities of Mutare, Chegutu, and Bulawayo.

Electricity shortages – reduced hydroelectric production resulted in load-shedding, rationing, and increased electricity tariffs, affecting the whole country. Load-shedding imposed particular costs on subsectors with batch or continuous processing whilst the system of electricity rationing imposed effectively discriminated against smaller manufacturers.

Input supply difficulties – shortages of agricultural inputs to the manufacturing sector were experienced, with adverse implications for most agroprocessors. However, larger food processing companies, such as grain millers, increased production as imports were channelled through urban plants rather than processed in smaller rural plants. Similarly, the meat processing industry faced increased supply of inputs as the drought forced up slaughtering rates.

Reductions in demand – demand for both agricultural inputs and other basic consumer goods, such as clothing and footwear, fell, in part because of the combined contractionary effects of the drought and an ongoing structural adjustment programme, as well as increased penetration of the Zimbabwean market by competitive imports following recent trade liberalisation.

Macroeconomic conditions – higher government domestic borrowing (in part to finance drought-related expenditure), higher rates of inflation, and higher nominal interest rates created an unfavourable macroeconomic operating environment. Subsectors where working capital requirements had increased sharply because of parastatal price rises (e.g., steel) were particularly severely affected.

Partly as a consequence of the drought, the International Finance Corporation identified the Zimbabwe Stock Market as the worst performer of fifty-four world stock markets in 1992, with a 62 per cent decline in value. Although increased costs of production were partly passed on to consumers, manufacturers faced a deterioration in their financial viability.

(Robinson 1993)

more widely, including into urban areas as senders of remittances were left with reduced income themselves (Hicks 1993).

Finally, although the extent of absolute poverty is likely to be lower in an intermediate than in a simpler economy and the nature of household vulnerability to drought is likely to have changed, absolute poverty may not necessarily be much reduced. There will still be some subsistence farming. Furthermore, vulnerability is not solely dependent on levels of poverty in nondrought years but also on the ability of households to cope with drought and other adverse conditions. Development involves some degree of specialisation, a decline in self-provisioning, and fuller integration into markets and financial systems, altering but not necessarily reducing a household's vulnerability to drought (Clay 1998).

Complex economies

The impacts of a drought are relatively easily absorbed in more complex economies, in part reflecting the typically smaller contribution of the agricultural sector to GDP, exports, and employment. Water resources are also likely to be better managed. In addition, complex economies are typically more open and have fewer foreign exchange constraints, facilitating the import of normally domestically sourced items in the event of a drought without forcing a decline in other imports. Real exchange rates may appreciate marginally as the price of agricultural commodities increases, but this will probably be temporary.

Average per capita incomes are higher and food items account for a smaller percentage share in total household expenditure, implying that even if prices of drought-affected food products rise, the purchasing power of most groups will not be significantly altered. Thus, the scale and cost of relief programmes will be limited, avoiding any substantial increase in government domestic or external borrowing. However, that small segment of the population that is affected – largely farmers in drought-affected areas – may be severely hurt in terms of loss of income, assets, and savings.[11]

Dualistic economies with large extractive sectors

Some drought-prone economies in sub-Saharan Africa exhibit a high degree of dualism, with a large capital-intensive extractive sector that features significantly in the trade account but which is weakly linked with other sectors of the economy. Indeed, a number of countries have achieved relatively high per capita levels of GDP through the development of these extractive sectors.

Unless the extractive sector is water-intensive and fails through lack of investment or poor management to insulate itself from variable water supply, the economic impact of drought in such economies is likely to be limited to variability in the agricultural sector with limited multiplier effects. Thus the macroeconomic impact of drought appears small, similar to that in a complex economy. But this impression is deceptive, overlooking the profound impacts within the agricultural sector (on which the majority of the population remains dependent). The potential impacts in terms of intensified food insecurity, water-related health risks, and loss of livelihoods in the agricultural sector are considerable. However, in contrast to simple economies, the broad revenue base and the scope for maintaining financial stability provided by taxing the extractive sector offer considerable opportunity for countervailing measures.[12]

The 'inverted U' hypothesis

In summary, features typical of a simple economy effectively contain the economic effects of drought, with the impact largely felt at the rural household level and within the informal economy. As an economy develops, with diversification into manufacture of technologically simple products using domestically produced raw materials, the growth of financial and commodity markets, and an expansion of the monetised consumption base and nonagricultural sectors, its economic vulnerability to drought shocks initially increases. Agricultural earnings increasingly take the form of cash as households grow a smaller proportion of crops for their own consumption, again spreading the impact of any downturn in the economy through the economy. The accompanying specialisation of labour and the breakdown of community and extended family ties may also reduce the ability of households to adapt to temporary shocks.

In the later stages of development, vulnerability to

drought shocks then declines again as the agricultural sector becomes decreasingly important both in GDP and as a source of employment, also implying weaker forward and backward linkages between the agricultural sector and the rest of the economy. Such economies are also relatively more open and do not face major foreign exchange constraints, ensuring that any domestic shortfalls can be met through imports without affecting other trade flows.

This conceptualisation of the interaction of drought and economic structure suggests an 'inverted U'-shaped relationship between the macroeconomic impacts of drought and the overall level of economic development of a country.[13] In other words, the economic impact of drought increases during the earlier stages of development before declining as an economy becomes more developed rather than, as conventionally assumed, continuously declining as an economy gradually becomes increasingly complex. However, as also indicated, a country's resource endowment, including its ecological diversity and mineral and water resource base, also influences the impact of a drought shock, potentially overriding any relationship between its level of development and the economic impacts of drought.[14]

The temporal dimensions of drought also vary between economies at intermediate stages of development and simpler, less complex economies. Basically, economic recovery in an agrarian rain-fed economy is largely dependent on the return of good rains and the timely and adequate provision of agricultural inputs. However, recovery in a more diversified developing economy is slower, requiring increased supplies of inputs to industries and the recovery of both effective demand and credit markets. This difference in the dynamics of drought shocks is captured by considering changes in real GDP attributable to changes in agricultural GDP against changes in GDP for major southern African economies between 1991 and 1993 (Figure 22.3).[15] In both Zimbabwe and South Africa, nonagricultural sectors continued to depress GDP in 1993 despite the more rapid recovery of agricultural output following the return of more favourable rains. In contrast, in the less complex economies of Malawi and Zambia, the agricultural sector accounted almost entirely for fluctuations in overall GDP, ensuring an immediate recovery of GDP as well as agricultural

GDP in 1993. Meanwhile, Namibia's performance demonstrates how the agricultural sector may have relatively little impact on overall GDP in a dualistic economy with a large extractive sector.

THE WIDER ECONOMIC IMPACTS OF DROUGHT: EVIDENCE FROM SIX SUB-SAHARAN AFRICAN ECONOMIES

The evidence presented below provides a more in-depth analysis of the economic impacts of drought, focusing particularly on the relationships between rainfall variability and macroeconomic and sectoral performance and drawing on evidence from Burkina Faso, Ethiopia, Kenya, Senegal, Zambia, and Zimbabwe. The factors determining economic sensitivity to drought shocks, the impact of drought shocks on trade and external debt, and the implications of drought for economic and development planning are examined. The budgetary impacts of drought and the particularly complex issues raised by droughts which coincide with the implementation of structural adjustment programmes are then explored at some length.

As will be seen, the six countries illustrate how a range of structural conditions interact with large differences in resource endowments to determine the economy-wide impact of a drought. These impacts broadly correspond to those suggested by the typology proposed above. Two of the economies, Burkina Faso and Ethiopia, can be stylised as simple economies. In both countries, as in many other sub-Saharan African countries, the agricultural sector forms a particularly substantial part of GDP, and the population is overwhelmingly rural. Kenya lies somewhere on the margin between a simple and intermediate economy, with an important agricultural sector as well as a relatively large services sector. Almost two-thirds of micro-enterprises (including forestry and textiles) are directly based on agriculture (Block and Timmer 1994), but the manufacturing sector is still relatively small. Senegal, the one lower-middle-income country considered, also has some characteristics of an intermediate economy, with relatively strong intersectoral linkages reflecting past French colonial policy. Zimbabwe, which has one of the more developed manufacturing sectors in sub-Saharan Africa, is the only economy that can be unambiguously classified as

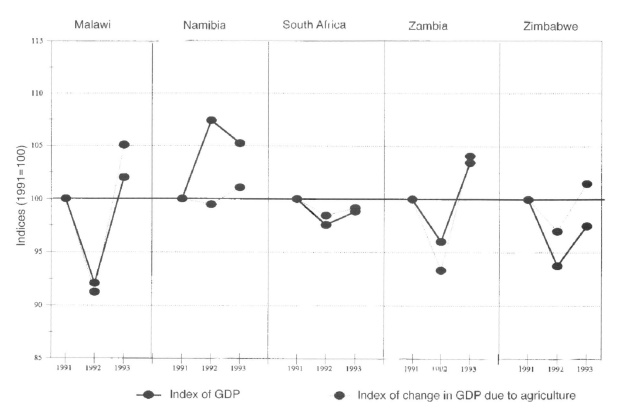

Figure 22.3 Economic performance and the 1991/92 drought in southern Africa (indices, 1991 = 100)
Source: Benson and Clay 1998

an intermediate economy. Zambia is more dualistic, with historically heavy dependence on copper production, particularly as a source of export earnings.

Economic sensitivity to drought

The sensitivity of sectoral economic performance to droughts since the early 1970s was examined quantitatively using ordinary least squares regression analysis. For each country, a drought series was constructed based either on rainfall or yields of major crops, depending on the availability of data for the former. This series was regressed against sectoral growth and the null hypothesis of no correlation between drought and sectoral performance tested.[16]

The regression results indicate that GDP and agricultural GDP in all six case study economies show some sensitivity to drought, with the statistically most significant results found for Ethiopia, Senegal, and

Zimbabwe. In terms of nonagricultural GDP, drought has had the least impact in proportional terms in the two lowest-income countries, Burkina Faso and Ethiopia. These results are broadly consistent with an 'inverted U' rather than an inverse relationship between drought vulnerability and the stage of economic development of a country. The behaviour of the Zambian economy also supports the hypothesis that a dualistic economy is partly cushioned from the impact of drought by the non-water-intensive extractive sector.[17] The one ambiguous case is Kenya, for which sectoral performance before the 1993 drought was only weakly correlated with rainfall, despite strong forward linkages between the agricultural and manufacturing sectors. Movements in international commodity prices and possibly the country's diverse agro-ecology appear to explain this finding (see below).[18]

Relatively speedy recovery was indicated by the generally statistically insignificant correlation between economic performance and lagged drought variables in the case study countries. However, there is some qualitative evidence that overall rates of recovery from a drought shock may be slower in relatively more complex economies, due to the initially greater impact of drought on the industrial sector, which is slower to recover than the agricultural sector. For example, following the 1991/92 drought, Zimbabwe's agricultural sector bounced back relatively rapidly in 1992–3, encouraged by good rains, incentive prices, and a massive free-input programme for small farmers. Maize production alone rose to its highest level since 1988. In contrast, the performance of the nonagricultural sector remained sluggish, depressed by lack of demand, high nominal interest rates, and tight credit conditions, which were in part a consequence of the drought (Benson 1998). Whereas agricultural GDP grew by 48 per cent, manufacturing output declined by 8.3 per cent in 1993 to its lowest level in real value terms since 1987, and overall GDP rose by only 0.9 per cent. This pattern of slower recovery in the industrial sector was paralleled in other economies affected by the 1991/92 drought, particularly Malawi, Zambia, and South Africa (Figure 22.3).

The case studies also indicate various ways in which the process of development may, as suggested by the country typology, make an economy more sensitive to the impact of drought. In Ethiopia, the small nonagricultural economy has been relatively drought insensitive to date, reflecting the low level of development and a war economy that discouraged market integration. The predominance of subsistence households, producing almost entirely for on-farm consumption, combined with poor market development and vertical sectoral integration has implied that impacts of drought have been largely contained within the rural economy and the immediately affected region. Poor vertical integration, in turn, reflects weak infrastructure, mountainous terrain increasing transport costs even further, and a very small domestic market. However, the wider Ethiopian economy is likely to become more vulnerable to drought as infrastructure is strengthened, integrating the economy nationally; as intersectoral linkages are developed; and as self-provisioning of rural households declines and households become increasingly drawn into monetised activities.

In the longer term, the impacts of drought are partly mitigated to the extent that drought-induced recessions are offset by higher growth during the recovery phase. However, some economic opportunities may be foregone – for example, to the extent that droughts distort investment portfolios and restrict rates of capital accumulation. Any such effects may be exacerbated if economic development objectives are set aside for the duration of a drought, weakening the links between relief and development as well as increasing the longer-term impacts. Indeed, in the most simple economies, such as Burkina Faso and Ethiopia, drought is an underlying long-term obstacle to growth rather than a short-term setback in growth rates and may even be emerging as an increasing impediment to development.

Drought and trade

One of the most serious shorter-term impacts of drought concerns its impact on merchandise trade and the balance of payments more broadly. The experience of the six case study countries indicates substantial increases in cereal imports during and in the aftermath of severe drought years. Such imports appear to have constrained noncereal imports, at least in the case of Burkina Faso. Demand for imports of capital and intermediate goods may also be dampened, as, for example, in Zimbabwe in 1992, to some extent easing the pressure on the balance of payments.

There are less clearly defined trends for exports, partly reflecting some lag between the production and export of a good. Nevertheless, examination of agricultural export data reveals some evidence of lower export earnings. The export destination may also be concerned about the drought-related increased possibility of disease in livestock, potentially resulting in reduced access to certain export markets for several years. In countries operating fixed exchange rates, a drought-related increase in the rate of domestic inflation can also imply a real appreciation of the exchange rate, discouraging exports and placing additional strains on foreign reserves. However, export earnings may be partly boosted to the extent that domestic demand declines and surplus supply is exported. For example, in Zimbabwe in 1992, producers of textiles, footwear, and furniture sought increased export outlets.

The policy environment is also important in determining the impact of drought on the external sector. Again in the case of Zimbabwe, the gradual build-up in stocks of imported inputs in 1990 and 1991, in turn reflecting uncertainty about the continuation of a more liberal import regime and speculation created by the unstable exchange rate, meant that producers entered the drought period with considerable inputs already in stock.

However, there is a danger inherent in placing too much emphasis on drought or, indeed, any form of adverse exogenous shock as the key factors determining economic performance. Such explanations of weak performance can serve to obscure more fundamental structural problems. For example, the 1982–4 drought in Zimbabwe occurred during a period of severe balance-of-payments difficulties. According to Davies (1992), the government initially viewed these difficulties as transitory, resulting from the drought. Rather than address more fundamental problems, a short-term quick-fix solution in the form of import controls was therefore employed to cope with immediate foreign exchange difficulties.

External and internal factors

The case study countries also indicate a number of externally determined and domestic factors that interact with rainfall variability to partly determine the extent and intensity of the economic impacts of a drought shock, irrespective of the type of economy.

Prevailing economic conditions

Perhaps most obviously, a weakened economy enhances the impact of drought, as demonstrated by the 1991/92 drought in southern Africa and the 1993 Kenyan crisis (Thomson 1995). The spread of the HIV/AIDS virus is also expected to heighten the economic fragility of a number of sub-Saharan African economies, again exacerbating their vulnerability to drought and other exogenous shocks.[19]

International commodity price movements

The six sub-Saharan African economies examined are all dependent on two or three export commodities for a significant part of their export earnings. Contemporaneous fluctuations in the prices of such commodities, as well as of major imports such as oil, can therefore play a major role in exacerbating or mitigating the impacts of a drought, particularly since trends in production in these countries, as in much of sub-Saharan Africa, typically have little influence on world production. Thus, the Zimbabwean economy was adversely affected by a weak international market for nonferrous metals as well as by drought in 1992–3. In contrast, improved groundnut prices together with strong growth in fish and fertiliser earnings counteracted the impact of Senegal's 1983–4 drought on its balance of payments. More generally, in Burkina Faso, annual rainfall patterns and international cotton prices were negatively correlated during the 1980s, with higher prices for the country's primary export partly offsetting the impact of lower rainfall. Movements in international commodity prices also partly explain the apparent insensitivity of the Kenyan economy to drought. During the severe drought year of 1984, when maize production declined by some 38 per cent, agricultural sector production fell by only 3.5 per cent. Tea and coffee production were little affected by the drought, and export earnings from these crops reached new all-time highs in 1984 and 1985, boosted by high world market prices and a rundown of domestically held stocks. Indeed, despite 'massive' drought-related food imports, Kenya's foreign exchange holdings reached a three-year high of US$422 million in the second quarter of 1984 and twelve months later had fallen by only 8 per cent (World Bank 1991).

The structure of the agricultural sector

Although agriculture is typically most directly sensitive to the level and timing of rainfall and dry spells relative to the agricultural cycle, the precise nature and extent of that vulnerability depend on a number of factors, including the types and varieties of crop grown; planting techniques; the proportions of rain-fed and irrigated production; the quality of cultivated land, including the scale of use of marginal lands; and the structure of land management and ownership. Government agricultural and food policies also play some role.

For example, in the 1980s the Zambian government promoted the production of maize at the expense of more drought-resistant crops through various input and output subsidies and other measures, resulting in a gradual increase in maize production to around 45 per cent of agricultural GDP by 1993. However, commercial farmers began to diversify into other crops, while smallholder and emergent farmers' shares in maize acreage rose, increasing the drought vulnerability of national maize production to the extent that the latter groups of farmers cultivate a higher proportion of their crops under rain-fed production and on more marginal lands. These farmers were also likely to have grown drought-resistant crops in the past. Meanwhile, the switch in production between the different categories of farmers was accompanied by the increasing cultivation of more moisture-sensitive hybrids. However, a more recent lifting of maize subsidies has seen a re-emergence of other crops, including more drought-resistant sorghum and millet.[20]

In Zimbabwe, the relative shift in maize and cotton production from the large-scale commercial sector to the communal sector (the latter of which is heavily concentrated in lower potential marginal areas) since 1980 has also been associated with increased rainfall-related variability in agricultural production. Over the period 1982–3 to 1992–3, regression analysis indicates that a rainfall level 10 per cent below the 1969–93 national mean would be associated with a 25 per cent reduction in maize yields from the communal sector, compared with only a 17 per cent drop in commercial sector yields. Meanwhile, a 30 per cent reduction in rainfall would be associated with declines of 62 per cent in communal and 47 per cent in commercial sector maize yields. These examples underscore the importance of a disaggregated approach in examining the sectoral impacts of drought, and of taking into account the effects of structural change in assessing the drought vulnerability of both individual sectors and the wider economy.

Environmental degradation

Increasing demographic pressures are resulting in the intensified use of more marginal lands in, for example, all the case study countries except Zambia.[21] These lands, by their very nature, are likely to be more vulnerable to adverse rainfall conditions. Furthermore, even less marginal lands are gradually losing productivity in a number of countries, such as Senegal, because of more intensive rain-fed cultivation, which again increases the sensitivity of crop yields to weather conditions. Sahelian countries have also experienced increased aridity over recent decades, as already indicated. There is no consensus on the mechanisms underlying increasing degradation and thus no scientific basis for ascertaining whether or not this trend will continue (Hulme 1992 and 1996).[22] However, it does imply that indigenous agricultural and other natural resource management practices that evolved to suit historical rainfall patterns may no longer be sustainable. Thus vulnerability to drought may increase in the shorter term, before households and economies have fully adapted to the changing climatic conditions (Davies 1995).

Management of water resources

The impact of drought on particular activities may be intensified if water resources have been poorly managed in the past, already lowering water 'stocks' and implicitly accepting greater risk exposure. The experience of Zambia and Zimbabwe in 1992 demonstrates how the rules on the use of water may leave supply at risk to extreme events (see Box 22.2). Various factors, including demographic pressures, improved domestic access to water, rising standards of living, the expansion of irrigation networks, industrialisation, and the growth of the tourism industry, are currently increasing levels of water consumption across sub-Saharan Africa, implying that the careful management of water resources will become increasingly important in determining the outcome of drought conditions in the future (Winpenny 1994).

Cereal reserves

Levels of food stocks held at the national and household levels are an important determinant of the short-term consequences of drought. They offer a timely response to impending food shortages and reduce short-term pressures on foreign exchange reserves. For example, maize stocks in excess of

---

BOX 22.2 LAKE KARIBA AND THE 1991/92 DROUGHT

Zambia and Zimbabwe rely on hydroelectric power generation for a major part of their electricity supply. During and in the aftermath of the 1991/92 drought, both countries experienced serious electricity shortages and also faced major threats to the continued supply of urban drinking water. However, the difficulties reflected less the impacts of the 1991/92 drought per se than the longer-term mismanagement of their common water resources. The drought simply proved to be the final trigger.

In the 1960s, climatologists had identified a statistically robust eighteen-year cycle in the summer rainfall region of southeastern Africa, and successfully forecast the wetter and drier periods of the 1970s and 1980s, respectively (Tyson and Dyer 1978). However, despite the predicted sequence of years of lower rainfall in the Kariba and Kafue catchments, during the 1980s the Zambian and Zimbabwean electricity generating authorities had continued to base levels of water offtake for power generation at Kariba on the average intake for the relatively more favourable 1970s. Thus, offtake exceeded the rate of inflow into the lake by an average 16 per cent during the 1980s, making the system increasingly vulnerable to further rainfall anomalies, as clearly demonstrated in the aftermath of the 1991/92 drought. The electricity curtailments in Zimbabwe alone were estimated to result in a Z$560 million (US$102 million at the 1992 rate of exchange) loss in GDP, a Z$200 million (US$36 million) loss in export earnings, and the loss of 3,000 jobs. Such reckless management may have partly reflected pressures to minimise short-run costs of power generation in the face of the large operating deficits of the Zimbabwe Electricity Supply Authority.

---

official minimum food security targets were important in ensuring adequate food availability in the aftermath of the 1984 and 1994 droughts in Zimbabwe. In contrast, much-reduced stocks necessitated large-scale food imports to Zambia and Zimbabwe in 1992, ahead of international relief. However, large carryover stocks are also very costly to maintain. Individual countries should therefore review acceptable levels of risk and the appropriate size of food reserves as well as the possibility of holding some reserves in a financial form instead.

Migration and remittances

Evidence from a number of sub-Saharan African economies highlights the important role that inflows of remittances from migrant workers can play in reducing vulnerability to drought. These often involve migration to a neighbouring country to work in the mining sector or to a coastal economy unaffected by drought, effectively spreading the benefits of drought-insensitive activities across borders. However, changing job opportunities also imply changes in the potential vulnerability of labour-exporting areas and economies to the risk of drought. In the case of Burkina Faso, for example, there was a marked decline in external workers' remittances in the early 1990s, owing to worsening economic conditions in neighbouring countries. Remittances represented an estimated 31 per cent of total export and private

transfer earnings in 1990–4, compared with 40 per cent in 1980–9, raising concerns about the country's future vulnerability to drought.

Internal or external conflict

A conflict will precipitate government expenditure in domestic war-related industries and services, effectively maintaining some level of economic activity even during periods of drought. Conflicts can also localise the impacts of drought to immediately affected regions by disrupting the flow of goods and services between regions. Such effects have been demonstrated in the case of drought in Ethiopia, as already noted. Moreover, conflict may also reinforce the impact of drought to the extent that it disrupts agricultural and other productive activities and renders affected populations more vulnerable to the impact of events that, in a more secure environment, were within the range of normal coping practices.

The policy environment

The existing policy framework can also play a fundamental role in determining the impact of drought as well as other exogenous shocks. In countries where large areas of the formal economy are highly regulated, thus effectively constraining levels of investment or imports, for example, the impact of a drought shock is minimised by existing binding constraints, as in Zimbabwe in the mid-1980s. The Zimbabwe government's trade policy also inadvertently influenced the impact of the 1991/92 drought, as uncertainty about the continuation of a more liberal import regime and speculation created by the unstable exchange rate had resulted in a gradual build-up in stocks of imported inputs in 1990 and 1991, so that producers entered the drought period with considerable inputs already in stock.

Conversely, government policies can exacerbate the impacts of drought. In Ethiopia, for example, the impacts of the 1982–4 drought were compounded by the Derg government's simultaneous implementation of a socialist system of collective ownership and centralised direction, which effectively undermined the ability of rural households to cope with the impacts of the drought. Namibia's experience in 1992 also highlights how a drought, in turn, can force other issues – in this case, chronic poverty – onto the government policy agenda, both increasing the costs of relief and entailing longer-term implications for levels of government expenditure (Thomson 1994, Devereux *et al.* 1995, Namibia 1997).

Governments can also use policy actions to influence the nature and scale of impact of drought events in a more deliberate fashion. Indeed, droughts pose certain policy choices, particularly relating to public finance and the external sector. These policy-related dimensions of a drought shock are illustrated with evidence from Zimbabwe and Namibia on the budgetary implications of drought.

Budgetary implications of drought

Droughts have potentially important implications for government policy, first and foremost via their impact on the budget deficit. A drought shock will be expected to result in lower tax revenue via a decline in income, employment, and exports. The revenue of utilities will also be adversely affected by the income impacts of the shock-induced recession on effective demand and increased nonpayment. Revenue from parastatal utilities in the water and hydroelectric power generation sectors will also fall as a result of some combination of lower output, recession-affected demand, and simultaneous upward pressures on costs from crisis provision of supply, whilst certain

other parastatals could be similarly affected.[23]

On the expenditure side, governments may be confronted by increased relief, social welfare, health, and water expenditure; consumption-related subsidies on food distribution; and the logistical costs of drought-related imports. Law-and-order services could also be put under greater pressure by a rise in crime, in turn associated with temporary unemployment, migration, and so forth. In addition, there are likely to be pressures for the increased provision of subsidies and credit to affected productive sectors, including public utilities, both because of the direct impact of water shortages on their operations and because of reduced demand. For example, the Zimbabwean government had to meet increased losses of the Agricultural Financial Corporation, the Grain Marketing Board (GMB), and the National Railways of Zimbabwe as a direct consequence of the 1991/92 drought.[24]

Increased budgetary pressures, resulting from lower revenues and higher expenditure, can be met by raising additional financing or reallocating planned government expenditure, or by a combination of the two. There are three basic potential sources of additional finance: borrowing, higher taxes, and increased charges for publicly provided goods and services.

Public borrowing and indebtedness

Government can increase borrowings from domestic and external official and private sources, although its ability to do so is in part determined by its existing level of indebtedness, its relationship with official lenders, and the confidence of private lenders in the economy. Indeed, there is evidence of increases in both external and internal borrowing during periods of drought.

The former is indicated in Figure 22.4, which shows increasing in-debt stocks in five of the six case study countries in the early 1990s as a consequence of drought. The exception was Zimbabwe, whose debt fell as a result of a deliberate longer-term policy of debt reduction. Increased indebtedness has obvious implications for future levels of debt servicing and thus for the availability of foreign exchange to finance capital imports. For example, in Ethiopia, forecast

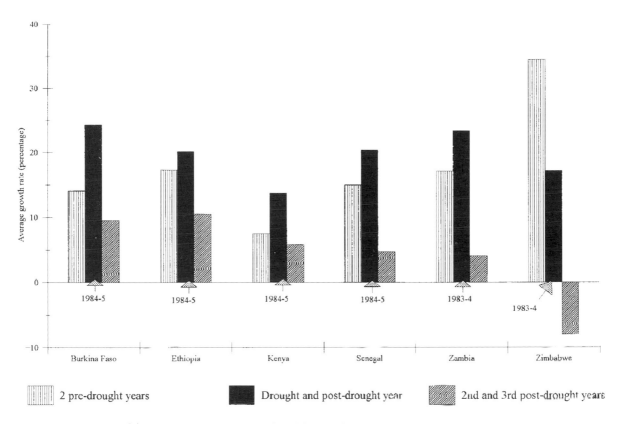

Figure 22.4. The Impact of drought on the growth rates of total debt stocks
Source: Benson and Clay 1998

debt interest payments alone, excluding amortisation, for 1985 increased by 9.2 per cent during the drought year of 1984.

A rise in internal borrowing is illustrated by the actions of the Zimbabwean government in 1992. As noted earlier, the government offset the implicit monetary expansion entailed in this increase in borrowing by maintaining the existing high levels of interest. This in turn contributed to a 5.2 per cent fall on the previous year in private sector investment, thus delaying the expected refurbishment of domestic industry at a time when barriers to external competition were removed.

Drought and taxation

Higher taxation is problematic as a source of additional government financing because of the direct and recessionary effects of the shock. In Zimbabwe, for example, drought levies were imposed on company taxes in both 1984–5 and 1987. However, the rate of company taxation was reduced to help alleviate financial difficulties that had arisen partly as a consequence of the drought. Higher electricity or water prices, despite supplies being temporarily less satisfactory, as well as recessionary pressures will be contentious but may be effective where demand is inelastic. Attempting to reduce subsidies for food and fertiliser or in the social sectors also involves challenging decisions in a crisis.

Reallocation of public expenditure and resources

Reallocation of planned government expenditure may occur within or between sectors and between capital and recurrent spending, with varying opportunity costs. In both Zimbabwe and Namibia in 1992, for instance, drought-related expenditures apparently led to a shift in the composition of the two countries' investment programmes, delaying some non-drought-related projects. In Zimbabwe, several non-water-related projects planned under the Second Five Year National Development Plan (1991–5) were delayed whilst the implementation of some planned water-related projects was brought forward and some additional programmes were begun. Additional government finance was transferred from capital to recurrent expenditure (Benson 1998). Similarly, in Namibia, it was announced that the initial funding of the drought relief programme would be met by postponing the upgrading of the trans-Caprivi highway, although, in the event, it was unclear precisely where the funds for the drought relief programme were drawn from (Thomson 1994). Further research would be required to analyse the precise long-term economic costs of such reallocations of government expenditure, but they almost certainly reduce rates of growth. For example, an estimated 58 per cent of the Namibian Drought Relief Programme expenditure involved the provision of goods, services, and financial transfers that would not have been provided in the absence of drought. These expenditures had no long-term benefit, although some elements of the programme – for example, in the area of water supply – fitted in with existing work and priorities (Thomson 1994).

There is also some evidence that levels of government staffing may not be increased sufficiently to deal with the extra drought-related workload, displacing normal activities and effectively entailing an additional, although intangible, switch of government expenditure. For example, in Zimbabwe in 1992, funding was switched from preventative health care, such as immunisation programmes, to emergency activities (Tobaiwa 1993).

Namibia's 1992 experience also highlights how a drought can force other issues – in this case, chronic poverty – onto the government policy agenda, both increasing the costs of relief and having longer-term implications for levels of government expenditure (Thomson 1994).

Drought and economic and development planning

The weather has invariably been cited *ex post*, in the case study countries considered, as an important variable determining overall patterns of growth. In contrast, drought risk and climatic variability have not been taken into account in forecasting growth rates, either for the agricultural sector or for the economy more broadly. Furthermore, the risk of drought had not been considered in identifying appropriate policies – for example, in agricultural pricing or in promoting particular growth strategies focusing on specific industries.

In some southern African countries, policy makers finally appear to be displaying a greater awareness of the economy-wide threat of drought. For example, the Zimbabwe government in its appeal for drought assistance in 1995 stated: 'Drought is now a permanent feature in Zimbabwe. It is therefore necessary that Government makes long-term strategies to deal with this phenomenon' (Zimbabwe 1995: 9). It then went on to list critical areas requiring action: promotion of appropriate economic activities in specific agroecological areas, consumption of small grains where these are the staple crop, construction of large-scale dams, establishment of a permanent drought mitigation unit to plan and implement long-term drought mitigation and recovery measures, and provision of adequate rations for those affected by droughts. However, even this remains a rather narrow perception of the impacts of drought, and further advancements to push drought onto the broader development agenda are required.

The implications for drought vulnerability of the increasing emphasis being placed in several countries on the agricultural sector is less clear-cut. In Kenya and Zambia, for example, agriculture is being promoted as a primary source of growth and increased export earnings as the scope for further short- to medium-term economic growth in other sectors (particularly public services) diminishes and pressure to secure long-term sustainable growth grows. However, food staples must not be neglected as governments and donors increasingly emphasise the development of other crops. Instead, considerable efforts should be made to reduce fluctuations in food staples, including subsistence and livestock production. Furthermore, drought risk should be properly incorporated into all agricultural plans. Work by Block and Timmer (1994) and others emphasises the

---

BOX 22.3   THE ROLE OF AGRICULTURE GROWTH MULTIPLIERS

The size of agricultural and nonagricultural multipliers plays an important role in determining the second- (and subsequent) round effects of drought shocks.

Recent studies have found that agricultural growth multipliers in sub-Saharan Africa may be much higher than previously calculated, possibly exceeding those of nonagricultural multipliers. In the case of Kenya, for example, Block and Timmer (1994) estimated that over a four-year period, a 100-million Kenyan shilling increase in agricultural value-added would increase nonagricultural value-added by a little more than 56 million shillings and agricultural value-added (via further investments in agriculture) by approximately 8 million shillings, implying an agricultural multiplier of 1.64. In contrast, they estimated a much lower nonagricultural multiplier of 1.23. In other words, according to these findings, a given increase in agricultural income will have a much greater impact on national income than an equivalent increase in nonagricultural income. In the event of a drought, these linkages will obviously work in reverse, with declines in the agricultural sector having severe impacts on other sectors.

---

potential pitfalls as well as the potential economy-wide benefits of higher agricultural growth. The challenge is to reduce vulnerability to drought (see Box 22.3).

Drought and structural adjustment programmes

Over the past fifteen years, many sub-Saharan African economies have adopted structural adjustment programmes, often at the behest and with the financial support of the international donor community. Indeed, there is even some evidence that natural disasters may be an important short-term trigger contributing to the adoption of reform programmes.[25] However, experience has also demonstrated that structural adjustment needs to occur against a backdrop of macroeconomic stability, a condition that does not hold during periods of major drought. Indeed, although partly dependent on the precise stage reached in a reform programme when a drought strikes, droughts can impede the progress of such a programme. In addition, they can exacerbate the adverse shorter-term impacts of reform because droughts typically reinforce the inflationary impact of the removal of basic food and other consumer subsidies (a common feature of many reform programmes) and contribute to job losses. Yet, despite the fact that droughts can have major implications for the progress and ultimate success of reform and also for the continued flow of multilateral and bilateral external assistance, which is increasingly conditional on continuing reform achievements, structural adjustment programmes typically do not anticipate droughts in their design.

The 1991/92 southern African drought offers some evidence of the ways in which a drought shock interacts with the progress of structural adjustment. In the case of Zambia, for example, the 1991/92 drought dampened the anticipated private sector response to the reform programme, which included the liberalisation of product and factor markets and the dismantling of price controls, and prevented the achievement of the programme's original economic targets. Partly drought-related inflationary concerns also led to the adoption of a cash budget at the end of 1992. The latter unfortunately reverberated on the recovery of the maize sector as the government reduced its maize marketing operations as part of its endeavour to reduce costs. At the same time, high domestic interest rates severely hindered the growth of private market operators. In consequence, a substantial quantity of maize was left unpurchased in 1993, in turn creating further hardships for farmers in addition to those inflicted by the previous year's drought. The government was consequently obliged to issue promissory notes to farmers for purchase and delivery of the crop during the 1993–4 marketing year (Anonymous 1994).

The progress of agricultural reform is perhaps most susceptible to fluctuations in weather conditions. Droughts rekindle overriding concerns with food security, weakening a government's resolve to proceed with reforms and reducing the willingness of the private sector to become involved in market reforms. In Kenya, for example, drought has clearly had a considerable effect on the pace of cereals market reform, with a discernible pattern of reluctant agreement to reform followed by retraction in the face of disruption to domestic cereal markets as a result of drought (Thomson 1995). However, it is less clear how this frustrating process of advance and retreat could have been avoided and how the current liberalisation process can be kept on track. Some way has to be found to strengthen the constituency for liberalisation while satisfying other powerful interests, particularly the producer lobby. This is made more difficult by the fact that the main opposition to intervention in Kenya is based on its financial costs.

In one of the six case study countries, Senegal, a drought even contributed to the abandonment of a reform programme. This instance is particularly ironic given that an earlier drought had been a major factor contributing to the decision to adopt the reform programme in the first place. More recently, the international financial institutions (IFIs) appear to be more willing to modify structural reform programmes in the aftermath of droughts, as indicated by experience in both Zambia and Zimbabwe.

Meanwhile, the existence of reform programmes and relationships with donors, particularly the IFIs, may have begun to play an important role in determining the nature and level of the international response to drought, partly reflecting the fact that donors are increasingly keen to ensure that structural reform programmes are not derailed, be it by droughts or other problems. An ongoing structural adjustment programme also implies that an economy's performance is already being closely monitored, providing early and credible indications of economic difficulties emerging as a consequence of a drought and thus highlighting economic as well as humanitarian concerns. Thus, for example, both the Zambian and Zimbabwean governments received balance-of-payments support as well as more conventional emergency food aid and other relief measures in response to the 1991/92 drought. These actions represent an important and positive precedent for future international responses to crises in sub-Saharan Africa.

In the longer term, the successful implementation of a structural reform programme should reduce the overall vulnerability of an economy to drought shocks by restoring economic growth and stability, thus making it more resilient to adverse shocks. Particular aspects of successful structural reform programmes could also play a more direct role in mitigating the impacts of drought. For example, a number of sub-Saharan African countries have already lifted regulations governing agricultural markets, prices, and imports, allowing private traders and millers to play a larger role. This could potentially reduce vulnerability to drought by permitting early market responses to droughts which could avoid substantial price increases and the need for large food aid imports. However, elimination of agricultural incentives could also stimulate shifts in agricultural cropping patterns toward patterns more appropriate to the prevailing climatological conditions, as, for example, has recently occurred in Zambia.

However, a structural adjustment programme is only one element of broader government plans and policies. If the latter do not incorporate proper management of natural and other resources and drought risks, then reform programmes alone may do little to reduce the vulnerability of an economy to drought.

CONCLUSIONS

This chapter has examined the potentially large, but often highly differentiated, economy-wide impacts of drought in various countries of sub-Saharan Africa. The likely scale and character of these impacts depends on the interaction of economic structure and resource endowments, as well as prevailing economic circumstances. Counterintuitively, some of the relatively more developed or complex economies, such as Senegal, Zambia, and Zimbabwe, may be more vulnerable to droughts than less developed, more arid economies, such as Burkina Faso, or countries experiencing conflict-related emergencies, such as Mozambique and Somalia. These observations suggest an 'inverted U'-shaped relationship between the level of complexity of an economy and its vulnerability to drought.

Both longer-term strategies to mitigate the impacts of drought and responses to specific drought events should be sensitive to these differences. Policies are likely to be poorly calibrated if they are based on Africa-wide, or even more general, prescriptions for drought mitigation. However, droughts in all sub-Saharan African economies will invariably have severe food security implications for at least some segments of the population as well. Concerns about meeting these needs raises questions of governance and the capacity and commitment of individual governments to undertake effective drought relief and rehabilitation efforts. Good governance implies a government genuinely committed to the well-being of all communities and regions, which will accord highest priority to efforts to address the social and economic threats posed by drought. The capacity to mitigate the effects of drought is also implied, a capacity that in certain circumstances, especially conflict, is severely curtailed. Taking into account both concerns of governance and the four-country typology indicated above, a broad hierarchy of appropriate aid instruments for responding to droughts can be summarised as follows.

First, as already noted, in *intermediate and complex economies*, the impacts of droughts are likely to be widely diffused through the economy, with more extreme droughts potentially precipitating a broader economic recession. Droughts will exert strong pressure on domestic revenue and expenditure and on foreign exchange resources. There will also be considerable social pressures for measures to assist affected populations.

In these economies, the disbursement of low-cost additional financial aid to provide balance-of-payments and budgetary support should have the highest priority. This aid should focus on meeting the direct costs of the drought response, but in such a way that the drought's recessionary effects are counteracted. It should also be rapidly disbursed to meet funding requirements relating to the much-increased food import bill and government relief expenditure, both of which could otherwise force increased public borrowing and cutbacks in non-essential expenditure and imports. In the context of a structural adjustment programme, flexibility in the programme's targets and in the use of funds already programmed is also important to avoid a drop in disbursement. If it can be rapidly committed and delivered, programme food aid is almost as effective as financial assistance. The main questions are whether it will be timely, cost-effective, or appropriate in terms of providing the type of food that can be readily absorbed in the recipient-country market.

Bilateral project aid, including technical cooperation and funding of local costs and import components of projects, can also play a role in sustaining the flow of project funds, thereby maintaining activities throughout the drought shock. There is also some scope for 'quick action' projects or the accelerated implementation of ongoing ones. Where there is good governance, there is a lower priority for either emergency food or emergency financial aid, both of which are relatively inflexible instruments since they are tied to direct relief. Moreover, emergency aid is costly to deliver, raises a number of targeting issues, and fails to address the economy-wide aspects of drought.

Second, in *simple and conflict-affected economies*, the impacts of a drought are likely to be concentrated in the rural sector, with potentially severe implications for those involved in self-provisioning and located in marginal environments. However, there may be relatively limited direct impacts beyond the rural economy, whilst the balance-of-payments implications will depend on the precise composition of exports and the scale of additional import requirements generated by the drought. In terms of governance, there is often limited awareness of the severity of the crisis in such countries because those in the capital city are insulated by subsidies and food imports from the drought's early impacts. At least in the first instance, a government may even choose to take no action. Indeed, unless there is *good governance*, sensitive to the impacts of the shock on the rural economy, there is then a real danger that a drought–famine syndrome could develop.

In these economies, large-scale targeted interventions should be the primary modality of response – for example, in the form of food distributions or rural works programmes in the immediately affected areas. Such measures are likely to be both more effective in providing relief and more cost-effective than indirect fiscal and monetary measures. Thin markets and lack of integration may also necessitate separate parallel distribution systems for relief transport, storage, and distribution. The most appropriate donor response is also strongly dependent on the governance situation. If there is an effective government, in which the donor has confidence, then general support with financial aid or programme food aid may still be an appropriate response to complement direct relief. Where a government is less effective or even nontherapeutic, the use of indirect channels is more appropriate. Examples of the latter appear to include Malawi and Mozambique in 1992–3, some of the Sahelian economies in the droughts of the early 1970s and 1980s, and the Horn of Africa up to the early 1990s.

Third, in *dualistic, extractive economies* it is important to establish the extent to which those economies with relatively high GDP per capita need emergency assistance on any substantial scale, taking into account issues of governance as well as the precise nature of the economic impacts of the droughts. For example, Botswana, Namibia, and South Africa would appear to no longer require substantial external assistance in response to a drought crisis. However, the interacting effects of conflict and economic decline may leave the populations of some countries with large extractive sectors vulnerable to any exogenous shock. Such groups may require targeted interventions in the event of a drought.

Drought mitigation activities more generally have typically received little sustained interest from either governments or donors, except with respect to food security. Moreover, even the latter strategies have traditionally been defined in terms of improving food security at the national and household level, often focusing on increasing long-run productivity of a country's main food crop rather than reducing annual fluctuations in yields. Yet there are a plethora of possible actions, ranging from increased cultivation of drought-tolerant plants to the provision of long-term weather forecasts and improved water conservation and management practices. Economic investment and water resource management strategies should also be formulated on the basis of the best available longer-term scientific rainfall data for the relevant region. More fundamentally, drought risks should be taken into account in budgetary exercises, investment programming, and the formulation of medium-term economic strategies, including structural adjustment programmes – an important weakness in current, or at least recent, policy practice. Food security and economic monitoring systems, both of which are likely to exist in a country, could also be improved by integrating the two systems. In addition, drought sensitivity analysis should be conducted before promoting particular sectors or subsectors, particularly as part of any diversification strategy, whilst drought mitigation considerations need to be incorporated into longer-term poverty programmes. In the least developed countries, droughts should even perhaps be treated less as exogenous shocks and more as a structural problem.

Ultimately, there is no single set of policies or mitigation and relief measures that will necessarily combat the impacts of drought. Success stories have owed much to chance occurrences, such as high commodity export prices, and to specific country circumstances as well as to deliberate policies and actions. Nevertheless, there are lessons to be learnt from country experiences in developing strategies to reduce the economy-wide impacts of droughts.

NOTES

1 This chapter is drawn from an Overseas Development Institute study, 'The Impact of Drought on Sub-Saharan African Economies and the Options for the Mitigation of such Impacts by National Governments and the International Community', reported more fully in Benson and Clay (1998), Benson (1998), and Clay (1998). The support of the UK Department for International Development (formerly Overseas Development Administration) and the World Bank in funding that study is gratefully acknowledged.

2 See, for example, Chen (1991), Downing *et al.* (1987), Drèze and Sen (1989), Glantz (1987), Sheets and Morris (1974).

3 For example, in 1992 the World Bank approved a US$150 million Emergency Recovery Loan to Zimbabwe and made additional drought-related modifications to credits of US$50 million for Malawi and US$100 million for Zambia. Some donors – for example, Germany – modified existing financial assistance to allow these funds to be used for procurement of drought-related food and other imports. The United States also organised large 'blended' packages of support for food imports including export credits, food aid credits, and grants to Zambia and Zimbabwe to address the direct balance-of-payments aspect of the drought (Callihan *et al.* 1994). Other food aid donors also provided a combination of programme aid to relieve balance-of-payments pressures as well as conventional relief for distribution to affected populations.

4 The study focused particularly on the drought experiences of Burkina Faso, Ethiopia, Kenya, Namibia, Senegal, Zambia, and Zimbabwe.

5   A number of other factors also play a role in determining crop yields, such as reduced input of fertiliser, lack of weeding, the presence of pest and crop diseases, lack of labour at critical periods in the growth cycle, unattractive producer prices, and overall market conditions. It may therefore be difficult to isolate the impact of reductions in moisture from the impact of other factors.

6   For purposes of statistical analysis of rainfall patterns, the Sahel is defined as the region lying between 9 and 15 degrees latitude and extending eastward to the Somali border; East Africa is defined as Uganda, Kenya, and Tanzania; and southeast Africa is defined as the region lying between −16 and −26 degrees latitude and east of the 23 degrees longitudinal line.

7   For example, S. Davies (1995) provides substantial evidence of such adaptation, which, at the level of household and specific groups, may imply transitional stress and impoverishment.

8   This typology builds on that initially presented in Nowlan and Jackson (1992). Those authors proposed a typology of subsistence, developing, and complex economies as a way of explaining the need for different forms of international response required by drought-affected economies in southern Africa in 1992.

9   The flow chart deliberately abstracts from the 'social' consequences of drought. Such effects are not directly considered because of the methodological difficulties entailed in trying to incorporate them.

10   Reductions in demand for labour are unlikely to be fully reflected in official statistics as these effects are partly met through restrictions on overtime, shorter working shifts, and laying off casual labour. Contract labour may also be laid off but permanent labour forces may be protected by stringent employment regulations such as significant redundancy payments, which prevent large declines in formal sector employment.

11   For example, Purtill et al. (1983) estimated that farm incomes for Australia's broadacre properties fell by an average of 45 per cent during the 1982–3 drought, with declines as high as 96 per cent in Victoria. Debt held by drought-afflicted farms increased fourfold over the period between June and November 1982. The drought also resulted in a 2 per cent fall in employment nationwide.

12   For example, in Botswana (Drèze and Sen 1989), and also Namibia in 1992–3 (Thomson 1994), the macro aggregates and trade account effects have been modest and governments have had the resources to finance substantial relief programmes. The Botswana example is particularly exceptional because the government managed its diamond revenue extremely well, treating high as well as low prices as temporary shocks.

13   Kuznets's 'inverted U' hypothesis was based on evidence that relative income inequality rises during the earlier stages of development, reaches a peak, and then declines in the later stages (Kuznets 1955).

14   See Benson and Clay (1998) for a more detailed exposition of the 'inverted U' hypothesis.

15   For example, a 50 per cent fall in agricultural GDP in an economy in which agricultural GDP had accounted for 20 per cent of total GDP in the predrought year would translate into a 10 per cent fall in GDP attributable to the decline in agricultural GDP.

16   The specification of the regression equations was highly simplified, ignoring other key factors determining economic performance such as the terms of trade or major political upheavals. However, fuller modelling of the determinants of economic performance was beyond the scope of this study. See Benson and Clay (1998) for a more detailed presentation of this analysis.

17   One of the most intriguing cases of dualism is South Africa, which is classified as an upper-middle income country in terms of per capita GDP and is the largest, most industrialised economy in Africa. The macroeconomic implications of the severe drought in 1991/92 were relatively modest despite maize import costs of some US$700 million. However, with only 1 per cent of white commercial farms accounting for 40 per cent of agricultural output, there was a large 'tail' of nonviable enterprises employing much migrant labour in drought-prone areas. Some 55 per cent of the black population living in the former homelands is dependent on a combination of self-provisioning and remittances, and is therefore food- and health-insecure in a drought.

18   This apparent insensitivity could also reflect data problems, relating in particular to the underreporting of activities in the closely integrated sectors of subsistence agriculture and rural informal manufacturing.

19   For example, Ainsworth and Over (1992) report studies that estimated that the rate of growth of per capita GDP would be reduced by 0.1 per cent in Tanzania and 0.3 per cent in Malawi under their most plausible set of assumptions about the AIDS epidemic.

20   This could also have important implications for levels of effective demand during periods of drought, as small farmers depended on maize for some 90 per cent of their cash income as well as for domestic consumption during the early 1990s (Banda 1993).

21   This may still be less an issue in Zambia because of its low rural population density and a high level of urbanisation for a relatively low-income country (Tiffen and Mulele 1993).

22   The relationship between the process of environmental degradation and demographic pressures is the subject of much controversy. There are even some counter-examples to the demographic pressures

hypothesis. For example, a study of Machakos District, Kenya, found that population growth was associated with a reversal of the process of environmental degradation in the medium to long term (Tiffen *et al.* 1994).

23 In the case of electricity generation, more costly thermal power plants may have to be used to provide a higher proportion of the load because of restrictions on hydroelectric supply. Meanwhile, load shedding could result in a reduction in revenue.

24 Before the deliberate run-down of maize stocks in 1990–1, the GMB had typically imposed heavier burdens on government finances during years of surplus than of deficit maize production, owing to particularly high storage and disposal costs.

25 For example, Killick and Malik (1992: 604) found in a survey of seventeen randomly selected developing countries with IMF programmes that in six cases, natural disasters (and in four, drought specifically) had been an 'important, perhaps dominant factor' in the decision to adopt a programme.

REFERENCES

Ainsworth, M. and Over, M. (1992) 'The economic impact of AIDS: Shocks, responses and outcomes', in M. Essex *et al.* (eds), *AIDS in Africa*, New York: Raven Press.

Anonymous (1994) 'Adjustment in Africa: Reforms, results and the road ahead – The Zambian experience', paper presented at the World Bank Seminar on Adjustment in Africa, May 1994, Harare, Zimbabwe.

Banda, A.K. (1993) 'Country assessment on the drought situation in Zambia', paper presented at SADC Regional Drought Management Workshop, Harare, Zimbabwe, 13–16 September, Ministry of Agriculture, Food and Fisheries, Policy and Planning Division, Lusaka, Zambia.

Benson, C. (1998) 'Drought and the Zimbabwe economy, 1980–93', in H. O'Neill and J. Toye (eds), *A World Without Famine?*, London: Macmillan.

Benson, C. and Clay, E.J. (1998) 'The impact of drought on Sub-Saharan African economies: A preliminary examination', Africa Technical Department, World Bank, Washington, DC.

Block, S. and Timmer, C.P. (1994) 'Agriculture and economic growth: Conceptual issues and the Kenyan experience', Cambridge, MA: Harvard Institute for International Development.

Borton, J., Stephenson, R.S., and Morris, C. (1988) 'ODA emergency aid to Africa 1983–86', Evaluation Report EV425, Overseas Development Administration, London.

Callihan, D.M., Eriksen, J., and Herrick, A. (1994) 'Famine averted: The United States government response to the 1991/92 Southern African Drought', Management Systems International, Washington, DC.

Chen, M. (1991) *Coping with Seasonality and Drought*, New Delhi: Sage Publications.

Clay, E.J. (1998) 'Responding to the human and economic consequences of natural disasters', in H. O'Neil and J. Toye (eds), *A World Without Famine?*, London: Macmillan.

Collins, C. (1993) 'Famine defeated: Southern Africa, UN win battle against drought', *Africa Recovery Briefing Paper* 9, New York: United Nations Department of Public Information.

Davies, R. (1992) 'Macroeconomic aspects of Zimbabwe's transition from socialism', University of Zimbabwe, Department of Economics, Harare.

Davies, S. (1995) *Adaptable Livelihoods: Coping with Food Insecurity in the Malian Sahel*, London: Macmillan.

Devereux, S., Rimmer, M., LeBeau, D., and Pendleton, W. (1995) 'The 1992/3 Drought in Namibia: An Evaluation of its Socio-Economic Impact on Affected Households', *Research Report* 7, Social Sciences Division, Multi-Disciplinary Research Centre, University of Namibia, Windhoek.

DHA (Department of Humanitarian Affairs) and SADC (1992) 'Drought Emergency in Southern Africa (DESA): Consolidated UN-SADC Appeal Mid Term Review', Geneva.

Downing, T.E., Gitu, K.W., and Kamau, C.M. (1987) *Coping with Drought in Kenya: National and Local Strategies*, Boulder, CO, and London: Lynn Rienner Publishers.

Drèze, J. and Sen, A. (1989) *The Political Economy of Hunger*, Oxford: Clarendon Press.

Glantz, M.H. (ed.) (1987) *Drought and Hunger in Africa: Denying Famine a Future*, Cambridge: Cambridge University Press.

Hicks, D. (1993) 'An evaluation of the Zimbabwe Drought Relief Programme 1992/1993: The roles of household level response and decentralized decision making', World Food Programme, Harare, Zimbabwe.

Hulme, M. (1992) 'Rainfall changes in Africa: 1931–60 to 1961–90', *International Journal of Climatology* 12: 685–99.

Hulme, M. (1995) 'Climatic trends and drought risk analysis in sub-Saharan Africa', University of East Anglia, Climatic Research Unit, Norwich.

Hulme, M. (ed.) (1996) 'Climate change and Southern Africa: An exploration of some potential impacts and implications for the SADC region', report commissioned by WWF International, Climatic Research Unit, University of East Anglia, Norwich.

IFAD (1994) 'Development and the vulnerability of rural households to drought: Issues and lessons from sub-Saharan Africa', paper for Technical Session: Managing Drought, World Conference on Natural Disaster Reduction, Yokohama, 23–7 May, Africa Division, International Fund for Agricultural Development, Rome.

Killick, T. and Malik, M (1992) 'Country experiences with IMF programmes in the 1980s', *The World Economy* 15, 5: 599–632.

Kuznets, S. (1955) 'Economic growth and income inequality', *American Economic Review* March, pp 1–28.

Namibia (Government of Republic of) (1997) 'Towards a drought policy for Namibia', papers prepared for National Workshop on Drought Policy, Windhoek.

Nowlan, J. and Jackson, B. (1992) 'Drought in Southern Africa', Version 5, US Agency for International Development, Harare, Zimbabwe.

Purtill, A., Backhouse, M., Abey, A., and Davenport, S. (1983) 'A study of the drought', *Supplement to Quarterly Review of the Rural Economy* (Supp) 5, 1: 3–11.

Robinson, P. (1993) 'Economic effects of the 1992 drought on the manufacturing sector in Zimbabwe', Overseas Development Institute, London.

Sheets, H. and Morris, R. (1974) *Disaster in the Desert: Failure of International Relief in West African Drought*, Washington, DC: Carnegie Endowment for International Peace.

Thompson, C. (1993) 'Drought emergency in Southern Africa: The role of international agencies', paper presented at SADC Regional Drought Management Workshop, Harare, Zimbabwe, 13–16 September, University of Zimbabwe, Harare.

Thomson, A. (1994) 'The impact of drought on government expenditure in Namibia in 1992/93', Overseas Development Institute, London.

Thomson, A. (1995) 'Drought and market liberalization in Kenya', Overseas Development Institute, London.

Tiffen, M. and Mulele, M.R. (1993) *The Environmental Impact of the 1991–2 Drought on Zambia*, Gland: International Union for the Conservation of Nature and Natural Resources.

Tiffen, M., Mortimore, M. and Gichuki, F. (1994) *More People, Less Erosion: Environmental Recovery in Kenya*, Chichester, United Kingdom: John Wiley.

Tobaiwa, C. (1993) 'Zimbabwe: The response to the 1992 drought in the context of long-term development objectives', paper presented at SADC Regional Drought Management Workshop, Harare, Zimbabwe, 13–16 September.

Tyson, P.D. and Dyer, T.G. (1978) 'The predicted above-normal rainfall of the seventies and the likelihood of droughts in the eighties in South Africa', *South African Journal of Science* 74: 372–7.

Wilhite, D.A. (ed.) (1993) *Drought Assessment, Management and Planning: Theory and Case Studies*, Boston, MA: Kluwer Academic Publishers.

Winpenny, J. (1994) *Managing Water as an Economic Resource*, London and New York: Routledge.

World Bank (1991) 'Food security and slow onset disasters in eastern Africa: Departmental action plan', Eastern Africa Department, Agriculture Operations Department, Washington, DC.

Zimbabwe, Ministry of Public Service, Labor and Social Welfare (1995) 'A state of disaster: Government of Zimbabwe appeal for assistance', Harare.

23
CANADIAN PRAIRIE DROUGHT IMPACTS AND EXPERIENCES

E.E. Wheaton

DROUGHTS OF THE CANADIAN PRAIRIES

Droughts occur in many parts of Canada; however, this hazard is neither as intense, as widespread, nor as frequent in other regions as it is in the Prairies. Neither are the effects of drought as dramatic and memorable in other regions. Drought is an intrinsic and noteworthy part of the Canadian Prairies' climate. Hardly a year goes by without some type of drought occurring somewhere in the Canadian Prairie Provinces.

Droughts are classified as major natural disasters. They affect Canada and the world, and their effects can be disastrous and surprising. Although the Prairie agricultural area is most famous for its droughts, even the northern boreal forest is susceptible to drought, especially in the Prairie Provinces. Droughts plague the forest with low river and lake levels and with many severe forest fires and insect infestations.

Prairie people have lived through some very dry times, including the classic droughts of the 1930s, 1961, the 1980s, and several others. Prairie people have become drought experts and this is a part of our character. The many newspaper headlines that appeared during our last great drought of 1987–8 are evidence of the wide range of effects of, our preoccupation and concern with, and our interest in droughts. The long list of drought themes headlined in the newspapers reflects this concern (Table 23.1). The diversity of the themes of drought effects is also amazing. They range from wind erosion to ducks, to cattle, to power generation, and to politics, for example.

This chapter explores the 'what, why, when, where, and who' of Prairie droughts; it examines their effects and gives some idea of what it is like to live through droughts. The nature of future droughts is also explored.

WHAT IS A DROUGHT?

Drought affects each area and each human activity differently, so each of us could write a unique definition according to our perspective. A major challenge in drought investigation is its definition and measurement. Many Prairie people, especially in rural areas, have been faced by water shortages that accompany droughts. It is a major concern when your well level is sinking sharply, when your crops are withering in the heat, or when your animals have no or poor-quality water and diminishing feed.

Each of these concerns could have a separate definition, and only scientists are worried about definitions when water supplies run short. So why define droughts? Scientific assessment of the nature of drought, including its frequency, intensity, and area, requires an objective way to measure droughts. A definition of drought and its effects is a first step in this process, and is a necessary prelude to actions.

Farm droughts

Meteorologists often refer to drought as a long-term lack of precipitation. An agrologist may consider a drought to be a period during which soil moisture is insufficient to support crops. Some plants are more drought tolerant than others, and other plants may be considered 'water hogs' because they require so much water. So droughts can also be specific to certain plants. For instance, a drought that might affect a

Table 23 1 List of newspaper articles about the 1987 and 1988 droughts

Date	Paper/magazine	Theme/headline
22 June 1987	Independent	Crop Report/no precipitation/soil erosion
25 June	Western Producer	Agriculture/drought
16 July	Western Producer	Dry weather/fewer disease and insect problems
19 Nov.	Western Producer	Old Wives Lake dry
19 Dec.	Leader Post	No snow cover
28 Jan. 1988	Western Producer	Program Re: soil + water pollution
17 Feb.	Star Phoenix	B.C. Drought (5th year)
3 Mar.	Western Producer	Alberta drought (agriculture)
17 Mar.	Western Producer	Prairie agriculture drought
21 Mar.	Leader Post	Canadian water diverted to US?
24 Mar.	Western Producer	World weather "bad"
26 Mar.	Star Phoenix	Water levels low
26 Mar.	Star Phoenix	Dry Forest Conditions
29 Mar.	Leader Post	Estevan dry
7 Apr.	Western Producer	American Drought
7 Apr.	Western Producer	Soil erosion
11 Apr.	L.A. Herald	American Drought
16 Apr.	Star Phoenix	Prairie Drought
23 Apr.	Star Phoenix	Costs of Drought
4 May	Leader Post	Waterfowl Wetlands
5 May	Western Producer	Low water for irrigation
5 May	Western Producer	Ranchers unload cattle
5 May	Western Producer	Greenhouse good for wheat?
5 May	Western Producer	3rd driest winter in Lethbridge
5 May	Western Producer	Old Wives Lake/alkali dust blowing
11 May	Leader Post	Editorial/Government aid
12 May	Western Producer	Normal rains? for Alberta
25 May	Leader Post	Forest fire + agriculture: Stock market
25 May	Leader Post	Drought vs waterfowl
31 May	Leader Post	Rain comes to North Battleford
31 May	Leader Post	Grassland fire near Elbow
June	Report on Business	Story of one farmer vs drought
1 June	Leader Post	Drought stops political squabbles
3 June	Star Phoenix	Next century weather forecasts
7 June	Star Phoenix	Heat more severe due to drought
13 June	Alberta Report	Costs for one farmer
14 June	Globe & Mail	Projected crop losses
20 June	Alberta Report	Omega block
20 June	Alberta Report	Poultry farming vs drought
20 June	The Independent	Editorial (agriculture)
20 June	Edmonton Journal	Ducks vs drought
22 June	Star Phoenix	Hydro-electric stations
23 June	Star Phoenix	Ground water vs drought
25 June	Star Phoenix	Sundance/raindance
25 June	Star Phoenix	1980s drier than 1930s
27 June	The Independent	Editorial: The drought IS real
27 June	The Independent	Drought & increase in soil erosion
27 June	Maclean's	North America's drought (agriculture, grain terminals, etc.)
29 June	Hydroline (Man)	Manitoba hydroelectric generation
29 June	Leader Post	Increase in electricity costs
29 June	Melfort Journal	Field erosion
30 June	Western Producer	Weed/Pesticides/Heat

Table 23.1 Continued

Date	Paper/magazine	Theme/headline
30 June	Western Producer	American Harvests Small
July	World Water	Drought on the Prairies
11 July	Alberta Report	Unemployment vs drought
14 July	Western Producer	Drought vs Prairie fires
16 July	Star Phoenix	Saskatoon climate breakdown
19 July	Shaunavon Standard	Shaunavon has a crop!!
3 Sept.	Leader Post – Special Report	Topics:
		Water value increases
		Why Prairies are dry
		Irrigation: consumptive water user
		World water crisis greenhouse effect
		Who should pay for water use
		Cloud seeding
		Sask. is well dependent?
		Lake Diefenbaker
		Small towns vs drought
		Efficient irrigation
		Inter-basin transfers
8 Sept.	Western Producer	Manitoba RM's vs soil erosion
8 Sept.	Western Producer	Canadian harvest
15 Sept.	Western Producer	Drought vs fall tillage
15 Sept.	Western Producer	African wheat vs drought
17 Sept.	Star Phoenix	Alberta bumper corn crop
19 Sept.	The Citizen-Kipling	1988 bird hunting regulations
19 Sept.	Grainews	Poor crop used as snow catch
19 Sept.	Grainews	Drought vs nutrients for cattle
22 Sept.	Western Producer	Lower bag limits for fowls
22 Sept.	Western Producer	Ont. farmers seek drought aid
23 Sept.	Leader Post	Duck populations
26 Sept.	The Independent	Drought vs costs
30 Sept.	Leader Post	Livestock payments (map)
Oct.	Ag News	Livestock payments
		Crop yields down
		Record amount of water assistance
3 Oct.	Alberta Report	Duck populations
5 Oct.	Estevan Mercury	Drought payments to cattle owners
5 Oct.	Estevan Mercury	Drought vs economy
6 Oct.	Western Producer	Be prepared for a drought
6 Oct.	Western Producer	Manitoba vs 2 year drought
6 Oct.	Western Producer	Farmers can learn to make do with lack of water
8 Oct.	Star Phoenix	Grain production
13 Oct.	Western Producer	Drought aid in limbo
24 Oct.	Grainews	Editorial – blowing dust
27 Oct.	Western Producer	Alberta and Saskatchewan yields
27 Oct.	Western Producer	No fall moisture
3 Nov.	Western Producer	Drought overreaction
10 Nov.	Western Producer	Quality of grain is high
21 Nov.	Alberta News	Political aid for farmers
1 Dec.	Western Producer	Drought & the environment
5 Jan. 1989	Western Producer	Sask. economy survived drought
9 Feb.	Western Producer	World temperature in 1988 highest
10 Feb.	Star Phoenix	World temperature in 1988 highest

16 Feb.	Western Producer	1988 drought effect on 1989
21 Feb.	Leader Post	Snow cover sporadic
23 Feb.	Western Producer	Farmers want better water
27 Feb.	Sask. Farm Life	Crop drought assistance
27 Feb.	Leader Post	World drought?
2 Mar.	Western Producer	El Niño/La Niña
9 Mar.	Western Producer	Weeds – winning the war?
9 Mar.	Western Producer	Drought helped increase nitrogen
9 Mar.	Western Producer	Federal drought aid allocations
13 Mar.	Scratching River Post Morris, Manitoba	Amount crops use in water
16 Mar.	Western Producer	Lake Head in for a slow year
16 Mar.	Western Producer	Grain prices
16 Mar.	Western Producer	Sask. Water's water relief programme
20 Mar.	The Globe & Mail	Drought leads to increased power cost
22 Mar.	Estevan Mercury	Drought zones defined
30 Mar.	Western Producer	Weyburn terminal handles less grain
1 Apr.	Winnipeg Free Press	Farmers plough dry wetlands
1 Apr.	Winnipeg Free Press	Editorial – Waterfowl catastrophe
12 Apr.	Leader Post	Sask. Credit Unions do well despite drought

Source: Wittrock and Wheaton 1989a

more susceptible crop, such as canola, may not be very harmful to a crop such as wheat.

Surface water supply droughts

A hydrological drought may mean a prolonged period of unusually low surface runoff and low levels in shallow wells (Maybank *et al.* 1995). So an agricultural crop drought may occur during a year with flooding problems on rivers. During the 1988 drought, for example, Manitoba Water Resources personnel drove through a dust storm to reach a flooded area that they were monitoring (A.A. Warkentin, personal communication, 1989).

Groundwater droughts

Groundwater is a very important supply of water in the Prairies, especially in rural areas. Groundwater has different responses to drought, depending on the level of the water-bearing strata and the type of drought. For example, a short drought affects shallow wells more quickly than deeper wells, which may not even be affected. The shallow wells, however, recharge more quickly when adequate rainfall and snowmelt occur. Longer droughts, lasting off and on for several years, may be required to produce changes in deeper wells (e.g., Wittrock and Wheaton 1989b).

HOW ARE DROUGHTS MEASURED?

The measurement of drought is almost as challenging as its definition. Unfortunately, no one has devised a 'drought metre' that we can hang up with the thermometer. The measurement of precipitation has several pitfalls, especially in the windy Prairies, where the rain and snow seem to fall sideways as much as downward. Drought measurement is even more difficult because it is a complex combination of several factors, including precipitation, evaporation, transpiration, and water use.

Why bother measuring droughts? The measurement of droughts is important for several reasons. Scientists need numeric descriptions of droughts for investigating the frequency and intensity of drought patterns. These numeric descriptors are called drought indices. If we can't measure drought, we can't find out how often, how bad, how long, or where it is. Drought assistance and monitoring programmes require drought measurements to be objective and effective. People who manage resources such as reservoirs, crops, forests, and pastures require specific information about droughts to make appropriate decisions. This is especially important in the drought-prone Prairies.

How are droughts characterised?

Many different methods are used to characterise the

nature, severity, and extent of drought. Precipitation variability is one indicator of an area's susceptibility to drought. The coefficient of variation (CV) is one of the best measures of precipitation variability. Higher CVs indicate greater precipitation variations, lower reliability of precipitation, and increased tendency toward droughts.

How does the Prairies' CV compare to CVs in other places on earth? Some areas have boringly similar amounts of rainfall from one year to the next. Coastal British Columbia tends to be one of them, with less than 10 per cent CV (Figure 23.1). This is definitely not true for places such as the Prairies. The highest values of CV are found in the most arid regions of the world, including the Sahara and Kalahari deserts of Africa and the southwestern part of the United States, with CVs in the 30–40 per cent range. The Prairie Provinces have the second highest values in Canada, with a large area having values higher than 20 per cent. These are second only to the high Arctic, which has values greater than 30 per cent.

Drought dynamics

Precipitation reliability, as measured by the CV, is poor in the Prairie Provinces as a whole (i.e., high CV). This is especially true compared with other areas in the world, and some areas in the Prairies are worse than others. The area of best growing-season precipitation reliability is around Edmonton, at about 20 per cent CV (Figure 23.2). The worst area is in the dry belt on the Alberta–Saskatchewan border near Swift Current (in southwestern Saskatchewan), which has a CV of more than 40 per cent.

Precipitation variability also changes with the seasons. This seasonality exacerbates drought problems in the Prairies. This is because variability is greatest during the summer months when the various needs (and uses) for water for agriculture, recreation, irrigation, and other activities are the highest. This is a very serious and unfortunate mismatch. It means that the water supply is most sporadic and uncertain just when the needs for water are the greatest.

The year-to-year variability makes planning very

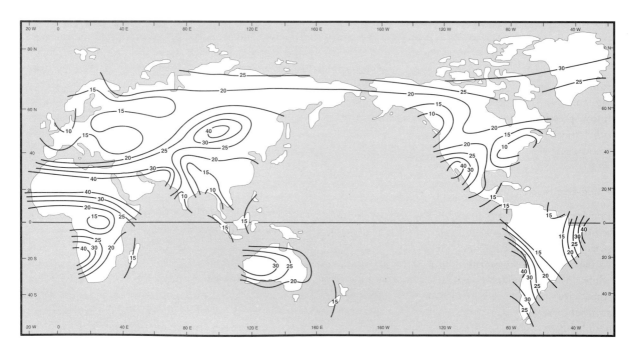

Figure 23.1 Continental distribution of coefficient of variation of annual precipitation (after Barry and Chorley 1976)

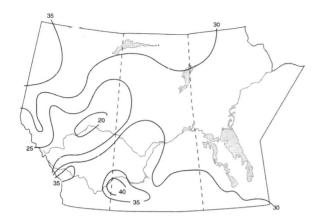

Figure 23.2 Coefficient of variation of growing season precipitation for the Canadian Prairies
Source: McKay 1963

difficult. We can go along for years without serious water shortages in a place. As a result, we can become very complacent about water conservation and almost 'forget' that we have droughts. The variability can fool us into thinking that our water worries are gone. Then another drought sneaks up and there go our precious water supplies again. There goes the boreal forest up in smoke again.

That is why the need for taking care of our water supplies is so critical in the Prairies. We must be very vigilant and good at this through conservation, pollution prevention, demand management, and various other mechanisms that really boil down to wise use of resources.

Place-to-place drought differences

Prairie precipitation is variable from month to month, season to season, and year to year. Summer thunderstorm rainfall is also notoriously different from place to place. One field may be deluged by a downpour while another remains bone dry. One part of even a small city may literally be filling with water while another part gasps in the dust. This is why Prairie people often ask even their neighbours 'how much rain did you get?' This is not just a polite form of conversation. This is curiosity to know how different the weird rainfall patterns can be. The sporadic rainfall patterns stretch the trustfulness of insurance

adjustors of various sorts too. When neighbouring farmers separated by only a few kilometres claim large losses from opposite causes (flood/drought), it usually is true.

The spatial and temporal characteristics of drought can be examined using many drought indices. Various indices have been used for this region, including forage drought early warning, climatic productivity, various crop yield, wind erosion, and crop moisture models. The Palmer Drought Severity Index (PDSI) is likely one of the most commonly used drought indices. It is used extensively in North America to monitor and study drought. The PDSI considers many factors, including precipitation, evaporation, transpiration, antecedent soil moisture, and runoff (Palmer 1965). Such an index is useful for examining the long-term year-to-year drought occurrences (Figure 23.3). Many years in the 1908–93 period have brought dry to drought conditions (PDSI less than − 2) to southern Saskatchewan. In contrast, few years have had wetter conditions (PDSI greater than 2).

The long-term (1908–93) pattern of drought (as measured by PDSI) in southern Saskatchewan emphasises the great year-to-year variability of drought (Figure 23.3). But longer trends appear to be embedded in this sporadic pattern. For example, if you drew a line through the overall trend for the 1974–89 period, the line would point downward. This means a trend toward increasing droughts. We should ask, is the region becoming drier? Conversely, an earlier trend (during the 1940s and 1950s) was upward, indicating fewer droughts and more wet spells.

What are the effects of droughts?

Very few people threshed anything in 1937. It was real dry until about the 10th of July. When the rain came, Russian thistle took over and choked out any grain that might have been left. That year Russian thistle was put up for feed and stock survived on it. By 1937, almost everyone in our municipality received some form of relief. By 1939, probably half the land had reverted back to weeds that thrived on uncultivated land . . . During the thirties life was difficult, but people managed to make the best of it and have many fond memories of that time.

(Handel New Horizons 1990: 33, 35)

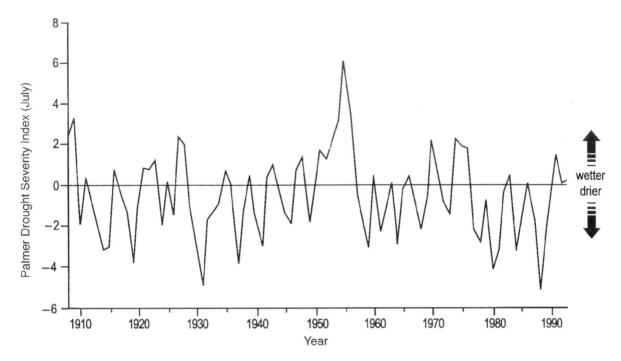

Figure 23.3 Average Palmer Drought Severity Index time series, 1908–93, for southern Saskatchewan
Source: Maybank *et al.* 1995

Droughts have major impacts on the Canadian economy, environment, and society. Drought is even thought to be a cause of an increase in heat-related health problems and deaths. Many activities related to agriculture, forestry, water resources, waterfowl, fisheries, recreation, energy, tourism, and transportation can be adversely affected by droughts (Table 23.1 shows newspaper titles reflecting such drought worries of the 1987–8 drought).

Drought years on the Prairies can be measured and compared by their effects. Droughts as measured by severity of effects on waterfowl, streamflow, and agriculture over the 1929–93 period are compared in Figure 23.4. Certain droughts can affect one sector (such as agriculture) severely and not another sector (such as water supply management).

The most severe and prolonged droughts, however, such as the one from 1987 to 1988, often affect many sectors severely. In other words, a 'mild' drought may only affect summer pastures, but a nasty drought may affect several sectors beyond agriculture as its effects ripple through the economy. Such a drought is very disruptive and costly. The early to

mid-1950s and 1970s had few or mild droughts, and they show large gaps in the graph (Figure 23.4).

Although we mostly see and hear and about the problems of drought, there are bright sides to it. These are as rare as rain during drought, but they do exist. The *benefits* (yes, there are benefits) of drought include its brilliant, sunny weather (especially for the beach lovers); larger beaches as lake levels retreat; lack of mosquitos; and more work for forest-fire fighters. Drought, with its bright blue skies and sparse rain, also provides great conditions for outdoor activities, from construction and haymaking to outdoor concerts. (The section on infamous droughts includes more about droughts' effects.)

Drought watches

Unlike many other hazards, droughts do not have a swift and attention-grabbing progression. They can sneak up on us and can catch us by surprise. We have a better idea of when droughts end than when they start. By the time crops start to wither and well levels plummet, it may be too late to take some precautions.

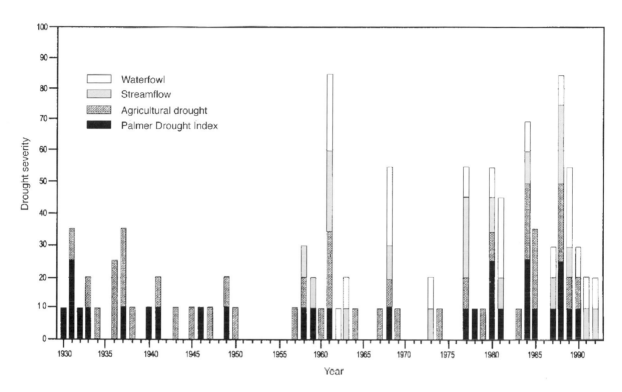

Figure 23.4 Comparison of different types of droughts, 1930–92
Source: Maybank et al. 1995

Drought early warning takes careful vigilance. Therefore, it is important to monitor for droughts and to have well-developed and tested water conservation and other drought-fighting methods ready much of the time.

When a 'budding' drought is detected, drought mitigation plans of various types, ranging from improved forest fire watches, grassland management, and soil conservation, must be initiated or enhanced to avoid adverse effects or maximise any benefits. Just as we have severe weather watches and warnings, we need to be alert to and prepared for droughts. This will reduce our vulnerability and the costs of droughts. Then perhaps we may learn to enjoy their benefits, rather than dread droughts.

Unfortunately, no formal drought monitoring programme currently exists. Before 1995, the Prairie Farm Rehabilitation Administration (PFRA) of Agriculture Canada had worked with several other agencies on a cooperative drought monitoring and reporting programme. It was a victim of staff and budget cuts (A.J. Cullen, personal communication, 1996), and perhaps

the improved moisture conditions of the agricultural region in the 1990s. This leaves the Prairie people in the precarious position of living in a very drought-prone region and being less than completely adapted to drought. Drought likely requires more careful monitoring than floods, for instance, because it is a 'creeping' phenomenon that develops over days or weeks and can sneak up on the nonmonitored and ill-prepared areas. Water and soil conservation is a continuous requirement for drought-prone areas. Prairie people have developed and applied water conservation techniques for years. However, we are still learning to do better as nature throws new surprises at us.

WHY DO PRAIRIE DROUGHTS OCCUR?

What causes Prairie droughts and why do they occur so often and over such wide areas? The cause of droughts is still not clear, and complete explanations are still out of reach. However, droughts are usually related to persistent high-pressure systems over the region. These conditions, in turn, are often linked with blocking of the westerly winds either by patterns in the general atmospheric circulation or by the Rocky Mountains, or by combinations of such factors. The patterns of climate in faraway places such as the Pacific Ocean also affect the Prairie climate, including drought (refer to the teleconnections section).

A long way from water

The position of the Prairie region, in the centre of a large continent far from large sources of water, such as the Pacific Ocean and the Gulf of Mexico, is also a cause of droughts. By the time the air masses reach the Prairies, their moisture has often been very depleted. If there were a large inland sea such as the Mediterranean reaching into Canada, as it does into Europe, droughts in the Canadian Prairies might be rare.

Drought's memory

It is thought that droughts 'feed on' droughts (e.g., Namais 1960). For example, dry spring conditions favour the formation of high-pressure systems over the area. Dry conditions also mean less local water vapour as a source for rain. This perpetuates the dry conditions for a season or longer. So, dry soil moisture conditions appear to prolong and amplify droughts. This effect is aptly termed 'persistence' or called 'memory' in the system.

Droughts result in drying soils and dying plants. The dry soils and sloughs and sparse vegetation of the 1988 drought likely increased its lifetime and intensity. So drought is linked with the surface conditions of an area, including soils and plants, for example. This link works in several ways. Evapotranspiration from moist soils and growing plants increases the local atmospheric water vapour. If this is occurring over a large area, it is a good local source for water vapour that may later become rain, if other conditions are appropriate.

Alternately, dry soils and water bodies and few plants contribute little water vapour to the air. The area then has to depend solely on water vapour coming from other regions for its rainfall. This situation increases the probability of drought occurrence and the lifetime of an existing drought. This can be

self-perpetuating because less rainfall leads to more dying plants, and drying soils and water bodies.

Teleconnections – the effect of faraway places

Climatic conditions in distant places are thought to be related to Prairie climatic anomalies such as drought. This phenomenon is termed 'teleconnections'. For instance, certain patterns of sea surface temperatures in the northern Pacific Ocean are associated with summer dry periods in the Prairies (e.g., Bonsal *et al*. 1993). For example, the weather pattern associated with the 1988 drought was a strong high-pressure system stalled over the American Midwest. Also, the jetstream and corresponding stormy weather systems were displaced northward of their 'usual' positions (Figure 23.5). The major shifts in the patterns of the general atmospheric circulation system were thought to play a larger role than the effect of the dry surface conditions.

INFAMOUS DROUGHTS

Each past Prairie drought is unique by several standards. Their characteristics differ in terms of intensity, timing, area of coverage, duration, causes, and effects. Each future drought will also be different from past droughts in some (or several) ways. This section introduces the infamous droughts, then provides details of experiences with these droughts, their effects, and people's responses.

The most notorious and devastating Prairie droughts in the 1900s are the classic droughts of the 1930s and 1980s – 'the dirty thirties and dirty eighties' – and the single drought year of 1961. During the 1930s, other places in the world experienced much more fortunate climates than the Prairies. Iceland, for instance, had what they call the 'golden thirties' (P. Bergthórsson, personal communication, 1984). During the winter, ice often covers the ocean surrounding Iceland. However, during the 1930s the ocean was warm enough that it was open, not ice covered, in many winters. The ice-free ocean resulted in a much warmer winter climate for Iceland. This was a bountiful time for Icelanders.

Droughts other than those of the 1930s and 1980s have been noteworthy, but not as famous. The

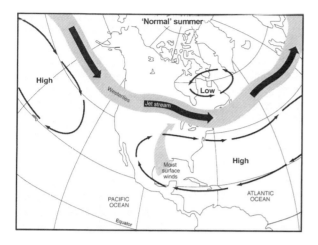

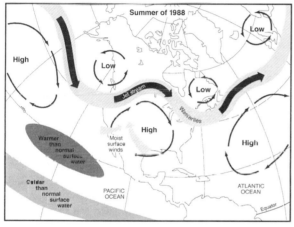

Figure 23.5 Atmospheric circulation patterns for a normal summer and for the summer of 1988
Source: Trenberth 1989

1930s and 1980s droughts gained their fame by occurring as a sequence of years and by covering large areas. For instance, the 1961 drought was extremely severe; crop drought conditions prevailed over most of agricultural Saskatchewan and Manitoba and in southeastern Alberta. That drought, however, was limited mostly to that single year. Few areas experienced drought in both 1960 and 1962 (AES 1986). Back-to-back yearly droughts, such as those in the 1930s and 1980s, are much more difficult to recover from than single-year droughts.

Although the worst agricultural droughts occurred in 1961, 1988, 1936–7, and 1984–5, crop yield droughts affecting parts of the Prairies occurred in *at*

least 32 other years during 1900–93. These years are 1910, 1914, 1917, 1918, 1919, 1920, 1924, 1929, 1931, 1933, 1934, 1938, 1941, 1943, 1945, 1947, 1949, 1950, 1957, 1958, 1960, 1964, 1967, 1968, 1969, 1974, 1977, 1979, 1980, 1983, 1989, and 1990 (O'Brien 1994). This number clearly shows the common occurrence of drought in the Prairies. Droughts as dry as the worst year of the 1930s are expected with an average frequency of one in twenty years. Less severe droughts are more common (Berry and Williams 1985).

Boreal forest droughts are less common and less noticeable because of the sparse population and climate stations in the north. The droughts of the 1980s, however, also affected the boreal forest of the Prairie Provinces. Unlike the agricultural droughts, which were more isolated in the 1990s, the northern drought continued into 1994 and 1995.

Droughts before the 1900s

Droughts have occurred since the Prairie climate became semiarid to subhumid following the last ice age. Weather records are usually less than 100 years for most Prairie climate stations. So other methods such as the use of tree ring records, historic records, and lake sediments have been used to study the recurrence of drought over longer periods. Most of these studies are for the United States, but droughts over large areas in the Prairies can be extensions of those in the US Great Plains.

Major droughts in the Great Plains during the 1700s to 1900 clustered in the late 1750s, early 1820s, early 1860s, and mid-1890s (Wilhite and Heim 1991). Selkirk settlers mention drought in 1820 and 1868 in the Red River Settlement of Manitoba. There are several historical references to droughts in the 1890s, but weather records are too scant for a comprehensive picture (Jones 1991).

The dirty thirties – the hungry thirties

As the thirties progressed, conditions on the Prairies became progressively worse. Grasshoppers, drought, Russian thistles, wind and many dust storms were real menaces to a continued livelihood there. Crops were practically 'choked' out. There was insufficient feed for animals, and the gardens were poor. Hardships set in. A very unpleasant memory I have is one when our milk cow died (just before freshening) due to lack of enough good feed. Mother really cried because she was looking forward to have this fresh milk for cooking better meals for us. Then as time went on, it became impossible to make payments on land and whatever else. These 'bright tomorrows' my parents, as many others, had, now went by the wayside. There was a hopelessness all around. People began moving out to northern parts or other places of hope where they could find a good and new future again. We, too, were among these people that dropped all we had hoped for in our 'Prairie home' and in October 1937 we left for the North, our destination being Goodsoil, Saskatchewan.

(Handel New Horizons 1990: 247)

The drought year of 1929 set the stage for the 1930s droughts. A wheat-yield-based drought indicator showed that 1929–38 was the worst long-term drought during the 52-year period from 1928 to 1980. The next year, 1930, was not considered a 'wheat drought' year, but moderately dry conditions prevailed in some areas such as southeast Saskatchewan (AES 1986).

Drought hit again in 1931, covering the central part of southern Alberta into the centre of agricultural Saskatchewan and in a small part of southwestern Manitoba (Figure 23.6). Adequate moisture conditions interrupted the drought in 1935, but a severe wheat-stem rust epidemic struck (AES 1986).

The 1936–8 period ensured that the 1930s drought would become infamous. Reported wheat yields during this period were lower than for any other three-year period from 1921 to 1974. The droughts of 1936, 1937, and 1938 were the second, third, and fourth worst during the 1928–80 period (AES 1986). Wheat yields are only a convenient scientific indicator of drought severity. They should also be used as a measure of human and animal suffering.

Books and scientific reports have been written on the human and environmental effects of this drought period (e.g., Berton 1990). The suffering comes to life in the letters written by the Prairie people then and in the community history books. Statistics can be drier than drought, but these statistics are staggering. The drought and economic depression combined to produce many devastating effects on people, the environment, and the economy. Farm abandonment in the thirties was unprecedented. In Saskatchewan, 4,907, 5,193, and 12,831 abandoned farms were reported during the 1926, 1931, and 1936 censuses,

Figure 23.6 Wheat yield drought during 1931 (AES 1986)
Note: Each grid-point number represents the ranking for the particular year's water-based yield estimate at that location. The ranking is in ascending order of yield for the fifty-three-year period, 1928–80. A rank of six means the sixth lowest yield in the period for that location. A 'wheat drought' is defined to exist when the water-based yield estimate for a year is among the sixth lowest in that period

respectively. Malnutrition became evident, especially among children. In 1936 the medical assistance area included most of the Saskatchewan wheat belt (AES 1986). The wheat belt had changed into the 'dust bowl'.

The following quote brings to life what living in these dust storm times felt like:

I think we left Handel [in western agricultural Saskatchewan] for the same reason that a lot of people did. The drought. We had acquired a model 'T' Ford and we got stuck in the dust on the road. The dust was so deep. The wind blew crops, seed and all, from a field on one side of the road to the field on the other side. The dust seeped into houses under doors and window sashes. After a few years of that, Dad decided enough is enough. The opportunity came to take up a homestead in northern Saskatchewan.

(Handel New Horizons 1990: 283)

Severe environmental effects were also noted, especially the serious problem of the 'black blizzards' or dust storms that blew for days during the thirties. Many thousands of hectares of land blew out of control and much valuable topsoil was lost (Gray 1978). The dust storms also increased the discomfort of people and animals. A roaring wind is bad enough but when it also carries tonnes of soil it is painful and unbearable. Dust storms also sandblast crops and other plants, destroying what was weakened by lack of water.

The dirty eighties

The eighties brought about numerous difficulties for farmers in the district. Drought, low farm prices, high production costs, combined with high interest rates caused a serious struggle, especially for young farmers. In addition, they were also plagued with grasshoppers and flea beetles . . . Moisture levels in the eighties were equivalent in comparison to the thirties. There was a trend to milder winters with less snowfall. Changes in farming methods, fertilization, herbicides and pesticides enabled farmers to produce reasonable yields. Farmers also relied on crop insurance, grain stabilization programs and Canadian Crop Drought Assistance program payment, as well as production loans for grain and cattle to help allay farm costs.

(Handel New Horizons 1990: 42)

True, there are desert areas in the Western Hemisphere, such as in Chile, where rain has not been recorded for many years. But by standards for the North American Great Plains, the droughts there during the 1980s were extreme. This section focuses on the most recent of the 'great droughts', the dirty eighties. The progression of this drought and its characteristics are described, and some of its many effects on health, agriculture, and soil and water resources are summarised.

The dry fall of 1987 initiated one of the worst droughts in North American history in 1988. The drought of 1988 is remembered for its viciousness because of its severity, persistence, effects, and extensiveness over the North American Great Plains. Above-average temperatures and well-below-average precipitation were reported for the winter of 1987–8 for all three Prairie Provinces (Wheaton and Wittrock 1989a).

Much of the agricultural portions of Alberta and Saskatchewan received less than 50 per cent of their normal precipitation in the winter of 1987–8. The minimal snow cover and high spring temperatures resulted in little or no spring runoff for prairie watersheds in the spring. By May and June 1988, nature's 'blast furnace' was turned on high and temperatures were soaring. Even nighttime temperatures were unbearable. Usually, the pastures form a wonderful green blanket by May. This was not so in May 1988 in most of the Prairies. The fields were brown, dry, and dusty; the wind roared; dust blew; and the grass crunched when stepped on.

June 1988 was the hottest June on record for most climate stations, with temperatures exceeding 40°C for several days in a row. Several stations broke records for extreme highs (Figure 23.7). The all-time record high temperature for Canada was almost broken when Kincaid reached 43.5°C that June.

However, the Saskatchewan towns of Yellow Grass and Midale still held the all-time record high. In fact, they are joint holders of the record for Canada at a blistering 45°C. This record was made many years ago during those dirty thirties, on 5 July 1937 (Phillips 1990).

Hot, dry, sunny, and dusty conditions prevailed over much of the agricultural Prairies in the summer of 1988. This combination of record hot and dry weather resulted in extreme drought conditions. A wedge of severe drought had moved northward from the United States almost to the boreal forest edge north of Prince Albert, Saskatchewan, by June 1988 (Figure 23.8). The drought continued to grip much of the Prairies, and soil moisture was still at a deficit at the end of September across the southern portion of western Canada.

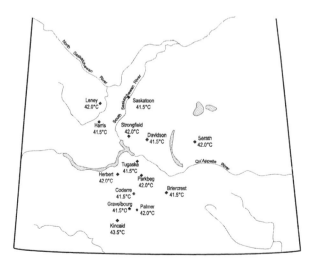

Figure 23.7 Climate stations with extreme temperatures greater than 41°C, June 1988, Saskatchewan (after Wheaton and Wittrock 1989a; data source: AES 1989)

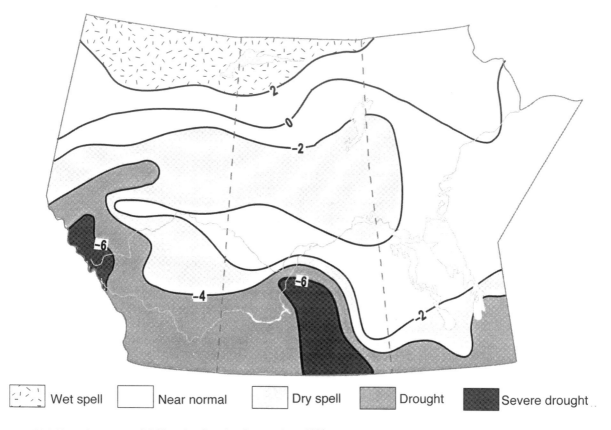

Wet spell   Near normal   Dry spell   Drought   Severe drought

Figure 23.8 Drought patterns (PDSI) in the Canadian Prairies, June 1988
Source: Wheaton and Wittrock 1989a

Hot spells and health

Hot spells can increase or exacerbate health problems, sometimes resulting in death. Humans can withstand a wide range of climatic conditions; we survive temperatures ranging from very hot (50°C) to very cold (−60°C). Most people, however, do best in the 'comfort zone' of a few degrees above or below the optimum annual average of about 10°C (Kalkstein 1989). For comparison, Saskatoon has an annual temperature of about 2°C (based on the 1961–90 period) (Beaulieu and Wittrock 1997).

The threshold temperature of this comfort zone is relative, however, and it is lower in cooler climates and higher in warmer climates. Therefore, people in cooler climates, such as the Prairies, are more vulnerable to heat waves than those in warmer climates,

and people in warmer climates are more vulnerable to cold spells (Kalkstein 1989).

The hot and dry summer of 1988 affected many people's health in North America. For example, twenty-eight people in Saskatchewan were affected badly enough to be hospitalised in the fiscal year 1987–8 because of problems related to the effects of heat and light. Eighty-eight were hospitalised for this problem in the fiscal year 1988–9. There was one fatality in the 1987–8 year, but none in 1988–9 (Wheaton and Wittrock 1992).

These people likely represented the 'tip of the iceberg'. Several others were also affected by respiratory problems complicated by the poor air quality during wind erosion and many larger-scale dust storms.

Agriculture effects

As you can imagine, the agricultural effects were devastating. Agriculture was one of the hardest hit sectors of the economy, although many aspects of both the environment and economy suffered greatly. Many farmers were unable to produce the eight bushels per acre required to meet harvesting costs. In Saskatchewan, more than half of the crop districts had crop yields less than 50 per cent of the ten-year average, and only one crop district had average yields more than 75 per cent of the ten-year average (Arthur and Chorney 1989a).

Saskatchewan was the hardest hit by the drought. This seems to be a common pattern during drought years. The lowest wheat production was in the central and west central parts of agricultural Saskatchewan (Figure 23.9). As compared to 1987, wheat production in 1988 dropped by 54.0 per cent in Saskatchewan, 38.8 per cent in Manitoba, and only 5.1 per cent in Alberta. Almost half of the Saskatchewan crop districts had spring wheat yields that were less than or equal to 50 per cent of the ten-year average (Arthur and Chorney 1989a).

The only plants that did well in this drought were

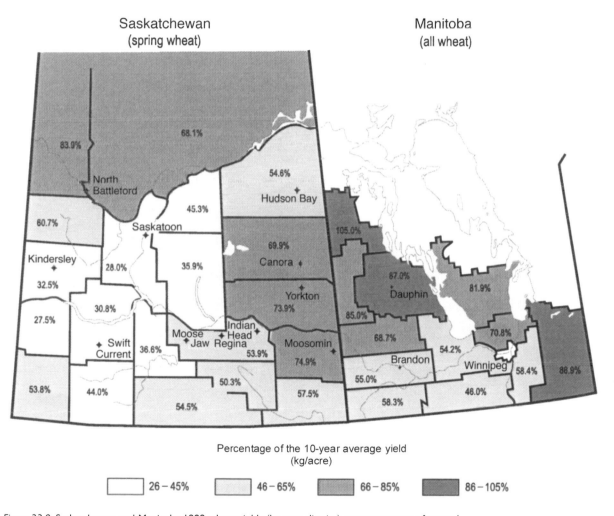

Figure 23.9 Saskatchewan and Manitoba 1988 wheat yields (by crop district) as a percentage of normal
Source: Arthur and Chorney 1989a

weeds. Thistle crops sprang up everywhere. Mounds of thistles filled dugouts and ditches. Thistles lined fences and redesigned the appearance of these structures for long distances. Kochia is a weed that flaunted its adaptability and drought tolerance remarkably during 1988. The plant germinated and just seemed to sit there and wait for its moment in the sun. Later during the year, rain finally fell, enough for the kochia to grow to remarkable proportions.

Livestock producers were also hard hit by the drought. The southern Canadian Prairies and northern US plains had the worst conditions for livestock because of dry pastures, poor hay and feed production, and shortages of good-quality water. Some cattle were moved to northern areas where pasture and water conditions were much better (Arthur and Chorney 1989a).

The economic effects of the 1988 drought were staggering. Canada's agricultural output decreased by 12.7 per cent, mostly because of the drought. Arthur and Chorney (1989a) estimated the drought to have caused a direct production loss of C$1.8 billion (in 1981 dollars), or 0.4 per cent of real gross domestic product (GDP).

Dust storms – the driest weather

Dust storms and their severe wind erosion were terrible in 1988. That year not only had some of the driest of weather, it also had about the dirtiest weather. The number of dust storms was at or above record numbers for several locations. The total number of dust storms ranged up to a maximum of fifteen at Kindersley in west central agricultural Saskatchewan (Figure 23.10). The area with the second-highest number of dust storms was around Winnipeg, Manitoba. The area with frequent dust storms covered a large portion of the agricultural Prairie. June saw the largest area affected by dust storms. June is usually the month with the most rainfall in the Prairie region, and therefore the greenest fields, so this condition was quite a contrast to that of other Junes.

Water resources

Most water supplies in the Prairies, even in the north, were affected by the 1988 drought (Figure 23.11).

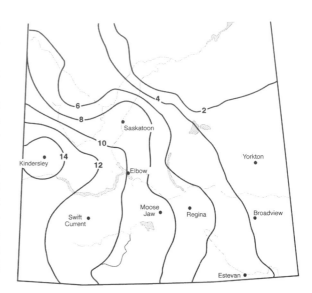

Figure 23.10 Dust storm days during 1988 in southern Saskatchewan
Source: Wheaton and Wittrock 1989b

Water supplies (ranging from farm supplies to municipal and hydroelectric reservoirs) shrunk. Most of the agricultural area of Saskatchewan had annual streamflows that were less than half of their average volumes. Almost 40 per cent of the stations measuring streamflow broke records for the lowest flows.

Forest fires

Drought impairs tree growth, especially of young trees, and it can foster disease and insect outbreaks, but the most noticeable, newsworthy, and dangerous connection is with fires. For example, the number of forest fires in Saskatchewan, at 1,038, was higher in 1988 than in any other year in the period of record since 1918 (Figure 23.12) (Wittrock and Wheaton 1997, Arthur et al. 1989). The area burned (81,000 ha), however, was surprisingly less than the long-term average of 130,000 ha per year. This was likely due to the extensive firefighting activities that year. Firefighting costs were high in both 1987 and 1988, at C$33.9 and C$31.8 million (Arthur et al. 1989).

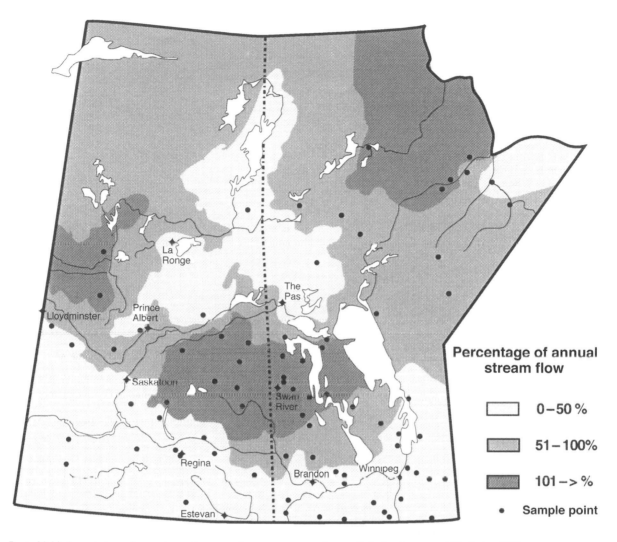

Figure 23.11 Annual streamflow volumes (expressed as a percentage of normal), Saskatchewan and Manitoba, 1988
Source: Whiting and Nicolichuk 1989

Waterfowl

Waterfowl, such as duck, and their habitat, such as sloughs, became scarce during the 1980s, as compared to normal (Figure 23.13). A record is kept of the number of sloughs in the Prairies because they are important to waterfowl. By July 1988, the number of sloughs counted in Saskatchewan and Manitoba was below half of normal (Wittrock and Wheaton 1989c).

Waterfowl were leaving for other places, such as farther north, to find habitat. The waterfowl numbers also diminished because of the increased incidence of disease thought to be related to dry conditions and the resulting crowding in the few remaining suitable areas. On the bright side, the waterfowl damage to crops was much less that year because of the low waterfowl numbers and the early, small harvest (Arthur and Chorney 1989b).

CONCLUSION

Recurrent droughts are a part of the Prairie climate.

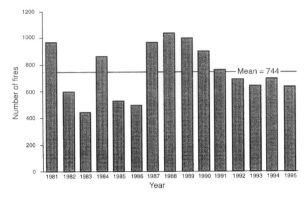

Figure 23.12 Annual number of forest fires in Saskatchewan
Source: Wittrock and Wheaton 1997

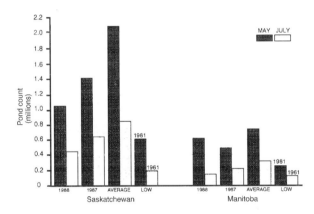

Figure 23.13 The number of sloughs counted in Saskatchewan and Manitoba, 1987–8, and the mean
Source: Wittrock and Wheaton 1989c

Some parts of the Prairies have a drought during most years. The consequences of the severe drought of 1988 were severe, numerous, and wide ranging. These effects were exacerbated because the 1988 drought followed other droughts during the 1980s, such as the drought of 1987. As in the 1930s, the timing of the drought in 1988 was bad in that it struck agriculturally dependent economies that were already weakened by years of low commodity prices. Unlike the 1930s, however, various programmes and policies were in place to help mitigate the effects of the 1988 drought.

The dirty eighties versus the dirty thirties

A common question (especially during the 1980s) was, 'was the drought of the 1980s as bad as the 1930s drought?' Were the 1930s droughts reincarnated? Society wanted to know if it had been through something like this before. As with most tough questions about complicated issues, that answer is yes and no.

The 1980s droughts are thought to have been more widespread in North America than the droughts of the 1930s, especially the 1988 drought. That year had the worst Palmer Drought Indices on record for many stations in the Prairies. Precipitation totals over the ten-year periods 1929–38 and 1979–88 were almost identical. However, the 1980s should be more renowned for their hot spells, as temperatures in the 1980s were much higher than in the 1930s (Lang and Jones 1988).

The 1930s also had much different winters than the 1980s. Winters during much of the 1980s were mild and had little snow cover. For example, the winter of 1988 had such a sparse snow cover that dust storms occurred. Dust storms are usually rare in winter because of the snow cover protection of the soil (Wheaton and Wittrock 1989b). In contrast, winters of the 1930s had considerable snow and were cold.

To answer the question, the 1930s and 1980s droughts were similar in intensity, but had several different characteristics, including the more severe winters of the 1930s and the worse hot spells of the 1980s. The 1980s droughts were also hard on the environment, economy, and people, but because of many drought programmes and policies, hardships did not appear to be as severe as in the 1930s. This is a lesson for dealing with future droughts – that we still have considerable risk to avoid and that drought planning and support as well as technological improvements can pay off in decreased hardship.

FUTURE DROUGHTS

The climate system consists of complex interactions among the land surfaces, oceans, atmosphere, and outer space. Although it is not possible, presently, to predict the date of the next drought, it is certain that

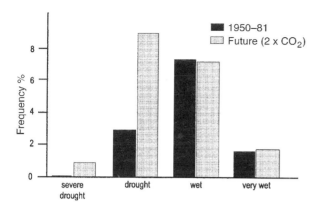

Figure 23.14 Current and future drought risks for Saskatchewan (data source: Williams *et al.* 1988)

they will recur, especially in the Canadian Prairies. It is possible, however, to use statistics on historical drought occurrences to determine the risk of different types of drought occurrence.

The risk of drought is high in the Prairies. The odds of having drought conditions during any month are about 23 per cent for Saskatchewan agricultural stations (Williams *et al.* 1988). This is twenty-three droughts during one hundred years, or almost one out of every four years.

It is thought that future warming will bring more frequent and more intense droughts by the middle of the next century (e.g., Williams *et al.* 1988). Reasons for this include (1) the higher temperatures that will increase the rate at which vegetation and soils and people use water and (2) the longer warm season over which water use can occur.

Drought risk is expected to increase into the future as the 'greenhouse effect' increases. We are or should be especially concerned about when either of the types of long-term droughts of the 1930s or 1980s will recur and how well we are prepared for and can cope with such extreme conditions (Figure 23.14).

ACKNOWLEDGEMENTS

This work is based on an earlier, less technical chapter that will appear in a forthcoming book on weather and climate of the Canadian Prairies (Fifth House Publishers).

REFERENCES

AES Drought Study Group (1986) *An Applied Climatology of Drought in the Canadian Prairie Provinces*, Downsview, Ontario: Canadian Climate Centre.

Atmospheric Environment Service (1989) *Monthly Record of Meteorological Observations*, Downsview, Ontario: AES, Environment Canada.

Arthur, L. and Chorney, B. (1989a) 'Impacts of the 1988 drought on agriculture – With emphasis on Saskatchewan and Manitoba', in E.E. Wheaton and L.M. Arthur (eds), *Environmental and Economic Impacts of the 1988 Drought: With Emphasis on Saskatchewan and Manitoba*, Volume 1, Saskatoon, Saskatchewan: Saskatchewan Research Council, Chapter 2.

—— (1989b) 'Migratory birds – Economic impacts', in E.E. Wheaton and L.M. Arthur (eds), *Environmental and Economic Impacts of the 1988 Drought: With Emphasis on Saskatchewan and Manitoba*, Volume 1, Saskatoon, Saskatchewan: Saskatchewan Research Council, Chapter 5, Part B.

Arthur, L., Thorpe, J., and Chorney, B. (1989) 'Impacts of the 1988 drought on forestry – Saskatchewan and Manitoba', in E.E. Wheaton and L.M. Arthur (eds), *Environmental and Economic Impacts of the 1988 Drought. With Emphasis on Saskatchewan and Manitoba*, Volume 1, Saskatoon, Saskatchewan: Saskatchewan Research Council, Chapter 3.

Barry, R.G. and Chorley, R.J. (1976) *Atmosphere, Weather and Climate – Third Edition*, Bungay, Suffolk: The Chaucer Press Ltd. (adapted by and cited in Maybank *et al.* 1995).

Beaulieu, C. and Wittrock, V. (1997) *Saskatoon SRC Climatological Reference Station – Annual Summary 1996*, Saskatoon, Saskatchewan: Saskatchewan Research Council.

Bergthórsson, P. (1984) Personal communication, Mr. P. Bergthórsson, Vedurstofa Islands, Bústadaregi 9, 150 Reykjavik, Iceland.

Berry, M.O. and Williams, G.D.V. (1985) 'Thirties drought on the Prairies – How unique was it?', in C.R. Harington (ed.), *Climatic Change in Canada 5 – Critical Periods in the Quaternary Climatic History of Northern North America*, Ottawa, Ontario: National Museums of Canada.

Berton, P. (1990) *The Great Depression*, Toronto, Ontario: Penguin Books.

Bonsal, B.R., Chakravarti, A.K., and Lawford, R.G. (1993) 'Teleconnections between North Pacific SST anomalies and growing season extended dry spells on the Canadian Prairies', *International Journal of Climatology* 13, 865–78.

Cullen, A.J. (1996) Personal communication, A.J. Cullen, Regional Director, Prairie Farm Rehabilitation Administration, Agriculture and Agri-Food Canada, Calgary, Alberta.

Gray, J.H. (1978) *Men against the Desert*, Saskatoon, Saskatchewan: Western Producer Prairie Books.

Handel New Horizons (1990) *Handel Notes and Half Notes*, Handel, Saskatchewan: Handel New Horizons.

Jones, K.H. (1991) 'Drought on the Prairies', in G. Wall (ed.), *Symposium on the Impacts of Climatic Change and Variability on the Great Plains*, 11–13 September 1990, Calgary, Alberta, Waterloo, Ontario: University of Waterloo, pp. 125–9.

Kalkstein, L.S. (1989) 'The impact of CO_2 and trace gas-induced climate changes upon human mortality', in J.B. Smith and D.A. Tirpak (eds), *The Potential Effects of Global Climate Change on the United States*, Washington, DC: US Environmental Protection Agency, Appendix G – Health.

Lang, T.A. and Jones, K. (1988) *A Comparison of the Meteorological Conditions during the Droughts of the 1930s and 1980s for the Prairie Provinces*, Regina, Saskatchewan: Canadian Climate program.

Maybank, J., Bonsal, B., Jones, K., Lawford, R., O'Brien, E.G., Ripley, E.A., and Wheaton, E. (1995) 'Drought as a natural disaster', *Atmosphere–Ocean* 33, 2: 195–222.

McKay, G.A. (1963) 'Climatic maps of the Prairie Provinces for agriculture', *Climatological Studies Number 1*, Figure 15, coefficient of variation of growing season precipitation, Toronto, Ontario: Department of Transport, Meteorological Branch.

Namais, J. (1960) 'Factors in the initiation, perpetuation and termination of drought', in *Publication 51, Association of Scientific Hydrology, International Union of Geodesy and Geophysics*.

O'Brien, E.G. (1994) 'Drought in Canada', in D. Burnett *et al.*, *Canadian National Report for the International Decade for Natural Disaster Reduction: 97–99*, Ottawa: The Royal Society of Canada/Canadian Academy of Engineering.

Palmer, W.C. (1965) 'Meteorological drought', *Research Paper* 45, Washington, DC: US Weather Bureau.

Phillips, D.W. (1990) *The Climate of Canada*, Ottawa, Ontario: Supply and Services Canada.

Trenberth, K.E. (1989) 'The wayward winds', *Natural History* 1: 44–5.

Warkentin, A.A. (1989) Personal communication, Mr. A. Warkentin, Hydrometeorologist, Water Resources Branch, Manitoba Natural Resources, Winnipeg, Manitoba.

Wheaton, E. and Wittrock, V. (1989a) 'An overview of the drought climate of 1988', in E.E. Wheaton and L.M. Arthur (eds), *Environmental and Economic Impacts of the 1988 Drought: With Emphasis on Saskatchewan and Manitoba*, Volume 1, Saskatoon, Saskatchewan: Saskatchewan Research Council, Chapter 1, Part A.

——— (1989b) 'Dust storms and wind erosion during 1988 – Saskatchewan and Manitoba', in E.E. Wheaton and L.M. Arthur (eds), *Environmental and Economic Impacts of the 1988 Drought: With Emphasis on Saskatchewan and Manitoba*, Volume 2, Appendices, Saskatoon, Saskatchewan: Saskatchewan Research Council, Appendix C.

——— (1992) 'Human health in Saskatchewan and global warming – A preliminary assessment', in E.E. Wheaton, V. Wittrock, and G.D.V. Williams (eds), *Saskatchewan in a Warmer World: Preparing for the Future*, Saskatoon, Saskatchewan: Saskatchewan Research Council.

Whiting, J. and Nicolichuk, N. (1989) 'Surface hydrology', in E.E. Wheaton and L.M. Arthur (eds), *Environmental and Economic Impacts of the 1988 Drought: With Emphasis on Saskatchewan and Manitoba*, Volume 1, Saskatoon, Saskatchewan: Saskatchewan Research Council.

Wilhite, D.A. and Heim, R.R. (1991) 'Drought incidence in the Great Plains of the United States', in G. Wall (ed.), *Symposium on the Impacts of Climatic Change and Variability on the Great Plains*, 11–13 September 1990, Calgary, Alberta, Waterloo, Ontario: University of Waterloo, pp. 119–24.

Williams, G.D.V., Fautley, R.A., Jones, K.H., Stewart, R.B., and Wheaton, E.E. (1988) 'Estimating effects of climatic change on agriculture in Saskatchewan, Canada', in M.L. Parry, T.R. Carter, and N.J. Konijn (eds), *The Impact of Climatic Variations on Agriculture*, Volume 1, *Assessments in Cool Temperate and Cold Regions*, Boston, MA: Kluwer Academic Publishers.

Wittrock, V. and Wheaton, E. (1989a) 'Newspaper articles and the drought of 1988', in E.E. Wheaton and L.M. Arthur (eds), *Environmental and Economic Impacts of the 1988 Drought: With Emphasis on Saskatchewan and Manitoba*, Volume 1, Saskatoon, Saskatchewan: Saskatchewan Research Council, Chapter 12.

——— (1989b) 'Groundwater', in E.E. Wheaton and L.M. Arthur (eds), *Environmental and Economic Impacts of the 1988 Drought: With Emphasis on Saskatchewan and Manitoba*, Volume 1, Saskatoon, Saskatchewan: Saskatchewan Research Council, Chapter 4, Part B.

——— (1989c) 'Impact of the 1988 drought on migratory birds – Saskatchewan and Manitoba', in E.E. Wheaton and L.M. Arthur (eds), *Environmental and Economic Impacts of the 1988 Drought: With Emphasis on Saskatchewan and Manitoba*, Volume 1, Saskatoon, Saskatchewan: Saskatchewan Research Council, Chapter 5, Part A.

——— (1997) *Climate Variations, Fire Characteristics and Budget Implications: Preliminary Analysis of their Relationships (Draft)*, Saskatoon, Saskatchewan: Saskatchewan Research Council.

24

THE IMPACTS OF DROUGHT IN CHINA

Recent experiences

Kerang Li, Yufeng Chen, and Chaoying Huang

BASIC CHARACTERISTICS OF DROUGHT IN CHINA

Spatial distribution of drought

Because drought is caused by the shortage of rainfall, the intensity of meteorological drought in China can be classified on the basis of departure-from-normal precipitation (Table 24.1). China can be divided into six subregions that represent the centres of drought in China (Figure 24.1), based on the total number of drought occurrences, the number of severe and extreme droughts, and the maximum number of drought months, according to information from meteorological stations during 1951–91. As shown in Figure 24.1, the six subregions are: north China, northwest China, northeast China, southwest China, the Middle and Lower Reaches of the Yangtze River (or central China), and south China. In terms of number, intensity, and duration, north China experiences the worst droughts, followed by south China and southwest China. In northeast China, drought mainly occurs in the middle and western part. Drought intensity in the Middle and Lower Reaches of the Yangtze River is relatively moderate; northwest China is subjected to drought throughout the year (Li *et al.* 1993).

Seasonal characteristics of drought

The main climatic features in China are that monsoon climate is evident and seasonal precipitation differs greatly, with summer rainfall usually sufficient and winter rainfall usually deficient. However, because the summer monsoon occurs from south to north, the time of occurrence of the rainy season varies from place to place. Generally, in mid-May, the rain belt arrives in south China. In mid-June, the rain belt shifts to the Yangtze River Valley, where plum rain or *Mei-yu* develops; in mid-July, when the plum season ends in the Yangtze Valley, the main rain belt moves across the Huai River so that north China enters into the rainy season. In mid-September, however, the rain belt begins to withdraw to south China, then gradually shifts toward southeast China. At the beginning of October, the winter monsoon begins to move southward, and the climate becomes dry with less rainfall. At the beginning of March, the winter monsoon becomes weak and gradually retreats from south to north. Because of the influence of monsoon climate and other factors causing such climate, the occurrence of drought in different regions of China has certain seasonal characteristics. However, with regard to any specific year, the occurrence of drought is also stochastic because the time of the rainy season, amount of precipitation, and temporal distribution of precipitation are random. For these reasons, severe drought can also occur in the moist part of southern China.

Briefly, in northern China, especially north China and northeast China, spring drought and spring–summer persistent drought occur most frequently, followed by summer drought, and spring–summer–autumn persistent drought occurs with the lowest frequency. In south China, autumn–winter drought and winter–spring drought occur most frequently, autumn–winter–spring persistent drought occurs only in isolated years, and summer drought occurs with

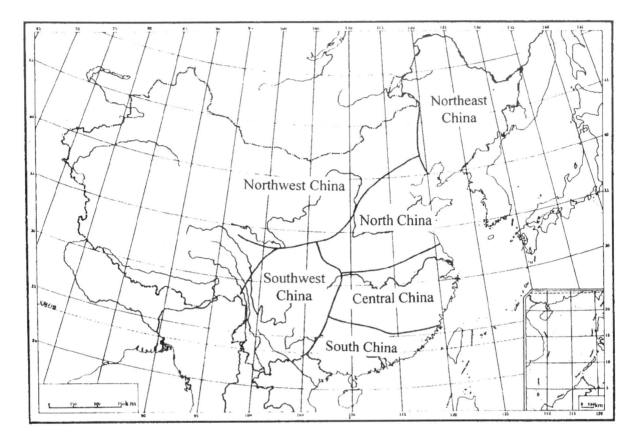

Figure 24.1 The major drought-prone regions in China (from Li *et al.* 1996)

Table 24.1 Drought intensity

Duration of drought	Moderate drought (%)	Severe drought (%)	Extreme drought (%)
One month	<−80		
Two months	−51 ~ −80	<−80	
Three months	−26 ~ −50	−51 ~ −80	<−80
Four months	−1 ~ −25	−26 ~ −50	−51 ~ −80
Five months		−1 ~ −25	−26 ~ −50
More than six months			−1 ~ −25

Source: Li *et al.* 1996

the lowest frequency. In the Middle and Lower Reaches of the Yangtze River basin, summer–autumn drought occurs most frequently, especially summer–autumn persistent drought, and spring drought occurs less frequently.

Temporal change of drought

To analyse the temporal change of drought in different regions as well as the country as a whole, a drought index (I_D) was used to calculate the relative dryness/wetness, using the following equation:

$$I_D = 2\frac{D}{N}$$

where I_D is the drought index, D is the total number of stations where all classes of drought were recorded in a given year, and N is the total number of stations. I_D then reflects the area affected by drought. In general, where the area affected by drought is larger, the losses caused by drought are more severe.

The time series of the drought index in different regions and the country as a whole from 1951 to 1991 is shown in Figure 24.2. In the past forty years, the driest year in China was 1972, followed by 1965, 1968, 1986, and 1991. The drought index of the entire country has a linear increase in the past forty years – that is, the climate of China is becoming more desiccated.

The equation of linear trend of the drought index of China is shown below.

$$I_D(t) = 7.64 \times 10^{-8}\, t - 14.25$$

where I_D is the drought index and t is the given year. The driest year and the drying trend varied among regions, with the drying trend of north China, northeast China, south China, and southwest China most evident.

The mean values of the drought index (I) and severe drought index (I_s) of different regions and the entire country from 1470 to 1992 are given in Table 24.2. In the six regions, the highest drought index occurred in northwest China, followed by north China and south China. The mean value of the three regions was higher than that of the country as a whole. The mean value of the other regions was lower than that of the entire country. Comparing the drought indexes of different centuries, drought in the twentieth century is the most severe, followed by the later years of the fifteenth and seventeenth centuries. The least severe drought occurs in the eighteenth century, followed by the nineteenth century. Of course, there were some differences among different regions in different centuries.

The above analyses show that the maximum drought index occurred in the twentieth century in all but two of the regions. In the twentieth century, the drought indexes showed an increasing trend, with

fluctuations (Figure 24.3). The drought indexes of the 1980s and early 1990s were the highest in most of the regions. Therefore, most regions in China are experiencing an increasing number of severe droughts. Meanwhile, many conditions, such as changes in water resources, glaciers, and streamflows and a tendency toward desertification, also indicate a drying trend, at least in the northern part of China (Li et al. 1993). If the drying tendency combines with impacts of future climate warming, particularly with the impacts of overpumping and overuse of water resources caused by population growth and rapid agricultural and industrial development, the consequences of drying will be extremely severe.

Teleconnection of drought

According to monthly climate data for the world (1965–90), Sun Guowu et al. (1997) first classified drought periods (Table 24.3) using precipitation data of selected typical stations in north Africa (A), the Middle East (B), middle Asia (C), and northwest China (D) in the range of the middle latitude of Asia and Africa (20° N–50° N, 20° W–110° E). They combined drought periods that were separated by less than three years and concentrated on drought periods occurring more than five years apart. They have analysed the relationships of drought in northwest China and other areas of Asia and Africa.

It was found that drought first started in northern Africa (A) and then extended eastward to northwest China (D) through the Middle East (B) and middle Asia (C). In the four regions, there have been three great droughts of more than ten years' duration since 1870: from the end of last century to 1910, the 1920s to the 1940s, the 1960s, and the 1980s. In middle Asia (C), there have been four great droughts of less than ten years' duration: from the end of the 1880s to the mid 1890s, from the end of the 1910s to the mid-1920s, the 1930s, and from the end of the 1940s to the beginning of the 1950s. These droughts were not synchronous with the droughts that occurred in the other three regions, which had the tendency of spreading out from Africa to Asia. In the last hundred years, the eastward progression of seven droughts shows that the droughts in northern Africa spread to the Middle East after 3.5 years. From the Middle

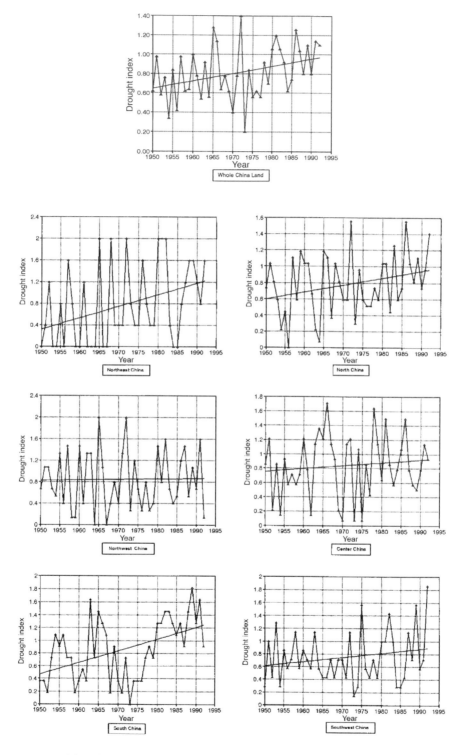

Figure 24.2 The time series of drought indices in different regions and the country as a whole (1951–91) (from Li *et al.* 1996)

Table 24.2 Mean values of drought indexes (I) and severe drought indexes (I_s) in China, 1470–1992

Century	China		Northeast China		North China		Northwest China		Middle and Lower Yangtze River		South China		Southwest China	
	I_s	I	I_s	I	I_s	I	I_s	I	I_s	I	I_s	I	I_s	I
The later period of:														
15th century	0.6	0.15	0.4	0.07	0.74	0.2	0.91	0.24	0.52	0.16	0.38	0	0.37	0.1
16th century	0.55	0.15	0.69	0.26	0.61	0.17	0.74	0.17	0.49	0.18	0.48	0.1	0.32	0.1
17th century	0.59	0.16	0.59	0.18	0.69	0.23	0.73	0.16	0.54	0.16	0.54	0.12	0.38	0.1
18th century	0.44	0.1	0.39	0.1	0.48	0.12	0.72	0.14	0.37	0.1	0.53	0.1	0.2	0.1
19th century	0.5	0.12	0.31	0.07	0.58	0.16	0.63	0.16	0.44	0.1	0.63	0.1	0.3	0.1
20th century	0.74	0.23	0.65	0.31	0.81	0.24	0.8	0.29	0.67	0.2	0.82	0.22	0.63	0.19
Total mean values	0.56	0.15	0.52	0.18	0.64	0.18	0.73	0.19	0.5	0.14	0.58	0.11	0.36	0.19

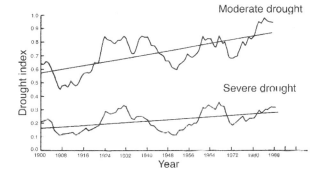

Figure 24.3 Ten-year running mean and linear trend of drought indexes of the twentieth century in China (the upper figure represents moderate drought, and the lower figure is severe drought)

East, the drought spread east to middle Asia after 20.4 years; from middle Asia, it spread to northwest China after 3.8 years. In other words, it took 25 to 29 years (mean 27.8 years) for the drought to spread from northern Africa to northwest China.

There are close connections between droughts in Asia and Africa and the abnormality of atmospheric circulation. In drought periods, the low-frequency teleconnection type (500 hPa) and the low-frequency wave train followed a great circle route: from North Africa (the centre of positive correlation), to the Mediterranean (the centre of negative correlation), to the Middle East (the centre of positive correlation), to middle Asia (the centre of negative correlation), to northwest China (the centre of positive correlation). This wave train indicates that not only does the occurrence of drought relate to the abnormality of atmospheric circulation in a large range, but there are also links among the abnormality of atmospheric circulation in different regions; the signs of correlation were the same in northern Africa, the Middle East, and northwest China, but were reversed in middle Asia.

A comparison of the number of earthquakes of

Table 24.3 Drought periods during 1870–1990

	A	B	C	D
Drought periods	1873	1874	1877–95	1890–1910
	1895–1906	1900–18	1903–7	1920–32
	1909–13	1927–37	1918–25	1938–42
	1924–7	1941–9	1931–41	1952–5
	1939–52	1959–68	1947–52	1968–82
	1957–61	1972–4	1965–7	1985–7
	1968–90		1982–4	

Source: Sun Guowu et al. 1997

≥ 6.0 magnitude (Richter scale) and drought periods in the four regions since 1870 shows that the more frequent drought periods usually correspond to a large number of earthquakes in each region and its neighbouring areas, while the nondrought periods usually correspond to a lower number of earthquakes. The occurrence of earthquakes often leads to a rise in ground temperature, which always influences the abnormality of atmospheric circulation. Since drought is the result of an abnormality of atmospheric circulation, drought persistence can affect ground temperature changes, and the rise in ground temperature usually is linked to activities of geothermal eddy – hence the active area of geothermal eddy is always the active area of an earthquake. Therefore, these complex physical processes are interconnected and related to the interactions between atmosphere and lithosphere, and the causal mechanism needs to be further studied.

IMPACTS OF DROUGHT ON WATER RESOURCES

Impacts on rainfall resources

Rainfall is the ultimate source of all kinds of water resources on earth. The impacts of drought on water resources are reflected in the reduction of rainfall. The average precipitation available each year in China is about 850 mm, which is equal to a water volume of $81,600 \times 10^8$ m^3, based on the territorial area of China (9.6×10^6 km^2). If it is assumed that a water depth of 1 mm is equal to the water volume of 1,000 m^3, the decrease in per-millimetre precipitation will lead to a drop in rainfall resources available in each 1 km^2 of 1,000 m^3. The rate of water volume decline in China would thus be 96×10^8 m^3. In twentieth-century China,

the lowest rainfall was recorded in 1978, when the annual average precipitation was only 767 mm. The volume of water resources was reduced by $8,352 \times 10^8$ m^3, amounting to a decrease of more than 10 per cent of the interannual average precipitation. In the subhumid and semiarid regions, the impacts of drought on rainfall resources are much greater because of great annual variations of precipitation. For example, the interannual average rainfall resource in Beijing, Tianjin, Hebei, and Shanxi was $1,993.78 \times 10^8$ m^3, but the five-year persistent drought from 1980 to 1984 resulted in an annual average rainfall volume of $1,683.38 \times 10^8$ m^3, which was reduced 250.4×10^8 m^3, or 13 per cent, compared to interannual mean values. Average reductions were 22 per cent in Beijing, 44 per cent in Tianjin, 21 per cent in Hebei, and 8 per cent in Shanxi. North China witnessed the most serious drought in 1972, when the volume of rainfall in Beijing, Tianjin, Hebei, and Shanxi was reduced by 31 per cent to the interannual mean values, causing serious shortages of water resources and bringing about critical consequences for socioeconomic development.

Impacts on surface water

The amount of surface water is usually denoted by surface runoff. Table 24.4 shows the annual runoff under different frequency regimes in China. It was found that in moderate drought years (accumulated frequency with 75 per cent), the total river discharge of the country was $24,533 \times 10^8$ m^3, a 7 per cent reduction from normal. In severe drought years (accumulated frequency with 95 per cent), the reduction from normal was about 15 per cent, equivalent to the 1978 reduction (about $22,730 \times 10^8$ m^3), 1978 being a severe drought year. In Beijing, the

Table 24.4 Runoff in China (10^8 cubic metres)

Accumulated frequency (%)	China	Beijing	Tianjin	Hebei	Shanxi	Henan	Jiangsu
20	28,490	33.30	16.40	232.0	142.0	445.0	390.0
50	26,116	22.50	10.50	156.0	109.0	297.0	255.0
75	24,533	13.70	6.50	110.0	86.3	206.0	161.0
95	22,423	7.79	1.68	59.3	63.6	110.0	48.4
Mean	26,380	23.6	11.2	169	114	322	269

Table 24.5 The mean (10^8 cubic metres) and ratio of mean to standard value of runoff in Beijing, Tianjin, Hebei, and Shanxi during different years

	1956–9 Mean	Ratio	1960–9 Mean	Ratio	1970–9 Mean	Ratio	1980–4 Mean	Ratio	Standard value (1956–84)
Beijing	47.3	2.06	20	0.87	21.8	0.95	12.3	0.53	23
Tianjin	9.8	0.97	9.9	0.98	12.2	1.21	6.4	0.63	10.1
Hebei	226.2	1.54	159.6	1.09	142.2	0.97	67.3	0.46	146.7
Shanxi	141.6	1.3	122.4	1.13	95.9	0.88	80.1	0.74	108.6

annual runoff was reduced by 42 per cent in moderate drought years and 85 per cent in severe drought years. In Henan Province, the annual runoff was reduced by 30 per cent in moderate drought years and 66 per cent in severe drought years. Therefore, it is clear that the impacts of drought on runoff varied in different regions.

Table 24.5 shows the mean and ratio of mean to standard value of runoff in Beijing, Tianjin, Hebei, and Shanxi in various years. A sharp decrease of the mean and ratio of mean occurred during 1980–4, in comparison to 1956–9. The degree of reduction was related to the reduction of rainfall. These changes in precipitation could lead to even greater changes in runoff.

To determine the hydrological regimes of the main rivers in China, the changing trend of the time series of natural runoff can be calculated on the basis of the data observed from the main controlled stations in the seven great rivers from southern China to northern China (Table 24.6).[1] It was found that in the past forty years, runoff of the above-mentioned rivers (except Songhuajiang River Valley and Pearl River Valley, whose runoff increased slightly) showed a decreasing trend. In particular, the reduction of runoff of the Haihe and Huaihe rivers was the largest. Compared to the changing tendency of surface temperature in China in the past forty years, surface temperature showed an increasing trend in areas north of 35°N, at the rate of 0.24°C every ten years. The Haihe River Valley had the greatest warm and dry climatic trend in the past forty years, followed by the Yellow River Valley; a cold and dry climatic trend appeared in the Yangtze Valley; and a warm and moist climatic trend appeared in the Songhuajiang River Valley.

Impacts on groundwater

Because rainfall infiltration is the main source of groundwater recharge, changes in that infiltration will be reflected in groundwater recharge rates. Table 24.7 shows rainfall infiltration in freshwater zones of the North China Plain in different years. Reductions in recharge rates were small from the 1950s to the beginning of the 1980s, but they increased rapidly in the 1980s as a result of drought. Because underground aquifers have a certain capacity to regulate groundwater, they can make up water from aquifers if low runoff or persistent low runoff lasting two to

Table 24.6 Runoff change tendency of main rivers of China in the past forty years

Valleys (Stations)	Songhuajiang-Liaohe River (Harbin)	Haihe River (Miyun)	(Huangbizhuang)	Yellow River (Huayuan kou)	Huaihe River (Bengbu)	(Sanhezha)	Yangtze River (Yichang)	Pearl River (Wuzhou)
Mean ($\times 10^8$ m³)	486.9	14	24	605	323.1	338.8	4465	2151
10-year trend	1.26	−22.5	−23.36	−0.45	−1	−19.34	−0.43	0.12
Standard deviation	150.3	8.06	13.34	119.4	147.1	187.2	428.5	370.9

three years occurs. However, when persistent low runoff of four to five (or more) years occurs, groundwater cannot be pumped normally. For instance, in the neighbouring areas of Beijing, the occurrence of a persistent drought of five years during 1980–4 caused the pumping volume of groundwater to exceed the rate of recharge during the same time period, resulting in an accumulative deficit of $47 \times 10^8 \, \mathrm{m}^3$ and a decline in the average groundwater level of 4.43 m. Moreover, the severe drought that occurred in Beijing in 1972 caused a 3–5 m decline in the average groundwater level, increasing to 6–7 m in some regions.

Impacts on total amount of water resource

The regional total amount of water resources refers to the yield of surface water and groundwater from rainfall. According to calculations by the Hydrological Department of the Ministry of Water Conservancy (1987), the total amount of water resources in China averaged over the years 1956–84 is $27,210 \times 10^8 \, \mathrm{m}^3$. The total amount of water resources in China is $25,100 \times 10^8 \, \mathrm{m}^3$ in drought years (four-year occurrence) and $23,100 \times 10^8 \, \mathrm{m}^3$ in severe drought years (twenty-year occurrence). The average total amount of water resources and the ratio to standard values in Beijing, Tianjin, Hebei, and Shanxi in different years

(given in Table 24.8) indicates that in the 1980s the average total amount of water resources was reduced about 40 per cent in Beijing and Hebei and 20–30 per cent in Tianjin and Shanxi.

The above analysis showed that rapid reductions in precipitation, runoff, and total amount of water resources all occurred in the 1980s. The reduction in runoff was the greatest, followed by reduction in total amount of water resources, reflecting the sensitivity of water resources to reductions in precipitation: the more severe the drought, the less water available and the more acute the conflict between supply and demand. China's annual per capita total rainfall availability is only 5,006 m³. Of the world's per capita water availability of 33,975 m³, China accounts for only 15 per cent. Rapid economic development, population increase, and urbanisation have increased the demand for water. Therefore, China is not only likely to experience drought, it is also easily threatened by drought. In addition, regional differences in China are very evident. For instance, in north China, with its developed economy and dense population, the total amount of water resource per capita is the lowest in the country, only about 500 m³, and this area is much more vulnerable to drought. Recently, the lower reaches of the Yellow River, the second largest river in China, dried up almost every year, and the duration of the dry period increased – 82 days in

Table 24.7 The rate of recharge in freshwater zones of the North China Plain (10⁸ cubic metres)

Years	1956–9	1960–9	1970–9	1980–4	Mean
Rate of recharge	140.87	130.73	124.15	91.42	123.08
Ratio to mean	1.14	1.06	1.01	0.74	1.0

Table 24.8 The mean (10⁸ cubic metres) and ratio of mean to standard value of water resources in Beijing, Tianjin, Hebei, and Shanxi

Station	1956–9 Mean	Ratio	1960–9 Mean	Ratio	1970–9 Mean	Ratio	1980–4 Mean	Ratio	Standard value (1956–84)
Beijing	65.3	1.76	33.3	0.9	36.6	0.99	23.0	0.62	37.1
Tianjin	14.3	1.01	14.0	0.99	16.3	1.16	10.0	0.71	14.1
Hebei	308.0	1.39	235.0	1.06	218.7	0.99	130.7	0.59	221.4
Shanxi	159.7	1.16	151.0	1.1	125.0	0.91	109.7	0.8	138.0

1992; 122 days in 1995; and, unexpectedly, 144 days in 1996. Drought and human factors are the reasons for this trend.

IMPACTS OF DROUGHT ON AGRICULTURE

China is a great agricultural country. A basic industry of the national economy, agriculture is easily affected by meteorological disasters (particularly drought and flooding), of which drought is the most serious.

In China, the annual average area affected by disasters is 4×10^8 mu.[2] Drought accounts for 60 per cent of this total, resulting in a loss of grain of about 1.5 billion kg every year. Table 24.9 gives the average area of flood- and drought-affected areas in different time periods in China. It was found that the drought-affected areas in different years were larger than the flood-affected areas. The drought-affected area has steadily increased since the 1950s. In the 1970s, the maximum was nearly 4×10^8 mu, and it was also close to 4×10^8 mu in the 1980s and 1990s. The drought-affected area exceeded 4×10^8 mu in ten years: 1972, 1973, 1976, 1977, 1978, 1986, 1988, 1989, 1992, and 1994, coming closer to 5×10^8 mu in 1988 and 1994 and reaching its largest area in 1978, almost 6×10^8 mu. It was estimated that grain production losses caused by drought in 1988, 1994, and 1978 were 230×10^8 kg, 263×10^8 kg, and 189×10^8 kg, respectively. Although the drought-affected areas of 1988 and 1994 were slightly smaller than that of 1978, the reduction of total grain production had gradually increased because of the improvement of per unit area grain production.

The periodicity of drought-affected and drought-damaged areas in China has been significant in the last forty years. During this time, three wet periods and three dry periods occurred. The periods 1958–62, 1971–81, and 1986–8 were observed as significant drought periods (i.e., more than 20 million ha were affected) (see Figure 24.4a). During the periods 1950–7, 1963–70, and 1981–5, less than 20 million ha were affected. The variability in the occurrence of drought-affected (E1) and drought-damaged (E2) areas seems to have increased during the last forty years (see Figure 24.4b). Averaged by decades, the drought-affected and drought-damaged areas in China increased from the 1950s to the 1990s, except for the 1970s (see Table 24.9). This trend is consistent with the general trend of aridisation in recent years in China.

The Huang-Huai-Hai region is the main grain-producing area in China, but it is also the area most seriously affected by drought. In the region, the drought-affected farming area accounts for 46.5 per cent of the national total, and loss of grain production due to drought damage amounts to 32.1 per cent. The Middle and Lower Reaches of the Yangtze Valley, where the drought-affected area makes up 22 per cent of the country's total, has the second highest loss of grain production at 27.5 per cent. This indicates that the greater the production, the more serious the losses (Li 1993).

IMPACTS OF DROUGHT ON ANIMAL HUSBANDRY AND FORESTRY

Impacts on animal husbandry

The pastoral areas in China such as Inner Mongolia, Xinjiang, Qinghai, and Tibet are mainly located in the arid-semiarid climate region and Qinghai-Xizang high frigid climate region, where the annual precipitation is mostly less than 400 mm – in most cases, less than

Table 24.9 Flood- and drought-affected areas (*mu*)

Years	Drought-affected	Drought-damaged	Flood-affected	Flood-damaged
1950–9	17,399	5,555	11,046	6,837
1960–9	32,466	15,038	14,130	8,780
1970–9	39,161	11,105	9,590	4,457
1980–9	36,856	17,558	15,629	8,290
1990–5	37,761	17,879	23,150	12,900

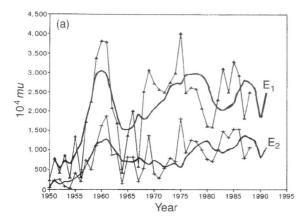

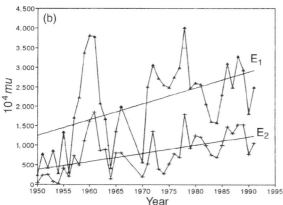

Figure 24.4 The time series of drought-affected (E1) and drought-damaged (E2) areas, their ten-year running mean (thick solid line) (a), and their linear trend (straight line) (b). From Li *et al.* 1996

200 mm. Drought is frequent in these areas. The impacts of drought on animal husbandry include grassland degradation, reduced grass biomass production, grass quality deterioration, and a shortage of drinking water for livestock.

The relationships between grassland production and precipitation in different grass zones are shown in Table 24.10, which indicates that the differences in precipitation bring about the diversity of grass types and grass production. In other words, in the pastoral areas of Inner Mongolia and Xinjiang, precipitation is the key factor to grass production. The relationship of positive correlation between grass production and precipitation means that the more serious drought is, the lower grass production is.

Decreasing groundwater levels, shrinking lake areas, dried-up springs, and cut-off of rivers caused by drought lead to a scarcity of water for human and livestock consumption. When water loss in animals reaches 8 per cent, animals experience a decrease in appetite and loss of disease resistance. When water loss reaches 10 per cent, serious metabolic disorders result, and when moisture loss exceeds 20 per cent, animals will die. For example, as a result of a drought lasting fifteen months (from May 1982 to August 1983) in the pastoral area of Inner Mongolia, precipitation was reduced by 30–80 per cent from normal, and the drought-affected grass area was $38 \times 10^4 \, \text{km}^2$. The shortage of water and grass caused the death of 10 million domestic animals. The number of calves decreased by 2,990,000 from the previous year, a reduction of 7.1 per cent.

Impacts on forestry

The impacts of drought on forestry are mainly concerned with afforestation, tree growth, forest fire, disease, and insect pests. Severe drought often makes the survival rate of afforested trees less than 50 per cent, and the influence on nursery trees is even greater, with a survival rate of only 10 per cent. Moreover,

Table 24.10 Grass production (kg/ha) and precipitation (mm) in different range zones

Range types	Poor year		Stable year		Good year	
	Precipitation	Grass production	Precipitation	Grass production	Precipitation	Grass production
Prairie	< 350	< 800	350–450	800–1,000	> 450	> 1,000
Steppe	< 300	< 600	300–350	600–800	> 350	> 800
Desert-steppe	< 150	< 400	150–300	400–600	> 300	> 600
Desert	< 50	< 200	50–150	200–300	> 150	> 300

tree growth is also affected, sometimes to the point of causing tree death. Forests in China are mainly located in the two great forest areas of northeast China and southwest China. The number of forest fires each year usually exceeds 10,000. Generally, in a drought year, the number of forest fires increases, and thus fire damage losses also increase. For instance, the greatest forest fire disaster in China in recent years occurred 6 May–1 June 1987. The fire covered 101×10^4 ha, burning down 855×10^4 m^3 of timber and causing 193 deaths. The direct economic loss exceeded 5×10^8 RMB yuan. During the sixteen months before the fire, precipitation was reduced by 40–50 per cent from normal. In March and April 1987, rainfall in the central region, where the fire disaster occurred, and its neighbouring areas was only 40–50 per cent of normal. There was no rainfall in the first three weeks of May. Under such meteorological and climatic conditions, drought plus high surface temperature caused the occurrence and rapid spread of the fire.

IMPACTS OF DROUGHT ON URBAN DEVELOPMENT AND INDUSTRY

Impacts on urban development

Of the more than 600 cities in China, half have water shortage problems and more than 100 are subject to serious water shortage problems. In these cities, the amount of water deficit exceeds 10 million m^3, and water supply shortage becomes even more difficult in drought years or persistent drought years. Since the 1980s, China has gone into a period of less rainfall, and 144 cities throughout the country are facing water shortage problems to differing degrees. Because of the shortage of surface water and the overpumping of groundwater, ground subsidence has occurred in many cities. For example, in Suzhou, Wuxi, and Changzhou (near Shanghai), cones of depression, with an area of about 7,000 km^2, have developed, resulting in the continuous decline of groundwater levels. In severe drought years, the supply of fresh and clean water, even drinking water, becomes much more difficult to maintain, causing great economic loss.

Impacts on industry

The impacts of drought on industry can be classified into two types: direct and indirect. In the processes of industrial production, water is an important source material or refrigerant, and no water means no production. The direct loss of output value as a result of water shortage impacts has been estimated at 120 billion RMB yuan. Water shortage due to drought often affects hydropower and thermal power generation. Especially for hydropower, greater rainfall means greater electricity generation; reduced rainfall means reduced electricity generation. For example, in northeast China, a severe drought occurred in 1982, and the amount of electricity generated was reduced by 15.7×10^8 kwh from that of 1981. Hydropower usually accounts for 50–60 per cent of the total amount of power in Hubei, and thus the occurrence of drought in the Yangtze Valley in 1985 resulted in the reduction of electricity generated – 7–8×10^8 kwh of average. Severe drought also seriously affects freshwater fishery, aquatics, and the development of navigation in inland rivers, resulting in great economic loss.

In brief, the impacts of drought are very far-ranging and far-reaching. They can cause chain reactions and result in a series of impacts on grain production, food processing, exports, prices, industrial development, and so on, even leading to inflation, unemployment, plant diseases and insect pests, and social disturbance. The impacts of severe drought in the Sahel in Africa and historical great severe droughts in China and India are typical (Li et al. 1993).

DROUGHT AND DESERTIFICATION

China is one of the few countries where desertification damage is more serious and the area of desertified lands is larger. China's desertified lands are mainly distributed in the arid, semiarid, and dry subhumid regions, affecting eleven provinces and autonomous regions, with a total area of 37.1×10^4 km^2, and accounting for 3.86 per cent of the whole territory (Zhu et al. 1994). These desertified lands are concentrated in the interlocking zone of pastures and farmlands, amounting to 63.2 per cent of the total nationwide area of desertified lands. According to statistics from Dong Yuxiang (1993), the total nationwide area of desertified lands increased annually by 15.6×10^4 ha with an annual growth rate of 1.01 per cent from the 1950s to the mid-1970s, and by 21.0×10^4 ha with an annual growth rate of 1.01 per cent from the mid-1970s to the mid-1980s. There is a trend of expansion in desertified land in recent years. The annual growth rate of desertified lands in Bashang of Hebei and five counties or banners in the southern part of Xilin Gol League reached 5–10 per cent, as shown in Table 24.11.

The impacts of desertification on the society and economy of China are very serious. First, available land area has been reduced. Since the 1950s, the annual average loss of available land has been 18.3×10^4 ha. Second, the productivity of land has fallen. For instance, because of desertification, grain yields have been reduced by 75–80 per cent and grass yields have been reduced by 30–40 per cent, causing estimated agricultural and animal husbandry losses of $17.4–20.4 \times 10^8$ RMB yuan. Moreover, desertification not only seriously threatens farmlands, grass ranges, towns and cities, villages, traffic routes and ways, hydraulic facilities, and so on, it also results in environmental pollution and health hazards. If the direct and indirect losses are estimated together, desertification in China causes an annual loss of $783–918 \times 10^8$ RMB yuan.

Both natural (mainly climate change and drought) and artificial factors are responsible for the formation and development of desertification. In the arid and semiarid areas and parts of subhumid areas of China, the natural factors constituting the eco-environment make these areas vulnerable to desertification. These factors include the following: (1) Drought and the high variability of precipitation. In most of northern China, annual precipitation is usually less than 600 mm and decreases to around 50 mm from east to west, where the annual variability of precipitation reaches 20–50 per cent. (2) Gales occur often, and the frequency of wind is usually very high. In the regions mentioned above, the wind speed is very high (more than 3 m/s) and the number of days with a wind speed exceeding the critical value for blowing sand is 200–300 days annually; the number of days with a wind velocity of force 8 is about 30–80 days. The more frequent and strong winds provide dynamic conditions for sand activity and formation and for the development of desertification. (3) Wind erosion occurs easily on ground surfaces with sufficient loose sand. It provides the physical basis for the formation and development of desertification. (4) Sparse and short vegetation and lower forest coverage do not provide effective ground cover to protect the sand from blowing, particularly in winter and spring. The vast areas of barren ground directly exposed to strong winds and insolation provide favourable conditions for wind erosion. In summary, the eco-environment of the regions mentioned above is vulnerable. Persistent drought, climate change, and human factors will likely lead to serious desertification problems.

The human dimensions of the formation and development of desertification are also very important. In recent years, rapid population growth has led

Table 24.11 Development of desertification in China in recent decades (km²)

Regions	Desertified land in mid-1970s	Desertified land in mid-1980s	Annual growth	
			Area	Rate
Horqin sandy land in Jirem League	28,917	32,851	323	1.05
Xili Gol steppe	13,194	16,408	267	1.8
Bashang region in Hebei province	2,612	4,514	158	4.66
Five counties or banners in Xilin Gol League	2,848	5,992	262	9.2
Houshan farming region in Ulanqab League	2,031	4,055	168	8.3
Ordos sandy desert in Ih Ju League	43,407	45,973	256	0.59
Yulin in Shaanxi province	15,307	13,219	−232	−1.6

Source: Zhu *et al.* 1994

to overuse of land resources (such as overfarming, overlogging, and overgrazing) in arid, semiarid, and subhumid areas of northern China. The serious stresses from human activities, animal husbandry, and excessive farming, grazing, and logging caused surface vegetation to suffer unprecedented destruction and lose ecological balance, thus inducing certain potential factors of desertification as well as the actual natural processes of desertification.

In recent years, China's desertification appears to be the result of rapid population growth. Besides the human dimensions, the drying and persistent warming of climate in northern China are very important natural factors. In the northern part of China, the average temperature in the 1980s was generally 0.3–0.5°C higher than that of the 1970s, even 1.0°C higher in some regions. Climatic warming can result in increased actual evaporation and an increase in aridity calculated by potential evapotranspiration. Persistent scarce rainfall or a drying tendency made the situation even more serious in northern China in recent years. The most evident reduction of precipitation occurred in north China. For instance, in some cities or provinces such as Beijing, Tianjin, Hebei, Shandong, Shanxi, and Liaoning, precipitation in the 1980s was 40–220 mm less than the mean of the previous thirty years, or 10–30 per cent less than the annual average value. Precipitation in the 1980s was reduced by 110 mm from that of the 1950s in Hebei Province, and by 139 mm in Shandong Province. Clearly, the intensity of drought was indeed considerable. In particular, it accelerated the development of desertification, extended the duration of spring drought, raised the probability of spring-summer persistent drought, decreased the soil moisture, and lengthened the duration of bare land. Meanwhile, because of lack of rain and increasing use of surface water, water in rivers dried up, the area of lakes shrunk, supplemental groundwater was lost, and vegetation died, accelerating the trend of desertification.

METHODOLOGY OF IMPACT ASSESSMENT OF DROUGHT AND DESERTIFICATION

Classification of drought impacts

The impacts of drought are far-ranging and far-reaching, mainly affecting natural environment, economy, and society. The classification of drought impacts is given in Table 24.12.

Main methods of drought impact assessment

On-the-spot investigation and news media

Information on drought and its impacts can be obtained from the news media; actual drought impacts can be determined through onsite investigation in drought-affected regions.

Drought monitoring

Drought is a creeping phenomenon, the extent of which appears gradually, thus offering the possibility for monitoring and early warning of drought. Drought monitoring can be classified roughly into five types. There are two ways to monitor droughts; one is based on a network system of stations, and another is by remote sensing, which offers fast, objective, economic, and large-range characteristics.

The components of monitoring include the following:

1 atmospheric parameters: precipitation, temperature, wind direction and speed, snow cover, cloud cover and all components of solar radiation, etc.
2 agricultural parameters: soil moisture, evaporation, soil temperature and methods of crop growing, etc.
3 hydrological parameters: runoff, groundwater level, water level of rivers and lakes, amount of water stored in reservoirs, etc.
4 satellite remote sensing parameters: vegetable cover, crop growing and all kinds of vegetation indexes, etc.
5 social and economic information: drought-affected area; loss of life and property; economic losses; economic indexes such as cultivated land area, grain production, population, etc.

Table 24.12 The classification of drought impacts

1   Impacts on natural environment
    Impacts on water resources
      rainfall and surface water reduction; water level of groundwater, rivers, reservoirs, lakes, and wetlands declining, even drying up; soil moisture loss; glaciers shrinking and attenuating; water quality worsening, etc.
    Impacts on land resources
      vegetation reduction; wind/water erosion strengthening; drop in grain production; land degradation; soil salinisation; desertification; loss of land resources, etc.
    Impacts on environmental quality
      decreased air quality; increase in dust; water and soil pollution; etc.
    Impacts on disasters
      high temperatures; heat waves; forest fires; hot-dry winds, etc.
2   Impacts on economy
    Impacts on agriculture
      reduced grain production; land productivity reduction; diffusion of diseases and pests; crop seeding delays, etc.
    Impacts on forestry
      tree growth, production, nursery affected; forest fires; diseases and pests; declining forest productivity, etc.
    Impacts on livestock husbandry
      grass growth and grazing affected; fodder, drinking water, milk and meat, etc. decreased
    Impacts on fishery and aquatics
      changes in eco-environment; polluting and worsening water quality; rivers and lakes drying up; fish kill, etc.
    Impacts on industry
      hydraulic power affected; work and production stopped by water shortage; work time shortened and work efficiency decreased, etc.
    Impacts on communication and transportation
      inland river shipping affected; river navigability decreased; drying and cracking of roadways, etc.
    Impacts on energy
      power consumption increased, etc.
3   Impacts on society
      famine, plague, diseases increased; declining quality of life; social disturbance and civil war increasing; etc.
    Main methods of drought impact assessment
      On-the-spot investigation and news media

Through remote sensing, station networks, and modern communications, including geographical information systems (GIS), a variety of information can be provided continuously before drought occurs. This information is useful for determining the possible range, period, and risk degree of drought, and it will help in the adoption of drought mitigation measures. During drought, the processes and status of drought can be monitored constantly to provide information to all drought response agencies. Drought losses can be determined quickly and precisely for large areas, and this information will facilitate response and recovery operations. The remote sensing method of drought monitoring will primarily track crop growth, status of soil moisture, evapotranspiration, status of the hydrological system, and precipitation. This technology, combined with station observations, can monitor the formation and development of droughts objectively, quickly, and economically for large areas.

Establishment of drought monitoring and early warning system

Before the drought monitoring and early warning systems are run, one or more objective and practical drought indexes should be provided. Then certain thresholds, also called the initial point, can be determined so that certain activities are adopted when the drought index(es) exceed the threshold. In the United States, the Palmer Drought Severity Index (PDSI) is often adopted, while the Surface Water Supply Index (SWSI) is also used. The SWSI was developed with historical data, data on the current water volume of reservoirs, stream runoff, and precipitation at all elevations.

Since no single index can be used to adequately evaluate the main factors of meteorological, agricultural, or hydrological droughts, all types of indexes should usually be combined. Meanwhile, the difference between the various regions and economic departments should also be considered.

A drought monitoring and early warning system should be established to provide timely information on the formation, development, persistence, alleviation, and end of drought to those responsible for drought response/recovery. To this end, the following steps should be undertaken: building a system that can capture, analyse, and transfer drought information in a timely fashion; setting up criteria to confirm drought-affected zones; monitoring the status of and estimating future available water and soil moisture; and establishing a special department to enforce the criteria and issue/cancel drought warnings.

Establishment of drought impact assessment system (DIAS)

DIAS includes the data base, statistics analysis software, methodology for impact assessment and appropriate models, graphics software, disaster search system, expert system to assess drought impacts, and so on.

Information is the basis of DIAS. In the processes of drought impact assessment, a wide variety of information, such as meteorological, agricultural, satellite remote sensed, and social and economic, must be collected. An information network must also be developed to analyse and deliver data and information.

Indices and models used in impact assessment can be classified as follows: precipitation indexes, such as production-moisture and crop-production; relative evapotranspiration models, such as the FAO model, Jensen's model, and CSDI model; and dynamic simulation models for crop growth.

Risk assessment of desertification

Desertified risk is the degree of desertification threatening or damaging a society and its economy. It can be defined in terms of potential threat or direct damage (Dong 1993).

Substance of risk assessment

Risk evaluation of desertification should include the following:

- All of the arid and semiarid areas and parts of subhumid areas where the surface is covered by loose sandy sediment and dry seasons coincide with windy seasons, where there are dynamic conditions and a greater inherent danger of desertification.
- Economic activities of varying intensities are key factors in the formation and development of desertification. People are both conductors and victims of desertification.
- The development of desertification is relative to the inherent risk of regional desertification and human and livestock stresses.

Therefore, desertification has both natural and man-made causes and has far-reaching impacts. Desertified risk assessment should include the following:

Inherent risk of desertification (IR) To evaluate the threat of desertification to society and the economy, desertified conditions must be understood. Inherent risk is one of the important conditions affecting the degree of the formation and development of desertification – that is, it is only in regions with an inherent risk of desertification that desertification can occur. The regional inherent risk of desertification is decided by many factors, such as soil, climate, and vegetation; the dominant factors include surface sandy content, wind speed, and precipitation.

Status of desertification (S) The status of desertification is the most direct expression of the damage caused by desertification and the basis for measuring the development of desertification. Indexes used to indicate the status of desertification measure the area of desertification, loss of surface soil layer, decreasing productivity, and so forth.

Rate of desertification (R) The rate of desertification expresses the intensity of desertification processes during a period (such as five to ten years), which indicates the predicted tendency and potential threat of desertification.

Population stress (PS) and *Livestock stress (LS)* Population and livestock stresses are among the conditions affecting the form and development of desertification.

The above five indexes can express and reveal the direct damages and potential threats caused by desertification. Therefore, the desertified risk (DR) can be expressed as

$$DR = S + R + IR + PS + LS$$

The desertified risk can be regarded as the quantitative index that indicates the degree of the threat of desertification to society and economy, and the five indexes are the major components of desertification risk assessment.

System and classes of assessing factors

Desertification is an outcome determined by many factors, and many factors can also affect the risk of desertification. If a single index is adopted to assess desertified risk, the results will be limited; on the other hand, if all indexes are selected, the results will be complex and confusing. Therefore, it is necessary to consider the two aspects of direct damage and potential threat of desertification and select the representative factors in the desertification risk assessment according to certain principles, forming a system of risk assessment.

According to the components of desertified risk assessment, a desertified risk assessment system should be set up, composed of classes of tools assessing the inherent risk of desertification, the status of desertification, population stress, and livestock stress:

Tools assessing the inherent risk of desertification include eco-environmental indexes indicating the physical and dynamic conditions leading to desertification, such as sand and clay content in soil, average wind speed, annual days of sandstorms, climate erosion index, and annual frequency of predominant wind.

Table 24.13 Ranking values of various factors of desertified risk

Factors	Risk classification			
	Slight	Moderate	Severe	Extreme
Sandy and clay content in soil (%)	<80	80–90	90–95	>95
Annual wind speed (m/s)	<2.60	2.60–4.55	4.55–5.85	>5.85
Annual number of days of sandstorms	<8	8–15	15–25	>25
Climatic erosion index	20–40	20–40	>40	>40
Annual frequency of predominant wind (%)	<5	5–15	15–25	>25
Ratio of shifting sand to cultivated land (%)	<5	5–25	25–50	>50
Percentage of vegetation cover (%)	>60	30–60	10–30	<10
Loss of surface soil layer (%)	<30	30–60	60–90	>90
Decreasing rate of land productivity (%)	<20	20–40	40–75	>75
Annual growth rate of desertified land (%)	<1	1–2	2–5	>5
Annual rate of increase of desertified land (%)	<0.25	0.25–1.00	1.00–2.00	>2.00
Annual decreasing rate of soil depth due to wind erosion (cm)	<2	2–5	5–10	>10
Annual decreasing rate of biomass (%)	<1.5	1.5–3.5	3.5–7.5	>7.5
Rate of population overcapacity (%)	–3.4	–3.4–0	0–50	>50
Rate of livestock overcapacity (%)	–34	–34–0	0–50	>50

Source: Dong 1993

Tools assessing the status of desertification express the current state of desertification, generally selecting the factors directly related to desertification, such as the ratio of shifting sand to cultivated land, percentage of vegetation cover, loss of surface soil layer, and decreasing ratio of land productivity.

Tools assessing the rate of desertification express the dynamic developing state of desertification, usually selecting measurements such as annual growth rate of desertified land, annual rate of increase of desertified land, and annual decreasing rate of soil depth by wind erosion and biomass.

Tools assessing population stress express the intensity and characteristics of human activities, selecting measurements such as ratio of population over-capacity.

Tools assessing livestock stress express the intensity and characteristics of livestock production and human activities that may affect grazing capacity.

According to the system of desertified risk assessment, desertified risk can be divided into four classes – slight, moderate, severe, and extreme, shown in Table 24.13. First, the four classes indicating desertified risk are evaluated, then the quantitative assessment of desertified risk can be given based on the above results.

NOTES

1 Private communication with Liu Chunzhen.
2 *Mu* is the Chinese unit of area. 1 *mu* = 0.0667 ha.

REFERENCES

Dong Yuxiang (1993) 'Evaluation on the risk potential of desertification', in *Methodology for Assessing Natural Disaster Risk of China* (in Chinese), Chapter 7, pp. 123–45, Beijing: China Science and Technology Press.

Li Kerang (1993) 'Evaluation on the risk potential of drought', in *Methodology for Assessing Natural Disaster Risk of China* (in Chinese), Chapter 4, pp. 58–86, Beijing: China Science and Technology Press.

Li Kerang and Lin Xianchao (1993) 'Drought in China: present impacts and future needs', in D.A. Wilhite (ed.), *Drought Assessment, Management, and Planning: Theory and Case Studies*, Chapter 15, pp. 263–89, Dordrecht, The Netherlands: Kluwer Academic Publishers.

Li Kerang, Yin Siming, and Sha Wanying (1996) Characters of time-space of recent drought in China (in Chinese), *Geographical Research* 15, 3: 6–14.

Sun Guowu, Yu Yaxun, and Feng Jianying (1997) 'The analysis and diagnosis of drought in northwest China and other areas of Africa since the late about 100 year (in Chinese)', in *The Research of Drought Climate in Northwest China*, pp. 7–15, Beijing: China Meteorological Press.

Zhu Zhenda, Chen Guangting, *et al.* (1994) *Sandy Desertification in China* (in Chinese), Beijing: China Science Press.

25

DROUGHT IN SOUTH AFRICA, WITH SPECIAL REFERENCE TO THE 1980–94 PERIOD

Coleen Vogel, Mike Laing, and Karl Monnik

INTRODUCTION

Although most people intuitively know what drought is, it is very elusive to define. In South Africa, there is no generally accepted drought definition or index, and so we will allude to the general definition given in the *Meteorological Glossary* (Meteorological Office 1991: 96).

> Drought is dryness due to the lack of rain. It is a relative term and any definition in terms of rainfall deficit must refer to the particular rainfall-related activity that is under discussion. For example, there may be a shortage of rainfall during the growing season of a particular crop (agricultural drought) or affecting the supply of water for domestic and industrial use (water supply drought). Such shortages need to be compared with the climatological expectation for the region and season.

Sakamoto (1989) refers to an 'operational' assessment process of providing real-time information on a drought situation to decision makers. The South African Weather Bureau uses this concept when employing a '75 per cent of normal rainfall' operational signal for drought alert in the several drought monitoring and assistance schemes running in this country.

A study by Tyson (1986) indicates that if a spatial average is taken for thirty-three widely distributed stations in the summer rainfall region (essentially all but southwest and southern South Africa), a clear oscillatory pattern is apparent in the rainfall series (Figure 25.1). This has a tendency to produce nine-year spells of generally wet and generally dry conditions in a quasi-cycle of about eighteen years. Thus the generally dry 1980s should be followed by generally wet 1990s.

Using 75 per cent of mean rainfall (519 mm) for the summer rainfall region of South Africa, Table 25.1 indicates the driest summer rainfall seasons in order of severity.

These rainfall figures clearly point to the severity of the 1982–3 and 1991–2 droughts in relation to the other severe dry summers. They also conform to the climatic characteristics of this region. The climate and rainfall of the semiarid subcontinent of southern Africa has been highly variable for millennia and will continue to be so in the future. All studies clearly indicate that drought of varying severity is a 'regular' feature over the entire region. All future planning should be predicated on the assumption that it is a land of drought rather than a land of plentiful rain. Indeed, only a very small part of the land along the eastern coastal regions and escarpments receives more than the world average of 1,000 mm rain per year.

DROUGHT OCCURRENCES

Since 1961, there have been nine seasons when the average rainfall for the entire summer rainfall area has been less than 80 per cent of normal. Although a rainfall deficit of 25 per cent of normal is regarded as severe drought, a shortfall of 20 per cent will cause crop and water shortfalls, accompanied by social and economic hardship, in many regions. Two or more consecutive dry summers substantially increase the adverse impacts. Dent *et al.* (1987) found that the drought of the two consecutive summers of the early 1980s was the most severe on record, according to the indices used. Other devastating droughts identified include those of the three consecutive summers ending in March 1933 and those of the late 1960s

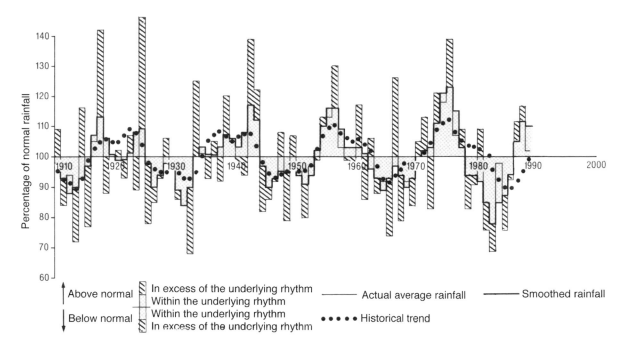

Figure 25.1 Time series of annual summer rainfall totals (after Tyson 1986)

Table 25.1 Driest summer rainfall seasons

Rank	Season	Mean total rain (mm)
1	1925–6	341
2	1923–4	342
3	1932–3	366
4	1921–2	375
5	1991–2	390
6	1982–3	394
7	1994–5	398
8	1951–2	401
9	1930–1	411
10	1946–7	415
11	1944–5	418

and early 1970s. The latter centred primarily on the central and western parts of the region, while that of the 1980s was more evident in the east (Figure 25.2).

According to Table 25.1, the 1991–2 and 1994–5 rainy seasons were the fifth and seventh driest in nearly seventy-five years. The three driest seasons since 1980 (Table 25.1), with surprisingly similar seasonal totals (all close to 75 per cent of normal), were

1991–2, 1982–3, and 1994–5. It appears that the earlier droughts this century were most severe over the western and central parts of the summer rainfall regions of South Africa. Since 1980, however, two of the three most severe droughts seem to have been worst over the eastern parts of the country, where the population is greatest and where the largest agricultural and commercial enterprises exist. The impact of these most recent droughts has therefore been much greater, striking at the most densely populated regions. In the 1994–5 season, large areas were again below 75 per cent of normal rainfall. However, in this season, crop yields in South Africa were less seriously affected, as the eastern and northeastern regions received 75–100 per cent of normal rainfall. This rainfall was just sufficient for crops to yield enough to supply home consumption. However, it proved woefully inadequate to supplement water storage and reserves. By the start of the next season, in October 1995, most of the eastern half of South Africa was experiencing water restrictions to some degree. The impact of droughts can thus be particularly severe, and it is to this important aspect that attention now shifts.

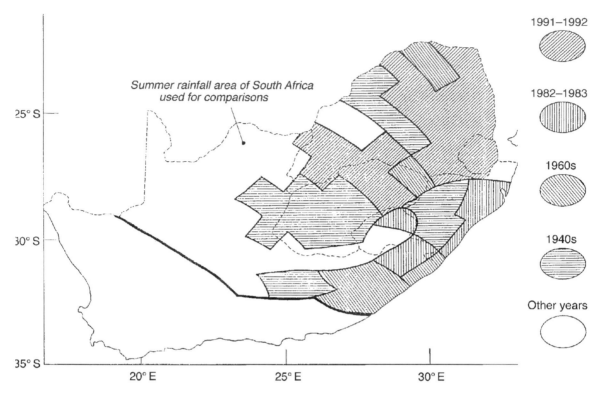

Figure 25.2 Summer rainfall regions: Area/years of the worst drought

DROUGHT IMPACTS

Drought has severe impacts on the social, environmental, and financial spheres of the country and in the broader region (Table 25.2). Drought impact extends to areas well beyond the area physically experiencing drought and often lingers for some time after the drought has ended. This is because drought disrupts the normal activities of people who directly and indirectly depend on the natural environment to provide them with food and/or income to sustain a living. Society's ability to cope with climate variability determines the level of risk and severity of drought impact. In this regard, social poverty plays an important role in many agricultural households. Major drought impacts, whether direct or indirect, are summarised in Table 25.2.

As indicated in Table 25.2, drought impacts are numerous and multifaceted. One of the most serious impacts, other than dwindling water reserves, are the effects on staple crops and commercial crops. Figure

25.3, showing the maize fluctuations against seasonal rainfall, indicates the close relationship between these two parameters. In 1992–3, maize had to be imported into South Africa (as well as the rest of southern Africa). This puts considerable downward pressure on the foreign reserves as well as on the gross domestic product (GDP) of the countries of this region. The ripple effect of crop failure can sometimes be seen in the population drift from some rural areas into the cities, farm labour layoffs and farm closures, and an increasing indebtedness in the agricultural sector. The downward trend that started in 1991–2 worsened in 1994–5 when yields of fruit orchards and water availability for irrigation declined, leading to farm closures in many cases.

The linkage between drought and development is also important. Development, and particularly a lack thereof, can seriously undermine drought mitigation initiatives and enhance vulnerability to a drought event. Drought impacts associated with water pro-

Table 25.2 Major drought impacts

Impact	Ripple effects
(a) *Social impacts*	
Lack or poor distribution of resources (food and water)	Migration, resettlement, conflicts between water users
Increased quest for water	Increased conflicts between water users
Marginal lands become unsustainable	Poverty, unemployment
Reduced grazing quality and crop yields	Overstocking
	Reduced quality of living
Employment layoffs	Reduced or no income
Food insecurity	Malnutrition and famine
	Civil strife and conflict
Increased pollutant concentrations	Public health risks
Inequitable drought relief	Social unrest, distrust
Increased forest and range fires	Increased threat to human and animal life
Urbanisation	Social pressure, reduced safety
(b) *Environmental impacts*	
Damage to natural habitats	Loss of biodiversity
Reduced forest, crop, and range land productivity	Reduced income and food shortages
Reduced water levels	Lower accessibility to water
Reduced cloud cover	Plant scorching
Increased daytime temperature	Increased fire hazard
Increased evapotranspiration	Crop withering and dying
More dust and sandstorms	Increased soil erosion
	Increased air pollution
Decreased soil productivity	Desertification and soil degradation (topsoil erosion)
Decreased water resources	Lack of feeding and drinking water
Reduced water quality	More waterborne diseases
	Increased salt concentrations
Increased incidence of animal diseases and mortality	Loss of income and food
	Reduced breeding stock
Soil desiccation	Increased soil 'blowability'
Degradation of landscape quality	Permanent loss of biological productivity of the landscape
Species concentration near water	Increased vulnerability to predation
(c) *Economic impacts*	
Reduced business with retailers	Increased prices for farming commodities
Food and energy shortages	Drastic price increases
	Expensive imports/substitutes
Loss of crops for food and income	Increased expense of buying food from shops
Reduction of livestock quality	Sale of livestock at reduced market price
Water scarcity	Increased transport costs
Loss of jobs, income, and property	Deepening poverty
	Increased unemployment
Less income from tourism and recreation	Increased capital shortfall
Forced financial loans	Increased debt
	Increased credit risk for financial institutions

vision, as will be illustrated below, are often compounded by poor water infrastructure and maintenance before and during a drought period. The following discussion highlights some of these local impacts of drought on the biophysical, agricultural, and social fabric of the country, illustrating the

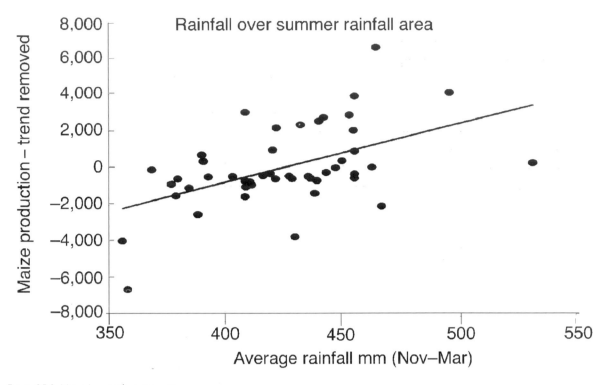

Figure 25.3 Maize harvest/summer rain

relationships and links between drought and other factors (e.g., agricultural policy, development policy and planning, the environment). For ease of discussion, drought impacts over the past twenty years for South Africa will be grouped into biophysical, agricultural, and social impacts.

BIOPHYSICAL IMPACTS

Several biophysical impacts can result from a drought. These include greatly reduced surface and ground-water supplies, diminished grass cover, and possible enhanced land degradation. One of the major impacts of drought in southern Africa relates to surface and underground water. There have been notable hydro-logical droughts in South Africa since 1920, including 1930–2, 1950–3, 1967–72, 1978–86, and 1989 (Alexander 1993). Water levels in several areas of the country were reduced during the 1980s and 1990s. In certain cases, dam levels dropped so notably during the 1990s drought that augmentation of water in some dams (such as the Vaal) was

necessary. Notwithstanding such measures, the inflow into the Vaal Dam during 1991–2 was still low at only 320 million m^3, and second lowest on record (Department of Water Affairs and Forestry 1993).

Although the state of the Vaal Dam, which serves industry in the Pretoria/Witwatersrand/Vereeneging (PWV) area, is critical, it is important to note that the levels of other dams, often located in remote rural areas in the country, are also drastically reduced during drought periods. Several dams in the former Bantustans were particularly low during the 1990s, and numerous cases of acute water shortages were noted (National Consultative Forum on Drought 1992). Recognising this important problem, an initiative known as the Water Supply Task Force of the National Consultative Forum on Drought, comprising engineers and field staff, actively monitored the water situation in rural areas and provided assistance where possible. It soon became evident that the severity of the drought impact in these areas was a result of reduced rainfall, lack of effective water management, lack of reliable data on water resources, and poor maintenance of water infrastructure and inadequate supply (National Consultative Forum on Drought 1992: 4).

Exploitation of groundwater, although a limited source of extractable water in South Africa, can help bridge such periodic water shortages associated with droughts. Problems such as uncertainty of yields, recharge rates, storage, and abstraction hamper the successful exploitation of this resource (Department of Water Affairs 1986). Furthermore, during periods of extreme demand, such as during severe drought, the strain on these supplies becomes excessive.

Groundwater recharge varies spatially and temporally over South Africa, depending on rainfall, evaporation, and surface conditions. The relationship between groundwater and rainfall variability is well documented (see, for example, Partridge 1985 and Braune 1992). Investigations for the Taung area, North West Province, for example, indicate that spring flow and rainfall show distinct oscillations (Partridge 1985). Wet periods significantly influence spring flow: although the period 1971–80 was only 1.5 times wetter than the previous drier spell, the spring flow increased 3.5 times, indicating the marked sensitivity of this geohydrological regime to rainfall variation.

These relationships between surface and groundwater, while lagged in some instances, directly affect decisions relating to the abstraction of water in climatically sensitive areas. Borehole water levels are lowered by a number of factors, including reduced yield, increased sand flow, borehole failure, and other management problems that can aggravate groundwater supplies: 'One or more of these problems can cause a rapidly declining water level which can at times be confused as a result of a drought' (Braune 1992).

Other drought impacts related to water supply are those that impinge more directly on urban and industrial water users. The threat of an electricity crisis and continued deterioration of water resources during a prolonged drought may result in the implementation of water restrictions (Schlemmer et al. 1989), which usually bring with them wider drought-impact ripple effects (Martins 1986, Van Zyl and Viljoen 1988, Schlemmer et al. 1989, Botha and Viljoen 1991). It has been shown in surveys in the Vaal River catch-

ment area, for example, that the greatest impact of water restrictions is on the householder, followed by industry and the agricultural sector (Botha and Viljoen 1991). Indirect and insidious impacts, such as demoralisation, job stress, and reduction of water-related recreational opportunities, usually downplayed in impact assessments, are nonetheless also important consequences associated with periods of water restrictions. Indirect impacts are often twice as important as the direct impacts of water restrictions (Botha and Viljoen 1991) but are difficult to quantify.

Another biophysical impact associated with drought is grassland or vegetation loss. Although few experimental data are available on the immediate and long-term effects of droughts on veld and grasses in South Africa, Danckwerts and Stuart-Hill (1988), Willis and Trollope (1987), Walker (1988), and Snyman and Van Rensburg (1990) have indicated that extensive grass mortality occurs during a drought period, with Decreaser species suffering as moisture content fluctuates.

Rainfall variability and grass species composition are also strongly related in the KwaZulu Natal coastal region (Van Wyk and Tomlinson, unpublished, in Walker 1988). Palatable grasses predominate in the drier periods and are replaced by sedges in the wetter spells. Changes in species composition in this area are expected every five to ten years, in accordance with rainfall cycle variations (Walker 1988). Periods of drought can also negatively affect the grasses in the central Free State (Snyman and Van Rensburg 1990). Damage to grasses includes species and basal cover mortality and increased veld degradation (Snyman and Van Rensburg 1990).

Grass mortality as a result of drought has also been linked to elements such as soil texture, degree of competition, and grazing intensity in an area (Scholes 1985). Grass mortality in the Klaserie Private Nature Reserve, adjacent to Kruger National Park, was thus higher on fine-textured soils than on coarser soils during times of below-normal rainfall. Grass mortality also increased in the area during the 1980s drought because of high tree densities, when grazing was intense and early summer rainfall was lowest (Scholes 1985).

Macroscale investigations, using satellite images of NDVI (Normalized Difference Vegetation Index), have been undertaken to assess the impact of rainfall variability on vegetation over the southwestern Cape from 1985 to 1988 (Jury 1992 and 1993). During 1987, a weak El Niño reduced rainfall to below normal, resulting in drought-stressed vegetation, poor crop yields, and inadequate grazing across Karoo, Kimberley, and Upington (Jury 1992). Rainfall also declined over the coastal plains. The response of vegetation during these periods of drought was surprisingly widespread (Jury 1992).

Another serious biophysical impact brought about by drought is devastating bush fires, which destroy large areas of grazing at a time when grass and fodder is already limited. Commercial timber and orchards are also vulnerable to fire damage. In 1992, following the failure of the summer rains, there were several wildfires, which destroyed thousands of hectares of grassland.

Drought periods may also enhance degradation of the landscape. Local farmers are well aware of the possible effects of drought, but they often fail to manage their farms correctly. Stocking rates also influence the period and probability of feed shortages and thus the overall production and grazing capacity of the land. Overstocking of farm land, for example, is regarded as the major problem hindering farming, with drought impacts secondary (De Klerk 1986). Ignorance and poor farm management have resulted in much of the natural veld (for the country as whole) being devastated by overstocking. Estimates given for overstocking indicate that 50–60 per cent of the country's veld is overgrazed (Bruwer 1989, Bruwer 1990c). The tall grass veld and thorn veld areas of Natal have been estimated to be overstocked by 55 per cent and 68 per cent, respectively (Bruwer 1990c).

During the 1980s drought, the condition of the veld in several areas of the country (a total of 110 of the 174 districts of the Highveld, Gauteng, Free State, and KwaZulu Natal) was described as poor (Department of Agriculture 1983), with certain areas described as critical. Water and stock conditions for this period were average, but the veld condition, for almost the entire eastern and central interior of the country, was critical. The role of continual degradation of this veld resource, through overgrazing and a lack of sufficient moisture and rainfall, is thus merely exacerbated during drought periods.

Drought can also cause a fundamental transformation of grasslands. In one study, a sward of mostly palatable perennial grasses was lost within the space of four years (O'Connor 1995). Drought seems to be the primary agent responsible for the initial restructuring of range land communities, but the extent of restructuring depends on the previous grazing history. In the same study, subsequent recovery was strongly constrained by grazing immediately before and during that period. The site with the most lenient history of grazing maintained its character of a perennial grassland of palatable species. Heavy grazing history resulted in a transition to an annual grass-forb community (O'Connor 1995).

In another study, the condition of the range land was found to be critical regarding its response to rainfall. Irrespective of increasing rainfall, range land in poor condition is unable to convert water into above-ground phytomass production efficiently. In contrast, production of veld in a good condition increases rapidly with increasing rainfall (Snyman and Fouché 1991). This was attributed to higher surface runoff due to low basal cover. The low production of veld in a poor condition leads to an *apparent* drought even during periods of reasonable rainfall (Snyman and Fouché 1991).

The adverse impacts of drought on natural vegetation, however, can be reduced by judicious management. If the veld is withdrawn from grazing, the species composition can recover rapidly (Danckwerts and Stuart-Hill 1988). Snyman (1985) has demonstrated, for example, that veld condition can very often reverse drought impacts, in that the veld governs water use efficiency. The response and resilience of the natural vegetation to the seasonality of rainfall therefore should not be underestimated (Roux and Vorster 1983, Hoffman and Cowling 1990).

AGRICULTURAL IMPACTS

Drought periods have negative impacts on agricultural production, particularly rain-fed agricultural production, in South Africa (Van Zyl *et al.* 1987, Van Zyl *et al.* 1988, Rimmer 1993). If the potential growth of the agricultural sector is estimated, then it is clear that negative deviations from the long-term trend in the value added by the agricultural sector are associated with periods of low rainfall (Pretorius and Smal 1992). The most prominent negative deviations, for example, were recorded in 1964–5, 1972–3, and 1982–4, all regarded as drought periods (Figure 25.4).

Changes in agricultural policy and the macroeconomic environment, including adjustments on the production level, diversification, and low maize profitability, also affect production. The macroeconomic environment, for example, encouraged maize production during the 1970s but turned negative in the 1980s. During the drought period of the 1980s, several structural changes in the agricultural industry combined with deteriorating parity of agriculture (Van Zyl et al. 1987) to enhance the impact of drought on the agricultural sector.

Although the agricultural sector's relative contribution to GDP is small (approximately 5–7 per cent), it plays an important role in wealth creation via its multiplier effects on the rest of the economy (Van Zyl 1993). The agricultural multipliers, for example, have been calculated as 1.6 (for every R1 million of agricultural production, additional output of R600,000 will be generated in all other sectors together) (Van Zyl 1993). The contribution of agriculture to the economy therefore usually is viewed in the light of a number of distinctive interrelated factors, such as the provision of employment, earning of foreign exchange, food supply, creation of a market for the products of other sectors, and contribution to the gross domestic product (Van Zyl and Nel 1988, Van Zyl et al. 1988, Lindesay 1990, Development Bank of Southern Africa 1992, Pretorius and Smal 1992).

The outputs (forward linkages) and inputs (backward linkages) of the maize industry at constant 1985 prices (Van Zyl and Nel 1988) indicate that the

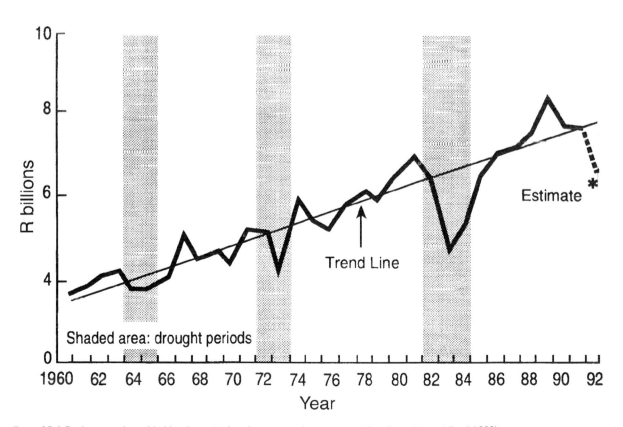

Figure 25.4 Real gross value added by the agricultural sector to the economy (after Pretorius and Smal 1992)

drought of the 1980s clearly had an adverse effect on industry's demand for inputs and final demand. Exports and the gross exporting surplus were hardest hit (Van Zyl and Nel 1988). Value added by the maize industry, in the form of employee remuneration and gross operating surplus, also dropped substantially during the drought years (Lindesay 1990). Van Zyl *et al.* (1987), furthermore, show that drought, general economic conditions, and structural inflation also affected the debt burden of the agricultural sector. The combined impacts of economic growth, average cost of capital, and the financial leverage of the farmer from the 1960s to the 1990s therefore weakened the position of the farmer.

Recurrent droughts therefore affect not only farmers and farm labourers but also the wider agricultural sector and other related sectors. Those areas particularly dependent on agriculture (for example, rural areas) are thus often the most negatively affected by a drought-induced multiplier effect in the agricultural sector. Delimiting the precise role that drought plays in such trends remains exceedingly difficult, especially when viewed against the myriad of other factors that contribute to agricultural production and obtaining a livelihood from the land (e.g., Sender 1994). Other effects of drought on society are similarly complex and difficult to isolate, particularly impacts (for example) on migration and employment.

SOCIAL IMPACTS

Food security

Droughts, such as those in the 1960s, 1980s, and early 1990s, have a number of negative sociological impacts, primarily loss of income, increased farmer debt, loss of property, and lack of farm work. Despite the impact of droughts on agriculture, South Africa is considered to be self-sufficient in most of the important staples (Kirsten and Van Zyl 1993). Notwithstanding this national level of food self-sufficiency, many households experience food insecurity. Excessive poverty, chronic malnutrition, and failed harvests are often the norm in certain areas (Mars 1984, Perlman 1984). Several people in the former Bantustans, for example, were estimated to be in need of emergency food aid during the 1990s drought. During this period, drought aid initiated by several NGOs (such as Operation Hunger and World Vision South Africa), several government intervention programmes, and donor agencies helped to contain cases of malnutrition and related diseases (AFRA 1992, Adams 1993).

Although numerous references are made to the impacts of droughts (such as the 1980s drought) on health, particularly in the press, determination of the precise nature of these impacts remains a difficult task (Vergnani 1984, Glatthaar 1992, Fincham *et al.* 1993, Natal Nutrition Working Group 1993). Few detailed assessments of local drought and health status therefore exist. Available assessments (Natal Nutrition Working Group 1993), however, do indicate that famine situations generally do not occur as a consequence of drought, but rather that endemic poverty and poor health prevail in several rural areas of the country (see, for example, Kustner 1983, Kustner *et al.* 1984), with these conditions greatly aggravated during drought years.

Drought heightens rural poverty and exposes cases of malnutrition rather than being the root cause of malnutrition (D'Souza *et al.* 1987, Natal Nutrition Working Group 1993). Malnutrition cases that have been particularly severe in the past, for example, were those in marginal agricultural areas or semidesert areas such as the North Cape and in areas that had previously been settled by relocated people who had little access to employment. Some villages had numbers of relocated families, all of whom had been dismissed from white farms as a result of drought and reduced labour requirements. Relocation, reduced income, and drought thus interacted to worsen the plight of those in remote rural areas. More recent investigations have shown that although high levels of stunting and wasting were evident in surveys of school children in areas of KwaZulu in October 1992, 'the conditions cannot be equated with a famine situation' (Natal Nutrition Working Group 1993: 29). Long-term development to counter the problem of widespread poverty and related poor nutrition has been recommended (Fincham *et al.* 1993). The interaction of drought and underlying socioeconomic influences is particularly evident in these studies, a trend that has also been noted for the past century (Vogel 1995).

The increased incidence of malnutrition and related disease therefore is not only linked to drought-induced crop failure: 'While drought clearly is an important factor it would seem vital to explore the extent to which rising unemployment . . . since at least the early 1980s, has shaped current conditions' (addenda by Perlman to D'Souza *et al.* 1987). The food question, entitlement of communities to food, monitoring of drought impact on food staples, and targeted investigations of the vulnerability of communities to drought require much more detailed local research.

Employment and migration

One of the harshest consequences of drought among farmers and farm labourers is the loss of employment during drought periods. Previous statistics show that the agricultural sector in South Africa generates employment for approximately one-tenth of the economically active portion of the population – approximately 1.2 million people, although if one includes migrant farm labour, then the estimate is probably higher (Development Bank of Southern Africa 1992).

Estimates indicate that for the agricultural sector, the drought of the 1990s may have resulted in the loss of livelihoods of approximately 245,000 people (Pretorius and Smal 1992). The impact of drought on employment, however, has to be seen against the larger canvas of national unemployment. Past estimates indicate that 50 per cent of the population live below the poverty line, and approximately 40 per cent of working-age people have no formal jobs (Development Bank of Southern Africa 1992), compared to only 4 per cent among the richest. As a result, 40 per cent of poor households and 50 per cent of ultra-poor households are dependent on pensions and remittances as their prime source of income (SALDRU 1995). The outcome of drought therefore has to be viewed against the broader canvas of national employment and the decreasing potential for self-employment, particularly in rural areas.

Some have argued that the lack of employment for migrants, increased retrenchment in the mining industry, and reduced remittances to those in rural areas have had consequences as important as the droughts of the 1980s and 1990s (D'Souza *et al.*

1987). By comparison, others have shown that employment in the agricultural sector remains relatively stable during drought periods (Pretorius and Smal 1992). Permanent employees on the farms are often encouraged to remain in farm accommodation, even during drought periods. In the past, the government has also assisted farmers with large subsidies, thereby enabling them to retain employees (Pretorius and Smal 1992). The pattern is different, however, for seasonal or temporary agricultural employees, as they are usually the first to become unemployed. Unfortunately, it is not possible to determine the quantitative impact of drought on temporary farm employment because official counts of black migrants who take up farm work are often inaccurate and underestimated owing to the seasonality of the movement of labour (Farmworkers Research and Resource Project 1991, Evans 1992). The seasonality of heightened vulnerability, however, is very important (e.g., Chambers *et al.* 1981), becomes acute during severe drought periods, and also requires further detailed investigation.

A possible consequence of increased unemployment caused by drought is the movement of people in search of alternative employment. The problem of poor data precludes a systematic national analysis of the effect of drought on migration patterns. Numerous anecdotal references from the media in the past and other more detailed sources (e.g., Cross *et al.* 1992), however, indicate that population movement during wetter and drier periods is a complicated process. There may be an influx into the cities, particularly during drought periods: 'Many seek employment in the towns' (*Diamond Fields Advertiser*, newspaper, Kimberley, 25 October 1965); 'Farmers are driven from the land, the drought is pushing some small farmers off the land' (*Star*, daily newspaper, Johannesburg, 14 May 1970). More recent research, however, has shown that the rate and directions of the movement of people as a direct response to drought is not as simple as previously thought, particularly in South Africa. Migration has been shown to vary spatially in the country, with some areas exhibiting a slow movement into towns and others a circular movement of people into towns (e.g., oscillating between a more rural settlement to a more urban settlement and back again) (e.g., Mabin

1991, Cross *et al.* 1996). Droughts and associated impacts therefore have to be viewed against this spatial and temporal movement of people.

Cases of migration from white farms are even more difficult to trace, but indications are that black farm workers affected by droughts may either remain on the farms and work for crops rather than wages or move back to rural areas (including former Bantustans). Some may also move in a stepwise fashion to cities (i.e., initially to other rural towns and not directly to cities). Farm transfer data provides a better indication of possible drought-induced movement from farms. Distinct changes in farm transfer, linked to drought periods, have been shown for areas in the Great Plains of the United States (Warrick 1980). In the local context, the relationship between drought and farm transfers is not a simple one to identify, and other factors such as land prices and inflation have to be carefully considered.

It is not clear from available data whether transfers of farmland are drought-induced; rather, the multi-dimensional effect of inflation, capital erosion, real debt reduction, and land price volatility have to be considered when examining land exchange in the agricultural sector (Van Zyl and Van Schalkwyk 1994). Possible drought-induced movements during the mid-1960s, early 1970s, 1980s, and early 1990s, however, are evident in the increased number of farm transfers during these periods (Figure 25.5). The impact of the extreme droughts, combined with increased financial stress and changes in agricultural assistance, surfaced more notably in the 1980s. Figures from the Land Bank on the attachment and sale of insolvent farms also show a rising trend in the 1980s and early 1990s (Rimmer 1993). An increased number of transfers occurred during this extreme drought, both nationally and regionally (Figure 25.5). Drought relief measures during the 1990s drought, however, did help prevent large-scale foreclosures. The number of foreclosures in 1991 was small – 267 out of 30,118 long-term accounts held at the Land Bank, or less than one in a hundred farmers (Rimmer 1993). Other official figures from the Department of Agriculture for the period 1991–2 also showed that the level of farm debt was small, increasing by only 1.6 per cent (Agrireview, Standard Bank 1994).

Several factors thus influence the movement of

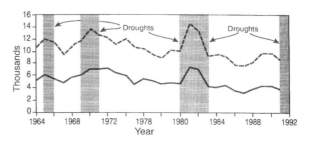

Figure 25.5 Farm transfers at national and regional scale. Numbers transferred at provincial level (Gauteng) = solid line, number transferred nationally = dashed line
Source: Central Statistical Services, Pretoria, Transfers of rural immovable property, 1964–93

farmers off their farms, with emergency measures often tiding certain farmers over through the droughts. Recent changes in state assistance to agriculture, decreasing subsidies to debt-ridden farmers, and the increase in the number of attacks on farmers are factors that also may influence farmers' options during and after droughts.

Although the preceding discussion about rural-urban migration as a result of drought reveals more complexity than was previously thought to exist about this issue, this must not be interpreted as stating that *no* migration may be triggered by a drought. Rather, it has been suggested that the mushrooming of squatter settlements in metropolitan areas in South Africa reflects both natural growth of the urbanised population and an urban migration influx (e.g., Crankshaw and Hart 1990, Crankshaw 1993, May 1993). Migration patterns are also strongly spatial in nature (Bank and Hobson 1993), and although certain areas may not experience out-migration, others, particularly in mining areas in the Free State and North West Province, have experienced movement during the droughts of the 1990s. If a severe, prolonged drought were to occur and agricultural and other sources of livelihood were greatly stressed, then outmigration possibly would occur, as suggested in the media. Overwhelming satisfactory evidence of this, however, has not been found.

Research on the issue of migration in South Africa, particularly rural–urban migration as a response to drought, is not conclusive. The movement of people in South Africa is complex. Instead of people moving from rural areas to urban areas, individuals and families 'appear to follow several routes in urban areas, and, once within the urban area, may shift several times' (May 1993: 10). Furthermore, it would appear that the dynamics of urbanisation are changing: 'As natural increase overtakes rural–urban migration as the major growth factor of metropolitan areas, the dynamics of urbanisation are changing' (May 1993: 5). Movement of people as a result of drought therefore has to be viewed against these long-term trends.

Apart from the political and economic factors influencing migration, cultural and local household factors influencing rural population movement also are often overlooked. For some people there is a reluctance to move during times of stress. The reluctance to move has been noted as early as the 1920s in South Africa and is well documented for other drought-stressed areas in Africa (Vogel 1995).

The impacts of drought on certain biophysical, sociological, and economic components have been shown to be linked to a host of interacting factors. Hidden and induced impacts are often underestimated in assessments of drought impact, and the interaction of a variety of causative factors is consequently often ignored. Water shortages and restrictions, for example, have been shown to be the result of both natural (drought) and human (mismanagement) factors. It has also been shown that the causes of drought impacts often are not always direct, and several of the physical, economic, and social impacts have been shown to have their roots in an already weakened resource base. Economic impacts of drought for large-scale commercial farmers, for example, are partly ascribed to the structural organisation of agriculture in the country as well as to the vagaries of weather. Thus on the one hand, biophysical units are weakened by activities not solely attributable to drought (for example, overgrazing and soil loss), and on the other hand, agricultural practices such as pricing policies, government diversification schemes (for example, structural changes in agriculture), and interest rates and inflation all heighten the impact of drought years.

MITIGATION OF DROUGHT IMPACTS

There are several methods and approaches that can be used when reducing drought impacts, including those that are related to the biophysical environment (such as improved forecasting and early warning) and those related to improved drought mitigation among communities. The latter embraces a number of socioeconomic issues such as reduction of vulnerability and risk to drought, food security issues, and ultimately a reduction in poverty. Several of these are discussed below.

The South African Weather Bureau, for example, currently employs two methods for helping to reduce the more physical impact of droughts. It is engaged in active research on extended weather outlooks for periods of up to six months ahead. Using numerical modelling for shorter periods and statistical methods for longer periods, bulletins are issued regularly, but especially from August on, when agricultural planning is most critical.

The close and significant correlation between low summer rainfall in South Africa and an El Niño (warm) event in the Pacific Ocean has led to increasing confidence for meaningful economic results from such extended weather outlooks. In collaboration with University Research Groups and by means of talks at farmers' meetings and workshops with potential clients, the Weather Bureau is bringing this knowledge to a widening segment of the population. Originally these outlooks were passed only to other scientists and to government and commercial enterprises involved in agriculture and water resource management. More recently, following a successful workshop for potential clients, a service named LOGIC (Long-Term Operational Group Information Centre) has been opened to provide extended outlooks and explanations on a far wider scale. The other method for remedying drought impact is the provision of up-to-date reports and assessments of rainfall deficits and regions where weather-related stress is highest. This is carried out by a climate monitoring section, which keeps drought assessment and agricultural organisations, the media, and the public constantly updated on the latest conditions.

Various models have also been developed by agricultural researchers to simulate the spatial occurrence of rainfall at a provincial level. These models are applied routinely to monitor the effect of abnormal climatic conditions, including drought, on agriculture. The value, however, is limited to the area for which it has been developed. Reliance on rainfall figures as a key input also puts a delay of approximately forty days to these models.

At a national level, advances have been made on the development of a real-time drought monitoring system using NOAA/AVHRR satellite data as the primary input data source. Daily satellite images are processed to decadal (ten-daily) composites on a routine basis. Vegetation index (NDVI, VCI) maps for the whole country are generated from information captured in the visible red and near-infrared parts of the electromagnetic spectrum. These indices are analysed as time series to follow the spatial and temporal development of abnormal conditions caused by drought.

A long-term data bank, containing all available historical NOAA/AVHRR imagery since 1985, will be used to develop severity threshold values for drought and disaster drought. These values will be used to gauge prevailing conditions anywhere in South Africa. This uniform data source should provide a more objective tool for real-time assessment of drought in South Africa. The ability to integrate with other spatial data sets (such as provincial models and vector overlays) in a GIS environment will enable the development of useful products for the decision-making process. It must be stressed, however, that ground-based data collection will always form an integral part of these products for proper calibration.

So-called Early Warning Systems (EWS) have been used in many African countries with limited success. When it comes to drought, EWS imply a certain ability to forecast or predict. As we have indicated, the large climate variability experienced in South Africa makes drought recurrence a certain but largely unpredictable phenomenon. Although research has indicated some correlation between the development of ENSO events and drought in certain parts of the world, not all drought events in South Africa can be explained by these teleconnections. Until more reliable relationships can be found to serve as early warning, certain efforts could be concentrated on early response systems using real-time information.

Despite the advances made in forecasting and warning, limitations do exist. These limitations include the number of rainfall stations available. Rainfall figures obtained from the local weather station network are used widely for the assessment of abnormal climatic conditions by comparing them with expected long-term rainfall figures calculated for specified locations and periods. Decisions are generally based on the current figures as well as precipitation amounts received for the previous three months. A shortcoming of this system is that rainfall stations are sparsely distributed in some semiarid regions of the country or, in the case of the former self-governing homelands, absent entirely. The irregular rainfall so typical of the larger part of South Africa is not adequately reflected by weather station recordings alone. A further disadvantage affecting real-time decision making is the time delay in receiving and processing the rainfall data. Efforts are being made, however, to integrate and improve the current early warning situation so that drought impacts can be reduced.

The dearth of information on social and other indicators of drought vulnerability is another major hindrance to effective drought mitigation in the country and the broader region. Enhancing the capacity of a rural community to respond to and mitigate drought is one way in which the risks of drought events can be reduced. Drought mitigation activities and programmes, through the engagement of local communities in drought mitigation both locally and in the region (e.g., Disaster Mitigation for Sustainable Livelihoods – Unit for Southern African Development Education and Policy Research, University of the Western Cape), are being undertaken. Additional and supportive ways of reducing community vulnerability in drought-prone regions of southern Africa through various drought initiatives (e.g., literacy and education projects, water management programmes, media products, conservation projects, etc.) need to be sought and expanded on. Developing more comprehensive early detection of drought-induced stress, including socioeconomic parameters and indicators, is also a much-needed area of research in the country. Despite some of the gaps and needs in drought monitoring and mitigation identified here, several proactive changes to drought management and drought policy have occurred and are currently being planned.

SOUTH AFRICAN DROUGHT POLICY – A PERSPECTIVE

Drought should be acknowledged as a normal feature of the climate in South Africa. Management of drought events, however, has varied in the past from a particularly skewed agricultural bias toward a more comprehensive strategy that includes an emphasis on national and household food security.

Past official response to drought

Drought policies from as early as 1923 (Union of South Africa 1923) have had an exclusively agricultural bias, particularly to white commercial farmers (Walters 1993, Adams 1993, Vogel 1994b):

> The pronounced agricultural bias of previous aid policies has led to insufficient consideration being given to the protection of the rural poor against threats posed to their security in terms of water supply, food and employment.
>
> (Walters 1993: 14)

> Current drought policy, distorted towards the commercial sector needs to be reviewed ... much of the programme (debt relief and drought relief of the 1990s) seeks to address problems related to inefficiency and low profitability rather than rainfall variations. For the future, drought policy will need to address the social and economic costs of drought induced vulnerability in a far more focused way than hitherto.
>
> (Rimmer 1993: 25)

Drought measures were largely countermeasures and were not very proactive. The history of the South African drought experience shows that droughts have been perceived as natural disasters that have usually necessitated large financial state payouts and subsidies.

Before the 1980s, drought assistance was given to stock farmers in areas proclaimed drought stricken. The purpose of these schemes was originally to assist farmers in the maintenance of a herd or flock during exceptionally dry times; this was later amended to the maintenance of a nucleus herd or flock. Seasonal droughts had to be accepted by farmers as their own

responsibility (Bruwer 1990a and 1990b). Drought assistance was given in successive phases: first, rebates on transport costs; then loans; and finally subsidies at increasing rates as drought persisted (the Phase Drought Relief Scheme).

Pre-1990 drought relief for stock farmers essentially encouraged veld degradation. The development of a new policy through the 1980s (which came into effect in 1990), however, began to reverse this trend. Drought disaster aid was linked to the farmers' adherence to stocking rate standards for their area. The effectiveness of the policy was linked to policing of range land conditions by the Directorate of Resource Conservation and the registration by farmers as a conservation farm. Drought aid was reserved only for farms that adhered to the conditions of a conservation farm. This included, inter alia, the submission of regular stock records to the local office of the Department of Agriculture. Through this 'carrot and stick' approach, a large proportion of stock farms were registered as conservation farms, resulting in the long term sustainability of the veld. Farms that exceeded the stocking rate norms were excluded from the scheme for at least five years. Once a drought was declared, conservation farmers had to reduce their stocking rate to one-third. Financial assistance was then available for farmers to maintain this 'nucleus heard' (Smith 1993).

Notwithstanding the changes in drought management over time, numerous forms of resources have been committed to disasters, particularly floods and droughts. Of the resources committed to drought, the debt relief programmes and broader agricultural relief programmes have been substantial. Arable farmers in the summer rainfall producing areas of the country have, for example, faced a growing debt burden (Rimmer 1993). Much of this assistance was in favour of the white commercial agricultural sector, with relatively little relief given to black farmers and the rural poor, who in several cases (the poorest and most marginal) may depend on agriculture to supplement their livelihoods (May *et al.* 1996).

Informal assistance outside the regular government channels, particularly to the rural communities and the poor, has often been undertaken by NGOs and other organisations during drought periods (e.g., through the Independent Development Trust, who launched a drought relief and development pro-gramme in 1992 [Loots and Roux 1993]; Mvula Trust; and Operation Hunger, amongst others). Private sector involvement has also occurred – for example, in the provision of food and food packages for distribution to the rural poor. The role of free food distribution as a drought relief measure, how-ever, is debatable, and alternatives such as vouchers, food stamps, and public works are other drought relief alternatives that are being considered in the region. A drought policy that acknowledges such varied dimensions of drought has thus begun to evolve.

The SARCCUS meeting in 1989 ushered in a period characterised by a more holistic approach to drought management. The call made at this meeting, for more proactive drought management strategy, was given added impetus by the harsh droughts of the early 1990s. Drought impacts on the environment and society were so extreme in South Africa during this period that a national drought forum (the first of its kind) was established as an emergency response to the drought of the time. For the first time, several sectors were involved in trying to manage the drought, including trade union movements, govern-ment sectors, and churches (Abrams *et al.* 1992, Adams 1993, Vogel 1994a and 1995). Much of the Consultative Forum's work on drought was devoted to coordinating and facilitating drought relief as well as providing information on the progress of the drought. Several task teams, including Nutrition, Employment, Water, and Agriculture, played essential roles in assisting and monitoring drought relief of the time (e.g., Hobson and Short 1993).

With the formation of the National Consultative Drought Forum after the 1992 drought and the changing political climate in the 1990s, evidence of some changes in the allocation of relief and drought management began to emerge. Unlike the previous drought programmes, when large white commercial farmers were the main beneficiaries, the programmes of the mid-1990s (e.g., 1994–5) appear to have been more equitable, with smaller farmers and farm workers being targeted for relief as well as support for rural water supply. An emphasis on reciprocity and the acknowledgment of a need to encourage sound farm and agricultural risk management has also

emerged with a move to encouraging farmers to farm in more self-reliant ways and to be prepared for and mitigate future drought impacts (Table 25.3).

The disastrous drought of the early 1990s thus once again brought local drought management under scrutiny. The foundations for a more proactive and wider-ranging drought management approach were established during this time. A drought strategy task team, comprising the heads of several departments (e.g., Department of Agriculture, Department of Water Affairs and Forestry, Department of National Health and Population Development, etc.), was formed (Drought Action Co-ordinating Centre 1993). Through this team, a proposal for drought manage-ment was drawn up and submitted to the National Consultative Forum (Drought Action Co-ordinating Centre 1993). Similar efforts to those begun by this Centre were revived in 1995, when the Cabinet approved the establishment of the National Disaster Management Committee (NDMC) at the national level. Supportive structures at provincial and local government levels with functions that include developing a national disaster management policy on a cross-functional basis, establishing an effective dis-aster management structure focusing on predisaster risk reduction, promoting community participation in disaster management, and promoting the establish-ment of an integrated disaster information system were also called for.

Problems of coordination and lack of capacity (amongst other problems at the various levels), how-ever, have dogged the progress of an effective drought 'management' strategy. Recent concerns about the need to galvanise a drought and disaster policy and the prospects of future El Niño events have resulted in a concerted effort toward developing more proactive drought management strategies at a national and local level. An Inter-Ministerial Com-mittee for the management of El Niño impacts, for example, has recently been established (1997) and a Green Paper on Disaster Management (due for comment in 1998) has been launched. At the same time as the preparation of the Green Paper, several task teams have been compiling inputs for a revised White Paper on Agriculture, including a reassessment of agriculture policy on drought and other agri-cultural disasters. Improved forecasts, early warning,

Table 25.3 Examples of drought mitigation methods

Appropriate farming systems	The selection of appropriate farming systems will reduce drought risk considerably. Information about the climate, soil type, and agricultural potential of most regions can be obtained from agricultural researchers or extension officers in each province. Farming methods that are generally useful include the following: Leave as much dead plant material (mulch) as possible on the soil surface to prevent soil heating and soil water loss to the atmosphere.
Improved grazing management	Information regarding recommended stocking rates and grazing strategies in different regions of the country is available from the National Department of Agriculture. Adherence to these recommendations will significantly reduce the drought risk faced by livestock farmers.
Improved crop production	Sorghum is more drought tolerant than maize, and millet is more tolerant than sorghum. Other crops that are reasonably drought tolerant are sunflower and sesame. Cassava can also be left in the ground for use if the rains cease. Although planting is usually dictated by rainfall and crop variety, it might be beneficial to plant during a cool time of the year.
Household gardens	Vegetables and crops can be grown on very small plots to provide food security and support to the family occupying a household.
Water harvesting and conservation	Several water harvesting and water conservation programmes are being carried on by both the government and NGOs in the country. Water laws and irrigation practise are also being revised.

monitoring of vulnerable areas and communities, and a move toward self-reliance and management of drought rather than dependence on the government during drought periods are also currently being considered.

Efforts are also being made to investigate other aspects of agricultural policy in promoting both national and household food security. Several policy initiatives, including the Land Reform Programme, Rural Infrastructure and the Farmer Settlement Programme, Land Tax and Trade Policy, Marketing Policy and the Balance of Payments, are being undertaken in a move toward greater food security for the country as a whole (Agrireview, Standard Bank 1997).

CONCLUSIONS

Drought is a normal feature of climate in South Africa, and it has occurred with varying intensity in several locations of the country. The impacts of drought, however, have often been compounded by poor preparedness and a lack of drought mitigation. The local physiographic, historic, and socioeconomic influences of a region are important in understanding a people's vulnerability to drought. Once a deeper understanding of local drought impact has been attained, appropriate drought policy can be made.

Determining local drought impacts thus requires a multifaceted, multidisciplinary approach that can determine the role that physical and socioeconomic factors have in contributing to drought impacts. It is important that the processes set up in the early 1990s to mitigate serious drought impacts are not allowed to fall apart during a period of sufficient rain. South Africa will continue to experience further droughts and must build on the knowledge of the previous events.

To be effective, however, the approach to managing droughts should cover all aspects of drought management and needs to include such aspects as prevention, mitigation, preparedness, response, recovery, and risk reduction to drought events (Pan American Health Organisation 1982, Adler 1988, Maskrey 1989). Some of the activities that would be required for effective preparation are vulnerability assessment, planning, information systems, institutional framework development, warning systems, public education and training, development of a short-term and longer-term mitigation strategy, and improved forecasts. An important aspect of long-term drought preparedness, however, is that such plans should not be counter to or hinder development.

During previous droughts it has been shown that the negative drought impacts, particularly for the rural poor, were often both the consequence of drought and a development problem. Measures to mitigate drought impacts should therefore focus on reducing vulnerability in the long term in these areas rather than (as has often been the case) giving short-term drought relief, which often creates situations of dependency.

Much positive work is currently being carried out to improve the management of drought at all levels in the country (national, provincial, and household) as well as in the SADC region. These efforts are forming an essential part of ensuring that South Africa and its people are better drought-proofed in the future.

REFERENCES

Abrams, L., Short, R., and Evans, J. (1992) *Root Cause and Relief Restraint Report*, Consultative Forum on Drought, Secretarial and Ops Room, Johannesburg, 8 October.

Adams, L. (1993) 'A rural voice: Strategies for drought relief', *Indicator South Africa* 10, 4: 41–6.

Adler, J. (1988) 'Assessment of disasters in the developing world', in P. Baskett and R. Weller (eds), *Medicine for Disasters*, London: John Wright, Butterworth.

AFRA (Association for Rural Advancement) (1992) 'Drought, relief and rural communities', Special Report No. 9, Pietermaritzburg.

Agrireview, Standard Bank (1994) 'A Quarterly Review: Drought, drought relief and agricultural debt', January.

—— (1997) 'A Quarterly Review: Government policies and food security', July.

Alexander, W.J.R. (1993) 'Floods or droughts', *Water Resource and Flood Studies Newsletter*, September, Department of Civil Engineering, University of Pretoria.

Bank, L. and Hobson, S. (1993) 'Between farm, village and location: Informal settlements and changing patterns of migration', in Informal Settlements in the Eastern Cape, Border and Transkei: A Pilot Study, unpublished report submitted to the Human Needs, Resources and the Environment Programme of the CSD, Pretoria, pp. 88–120.

Botha, S.J. and Viljoen, J.F. (1991) 'The financial implications of water restrictions of 1983 to 1987 for the Vaal and Riet River water catchments Part 1', *Report of the Water Research Commission, WRC 288/1/91*, Department of Agricultural Economics, University of the Orange Free State, Bloemfontein.

Braune, E. (1992) 'Focus on groundwater aspects of the 1992/93 drought', *Drought Update No. 5*, National Consultative Forum on Drought, Johannesburg, pp. 21–4.

Bruwer, J.J. (1989) 'Drought policy in the Republic of South Africa, Part I', *Drought Network News* 1, 3: 14–16.

—— (1990a) 'Drought policy in the Republic of South Africa, Part II', *Drought Network News* 2, 1: 10–11.

—— (1990b) 'Drought policy in the Republic of South Africa', *Drought Network News*, 2, 2: 10–12.

—— (1990c) 'Drought policy in the Republic of South Africa', in A.L. DuPisani (ed.), *Workshop on Drought. Proceedings of the SARCCUS Workshop on Drought*, pp. 23–38.

Chambers, R., Longhurst, R., and Pacey, A. (eds) (1981) *Seasonal Dimensions to Rural Poverty*, London: Francis Pinter.

Crankshaw, O. and Hart, T. (1990) 'The roots of homelessness: Causes of squatting in the Vlakfontein settlement south of Johannesburg', *South African Geographical Journal* 72: 65–70.

Crankshaw, O. (1993) 'Squatting, apartheid and urbanisation on the southern Witwatersrand', *African Affairs* 92: 31–51.

Cross, C.R., Bekker, S., and Clark, C. (1992) 'Fresh starts: Migration streams in the southern informal settlements of the Durban Functional region', *Natal Town and Regional Planning Supplementary Report*, Vol. 40, Pietermaritzburg.

Cross, C., Luckin, L., Mzimela, T., and Clark, C. (1996) 'On the edge: Poverty, livelihoods and natural resources in rural KwaZulu-Natal', in Michael Lipton, F. Ellis, and Merle Lipton (eds), *Land, Labour and Livelihoods in Rural South Africa*, Durban, South Africa: Indicator Press, pp. 173–213.

Danckwerts, J.E. and Stuart-Hill, G.C. (1988) 'The effect of the severe drought and management after drought on mortality and recovery of semi-arid grassveld', *Journal of the Grassland Society of Southern Africa* 5: 218–22.

DeKlerk, C.H. (1986) 'An investigation into the factors that stand in the way of the acceptance of recommended grassland management', Department of Agriculture and Water Affairs, Pretoria.

Dent, M.C., Schulze, R.E., Wills, H.M.M., and Lynch, S.D. (1987) 'Spatial and temporal analysis of the recent drought in the summer rainfall region of S.A.', *Water SA* 13, 1: 37–42.

Department of Agriculture (1983) 'Drought report for the season', Department of Agriculture, Pretoria.

Department of Water Affairs (1986) *Management of the Water Resources of South Africa*, Government Printer, Pretoria.

Department of Water Affairs and Forestry (1993) Dam level data (1980–92), Department of Water Affairs and Forestry, Pretoria.

Development Bank of South Africa (1992) 'Survey of current drought and poverty relief initiatives', unpublished report, Midrand.

Drought Action Co-ordinating Centre (1993) A proposal for a National Drought Management Strategy, presented to the National Consultative Forum on Drought, Pretoria, 23 March.

D'Souza, F., Mashinini, M., and Mashinini, T. (1987) 'First report on estimating vulnerability in black rural communities in South Africa', Operation Hunger, Johannesburg.

Evans, J. (1992) 'Farmworkers in the drought', paper presented at the Conference on Drought, University of the Witwatersrand, Johannesburg, 13–14 June 1992.

Farmworkers Research and Resources Project (1991) 'Taung farmer/migrant labour', unpublished project, Johannesburg.

Fincham, R., Harrison, D., Khosa, M., and LeRoux, I. (1993) 'Nutrition and health in South Africa: The state of nutrition and the development of nutrition policy', report presented to the World Bank as part of the Project for Statistics and Living Standards and Development, *Investigational Report* 89, Institute of Natural Resources, Natal.

Glatthaar, I.I. (1992) 'Protein-energy malnutrition in South Africa pre-school children', *South Africa's Continuing Medical Education Monthly* 10: 1,329–40.

Hobson, S. and Short, R. (1993) 'A perspective on the 1991–92 drought in South Africa', *Drought Network Newsletter* 5, 1: 3–6.

Hoffman, M.T. and Cowling, R.M. (1990) 'Vegetation change in the semi-arid eastern Karoo over the last 200 years: An expanding Karoo fact or fiction', *South African Journal of Science* 86: 286–94.

Jury, M.R. (1992) 'Vegetation changes over Southern Africa', *Conserva* (Department of Environment Affairs, Pretoria) 7: 10–11.

—— (1993) 'A preliminary note on rainfall and vegetation trends in the south-western Cape', *South African Journal of Botany* 59: 265–9.

Kirsten, J. and Van Zyl, J. (1993) 'Agriculture, land and food security in South Africa', paper presented at UNICEF Conference on Food Security in South Africa, 14–15 June 1993, Johannesburg.

Kustner, H.G.V. (1983) 'Studies to determine the risk of malnutrition attributable to the present drought, Part 1 and 2', *Epidemiological Comments* 10, 7: 1–30 and 10, 8: 1–24.

Kustner, H.G.V., Whitehorn, R., Wittner, H., Hignett, V.M., Rawlinson, J.L., Raubenheimer, W.J.J., and Van der Merwe, C.A. (1984) 'Weight-for height nutritional surveys in rural Kwa-Zulu and Natal', *South African Medical Journal* 65: 470–4.

Laing, M. (1992) 'Drought update 1991–92, South Africa', *Drought Network News* 4, 2: 15–17.

Lindesay, C.J. (1990) 'Economic and socio-political impacts of rainfall variations', unpublished MBA Report, University of Witwatersrand.

Loots, L. and Roux, A. (1993) An evaluation of the Relief and Development Programme of the Independent Development Trust, University of the Western Cape, Cape Town.

Mabin, A. (1991) 'The dynamics of urbanisation since 1960', in M. Swilling, R. Humphries, and K. Shubane (eds), *Apartheid City in Transition*, Cape Town: Oxford University Press, pp. 33–47.

Mars, I. (1984) 'The Red Cross Relief Fund, Rural Monitor', *Indicator South Africa* 2, 1: 4.

Martins, J.H. (1986) 'Financial and social implications of water restrictions for householders in selected areas', *Report of the Water Research Commission, WRC*, 169/1/86, Buro of Market Research, Pretoria.

Maskrey, A. (1989) *Disaster Mitigation – A Community Based Approach: Approaches to Mitigation*, Oxford: Oxfam.

May, J. (1993) 'Development options for peri-urban agriculture', unpublished report prepared for the World Bank, 10 September.

May, J., Carter, M., and Posel, D. (1996) 'The composition and persistence of poverty in rural South Africa', *Land and Agriculture Policy Paper* 15, Johannesburg.

Meteorological Office (1991) *Meteorological Glossary*, 6th Edition, London: HMSO Publication Centre.

Natal Nutrition Working Group (1993) 'The evaluation and monitoring of the National Nutrition and Social Development Programme (NNSDP), Natal Region', unpublished final report submitted to the Department of National Health and Population Development, Natal Region.

National Consultative Forum on Drought (1992) *Drought Update No. 2*, Operations Room, Johannesburg.

O'Connor, T.G. (1995) 'Transformation of a savanna grassland by drought and grazing', *African Journal of Range and Forage Science* 12, 2: 53–60.

Pan American Health Organisation (1982) *Environmental Health Management after Natural Disasters*, Scientific Publication No. 430, PAHO, Washington, DC.

Partridge, T.C. (1985) 'Spring flow and tufa accretion at Tang', in P.V. Tobias (ed.), *Hominid Evolution: Past, Present and Future*, New York: Alan Liss, pp. 171–87.

Perlman, I. (1984) 'Operation Hunger, Rural Monitor', *Indicator South Africa* 2, 1: 5.

Pretorius, C.I. and Smal, M.M. (1992) 'Notes on the macro-economic effects of the drought', *South African Reserve Bank Quarterly Bulletin*, June, pp. 31–8.

Rimmer, M. (1993) 'Debt relief and the South African Drought Relief Programme', *Land and Agricultural Policy Centre*, Policy Paper 1, Johannesburg.

Roux, P.W. and Vorster, M. (1983) 'Vegetation changes in the Karoo', *Proceedings of the Grassland Society of Southern Africa* 18: 25–9.

Sakamoto, C.M. (1989) 'Tools for an operational drought impact assessment system', in A.L. DuPisani (ed.), *Workshop on Drought. Proceedings of the SARCCUS Workshop on Drought*, pp. 12–22.

SALDRU (Southern Africa Labour and Development Research Unit) (1995) 'Key indicators of poverty in South Africa', prepared for the Office of Reconstruction and Development (RDP), Pretoria.

Schlemmer, L., Stewart, G., and Whittles, J. (1989) 'The socio-economic effects of water restrictions on local authorities, selected industrial and commercial establishments and other private agencies', *Report to the Water Research Commission*, WRC, 168/1/89, Centre for Social and Development Studies, University of Natal, KwaZulu, Natal.

Scholes, R.J. (1985) 'Drought-related grass, tree and herbivore mortality in a southern African Savanna', in J.C. Tothill and J.H. Mott (eds), *Ecology and Management of the World's Savannas*, Canberra: Australian Academy of Science, pp. 350–3.

Sender, J. (1994) 'Rural poverty and land redistribution: Some macroeconomic issues', paper presented at the Land and Agriculture Policy Centre Land Redistribution Option Conference, 12–15 October 1993; proceedings published by Land and Agriculture Policy Centre, Johannesburg, June, pp. 71–84.

Smith, D.I. (1993) 'Drought policy and sustainability: Lessons from South Africa', *Search* 24, 10: 292–5.

Snyman, H.A. (1985) 'Moisture balance on natural veld of the Central Orange Free State', unpublished Ph.D Thesis, University of the Orange Free State, Bloemfontein.

Snyman, H.A. and van Rensburg, W.L.J. (1990) 'Short-term influence on severe drought on veld conditions and water usage effectiveness of grasses in the Central Orange Free State', *Journal of the Grassland Society of Southern Africa* 7: 249–56.

Snyman, H.A. and Fouché, H.J. (1991) 'Production and water use efficiency of semi-arid grasslands of South Africa as affected by veld condition and rainfall', *Water SA* 17: 263–8.

Tyson, P.D. (1986) *Climate Change and Variability in Southern Africa*, Cape Town: Oxford University Press.

Union of South Africa (1923) *Final Report of the Drought Investigation Commission, U.G. 49– '23*, Cape Town: Government Printer.

Van Zyl, J. (1993) 'The last straw: Drought and economy', *Indicator South Africa* 10, 4: 47–51.

Van Zyl, J. and Nel, H.J.G. (1988) 'The role of the maize industry in the South African economy', *Agrekon* 27, 2: 10–16.

Van Zyl, J.F. and Viljoen, M.F. (1988) 'Summary report of the socio-economic consequences of water restrictions 1983 to 1985', *Report to the Water Research Commission*, WRC 167/2/88, Institute of Social and Economic Research, University of the Orange Free State, Bloemfontein.

Van Zyl, J. and Van Schalkwyk, H. (1994) 'Aspects of the South African land market and its role in a rural restructuring programme in South Africa', paper presented at the Land and Agriculture Policy Centre Land Redistribution Option Conference, 12–15 October 1993; proceedings published by Land and Agriculture Policy Centre, Johannesburg, June, pp. 33–40.

Van Zyl, J., Van der Vyver, A., and Groenewald, J.A. (1987) 'The influence of drought and general economic effects on agriculture: A macro-analysis', *Agrekon* 26, 1: 8–12.

Van Zyl, J., Nel, H.J.G., and Groenewald, J.A. (1988) 'Agriculture's contribution to the South African Economy', *Agrekon* 27, 2: 1–9.

Vergnani, T. (1984) 'Malnutrition in South Africa', *Indicator South Africa* 2, 1: 9–10.

Vogel, C.H. (1994a) '(Mis)management of droughts in South Africa', *South African Journal of Science* 90: 4–5.

—— (1994b) 'South Africa', in M.H. Glantz (ed.), *Drought Follows the Plough: Cultivating Marginal Areas*, Cambridge: Cambridge University Press, pp. 151–70.

—— (1995) 'Human response to the environment', in T. Binns (ed.), *People and Environment in Africa*, Chichester, UK, and New York: Wiley, pp. 249–56.

Walker, R.S. (1988) 'Long-term data series from South African grasslands', in I.A.W. MacDonald and R.J.M. Crawford (eds), 'Long-term data series relating to South Africa's renewable natural resources', *South African National Scientific Programme Reports* 157: 253–67.

Walters, M. (1993) 'Present state drought policy in the RSA and possible areas of adaptation', paper presented at a seminar, Planning for Drought as a Natural Phenomenon, Mmabatho, North West Province.

Warrick, R.A. (1980) 'Drought in the Great Plains: A case study of research on climate and society in the USA', in J. Ausubel and A. Biswas (eds), *Climatic Constraints and Human Activities*, New York: Pergamon, pp. 93–123.

Willis, M.J. and Trollope, W.S.W. (1987) 'Use of key grass species for assessing veld condition in the Eastern Cape', *Journal of the Grassland Society of Southern Africa* 4: 113–15.

26

THE DROUGHT OF 1991–5 IN SOUTHERN SPAIN

Analysis, economic repercussions, and response measures

C. Peral Garcia, A. Mestre Barceló, and J.L. Garcia Merayo

INTRODUCTION

The Iberian Peninsula, located in extreme south-western Europe, is ideal for climatological studies. The factors that influence the climate are so varied that in an area of almost 500,000 km², one can find all types of subclimates. According to the Köppen classification, they range from the Dfb (wet cold climate with hot summers) to the BW (desert climate). Tracing a line along a meridian from north to south, climate conditions change from wet temperate to subtropical dry. Following the 40°N parallel that crosses the Peninsula from west to east, the wet Atlantic climate changes to a dry Mediterranean one.

Therefore, the Iberian Peninsula offers climatologists a wide range of climate regimes to study. One of the common features of all the subclimates of the Peninsula, wet as well as dry, is the existence of protracted drought periods. Each subclimate has a unique set of dry conditions (defined by the quantity of precipitation and by the length of the period without rain) that demands separate study. One of the most common features of the atmospheric circulation in the North Atlantic is the occurrence of a high pressure system approximately centred in the Azores islands. During a major part of the year, the Iberian Peninsula falls within the range of the Azores high pressure system. Therefore it is frequently affected by the prevailing atmospheric conditions: stability, air subsidence, and absence of clouds and rainfall.

The Iberian Peninsula is located in the southern part of the zone over which the northern hemisphere's circumpolar vortex flows. The Peninsula's weather depends on the jetstream location and wave shape (upper circulation). The typically favourable atmospheric conditions that bring rainstorms correspond with low zonal circulation or meridian circulation in which the trough axis is located slightly to the west of the Peninsula. With these conditions in the high troposphere, the fronts associated with the low pressure systems sweep the Peninsula from west to east. This type of synoptic situation can affect the whole territory and bring rain to all of it, but in most cases, rain would reach just a small area located in the northwest. Frequently the fronts associated with the low pressure systems that are associated with the jetstream affect only the northern part of the Iberian Peninsula, where they produce abundant rains, while the rest of the territory remains under the effect of the high pressure systems and therefore has dry weather.

The area's orography, which modulates the influence of the low pressure systems, and the occurrence of the mesoscale convective phenomena help determine how much water is collected in each zone. These two factors are responsible for the great spatial variability of rainfall in the Iberian Peninsula. A good portion of the territory is above 1,000 m in altitude, and the orientation of all the mountain chains but one is approximately west to east. There is a difference, clearly noticeable in the vegetation, between slopes facing north and slopes facing south. Geography books frequently divide the Spanish Peninsula into two zones: wet and dry. The wet area, with total annual rains of more than 600 mm, encompasses the mountainous part of the north; the dry area covers the rest of the country. It is a schematic division, simple and useful. In reality, it is much more complex. Parts of the dry area (specifically, the higher elevations) have total rainfall of more than 600 mm. In contrast, some parts of the wet area have summer drought despite total rainfall amounts of more than 600 mm. Because of the type of vegetation that grows in these areas, the climate could be considered Mediterranean.

The study area of this chapter is the southern half of the Peninsula (within the dry part of Spain), an area that includes the basins and rivers that flow into the Atlantic and the Alborán Sea. Figure 26.1 shows the selected area, which encompasses approximately 200,000 km². This area was chosen because of its uniform rainfall patterns. The entire area has a rainy period from October to April, and it has a very distinct summer minimum. The atmospheric situations responsible for the rains are the same throughout the area and, as a rule, they operate at the same time, except in the southern strip that borders the Alborán Sea. This strip of land shares some conditions with the study area, but it also has some characteristics of a coastal Mediterranean climate. It has been included in the study because in the 1991–5 period, it was

intensely affected by the drought. It is important to emphasise that these were not the only regions affected by the drought during that time period. The drought also occurred in other basins – for example, it struck the southeast with great intensity, but not with the same persistence as in the studied area. The serious aridity problems of the study area are not only due to the rain temporal pattern (scarcity in some years and floods in others), they are also a result of human activity.

This study has been limited to the southern Spanish part of the Iberian Peninsula. However, we must point out that to add Portugal would not change the conclusions. Southern Portugal lies within two of the basins that flow into the Atlantic and is affected by the same phenomena as the Spanish contiguous area.

The rainfall in the studied area has among its characteristics a clear seasonality. Taking monthly precipitation into account, the year can be divided into four rainfall periods. The dry season occurs from June to September; it barely reaches 13 per cent of the annual rainfall. There are two periods of two months in which the rains usually fall as heavy showers; one corresponds to autumn (October and

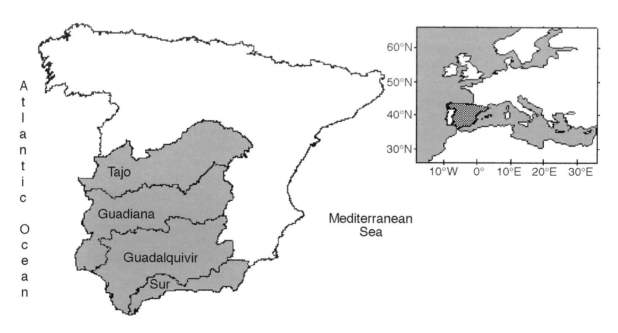

Figure 26.1 The study zone

November) and the other to spring (April and May). These two periods represent approximately 43 per cent of the annual rainfall. The most regular rainy season occurs from December to March and supplies 46 per cent of the total annual rainfall. This study must take into account the temporal pattern of the annual rainfall and consider the seasonal distribution. Therefore, the study uses two time units to calculate the quantity of precipitation. The first unit is the hydrological year, which in this part of the world starts 1 October, because this cycle adjusts better than that of the calendar year to the planning needs of hydrologists and agronomists. The second unit is the winter period, from December to March, because it is the rainiest period. In fact, winter rainfall is very important because of its amount and regularity; it usually fills the soil and reservoirs. It is in the winter that the greatest variations have taken place (at least in the years of available data), and this should be called to the planners' attention.

DATA

The precipitation volume data used in this study were calculated by the Climatic Studies Section of the Instituto Nacional de Meteorología (INM, National Institute of Meteorology), based on a method that uses the software SURFER for interpolation and drawing isolines. The method calculates the volumes (of precipitated water) of each basin using monthly data from the pluviometric stations within the basin. It makes use of every available station.

All of the available stations have been used to calculate the monthly volumes from 1930 on. Using a fixed number of stations, estimates of volumes can only be made starting from 1947; before this year, the majority of the stations have no precipitation record. Adding the limitation of using a minimum number of pluviometric stations (in this case, there were 352 stations), estimates can only be made starting from 1956. Even after that year, in order to use the same number of stations, it was necessary to substitute monthly data from other nearby stations for some of the selected stations. The Climatic Studies Section also carried out a study to compare the volumes obtained using all the available stations and the volumes obtained using a fixed number of selected stations. The results show that there were important differences (in some instances, more than 20 per cent) between the monthly volumes of some basins; however, the results were very similar when dealing with the annual volumes for the basins (in this case, the differences were all less than 2 per cent).

The main objective of the present study is to place the last drought period (1991–5) in context within the available volume data series, so the core data are those obtained by the Climatic Studies Section using the same method (SURFER, Simpson[1]) and the same number of stations (because they are considered to be more consistent and therefore much more comparable). In total there are forty years of reliable data (the period between the hydrological years 1955–6 and 1994–5).

Nevertheless, because the comparison of data (those obtained using all the available stations and those obtained using the same number) showed such small differences, it has been determined that, with respect to the annual data study, the series of precipitation volumes can be extended back to the hydrological year 1930–1 – if not to obtain statistics, then to get an idea of the general evolution of rainfall and the existence (or not) of similar drought periods. As such, the data for the period from 1930–1 to 1954–5 have been obtained from all of the available pluviometric stations (SURFER, Simpson).

In an attempt to extend the qualitative analysis further back in time, the annual rainfall data from the stations with the longest precipitation records pertaining to the basins under study were analysed. These stations are: Madrid (Tajo basin), with rainfall data from 1859; Badajoz (Guadiana basin), with data from 1876; S. Fernando (Guadalquivir basin), with data from 1839; and Malaga (representative of the Sur basins and rivers that flow into the Alborán Sea), with data from 1887. The data from these stations are annual rainfall data (calendar year) and have been statistically treated by the Statistics Technic Section of the INM for homogenisation and filling in missing data.

Sources for data concerning drought impacts include the following: water reserve data comes from the Department of Hydraulic Works and Quality of Water (Dirección General de Obras Hidráulicas, Environment Ministry); data for the agrarian sector comes from the Ministry of Agriculture, Fishing and Nourishment; and data on surfaces affected by forest fires comes from the Department of Nature Conservation (Direct Gen. de Conservación de la Naturaleza, Environment Ministry).

STUDY

Rainfalls in the study area occur mainly in the period beginning in late autumn and ending in mid-spring. As shown in the graph of average monthly rainfall (Figure 26.2a) corresponding to the 1956–95 period, the rainiest months are November, December, January, and February. During these months, the circulation in the high troposphere is sufficiently low in latitude and sufficiently meridian so that all the Peninsula is affected by the passing of the low pressure system associated with the jetstream. In the Atlantic to the southwest of the Peninsula, cut-off lows that cause intense rainfalls are relatively frequent. Blocking anticyclones that provoke long spells of dry weather are also relatively frequent in winter and spring. In what could be designated as the dry season (from May to September), the jetstream bypasses higher latitudes. Consequently, rainfalls are scarce and, in general, are caused by isolated storms provoked by convective phenomena that develop within the Iberian Peninsula.

Analysis of the evolution of annual rainfall volume

The interannual variability of rainfall is very high. The variation range in this forty-year period (1956–95) is 104,622 hm³ (maximum: 174,883 hm³, in the hydrological year 1962–3; minimum: 70,260 hm³, in 1994–5). This range is very close to the median and the average. The form of the frequency distribution (Figure 26.3) is bimodal, with a very low frequency for volumes close to the average, which suggests that the atmospheric processes (circulation patterns) that cause rainfall could be grouped in two principal groups. Therefore, using the average as reference, the years are quite rainy or quite dry. Planners used to dealing with data that adjust to the gaussian distribution should be aware that what is usually considered 'normal' (i.e., values near the average) is in this case rare. The distribution shape also shows that the

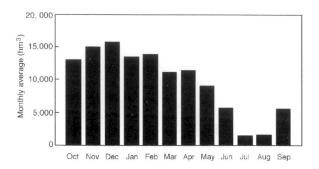
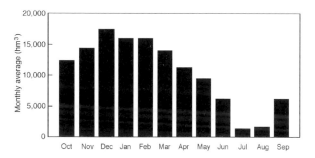
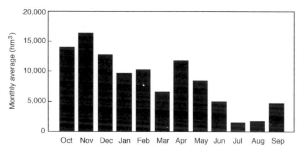

Figure 26.2 Monthly mean rainfall volumes collected in the study zone during the hydrological year. Data periods: (a) 1955–6, 1994–5; (b) 1955–6, 1979–80; (c) 1980–1, 1994–5 (data from the archives of Instituto Nacional de Meteorologiá [INM])

highest frequencies appear in amounts a little below the median. There is an agglomeration of data around the median and just below it. Between the median (107,154 hm³) and the second quintile (104,124 hm³) there is a difference of only 3,030 hm³, while between the median and the third quintile (125,890 hm³) there is a 18,736 hm³ difference, higher than the one between the median and the first quintile.

As the annual evolution graph (Figure 26.4) shows, there is a negative trend from the mid-1960s in the amount of rainfall volume. A purely statistical study of this data would verify the decreasing trend in

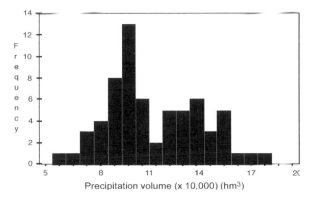

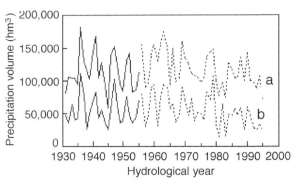

Figure 26.3 Frequency distribution of the annual rainfall volumes (hydrological year) in the study zone. Data period 1930–1, 1994–5 (data INM)

Figure 26.4 Rainfall volume evolution in the southern half of Spain from 1931–2 to 1994–5: (a) annual evolution; (b) winter (December, January, February, March) evolution. Data are obtained by the same method, using same number of pluviometric stations (thick line) or using all available pluviometric stations (thin line). Data from INM

rainfall and, consequently, would conclude that possibly there will be smaller volumes of rainfall for the coming years. However, this type of forecast cannot be made with such a low number of years of data. Fortunately, in addition to the forty years of data, there are other data that, although not as reliable and representative, can give an idea of what has happened and show that the last 150 years have had several positive and negative trends, and that any such trends could be broken. The hydrological year 1995–6 and the beginning of 1996–7 provide an example of how a trend of successive dry years can be broken with at least two rainy years.

To get a better idea of the annual evolution, volume data from 1930–1 to 1954–5 have been calculated using the homogeneous method and added to the volume data of the forty-year period to make a total of sixty-four years of data. These added data are less reliable, and indeed the numbers should be taken only as an approximation, but they give a good idea of the evolution and a better perspective. Figure 26.4 represents the evolution and shows that (1) dry and wet years alternate, with the sequence of two consecutive rainy or dry years occurring frequently; and (2) from 1980 on there is a change with respect to the evolution of the previous years: the variability range is reduced (mainly because the rainy years are no longer so rainy), and drought periods are more persistent.

To provide a better historical perspective, Figure

26.5 represents the annual evolution of rainfall (moving averages) for the four stations with longer records located inside the study zone. Evidently, specific conclusions referring to the rainfall volumes for all the basins cannot be drawn from the data from these four stations, but these data are representative, and, as the volume data for the period 1956–95 demonstrates, the annual precipitation data of these stations bear a high correlation with the volume series. Thus it can be said with a high degree of confidence that (1) the alternation of dry and wet years from the middle of the past century is similar to that of the last forty years; (2) in the last one hundred years, there have been two dry periods (in which the rainfalls have been below the median for each of the four stations with long records) and two rainy periods; and (3) to find similarity with the last fifteen years in terms of rainfall shortage and dry and rainy period alternation (duration of drought periods), one must go back some 120 years, around 1870.

To quantify the intensity of drought, it is necessary to establish thresholds. This has been done using the quintile method, which is customarily practised in the INM and in the hydrological sector. We consider dry periods (consecutive years) those in which the rainfall was below the median; very dry periods are those with two or more consecutive years in which the rainfall was below the second quintile; and periods of severe drought are those with two or more

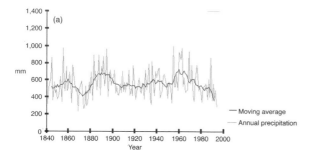

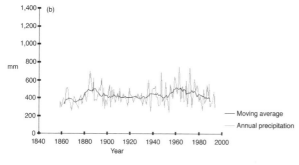

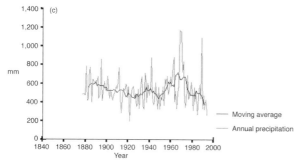

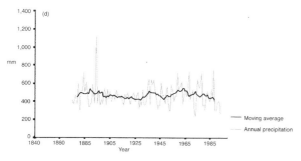

Figure 26.5 Annual rainfall evolution (simple moving average, eleven terms) in four principal stations with long records, each one located in one of the basins considered in the present work. Stations: (a) S. Fernando (Guadalquivir), (b) Madrid (Tajo), (c) Málaga (Sur), (d) Badajoz (Guadiana). Data from INM

consecutive years in which the rainfall was below the first quintile. In this case, taking into account that the difference between the median (107,154 hm³) and the second quintile (104,124 hm³) is very small, one can simplify the classification and in practise consider two types of periods: dry periods (two or more consecutive years with rainfall volumes below the median) and those of severe drought (two or more consecutive years with rainfall volumes below the first quintile). According to this classification, between 1956 and 1995, there have been three periods of severe drought (1957–8, 1981–3, and 1992–3) and three dry periods (1974–6, 1980–3, 1991–5). Considering, as the hydrologic planner does, the average as a reference amount to design an adequate substructure for water resources management, great water deficits occurred in these drought periods. In the biennium 1957–8 (hydrological years 1956–7 and 1957–8), there was a rainfall deficit of 51,196 hm³ (approximately 24 per cent of the volume that would fall in two average consecutive years); in the three years 1981–1982–1983, there was a deficit of 104,445 hm³ (which equals the volume that falls in an average year); and in the biennium 1992–3, there was a deficit of 50,761 hm³ (again, 24 per cent of the volume that would fall in two average consecutive years). The rain deficit accumulated in the period of persistent drought (1991–5) was approximately 128,558 hm³.

The fifteen hydrological years spanning 1980 to 1995 are characterised by persistent drought periods. The consecutive biennia 1980–1 and 1982–3 could be considered a period of severe drought; the deficit accumulated in those four years totals 123,258 hm³. The period 1991–5 starts with the dry 1991–2 biennium, followed by a very dry year in 1993, a mildly dry year in 1994 (in which rainfall quantity is slightly inferior to the median); and a very dry year in 1995 (in fact, the driest of the 1956–95 period).

With all the available data, it can be said with confidence that, from the purely climatic point of view, the longest drought occurred from 1990 to 1995. The 1980–3 period was a shorter but more intensive drought period. Drought was also severe in the biennia 1953–4, 1949–50, and 1944–5. In the hydrologic year 1944–5, the volume of rain was approximately half of the average in the southern part of the Peninsula.

Analysis of the evolution of rainfall distribution within the year

Concerning the evolution of the rainfall throughout the period 1956–95, a decrease is observed in the 1980–95 period, but what catches one's attention is the change in the seasonal rainfall distribution. The monthly averages of the 1956–80 period (Figure 26.2b) and the 1981–95 period (Figure 26.2c) are considerably different. In the earlier period, rainfall was at a maximum in the four winter months (December, January, February, and March), with a maximum in December and a gradual decrease until the dry months of the summer; in the later period, winter rainfall had a notable decrease and the months with greater rainfall were November, December, October, and April. So an increase of autumn and spring rainfall as a percentage of the annual total has been detected. In reality, there has not been a significant increase in autumn and spring rainfall, but there has been a dramatic decrease in winter rainfall. Winter precipitation dropped from an average of approximately 60,000 hm^3 to an average of about 40,000 hm^3; autumn rainfall increased slightly, approximately 10 per cent, while spring rainfall remained around 20,000 hm^3. Figure 26.4b shows the evolution of rainfall in the winter months, and one can clearly notice the decrease in the period 1981–95. Winter rainfall went from representing approximately 50 per cent of the annual rainfall to representing less than 40 per cent, while autumn and spring rainfall (October, November, April, and May) together increased from 38 per cent of the annual precipitation to approximately 50 per cent. Rainfall in the summer months was reduced, but its proportion in the set of years remained at about 12 per cent of the annual precipitation.

This matter is especially worrisome. If this trend were to continue in the next few years, it would force important changes in water management policy. Making plans based on abundant rainfall in the winter months, in which rain falls more or less uniformly and in the form of snow in the summits, is simpler than planning based on more irregular (in time and space) rainfall patterns. In the case of spring rainfall, although the total amount has not varied, a change in rainfall intensity (quantity of water per minute) has

probably occurred. Although this cannot be confirmed yet (it is the subject of an ongoing study), it coincides with the expected alterations of climate because of anthropogenic factors.

Analysis of atmospheric circulation in 1991–5

From 1981 to 1995, the winter months (December to March) have been characterised by a positive NAO (North Atlantic Oscillation) index (Figure 26.6). In particular, since 1988, there have been eight consecutive winters with the same circulation state – positive NAO index and scarce rainfalls. This extreme persistence ended in the winter of 1996, when the NAO index had a negative value and rainfalls were abundant. One of the characteristic features of circulation with a positive NAO index is a northward shift in the mean jetstream. This type of circulation of the westerlies is related to rainfall deficits in the Mediterranean zone.

A change is also observed in winter rainfall volume anomalies (Figure 26.7), beginning in 1980. From this time until 1995, the anomaly is quite negative, except for four years in which the sign is feebly positive. Focusing on the study period, 1991–5, and more specifically on the winter months, the NAO index is positive and the volume anomaly is negative. One can conclude that the NAO index series is consistent with the volume anomaly series, which reinforces the hypothesis that between 1980 and 1995, winter atmospheric circulation on the western part of the North Atlantic and southwestern Europe was different from that of the previous thirty years. This

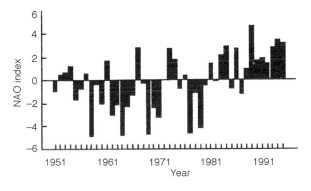

Figure 26.6 NAO index for winters between 1951 and 1995

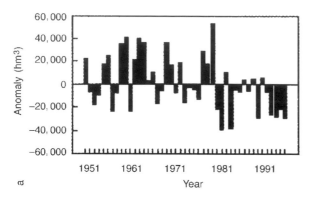

Figure 26.7 Precipitation volume anomalies for winters between 1951 and 1995 (data INM)

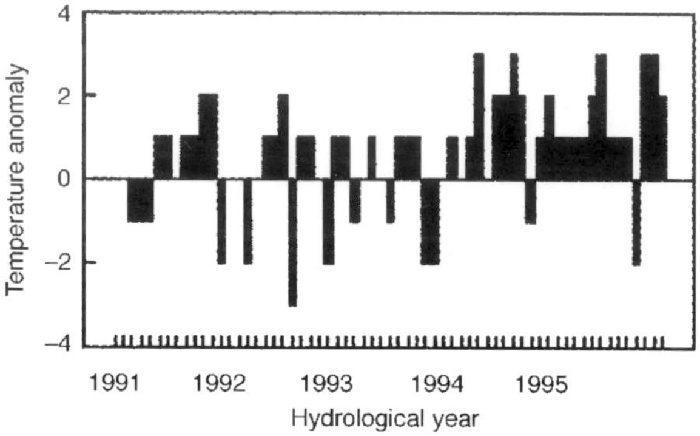

Figure 26.9 Monthly temperature anomaly, October 1990–September 1995 (data INM)

circulation pattern has produced the abnormally dry winters.

During the 1991–5 period, there were three exceptionally dry intervals: (1) November 1991–March 1992, (2) November 1992–March 1993, and (3) November 1994–May 1995 (Figure 26.8). A very important feature common to these intervals is that the rainfall deficit took place during the winter months, which are on average the rainiest of the whole period (1956–95). The seasonal nature of this drought makes it even more severe. The last of these three periods experienced the most intensive drought. In addition to having lasted longer (seven months), it also experienced positive temperature anomalies during eleven months, from October 1994 to August

1995 (Figure 26.9). This added to the adverse consequences of the water deficit.

IMPACTS OF THE 1991–5 DROUGHT: RESPONSE MEASURES

The long period of rainfall deficit greatly affected the activities of various productive sectors in the country – particularly those related to water resources management and the agrarian sector – and caused important economic losses and severe environmental damages that forced authorities to take emergency measures, especially in the communities of Andalucía, Castilla–La Mancha, and Extremadura. This part of the study evaluates the different impacts of the drought, grouped by specific sectors, as well as the actual measures carried out to alleviate its effects, during 1991–5.

Impacts on the water resources sector

The hydrological drought that accompanied the meteorological drought during 1991–5 reached a high degree of severity in wide zones of the nation, especially in the Tajo, Guadiana, Guadalquivir, and Sur basins. It was the hydrological drought that caused the greatest impacts.

One of the reasons for the intensity of the hydrological drought was the persistent rainfall deficit and its cumulative effects in the southwest Peninsula. This deficit was concentrated in the winter period, which is

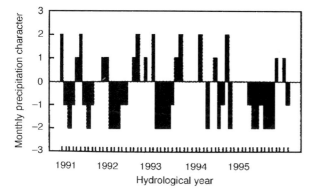

Figure 26.8 Monthly precipitation character (defined by quintiles), October 1990–September 1995. Data from INM

when rainfall is more effective in creating surface runoff. These conditions caused the large peninsular rivers to reach very low levels during the quinquennium, especially in the hydrological year 1994–5, when in some cases inflow was less than 25 per cent of the annual average. In addition, as we have noted, the average temperatures of the period were higher than normal (Figure 26.9), especially during 1994 and 1995. This caused extremely high evaporation rates that contributed to a more rapid depletion of water resources. For example, an estimated increase of 20 per cent occurred in the mean evapotranspiration rate throughout the 1994 season in irrigated areas where corn is cultivated in Castilla–La Mancha.

The impact of the drought on the water resources sector has been evaluated using the total volume of water stored in the reservoirs for domestic consumption as an indicator. Figure 26.10 represents the evolution of water reserves for September 1991–May 1996 for all of the study basins. It shows the progressive effects of drought on available resources, reaching the most critical point in September 1995, when the Tajo, Guadiana, Guadalquivir, and Sur basins had a storage of only 2,400 hm³, or 10.6 per cent of the maximum storage capacity. Storage in the latter three basins fell below 10 per cent of capacity. The situation abruptly changed in November 1995, when an abundant and persistent rainfall began in the

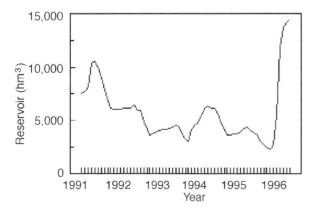

Figure 26.10 Evolution of water resources in surface reservoirs (for domestic water consumption) during the period 1992–6. Based on data from the Ministry of Public Works

Iberian Peninsula, especially in the southwest regions, which had been the most affected by the drought. This caused the soils to reach moisture saturation toward the middle of December. The persistence of strong rainfall generated a large surface runoff in all the basins in the western half of Spain, producing an extraordinary increase in water reserves within five weeks.

Because water supply was so limited for such a long period, various productive sectors experienced a number of direct impacts. These are discussed below:

Domestic water supply problems During the entire drought period, numerous urban areas of Castilla–La Mancha, Andalucía, and Extremadura, including most of the provincial capitals and populations of more than 50,000, suffered some type of limitation and partial shortage in domestic water supply. The situation worsened by the end of the hydrological year 1994–5, when the reservoirs that supply large urban areas in the southwestern zone of Spain fell to 5–10 per cent of their total capacity. In some places there was hardly any useable water left. At the beginning of autumn 1995, just before the abrupt end of the drought, 15 per cent of the Spanish population was experiencing water shortages, and another 15 per cent was facing reduced water supply.

Overexploitation of aquifers By 1995, the shortage of surface water resources had forced a greater exploitation of hydrogeological resources, especially for agricultural uses, but also for municipal water supply systems. This caused a rapid decrease in groundwater levels, thereby draining wetlands in the interior southern half of the Peninsula and increasing salinisation by allowing marine water intrusion in the coastal zone aquifers of the southeast.

Reduction of irrigated land During the entire 1992–5 period, strong restrictions were placed on irrigation because of the water shortage in the reservoirs and the depletion of aquifers. This seriously affected irrigated herbaceous crops, reducing them by more than 200,000 ha (about 18 per cent of the total area of land in these crops) between 1992 and 1993.

To evaluate the impact of the drought on the size of irrigated lands, areas planted with rice, cotton, and corn were used. These are the three principal irrigated

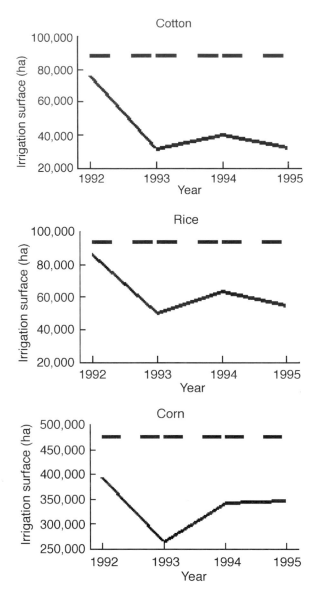

Figure 26.11 Evolution of irrigated area for certain crops (cotton, corn, rice), 1992–5. Dotted line represents the mean for the previous five-year period (1986–91). Based on data from the Ministry of Agriculture, Fisheries and Food

crops in south and southwest Spain. Figure 26.11 shows the evolution of these crops in the study area during 1992–5. Nationally, during the 1992–5 period (compared to a normal hydric situation [1986–91]), the average area in corn was reduced by 30 per cent (about 140,000 ha), the area in cotton was reduced

by 51 per cent (45,000 ha), and the area in rice was reduced by 33 per cent (30,000 ha).

Decreased hydroelectrical energy production The shortage of water resources also affected the hydroelectric reservoir during the entire quinquennium, causing a reduction in hydroelectric production. The average production of hydroelectric energy for the four hydrological years from 1991–2 to 1994–5 was 14.5 per cent less than the average during the five-year period 1986–91, despite the gradual increase in the total capacity of the reservoirs for electrical production throughout this period. In this respect, 1992 was an extremely unproductive year, with production 30 per cent lower than the 1986–91 average. This production deficit, which caused serious economic losses for electrical companies, had to be compensated by an increase in thermal energy production of about 7 per cent.

Drought impact on crop production, forests, and cattle raising

The persistent rainfall shortages had great repercussions on the agrarian sector. The shortages were centred in certain areas and crops, affecting the entire southern half of the Peninsula; other zones of Spain were also affected, although not for the entire length of the period. In this regard, it can be asserted that the growing diversification of the agrarian sector in Spain tends to limit adverse climatic impacts on agricultural production at the national level. Thus, the value of the agrarian final production (AFP) in Spain (expressed in 1980 pesetas [pta]) is maintained throughout 1991 and 1992 with values similar to the average of the previous five-year period (about 1.74×10^9 pta), while the 1993 AFP is about 3.2 per cent less than the five-year average; the 1994 AFP, about 5 per cent less; and the 1995 AFP, about 10 per cent less – primarily because of the soil moisture deficit and the decrease in irrigated lands.

During 1992–5, the main crops affected were irrigated herbaceous crops, particularly cereals and beans, because of the previously mentioned reduction in irrigated lands, especially in Andalucía (out of approximately 200,000 ha taken out of irrigation nationwide, around 90,000 ha was in Andalucía) and

Extremadura (with an average reduction of about 50,000 ha). Also, the lack of soil moisture during the entire vegetative cycle caused a serious reduction in rainfed crop yields. In the cereal-producing sector, yields were about 1.7 t/ha in 1995, a decrease of about 30 per cent compared to the average of 20.5×10^6 t in the quinquennium 1987–91. The minimum harvest occurred in 1995 – only 11.2×10^6 t, a little more than half of normal.

Perennial crops were not severely affected by the rainfall shortage in the first three years of the quinquennium 1991–5, but with the persistence of drought, crops like vines, olives, and citrus fruits were affected from 1994 on. For instance, in the 1994–95 season, olive oil production was reduced by 20 per cent from the average of the previous four seasons. The vinicultural sector was also affected. Average wine production decreased in 1994 and 1995 by 25 per cent compared to 1993 and by 40 per cent compared to 1992.

Cattle production was also affected by the decrease in the capacity of the pasture lands to sustain cattle, which lead to a 5 per cent increase in the use of concentrated fodders for livestock during this period.

In addition to its direct effects, the drought had a number of indirect effects on the agricultural sector. Since reduced production was expected, agricultural machinery was not maintained as often as usual, and maintenance and repair costs subsequently increased. Fertiliser production industries and industries manufacturing products to prevent and fight plant pests and diseases were also affected; consumption of these products was reduced by 5–7 per cent.

The prolonged drought seriously affected the forested areas within the Peninsula, especially those located in the mountains of Andalucía, where it caused a high mortality of maritime pines (*Pinus pinaster*) and severe withering symptoms in oak groves, scrub, gall oaks, wild olives, stone pines (*Pinus pinea*), and, above all, cork oak, especially among the recently uncorked.

The weakening of trees in forests, which in Andalucía, Extremadura, and other zones of east and southeast Spain reached the limit of their survival capacity at the end of the drought period, also increased the risk of forest fires, because of the higher combustibility level of live vegetation with reduced water content and the greater accumulation of flammable dead vegetation. The climatic characteristics of the summer periods during 1991–5 were also very favourable to the starting and spreading of fires, since rainfall was scarce and temperatures were above average. The temperature anomaly reached a peak during the summer of 1994, when temperatures in July and August were 2–3°C above average in the entire southern half of the Peninsula. Nationwide, the area of forest affected by fires increased 6.8 per cent in the 1991–5 period in comparison with the previous ten-year period. In the study zone, the zone most severely affected by the drought, the area affected by fires increased 63 per cent.

Measures adopted to mitigate drought effects

The dramatic situation created by the drought in certain sectors forced the adoption of urgent measures, beginning in 1992 and continuing for three subsequent years. These measures were created to reduce water consumption and to provide extraordinary credits for new water catchments. The government also approved a series of economic and administrative measures to mitigate the effects of the drought on agricultural activities and production and marketing cooperatives. The measures are described below:

Water rationing The government adopted short-term measures giving domestic consumption first priority and also began a series of mid- and long-term plans. Short-term measures included the following:

- Irrigation suspension in areas where water reserves fell below the admissible threshold, especially in the irrigated lands of the Guadiana and Guadalquivir rivers. The cultivation of crops with high levels of water consumption was greatly reduced, and other crops more resistant to drought, in particular wheat and sunflower, were substituted. Nevertheless, at least minimal irrigation was maintained for crops considered of strategic interest, particularly fruit-bearing trees.
- The establishment of consumption quotas for municipalities by the public institutions in charge of water resources management. These institutions were responsible for adopting a number of actions to decrease domestic consumption.

- Limitations and even total bans (in certain municipalities) on the irrigation of parks and public and private gardens.

These measures were accompanied by an intensive campaign, using widespread media coverage, to increase public awareness of the need for reducing domestic consumption. In Madrid, which reached its most critical situation with water resources in the summer of 1993, domestic water consumption was reduced to about 20 per cent, preventing further restrictions and supply losses. One of the long-term measures was the establishment of extra-budgetary funds to help irrigation communities improve and modernise irrigation systems, mainly through reduction of leakage and volume losses from channels. Another high priority was the review and modification of irrigation systems, eliminating aspersion irrigation in favour of computer drip control. Like the establishment of progressive tariffs for progressive levels of water consumption, the shift from a tariff depending on the area of irrigated land (which was the traditional practice in Spain) to a tariff depending on consumed water volume reflects the scarcity of water resources.

New water resources catchment   Throughout 1992–5, extraordinary credits were approved to carry out emergency construction of new reservoirs as well as interconnections for existing supply systems in the southern half of Spain. Numerous towns and cities in the centre and southern parts of the country (including Madrid) incorporated groundwater into their supply systems, authorised new hydrogeological catchments, and approved measures that allowed seizure of water from private wells and galleries, if the drought situation persisted.

During summer 1995 in coastal areas of south and southeast Spain, the progressive depletion of superficial water reserves and the realisation that underground reserves were limited led to the development of a project to build more seawater desalinisation plants as well as modernise and expand existing desalinisation facilities. The abrupt end of the drought in autumn 1995 halted this project.

Economic and administrative measures to alleviate losses to producers   To reduce the social and economic impacts caused by the drought in the agrarian sector, the government approved exceptional measures during 1992–5 that aided both dryland and irrigated farming. They also approved complementary measures to maintain agricultural production and production and marketing cooperatives. Producers were given financial assistance if their harvest was reduced by more than 50 per cent for unirrigated cultivation or, in the case of irrigated cultivation, if their water quota was reduced by more than 50 per cent.

The principal measures adopted were:

- Providing water supplies for cattle producers through construction of supply points.
- Special tax policies for producers affected by drought, including a one-year moratorium on tariff payments for water use, a moratorium on the payment of social security quotas, and a set of modifications to decrease tax quotas and create fiscal exemptions.
- Measures to promote low-rate interest loans as financial alternatives.
- Providing low-cost cereal fodder to affected farmers for cattle feed in the absence of pasture.
- Modifying rural employment plans by increasing the number of investment projects to be financed, to compensate for the possible decrease in farm employment caused by the reduction of the irrigated area.

CONCLUSIONS

- From the precipitation volume data corresponding to the period 1930–95, the following can be concluded:

1 The annual volume distribution frequency is bimodal. This suggests that the atmospheric circulation modes affecting this zone are such that the higher frequencies are either well below or well above the average precipitation volume, but not near the average.

2 Monthly precipitation distribution has a seasonal character.

3 There is a wide interannual variability range, and the occurrence of two consecutive dry or rainy years is frequent.

4 In the period 1981–95, drought persistency has increased. There were two drought periods;

these lasted four and five years, for a total of nine dry years out of fifteen. There has been a negative trend in the annual precipitation volume, as well as a decrease in the interannual variability.

- Focusing on the intra-annual pattern, it appears that the negative trend of the 1981–95 period is mainly due to a marked decrease in what could be called winter precipitation (December, January, February, and March). Winter precipitation represents approximately 40 per cent of the total precipitation for the 1981–95 period; for the 1956–80 period, winter precipitation was closer to 50 per cent of the total. This indicates the occurrence of a northward shift in the atmospheric circulation over the northeast Atlantic and southwestern Europe in the period 1981–95, compared to the previous thirty years.

- The 1991–95 drought has been the most persistent drought in the period for which there are precipitation volume data (1930–95). Based on the longest available pluviometric records, it appears that there is an irregular succession of dry and rainy periods. The dry intervals are longer and show a lesser annual volume variability than the rainy periods. Around 1870, these longest records show similar events (in persistency and intensity) to those that occurred in the 1981–95 period.

- The impacts of a persistent and intense drought are severe and constitute a hard test for the country's response capacity. At the same time, they force the government to make decisions that will affect the entire country's economy for a long time. To evaluate these drought impacts, two important issues have to be taken into account. The first issue is that this period of scarce rains happened simultaneously with a marked increase in the demand for water. The second is that a good part of our substructure and planning was done in the last thirty years of economic development, and it was based on climatological data corresponding to the rainy period around 1960.

- The point that we would like to stress in this study is the need for a drought monitoring programme for Spain. We think it is of vital importance,

regardless of the nature of precipitation in the next few years. It does not matter whether this low-frequency dry phase continues or if the general circulation model scenarios (hydrological cycle enhancement bringing frequent and more intense floods and droughts in temperate latitudes) materialise, or if the dry period abruptly ends and a rainy one takes its place; there will always be a drought threat in Spain. Planners should be aware of climatic features and fluctuations, and climatologists should provide them with the best information to understand and plan for drought.

NOTE

1 A computer program enabling the computation of volumes by the use of Simpson's Rule (among other methods).

REFERENCES

Carleton, A.M., Carpenter, D.A., and Weser, P.J. (1990) 'Mechanisms of interannual variability of the Southwest United States summer rainfall maximum', *Journal of Climate* 3, 9: 999–1,015.

CEDEX (1995) 'Las sequias en España', Direccion General de Obras Hidraulicas, Madrid.

Climatic Prediction Center (NCEP, USA) (ongoing) Teleconnection indexes: NAO monthly values.

Hurrell, J.W. (1995) 'Decadal trends in the North Atlantic oscillation regional temperatures and precipitation', *Science* 269, 5224: 676–9.

Klein Tank, A. (1996) 'How does the cold winter of 1996 fit in with global warming?', *Change* 29.

Lamb, P.J. and Peppler, R. (1987) 'North Atlantic Oscillation: Concept and application', *Bulletin of the American Meteorological Society* 68.

Lupo, A.R. and Smith, P.J. (1995) 'Climatological features of blocking anticyclones in the Northern Hemisphere', *Tellus* 47A, 4.

Ministerio de Agricultura, Pesca y Alimentacion. La agricultura, la pesca y la alimentacion españolas (Anuarios 1991, 1992, 1993, 1994 y 1995).

Ministerio de Medio Ambiente. Direccion General de Conservacion de la Naturaleza (1996) Los incendios forestales en España durante el decenio 1986–1995 (Informe tecnico).

Ministerio de Obras Publicas, Transportes y Medio Ambiente. Boletines hidrologicos semanales (correspondientes a los años 1991 a 1996).

Mock, C.J. (1996) 'Climatic controls and spatial variations of precipitation in the western United States', *Journal of Climate* 9, 5: 1,111–25.

Pfister, C. (1992) 'Monthly temperature and precipitation in Central Europe 1525–1979: Quantifying documentary evidence on weather and its effects', in R.S. Bradley and P.D. Jones (eds), *Climate since A. D. 1500*, London: Routledge.

Servicio de Aplicaciones, 1995. 'Analisis del volumen de agua recogida en las cuencas meridionales de la Peninsula Iberica', INM, Madrid.

Trenberth, K.E. and Guillemot, C.J. (1996) 'Physical processes involved in the 1988 drought and 1993 floods in North America', *Journal of Climate* 9, 6: 1,288–98.

Wilhite, D.A. and Easterling, W.E. (eds) (1987) *Planning for Drought: Toward a Reduction of Societal Vulnerability*, Boulder, CO: Westview Press.

Wilhite, D.A. (1993) *Drought Assessment, Management, and Planning: Theory and Case Studies*, Dordrecht, The Netherlands: Kluwer Academic Publishers.

Zorita, E., Kharin, V., and von Storch, H. (1992) 'The atmospheric circulation and sea surface temperature in the North Atlantic area in winter: Their interaction and relevance for Iberian precipitation', *Journal of Climate* 5, 10: 1,097–108.

27

THE VIRGIN LANDS SCHEME IN THE FORMER SOVIET UNION[1]

Igor Zonn, Michael H. Glantz, and Alvin Rubinstein

To the expanding list of examples of the encroachment of human activities on marginal lands must be added the initial attempts at agricultural development of the virgin lands in the 1950s and 1960s in northern Kazakhstan and western Siberia. The 1964 edition of the Soviet Geographical Encyclopedia referred to such lands as 'untilled, but suitable for tillage and sowing of agricultural crops, which either never were tilled [i.e., virgin lands] or had not been cultivated for a long period of time [i.e., idle lands]'. In this region, between 1954 and 1958, more than 40 million hectares of new land (larger than three times the size of Great Britain) were put into cultivation (Lydolph 1979). These lands straddle the northern edge of an arid zone where soils are marginal for rain-fed agricultural production. Experience later showed that such lands could not be developed for sustained agricultural production without resorting to appropriate scientifically based land-use practices.

The catalyst for the development of virgin and idle lands was the pressing need to sharply increase grain and meat production in the Soviet Union. The agricultural sector had clearly been neglected since the Bolshevik Revolution in 1917; most resources went toward industrialisation efforts. With regard to increasing agricultural production, options available to the Soviet government were few: increase productivity (e.g., crop yields) on existing farmlands, such as in the highly productive Ukraine, or extend agricultural activities into seemingly unused, potential arable lands.

The Virgin Lands Scheme was Nikita Khrushchev's pet project. Its roots can be found in the 'court' politics of the final years of the Stalin era, and in the Soviet leadership's search for a way of expanding domestic food production. Although made a member of the Politburo of the Central Committee of the CPSU (Communist Party of the Soviet Union) in 1939, Khrushchev was kept in the Ukraine until December 1949, when Stalin brought him to Moscow for political reasons.

In 1949, the Soviet Union's food production was barely able to meet the country's essential needs. Grain production, in fact, was lower than it had been in 1928, on the eve of collectivisation. Soviet farmers had paid a heavy price for (1) the forced and rapid collectivisation in the late 1920s and early 1930s, and (2) the dislocation of millions during the Soviet purges of the late 1930s, and the high number of casualties of the Second World War. As a consequence, agriculture, when compared with industry, was a relative wasteland.

From 1950 to 1964, Khrushchev chose to engage in agropolitics and played a key role in trying different policies in an attempt to raise the level of Soviet food production. His successes were evident, but exaggerated, during his period in power; only after 1964 when he was ousted by Leonid Brezhnev, whom he had promoted, were the benefits and costs of his agricultural policies to become clear and evaluated. Many of the virgin lands problems encountered during Khrushchev's tenure in office were addressed after his ouster. McCauley noted that 'the considerable successes scored by the virgin lands since 1966 underlines the wisdom [to stay in these lands]' (McCauley 1976).

The main climatic characteristics of the virgin

lands are their continentality (i.e., hot summers, cold winters and aridity). The degree of continentality is greater than for other parts of the Russian plain at similar latitudes. Winters are lengthy and cold with January temperatures averaging about –19°C. Summers are short and hot with regional July temperatures averaging about 22°C. The average length of the growing season is about 165 days. Average annual precipitation ranges from about 250 mm in the southern part of the region to 300 mm in the north; in summer evaporation is much higher than precipitation. Precipitation in such regions is highly variable from one year to the next, bringing a high risk to rain-fed agricultural activities.

Thus, those seeking to engage in dryland farming would be at high risk to meteorological drought with the added risk of strong dry winds during winter and spring and hot dry winds in summer. Winter winds scour snow cover off the cultivated fields, removing a protective blanket for seed and soil during harsh winters. The winds also accelerate the desiccation of soils in springtime and in summer. Thus, soil erosion is a major regional environmental problem. Earlier this century, it was generally believed that the dry winds in Kazakhstan came from Central Asia to the south. More recently, however, the view is that dry air masses originate from the Arctic north. During spring and summer when air masses shift toward the south, the warmed air masses can hold more moisture. Higher air temperatures increase evaporation, thereby reducing soil moisture. Drought-like conditions often follow.

The interaction between natural conditions in the region and human activities that do not match the ecological conditions sparks dust storms. The total number of dust storms within the steppelands of Kazakhstan ranges from 20 to 80 per year, many of which usually occur between May and July. Sdobnikov noted in 1958 that 'wind erosion of soils originated in connection with the ploughing of large areas of virgin lands and the use of fine textured soils in widespread crop production. Already in regions of northern, northeastern and western Kazakhstan, especially in the Pavlodar and Aktyubinsk Regions, dust storms have damaged or completely destroyed sowings across large areas' (Kuznetsov 1959).

Precipitation varies widely from year to year throughout the region. For example, eight of the years between 1948 and 1958 were dry ones. In 1911, a dreadful drought year, precipitation was only 52 mm. In 1957, in the midst of the development of the Virgin Lands Scheme, only 9 mm of rainfall were recorded for the entire growing season. Soil temperatures can also be exceedingly high, reaching 63°C, adversely affecting agricultural productivity.

Although physical features, such as the high degree of climate variability of the region encompassing the virgin and idle lands, may have been well understood by technical people trained in a variety of physical science disciplines, they were less understood by specialists in other fields and even less so by policy makers responsible for agricultural development. This condition exists in many parts of the world and was not unique to the former Soviet Union. Hutchinson and colleagues in an article about land use in western Africa noted that 'although the inherent variability of climates is understood by climatologists, it seems to be routinely ignored or underestimated by developers' (Hutchinson *et al.* 1992). With regard to the Virgin Lands Scheme, Khrushchev pursued land-use policies based on his experiences in the better-watered Ukraine and on wishful thinking.

POLITICAL DECISIONS

References to considerations of ploughing the steppe-lands in the eastern part of the Soviet Union appeared in one of Lenin's Plans in which it was suggested that 'if farming is raised at least to the level of those parts of European Russia where climate and soils are similar, it would be possible to provide 40 to 60 million people with food'.

The first actions to develop the new lands were taken at the end of the 1920s, and particularly in 1928, when the Communist Party and the Soviet Government made a historical decision to produce grain by creating state farms on previously uncultivated lands (the 'virgin lands') in several parts of the country, including northern Kazakhstan and western Siberia. Ultimately, 19 state farms in only two of Kazakhstan's northern districts – Kustanai and Petropavolvsk – were organised, covering an area of about 500,000 hectares.

The second stage of the development of the virgin

lands occurred in the 1930s, when the XVIII Communist Party Congress decided to develop the country's industrial and agricultural base in the eastern regions. At that time the objective was to increase within two to three years the area of tillage by 4.5 million hectares, including more than 1 million hectares in Kazakhstan. However, the outbreak of the Second World War thwarted such a plan (Baishev 1979).

A plan to exploit the virgin land area was proposed again in 1930. Although the plan was not implemented, a brief review of it provides some interesting history to the Virgin Lands Scheme that was ultimately pursued. Ya. A. Yakovlev, the People's Commissar for Agriculture, at the XVI Party Congress of the Bolshevik Party in the summer of 1930, proposed a programme to develop 20 to 25 million hectares in Kazakhstan, western Siberia and other regions in order to cultivate wheat (McCauley 1976). He suggested supplying local people with enough equipment to avoid the need to bring in large numbers of farm workers from other parts of the country: 'each human force should be used at least fifteen times more efficiently than is now done'. The model for such a plan for the virgin lands was based on Canadian farming in arid and semiarid areas. Yakovlev wrote that, as in Canada, 'the entire area should be subdivided into farms by roads passing from north to south and from east to west with each farmer tending to 200 ha of land'. If the dry soils of the Canadian prairies could successfully produce grain, why not the virgin lands with analogous soil, temperature, and rainfall conditions? The XVI Party Congress report realistically noted that 'for the time being there are no guarantees against crop failures. Guarantees should not be against crop failures but against hunger.' Thus, planners in the 1930s realised that adverse, natural environmental conditions could hamper attempts to increase food production in the region each and every year, but that those risks were worthwhile in an attempt to alleviate hunger throughout the country. It is important to note that the Russian fear of famine still persisted from the early 1920s when famine conditions prevailed in the Soviet Union, requiring that the new Bolshevik government seek international food assistance from capitalist countries.

In October 1948 Stalin developed his 'State Plan for Remaking Nature'. It represented a wide-ranging programme focused on the exploitation of nature by, for example, constructing large hydraulic works. The part of the plan dealing with the improvement of soil quality focused only on the existing farming areas in the European territory of the Soviet Union, especially the Ukraine. Stalin, however, oblivious to the problems associated with such improvements, was intent on raising food production and of doing so within an ideological framework that was congenial to the collectivisation of agriculture and the totalitarian rule that he had used to fashion Soviet society. Khrushchev had a sense of what Stalin's vision was for mobilising and organising the countryside in much the same way he had succeeded in doing for industry – the politics of gigantism. Khrushchev also understood that no one in the Politburo wanted to tackle such a high-risk assignment. Postwar economic difficulties, struggles between factions within the biological sciences, inadequate technical support and, not the least important, the death of Stalin in 1953, resulted in the shelving of Stalin's Plan.

A persistent, grave shortage of grain and meat in the Soviet Union continued into the early 1950s. This suggested that, after several decades of great technological achievements, Soviet communism could not adequately feed the Soviet people. For example, in 1953 only 31 million metric tons of grain were purchased by the state but more than 32 million tons were needed that year (Maslov 1980). In this instance the government was forced to draw on its state grain reserves to cover the deficit. Sparked by such chronic food shortages, the government sought to increase crop yields in the traditional grain-producing regions in the European territory of the Soviet Union (i.e., the Soviet breadbasket) and at the same time sought to expand the area under cultivation.

When Khrushchev gained responsibility for Soviet agriculture in 1950, he proposed a programme to amalgamate collective farms and villages into *agrogorods* (agricultural towns). His aims were commendable: to reduce bureaucracy, eliminate waste, encourage specialisation, optimise the use of farm machinery and, in the process, enhance the Party's control over the countryside. Khrushchev's model towns, however, existed only on paper. In reality, their creation required investment, resources, personnel, and time – none of which Khrushchev had (McCauley 1976). While flattering to 'Stalin's obsession with regimentation', Khrushchev's plan soon proved to be unworkable but, with rare political perceptiveness,

> Khrushchev knew . . . that any publicity is better in the long run than no publicity. He had established himself as the only man in the country besides Stalin who could act, apparently, on his own initiative and get away with it. He had *also sown the seed of an idea, which was to recur again and again after his enlargement and flower briefly in the spectacular opening of the Virgin Lands in 1954.*
> (Crankshaw 1966, italics added)

His main political rival, Malenkov, favoured improving existing agricultural lands, whereas Khrushchev favoured extending agriculture into the virgin and idle lands (McCauley 1976).

At the February 1954 Plenary Session of the Central Committee of the CPSU, a report by Khrushchev was adopted 'on the further increase of grain output in the country and on the development of the virgin and idle lands'. As a direct result, a task was set forth to extend wheat cultivation in 1954–5 into 13 million hectares of the virgin and idle lands. 'The adoption of this policy in March 1954 was', according to G.A.E. Smith, 'a radical turning point in post-war Soviet agricultural policy and signified the leadership's acceptance that further economic growth could no longer be based on extracting a "surplus" from agriculture regardless of the effects on its development' (Smith 1987). A slogan used for launching this major agricultural campaign stated that 'We cannot wait for favors from nature; our goal is to take them from it!'

At the time (1954) the amount of virgin and idle lands in the Soviet Union that had been assimilated into the production system of existing cultivated land was about 19 million hectares. In an August 1954 resolution of the Central Committee of the CPSU and the Council of Ministers it was decided to bring the area sown to cereals up to 28 to 30 million hectares by 1956. The total area of newly cultivated lands was increased between 1954 and 1962 to about 42 million hectares. Smith noted that 'by 1960 the possibilities of further significant increases in sown land had come to an end (the limiting factor being the lack of precipitation in the virgin lands regions)

and further increases could only be achieved by assimilating submarginal virgin land or by draining and clearing idle land in established agricultural regions' (Smith 1987).

The first detachment of farmers and ordinary citizens was sent to the virgin lands in Kazakhstan in 1954. During the first two years of the programme about 650,000 new settlers went to these lands. According to Wheeler, the cultivation of the virgin lands was 'unpopular among the Kazakhs, partly because it seemed, perhaps wrongly, to threaten their traditional industry of stock breeding, and partly because it resulted in the introduction of a further 600,000 or more non-Asian immigrants' (Wheeler 1964).

Up to that time history had not witnessed on such a large scale the ploughing up of new lands over such a short period of time. Some researchers have argued that many of the problems encountered in carrying out the Virgin Lands Scheme resulted not from what Khrushchev was trying to achieve but the rapid pace at which he tried to achieve it. Steppe regions require considerable care in their usage. The development of appropriate land tillage technologies and techniques for the purpose of rain-fed cultivation in such regions had evolved as a result of trial and error over many centuries. Yet, with the rush to cultivate virgin and idle lands, little regard was given to these traditional land-use practices or to the fragility of the soils and the harshness of the region's climate. Instead, blind faith was placed in existing technology from other agricultural regions as well as in the belief that humans could dominate nature.

In his excellent review of the Virgin Lands Scheme, McCauley succinctly stated this problem:

> It is not surprising to discover that traditional European methods were adopted when the cultivation of the new expanses in the East began. After all, the operatives came from areas with a higher level of precipitation, which results in heavier soils, so they treated the whole operation as an extension of their own traditional areas.
> (McCauley 1976)

These attitudes led to several adverse impacts such as the breakdown of the physical properties of the soil and the loss of soil fertility. Even the seeds brought into these newly cultivated areas for sowing were poorly adapted to the region's harsh environmental conditions (severe winds, heat, moisture stress).

During the first two years of the scheme (1954–6), agricultural development in northern Kazakhstan and western Siberia had both positive and negative impacts. With regard to the latter, soil degradation processes were initiated (e.g., clearing a large expanse of a sandy plain of its natural vegetation) that set the stage for the widespread, highly visible soil erosion drama that eventually took place in the virgin lands. Yet, this should have come as no surprise to Soviet leaders as history is rent with examples of failed attempts by governments to plant what they wanted to plant, where and how they wanted to plant it, with little consideration given to prevailing environmental constraints. For example, during the drought-plagued 1930s, the Canadian prairie provinces (especially Saskatchewan, which Soviet planners used as their model), witnessed Dust-Bowl-like conditions similar to those which occurred in the US Great Plains to the south. The environment of the virgin lands (and local inhabitants) would pay for the lack of attention by decision makers to existing environmental constraints on long-term sustainable development prospects of the virgin lands. In just a few years, following the introduction of the moldboard plough (to turn the soil and bury natural grasses of the Kazakh steppe), soils became subject to desiccation and severe wind erosion. On some days, farmers in the area could not see the sun even at midday, because of the amount of dust put into the atmosphere as a result of ploughing fragile soils. The use of modern tractors only served to accelerate and intensify soil degradation on time and space scales that had not been witnessed throughout the history of farming. The plan was not realised, in large measure because of considerable political opposition to diverting capital from industrialisation to the agricultural sector.

Before the large-scale development of virgin lands, erosion of the topsoil by wind action (deflation) in northern Kazakhstan was limited; it appeared as isolated minor dust storms on ploughed land. In the Pavlodar Region, for example, dust storms were observed in 1922 on only one collective farm, in 1929 on about 30,000 hectares and by 1930 on even larger areas. The low level of wind erosion in the early decades of the century was because there was no widespread ploughing of the land. Where it had been

done, it had been as part of a fallow system which left land uncultivated for 5 to 7 years in order to restore nutrients and structure to the soils. While such a fallow system may have been less productive in economic terms, it was environmentally prudent because the risk of deflation was considerably lowered. Khrushchev paid little attention to the need for and value of letting such lands lie fallow. To him this land was not being used to its full potential. But the fragility of the soils required lengthy fallow periods, if sustainable productivity was to be achieved.

IMPACTS ON THE VIRGIN LANDS

As a result of widespread ploughing with little regard for the fragility of the virgin and idle lands, especially on those areas with finely textured soils, the frequency and intensity of dust storms increased. Many of the storms were so large in spatial terms that they encompassed entire administrative regions in northern Kazakhstan. Dust storms robbed arable land not only of good topsoil but also of nutrients; for example, the not-infrequent loss of 3 cm of topsoil meant that the winds would have also carried away about 800 kg of nitrogen per hectare, about 200 kg of phosphorous and 6 metric tons of potassium. In the absence of human intervention it would take several centuries to replenish these soil nutrients through natural processes.

Dust storms appeared even during the first few years of ploughing. As early as 1955 one could see the proverbial writing on the wall, when wind erosion caused the degradation of about 500,000 hectares of sown land with about 50,000 hectares being completely lost to agricultural production in the Kustanai Region. Deflation in 1957 on areas subjected to large-scale sowing (e.g., on state farms) reduced state farm yields of 370 kg per hectare. The average crop yield on collective farms that year was only 200 kg per hectare. In fact, crop yields throughout the virgin and idle lands were much lower than expected, which made grain produced in the region more expensive than the same amount of grain produced in other parts of the USSR.

Because of the problems caused by ploughing up large expanses of steppelands, local authorities had to make frequent requests to the State Planning

Committee of Kazakhstan to convert the newly culti-vated areas to other types of agricultural production. In fact, not an insignificant portion of these lands had become so degraded in such a short period of time that they had to be removed from grain production altogether. Nevertheless, authorities seeking to pro-duce the best statistics (if not the best output) for their agricultural activities (e.g., with regard to area ploughed, area sown, and desired yield levels) insisted on the continued ploughing of virgin and idle lands, including areas with finely textured, fragile soils, and an opening up of additional lands to make up for the loss of production from the retired areas. In most cases ploughing continued on areas already subjected to blowing sands as well as on lands unsuitable for farming and known to be at high risk of severe wind erosion. A constant target for continual cropping was the fallow lands. Scientists debated the various ways these lands might be incorporated on a full-time basis into crop production.

Commenting on the development of the virgin lands, Leonid Brezhnev (who at that time had been second secretary of the Central Committee of the Communist Party of Kazakhstan) stated that 'we knew, of course, that heat and aridity in that region were not unusual. But we did not yet know the ominous inexorability of the steppe calendar in which there is an especially severe disastrous drought once every ten years' (Brezhnev 1979).

Cereal production in the Soviet Union did increase as a result of the Virgin Lands Scheme. The years 1954–8 were good years with favourable weather conditions for grain production. In fact, 1958 was a record-setting year. In the several years that followed, however, years of average crop production were inter-spersed with major drought-related failures (McCauley 1976).

In sum, for a short time production of cereals on these newly cultivated lands increased but success was short-lived. With a variety of weather-related prob-lems, such as unusually wet springs, early frost, increased freezing of seeds in the ground and intensification of wind erosion, parts of the newly cultivated virgin lands had to be returned for use only as livestock pastures. Ploughing up grassland that had traditionally been used as range lands had depleted nutrients from the soil, making them less productive

in the future even for use by livestock. Cultivation of the virgin lands in the 1950s and early 1960s led to widespread land degradation and desertification throughout the region.

At the time (in the 1950s) many officials blamed meteorological factors for the degradation of the land and for the false start of the cultivation of the virgin and idle lands. However, human activities (e.g., ploughing) had degraded the fragile vegetative cover and the surface layer of soils. At that time Izmailsky identified the cause of the drying out of the steppe-lands as the disappearance of the rich grass cover resulting from ploughing. Ploughing such soils reduces their ability to accumulate much-needed moisture. According to Russian soil scientist Dokuchaev, as quoted by P.N. Pilatov, 'there is no ground to blame climate change in the steppe region in order to explain (1) the deficiency of groundwater in the steppe area or (2) the frequent occurrence of crop failures related to drought. Only the changes in the surface properties of the steppe soils due to plough-ing and compaction [from heavy machinery] . . . could radically change the soil moisture relationship' (Pilatov 1966).

Droughts in the steppes are a part of the regional climate and are to be expected. In the early years of the virgin lands project, few planners or policy makers gave any consideration to the fact that alterations in the land's surface would increase albedo (reflectivity of the earth's surface) which in turn would alter the regional climate. Perhaps these initial large-scale, land-surface changes increased the frequency or intensity of meteorological drought in the region. Actually, some scientists did take into account the potential impacts of drought on grain production, but key people (or agricultural planners) seemed to have discounted their importance. Brezhnev wrote that 'when economic calculations were made on virgin land development, scientists considered that even if two extremely dry years were to take place during each five-year plan, we would still be able to get [favourable] grain yields in the steppe' (Brezhnev 1979).

In the first century AD, historian and farmer Kolumella commented on persistent regional crop failures. He wrote that

I often hear the leaders of our state accuse either the earth of barrenness or the climate for the poor and irregular yields. Some of them refer to the process as if it were a law; in their opinion the earth, tired and depleted by the luxuriant yields in ancient times, is no longer capable of providing people with the earth's previous generosity. I am sure that these reasons are far from the truth. The problem is not with heavenly wrath but with our own faults.

The euphoria generated by expected large grain outputs from the virgin and idle lands diminished quickly after 1958, in the face of recurrent drought, dust storms, and declining crop yields. It took about ten years before those planners and scientists who knew that new methods of cultivation attuned to regional environmental conditions were needed won the day. At first the Soviets looked for examples to the United States and Canada, both of which had emerged from the Dust Bowl days in the 1930s with greatly improved agricultural production systems. Zero or minimum tillage resulted in higher grain yields and reduced wind erosion and dust storms, especially during very dry years. In addition to these practices borrowed from North American agriculture, the Soviets supplemented their land-use activities with a system of tillage designed especially for the virgin lands, referred to as the conservation cropping system. Principal elements of this system were as follows: stubble mulching (preserving stubble and straw on the soil's surface), band tillage (with a distribution of bare fallow and sowing annual crops in rows perpendicular to the prevailing winds), crop rotation (grain–fallow–arable crop rotation), alternating sections of annual crops with sections of perennial grasses, sowing alternating strips of high-stem plants, and the reseeding of grassy areas that had been eroded. In addition, forest belts (called shelterbelts) would be planted (as in North America in the Dust Bowl days) to protect the stubble, band fallow and reseeded areas.

Soil-protecting cropping systems were introduced over about 20 million hectares. For example, the Tselinograd Region produced grain yields of about 600 kg per hectare before soil conservation measures had been put into place (this was the average yield from 1961 to 1965). As the system was being put into place (1966–70), yields increased to 700 kg per hectare and by 1971–3 yields had increased to 1,190 kg per hectare.

The development of the virgin lands was of major social and economic as well as political importance. In the sparsely populated steppes of Kazakhstan, highly mechanised socialist state farms were established, settlements constructed, transportation infrastructure (rail and road ways) were built, and power plants erected. These were major accomplishments, but were achieved at great sacrifice by 'immigrants' into the region as well as by indigenous inhabitants of the steppes whose livestock herds had been displaced from their traditional range lands. The truth is that these lands were neither virgin nor idle. According to Martha Olcott 'the term "virgin lands" was itself a misnomer, probably deliberate. The six Kazakh oblasts included in the virgin lands territory may have produced little grain but were not unexploited, for they were Kazakh pasturelands' (Olcott 1987).

What happened in the virgin and idle lands of the Soviet Union in the 1950s and 1960s was in many ways a repeat of the 'Dirty Thirties' in the US Great Plains and the Canadian prairie provinces. The ensuing degradation represents a response by natural environmental processes to inappropriate land-use practices (including inappropriate technology) in agriculturally marginal areas. It represents a good example of drought following the plough in the early decades of exploitation of these 'virgin and idle' lands. Only with improved land-use practices and technology appropriate to regional environmental conditions might sustained agriculture take place. The harsh lessons of the early years of carrying out the virgin and idle lands scheme stand out as a reminder to Russian leaders and, now, the leaders of newly independent Kazakhstan that marginal lands must be treated with care and require considerable understanding before exploitation. To do less would be to set up such lands for highly destructive desertification processes.

NOTE

1 This chapter is reprinted from *Drought Follows the Plow* (Michael H. Glantz, ed.), Cambridge: Cambridge University Press, 1994.

REFERENCES

Baishev, S.B. (1979) 'The historical significance of opening up the virgin and idle lands', *Voprosy Ekonomiki* 3, 52–8.

Brezhnev, L. (1979) *The Virgin Lands*, Moscow: Progress Publishers.

Crankshaw, E. (1966) *Khrushchev: A Career*, New York: Viking Press, pp. 179–80.

Hutchinson, C.F., Warshall, P., Arnould, E.J., and Kindler, J. (1992) 'Development in arid lands: Lessons from Lake Chad', *Environment* 34, 6: 41.

Kuznetsov, A.T. (1959) 'Climatic zones', in A.T. Kuznetsov, *Climate of Kazakhstan*, Leningrad: L. Gidrometeoizdat, pp. 76–7.

Lydolph, P.E. (1979) *Geography of the U.S.S.R.: Topical Analysis*, Elkhart Lake, Wisconsin: Misty Valley Publishing, p. 222.

Maslov, N. (1980) 'Virgin lands: 25 years later', *Soviet Life*, May, p. 6.

McCauley, M. (1976) *Khrushchev and the Development of Soviet Agriculture*, New York: Holmes & Meier Publishers, p. xii.

Olcott, M.G. (1987) *The Kazakhs*, Stanford, CA: Hoover Institution Press, p. 237.

Pilatov, P.N. (1966) *Steppes of the USSR as a Condition of the Material Life of Society*, USSR: Yaroslavl State University, p. 118.

Smith, G.A.E. (1987) 'The Stalinist legacy and the pressure for reform', in M. McCauley (ed.), *Khrushchev and Khrushchevism*, Bloomington, IN: Indiana University Press, p. 103.

Wheeler, G. (1964) *The Modern History of Soviet Central Asia*, Westport, CT: Greenwood Press, p. 162.

INDEX